Studies in International Corporate Finance and Governance Systems

A Comparison of the U.S., Japan, and Europe

Edited by
DONALD H. CHEW

New York   Oxford ■ OXFORD UNIVERSITY PRESS ■ 1997

Oxford University Press

Oxford   New York
Athens   Auckland   Bangkok   Bogota   Bombay
Buenos Aires   Calcutta   Cape Town   Dar es Salaam
Delhi   Florence   Hong Kong   Istanbul   Karachi
Kuala Lumpur   Madras   Madrid   Melbourne
Mexico City   Nairobi   Paris   Singapore
Taipei   Tokyo   Toronto

and associated companies in
Berlin   Ibadan

Published by Oxford University Press, Inc.,
198 Madison Avenue, New York, New York 10016

Oxford is a registered trademark of Oxford University Press

Library of Congress Cataloging-in-Publication Data
Studies in international corporate finance and governance systems:
a comparison of the U.S., Japan, and Europe / edited by Donald H. Chew.
p.   cm.
A collection of articles most of which were originally published
in the Journal of applied corporate finance.
Includes bibliographical references.
ISBN 0-19-510795-0
1. Corporations—Finance. 2. Corporate governance.
3. Corporations—United States—Finance.
4. Corporate governance—United States.
5. Corporations—Japan—Finance.
6. Corporate governance—Japan.
7. Corporations—Europe—Finance.
8. Corporate governance—Europe.
I. Chew, Donald H.
HG4026.S768   1997
658.15'99—dc20   96-34701

9 8 7 6 5 4 3 2 1

Printed in the United States of America
on acid-free paper

To my wife of unconstrained affections,
Susan Emerson,
for enduring our ten years' trial

■ CONTENTS

■ I. INTRODUCTION

The past decade has given rise to a growing debate over the relative efficiency of different national economic systems. At the risk of oversimplifying, there are two basic corporate finance and governance systems that predominate in developed economies today. One is the Anglo-American "market-based" model, with widely dispersed shareholders and a fairly vigorous corporate control (or takeover) market. The other can be represented by the Japanese and German "relationship-based" systems, with their large bank and intercorporate holdings (and conspicuous absence of takeovers). Given the increasing globalization of business, which of these two systems can be expected to prevail over time? Or will both systems continue to coexist, while seeking to adopt some aspects of the other?

Throughout the 1980s and well into the 1990s, the popular business press was telling us that U.S. companies were falling farther behind their global competitors—even as U.S. stock prices were climbing ever higher. We were also told that the corporate restructuring movement was adding to the American competitiveness problem by reducing investment and otherwise reinforcing the "short termism" of U.S. managers. At the same time, Japanese companies were pronounced the victors in the competitive wars, and U.S. managers and investors were urged to cultivate the "patience" of their Japanese counterparts.

Over the same period, however, academic research in corporate finance (much of which was reviewed in Bank of America's *Journal of Applied Corporate Finance*, which I serve as editor) was telling a quite different story. The average stock price reactions to announcements of all variety of U.S. corporate restructurings—takeovers, LBOs, spin-offs, and large stock buybacks—were consistently positive. A follow-up set of studies examining the operating performance of restructured companies have by and large vindicated the market's initial endorsement of such restructurings. Moreover, a 1993 study published by Morgan Stanley showed U.S. companies accounting for an impressive 48% of worldwide total profits and 37% of total sales in 19 major global industries over the period 1986-1992 (as compared to only 15% of profits and 32% of sales for Japanese companies over the same period, and 37% of profit and 31% of sales for European firms).

At the same time research in corporate finance was furnishing evidence in support of the Anglo-American market for corporate control, some financial economists were also beginning to question at least some aspects of the Japanese relationship-based system. At the end of 1990, we published an article by Harvard's Japanese corporate finance specialist Carl Kester entitled "*The Hidden Costs of Japanese Success.*" That article identified a fundamental problem with the Japanese corporate governance system that was being masked by Japanese companies' gains in market share and the growing Japanese trade surplus. The problem, which has been called "the agency costs of free cash flow" by Harvard professor Michael Jensen, comes down to this: the Japanese system's ineffectiveness in forcing its large, mature companies to return excess capital to investors (dividends are minimal and stock repurchases were prohibited until quite recently) was leading to widespread, value-reducing corporate diversification as well as massive overcapacity in many industries.

Our analysis received confirmation of sorts in a 1992 report on the Japanese economy by the prestigious Nomura Research Institute. As summarized in a speech by Toshiba's Chairman Joichi Aoi (which appears in this book), the NRI's principal conclusions were as follows:

■ *The declines in* [Japanese] *corporate earnings and share prices have by far exceeded those that would have been expected in a purely "cyclical" downturn, and the NRI has attributed such declines to a "structural" overcapacity stemming from lax investment criteria employed by Japanese companies.*

■ *In addition to denying shareholders any means of effective oversight or control over their investment policies, Japanese companies also tend to compound the problem by retaining excess capital rather than returning it to shareholders in the form of higher dividends or share repurchases. Failure to pay out excess capital leads to inefficiency.*

Since publication of this report, calls for reform of both the Japanese corporate governance system and stock market regulations have intensified. One consequence of such pressures for reform was the lifting, in 1995, of the ban on stock repurchases by Japanese companies. And similar Anglo-American style corporate governance challenges have recently been launched in countries like Germany and France.

But if the world appears to be moving toward a more market-based system, does this mean that all is well with U.S. corporate governance and that the relationship-based system is doomed to obsolescence? The story now being told by economists and management experts—the one that this book attempts to present—is considerably more complicated.

1

For example, in the first article in the book, "*Capital Choices: Changing the Way America Invests in Industry,*" corporate strategist Michael Porter states that "the U.S. system of allocating capital both within and across companies appears to be failing," thereby putting "American companies in a range of industries at a serious disadvantage in global competition." As noted earlier, the most voluble critics of U.S. industry have long decried the short termism foisted upon American management by U.S. *financial* markets. According to the most popular version of this argument, the quarter-to-quarter focus of now dominant institutional investors pressures American companies into passing up valuable R&D and other long-term investments—investments that were allowing Japanese and German competitors to prevail in the international marketplace.

Such claims, to be sure, have been largely discredited by research attesting to the willingness of U.S. investors to respond positively to announcements of a variety of long-term projects: major capital expenditure programs, joint ventures, and increases in R&D spending. Assertions of the myopia of U.S. capital markets also seem unconvincing when set against the current level of U.S. stock prices, not to mention the recent booms in the U.S. IPO and venture capital markets. As Porter himself concedes, investors as eager to fund biotechnology start-ups as our IPO markets have shown themselves hardly deserve to be branded craven or short-sighted.

But Porter's story is both more complex and more persuasive. Porter's argument, stated briefly, is that U.S. companies face both *external* (capital market) and *internal* (corporate) pressures to underinvest in relatively intangible assets—things like stronger supplier relationships, market penetration, process improvements, employee training, and other corporate capabilities. Not only are such assets difficult for investors on the outside to appreciate (and reflect in higher share prices), but their value also tends to elude measurement by most internal corporate capital budgeting and management compensation systems. Under most capital budgeting systems, managers in large, decentralized corporations typically have incentives to skimp on investments in capabilities. Whereas the benefits of such investments take time to materialize and are generally shared throughout the company, the costs are expensed immediately rather than capitalized and are generally charged to particular units.

Such a tendency to underinvest could be counteracted by partly "centralizing" authority and by

accounting properly for (say, by capitalizing rather than expensing) corporate investments in capabilities. But, according to Porter, the source of the U.S. corporate investment problem is far more fundamental—a flaw at the core of the entire ownership and corporate governance structure. As a result of laws and regulations passed since the 1930s aimed at curbing abuses and concentration of power, there has been a progressive widening of the gap between the ownership and control of large U.S. corporations. The major institutional investors that today dominate ownership of U.S. companies are essentially powerless to intervene when management neglects shareholder interests. And corporate boards, the nominal defenders of such interests, have until quite recently been almost completely ineffectual. Most institutions respond to these constraints by keeping American managements "on a short leash," demanding that their companies produce steady increases in earnings or dumping the shares and thereby driving down stock prices. The U.S. system is said to accentuate conflicts among shareholders, lenders, managers, and employees. As a result, in Porter's words, "even though all parties to the corporate contract are acting rationally, none is satisfied."

The stocks of Japanese and German companies, by contrast, are said to be held by "dedicated, permanent" owners whose aims are "perpetuation of the enterprise" and building "corporate position" rather than maximizing period-by-period profit. The greater concentration of ownership and investor participation encouraged by the Japanese and German systems reduces the large "agency costs"—notably, the conflicts of interest among management, shareholders, and lenders— and the "information costs"—the inability of outsiders to know what insiders know—faced by U.S. investors. Lower agency and information costs in turn mean less perceived risk for investors; and lower risk, all else equal, translates into lower investor required rates of return and higher stock prices.

All this, of course, *looks like* a lower cost of capital for Japanese and German companies; but it is not so in reality. Rather, U.S. investors are simply, and rationally, charging normal premiums for the higher risks imposed by the fragmented U.S. corporate governance system.

But, for all their strengths, the Japanese and German systems also have their own problems: overinvestment in declining industries, failure to abandon unprofitable activities, and excessive insistence on growth and market share. Indeed, most economists would likely agree that holding up "self-perpetuation" as the primary goal for any enterprise is a prescription for chronic inefficiency. And Porter concedes as much, if only implicitly, when he argues for the current advantages of the U.S. system: "efficiency, flexibility, responsiveness, and high rates of corporate profit."

What Porter accordingly ends up proposing is, in effect, a blending of the strengths of the two systems—one that combines the near-term efficiency of the U.S. system with the greater willingness to invest in long-term capabilities that is said to distinguish Japanese and German companies. Such system-wide changes would aim to transform America's "EPS-enthralled," largely passive institutional investors into active, longer-term owners. This would be accomplished in part by giving board seats to major stockholders—and to representatives of other corporate constituencies such as major suppliers, customers, and employees. As in Japan and Germany, bankers and other lenders would also be encouraged to hold large equity stakes (now prevented, of course, by Glass Steagall). With the active, long-term owners envisioned by Porter, corporations would in turn be encouraged to make internal capital budgeting changes leading to more far-sighted investment decisions. The net consequence of such changes to corporate as well as capital market behavior, Porter suggests, would be a "system superior to that in Japan and Germany."

While endorsing some of Porter's proposed changes, one can disagree strongly with parts of the analysis. Perhaps the most troubling aspect of Porter's statement is its failure to lay sufficient emphasis on important adjustments in U.S. ownership and governance that were accomplished by capital markets in the 1980s—notably, the increased concentration of ownership achieved by the leveraged restructuring movement—and the stepped-up activism of institutional shareholders in the 1990s.

As Michael Jensen argues in "*The Modern Industrial Revolution, Exit, and the Failure of Internal Control Systems*" (which follows Porter's article), the leveraged restructuring of the 1980s has helped produce sharply increased levels of productivity and export growth among U.S. manufacturers by squeezing excess capacity out of mature industries. In short, restructuring has helped curb the U.S. *over*investment problem—a problem that may well be as harmful to competitiveness as the underinvestment problem that troubles Porter.

Indeed, Jensen goes so far as to suggest that squeezing out excess capital and capacity is the most formidable challenge now facing the U.S. economy—and, indeed, the economies of all industrialized nations. In making this argument, Jensen draws striking parallels between the 19th-century industrial revolution and worldwide economic developments in the last two decades. In both periods, technological advances led not only to sharp increases in productivity and dramatic reductions in prices, but also to massive obsolescence and overcapacity. And much as the great M & A wave of the 1890s reduced capacity (by consolidating some 1800 U.S. firms into roughly 150), the leveraged takeovers, LBOs, and other leveraged recapitalizations of the 1980s provided "healthy adjustments" to overcapacity that was building in many sectors of the U.S. economy: for example, oil and gas, tires, tobacco, commodity chemicals, food processing, paper and forest products, financial services, publishing, and broadcasting.

Jensen interprets the shareholder gains from corporate restructuring transactions of the 1980s (which he estimates at $750 billion) as evidence of the failure of U.S. *internal* corporate control systems—that is, managements as supervised by boards of directors—to deal *voluntarily* with the problem of excess capacity. And, given the shutdown of the takeover market in the early 1990s, together with intensifying global competition, worldwide protectionism, and other causes of future overcapacity, Jensen views reform of the U.S. corporate governance system as an urgent matter. Notable among his proposals is that large public companies should seek to replicate certain governance features of venture capital and LBO firms like Kleiner Perkins and KKR—specifically, significant equity ownership by managers and directors, greater participation by outside "active" investors, and smaller and better informed boards.

In "*Is American Corporate Governance Fatally Flawed?*", Nobel-Prize economist Merton Miller answers both critics of U.S. underinvestment and Jensen's pessimism about U.S. control systems with a classic defense of the "shareholder-value principle." That U.S. managers are more concerned than Japanese managers about stock prices, says Miller, is not a flaw, but rather "one of the primary strengths" of the U.S. economy. "Myopia," as he points out,

is not the only disease of vision afflicting business managers. They may suffer from astigmatism or even from excessive far-sightedness or hyperopia. Over the last 20 years, one will find cases in which

American firms facing strong stockholder pressures to pay out funds invested too little. But many Japanese firms, facing no such pressures, have clearly overinvested during the same period.

Japanese managers, adds Miller, are justly skeptical about using stock prices to guide their investment decisions. Because of "the heroic scale of financial intervention by the Ministry of Finance, Japanese managers can be pardoned for wondering whether the stock market may be just a Bunraku theater, with the bureaucrats from MOF backstage manipulating the puppets."

In the fourth article, however, corporate strategist C.K. Prahalad remains unconvinced by the arguments of both Miller and Jensen. In contrast to Jensen's focus on the importance of efficient exit, Prahalad asserts that the greater challenge facing large corporations today is ensuring continuous *renewal*—that is, finding new *growth* opportunities based on core competencies while still seeking efficiencies in mature businesses. To accomplish this end, moreover, corporate America must seek to balance its single-minded commitment to shareholder interests with greater concern for other corporate stakeholders such as employees and critical suppliers (especially those supplying access to key technology). At the same time, Japanese firms are urged to balance *their* traditional commitments to employees and suppliers with greater attention to shareholder interests.

Prahalad is also the featured speaker in the "*Continental Bank Roundtable on Corporate Competition in the 1990s*" that concludes the opening section of the book. There Prahalad argues that corporate restructuring—that is, the pruning back of excessive or misdirected corporate growth—is only part of the corporate process of adding value and creating social wealth. For American companies to meet global competitors such as the Japanese, near-term restructuring must be accompanied by far-sighted strategic investment designed to develop a company's core competencies. Such competencies, according to Prahalad, can and should then be "leveraged" across *multiple* businesses to create new growth opportunities for otherwise mature companies.

After exploring these strategic ideas with six top corporate executives (from companies ranging

on a technology continuum from semiconductors and mainframes to grocery retailing and close-outs) with interesting effect, Prahalad then calls for a general re-examination of the principle that corporations be run to maximize shareholder value. This in turn provokes shareholder value advocate Bennett Stewart into a defense of leveraged restructuring, corporate specialization, and the shareholder gains of the '80s—and a challenge of the diversification strategies still being pursued by the largest Japanese companies. The resulting exchange between Stewart and Prahalad is one of the highlights of the book.

A WORD ABOUT THIS BOOK

This book consists of 28 articles and two roundtable discussions on aspects of corporate governance. The articles are divided into five sections. Following the "Overview" whose contents are summarized above, the next three sections are devoted to corporate governance issues in, respectively, the United States, Japan, and Europe. The fact that articles focusing on the U.S. experience make up more than half of the book reflects not (I hope) the provincialism or chauvinism of this writer, but rather the relative scarcity of research (and data) on companies outside the U.S. The fifth and concluding section consists of two articles on the "EVA® financial management system," an approach to corporate performance measurement and incentive compensation that has recently attracted strong interest in the U.S., Europe, Australia, and South Africa.

All but four of these articles were originally published in the *Journal of Applied Corporate Finance*, which is sponsored by Bank of America and published by Stern Stewart & Co. The aim of this publication is to "translate" outstanding academic research into relatively plain English for practicing businessmen. As such, this book should prove useful for MBA and corporate executive development programs.

In closing, I would like to thank Joel Stern and Bennett Stewart for their collaboration in what has become a 15-year publishing effort. My greatest debt, however, is to all the financial economists who have contributed to our journal.

Donald H. Chew
New York City
October 22, 1996

CAPITAL CHOICES: CHANGING THE WAY AMERICA INVESTS IN INDUSTRY

*by Michael E. Porter,
Harvard Business School**

The Project on Capital Choices, sponsored by the Harvard Business School and the Council on Competitiveness, initially set out to determine the extent to which the competitiveness of American industry is being undermined by a short time horizon. The project has since evolved into a broader examination of how private capital is allocated in the United States, Japan, and Germany and an assessment of the relative effectiveness of the American corporate governance system. Eighteen research papers were prepared by 25 prominent scholars in a wide range of disciplines. Professor Porter's paper, from which the following article is excerpted, develops an overall framework for understanding national investment systems and their consequences, drawing on the project papers and his own research. The complete paper is available through the Council on Competitiveness. A book containing all the project papers will be published by the Harvard Business School Press.

To compete effectively in international markets, companies must continuously innovate and upgrade their competitive advantages. This requires sustained investment in a wide variety of forms, including not only physical assets but also intangible assets such as R&D, employee training and skills development, information systems, organizational development, and close supplier relationships. Today, the changing nature of competition and the increasing pressure of globalization make investment the most critical determinant of competitive advantage.

Yet the U.S. system of allocating investment capital both within and across companies appears to be failing.[1] Although the system has many strengths, including efficiency, flexibility, responsiveness, and high rates of corporate profit, it does not seem to be effective in directing capital to companies that can deploy it most productively and, within companies, to the most productive investment projects. As a consequence, many American companies invest too little in assets and capabilities critical for competitiveness (such as employee training), while others waste capital on investments with limited financial or social rewards (such as unrelated acquisitions). This distortion of corporate investment priorities puts American companies in a range of industries at a serious disadvantage in global competition and, ultimately, threatens the long-term growth of the U.S. economy.

---

*This article draws heavily on the research and commentary of my colleagues in the Project on Capital Choices, which was co-sponsored by the Harvard Business School and the Council on Competitiveness. Rebecca Wayland's research assistance and insights have contributed greatly to the study.

[1]. Although this report focuses on private sector investment behavior, public sector investment in education and in efficient transportation, communication, and information networks is also critical to industrial competitiveness.

Although critics frequently blame the shortcomings of American industry on a short time horizon, ineffective corporate governance, or a high cost of capital, these concerns are just symptoms of a larger problem. What is at issue here is the effectiveness of the entire U.S. system of allocating investment capital both among and within companies—a system that includes shareholders, lenders, investment managers, corporate directors, managers, and employees.

The U.S. system of capital allocation creates a divergence of interests between owners and corporations that interferes with the flow of capital to those corporate investments that offer the highest long-run payoffs. American owners, investment managers, directors, managers, and employees are thus trapped in a system in which all are acting rationally, but none is satisfied. The U.S. system also has difficulty aligning the interests of private investors and corporations with those of society as a whole, including employees, suppliers, and local educational institutions.

The problems with the U.S. system are largely of our own making and have been building over a long period of time. Yet the investment problem has surfaced particularly in the last two decades. Through a series of regulatory decisions and other choices with unintended consequences, important changes have occurred in such areas as the pattern of corporate ownership, stock valuation and trading practices, and capital budgeting practices—all of which have fundamentally altered the way corporate investment choices are made.

At the same time, the nature of competition has shifted in ways that make investment more critical to success—especially in forms of investment like employee training and development of close supplier relationships that are most heavily penalized by the U.S. system. Also, globalization has brought American firms into more frequent contact with firms based in nations with different capital allocation systems, intensifying the impact of U.S. investment practices.

Reform is needed to shore up the weaknesses in the U.S. system, while preserving its strengths. Meaningful change will be difficult because the U.S. investment problem is far more complex than conventional wisdom suggests. Most current proposals aimed at addressing America's investment problem fail to recognize the interdependencies among the different parts of our capital allocation system. Proposals to tax transactions or eliminate quarterly financial reports address the symptoms of the investment problem rather than its underlying causes. Other proposals seek to deal with the investment problem indirectly, through government support for investment in particular sectors and the encouragement of widespread collaboration among competitors. These, too, treat symptoms and risk unintended and unwanted consequences.

Reform must address many aspects of the U.S. system, ideally all at once. Policymakers, institutional investors, and corporate managers must all play a role in instituting necessary changes.

THE IMPORTANCE OF INVESTMENT IN A COMPETITIVE ECONOMY

The appropriate rate of investment in one form often depends on making complementary and sequential investments in others. A physical asset such as a new factory, for example, may not reach its potential level of productivity unless there are parallel investments in intangible assets such as employee training and product redesign.[2] Such "softer" investments are of growing importance to competition, and are also the most difficult to measure and evaluate using traditional approaches to evaluating investment alternatives.

The optimal rate of investment for society may also differ from that of an individual firm because of the presence of "externalities" or "spillovers" from private investment. These spillovers create benefits for the economy as a whole (referred to as "social returns") above and beyond the private returns accruing to a firm's shareholders.[3] Social returns include such things as potentially higher wages of employees or benefits to local suppliers that result from productivity-increasing technology investments. One important test of national systems for allocating investment capital is the extent to which such social benefits are created and captured.

2. See Carliss Y. Baldwin and Kim B. Clark, "Capabilities and Capital Investment: New Perspectives on Capital Budgeting," in the project on Capital Choices, Harvard Business School and Council on Competitiveness, 1992. The article also appears in this issue.

3. For example, the social returns from R&D have been documented to be 50 to 100% higher than private returns to investors. See J.I. Bernstein and M.I. Nadiri,

"Research and Development and Intra-industry Spillovers: An Empirical Application of Dynamic Duality," *Review of Economic Studies*, Vol. 56, 1989, pp. 249-269. The difference between private and social returns varies by form of investment and tends to be higher for intangible forms of investment such as R&D than for investments in physical assets such as plant and equipment.

Evidence (and Complexities) of the U.S. Investment Problem

Ideally, we could test directly whether the rate and mix of investment in the United States are optimal. Unfortunately, the lack of available data, coupled with the many influences on the optimal rate of investment, rule out such a direct test. Instead, we are forced to proceed indirectly, and examine a variety of measures of the comparative outcomes, rates, and patterns of U.S. investment and the behavior of American investors.

Although there are important complexities, as described below, there is a great deal of evidence that supports the view that American industry invests at a lower rate and on a shorter-term basis than German and Japanese industry in many areas:

■ The competitive position of significant parts of the U.S. economy seems to have declined relative to those of other nations.
■ Aggregate investment in property, plant, and equipment, civilian R&D, and intangible assets such as corporate training and related forms of human resource development is lower in the U.S. than in Japan and Germany.
■ Leading American firms in many industries, including automobiles, computers, and tires, are outinvested by their Japanese counterparts.
■ Anecdotal evidence suggests that American firms invest at a lower rate than both Japanese and German firms in non-traditional forms such as human resource development, relationships with suppliers, and start-up losses to enter foreign markets.
■ The R&D portfolios of American firms include a smaller share of long-term projects than those of European and Japanese firms.[4]
■ The hurdle rate used by U.S. firms to evaluate investment projects appears to be higher than estimates of the cost of capital.[5]

■ American CEOs believe that their firms have shorter investment horizons than their international competitors.
■ The average holding period of stocks has declined from over seven years in 1960 to about two years.
■ Long-term growth has become a less important influence on U.S. stock prices.[6]
■ Many recent U.S. policy proposals such as government funding of specific industries, R&D consortia, and joint production ventures implicitly reflect a private investment problem.

Although these findings present a broadly consistent picture of lagging U.S. investment, there are some interesting and important complexities that seem to defy the overall pattern. These puzzles contradict many simple explanations of why America invests less or has a shorter time horizon:

■ The U.S. investment problem varies by industry and even by company. Understanding why there are differences across industries and companies is crucial to telling a convincing story.[7]
■ The United States does well in funding emerging industries and high-risk start-ups that require investments of five years or more. How does a low-investing, short-horizon nation achieve such performance?
■ The average profitability of American industry is higher than that in Japan and Germany,[8] yet American shareholders have consistently achieved no better or lower returns.[9] There is thus no simple connection between average corporate returns on investment and long-term shareholder returns, as much American thinking about shareholder value seems to suggest.
■ American industry seems clearly to have overinvested in some forms, such as unrelated acquisitions.[10] How this overinvestment can be reconciled with a lower average rate of investment in crucial forms such as intangible assets is important to fully understanding U.S. investment behavior.

---

4. A recent survey of CEOs in the United States, Japan, and Germany provides insights into the composition of R&D portfolios, hurdle rates, and CEO perceptions of the relative investment time horizons of their competitors. See James M. Poterba and Lawrence H. Summers, "Time Horizons of American Firms: New Evidence from a Survey of CEOs," in the project on Capital Choices, Harvard Business School and Council on Competitiveness, 1992.

5. See Poterba and Summers, cited in the previous note.

6. See Burton G. Malkiel, "The Influence of Conditions in Financial Markets on the Time Horizons of Business Managers: An International Comparison," in the project on Capital Choices, Harvard Business School and Council on Competitiveness, 1992.

7. Although leading U.S. firms in industries such as construction equipment and steel invest less in R&D and capital expenditures than their Japanese or German counterparts, those in telecommunications and, compared to Japan, in pharmaceuticals, seem to invest as much or even more.

8. See R. Z. Lawrence, "Time Horizons of American Management: The Role of Macroeconomic Factors," in the project on Capital Choices, Harvard Business School and Council on Competitiveness, 1992.

9. The average return to shareholders in the first section of the Tokyo Stock Exchange between 1980 and 1990 was 13.0%, while the average return of shareholders of the NYSE for the same period was 11.8%. Results for the period 1960-1990 were 12.6% for the Tokyo Stock Exchange and 10.3% for the NYSE. For the periods 1960-1970 and 1970-1980, average returns were 8.2% and 15.2% for the TSE and 8.5% and 9.5% for the NYSE. Returns include dividend payments and price appreciation using year-end figures. They are not adjusted for inflation or the relative risk of the two markets. The generally lower rates of inflation in Japan and Germany strengthen this finding.

10. See M.E. Porter, "From Competitive Advantage to Corporate Strategy," *Harvard Business Review*, May-June 1987, and D. J. Ravenscraft and F.M. Scherer, *Mergers, Sell-offs, and Economic Efficiency*, Brookings Institute, 1987.

The nature of competition has shifted in ways that make investment more critical to success—especially in forms of investment like employee training and development of close supplier relationships that are most heavily penalized by the U.S. system.

■ There is persuasive evidence of systematic overinvestment by some companies in studies documenting significant shareholder gains from takeovers.[11] Why do some firms underinvest while others apparently invest too much?

■ The United States has the most efficient capital markets of any nation. How can such efficient capital markets be guilty of apparently sub-optimal investment behavior?

■ The investment problem seems to have become more significant today than it was several decades ago. Why this is so is another puzzle that must be addressed in understanding the investment problem.

Clearly, it is not so simple as concluding that the U.S. underinvests or that the U.S. has a short time horizon. Yet many of these complexities only reinforce the notion that the U.S. system is missing the mark by failing to invest the appropriate amount in the appropriate forms. Explaining these paradoxes, as well as the differences in investment behavior across industries, companies, and forms of investment, is essential to gaining a full understanding of the U.S. investment problem.

THE DETERMINANTS OF INVESTMENT

The determinants of investment can be grouped into three broad categories: the macroeconomic environment; the allocation mechanisms by which capital moves from its holders to investment projects; and the conditions surrounding specific investment opportunities themselves.

The *macroeconomic environment* establishes the context in which investment by all firms in a nation takes place. Investment tends to flourish in a fiscally stable and growing economy; the expectation of stability and future economic growth reassures investors of adequate returns over the long term. In the United States, high federal budget deficits, low national savings rates, sporadic and unpredictable changes in tax policy, and a tax code favoring consumption over investment have dampened both private and public sector investment over the past two decades.[12]

The *capital allocation mechanisms* in an economy work through two distinct but related channels: the *external* capital market, in which

holders of equity and debt provide capital to particular companies; and the *internal* capital market, in which companies allocate the internally and externally generated funds at their disposal to particular investment programs. Previous work has focused on individual aspects of these markets but has not addressed them as a whole. Our research focuses on the dual markets and their effects on investment behavior.

Project-specific conditions reflect the different payoffs that can be gained from a particular investment project. The potential returns of an investment can be affected by the nature of the industry, the competitive position of the company, and the nation or region in which the investment is made. My previous research suggests that the capacity to invest and innovate effectively depends largely upon the following factors: the presence of specialized skills, technology, and infrastructure; sophisticated and demanding local customers; capable local suppliers; competitive local companies in industries closely related by technology, skills, or customers; and a local environment that encourages sustained investment and vigorous competition.[13] These attributes combine to form a self-reinforcing system. Competitive advantage, then, grows not from a comfortable home environment but out of the pressure and challenges generated by these elements.

Sustained private investment can not only improve the skills of employees, increase the capabilities of supporting industries, or upgrade the sophistication of consumer demand, but also generates local "externalities" that develop and reinforce other parts of the system. Such "spillovers" from investment play a crucial role in building competitiveness.

The External Capital Market

Four attributes of the external capital market are of principal importance for investment behavior. The first is the pattern of share ownership and agency relationships, which refers to the nature of the owners, the extent of their representation by agents, and the size of the stakes held in companies. The second is the goals of owners and agents, which influence their desired investment outcomes. The ability to hold debt and equity jointly is one important

---

11. For a discussion of the corporate overinvestment problem and the role of corporate restructuring in addressing it, see Michael C. Jensen, "Corporate Control and the Politics of Finance," *Journal of Applied Corporate Finance*, Summer 1991.

12. See Lawrence, cited in note 8.
13. See M.E. Porter, *The Competitive Advantage of Nations*, New York: Macmillan, The Free Press, 1990.

influence on goals, as is the existence of a principal-agent relationship. The third attribute is the approach and information used by owners or their agents in monitoring and valuing companies. There is a spectrum of approaches to valuation ranging from fundamental research based on company-specific information to investing in index funds. The approach used by owners or agents will depend on their goals, the information available, and their incentives for information-gathering. The final important attribute is the ways in which owners or their agents influence management behavior in the companies whose shares they own. These four attributes are interrelated and, over time, mutually reinforcing.

The predominant configuration of the U.S. external capital market is very different from that in Japan and Germany. Although exceptions exist in all three nations, in each case there is a set of circumstances that affect the majority of large companies.

Fluid Capital. In the U.S., the attributes combine to create a system distinguished by fluid capital. Funds supplied by external capital providers move rapidly from company to company, usually based on perceptions of opportunities for near-term appreciation. Publicly traded companies increasingly rely on a transient ownership base comprised of institutional investors such as pension funds, mutual funds, or other money managers, which act as agents for individual investors. Such owners have increased their holdings from 8% of total equity in 1950 to 60% in 1990. The performance of U.S. money managers is typically evaluated based on quarterly or annual appreciation relative to stock indices, and they thus seek near-term appreciation of their shares, holding stock for an average of only 1.9 years. Due to legal constraints on concentrated ownership, fiduciary requirements that encourage extensive diversification, and a strong desire for liquidity, these investors hold portfolios involving small stakes in many, if not hundreds, of companies.

Because of their fragmented stakes in numerous companies, short expected holding periods, and lack of access to "inside" information through disclosure or board membership, institutional investors tend to base their buy and sell decisions heavily on relatively limited information oriented toward pre-dicting near-term share price movements. Those investors that do conduct fundamental research are still highly sensitive to the timing of purchases and sales, given the pressure to show near-term appreciation. Investors are driven by the system to focus on measurable company attributes, such as current earnings or patent approvals, as proxies of a company's value. The value proxies employed vary among different classes of companies and can lead to underinvestment in some industries, or in certain kinds of investment, while allowing overinvestment in others.[14]

We can divide companies in the American market into three broad groups: (1) established companies in relatively mature industries; (2) companies in emerging or obviously high-technology sectors; and (3) companies in the throes of a clearly visible discontinuity. In the first category, the dominant value proxy is current earnings, which have a strong effect on share prices. For companies in the latter two groups, the value proxies are different. In such cases, current earnings are clearly an inappropriate indicator, and thus investments are based on value proxies such as scientific successes, regulatory decisions, and perceived rapid growth prospects. In such sectors, current earnings play a limited role until the firm is seen as "established."

Owing to the inability of many proxy-based approaches to outperform the market, some institutions have moved to invest as much as 70% to 80% of their equity holdings in index funds, which simply attempt to match the performance of the broad market and thus involve no use of company-specific information.

Despite their large aggregate holdings, U.S. institutional investors do not sit on corporate boards and have virtually no real influence on management behavior.

Dedicated Capital. The Japanese and German systems are fundamentally different from the U.S. system. Overall, Japan and Germany have systems defined by dedicated capital in which the funds of principal owners remain invested in companies over long periods of time. The dominant owners are principals rather than agents and hold significant ownership stakes. They are virtually perma-

---

14. Studies find that the stock market responds positively, on average, to announcements of increases in capital expenditures, R&D, and joint ventures. But because such studies examine broad populations of companies, they do not address the question of whether there are biases in particular subpopulations, which our theory would suggest is the proper question. For one of the few studies that attempts to address this issue, see Su H. Chan, John A. Martin, and John W. Kensinger, "The Market Rewards Promising R&D—and Punishes the Rest," in this issue.

> **Japan and Germany have systems defined by dedicated capital in which the funds of principal owners remain invested in companies over long periods of time. The dominant owners are principals rather than agents and hold significant ownership stakes.**

nent owners who seek long-term appreciation, and their goals are more relationship- than transaction-driven. Suppliers and customers own stakes in each other, with the aim not of profiting from share ownership so much as cementing their business relationships.

Because principal Japanese and German owners hold significant shares for long periods, they have both the incentive and the ability to engage in extensive and ongoing information-gathering about the companies they own. Unlike the American system, principal Japanese and German owners are driven not by the need to make quick decisions on buying or selling stock for profit taking, but by the desire to assess the ongoing prospects of the company. They therefore command the respect of management, have access to inside information, and, particularly in Germany, exert considerable influence on management behavior.

Interestingly, the non-permanent owners/agents in Japan trade as much or even more frequently than those in the United States, and base buy and sell choices on even less information.[15] Yet it is important to recognize that, in both Japan and Germany, share prices and pressure from non-permanent owners/agents have virtually no influence on management.

The Internal Capital Market

The internal capital market is the system by which corporations allocate the capital available from both internal and external sources among competing investment projects within and across business units. The most important influences on the internal capital market can be divided into four categories that parallel those that shape the external market: corporate goals; organizational principles governing the relationship between senior management and business units; the information and methods used to value and monitor internal investment options; and the nature of intervention by senior managers into investment projects. Again, the predominant U.S. system of allocating capital internally differs markedly from those in Japan and Germany.

Maximizing Investment Returns. The U.S. internal system can be characterized as one structured to maximize measurable investment returns. It is organized to motivate management to achieve such returns, to raise accountability for unit financial performance, and to base decision-making and investment allocation heavily on financial criteria.

In the U.S. system, corporate goals are centered on earning high financial returns. Maximizing "shareholder value," *as measured by current stock price*, is explicitly codified in many companies as the corporate goal. The dominant influence on corporate goals is management, who are often subject to limited direct influence either by boards, which are dominated by outside directors with no other links to the firm, or by owners, who typically hold fragmented stakes in hundreds of different companies. The goals set by American managers are typically framed in terms of ROI or increasing stock price. The frequency with which managers meet with investors and analysts (once per week for CEOs, three times per week for CFOs) is both a cause and an indication of their attention to stock prices. Compensation and reward practices, based largely on current accounting profits and unrestricted stock options, only accentuate their importance.

Over the last two decades, many American companies have adopted a form of decentralization involving highly autonomous business units and limited information flow both vertically and horizontally. This is accentuated by the tendency for senior management to have little knowledge or experience in many of the company's businesses and to lack the technical background essential to understanding the substance of products or processes (partly because such background and experience are unnecessary in the typical decision-making process). Decision-making involves limited dialogue among business units or across different functions, and little consensus building. All of these factors have distanced management from the details of the business. Extensive diversification into unrelated areas has accentuated these tendencies and further restricted the flow of information throughout the organization.

---

15. The very high turnover rate of this rapidly traded portion of the Tokyo Stock Exchange is in stark contrast to the long holding periods of principal Japanese investors. The rapidly traded portion of the market lowers the average turnover on the TSE to 2.6 years, which is actually higher than the turnover of 2.8 years in the United States reported by Froot, Shleifer, and Stein (1992). But this comparison obscures the important difference that 70% of Japanese equity is comprised of holdings that were held, on average, over five years. Indeed, the most stable group of Japanese shareholders, insurance companies (accounting for 4% of total equity)

and corporations (30%) held their shares for 18.3 and 7.4 years, on average, including shares that are actively traded. By contrast, no single group of U.S. stockholders had average holdings over five years.

For a comparison of Japanese and U.S. shareholder practices, see Kenneth Froot, Andrei Sheifer, and Jeremy Stein, "Shareholder Trading Practices and Corporate Investment Horizons," in the project on Capital Choices, Harvard Business School and Council on Competitiveness, 1992. The article also appears in this issue.

Both as a cause and an effect of the limited information available to top management, capital budgeting takes place largely through "by the numbers" systems in which unit or functional managers are required to justify investment projects quantitatively. Important investments such as R&D, advertising, or market entry are often not treated as capital investments at all; rather they are negotiated as part of the annual budgeting process, which is driven by a concern for current profitability. Intangible investments such as training may not even be tracked by the financial system and fall prey to deferral in the name of increasing near-term profits. Central control is exerted infrequently and occurs through strict financial budgeting and control systems that focus on financial measures of the unit's performance. Investment projects are placed on accelerated schedules under tight budgets, and senior managers intervene only when financial measures indicate a project is failing.

Securing Corporate Position. The Japanese and German internal capital allocation systems are significantly different from those in the United States, most notably in corporate goals and the flow of information. In both Japanese and German companies, the dominant goal is to ensure the perpetuation of the enterprise. Both Japanese and German companies practice a form of decentralization involving much greater information flow among multiple units in the company as well as with customers and suppliers. They tend to be less diversified than their American counterparts and diversification occurs into more closely related businesses. Managers are more likely to have a technical background and long tenure in the business of the firm. Top managers get involved in all important decisions, which are usually made after extensive face-to-face consultation and discussions aimed at building consensus.

Financial control and capital budgeting are practiced in Japan and Germany, but investments are heavily driven by technical considerations and the desire to ensure the firm's long-term position in the business. German companies are particularly oriented toward attaining technical leadership. Japanese companies place special value on market share, new product development, technological position, and participation in businesses and technologies that will be crucial in the next decade.

It is interesting to note that American innovations in management practices have, by and large, reduced the amount of face-to-face consultation, information flow, and direct involvement of management in the name of responsiveness and management efficiency. Many of these innovations were the American solutions to the problems of size and diversity that arose during the diversification boom of the 1960s. They preceded the major changes that occurred in the external capital markets. In contrast, Japanese innovations in management, such as total quality management and greater cross-functional coordination, result in much greater vertical and horizontal flows of information in support of management decision-making. This comes at the expense of efficiency in the short run but often results in greater effectiveness and efficiency over time as knowledge and abilities cumulate.

COMPARATIVE CAPITAL ALLOCATION SYSTEMS

The external and internal capital markets are linked and form a self-reinforcing national system for allocating investment capital. The way corporations allocate capital internally will be influenced by their perceptions of how equity holders and lenders value companies. At the same time, investors' process of valuation will be affected by their perceptions of how companies are managed and how they allocate their funds internally, thus creating a circular chain of influence. Reinforcing this effect, the use of stock options in management compensation creates a direct link between stock market valuation and management behavior.

Effects on Investment Behavior

The U.S. system for allocating investment capital creates the following tendencies and biases in investment behavior, which differ from those in Japan and Germany.

■ The U.S. system is less supportive of investment overall, because of its sensitivity to current returns for many established companies combined with corporate goals that stress current stock price over long-term corporate value. This explains why the average level of investment in U.S. industry lags that in Japan and Germany.

■ The U.S. system favors those forms of investment for which returns are most readily measurable due to the importance of financial returns and the limited information available to investors and managers. This helps explain why the United States underinvests, on average, in intangible assets, where returns are more difficult to measure.

- The U.S. system favors investment in discrete projects as opposed to ongoing programs of complementary investment that yield sustained capability improvements. This helps explain why the United States underinvests in areas such as employee training and supplier relationships.

- While the U.S. system is prone to underinvest in some forms, it simultaneously overinvests in others. The U.S. system heavily favors acquisitions, which involve assets that can be easily valued, over internal development projects that are more difficult to value and that constitute a drag on current earnings.

- The U.S. system encourages investment in some sectors while limiting it in others. It is at its best with companies in obviously high technology or emerging industries, especially those with rapid growth and high upside potential. The American system also supports investment in turnarounds or other situations of clear discontinuity. In these cases, investors recognize that current earnings are irrelevant and seek other value proxies, such as patents, new product announcements, and the track records of new management, that are more supportive of investment. This helps explain why the United States invests more than its competitors in some industries but less in others, why it performs well in funding emerging companies, and why it often awards high stock prices to turnarounds with current losses.

- The U.S. system allows some types of companies to overinvest. For example, case studies of takeovers demonstrate a tendency by target company managements to continue investing (or accumulating cash) despite few profitable opportunities as long as current earnings are satisfactory or until a company's situation so clearly deteriorates that it changes hands.[16] This helps explain why some companies waste resources while U.S. industry as a whole lags in investment.

There are companies and owners that operate differently from the predominant U.S. system and that achieve superior results. Firms with permanent family ownership, such as Hallmark, Hewlett-Packard, Motorola, and others seem to enjoy competitive advantages in investing. Investors such as Warren Buffett's Berkshire Hathaway have thrived by becoming, in effect, permanent owners of acquired companies, supporting well-performing current management, and concentrating on franchise building. Such investors seem to have devised their own alternative ownership and governance systems to overcome many of the weaknesses of the U.S. system.

Venture capital firms and leveraged buyout groups are also structured in ways designed to overcome some of the problems that trouble the dominant U.S. system. In both cases, investors with concentrated stakes receive inside information, participate actively on corporate boards, and exert strong influence over management. Yet neither venture capital firms nor LBOs represent the ideal solution. In both cases, the term of the investment is limited. Rather than being long-term, quasi-permanent owners, most American venture capital and LBO firms are at best medium-term owners who feel intense pressure to sell companies or take them public. This leads to a tendency to emphasize the rapid achievement of profits, and the company enters or reenters the mainstream system (perhaps prematurely) with its attendant problems.

Trade-Offs Among Systems

The U.S. system for allocating investment capital has major disadvantages, yet the Japanese and German systems are not ideal in every respect. While reform of the U.S. system is sorely needed, our system has important strengths that should be preserved. The U.S. system is good at reallocating capital among sectors, funding emerging fields, shifting resources out of "unprofitable" industries, and achieving high private returns each period, as measured by higher corporate returns on investment. Such responsiveness and flexibility, however, are often achieved at the price of failing to invest enough to secure competitive positions in existing businesses, investing in the wrong forms, and overinvesting in some circumstances.

The Japanese and German systems encourage aggressive investment to upgrade capabilities and productivity in existing fields. They also encourage

---

16. The slow-growth, mature industries (particularly those facing strong international competition) which our theory identifies as most vulnerable to overinvestment are those which Hall (1992) identifies as experiencing the predominant share of financial restructurings and control changes. See Bronwyn

H. Hall, "Corporate Restructuring and Investment Time Horizons," in the project on Capital Choices, Harvard Business School and Council on Competitiveness, 1992.

internal diversification into related fields—the kind of diversification that builds upon and extends corporate strengths. This comes at the cost, however, of a tendency to overinvest in capacity, to produce too many products, and to maintain unprofitable businesses indefinitely. For this reason, the U.S. system may come closer to optimizing short-term private returns.

The Japanese and German systems, however, appear to come closer to optimizing long-term private and social returns. Their greater focus on long-term corporate position—encouraged by an ownership structure and governance process that incorporate the interests of employees, suppliers, customers, and the local community—allow the Japanese and German economies to better capture the social benefits of private investment.

DIRECTIONS FOR SYSTEM-WIDE REFORM

The aim of reform should be to create an environment in which managers make investments that maximize the long-term value of their corporations. Capital providers must have interests aligned with those of the corporation and the information necessary to make sound valuation decisions and appropriate corporate investment choices. Corporations must be organized and managed in ways that encourage investment in the forms essential to building competitiveness. Finally, public policymakers must identify those areas in which private returns diverge from those of society as a whole, and craft laws and regulations to better align them. Constructive pressures from capital providers are beneficial and necessary, provided that they have the proper goals and information. Regulators must refrain from creating "protective" measures that insulate firms from such pressures.

Reform of the U.S. system must recognize it is an internally consistent system involving many parts. A series of changes must be made, ideally all at once. Altering one aspect of the system without simultaneously altering others may well lead to unwanted consequences. Giving institutional investors more power over management without changing their goals, for example, may heighten pressures toward

underinvestment. Appropriate reform will also require that each important constituency give up some of its perceived benefits under the current system. Institutions should not expect to gain greater influence over management without giving up some of their trading flexibility, while management should not expect informed and committed owners without giving them a real voice in corporate decisions.

Many current proposals for improving the U.S. system are counterproductive. They suffer from a partial view of the problem and address symptoms rather than causes. Taxing stock transactions, for example, will make stock markets less efficient without addressing the underlying reasons that investors trade. Similarly, eliminating quarterly financial reports will make investors less informed and will have little impact on the forces that make current earnings so important. Increasing the use of stock options in management compensation only heightens pressure to maximize current stock price unless restrictions are placed on managers' ability to exercise those options. Finally, providing government subsidies for particular sectors or creating joint production ventures allows companies to economize on investment but deals only indirectly with the underlying problem. These approaches do not address the reasons that companies are seemingly unable to make the investments needed for competitiveness. Moreover, they run the risk of blunting innovation and undermining competitiveness. The only real solution to the failure of the U.S. capital allocation system is to address it as a "system."

We can create a more appropriate system of capital allocation if we choose to do so. Improving the U.S. system for capital allocation will require complementary changes in public policy, the behavior of institutional investors, and the practices of management. Reform is needed in the five broad areas listed below. Such changes will not only reduce underinvestment but also limit overinvestment in those companies and those forms prone to it.

Improve the macroeconomic environment. Steps are needed to increase the stability of the macroeconomic environment and to enlarge the pool of savings in order to reduce risk premiums and lower the cost of capital.[17] A more supportive macroeconomic

---

17. It is important to note that the most relevant cost of capital for investment is not the hypothetical average cost of capital for a nation, but the cost of capital for a particular firm and for a particular form of investment. The perceived cost of capital for an individual firm or project is affected by the macroeconomic

environment but not determined by it. The capital allocation process itself exerts an equally important effect through its influence on how investors and managers perceive companies and value projects.

Venture capital firms and leveraged buyout groups are structured in ways designed to overcome some of the problems that trouble the dominant U.S. system. In both cases, investors with concentrated stakes receive inside information, participate actively on corporate boards, and exert strong influence over management.

environment will provide a foundation for the other systemic changes needed, but this alone will not change the structure of incentives and information that underlie the true capital allocation problem.

Expand true ownership throughout the system. The current concept of ownership in the U.S. system is too limited, and ownership is largely restricted to outside shareholders. Outside owners should be encouraged to hold larger stakes and to take a more active and constructive role in companies. Ownership should be expanded to include directors, managers, employees, and even customers and suppliers. Expanded ownership will foster commonality of interest and help make investors more aware of the value of investment spillovers, such as more highly skilled workers, that strengthen firms and benefit related industries and the economy as a whole.

Better align the goals of capital providers, corporations, directors, managers, employees, customers, suppliers, and society. More ownership *per se* will not be sufficient if the goals of owners, corporations, and others are not aligned with each other and with maximizing the long-term value of corporations. It is possible to create a system of incentives and to alter rules in a way that helps align the goals of all corporate constituencies.

Improve the information used in decision-making. Even if goals are better aligned, the quality of information used to allocate capital throughout the system will affect investment choices. The U.S. system of investment should offer greater access to information that better reflects actual corporate performance. Both investors and managers should be encouraged to supplement strictly quantitative measures of investment and performance with assessments of qualitative factors, such as the quality of the firm's work force or its level of technological sophistication.

Foster more productive modes of interaction and influence among capital providers, corporations, and business units. Appropriate investment choices require effective systems and processes by which owners interact with corporate management and corporate management interacts with business and functional units.

Implications for Public Policy

Government policies, laws, and regulations play a decisive role in defining the macroeconomic environment and both the external and the internal capital markets. The weaknesses of the U.S. system and the importance of regulation in defining that system suggest that those policy areas that affect investment behavior (and thus corporate performance) should be reexamined.

The current American system is the result of explicit regulatory choices typically designed to promote goals other than growth in corporate investment. They have developed out of the regulatory regime established in the 1930s to deal with the perceived abuses occurring in financial markets at that time. Yet the record shows a near total failure by legislators from the 1930s to the 1980s to consider the effects of regulation on corporate investment behavior.

The principles guiding U.S. regulation address some legitimate and commendable purposes, and have achieved the goal of keeping abuses to a bare minimum. Nevertheless, the cumulative pattern of regulation has had unfortunate, unintended consequences for investment behavior. Through diversification requirements and the threat of lawsuits, the U.S. system encouraged excessive diversification and the holding of many small stakes in companies, which in turn has led to frequent trading and heightened the influence of accounting earnings on buy and sell decisions.

Some of the most important directions for public policy change are outlined in a table below. These reforms rest on principles that differ markedly from those which have defined the regulatory framework of the traditional U.S. system. They seek to create incentives that support corporate investment rather than focus on avoiding abuses through regulatory restraints with unintended consequences for corporate investment. For example, broadening corporate ownership and allowing investors to hold larger stakes will better align the goals of capital providers, corporations, managers, employees, and society; it will create a constructive tension among these groups that prevents unilateral, self-interested action by either investors or managers. Capital providers thus become knowledgeable and constructive participants rather than adversaries. Under this provision, the market would continue to have the strength of a wide investor base, while gaining the benefit of owners with larger stakes in particular companies. At the same time, the large number of substantial U.S. institutional investors will prevent any undue concentration of economic power.

Implications for Institutional Investors

The U.S. system of capital allocation creates perverse outcomes for institutional investors, especially pension funds. Such institutions should be the ideal long-term investors. Instead, we have the paradoxical situation in which many institutions, especially pension funds, are entrusted with funds for extremely long periods yet trade actively. Institutions are at odds with management, whom they see as misapplying corporate resources while they feel powerless to do anything about it. Many institutions relish takeovers, not only because stock prices rise quickly but also because they are a way to dislodge entrenched managements. Worst of all, institutions are trapped as crucial actors in a system that undermines the long-term earning power of the American companies on which they must ultimately depend for the bulk of their portfolio investments.

While the U.S. system is partly the result of regulation, there are positive steps that can be taken by institutions without the need for public policy changes (see table below). First and foremost, institutions must begin to understand why managements view them as adversaries. They must understand the subtle consequences of their monitoring and valuation practices on corporate investment behavior. They must also recognize that greater influence over management will come only at the price of less flexibility, less trading, and greater knowledge of and concern with company fundamentals.

The new breed of institutional investor that we envision will have a larger stake in the corporations in its portfolio, greater knowledge about the companies, and a more important role in corporate oversight and decision-making. Index funds, which might be seen as long-term investors, cannot play this role effectively. With their investment philosophy, extreme fragmentation of ownership, and lack of incentive to invest in information, index funds have little realistic prospect of credibly monitoring and influencing management behavior.

These needed reforms are likely to be resisted by some institutional investors who have grown up in the current system, perceive the risks of a more active role as investors, and are currently ill-equipped to move to new investment practices. Despite these challenges, the end result of systemic reform will prove to be far superior to the situation today.

Implications for Corporations

The U.S. system of capital allocation raises challenging questions for the directors and managers of American companies, particularly those that are publicly traded. Stated most boldly, our research suggests the need to reexamine much of what constitutes the U.S. system of management, with its extreme approach to managing decentralization, its limited flow of information, and its reliance on financial control and quantitative capital budgeting processes. This system, a post-war innovation that has been widely diffused to other countries, carries subtle costs for investment behavior, particularly investments in intangible and non-traditional forms.

Managers are not simply victims of the U.S. system, but have helped to create it. They have not only shaped internal capital allocation practices, but they have defined their relationship with the external market through their board selections, disclosure practices, and the nature of their discussions with investors. American managers are the group best positioned to make changes in the current system, and to benefit most from reform.

While it is not possible here to explore fully all the potential implications of our research for corporations, some of the most significant directions for change are listed in the table opposite. Moving in the appropriate directions may be uncomfortable for some managers who have grown up in the current system. Directors may have to take the lead in some companies to push through needed reforms, not only in corporate governance but also in internal management practices.

TOWARD A SUPERIOR AMERICAN SYSTEM

Corporate investment behavior defies simple explanations. Its causes go to the very heart of how corporations are owned, how capital markets function, and how companies are managed in a world of international competition. Although our research on corporate investment behavior is by no means the final word on the subject, the evidence does suggest that moving in the directions described promises to

RECOMMENDATIONS FOR CORPORATIONS

- Seek long-term owners and give them a direct voice in governance

- Refrain from erecting artificial anti-takeover defenses that insulate management from competitive pressures

- See management buy-outs as a fallback solution

- Nominate significant owners, customers, suppliers, employees, and community representatives to the board of directors

- Link incentive compensation to measures of competitive position

- Move away from unrelated diversification

- Shift from fragmented to integrated organizational structures

- Transform financial control systems into position-based control systems based on
  - broader definition of assets
  - measurement of asset quality and productivity in addition to quantity
  - relative instead of absolute measures

- Move to universal investment budgeting by
  - evaluating investment programs instead of discrete projects
  - unifying treatment of all forms of investment
  - separating the determination of required asset position from evaluation of the means of achieving it

yield more appropriate investment behavior in American industry without threatening those aspects of the current system that represent advantages.

The Convergence of National Systems

There is evidence that Japan and Germany may be moving toward a more American-like system in certain respects, but actual changes have thus far been modest. Observers note, for example, the declining influence of Japanese banks as companies rely less on debt capital and the impending liquidity standards that may require that Japanese banks to sell some of their equity holdings. In the internal market, observers have recently noted shifts toward greater emphasis on profitability and the beginnings of unrelated diversification. In Germany there are proposals to limit bank ownership of equity. Yet even if banks are forced to sell some of their equity holdings, they will first sell their non-permanent shares, which are actively traded and have little influence on corporate behavior. Internally, Japanese firms have long been concerned with profits insofar as they help fund their investment programs. The increased profit consciousness of Japanese firms today thus reflects the need to raise cash flow during a time of depressed market conditions, not a concern with stock prices. If major changes were to occur in the Japanese or German systems, the threat to these nations' economies would be substantial due to the relatively uninformed traded capital markets.

The U.S. system is also experiencing changes in several areas. Some institutional investors are having discussions with management, some boards are taking a more active role in corporations, and some firms are developing closer relationships with customers, suppliers, and employees. Yet these changes are occurring only at the margin and, in the U.S., reflect frustration at the current situation rather than a shift in the goals of investors, boards, or managers. The underlying causes of our investment problem—particularly the goals and information that guide the decisions of investors, directors, and managers—remain unchanged. We should not let isolated improvements nor hope that Japan and Germany are changing prevent reform of our national system. It exacts a cost on our corporations and our economy that will remain even if Japan's and Germany's systems evolve to match our own.

The Promise of Reform

The suggested changes can be expected to produce the following benefits:
- increase true ownership in the economy by giving owners a long-term, active role in companies;
- better align the goals of American shareholders, corporations, managers, employees, and society;
- improve the quality of information used in investment decisions;
- allow investors more effectively to scrutinize management performance based on criteria more appropriate to competitiveness; and
- make internal management processes more consistent with the sources of competitive advantage.

Such changes will not only encourage investment in more appropriate forms, but also reduce wasted investment in companies most liable to it.

If progress can be made on these fronts, it will not only reduce the disadvantages of the U.S. system but could result in a system superior to that in Japan and Germany. A reformed U.S. system would be more flexible, more responsive, and even better informed in allocating capital than those in Japan and Germany. Investors in a reformed U.S. system would be long-term owners, though not necessarily permanent ones. This would provide more flexibility to withdraw capital if long-term prospects were genuinely unattractive than exists in Japan or Germany. In a reformed U.S. system, the substantial number of sophisticated American investors would redirect their valuation methods and make investment choices that would be better informed than those in Japan and Germany. Owners would have the incentive to gather more information that is useful in evaluating the creation of long-term private and social value.

A reformed U.S. system would also produce more careful monitoring of management and more pressure on poor performers than exists in Japan or Germany. The result should be less wasted investment. With greater incentives for individual employee performance and less tolerance of non-performers, a reformed U.S. system would avoid some of the internal inefficiencies of the Japanese and German systems. Finally, a reformed U.S. system, with its already higher levels of disclosure and transparency, promises to be fairer to all shareholders than the Japanese and German systems.

But changing the U.S. system of capital allocation will be made difficult by the need for all the major corporate constituencies to sacrifice some of their interests in the pursuit of a more satisfying overall system. We must avoid the tendency to take half-measures and tinker at the margin. The widespread concern and dissatisfaction with the status quo suggests that system-wide reform may be possible. The gains will accrue not only to investors and firms, but will increase the rate of long-term productivity growth, competitiveness, and prosperity of the U.S. economy.

- MICHAEL PORTER

is C. Roland Christensen Professor of Business Administration at the Harvard Business School.

THE MODERN INDUSTRIAL REVOLUTION, EXIT, AND THE FAILURE OF INTERNAL CONTROL SYSTEMS

*by Michael C. Jensen,
Harvard Business School**

undamental technological, political, regulatory, and economic forces are radically changing the worldwide competitive environment. We have not seen such a metamorphosis of the economic landscape since the industrial revolution of the 19th century. The scope and pace of the changes over the past two decades qualify this period as a modern industrial revolution, and I predict it will take decades more for these forces to be worked out fully in the worldwide economy.

Although the current and 19th-century transformations of the U.S. economy are separated by almost 100 years, there are striking parallels between them—most notably, rapid technological and organizational change leading to declining production costs and increasing average (but decreasing marginal) productivity of labor. During both periods, moreover, these developments resulted in widespread excess capacity, reduced rates of growth in labor income, and, ultimately, downsizing and exit.

The capital markets played a major role in eliminating excess capacity both in the late 19th century and in the 1980s. The merger boom of the 1890s brought about a massive consolidation of independent firms and closure of marginal facilities. In the 1980s the capital markets helped eliminate excess capacity through leveraged acquisitions, stock buybacks, hostile takeovers, leveraged buyouts, and divisional sales.

And much as the takeover specialists of the 1980s were disparaged by managers, policymakers, and the press, their 19th-century counterparts were vilified as "robber barons." In both cases, the popular reaction against "financiers" was followed by public policy changes that restricted the capital markets. The turn of the century saw the passage of antitrust laws that restricted business combinations; the late 1980s gave rise to re-regulation of the credit markets, antitakeover legislation, and court decisions that all but shut down the market for corporate control.

*This is a shortened version of a paper by the same title that was originally published in the *Journal of Finance* (July 1993), which was based in turn on my Presidential Address to the American Finance Association in January 1993. It is reprinted here by permission of the American Finance Association. I wish to express my appreciation for the research assistance of Chris Allen, Brian Barry, Susan Brumfield, Karin Monsler, and particularly Donna Feinberg, the support of the Division of Research of the Harvard Business School, and the comments of and discussions with George Baker, Carliss Baldwin, Joe Bower, Alfred Chandler, Harry and Linda DeAngelo, Ben Esty, Takashi Hikino, Steve Kaplan, Nancy Koehn, Claudio Loderer, George Lodge, John Long, Kevin Murphy, Malcolm Salter, Rene Stulz, Richard Tedlow, and, especially, Robert Hall, Richard Hackman, and Karen Wruck.

Although the vast increases in productivity associated with the 19th-century industrial revolution increased aggregate welfare, the resulting obsolescence of human and physical capital caused great hardship, misunderstanding, and bitterness. As noted in 1873 by Henry Ward Beecher, a well-known commentator and influential clergyman of the time,

The present period will always be memorable in the dark days of commerce in America. We have had commercial darkness at other times. There have been these depressions, but none so obstinate and none so universal... Great Britain has felt it; France has felt it; all Austria and her neighborhood has experienced it. It is cosmopolitan. It is distinguished by its obstinacy from former like periods of commercial depression. Remedies have no effect. Party confidence, all stimulating persuasion, have not lifted the pall, and practical men have waited, feeling that if they could tide over a year they could get along; but they could not tide over the year. If only one or two years could elapse they could save themselves. The years have lapsed, and they were worse off than they were before. What is the matter? What has happened? Why, from the very height of prosperity without any visible warning, without even a cloud the size of a man's hand visible on the horizon, has the cloud gathered, as it were, from the center first, spreading all over the sky?[1]

Almost 20 years later, on July 4, 1892, the Populist Party platform adopted at the party's first convention in Omaha reflected continuing unrest while pointing to financiers as the cause of the current problems:

We meet in the midst of a nation brought to the verge of moral, political, and material ruin... The fruits of the toil of millions are boldly stolen to build up colossal fortunes for the few, unprecedented in the history of mankind; and the possessors of these in turn despise the republic and endanger liberty. From

the same prolific womb of government injustice are bred two great classes of tramps and millionaires.[2]

Technological and other developments that began in the mid-20th century have culminated in the past two decades in a similar situation: rapidly improving productivity, the creation of overcapacity, and, consequently, the requirement for exit. Although efficient exit has profound import for productivity and social wealth, research on the topic[3] has been relatively sparse since the 1942 publication of Joseph Schumpeter's famous description of capitalism as a process of "creative destruction." In Schumpeter's words,

Every piece of business strategy...must be seen in its role in the perennial gale of creative destruction... The usual theorist's paper and the usual government commission's report practically never try to see that behavior... as an attempt by those firms to keep on their feet, on ground that is slipping away from under them. In other words, the problem that is usually being visualized is how capitalism administers existing structures, whereas the relevant problem is how it creates and destroys them.[4]

Current technological and political changes are bringing the question of efficient exit to the forefront, and the adjustments necessary to cope with such changes will receive renewed attention from managers, policymakers, and researchers in the coming decade.

In this paper, I begin by reviewing the industrial revolution of the 19th century to shed light on current economic trends. Drawing parallels with the 1800s, I discuss in some detail worldwide changes driving the demand for exit in today's economy. I also describe the barriers to efficient exit in the U.S. economy, and the role of the market for corporate control—takeovers, LBOs, and other leveraged restructurings—in surmounting those barriers during the 1980s.

1. Walter W. Price, *We Have Recovered Before!* (Harper & Brothers: New York, 1933), p. 6.

2. Donald L., McMurray, *Coxey's Army: A Study of the Industrial Army Movement of 1894* (Little, Brown: Boston, 1929), p. 7.

3. For a rare study of exit in the finance literature, see the analysis of the retrenchment of the U.S. steel industry in Harry DeAngelo and Linda DeAngelo, "Union Negotiations and Corporate Policy: A Study of Labor Concessions in the Domestic Steel Industry during the 1980s," *Journal of Financial Economics* 30 (1991), 3-43. See also Pankaj Ghemawat and Barry Nalebuff, "Exit," *Rand Journal of Economics* 16 (Summer, 1985), 184-194. For a detailed comparison of U.S. and Japanese retrenchment in the 1970s and early 1980s, see Douglas Anderson,

"Managing Retreat: Disinvestment Policy," in Thomas K. McCraw, ed., *America Versus Japan* (Harvard Business School Press: Boston, 1986), 337-372. Joseph L. Bower analyzes the private and political responses to decline in the petrochemical industry in *When Markets Quake* (Harvard Business School Press: Boston, 1986). Kathryn Harrigan presents detailed firm and industry studies in two of her books: *Managing Maturing Businesses: Restructuring Declining Industries and Revitalizing Troubled Operations* (Lexington Books, 1988) and *Strategies for Declining Businesses* (Lexington Books, 1980).

4. Joseph A., Schumpeter, *Capitalism, Socialism, and Democracy* (Harper Torchbook Edition: New York, 1976), p. 83.

With the shutdown of the capital markets in the 1990s, the challenge of accomplishing efficient exit has been transferred to corporate internal control systems. With few exceptions, however, U.S. managements and boards have failed to bring about timely exit and downsizing without external pressure. Although product market competition will eventually eliminate overcapacity, this solution generates huge unnecessary costs. (The costs of this solution have now become especially apparent in Japan, where a virtual breakdown of the internal control systems, coupled with a complete absence of capital market influence, has resulted in enormous overcapacity—a problem that Japanese companies are only beginning to address.)

At the close of the paper, I offer suggestions for reforming U.S. internal corporate control mechanisms. In particular, I hold up several features of venture capital and LBO firms such as Kleiner Perkins and KKR for emulation by large, public companies—notably (1) smaller, more active, and better informed boards; and (2) significant equity ownership by board members as well as managers. I also urge boards and managers to encourage larger holdings and greater participation by people I call "active" investors.

THE SECOND INDUSTRIAL REVOLUTION[5]

The Industrial Revolution was distinguished by a shift to capital-intensive production, rapid growth in productivity and living standards, the formation of large corporate hierarchies, overcapacity, and, eventually, closure of facilities. Originating in Britain in the late 18th century, the First Industrial Revolution witnessed the application of new energy sources to methods of production. The mid-19th century saw another wave of massive change with the birth of modern transportation and communication facilities, including the railroad, telegraph, steamship, and cable systems. Coupled with the invention of high-speed consumer packaging technology, these innovations gave rise to the mass production and distribution systems of the

late 19th and early 20th centuries—the Second Industrial Revolution.

The dramatic changes that occurred from the middle to the end of the century clearly warrant the term "revolution." Inventions such as the McCormick reaper in the 1830s, the sewing machine in 1844, and high-volume canning and packaging devices in the 1880s exemplified a worldwide surge in productivity that "substituted machine tools for human craftsmen, interchangeable parts for hand-tooled components, and the energy of coal for that of wood, water, and animals."[6] New technology in the paper industry allowed wood pulp to replace rags as the primary input material. Continuous rod rolling transformed the wire industry: within a decade, wire nails replaced cut nails as the main source of supply. Worsted textiles resulting from advances in combing technology changed the woolen textile industry. Between 1869 and 1899, the capital invested per American manufacturer grew from about $700 to $2,000; and, in the period 1889-1919, the annual growth of total factor productivity was almost six times higher than that which had occurred for most of the 19th century.[7]

As productivity climbed steadily, production costs and prices fell dramatically. The 1882 formation of the Standard Oil Trust, which concentrated nearly 25% of the world's kerosene production into three refineries, reduced the average cost of a gallon of kerosene by 70% between 1882 and 1885. In tobacco, the invention of the Bonsack machine in the early 1880s reduced the labor costs of cigarette production by 98%. The Bessemer process reduced the cost of steel rails by 88% from the early 1870s to the late 1890s, and the electrolytic refining process invented in the 1880s reduced the price of aluminum by 96% between 1888 and 1895. In chemicals, the mass production of synthetic dyes, alkalis, nitrates, fibers, plastics, and film occurred rapidly after 1880. Production costs of synthetic blue dye, for example, fell by 95% from the 1870s to 1886.[8]

Such sharp declines in production costs and prices led to widespread excess capacity—a problem that was exacerbated by the fall in demand that

---

5. This section draws extensively on excellent discussions of the period by Alfred Chandler, Thomas McCraw, and Naomi Lamoreux. See the following works by Chandler: "The Emergence of Managerial Capitalism," Harvard Business School #9-384-081, revised by Thomas J. McCraw, July 1, 1992; *Scale and Scope, The Dynamics of Industrial Capitalism* (Harvard University Press, 1990); and *The Visible Hand: The Managerial Revolution in American Business* (Harvard University Press, 1977). See also Naomi R. Lamoreaux, *The Great Merger Movement in American Business, 1895-1904* (Cambridge University Press: Cambridge, England,

1985); and Thomas K. McCraw, "Antitrust: The Perceptions and Reality in Coping with Big Business," Harvard Business School #N9-391-292 (1992), and "Rethinking the Trust Question," in T. McCraw, ed., *Regulation in Perspective* (Harvard University Press, 1981).

6. McCraw (1981), p. 3.

7. McCraw (1981), p. 3.

8. For most of the examples of cost reduction cited in this paragraph, see Chandler (1992), pp. 4-6.

accompanied the recession and panic of 1893. Although attempts were made to eliminate excess capacity through pools, associations, and cartels, the problem was not substantially resolved until the capital markets facilitated exit by means of the 1890s' wave of mergers and acquisitions. Capacity was reduced through consolidation and the closing of marginal facilities in the merged entities. From 1895 to 1904, over 1,800 firms were bought or combined by merger into 157 firms.[9]

THE MODERN INDUSTRIAL REVOLUTION

The major restructuring of the American business community that began in the 1970s and continues in the 1990s is being driven by a variety of factors, including changes in physical and management technology, global competition, new regulation and taxes, and the conversion of formerly closed, centrally planned socialist and communist economies to capitalism, along with open participation in international trade. These changes are significant in scope and effect; indeed, they are bringing about the Third Industrial Revolution. To appreciate the challenge facing current control systems in light of this change, we must understand more about these general forces sweeping the world economy, and why they are generating excess capacity and thus the requirement for exit.

What has generally been referred to as the "decade of the '80s" in the United States actually began in the early 1970s, with the 10-fold increase in energy prices from 1973 to 1979, and the emergence

of the modern market for corporate control and high-yield, non-investment-grade ("junk") bonds in the mid-1970s. These events were associated with the beginnings of the Third Industrial Revolution which—if I were to pick a particular date—would be the time of the oil price increases beginning in 1973.

The Decade of the '80s: Capital Markets Provide an Early Response to the Modern Industrial Revolution

The macroeconomic data for the 1980s show major productivity gains. In fact, 1981 was a watershed year. Total factor productivity growth in the manufacturing sector more than doubled after 1981, from 1.4% per year in the period 1950-1981 (including a period of zero growth from 1973-1980) to 3.3% in the period 1981-1990.[10] Over the same period, nominal unit labor costs stopped their 17-year rise, and real unit labor costs declined by 25%. These lower labor costs came not from reduced wages or employment, but from increased productivity: nominal and real hourly compensation increased by a total of 4.2% and 0.3% per year, respectively, over the 1981-1989 period.[11] Manufacturing employment reached a low in 1983, but by 1989 had experienced a small cumulative increase of 5.5%.[12] Meanwhile, the annual growth in labor productivity increased from 2.3% between 1950-1981 to 3.8% between 1981-1990, while a 30-year decline in capital productivity was reversed when the annual change in the productivity of capital increased from -1.0% between 1950-1981 to 2.0% between 1981-1990.[13]

9. Lamoreux (1985), p. i.

10. Measured by multifactor productivity, as reported in Table 3 of U.S. Department of Labor, Bureau of Labor Statistics, 1990, *Multifactor Productivity Measures*, Report #USDL 91-412. Manufacturing labor productivity also grew at an annual rate of 3.8% in 1981-1990, as compared to 2.3% in the period 1950-1981 (U. S. Department of Labor, 1990, Table 3). By contrast, productivity growth in the overall (or "non-farm") business sector actually fell from 1.9% in the 1950-1981 period to 1.1% in the 1981-1990 period (U. S. Department of Labor, 1990, Table 2). The reason for the fall apparently lies in the relatively large growth in the service sector relative to the manufacturing sector and the low measured productivity growth in services. But there is considerable controversy over the adequacy of the measurement of productivity in the service sector. For example, the U.S. Department of Labor has no productivity measures for services employing nearly 70% of service workers, including, among others, health care, real estate, and securities brokerage. In addition, many believe that service sector productivity growth measures are downward biased. Service sector price measurements, for example, take no account of the improved productivity and lower prices of discount outlet clubs such as Sam's Club. As another example, the Commerce Department measures the output of financial services as the value of labor used to produce it. Because labor productivity is defined as the value of total output divided by total labor inputs, it is impossible for measured productivity to grow. Between 1973 and 1987, however, total equity shares traded daily grew from 5.7 million to 63.8 million, while employment only doubled, thus implying considerably more productivity growth than the zero growth reflected in the statistics.

11. Nominal and real hourly compensation, *Economic Report of the President*, Table B42 (1993).

12. U.S. Department of Labor, Bureau of Labor Statistics, 1991, *International Comparisons of Manufacturing Productivity and Unit Labor Cost Trends*, Report #USDL 92-752.

13. U.S. Department of Labor (1990). Trends in U.S. productivity have been controversial issues in academic and policy circles in the last decade. One reason, I believe, is that it takes time for these complicated changes to show up in the aggregate statistics. For example, in their recent book Baumol, Blackman, and Wolff changed their formerly pessimistic position. In their words: "This book is perhaps most easily summed up as a compendium of evidence demonstrating the error of our previous ways... The main change that was forced upon our views by careful examination of the long-run data was abandonment of our earlier gloomy assessment of American productivity performance. It has been replaced by the guarded optimism that pervades this book. This does *not* mean that we believe retention of American leadership will be automatic or easy. Yet the statistical evidence did drive us to conclude that the many writers who have suggested that the demise of America's traditional position has already occurred or was close at hand were, like the author of Mark Twain's obituary, a bit premature... It should, incidentally, be acknowledged that a number of distinguished economists have also been driven to a similar evaluation..." William Baumol, Sue Anne Beattey Blackman, and Edward Wolff, *Productivity and American Leadership* (MIT Press, Boston, 1989), pp. ix-x.

Reflecting these increases in the productivity of U.S. industry, the real value of public corporations' equity more than doubled during the 1980s from $1.4 to $3 trillion.[14] In addition, real median income increased at the rate of 1.8% per year between 1982 and 1989, reversing the 1.0% per year decline that occurred from 1973 to 1982.[15] Contrary to generally held beliefs, real R&D expenditures set record levels every year from 1975 to 1990, growing at an average annual rate of 5.8%.[16] In one of the media's few accurate portrayals of this period, a 1990 issue of The Economist noted that from 1980 to 1985, "American industry went on an R&D spending spree, with few big successes to show for it."[17]

Regardless of the gains in productivity, efficiency, and welfare, the 1980s are generally portrayed by politicians, the media, and others as a "decade of greed and excess." The media attack focused with special intensity on M&A transactions, 35,000 of which occurred from 1976 to 1990, with a total value of $2.6 trillion (in 1992 dollars). Contrary to common belief, only 364 of these offers were contested, and of those only 172 resulted in successful hostile takeovers.[18]

The popular verdict on takeovers was pronounced by prominent takeover defense lawyer Martin Lipton, when he said,

The takeover activity in the U.S. has imposed short-term profit maximization strategies on American Business at the expense of research, development, and capital investment. This is minimizing our ability to compete in world markets and still maintain a growing standard of living at home.[19]

But the evidence provided by financial economists, which I summarize briefly below, is starkly inconsistent with this view.

The most careful academic research strongly suggests that takeovers—along with leveraged restructurings prompted (in many, if not most cases) by the threat of takeover—have produced large gains for shareholders and for the economy as a whole. Based on this research,[20] my estimates indicate that over the 14-year period from 1976 to 1990, the $1.8 trillion volume of corporate control transactions—that is, mergers, tender offers, divestitures, and LBOs—generated over $750 billion in market value "premiums"[21] for selling investors. Given a reasonably efficient market, such premiums (the amounts buyers are willing to pay sellers over current market values) represent, in effect, the minimum increases in value forecast by the buyers. This $750 billion estimate of total shareholder gains thus neither includes the gains (or the losses)[22] to the buyers in such transactions, nor does it account for the value of efficiency improvements by companies pressured by control market activity into reforming without a visible control transaction.

Important sources of the expected gains from takeovers and leveraged restructurings include synergies from combining the assets of two or more organizations in the same or related industries (especially those with excess capacity) and the replacement of inefficient managers or governance systems.[23] Another possible source of the premiums, however, are transfers of wealth from other corporate stakeholders such as employees, bondholders, and the IRS. To the extent the value gains are merely wealth transfers, they do not represent efficiency improvements. But little evidence has been found to date to support substantial wealth transfers from any group,[24] and thus most of the reported gains appear to represent increases in efficiency.

Part of the attack on M&A and LBO transactions has been directed at the high-yield (or "junk") bond

---

14. As measured by the Wilshire 5,000 index of all publicly held equities.

15. Bureau of the Census, Housing and Household Economic Statistics Division (1991).

16. *Business Week* Annual R&D Scoreboard, 1991.

17. "Out of the Ivory Tower," *The Economist*, February 3, 1990.

18. *Mergerstat Review*, 1991, Merrill Lynch, Schaumburg, Illinois.

19. Martin Lipton, "Corporate Governance: Major Issues for the 1990's," Address to the Third Annual Corporate Finance Forum at the J. Ira Harris Center for the Study of Corporate Finance, University of Michigan School of Business, April 6, 1989, p. 2.

20. For a list of such studies, see the Appendix at the end of this article.

21. Measured in 1992 dollars. On average, selling-firm shareholders in all M&A transactions in the period 1976-1990 were paid premiums over market value of 41%. Annual premiums reported by *Mergerstat Review* (1991, Fig. 5) were weighted by value of transactions in the year for this estimate.

In arriving at my estimate of $750 billion of shareholder gains, I also assumed that all transactions without publicly disclosed prices had a value equal to 20% of the value of the average publicly disclosed transaction in the same year, and that they had average premiums equal to those for publicly disclosed transactions.

22. In cases where buyers overpay, such overpayment does not represent an efficiency gain, but rather only a wealth transfer from the buying firm's claimants to those of the selling firm. My method of calculating *total* shareholder gains effectively assumes that the losses to buyers are large enough to offset all gains (including those of the "raiders" whose allegedly massive "paper profits" became a favorite target of the media).

23. A 1992 study by Healy, Palepu, and Ruback estimates the total gains to buying- and selling-firm shareholders in the 50 largest mergers in the period 1979-1984 at 9.1% of the total equity value of both companies. Because buyers in such cases were typically much larger than sellers, such gains are roughly consistent with 40% acquisition premiums. They also find a strong positive cross-sectional relation between the value change and the operating cash flow changes resulting from the merger. See Paul Healy, Krishna Palepu, and Richard Ruback, "Does Corporate Performance Improve After Mergers?," *Journal of Financial Economics* 31, vol. 2 (1992), 135-175.

market. Besides helping to provide capital for corporate newcomers to compete with existing firms in the product markets, junk bonds also eliminated mere size as an effective takeover deterrent. This opened America's largest companies to monitoring and discipline from the capital markets. The following statement by Richard Munro, while Chairman and CEO of Time Inc., is representative of top management's hostile response to junk bonds and takeovers:

Notwithstanding television ads to the contrary, junk bonds are designed as the currency of 'casino economics'... they've been used not to create new plants or jobs or products but to do the opposite: to dismantle existing companies so the players can make their profit... This isn't the Seventh Cavalry coming to the rescue. It's a scalping party.[25]

As critics of leveraged restructuring have suggested, the high leverage incurred in the 1980s did contribute to a sharp increase in the bankruptcy rate of large firms in the early 1990s. Not widely recognized, however, is the major role played by other, external factors in these bankruptcies. First, the recession that helped put many highly leveraged firms into financial distress can be attributed at least in part to new regulatory restrictions on credit markets such as FIRREA—restrictions that were implemented in late 1989 and 1990 to offset the trend toward higher leverage.[26] And when companies did get into financial trouble, revisions in bankruptcy procedures and the tax code made it much more difficult to reorganize outside the courts, thereby *encouraging* many firms to file Chapter 11 and increasing the "costs of financial distress."[27]

But, even with such interference by public policy and the courts with the normal process of private adjustment to financial distress, the general economic consequences of financial distress in the high-yield markets have been greatly exaggerated. While precise numbers are difficult to come by, I estimate that the total bankruptcy losses to junk bond and bank HLT loans from inception of the market in the mid-1970s through 1990 amounted to less than $50 billion. (In comparison, IBM alone lost $51 billion—almost 65% of the total market value of its equity—from its 1991 high to its 1992 close.[28]) Perhaps the most telling evidence that losses have been exaggerated, however, is the current condition of the high-yield market, which is now financing record levels of new issues.

Of course, mistakes were made in the takeover activity of the 1980s. Indeed, given the far-reaching nature of the restructuring, it would have been surprising if there were none. But the popular negative assessment of leveraged restructuring is dramatically inconsistent with both the empirical evidence and the near-universal view of finance scholars who have studied the phenomenon. In fact, takeover activities were addressing an important set of problems in corporate America, and doing it before the companies faced serious trouble in the product markets. They were providing, in effect, an early warning system that motivated healthy adjustments to the excess capacity that was building in many sectors of the worldwide economy.

Causes of Excess Capacity

Excess capacity can arise in at least four ways, the most obvious of which occurs when market demand falls below the level required to yield returns that will support the currently installed production capacity. This *demand-reduction* scenario is most familiarly associated with recession episodes in the business cycle.

24. A 1989 study by Laura Stiglin, Steven Kaplan, and myself demonstrates that, contrary to popular assertions, LBO transactions resulted in increased tax revenues to the U. S. Treasury—increases that average about 60% per annum on a permanent basis under the 1986 IRS code. (Michael C. Jensen, Steven Kaplan, Laura Stiglin, "Effects of LBOs on Tax Revenues of the U.S. Treasury," *Tax Notes*, Vol. 42, No. 6 (February 6, 1989), pp. 727-733.)

The data presented by a study of pension fund reversions reveal that only about 1% of the premiums paid in all takeovers can be explained by reversions of pension plans in the target firms (although the authors of the study do not present this calculation themselves). (Jeffrey Pontiff, Andrei Shleifer, and Michael S. Weisbach, "Reversions of Excess Pension Assets after Takeovers," *Rand Journal of Economics*, Vol. 21, No. 4 (Winter 1990), pp. 600-613.)

Joshua Rosett, in analyzing over 5,000 union contracts in over 1,000 listed companies in the period 1973 to 1987, shows that less than 2% of the takeover premiums can be explained by reductions in union wages in the first six years after the change in control. Pushing the estimation period out to 18 years after the change

in control increases the percentage to only 5.4% of the premium. For hostile takeovers only, union wages *increase* by 3% and 6% for the two time intervals. (Joshua G. Rosett, "Do Union Wealth Concessions Explain Takeover Premiums? The Evidence on Contract Wages," *Journal of Financial Economics*, Vol. 27, No. 1 (September 1990), pp. 263-282.)

25. J. Richard Munro, "Takeovers: The Myths Behind the Mystique," May 15, 1989, published in *Vital Speeches*, p. 472.

26. See the collection of articles on the "credit crunch" in Vol. 4 No. 1 (Spring 1991) of the *Journal of Applied Corporate Finance*.

27. I make this case in "Corporate Control and the Politics of Finance," *Journal of Applied Corporate Finance* (Summer, 1991), 13-33. See also Karen Wruck, "Financial Distress, Reorganization, and Organizational Efficiency," *Journal of Financial Economics* 27 (1990), 420-444.

28. Its high of $139.50 occurred on 2/19/91 and it closed at $50.38 at the end of 1992.

Excess capacity can also arise from two types of technological change. The first type, *capacity-expanding* technological change, increases the output of a given capital stock and organization. An example of the capacity-expanding type of change is the Reduced Instruction Set CPU (RISC) processor innovation in the computer workstation market. RISC processors have brought about a ten-fold increase in power, but can be produced by adapting the current production technology. With no increase in the quantity demanded, this change implies that production capacity must fall by 90%. Of course, such price declines increase the quantity demanded in these situations, thereby reducing the extent of the capacity adjustment that would otherwise be required. Nevertheless, the new workstation technology has dramatically increased the effective output of existing production facilities, thereby generating excess capacity.

The second type is *obsolescence-creating* change—change that makes obsolete the current capital stock and organization. For example, Wal-Mart and the wholesale clubs that are revolutionizing retailing are dominating old-line department stores, thereby eliminating the need for much current retail capacity. When Wal-Mart enters a new market, total retail capacity expands, and some of the existing high-cost retail operations must go out of business. More intensive use of information and other technologies, direct dealing with manufacturers, and the replacement of high-cost, restrictive work-rule union labor are several sources of the competitive advantage of these new organizations.

Finally, excess capacity also results when many competitors simultaneously rush to implement new, highly productive technologies without considering whether the aggregate effects of all such investment will be greater capacity than can be supported by demand in the final product market. The winchester disk drive industry provides an example. Between 1977 and 1984, venture capitalists invested over $400 million in 43 different manufacturers of winchester disk drives; initial public offerings of common stock infused additional capital in excess of $800 million. In mid-1983, the capital markets assigned a value of $5.4 billion to twelve publicly-traded, venture-capital-backed hard disk drive manufacturers. Yet, by the end of 1984, overcapacity had caused the value assigned to those companies to plummet to $1.4 billion. My Harvard colleagues William Sahlman and Howard Stevenson have attributed this overcapacity to an "investment mania" based on implicit assumptions about long-run growth and profitability "*for each individual company* [that,]...had they been stated explicitly, would not have been acceptable to the rational investor."[29]

Such "overshooting" has by no means been confined to the winchester disk drive industry.[30] Indeed, the 1980s saw boom-and-bust cycles in the venture capital market generally, and also in commercial real estate and LBO markets. As Sahlman and Stevenson have also suggested, something more than "investment mania" and excessive "animal spirits" was at work here. Stated as simply as possible, my own analysis traces such overshooting to a gross misalignment of incentives between the "dealmakers" who promoted the transactions and the lenders, limited partners, and other investors who funded them.[31] During the mid to late'80s, venture capitalists, LBO promoters, and real estate developers were all effectively being rewarded simply for doing deals rather than for putting together successful deals. Reforming the "contracts" between dealmaker and investor—most directly, by reducing front-end-loaded fees and requiring the dealmakers to put up significant equity—would go far toward solving the problem of too many deals. (As I argue later, public corporations in mature industries face an analogous, though potentially far more costly (in terms of shareholder value destroyed and social resources wasted), distortion of investment priorities and incentives when their managers and directors do not have significant stock ownership.)

Current Forces Leading to Excess Capacity and Exit

The ten-fold increase in crude oil prices between 1973-1979 had ubiquitous effects, forcing contraction in oil, chemicals, steel, aluminum, and

---

29. See William A. Sahlman and Howard H. Stevenson, "Capital Market Myopia," *Journal of Business Venturing* 1 (1985), p. 7.

30. Or to the 1980s. There is evidence of such behavior in the 19th century, and in other periods of U.S. history.

31. Stated more precisely, my argument attributes overshooting to "incentive, information, and contracting" problems. For more on this, see Jensen (1991), cited in note 27, pp. 26-27. For some supporting evidence, see Steven N. Kaplan and Jeremy Stein, 1993, "The Evolution of Buyout Pricing and Financial Structure in the 1980s, *Quarterly Journal of Economics* 108, no. 2, 313-358. For a shorter, less technical version of the same article, see Vol. 6 No. 1 (Spring 1993) of the *Journal of Applied Corporate Finance*.

international shipping, among other industries. In addition, the sharp crude oil price increases that motivated major changes to economize on energy had other, longer-lasting consequences. The general corporate re-evaluation of organizational processes stimulated by the oil shock led to dramatic increases in efficiency above and beyond the original energy-saving projects. (In fact, I view the oil shock as the initial impetus for the corporate "process re-engineering" movement that still continues to accelerate throughout the world.)

Since the oil price increases of the 1970s, we have again seen systematic overcapacity problems in many industries similar to those of the 19th century. While the reasons for this overcapacity appear to differ somewhat among industries, there are a few common underlying causes.

Macro Policies. Major deregulation of the American economy (including trucking, rail, airlines, telecommunications, banking, and financial services industries) under President Carter contributed to the requirement for exit in these industries, as did important changes in the U.S. tax laws that reduced tax advantages to real estate development, construction, and other activities. The end of the Cold War has had obvious consequences for the defense industry and its suppliers. In addition, I suspect that two generations of managerial focus on growth as a recipe for success has caused many firms to overshoot their optimal capacity, thus setting the stage for cutbacks. In the decade from 1979 to 1989, *Fortune* 100 firms lost 1.5 million employees, or 14% of their workforce.[32]

Technology. Massive changes in technology are clearly part of the cause of the current industrial revolution and its associated excess capacity. Both within and across industries, technological developments have had far-reaching impact. To give some examples, the widespread acceptance of radial tires (which last three to five times longer than the older bias ply technology and provide better gas mileage) caused excess capacity in the tire industry; the personal computer revolution forced contraction of the market for mainframes; the advent of aluminum and plastic alternatives reduced demand for steel and glass containers; and fiberoptic, satellite, digital (ISDN), and new compression technolo-

gies dramatically increased capacity in telecommunication. Wireless personal communication such as cellular phones and their replacements promise further to extend this dramatic change.

The changes in computer technology, including miniaturization, have not only revamped the computer industry, but also redefined the capabilities of countless other industries. Some estimates indicate the price of computing capacity fell by a factor of 1,000 over the last decade. This means that computer production lines now produce boxes with 1,000 times the capacity for a given price. Consequently, computers are becoming commonplace—in cars, toasters, cameras, stereos, ovens, and so on. Nevertheless, the increase in quantity demanded has not been sufficient to avoid overcapacity, and we are therefore witnessing a dramatic shutdown of production lines in the industry—a force that has wracked IBM as a high-cost producer. A change of similar magnitude in auto production technology would have reduced the price of a $20,000 auto in 1980 to under $20 today. Such increases in capacity and productivity in a basic technology have unavoidably massive implications for the organization of work and society.

Fiberoptic and other telecommunications technologies such as compression algorithms are bringing about similarly vast increases in worldwide capacity and functionality. A Bell Laboratories study of excess capacity indicates, for example, that, given three years and an additional expenditure of $3.1 billion, three of AT&T's new competitors (MCI, Sprint, and National Telecommunications Network) would be able to absorb the entire long-distance switched service that was supplied by AT&T in 1990.[33]

Organizational Innovation. Overcapacity can be caused not only by changes in physical technology, but also by changes in organizational practices and management technology. The vast improvements in telecommunications, including computer networks, electronic mail, teleconferencing, and facsimile transmission are changing the workplace in major ways that affect the manner in which people work and interact. It is far less valuable for people to be in the same geographical location to work together effectively, and this is encouraging smaller,

---

32. Source: Compustat.
33. Federal Communications Commission, *Competition in the Interstate Interexchange Marketplace*, FCC 91-251 (Sept. 16, 1991), p. 1140.

more efficient, entrepreneurial organizing units that cooperate through technology.[34] This in turn leads to even more fundamental changes. Through competition, "virtual organizations"—networked or transitory organizations in which people come together temporarily to complete a task, then separate to pursue their individual specialties—are changing the structure of the standard large bureaucratic organization and contributing to its shrinkage. Virtual organizations tap talented specialists, avoid many of the regulatory costs imposed on permanent structures, and bypass the inefficient work rules and high wages imposed by unions. In so doing, they increase efficiency and thereby further contribute to excess capacity.

In addition, Japanese management techniques such as total quality management, just-in-time production, and flexible manufacturing have significantly increased the efficiency of organizations where they have been successfully implemented throughout the world. Some experts argue that such new management techniques can reduce defects and spoilage by an order of magnitude. These changes in managing and organizing principles have contributed significantly to the productivity of the world's capital stock and economized on the use of labor and raw materials, thus also contributing to excess capacity.

Globalization of Trade. Over the last several decades, the entry of Japan and other Pacific Rim countries such as Hong Kong, Taiwan, Singapore, Thailand, Korea, Malaysia, and China into worldwide product markets has contributed to the required adjustments in Western economies. And, competition from new entrants to the world product markets promises only to intensify.

With the globalization of markets, excess capacity tends to occur worldwide. The Japanese economy, for example, is currently suffering from enormous overcapacity caused in large part by what I view as the "breakdown" of its corporate control system.[35] As a consequence, Japan now faces a massive and long-overdue restructuring—one that includes the prospect of unprecedented (for Japanese companies) layoffs, a pronounced shift of corporate focus from market share to profitability, and even the adoption of pay-for-performance executive compensation contracts (something heretofore believed to be profoundly "un-Japanese").

Yet even if the requirement for exit were isolated in just Japan and the U.S, the interdependency of today's world economy would ensure that such overcapacity would have global implications. For example, the rise of efficient high-quality producers of steel and autos in Japan and Korea has contributed to excess capacity in those industries worldwide. Between 1973 and 1990, total capacity in the U.S. steel industry fell by 38% from 157 to 97 million tons, and total employment fell over 50% from 509,000 to 252,000 (and had fallen further to 160,000 by 1993). From 1985 to 1989 multifactor productivity in the industry increased at an annual rate of 5.3%, as compared to 1.3% for the period 1958 to 1989.[36]

Revolution in Political Economy. The rapid pace of development of capitalism, the opening of closed economies, and the dismantling of central control in communist and socialist states is occurring in various degrees in Eastern Europe, China, India, Indonesia, other Asian economies, and Africa. In Asia and Africa alone, this development will place a potential labor force of almost a billion people—

---

34. The *Journal of Financial Economics*, which I have been editing with several others since 1973, is an example. The *JFE* is now edited by seven faculty members with offices at three universities in different states, and the main editorial administrative office is located in yet another state. The publisher, North Holland, is located in Amsterdam, the printing is done in India, and mailing and billing is executed in Switzerland. This "networked organization" would have been extremely inefficient two decades ago without fax machines, high-speed modems, electronic mail, and overnight delivery services.

35. A collapse I predicted in print as early as 1989. (See Michael C. Jensen, "Eclipse of the Public Corporation," *Harvard Business Review*, Vol. 89, No. 5 (September-October, 1989), pp. 61-74.)

In a 1991 article published in this journal, I wrote the following: "As our system has begun to look more like the Japanese, the Japanese economy is undergoing changes that are reducing the role of large active investors and thus making their system resemble ours. With the progressive development of U.S.-like capital markets, Japanese managers have been able to loosen the controls once exercised by the banks. So successful have they been in bypassing banks that the top third of Japanese companies are no longer net bank borrowers. As a result of their past success in product market competition, Japanese companies are now "flooded"

with free cash flow. Their competitive position today reminds me of the position of American companies in the late 1960s. And, like their U.S. counterparts in the 60s, Japanese companies today appear to be in the process of creating conglomerates.

My prediction is that, unless unmonitored Japanese managers prove to be much more capable than American executives of managing large, sprawling organizations, the Japanese economy is likely to produce large numbers of those conglomerates that U.S. capital markets have spent the last 10 years trying to pull apart. And if I am right, then Japan is likely to experience its own leveraged restructuring movement." ("Corporate Control and the Politics of Finance," *Journal of Applied Corporate Finance*, Vol. 4 No. 2, p. 24, fn. 47.)

For some interesting observations attesting to the severity of the Japanese overinvestment or "free cash flow" problem, see Carl Kester, "The Hidden Costs of Japanese Success," *Journal of Applied Corporate Finance* (Volume 3 Number 4, Winter 1990).

36. See James D. Burnham, *Changes and Challenges: The Transformation of the U.S. Steel Industry*, Policy Study No. 115 (Center for the Study of American Business, Washington University: St. Louis, 1993), Table 1 and p. 15.

When left to the product markets, the adjustment process [to excess capacity] is greatly protracted and ends up generating enormous additional costs. This is the clear lesson held out by the most recent restructuring of the U.S. auto industry— and it's one that many sectors of the Japanese economy are now experiencing firsthand.

whose current average income is less than $2 per day—on world markets. The opening of Mexico and other Latin American countries and the transition of some socialist Eastern European economies to open capitalist systems could add almost 200 million more laborers with average incomes of less than $10 per day to the world market.

To put these numbers into perspective, the average daily U.S. income per worker is slightly over $90, and the total labor force numbers about 117 million, and the European Economic Community average wage is about $80 per day with a total labor force of about 130 million. The labor forces that have affected world trade extensively in the last several decades (those in Hong Kong, Japan, Korea, Malaysia, Singapore, and Taiwan) total about 90 million.

While the changes associated with bringing a potential 1.2 billion low-cost laborers onto world markets will significantly increase average living standards throughout the world, they will also bring massive obsolescence of capital (manifested in the form of excess capacity) in Western economies as the adjustments sweep through the system. Such adjustments will include a major redirection of Western labor and capital away from low-skilled, labor-intensive industries and toward activities where they have a comparative advantage. While the opposition to such adjustments will be strong, the forces driving them will prove irresistible in this day of rapid and inexpensive communication, transportation, miniaturization, and migration.

One can also confidently forecast that the transition to open capitalist economies will generate great conflict over international trade as special interests in individual countries try to insulate themselves from competition and the required exit. And the U.S., despite its long-professed commitment to "free trade," will prove no exception. Just as U.S. managers and employees demanded protection from the capital markets in the 1980s, some are now demanding protection from international competition in the product markets, generally under the guise of protecting jobs. The dispute over NAFTA is but one general example of conflicts that are also occurring in the steel, automobile, computer chip, computer screen, and textile industries.

It would not even surprise me to see a return to demands for protection from *domestic* competition. This is currently happening in the deregulated airline industry, an industry faced with significant excess capacity.

We should not underestimate the strains this continuing change will place on worldwide social and political systems. In both the first and second industrial revolutions, the demands for protection from competition and for redistribution of income became intense. It is conceivable that Western nations could face the modern equivalent of the English Luddites, who destroyed industrial machinery (primarily knitting frames) in the period 1811-1816, and were eventually subdued by the militia. In the U.S. during the early 1890s, large groups of unemployed men (along with some vagrants and criminals), banded together in a cross-country march on Congress. The aim of "Coxey's industrial army," as the group became known, was to demand relief from "the evils of murderous competition; the supplanting of manual labor by machinery; the excessive Mongolian and pauper immigration; the curse of alien landlordism."[37]

Although Coxey's army disbanded peacefully after arriving in Washington and submitting a petition to Congress, some democratic systems may not survive the strain of adjustment, and may revert under pressure to a more totalitarian system. We need look no farther than current developments in Mexico or Russia to see such threats to democracy in effect.

The bottom line, then, is that with worldwide excess capacity and thus greater requirement for exit, the strains put on the internal control mechanisms of Western corporations are likely to worsen for decades to come. The experience of the U.S. in the 1980s demonstrated that the capital markets can play an important role in forcing managers to address this problem. In the absence of capital market pressures, competition in product markets will eventually bring about exit. But when left to the product markets, the adjustment process is greatly protracted and ends up generating enormous additional costs. This is the clear lesson held out by the most recent restructuring of the U.S. auto industry— and it's one that many sectors of the Japanese economy are now experiencing firsthand.

---

37. McMurray (1929), pp. 253-262, cited in note 2.

THE DIFFICULTY OF EXIT

The Asymmetry between Growth and Decline

Exit problems appear to be particularly severe in companies that for long periods enjoyed rapid growth, commanding market positions, and high cash flow and profits. In these situations, the culture of the organization and the mindset of managers seem to make it extremely difficult for adjustment to take place until long after the problems have become severe and, in some cases, even unsolvable. In a fundamental sense, there is an "asymmetry" between the growth stage and the contraction stage in the corporate life cycle. Financial economists have spent little time thinking about how to manage the contracting stage efficiently or, more important, how to manage the growth stage to avoid sowing the seeds of decline.

In industry after industry with excess capacity, managers fail to recognize that they themselves must downsize; instead they leave the exit to others while they continue to invest. When all managers behave this way, exit is significantly delayed at substantial cost of real resources to society. The tire industry is an example. Widespread consumer acceptance of radial tires meant that worldwide tire capacity had to shrink by two thirds (because radials last 3 to 5 times longer than bias ply tires). Nonetheless, the response by the managers of individual companies was often equivalent to: "This business is going through some rough times. We must invest so that we will have a chair when the music stops."

The Case of Gencorp. William Reynolds, Chairman and CEO of GenCorp, the maker of General Tires, illustrates this reaction in his 1988 testimony before the U.S. House Committee on Energy and Commerce:

The tire business was the largest piece of GenCorp, both in terms of annual revenues and its asset base. Yet General Tire was not GenCorp's strongest performer. Its relatively poor earnings performance was due in part to conditions affecting all of the tire industry... In 1985 worldwide tire manufacturing capacity substantially exceeded demand. At the same time, due to a series of technological improvements in

the design of tires and the materials used to make them, the product life of tires had lengthened significantly... The economic pressure on our tire business was substantial. Because our unit volume was far below others in the industry, we had less competitive flexibility... We made several moves to improve our competitive position: We increased our investment in research and development. We increased our involvement in the high performance and light truck tire categories, two market segments which offered faster growth opportunities. We developed new tire products for those segments and invested heavily in an aggressive marketing program designed to enhance our presence in both markets. We made the difficult decision to reduce our overall manufacturing capacity by closing one of our older, less modern plants... I believe that the General Tire example illustrates that we were taking a rational, long-term approach to improving GenCorp's overall performance and shareholder value...

Like so many U.S. CEOs, Reynolds then goes on to blame the capital markets for bringing about what he fails to recognize is a solution to the industry's problem of excess capacity:

As a result of the takeover attempt... [and] to meet the principal and interest payments on our vastly increased corporate debt, GenCorp had to quickly sell off valuable assets and abruptly lay off approximately 550 important employees.[38]

Without questioning the genuineness of Reynolds' concerns about his company and employees, it nevertheless now seems clear that GenCorp's increased investment was neither going to maximize the value of the firm nor to be a socially optimal response in a declining industry with excess capacity. In 1987, GenCorp ended up selling its General Tire subsidiary to Continental AG of Hannover, thus furthering the process of consolidation necessary to reduce overcapacity.

Information Problems

Information problems hinder exit because the high-cost capacity in the industry must be eliminated

---

38. A. William Reynolds, in testimony before the Subcommittee on Oversight and Investigations, U.S. House Committee on Energy and Commerce, February 8, 1988.

> In industry after industry with excess capacity, managers fail to recognize that they themselves must downsize; instead they leave the exit to others while they continue to invest. When all managers behave this way, exit is significantly delayed at substantial cost of real resources to society.

if resources are to be used efficiently. Firms often do not have good information about their own costs, much less the costs of their competitors. Thus, it is sometimes unclear to managers that they are the high-cost firm that should exit the industry.[39]

But even when managers do acknowledge the requirement for exit, it is often difficult for them to accept and initiate the shutdown. For the managers who must implement these decisions, shutting plants or liquidating the firm causes personal pain, creates uncertainty, and interrupts or sidetracks careers. Rather than confronting this pain, managers generally resist such actions as long as they have the cash flow to subsidize the losing operations. Indeed, firms with large positive cash flow will often invest in even more money-losing capacity—situations that illustrate vividly what I call the "agency costs of free cash flow."[40]

Contracting Problems

Explicit and implicit contracts in the organization can become major obstacles to efficient exit. Unionization, restrictive work rules, and lucrative employee compensation and benefits are other ways in which the agency costs of free cash flow can manifest themselves in a growing, cash-rich organization. Formerly dominant firms became unionized in their heyday (or effectively unionized in organizations like IBM and Kodak) when managers spent some of the organization's free cash flow to buy labor peace. Faced with technical innovation and worldwide competition—often from new, more flexible, and non-union organizations—these dominant firms have not adjusted quickly enough to maintain their market dominance. Part of the problem is managerial and organizational defensiveness that inhibits learning and prevents managers from changing their model of the business.

Implicit contracts with unions, other employees, suppliers, and communities add to formal union barriers to change by reinforcing organizational defensiveness and delaying change long beyond the optimal time—often even beyond the survival point for the organization. While casual breach of implicit contracts will destroy trust in an organization and seriously reduce efficiency, all organizations must retain the flexibility to modify contracts that are no longer optimal.[41] In the current environment, it takes nothing less than a major shock to bring about necessary change.

THE ROLE OF THE MARKET FOR CORPORATE CONTROL

The Four Control Forces Operating on the Corporation

There are four basic control forces bearing on the corporation that act to bring about a convergence of managers' decisions with those that are optimal from society's standpoint. They are (1) the capital markets, (2) the legal, political, and regulatory system, (3) the product and factor markets, and (4) the internal control system headed by the board of directors.

The capital markets were relatively constrained by law and regulatory practice from about 1940 until their resurrection through hostile tender offers in the 1970s. Prior to the 1970s, capital market discipline took place primarily through the proxy process.

The legal/political/regulatory system is far too blunt an instrument to handle the problems of wasteful managerial behavior effectively. (Nevertheless, the break-up and deregulation of AT&T is one of the court system's outstanding successes; I estimate that it has helped create over $125 billion of increased value between AT&T and the Baby Bells.[42])

While the product and factor markets are slow to act as a control force, their discipline is inevitable; firms that do not supply the product that customers desire at a competitive price will not survive. Unfor-

---

39. Total quality management programs strongly encourage managers to benchmark their firm's operations against the most successful worldwide competitors, and good cost systems and competitive benchmarking are becoming more common in well-managed firms.

40. Briefly stated, the "agency costs of free cash flow" means the loss in value caused by the tendency of managements of large public companies in slow-growth industries to reinvest corporate cash flow in projects with expected returns below the cost of capital. See Michael Jensen, "The Agency Costs of Free Cash Flow: Corporate Finance and Takeovers," *American Economic Review* 76, no. 2 (May,1986), 323-329.

41. Much press coverage and official policy seems to be based on the notion that *all* implicit contracts should be immutable and rigidly enforced. But while I agree that the security of property rights and the enforceability of contracts are essential to the growth of real output and efficiency, it is also clear that, given unexpected and unforeseeable events, *not all* contracts, whether explicit or implicit, can (or even should) be fulfilled. (For example, bankruptcy is essentially a state-supervised system for breaking (or, more politely, rewriting) explicit contracts that have become unenforceable. All developed economies devise such a system.) Implicit contracts, besides avoiding the costs incurred in the writing process, provide the opportunity to revise the obligation if circumstances change; presumably, this is a major reason for their existence.

42. For this calculation, see the original version of this article in the *Journal of Finance* (Jensen (1993)).

tunately, by the time product and factor market disciplines take effect, large amounts of investor capital and other social resources have been wasted, and it can often be too late to save much of the enterprise.

Which brings us to the role of corporate internal control systems and the need to reform them. As stated earlier, there is a large and growing body of studies documenting the shareholder gains from corporate restructurings of the '80s.[43] The size and consistency of such gains provide strong support for the proposition that the internal control systems of publicly held corporations have generally failed to cause managers to maximize efficiency and value in slow-growth or declining industries.

Perhaps more persuasive than the formal statistical evidence, however, is the scarcity of large, public firms that have voluntarily restructured or engaged in a major strategic redirection without either a challenge from the capital markets or a crisis in product markets. By contrast, partnerships and private or closely held firms such as investment banking, law, and consulting firms have generally responded far more quickly to changing market conditions.

Capital Markets and the Market for Corporate Control

Until they were shut down in 1989, the capital markets were providing one mechanism for accomplishing change before losses in the product markets generated a crisis. While the corporate control activity of the 1980s has been widely criticized as counterproductive to American industry, few have recognized that many of these transactions were necessary to accomplish exit over the objections of current managers and other corporate constituencies such as employees and communities.

For example, the solution to excess capacity in the tire industry came about through the market for corporate control. Every major U.S. tire firm was either taken over or restructured in the 1980s.[44] In

total, 37 tire plants were shut down in the period 1977-1987, and total employment in the industry fell by over 40%.

Capital market and corporate control transactions such as the repurchase of stock (or the purchase of another company) for cash or debt accomplished exit of resources in a very direct way. When Chevron acquired Gulf for $13.2 billion in cash and debt in 1984, the net assets devoted to the oil industry fell by $13.2 billion as soon as the checks were mailed out. In the 1980s the oil industry had to shrink to accommodate the reduction in the quantity of oil demanded and the reduced rate of growth of demand. This meant paying out to shareholders its huge cash inflows, reducing exploration and development expenditures to bring reserves in line with reduced demands, and closing refining and distribution facilities. Leveraged acquisitions and equity repurchases helped accomplish this end for virtually all major U.S. oil firms.

Exit also resulted when KKR acquired RJR-Nabisco for $25 billion in cash and debt in its 1986 leveraged buyout. The tobacco industry must shrink, given the change in smoking habits in response to consumer awareness of cancer threats, and the payout of RJR's cash accomplished this to some extent. RJR's LBO debt also prevented the company from continuing to squander its cash flows on wasteful projects it had planned to undertake prior to the buyout. Thus, the buyout laid the groundwork for the efficient reduction of capacity and resources by one of the major firms in the industry. The recent sharp declines in the stock prices of RJR and Philip Morris are signs that there is much more downsizing to come.

The era of the control market came to an end, however, in late 1989 and 1990. Intense controversy and opposition from corporate managers—assisted by charges of fraud, the increase in default and bankruptcy rates, and insider trading prosecutions—led to the shutdown of the control market through court decisions, state antitakeover amendments, and regulatory restrictions on the availability of financ-

---

43. For a partial list of such studies, see the Appendix at the end of this article.

44. In May 1985, Uniroyal approved an LBO proposal to block hostile advances by Carl Icahn. About the same time, BF Goodrich began diversifying out of the tire business. In January 1986, Goodrich and Uniroyal independently spun off their tire divisions and together, in a 50-50 joint venture, formed the Uniroyal-Goodrich Tire Company. By December 1987, Goodrich had sold its interest in the venture to Clayton and Dubilier; Uniroyal followed soon after. Similarly, General Tire moved away from tires: the company, renamed GenCorp in 1984, sold its tire division to Continental in 1987. Other takeovers in the industry

during this period include the sale of Firestone to Bridgestone and Pirelli's purchase of the Armstrong Tire Company. By 1991, Goodyear was the only remaining major American tire manufacturer. Yet it too faced challenges in the control market: in 1986, following three years of unprofitable diversifying investments, Goodyear initiated a major leveraged stock repurchase and restructuring to defend itself from a hostile takeover from Sir James Goldsmith. Uniroyal/Goodrich was purchased by Michelin in 1990. See Richard Tedlow, "Hitting the Skids: Tires and Time Horizons," Unpublished manuscript, Harvard Business School, 1991.

Capital market and corporate control transactions such as the repurchase of stock (or the purchase of another company) for cash or debt accomplished exit of resources in a very direct way. When Chevron acquired Gulf for $13.2 billion in cash and debt in 1984, the net assets devoted to the oil industry fell by $13.2 billion as soon as the checks were mailed out.

ing.[45] In 1991, the total value of transactions fell to $96 billion from $340 billion in 1988.[46] Leveraged buyouts and management buyouts fell to slightly over $1 billion in 1991 from $80 billion in 1988.[47]

The demise of the control market as an effective influence on American corporations has not ended the restructuring. But it has allowed many organizations to postpone addressing major problems until forced to do by financial difficulties generated by the product markets. Unfortunately, the delay means that some of these organizations will not survive—or will survive as mere shadows of their former selves.

THE FAILURE OF CORPORATE INTERNAL CONTROL SYSTEMS

With the shutdown of the capital markets as an effective mechanism for motivating change, exit, and renewal, we are left to depend on the internal control system to act to preserve organizational assets, both human and otherwise. Throughout corporate America, the problems that motivated much of the control activity of the 1980s are now reflected in lackluster performance, financial distress, and pressures for restructuring. General Motors, Kodak, IBM, Xerox, Westinghouse, ITT, and many others have faced or are now facing severe challenges in the product markets. We therefore must understand why these internal control systems have failed and learn how to make them work.

By nature, organizations abhor control systems. Ineffective governance is a major part of the problem with internal control mechanisms; they seldom respond in the absence of a crisis. The recent GM board "revolt," which resulted in the firing of CEO Robert Stempel, exemplifies the failure, not the success, of GM's governance system. Though clearly one of the world's high-cost producers in a market with substantial excess capacity, GM avoided making major changes in its strategy for over a decade. The revolt came too late; the board acted to remove the CEO only in 1992, after the company had reported losses of $6.5 billion in 1990 and 1991.

Unfortunately, GM is not an isolated example. IBM is another testimony to the failure of internal

control systems. The company failed to adjust to the substitution away from its mainframe business following the revolution in the workstation and personal computer market—ironically enough, a revolution that it helped launch with the invention of the RISC technology in 1974. Like GM, IBM is a high-cost producer in a market with substantial excess capacity. It too began to change its strategy significantly and removed its CEO only after reporting huge losses—$2.8 billion in 1991 and further losses in 1992—while losing almost 65% of its equity value.

Eastman Kodak, another major U.S. company formerly dominant in its market, also failed to adjust to competition and has performed poorly. Largely as a result of a disastrous diversification program designed to offset the maturing of its core film business, its $37 share price in 1992 was roughly unchanged from 1981. After several reorganizations attempting relatively modest changes in its incentives and strategy, the board finally replaced the CEO in October 1993.

General Electric is a notable exception to my proposition about the failure of corporate internal control systems. Under CEO Jack Welch since 1981, GE has accomplished a major strategic re-direction, eliminating 104,000 of its 402,000 person workforce (through layoffs or sales of divisions) in the period 1980-1990 without a threat from capital or product markets. But there is little evidence to indicate this is due to the influence of GE's governance system; it appears attributable almost entirely to the vision and leadership of Jack Welch.

General Dynamics provides another exceptional case. The appointment of William Anders as CEO in September 1991 resulted in a rapid adjustment to excess capacity in the defense industry—again, with no apparent threat from any outside force. The company generated $3.4 billion of increased value on a $1 billion company in just over two years. One of the key elements in this success story, however, was a major change in the company's management compensation system[48] that tied bonuses directly to increases in stock value (a subject I return to later).

My colleague Gordon Donaldson's account of General Mills' strategic redirection is yet another

---

45. For a more detailed account, see my article in this journal, "Corporate Control and the Politics of Finance," Summer 1991.

46. In 1992 dollars, calculated from *Mergerstat Review*, 1991, p. 100f.

47. In 1992 dollars, *Mergerstat Review*, 1991, Figs. 29 and 38.

48. See Kevin J. Murphy and Jay Dial, "Compensation and Strategy at General Dynamics (A) and (B)," Harvard Business School #N9-493-032 and N9-493-033, 1992.

case of a largely voluntary restructuring.[49] But the fact that it took more than ten years to accomplish raises serious questions about the social costs of continuing the waste caused by ineffective control. It appears that internal control systems have two faults: they react too late, and they take too long to effect major change. Changes motivated by the capital market are generally accomplished quickly—typically, within one to three years. No one has yet demonstrated social benefits from relying on internally motivated change that would offset the costs of the decade-long delay in the restructuring of General Mills.

In summary, it appears that the infrequency with which large corporate organizations restructure or redirect themselves solely on the basis of the internal control mechanisms—that is, in the absence of intervention by capital markets or a crisis in the product markets—is strong testimony to the inadequacy of these control mechanisms.

[At this point, the original Journal of Finance *paper contains a section, omitted here because of space constraints, called "Direct Evidence of the Failure of Internal Control Systems." It presents estimates of the productivity of corporate capital expenditure and R & D spending programs of 432 firms that suggest "major inefficiencies in a substantial number of firms."]*

REVIVING INTERNAL CORPORATE CONTROL SYSTEMS

Remaking the Board as an Effective Control Mechanism

The problems with corporate internal control systems start with the board of directors. The board, at the apex of the internal control system, has the final responsibility for the functioning of the firm. Most important, it sets the rules of the game for the CEO. The job of the board is to hire, fire, and compensate the CEO, and to provide high-level counsel. Few boards in the past decades have done this job well in the absence of external crises. This is particularly unfortunate, given that the very purpose of the internal control mechanism is to provide an early warning system to put the organization back on track before difficulties reach a crisis stage.

The reasons for the failure of the board are not completely understood, but we are making progress toward understanding these complex issues. The available evidence does suggest that CEOs are removed after poor performance;[50] but this effect, while statistically significant, seems too late and too small to meet the obligations of the board. I believe bad systems or rules, not bad people, are at the root of the general failings of boards of directors.

Board culture. Board culture is an important component of board failure. The great emphasis on politeness and courtesy at the expense of truth and frankness in boardrooms is both a symptom and cause of failure in the control system. CEOs have the same insecurities and defense mechanisms as other human beings; few will accept, much less seek, the monitoring and criticism of an active and attentive board.

The following example illustrates the general problem. John Hanley, retired Monsanto CEO, accepted an invitation from a CEO

... to join his board—subject, Hanley wrote, to meeting with the company's general counsel and outside accountants as a kind of directorial due diligence. Says Hanley: "At the first board dinner the CEO got up and said, 'I think Jack was a little bit confused whether we wanted him to be a director or the chief executive officer.' I should have known right there that he wasn't going to pay a goddamn bit of attention to anything I said." So it turned out, and after a year Hanley quit the board in disgust.[51]

The result is a continuing cycle of ineffectiveness. By rewarding consent and discouraging conflicts, CEOs have the power to control the board, which in turn ultimately reduces the CEO's and the company's performance. This downward spiral makes corporate difficulties likely to culminate in a crisis

49. See Gordon Donaldson, "Voluntary Restructuring: The Case of General Mills," *Journal of Financial Economics* 27, no. 1 (1990), 117-141. For a shorter, less technical version of the same article, see Vol. 4 No. 3 (Fall 1991) of the *Journal of Applied Corporate Finance*.

50. CEO turnover approximately doubles from 3% to 6% after two years of poor performance (stock returns less than 50% below equivalent-risk market returns, Weisbach (1988)), or increases from 8.3% to 13.9% from the highest to the lowest performing decile of firms, Warner, Watts, and Wruck (1988). See Michael Weisbach, "Outside Directors and CEO Turnovers," *Journal of Financial Economics* 20 (January-March, 1988), 431-460. and Jerold Warner, Ross Watts, and Karen Wruck, "Stock Prices and Top Management Changes," *Journal of Financial Economics* 20 (1989), 461-492.

51. Myron Magnet, "Directors, Wake Up!," *Fortune* (June 15, 1992), p. 86.

Much of corporate America's governance problem arises from the fact that neither managers nor board members typically own substantial fractions of their firm's equity. While the average CEO of the 1,000 largest firms owned 2.7% of his or her firm's equity in 1991, the median holding was only 0.2%—and 75% owned less than 1.2%.

requiring drastic steps, as opposed to a series of small problems met by a continuously self-correcting mechanism.

Information Problems. Serious information problems limit the effectiveness of board members in the typical large corporation. For example, the CEO almost always determines the agenda and the information given to the board. This limitation on information severely restricts the ability of even highly talented board members to contribute effectively to the monitoring and evaluation of the CEO and the company's strategy.

Moreover, board members should have the financial expertise necessary to provide useful input into the corporate planning process—especially, in forming the corporate objective and determining the factors which affect corporate value. Yet such financial expertise is generally lacking on today's boards. And it is not only the inability of most board members to evaluate a company's current business and financial strategy that is troubling. In many cases, boards (and managements) fail to understand that their basic mission is to maximize the (long-run) market value of the enterprise.

Legal Liability. The incentives facing modern boards are generally not consistent with shareholder interests. Boards are motivated to serve shareholders primarily by substantial legal liabilities through class action suits initiated by shareholders, the plaintiff's bar, and others—lawsuits that are often triggered by unexpected declines in stock price. These legal incentives are more often consistent with minimizing downside risk than maximizing value. Boards are also concerned about threats of adverse publicity from the media or from the political or regulatory authorities. Again, while these incentives often provide motivation for board members to reduce potential liabilities, they do not necessarily provide strong incentives to take actions that create efficiency and value for the company.

Lack of Management and Board-Member Equity Holdings. Much of corporate America's governance problem arises from the fact that neither managers nor board members typically own sub-

stantial fractions of their firm's equity. While the average CEO of the 1,000 largest firms (measured by market value of equity) owned 2.7% of his or her firm's equity in 1991, the median holding was only 0.2%—and 75% of CEOs owned less than 1.2%.[52] Encouraging outside board members to hold substantial equity interests would provide better incentives.

Of course, achieving significant direct stock ownership in large firms would require huge dollar outlays by managers or board members. To get around this problem, Bennett Stewart has proposed an interesting approach called the "leveraged equity purchase plan" (LEPP) that amounts to the sale of slightly (say, 10%) in-the-money stock options.[53] By requiring significant out-of-pocket contributions by managers and directors, and by having the exercise price of the options rise every year at the firm's cost of capital, Stewart's plan helps overcome the "free-option" aspect (or lack of downside risk) that limits the effectiveness of standard corporate option plans. It also removes the problem with standard options that allows management to reap gains on their options while shareholders are losing.[54]

Boards should have an implicit understanding or explicit requirement that new members must invest in the stock of the company. While the initial investment could vary, it should seldom be less than $100,000 from the new board member's personal funds; this investment would force new board members to recognize from the outset that their decisions affect their own wealth as well as that of remote shareholders. Over the long term, the investment can be made much larger by options or other stock-based compensation. The recent trend to pay some board-member fees in stock or options is a move in the right direction. Discouraging board members from selling this equity is also important so that holdings will accumulate to a significant size over time.

Oversized Boards. Keeping boards small can help improve their performance. When boards exceed seven or eight people, they are less likely to function effectively and are easier for the CEO to

52. See Kevin Murphy, *Executive Compensation in Corporate America, 1992,* United Shareholders Association, Washington, DC, 1992. For similar estimates based on earlier data, see also Michael Jensen and Kevin Murphy, "Performance Pay and Top-Management Incentives," *Journal of Political Economy* 98, no. 2 (1990), 225-264; and Michael Jensen and Kevin Murphy, "CEO Incentives—It's Not How Much You Pay, But How," *Harvard Business Review* 68, no. 3 (May-June, 1990).

53. See G. Bennett Stewart III, "Remaking the Public Corporation From Within," *Harvard Business Review* 68, no. 4 (July-August, 1990), 126-137.

54. This happens when the stock price rises but shareholder returns (including both dividends and capital gains) are less than the opportunity cost of capital.

control.[55] Since the possibility for animosity and retribution from the CEO is too great, it is almost impossible for direct reports to the CEO to participate openly and critically in effective evaluation and monitoring of the CEO. Therefore, the only inside board member should be the CEO; insiders other than the CEO can be regularly invited to attend board meetings in an unofficial capacity. Indeed, board members should be given regular opportunities to meet with and observe executives below the CEO—both to expand their knowledge of the company and CEO succession candidates, and to increase other top-level executives' exposure to the thinking of the board and the board process.

The CEO as Chairman of the Board. It is common in U.S. corporations for the CEO also to hold the position of Chairman of the Board. The function of the Chairman is to run board meetings and oversee the process of hiring, firing, evaluating, and compensating the CEO. Clearly, the CEO cannot perform this function apart from his or her personal interest. Without the direction of an independent leader, it is much more difficult for the board to perform its critical function. Therefore, for the board to be effective, it is important to separate the CEO and Chairman positions.[56] The independent Chairman should, at a minimum, be given the rights to initiate board appointments, board committee assignments, and (jointly with the CEO) the setting of the board's agenda. All these recommendations, of course, should be made conditional on the ratification of the board.

An effective board will often experience tension among its members as well as with the CEO. But I hasten to add that I am not advocating continuous war in the boardroom. In fact, in well-functioning organizations the board will generally be relatively inactive and will exhibit little conflict. It becomes important primarily when the rest of the internal control system is failing, and this should be a relatively rare event. The challenge is to create a system that will not fall into complacency during periods of prosperity and good management, and therefore be unable to rise early to the challenge of correcting a failing management system. This is a difficult task because there are strong tendencies for boards to develop a culture and social norms that reflect optimal behavior under prosperity, and these norms make it extremely difficult for the board to respond early to failure in its top management team.

Attempts to Model the Process on Political Democracy. There have been a number of proposals to model the board process after a democratic political model in which various constituencies are represented. Such a process, however, is likely to make the internal control system even less accountable to shareholders than it is now. To see why, we need look no farther than the inefficiency of representative political democracies (whether at the local, state or federal level) and their attempts to manage quasi-business organizations such as the Post Office, schools, or power-generation entities such as the TVA.

Nevertheless, there would likely be significant benefits to opening up the corporate governance process to the firm's largest shareholders. Proxy regulations by the SEC severely restrict communications between management and shareholders, and among shareholders themselves. Until recently, for example, it was illegal for any shareholder to discuss company matters with more than ten other shareholders without previously filing with and receiving the approval of the SEC. The November 1992 relaxation of this restriction now allows an investor to communicate with an unlimited number of other stockholders provided the investor owns less than 5% of the shares, has no special interest in the issue being discussed, and is not seeking proxy authority. But these remaining restrictions still have the obvious drawback of limiting effective institutional action by those investors most likely to pursue it.

As I discuss below, when equity holdings become concentrated in institutional hands, it is easier to resolve some of the free-rider problems that limit the ability of thousands of individual shareholders to engage in effective collective action. In principle, such institutions can therefore begin to exercise corporate control rights more effectively.

---

55. In their excellent analysis of boards, Martin Lipton and Jay Lorsch also criticize the functioning of traditionally configured boards, recommend limiting membership to 7 or 8 people, and encourage equity ownership by board members. (See Lipton and Lorsch, "A Modest Proposal for Improved Corporate Governance," *The Business Lawyer* 48, no. 1 (November, 1992), 59-77. Research supports the proposition that, as groups increase in size, they become less effective because the coordination and process problems overwhelm the advantages gained from having more people to draw on. See, for example, I. D. Steiner, *Group Process and Productivity* (Academic Press: New York, 1972) and Richard Hackman, ed., *Groups That Work* (Jossey-Bass: San Francisco, 1990).

56. Lipton and Lorsch (1992) stop short of recommending appointment of an independent chairman, recommending instead the appointment of a "lead director" whose function would be to coordinate board activities.

> **Wise CEOs can recruit large block investors to serve on the board. Active investors are important to a well-functioning governance system because they have the financial interest and independence to view firm management and policies in an unbiased way. They have the incentives to buck the system to correct problems early rather than late when the problems are obvious but difficult to correct.**

Legal and regulatory restrictions, however, have prevented financial institutions from playing a major corporate monitoring role. Therefore, if institutions are to aid in effective governance, we must continue to dismantle the rules and regulations that have prevented them and other large investors from accomplishing this coordination.

Resurrecting Active Investors

A major set of problems with internal control systems are associated with the curbing of what I call "active investors."[57] Active investors are individuals or institutions that hold large debt and/or equity positions in a company and actively participate in its strategic direction. Active investors are important to a well-functioning governance system because they have the financial interest and independence to view firm management and policies in an unbiased way. They have the incentives to buck the system to correct problems early rather than late when the problems are obvious but difficult to correct. Financial institutions such as banks, pension funds, insurance companies, mutual funds, and money managers are natural active investors, but they have been shut out of boardrooms and firm strategy by the legal structure, by custom, and by their own practices.

Active investors are important to a well-functioning governance system, and there is much we can do to dismantle the web of legal, tax, and regulatory apparatus that severely limits the scope of active investors in this country.[58] But even without such regulatory changes, CEOs and boards can take actions to encourage investors to hold large positions in their debt and equity and to play an active role in the strategic direction of the firm and in monitoring the CEO.

Wise CEOs can recruit large block investors to serve on the board, even selling new equity or debt to them to encourage their commitment to the firm. Lazard Freres Corporate Partners Fund is an example of an institution set up specifically to perform this function, making new funds available to the firm

and taking a board seat to advise and monitor management performance. Warren Buffet's activity through Berkshire Hathaway provides another example of a well-known active investor. He played an important role in helping Salomon Brothers through its recent legal and organizational difficulties following the government bond bidding scandal.

Learning from LBOs and Venture Capital Firms

Organizational Experimentation in the 1980s. The evidence from LBOs, leveraged restructurings, takeovers, and venture capital firms has demonstrated dramatically that leverage, payout policy, and ownership structure (that is, who owns the firm's securities) affect organizational efficiency, cash flow, and hence value.[59] Such organizational changes show that these effects are especially important in low-growth or declining firms where the agency costs of free cash flow are large.

Evidence from LBOs. LBOs provide a good source of estimates of the value increases resulting from changing leverage, payout policies, and the control and governance system. After the transaction, the company has a different financial policy and control system, but essentially the same managers and the same assets. Leverage increases from about 18% of value to 90%, there are large payouts to prior shareholders, and equity becomes concentrated in the hands of managers and the board (who own about 20% and 60%, on average, respectively). At the same time, boards shrink to about seven or eight people, the sensitivity of managerial pay to performance rises, and the companies' equity usually becomes private (although debt is often publicly traded).

Studies of LBOs indicate that premiums to selling-firm shareholders are roughly 40% to 50% of the pre-buyout market value, cash flows increase by 96% from the year before the buyout to three years after the buyout, and value increases by 235% (96% adjusted for general market movements) from two months prior to the buyout offer to the time of going-

---

57. See my article in this journal, "LBOs, Active Investors, and the Privatization of Bankruptcy," *Journal of Applied Corporate Finance* (Spring 1989).

58. For discussions of such legal, tax, and regulatory barriers to active investors (and proposals for reducing them), see Mark Roe, "A Political Theory of American Corporate Finance," *Columbia Law Review* 91 (1991) 10-67; Mark Roe, "Political and Legal Restraints on Ownership and Control of Public Companies," *Journal of Financial Economics* 27, No. 1 (September, 1990); Bernard Black,

"Shareholder Passivity Reexamined," *Michigan Law Review* 89 (December, 1990), 520-608; and John Pound, "Proxy Voting and the SEC: Investor Protection versus Market Efficiency," *Journal of Financial Economics* 29, no. 2, 241-285.

59. See the Appendix at the end of this article for a listing of broad-based statistical studies of these transactions, as well as detailed clinical and case studies that document the effects of the changes on incentives and organizational effectiveness.

public, sale, or recapitalization (about three years later, on average).[60] Large value increases have also been documented in voluntary recapitalizations—those in which the company stays public but buys back a significant fraction of its equity or pays out a significant dividend.[61]

A Proven Model of Governance Structure. LBO associations and venture capital funds provide a blueprint for managers and boards who wish to revamp their top-level control systems to make them more efficient. LBO firms like KKR and venture capital funds such as Kleiner Perkins are among the pre-eminent examples of active investors in recent U.S. history, and they serve as models that can be emulated in part or in total by most public corporations. The two have similar governance structures, and have been successful in resolving the governance problems of both slow-growth or declining firms (LBO associations) and high-growth entrepreneurial firms (venture capital funds).

Both LBO associations and venture capital funds tend to be organized as limited partnerships. In effect, the institutions that contribute the funds to these organizations are delegating the task of being active investors to the general partners of the organizations. Both governance systems are characterized by the following:
- limited partnership agreements at the top level that prohibit headquarters from cross-subsidizing one division with the cash from another;
- high equity ownership by managers and board members;
- board members (mostly the LBO association partners or the venture capitalists) who in their funds directly represent a large fraction of the equity owners of each subsidiary company;
- small boards (in the operating companies) typically consisting of no more than eight people;
- CEOs who are typically the only insider on the board; and
- CEOs who are seldom the chairman of the board.

LBO associations and venture funds also solve many of the information problems facing typical boards of directors. First, as a result of the due diligence process at the time the deal is done, both the managers and the LBO and venture partners have extensive and detailed knowledge of virtually all aspects of the business. In addition, these boards have frequent contact with management, often weekly or even daily during times of difficult challenges. This contact and information flow is facilitated by the fact that LBO associations and venture funds both have their own staffs. They also often perform the corporate finance function for the operating companies, providing the major interface with the capital markets and investment banking communities. Finally, the close relationship between the LBO partners or venture fund partners and the operating companies encourages the board to contribute its expertise during times of crisis. It is not unusual for a partner to join the management team, even as CEO, to help an organization through such emergencies.

CONCLUSION

Beginning with the oil price shock of the 1970s, technological, political, regulatory, and economic forces have been transforming the worldwide economy in a fashion comparable to the changes experienced during the 19th-century Industrial Revolution. As in the 19th century, technological advances in many industries have led to sharply declining costs, increased average (but declining marginal) productivity of labor, reduced growth rates of labor income, excess capacity, and the requirement for downsizing and exit.

Events of the last two decades indicate that corporate internal control systems have failed to deal effectively with these changes, especially excess capacity and the requirement for exit. The corporate control transactions of the 1980s—mergers and acquisitions, LBOs, and other leveraged recapitalizations—represented a capital market solution to this problem of widespread overcapacity. But because of the regulatory shutdown of the corporate control markets beginning in 1989, finding a solution to the problem now rests once more with the internal control systems, with corporate boards, and, to a lesser degree, with the large institutional shareholders who bear the consequences of corporate losses in value. Making corporate internal control systems work is the major challenge facing us in the 1990s.

---

60. For a review of research on LBOs, their governance changes, and their productivity effects, see Krishna Palepu, "Consequences of Leveraged Buyouts," *Journal of Financial Economics* 27, no. 1 (1990), 247-262.

61. See David and Diane Denis, "Managerial Discretion, Organizational Structure, and Corporate Performance: A Study of Leveraged Recapitalizations,"

Journal of Accounting and Economics (January 1993); and Karen Wruck and Krishna Palepu, "Consequences of Leveraged Shareholder Payouts: Defensive versus Voluntary Recapitalizations," Working paper, Harvard Business School, 1992.

APPENDIX:
Studies Documenting The Shareholder Wealth Effects of Capital Market Transactions

■ **Baker, George and Karen Wruck**, 1989, "Organizational Changes and Value Creation in Leveraged Buyouts: The Case of O.M. Scott and Sons Company," *Journal of Financial Economics* 25, no. 2, 163-190. For a shorter, less technical version of the same article, see Vol. 4 No. 1 (Spring 1991) of the *Journal of Applied Corporate Finance*.

■ **Brickley, James A., Gregg A. Jarrell, and Jeffrey M. Netter**, 1988, "The Market for Corporate Control: The Empirical Evidence Since 1980," *Journal of Economic Perspectives* 2, no. 1, 49-68, Winter.

■ **Dann, Larry Y. and Harry DeAngelo**, 1988, "Corporate Financial Policy and Corporate Control: A Study of Defensive Adjustments in Asset and Ownership Structure, *Journal of Financial Economics* 20, 87-127.

■ **DeAngelo, Harry, Linda DeAngelo, and Edward Rice**, 1984, "Going Private: Minority Freezeouts and Stockholder Wealth,"*Journal of Law and Economics* 27, 367-401.

■ **David and Diane Denis**, 1993, "Managerial Discretion, Organizational Structure, and Corporate Performance: A Study of Leveraged Recapitalizations,"*Journal of Accounting and Economics* (January). For a shorter, less technical version of the same article, see Vol. 6 No. 1 (Spring 1993) of the *Journal of Applied Corporate Finance*.

■ **Denis, David J.**, 1994, "Organizational Form and the Consequences of Highly Leveraged Transactions: Kroger's Recapitalization and Safeway's LBO," *Journal of Financial Economics*, forthcoming.

■ **Donaldson, Gordon**, 1990, "Voluntary Restructuring: The Case of General Mills," *Journal of Financial Economics* 27, no. 1, 117-141. For a shorter, less technical version of the same article, see Vol. 4 No. 3 (Fall 1991) of the *Journal of Applied Corporate Finance*.

■ **Healy, Paul M., Krishna G. Palepu, and Richard S. Ruback**, 1992, "Does Corporate Performance Improve After Mergers?," *Journal of Financial Economics* 31, vol. 2, 135-175.

■ **Holderness, Clifford G. and Dennis P. Sheehan**, 1991, "Monitoring An Owner: The Case of Turner Broadcasting," *Journal of Financial Economics* 30, no. 2, 325-346.

■ **Jensen, Michael C. and Brian Barry**, 1992, "Gordon Cain and the Sterling Group (A) and (B)," Harvard Business School, #9-942-021 and #9-942-022, 10/15.

■ **Jensen, Michael C., Willy Burkhardt, and Brian K. Barry**, 1992, "Wisconsin Central Ltd. Railroad and Berkshire Partners (A): Leverage Buyouts and Financial Distress," Harvard Business School #9-190-062, 11/13.

■ **Jensen, Michael C., Jay Dial, and Brian K. Barry**, 1992, "Wisconsin Central Ltd. Railroad and Berkshire Partners (B): LBO Associations and Corporate Governance," Harvard Business School #9-190-070, 11/13.

■ **Jensen, Michael C.**, 1986, "The Agency Costs of Free Cash Flow: Corporate Finance and Takeovers," *American Economic Review* 76, no. 2, 323-329, May.

■ **Jensen, Michael C.**, 1986, "The Takeover Controversy: Analysis and Evidence," *The Midland Corporate Finance Journal*, 4, no. 2, 6-32, Summer.

■ **Kaplan, Steven N.**, 1993, "Campeau's Acquisition of Federated: Post-bankruptcy Results," *Journal of Financial Economics* 35, 123-136.

■ **Kaplan, Steven N.**, 1989, "The Effects of Management Buyouts on Operating Performance and Value," *Journal of Financial Economics* 24, 581-618.

■ **Kaplan, Steven N.**, 1989, "Campeau's Acquisition of Federated: Value Added or Destroyed," *Journal of Financial Economics* 25, 191-212.

■ **Kaplan, Steven**, 1989, "Management Buyouts: Evidence on Taxes as a Source of Value," *Journal of Finance* 44, 611-632.

■ **Kaplan, Steven N. and Jeremy Stein**, 1993, "The Evolution of Buyout Pricing and Financial Structure in the 1980s," *Quarterly Journal of Economics* 108, no. 2, 313-358. For a shorter, less technical version of the same article, see Vol. 6 No. 1 (Spring 1993) of the *Journal of Applied Corporate Finance*.

■ **Kaplan, Steven N. and Jeremy Stein**, 1990, "How Risky is the Debt in Highly Leveraged Transactions?," *Journal of Financial Economics* 27, no. 1, 215-245.

■ **Lang, Larry H.P., Annette Poulsen, and Rene M. Stulz**, 1994, "Asset Sales, Leverage, and the Agency Costs of Managerial Discretion,"*Journal of Financial Economics*, forthcoming.

■ **Lichtenberg, Frank R.**, 1992, *Corporate Takeovers and Productivity*, (MIT Press: Cambridge, MA). For a shorter, less technical summary of the findings, see Vol. 2 No. 2 (Summer 1989) of the *Journal of Applied Corporate Finance*.

■ **Lichtenberg, Frank R. and Donald Siegel**, 1990, "The Effects of Leveraged Buyouts on Productivity and Related Aspects of Firm Behavior," *Journal of Financial Economics* 27, volume 1, 165-194, September.

■ **Mann, Steven V. and Neil W. Sicherman**, 1991, "The Agency Costs of Free Cash Flow: Acquisition Activity, and Equity Issues," *Journal of Business* 64, no. 2, 213-227.

■ **Murphy, Kevin J. and Jay Dial**, 1992, "Compensation and Strategy at General Dynamics (A) and (B)," Harvard Business School #N9-493-032 and N9-493-033, Boston, MA, 11/19.

■ **Palepu, Krishna G.**, 1990, "Consequences of Leveraged Buyouts," *Journal of Financial Economics* 27, no. 1, 247-262.

■ **Rosett, Joshua G.**, 1990, "Do Union Wealth Concessions Explain Takeover Premiums? The Evidence on Contract Wages," *Journal of Financial Economics* 27, no. 1, 263-282.

■ **Smith, Abbie J.**, 1990, "Corporate Ownership Structure and Performance: The Case of Management Buyouts," *Journal of Financial Economics* 27, 143-164.

■ **Tedlow, Richard**, 1991, "Hitting the Skids: Tires and Time Horizons," Unpublished manuscript, Harvard Business School, Cambridge, MA.

■ **Tiemann, Jonathan**, 1990, "The Economics of Exit and Restructuring: The Pabst Brewing Company," Unpublished manuscript, Harvard Business School.

■ **Wruck, Karen H.**, 1991, "What Really Went Wrong at Revco?," *Journal of Applied Corporate Finance* 4, 79-92, Summer.

■ **Wruck, Karen H.**, 1990, "Financial Distress, Reorganization, and Organizational Efficiency,"*Journal of Financial Economics* 27, 420-444.

■ **Wruck, Karen H.**, 1994, "Financial Policy, Internal Control, and Performance: Sealed Air Corporation's Leveraged Special Dividend," *Journal of Financial Economics*, forthcoming.

■ **Wruck, Karen H. and Krishna Palepu**, 1992, "Consequences of Leveraged Shareholder Payouts: Defensive versus Voluntary Recapitalizations," Working paper, Harvard Business School, August.

■ **Wruck, Karen H. and Steve-Anna Stephens**, 1992, "Leveraged Buyouts and Restructuring. The Case of Safeway, Inc.," Harvard Business School Case #192-095.

■ **Wruck, Karen H. and Steve-Anna Stephens**, 1992, "Leveraged Buyouts and Restructuring: The Case of Safeway, Inc.: Media Response," Harvard Business School Case #192-094.

IS AMERICAN CORPORATE GOVERNANCE FATALLY FLAWED?

by Merton H. Miller,
University of Chicago*

Are the investment horizons of U.S. firms too short? Yes, was the conclusion of *Capital Choices*, a report published in August 1992 by 25 academic scholars under the leadership of Professor Michael Porter of the Harvard Business School. The Porter Report was widely acclaimed not only by the U.S. financial press, but by many Japanese observers. Mr. Katsuro Umino, for one, Vice President of the Osaka-based Kotsu Trading Company, was quoted in the Chicago *Tribune* of August 24, 1992 as saying:

It's interesting to see that somebody in America is finally waking up to the real culprit behind the decline of American corporate competitiveness. I think many of us in Japan have known for a long time that America's capital allocation system is inherently flawed.

The flaw seen by Messrs. Porter and Umino and ever so many others is the overemphasis on stock prices and shareholder returns in the American system of corporate governance. By contrast, a survey of 1,000 Japanese and 1,000 American firms by Japan's Economic Planning Agency, reported in the same Chicago *Tribune* story, finds that on a scale of 0 to 3—3 being most important—Japanese firms give "Higher Stock Price" a rating of only 0.02. "Increasing Market Share" gets a reported rating of 1.43 in Japan, almost twice its rating in the United States.

Surveys must never be taken too literally, of course. Japanese managers surely cannot believe that increasing market share is the overriding corporate goal. Achieving a 100 percent market share for your product is too easy: just give it away! Profitability must also and always be considered. And, indeed, the Japanese firms surveyed did give a rating of 1.24 to Return on Investment—far less than the 2.43 rating given by the American firms, but still much much more than the virtually zero weight given to Higher Stock Prices.

For all its technical limitations, however, the survey does, I believe, accurately reflect differences in managerial behavior in the two countries. American managers *are* more concerned with current movements in their own stock prices than are Japanese managers. And rightly so. The emphasis American managers place on shareholder returns is not a flaw in the U.S. corporate governance system, but one of its primary strengths.

Some of my academic colleagues believe, in fact, that American big-business management has been putting put too *little* weight on stockholder returns, leading to massive waste of both shareholder and national wealth. Their argument has not, in my view, been convincingly established. The billion-dollar losses of companies like IBM and General Motors in recent years, offered by such critics as evidence for their case, testify less to failures in the U.S. governance system than to the vigorously competitive environment in which U.S. firms must operate.

*My thanks for helpful comments from my colleagues Steven Kaplan and Anil Kashyap and from Donald Chew.

MAXIMIZING SHAREHOLDER VALUE AS THE PRIMARY OBJECTIVE OF THE BUSINESS CORPORATION

Let me begin my defense of U.S. corporate governance by emphasizing that managerial concern with shareholder value is merely one specific application of the more general proposition that in American society the individual is king. Not the nation, not the government, not the producers, not the merchants, but the individual—and especially the individual consumer—is sovereign. Certainly that has not been the accepted view of ultimate economic sovereignty here in Japan, though the first signs of change are beginning to appear.

The connection between consumer sovereignty and corporate governance lies not just in the benefits customers derive from the firm's own output. The customers are not the only consumers the firm serves. The shareholders, the investors, the owners—however one chooses to call them—are also consumers and their consumption, actual and potential, is what drives the shareholder-value principle.

To see how and why, consider the directors of a firm debating how much of the firm's current profits, say $10 million, to pay out as dividends to the shareholders. If the $10 million is paid as dividends, the shareholders clearly have an additional $10 million in cash to spend. Suppose, however, that the $10 million is not paid out, but used instead for investment in the firm—buying machinery, expanding the factory, setting up a new branch, or what have you. The stockholders now do not get the cash, but they need not be disadvantaged thereby. That will depend on how the stock market values the proposed new investment projects.

If the market believes the firm's managers have invested wisely, the value of the shares may rise by $10 million or even more. Stockholders seeking to convert this potential consumption into actual consumption need only sell the shares and spend the proceeds. But if the market feels that the managers have spent the money foolishly, the stock value will rise by less than the forgone dividend of $10 million—perhaps by only $5 million, or possibly not at all. Those new investments may have expanded the firm's market share; they may have vastly improved the firm's image and the prestige of its managers. But they have not increased shareholder wealth and potential consumption. They have reduced it.

Current Market Values and Future Earnings

Using the stock market's response to measure the true worth of the proposed new investments may strike many here in Japan as precisely the kind of short-termism that has led so many American firms astray. Let it be clearly understood, therefore, that, in a U.S.-style stock market, focusing on current *stock* prices is not short-termism. Focusing on current *earnings* might be myopic, but not so for stock prices, which reflect not just today's earnings, but the earnings the market expects in all future years as well.

Just how much weight expected future earnings carry in determining current stock prices always surprises those not accustomed to working with present-value formulas and, especially, with growth formulas. Growth formulas, however, whether of dividends or earnings, rarely strike my Japanese friends or my Japanese students as very compelling. Many Japanese firms, after all, pay only nominal dividends, and the formulas don't make sufficiently clear what investors are really buying when they buy a stock.

Let me therefore shift the focus from a firm's rate of sales or earnings growth to where it ought to be— namely, to the competitive conditions facing the firm over meaningful horizons. And let me, for reasons that will become clear later, measure the strength of those competitive conditions by the currently fashionable market value-to-book value ratio (also known as the "market-to-book" or "price-to-book" ratio). The book-value term in the ratio, based as it is on original cost, approximates what management actually spent for the assets the market is valuing. A market-to-book ratio of 1.0 (abstracting from any concerns about pure price inflation) is thus a natural benchmark, signifying a firm with no competitive advantage or disadvantage. The firm is expected to earn only normal profits in the economists' sense of that term, that is, profits just large enough to give the stockholders the average, risk-adjusted return for equities generally.

To sell for more than an unremarkable market-to-book ratio of 1.0—that is, to have a positive "franchise value," as some put it—a firm must have long-term competitive advantages allowing it to earn a higher than normal rate of return on its productive assets. And that's not as easy to do as it may seem. Above-normal profits always carry with them the seeds of their own decay. They attract competitors, both from within a country and from abroad, driving profits and share prices relentlessly back toward the competitive norm. Investors buying into a firm are thus making judgments not only about whether the firm and its managers have produced a competitive advantage over their rivals, but also about how far into the future that competitive advantage can be expected to last.

Some specific numbers may help to fix ideas.[1] Consider a U.S. firm with a market-to-book ratio of 3.0—and there still are many such. And suppose, further, that it will be plowing back its entire cash flow into investments expected to earn *twice* the normal competitive rate of return. By paying three times book value for the shares, investors are in effect anticipating that the firm will expand and stay that far ahead of its competitors *for the next 20 years*!

That's *really* forward-looking—much too forward looking, some would say, in this highly uncertain world. And perhaps that's why so many Japanese managers are instinctively skeptical about using the stock market to guide or evaluate managerial decision-making. They don't really trust the prices in the Japanese stock market where, at the height of the stock market boom of 1989, market-to-book ratios were not just 3.0 but, even after adjusting for real estate and for other corporate shares in crossholdings, ran routinely to 5.0 or even 10.0. Such ratios implied that investors saw opportunities for these companies to earn above-normal, competitor-proof returns for centuries to come!

Prices and market-to-book ratios have fallen substantially since then, but are still hard to take seriously because they are not completely free-market prices. The values are not only distorted by the pervasive cross-holdings of nontraded shares, but the prices of the thinly-traded minority of shares in the floating supply often reflect the heroic scale of market intervention by the Ministry of Finance (MOF). Japanese managers can be pardoned for wondering whether the stock market may be just a *Bunraku* theater, with the bureaucrats from MOF backstage manipulating the puppets.

MOF's notorious market support activities also interact in other ways with the issue of corporate governance in Japan. Many academic observers in the U.S. (myself, in particular)[2] have attributed MOF's famous P.K.O. (Price Keeping Operations, and a Japanese pun on the country's participation in the U.N.'s Peace Keeping Operations in Cambodia) to its role as cartel manager for the Japanese brokerage industry. Another motivation traces, however, to the Japanese banking industry. Japanese banks, unlike those in the U.S., can hold equity positions in the companies to which they are also lending—a dual role that, in turn, has often been cited as the real key to Japanese managerial success. The bank connection is said to reduce corporate agency costs, provide better monitoring of corporate decisions, and, above all, allow management to undertake profitable but risky long-run ventures while confident of having the continued financial support needed to carry projects through to completion.

But any gains to the Japanese economy on the governance front have come at a substantial cost on other fronts. Corporate equities can be great assets for banks when the stock market is booming as it was in Japan in the 1980s. The price appreciation then provides the banks with substantial regulatory capital to support their lending activities. But when the stock market collapses, as it did in Japan after 1989, the disappearance of those hidden equity reserves can threaten the solvency of the banks and the integrity of the country's payment system.

The prospect becomes even more frightening when we remember that shareholdings in Japan run in both directions. Not only do banks hold the firm's shares but the firms—again, presumably with a view to better governance—also hold the *banks'* shares. The result is a classic, unstable, positive-feedback asset pyramid. No wonder MOF must keep supporting stock prices and always seems to be running around, like the proverbial Dutch boy on the dikes, plugging holes and leaks in its regulations.

Stock Prices and Information

To say that the stock market in the U.S. is much closer to the free-market ideal than the Japanese

1. The calculations to follow are adapted from the finite growth model presented in Merton H. Miller and Franco Modigliani, "Dividend Policy, Growth and the Valuation of Shares," *Journal of Business*, Vol. 24, No. 4 (October 1961), pp. 411-433. I have taken the value of *rho* (the risk-adjusted cost of capital) as 10 percent (what else?) and the value of *k* (the investment-to-earnings ratio) as 1.0. A firm with a market-to-book ratio of 1.0 corresponds to a "no growth-premium firm" with average internal rate of return (*rho-star*) just equal to the cost of capital.

2. For an account of how MOF systematically uses its regulatory powers to sustain the Japanese brokerage industry cartel and to support the level of stock prices, see my articles, "The Economics and Politics of Index Arbitrage in the U.S. and Japan," *Pacific-Basin Finance Journal*, Vol. 1, No. 1 (May 1993), pp. 3-11; and "Japanese-American Trade Relations in the Financial Services Industry," Working Paper, Graduate School of Business, University of Chicago (September 1993).

Japanese stock prices, even at current levels, are still hard to take seriously because
they are not completely free-market prices. Japanese managers can be pardoned for
wondering whether the stock market may be just a *Bunraku* theater, with the
bureaucrats from MOF backstage manipulating the puppets.

stock market is not to suggest that valuations in the U.S. are always correct. But at least those investors with bearish opinions about particular stocks or the market as a whole can express their pessimism by selling, even selling short, without encountering the kind of anti-selling rules and taboos for which MOF has become notorious. Those pessimists may well be wrong, of course. And so in their turn may be those who are optimistically anticipating a rise in future earnings and prices.

No serious student of stock markets has ever suggested that stock prices always "correctly" measure the true "fundamentals," whatever those words might mean. The most claimed is that the prices are not systematically distorted, like those in Japan where MOF's heavy thumb often tilts the scales against selling. Nor are the prices in the U.S. just some artificial numbers driven by whims and fads, as some academics have argued (and quite unsuccessfully so, in my opinion). The evidence overwhelmingly supports the view that prices reflect in an unbiased way all the information about a company that is available to the investing public.

The word "available" is worth stressing, however. Stockholders and potential outside investors can't be expected to value management's proposed investment projects properly if they don't have the information on which management has based those plans. And management may well hesitate to disclose that information for fear of alerting competitors. This inevitable "asymmetry" in information, to use the fashionable academic jargon, is what many see as the real flaw in the shareholder-value principle. Projects with positive net present values, possibly even with substantial net present values, may not be undertaken because outside investors cannot value the projects properly and will condemn management for wasting the stockholders' money. That, essentially, is the Porter position. As one way to deal with it, the Porter study recommends that U.S. governance rules be changed to permit firms to disclose proprietary, competitively-sensitive information *selectively* to that subset of the stockholders willing to commit to long-term investing in the company.

Can investment be discouraged by inability to disclose selectively? Possibly. Has it happened? And on what scale? That is much harder to say. The main evidence cited for its pervasiveness in the U.S. is the supposedly superior earnings and growth performance of bank-disciplined Japanese manufacturing firms relative to their impatient American stock-

holder-disciplined counterparts. Note that I stress Japanese *manufacturing* firms. No one has ever suggested that Japanese market-share-oriented firms were superior in the service industries, notably retailing, or in commercial banking.

And I should say that manufacturing *was* the main evidence for Japanese governance superiority cited before the current recession hit Japan. That recession, painful as has been and still is its impact on the Japanese economy, has at least served to remind us that myopia is not the only disease of vision afflicting business managers. They may suffer from astigmatism (distorted vision) or even from hyperopia or excessive far-sightedness. Looking back over the last 20 years, one may well find cases in which American firms facing strong stockholder pressures to pay out funds invested too little in some kinds of capital-intensive technology. But many Japanese firms, facing no such pressures, have clearly *over*invested during that same period in highly capital-intensive plants that will never come close to recovering their initial investment, let alone earning a positive rate of return. And I won't even mention the trillions of yen poured into land and office buildings both at home and abroad.

No form of corporate governance, needless to say, whether Japanese or American, can guarantee 20-20 vision by management. Mistakes, both of omission and of commission, will always be made. My claim is only that those American managers who *do* focus on maximizing the market value of the firm have a better set of correcting lenses for properly judging the trade-off between current investment and future benefits than those who focus on maximizing growth, market share, or some other, trendy, presumed strategic advantage.

MANAGEMENT OBJECTIVES AND STOCKHOLDER INTERESTS

Glasses help you see better, of course, only if you wear them. And the complaint of at least one wing of American academic opinion, especially in the field of finance, is precisely that U.S. managers don't always wear their stockholder-corrected lenses to work. Because ownership of American corporations is so widely dispersed among a multitude of passive individual and institutional investors, U.S. managers, so the argument runs, are left free to pursue objectives that may, but need not, conform to those of the stockholders.

Shareholders, however, are not powerless. Although neither able nor willing to perform day-by-day monitoring of management operating decisions, shareholders do have the right to elect the company's Board of Directors. And the Board, in turn, by its power to unseat management, and even more by its power to design the program for executive compensation, has command over important levers for aligning management's objectives with those of the shareholders.

Compensation Packages and Management Incentives

The Board of Directors has a tool-box full of levers but not, alas, any simple or fool-proof set of instructions for using them. In fact, academic "agency cost" theory suggests that *no* all-purpose optimal scheme—no "first-best" as opposed to, say, second-best or even lower-best solution—really exists for aligning interests when success depends on luck as well as skill.

To see why, ask yourself how the directors could make the managers accept the stockholders' attitudes toward risk. Suppose, to be specific, that the directors try what may seem the obvious performance-based compensation strategy of giving the managers shares in the company. Will that make managers act like the shareholders would? More so, probably, than if the directors just offered a flat—and presumably high—salary supplemented with generous retirement benefits. Managers so compensated are more likely to be working for the bondholders than for the stockholders. Salaried managers clearly have little incentive to consider projects with serious downside risk.

Giving managers stock at least lets them participate in the gains from their successful moves, but still does not solve the problem of excessive managerial timidity—excessive, that is, relative to the interests of the outside stockholders. Those stockholders are, or at least in principle ought to be, well diversified. They can thus afford risking their entire investment in the company even for only 50:50 odds because their stockholding is only a small part of their total wealth. That, after all, is a key social benefit of the corporate form with fractional and easily transfer-able ownership interests: more efficient sharing of the business risks. But the managers are typically *not* diversified. A major fraction of their personal wealth and their human capital is tied to the corporation. Caution, not boldness, inevitably becomes their watchword.

The executive stock option was invented in the U.S. in the 1950s precisely to offset the play-it-safe tendencies of underdiversified corporate managers (though tax considerations and accounting conventions have since blurred the original incentive-driven motivation for options).[3] Stock options, suitably structured, work by magnifying the upside potential for the manager relative to the down. A bet paying $1,000 if a coin comes up heads and losing $1,000 if tails would hardly be tempting to the typical risk-averse manager. But tossing a fair coin might well seem attractive if heads brought $5,000 and tails cost only $500.

Options and their many variations—including option-equivalents like highly leveraged corporate capital structures—not only can reduce management's natural risk-aversion, but may overdo it and tempt managers into excessively risky ventures. If these long-odds strategies do happen to pay off, the managers profit enormously. If not, the bulk of the losses are borne by the shareholders, and probably the bondholders and other prior claimants as well. Many observers feel that a payoff asymmetry of precisely this kind for undercapitalized owner-managers was the root cause of the U.S. Savings and Loan disaster.

The inability to align management interests and risk attitudes more closely with those of the stockholders shows up most conspicuously, some academic critics would argue, in the matter of corporate diversification. Corporate diversification does reduce risk for the managers. But because stockholders can diversify directly, they have little to gain—except perhaps for some tax benefits, large in some cases, from internal offsetting rather than carryforward of losses—when a General Motors, say, uses funds that might otherwise have been paid as dividends to buy up Ross Perot's firm, Electronic Data Services (EDS). In fairness, however, let it be noted that the stockholders, by the same token, would have little to lose by such acquisitions unless the acquiring firm

3. See Merton Miller and Myron Scholes, "Executive Compensation, Taxes and Incentives," in *Financial Economics: Essays in Honor of Paul Cootner,* William Sharpe and Catheryn Cootner (Eds.), Prentice-Hall, Englewood Cliffs, NJ, 1982.

Myopia is not the only disease of vision afflicting business managers. They may suffer from astigmatism or even from excessive far-sightedness. Looking back over the last 20 years, one will find cases in which American firms facing strong stockholder pressures to pay out funds invested too little. But many Japanese firms, facing no such pressures, have clearly over*invested during that same period.*

FIGURE 1
SOCIAL VERSUS PRIVATE
COSTS OF LOSING
A CORPORATE
FRANCHISE PREMIUM

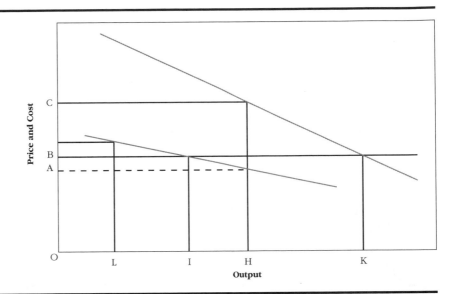

were to pay too high a price for control—which certainly has been known to happen.

Stockholders could also lose if diversification predictably and consistently means sacrificing the efficiencies from specialization. Some evidence suggests that it does—although hardly enough, in my view, to justify claims by some academic critics of corporate diversification that loss of corporate focus and related failures of governance by GM or IBM or Sears in recent years have destroyed *hundreds of billions* of dollars of their stockholders' and, by extension, of the nation's wealth.

For those firms, certainly, aggregate stock market values have declined substantially. But to treat such declines as a national disaster like some gigantic earthquake is to overlook the distinction between social costs and private costs. Consider, for example, the story told in Figure 1, which pictures an IBM-type firm about to be hit unexpectedly with an anti-trust suit (and let it be clearly understood that this is an illustration, and not necessarily a recommendation). The company's initial demand curve is d_1d_1, and its long-run marginal cost is BJ (assumed, for simplicity, to be constant and hence equal to its average cost). Because the firm had "market power," it set its product price at OC (i.e., above average and marginal cost), earning thereby the above-normal profits indicated by the rectangle BCDF. Those above-competitive profits will be capitalized by the stock

market and the company will sell for a high market-to-book value premium.

Now let the government win its anti-trust suit against the company and immediately force the company's price and output to their competitive levels (OB for price and OK for quantity). The abnormal profits will vanish, the stock price will fall, and the market-to-book value premium will disappear. Yet no net loss in *national* wealth or welfare has occurred in this instance. Wealth and economic welfare have simply been transferred from the company's shareholders to its customers; producer surplus has been transformed into consumers' surplus. In fact, in the case pictured, society is better off on balance, not worse off. Because output increases to the competitive level, consumers gain additional consumers' surplus in the form of the ("Harberger") triangle DFN.

The social and private consequences are easily distinguished in this anti-trust scenario. But what if the decline in stock-market value is a self-inflicted wound? IBM, after all, did *not* lose its anti-trust case. Its market value was eroded by the entry of new firms with new technologies.

That kind of value erosion, however, surely cannot be the national disaster to which the governance critics are pointing. Why, after all, should society's consumers care whether the new products were introduced by IBM or by Intel or Apple; by

Wal-Mart or by Sears; or, for that matter, by General Motors or by Toyota? The complaint of the critics may be rather that the managements of those firms have failed to downsize and restructure fast enough even *after* the new competition had penetrated the market. Entrenched managements, unchecked by the hand-picked sycophants on their Boards, kept pouring money into the old, money-losing lines of the firm's business rather than letting their stockholders redeploy the funds to better advantage elsewhere.

But continuing to make positive investments in a declining industry—"throwing good money after bad," as the cliché would have it—cannot automatically be taken as evidence of economic inefficiency, and certainly not of bad management. Nothing in economic logic or commonsense suggests the best exit path is always the quickest one. A firm withdraws its capital by making its *net* investment negative, that is, by holding its rate of gross investment below the rate of depreciation. The marginal rate of return on that gross investment may well be high even though the average rate of return on the past capital sunk in the division or the firm as a whole is low or even negative. When the direct costs of exit (such as severance payments) are high, and when the firm is at least covering its variable costs (unlike many in Russia, so we are told), investing to reduce a loss can often be a highly positive net-present-value project indeed.

Suppose, however, for the sake of argument that some entrenched managers *were* too slow in downsizing. The losses reported by their firms still cannot be equated dollar for dollar with the social costs of bad governance. To see why, turn again to Figure 1, which can also be used to show the new condition of our original firm—that is, after the entry of the new competition attracted by its earlier high profits. The firm's demand curve is now the much more elastic demand curve d_2d_2, and its new long-run equilibrium level of output will be OL, smaller than its earlier equilibrium output level OH.

Should the firm seek to maintain its earlier market share of OH, however, net losses of ABFG will be incurred, exactly as the critics insist. But only the triangle MFG represents the social cost of the failure to downsize. The rest, given by the area ABMG is, again, merely a transfer to consumer surplus. How much of the reported loss goes one way and how much goes the other cannot be settled, of course, merely from a schematic diagram. That

requires specific empirical research of a kind not yet found in the recent academic literature so critical of U.S. corporate governance.

That the losses suffered in recent years by firms like IBM or Sears or General Motors may not be social losses will be of little comfort, of course, to those stockholders who have seen so much of their retirement nest eggs in those companies vanish. One can hardly blame them for wishing that the directors had somehow prodded management to abandon their formerly successful strategies *before* the success of the newer competitive strategies had been so decisively confirmed. Fortunately, however, shareholders whose personal stake is too small to justify costly monitoring of management have another and well-tested way to protect their savings from management's mistakes of omission or commission: diversify! A properly diversified shareholder would have the satisfaction of knowing that his or her loss on IBM shares or Sears or General Motors was not even a *private* loss since it was offset in the portfolio by gains on Microsoft, Intel, Apple, WalMart and other new-entrant firms, foreign and domestic, that did pioneer in the new technologies.

CONCLUSION

Summing up, then, we have seen two quite different views of what is wrong with American corporate management. One view, widely accepted in Japan and by the Michael Porter wing of academic opinion, is that American managers pay too much attention to current shareholder returns. The other view, widely held among U.S. academic finance specialists, is that American managers pay too little attention to shareholder returns.

Which view is right? Both. And neither. Both sides can point to specific cases or examples seeming to support their positions. But both are wrong in claiming any permanent or systematic bias for U.S. firms in the aggregate toward myopia or hyperopia, toward underinvestment or overinvestment relative either to the shareholders' or to society's best interests. There is no inherent bias because market forces are constantly at work to remove control over corporate assets from managers who lack the competence or the vision to deploy them efficiently.

We saw those forces most dramatically perhaps in the takeover battles, leveraged buyouts, and corporate restructurings of the 1980s and, more recently, in many well-publicized board-led insur-

> **There is no permanent or systematic bias for U.S. firms in the aggregate toward myopia or hyperopia, toward underinvestment or overinvestment, because market forces are constantly at work to remove control over corporate assets from managers who lack the competence or the vision to deploy them efficiently.**

gencies. But, for all their drama, those events (which often seem little more than struggles over how the corporate franchise premium is to be shared between the executives and the shareholders) represent only one part—and by no means the most important part—of the process of allocating society's productive capital among firms. The ultimate disci-

pline for the managers of one firm in the U.S. will always be the managers of other firms, including foreign firms, competing with them head to head for customer business. As long as we continue to have plenty of *that* kind of competition in the U.S., I, for one, can't become terribly concerned about the supposedly fatal flaws in our governance system.

■ MERTON MILLER

is the Robert R. McCormick Distinguished Service Professor Emeritus at the University of Chicago's Graduate School of Business. Professor Miller won the Nobel Prize in Economics in 1990.

CORPORATE GOVERNANCE OR CORPORATE VALUE ADDED?: RETHINKING THE PRIMACY OF SHAREHOLDER VALUE

by C. K. Prahalad,
University of Michigan*

Accounts of the much-publicized troubles of CEOs at companies like IBM, General Motors, Kodak, and Sears have focused almost exclusively on the balance of power and struggle for control between top management and investors. Boards of directors are caught in the middle of such control "contests," and when and how they should perform their mediating function is now being widely debated. Large pension funds such as CalPERS and other investor advocates are viewed as saviors by some and villains by others.

But, in spite of all the emotion and energy behind the debate, the real problem has not been correctly identified—and so the recommended cures are often worse than the disease. We may need to rethink what we mean by "corporate governance."

The popular understanding of the U.S. corporate governance problem is grounded in financial economists' theory of capital markets. This theory, which begins with the assumption that stockholders are the owners of the firm,[1] is preoccupied with the efficiency of the *market* in allocating capital *among firms*. In this view of the world, the efficiency of firms in general is maintained by investors' ability to move their capital and, by denying capital or making it expensive, to punish errant managers. The theory offers managers little guidance, however, about the means of increasing the efficiency of *specific firms within that market.*

The capital market focus also leads to an easily understood and readily communicated *scorecard* of corporate performance—that is, a company's market value as measured by its current stock price. Using stock price as their yardstick, financial economists profess to be able to tell us which companies are "winning the game" and which are losing. Almost no attention is paid, however, to the process by which wealth is created in a large firm—that is, *how the game is played.* Financial economists, analysts, and investors have all, for the most part, been content to treat the internal process of wealth creation—what I think of as *the game itself*—as a "black box."

In my talk today, I approach the corporate governance issue from the *perspective of the individual firm*; that is, I concentrate on *the game itself*, as opposed to the capital market's latest pronouncements on winners and losers. This focus provides an alternative to the "control-oriented" perspective provided by financial economists—one that I believe will lead to more effective crisis avoidance, fewer unpleasant surprises for shareholders, and, over time, greater wealth creation for investors and society at large.

I begin by arguing that the reality of capital markets in the 1990s—notably, the changing patterns of share ownership and the slowdown of the takeover market—is very different from that which existed during the development of capital market theory, and that some of the critical assumptions on which this theory rests are no longer tenable. I then go on to demonstrate that the quality of *internal* governance depends critically on the nature of stockholder activism. In brief, my message here is that greater information-sharing and cooperation among boards, managers, and major investors are more likely to lead to sustained wealth creation than the adversarial relationships that prevailed during the 1980s.

*The author gratefully acknowledges the research assistance provided by Ms. Karen Schnatterly, Ph.D. student, at the University of Michigan.

1. More precisely, finance shareholders are the "residual claimants" entitled to all earnings and assets once all other prior claimants are fully compensated.

In closing, I present my conception of the *process of wealth creation* as a *balancing act* that attempts to meet simultaneously the demands of various corporate "stakeholders"—customers, employees, suppliers, as well as investors. This is quite different from the financial economist's prescription that managers attempt single-mindedly to maximize shareholder value. In place of shareholder-value maximization, I offer my own concept of *corporate value added*—a corporate objective more attuned to the economic and competitive realities of the 1990s.

WHY THIS DEBATE NOW?

Although we may continue to debate the effectiveness of the takeovers and LBOs of the 1980s, these capital market solutions to corporate inefficiency are no longer as readily available today. Managers now have at their disposal a wide variety of anti-takeover measures. Poison pills, shark repellants, state anti-takeover laws, and other such roadblocks to control transactions have sharply increased the costs of imposing the discipline of the capital market on poor performers.

The activity of the "corporate control" market during the 1980s was not an indication of the success of the U.S. corporate governance system, but rather a clear sign of its failure. The stockholder activism of the '80s was a response of last resort, and it therefore functioned as a very blunt instrument of corporate reform.[2] Although large shareholder gains were achieved through takeovers in the short run, much longer-term corporate value—which consists, as I will argue, in no small part of the quality of management relations with employees, suppliers, and investors—was lost in the process.

Efforts to discipline inefficient managers using market mechanisms during the 1980s followed a predictable sequence. The first sign of investor unrest was often triggered by persistent, typically unanticipated, profit declines that led in turn to sharp stock price declines. If things deteriorated far enough, a hostile takeover bid emerged.

One major problem with this capital market "solution" is that, by the time outsiders intervene, it is often too late to take meaningful corrective action. In any large diversified firm, profit declines are typically preceded by several years of inefficient management. Sheer momentum in such firms can insulate profits for quite some time before clear evidence of managerial inefficiencies begins to show through the veil of corporate size and scope. (The opposite is true as well; it generally takes several years for even the best managers to turn around the financial performance of badly run firms.) For example, when did the impending crisis first become apparent to investors in firms such as IBM, DEC, Wang, Philips, and General Motors?

The most sophisticated observers of corporate behavior are those able to distinguish *strategic vulnerability* from *financial results*. Such people pay attention to not only profit and cash flow numbers, but also to changes in product portfolios, productivity, cycle times, and quality of products and services. In many of the cases of corporate decline just cited, sophisticated corporate strategists were expressing doubts about the efficiency of top management long before sharp declines in stock prices and financial performance exposed the extent of the problem to all. Consider that, as recently as 1987, IBM's stock, now under $60, was selling for $175; at the same time DEC, now trading for less than $35, was adjudged by the stock market to be worth $200.

After stock prices decline and the extent of managerial inefficiency is revealed, shareholders have two basic choices. One, they can sell their stock and move on to better-managed alternatives (although, as we shall see, this option is less feasible today for large institutional holders than it once may have been). Or two, they can attempt to replace the top managers. But this is a very costly process, especially since managers have found many ways to use the legal and regulatory system to set up roadblocks. And even if managers are replaced, there is no guarantee that efficiency will be restored soon.

The severity of the corporate governance problem confronting investors today can be seen, in part, as an after-effect of the "vicious cycle" of the 1980s. In that period, stockholder activists and top managers alike devoted more time and energy to legal maneuvers designed to outwit one another than to improving the long-run prospects of the business. And while the issue of corporate governance became mired in legal debates, attention was diverted

---

2. While the process allowed for some rationalization of efficiency, it came at a significant cost. I estimate the costs of restructuring in the U.S. to have exceeded $400 billion during the 1980s.

away from the substantive economic issues—notably, the process of *continuous corporate renewal* and *sustained wealth creation.*

ARE OUR ASSUMPTIONS INCOMPLETE?

It is my contention that the underlying assumptions of financial economics are neither appropriate nor adequate for dealing with the wealth-creation process and its demands on corporations in the 1990s. As a consequence, the finance literature offers at best partial explanations of the corporate governance issues that now confront us. To see why the current governance debate misses the mark, and why the proposed solutions are inadequate, let's examine the assumptions themselves.

The interests of owners and managers are divergent. The theory of "agency costs" that pervades the finance literature suggests that the relationship between shareholders and management in large public companies is inevitably adversarial. There is thus a need to align the interests of owners (investors) and managers, primarily by creating appropriate financial incentives for top managers. In practice, this means tying the pay of CEOs and other top managers more strongly to financial measures of performance, especially share price. The underlying assumption is that changing incentives will cause the firm to increase its market value or, in my terms, to become more effective in "playing the game."

As I suggested earlier, however, very little attention is paid to the actual wealth creation process; in effect, the firm is still treated as a black box.

Very large firms and widely distributed ownership leads to "powerless shareholders." The popular image of shareholders as "poor old men and women in tennis shoes" unable to rein in CEOs who fly around in Lear jets and enjoy country club memberships is difficult to dispel. The reality, however, is not nearly as one-sided. Today, more than 60% of the shares of the Fortune 200 are held by institutional investors.[3] Moreover, many individual institutional investors are increasingly likely to hold concentrated blocks in large companies. CalPERS, for example, held almost 2% of Kodak throughout most of 1993.

This evolving pattern of more concentrated shareholdings has created a new problem for institutional investors. They cannot sell such large holdings in a company without significantly reducing the price of the stocks being sold. Such illiquidity in turn creates a two-way dependence between managers and large investors. Top managers depend on the goodwill of institutional investors who evaluate their performance through their portfolio choices. At the same time, investors depend on managers to produce the superior operating performance necessary for them to show adequate investment returns.

Given such mutual dependence, one wonders why a more cooperative relationship between the two groups has not evolved. Institutional investors, for example, should play a much larger role in crisis prevention than they now do; they should intervene long before the problems escalate to the point where companies like IBM and General Motors are reporting billion-dollar losses. Institutional investors have the resources and sophistication necessary to play such a role.

Boards are protectors of shareholder interests. While the ownership and management debate goes on, corporate boards are seen as providing the necessary checks and balances to make the system work. In practice, however, the capacity of boards to perform this function is debatable. The sympathies of most board members are much more closely aligned with the interests of top managers, whom they know, than with those of stockholders, who are faceless. Even when boards have acted, as in the cases of GM and Kodak, the action has come only after huge losses in value. GM's problems were obvious to sophisticated outsiders by the mid-1980s. Why then wait until 1992? Whose interest was the board protecting? Clearly not the shareholders'.

All three of the above assumptions limit our ability to think clearly about the role and reform of U.S. corporate governance. In reality, the relationship between investors and managers is far more complex than these simple assumptions would suggest. Nevertheless, most academics and other experts appear to cling to them with the same fervor that a captain holds onto a sinking ship.

LIMITATIONS OF THE CURRENT APPROACH

The investor control-oriented solutions to the corporate governance problem endorsed by financial economists are, in effect, "crisis-driven"—they

---

3. SEC filings, form 13-F, data processed by Spectrum.

are means of dealing with crises in profitability that have already happened. A better approach would aim at *crisis prevention*, in part through more open and regular communication among managers, boards, and major investors.

Large corporations are confronted with three interrelated challenges that are all essential to the corporate process of creating value:

The Performance Gap

Most companies evaluate their performance by "benchmarking" themselves against their competitors along a set of dimensions that include product quality, cycle time, costs, head count reductions, productivity levels, and administrative costs. Their aim in so doing is generally to put themselves at least on a par with the "best in their class." Eliminating the performance gap has been the focus of the reengineering and restructuring efforts of most firms.

It is common knowledge, however, that most firms that have focused only on the performance gap are forced to revisit the restructuring issue every two or three years. Focusing on the performance gap allows firms to get the obvious waste out of their operations, buy some time, and hopefully create an investment pool. But no company should depend only on this approach. The limitation of this approach is that, while firms strive to achieve par, the "best" of their competitors have already moved on. To keep up, companies focused totally on performance-gap measures must repeatedly force themselves on crash diets in which corporate muscle is very likely to be mistaken for fat.

Clearly, then, focusing on the performance gap is a necessary but not a sufficient condition for wealth creation.

Adaptability Gap

Most, if not all, the performance problems in large firms are a combination of "undermanaging" the performance parameters and not responding in a timely way to structural change within the industry. Structural changes are continually taking place in most industries. Such changes can be attributed to a wide variety of forces: deregulation (in telecommunications, for example), global excess capacity (earth-moving equipment), mergers and acquisitions (financial services), reduced protectionism (state-owned enterprises all around the world),

changing customer expectations (consumer electronics) and technological discontinuities (PCs).

As a result of such continuous change, large firms are often confronted by the dilemma of cannibalizing existing businesses or having the world move on without them. IBM, for example, stayed with its vertically integrated system and commitment to mainframes too long (and the same was true of the large Japanese computer makers, Fujitsu and Hitachi). In the meantime, however, the industry was effectively "de-verticalising." The emergence of dominant specialist suppliers such as Intel and Microsoft, together with a wide variety of new distribution channels, led to the fragmentation of the industry. Ironically, many of these trends were initiated by IBM; but once they were launched, IBM watched the industry pass them by.

In Europe, the cases of Siemens, Daimler Benz, and Philips are much the same. Each of these companies failed to prepare itself fully for an "open" European market.

The challenge of responding to structural change is made much more difficult because management must also continue to address the performance gap *at the same time*. That is, the firm must continue to seek out new sources of growth even while cutting out inefficiencies in existing ones. This dual task is particularly formidable because of the tendency of stock analysts to focus primarily on the performance gap. And such a tendency is not difficult to understand—after all, information about corporate success in managing the performance gap can be readily identified, quantified, and communicated through the simplistic medium of brokerage research reports.

But management's job, as suggested, is much more complex than squeezing out inefficiencies through cost-cutting. No amount of performance improvement will help if management fails to anticipate structural changes and adapt its strategy and organization to meet the new demands. Neither IBM nor GM can simply restructure its way to health. They must undertake a fundamental rethinking of their "business model" or "profit engine."

In sum, although failure to anticipate industry transformation results in a "performance gap," corporate restructuring provides only a surface solution to such problems. An effective long-run corporate governance system must provide timely and reliable signals that indicate how well management is anticipating and responding to continuous structural change in industries.

FIGURE 1
TOWARD A NEW
SCORECARD FOR TOP
MANAGEMENT: VALUE
(WEALTH) CREATION

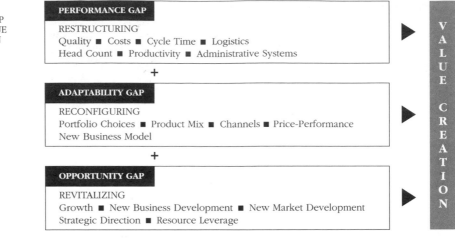

PERFORMANCE GAP

RESTRUCTURING
Quality ■ Costs ■ Cycle Time ■ Logistics
Head Count ■ Productivity ■ Administrative Systems

\+

ADAPTABILITY GAP

RECONFIGURING
Portfolio Choices ■ Product Mix ■ Channels ■ Price-Performance
New Business Model

\+

OPPORTUNITY GAP

REVITALIZING
Growth ■ New Business Development ■ New Market Development
Strategic Direction ■ Resource Leverage

VALUE CREATION

Opportunity Gap

While structural changes force a redeployment (and, in some cases, a reduction) of firm resources, they can also present new opportunities. Indeed, the potential for growth is limited, in some sense, only by the imagination of management. Current developments in multimedia, for example, have opened up major investment opportunities for industries as diverse as retailing, publishing, office equipment, and consumer electronics. Those companies with the vision to invest in such opportunities will reap huge profits. Hewlett-Packard and Motorola are good examples of companies whose continuous commitment to new markets and opportunities has paid off richly.

Summing Up

The process of value creation, then, requires that firms simultaneously manage three dimensions: performance in the existing businesses ("the performance gap"), adaptation to structural changes in the industries in which they operate ("the adaptability gap"), and growth in new directions based on their resource and competence endowments ("the opportunity gap"). As illustrated in Figure 1, sustained competitiveness requires that top managers focus on all three aspects of value creation.

This view of the wealth creation process, moreover, has considerable import for the current debate on corporate governance. As stated earlier, the finance literature tends to focus primarily on the performance gap. As I will now go on to argue, however, this traditional finance-oriented focus must be expanded to consider the quality of the relationship between management and investors, and its potential for increasing companies' effectiveness in identifying and making the most of growth opportunities.

Such an expansion of focus means that management should put current stock prices in proper perspective; that is, it should not be overly influenced by short-term stock price fluctuations. At the very least, management should give more consideration to limitations on outside investors' ability to detect underlying changes in long-run corporate profitability before they are confirmed by changes in reported earnings. As financial economists themselves have recently begun to emphasize, there is an inevitable information gap (or "asymmetry") between management and outside investors. Publicly available information can tell us only so much about what is really going on inside companies and, as mentioned earlier, generally only with a significant lag in time. (This information problem is made worse, moreover, by SEC regulations that restrict selective corporate communications with investors.)

This expanded view of value creation also raises a more fundamental question: Is the governance crisis in large firms an *internal* governance crisis? Public debate on corporate governance has focused on the nature of the relationship among sharehold-

Publicly available information can tell us only so much about what is really going on inside companies and generally only with a significant lag in time. For this reason, we need to explore alternative, non-financial indicators that would help reduce the time lag between actual declines in managerial performance and their confirmation by financial statements.

ers, boards, and top management. But what about the *quality of management* inside the large firm and conventional methods for evaluating it? Does the internal governance system provide investors with useful early warning signals to alert them to what is likely to happen to financial performance?

Investors must spend as much effort in attempting to understand and monitor the quality of internal governance as they do in poring over financial statements. As I have said several times now—and this message cannot be insisted upon too strongly—a crisis in profitability is too late for active stockholder intervention. For this reason, we need to explore alternative, *non-financial* indicators that would help reduce the time lag between actual declines in managerial performance and their confirmation by financial statements. Adopting a new performance scorecard (for which Figure 1 could serve as a model) could be an important first step in this undertaking.

A PERSPECTIVE ON THE ROLE OF TOP MANAGEMENT

The finance literature assumes that the *primary market discipline* on top managers comes from the capital market. As providers of equity capital, shareholders are the "residual claimants" who bear most of the risk, and they accordingly receive the lion's share of the reward for corporate success. Other corporate "stakeholders"—customers, employees, suppliers, local communities—should be adequately compensated, but no more. Finance theory says, in effect, that corporations should devote resources to such stakeholders only to the point where the marginal dollar spent yields at least a dollar in return to the shareholders.

Implicit in this view is thus a clear hierarchy of objectives. The primary objective of management is to maximize shareholder value, and the ultimate scorecard for managers becomes the current stock price—or, more precisely, stockholder returns over a definite time horizon.

As we approach the 21st century, however, this view may no longer be appropriate. Shareholder priority was clearly a valid view of a large enterprise when the scarce resource was capital. In the days when access to capital was essential to achieve large economies of scale in manufacturing, the ability to raise and allocate capital effectively were the defining characteristics of superior top management. At this time in our history, there was a plentiful, undifferentiated supply of labor, customers, and suppliers; capital was the resource in relatively short supply.

But the world has changed. Capital, of course, is still essential for growth, and capital markets will continue to impose a certain discipline in the form of required rates of return on firms that make use of it (although investor time horizons may require some adjustment). What is relatively new, however, is the intensity of the global competition for other key stakeholders. While capital remains a necessary ingredient, access to specialized talent (labor) and to a specialized supplier infrastructure (including technology) have become much more important factors in corporations' ability to compete in increasingly sophisticated and global consumer markets.

And, just as capital has long been viewed by economists as trading in a distinct "market," I will argue that the services of stakeholder groups such as consumers, employees, and suppliers now each deserve to be regarded as trading in a separate "market" in its own right, each with its own distinctive set of characteristics and internal dynamics. Of course, there are important differences in the stages of development and level of efficiency of each of these markets—particularly across national boundaries (some of which will be discussed later). The point of viewing non-investor corporate stakeholders as markets is to encourage recognition that key stakeholders, like capital markets, also impose a unique set of internal disciplines on firms. To create long-run value and social wealth, firms must compete effectively in *all* of these markets.

The Product Markets

That consumers constitute a distinct market has, of course, long been recognized by economists. Through the operation of product markets, consumers impose their own kind of discipline on firms—one that operates even in the absence of capital market pressures. Consider a state-owned enterprise such as Thomson of France, which produces electronic equipment. Even though relatively insulated from capital markets by government funding, Thomson must *ultimately* meet the demands imposed on it by the consumer electronics market if it is to survive.

Consumers worldwide have become more sophisticated, and the discipline of global product market competition far more demanding, in recent years. For example, in the past, large multinationals expanded by employing a concept known as the "product life cycle." In practice, this meant achieving growth by marketing mature, lower-quality, or less sophisticated products to consumers in developing countries. Today such a strategy is bound to fail. Any firm that has tried to sell low-quality or previous-generation products in the emerging markets of southeast Asia has learned this lesson the hard way. Consumers of TVs, camcorders, PCs, and cellular telephones everywhere demand the same level of quality.

Much, then, as capital markets have become globally integrated, advances in technology are also bringing about a single worldwide market for many products and services.

The Market for Technology

The intensity of global competition has elevated the importance of technological capability. In today's world of increasing specialization, technology is often effectively bundled and sold by specialist "suppliers" to a global set of customers. Sharp, for example, makes liquid crystal displays (LCDs) for products such as laptops and PDAs manufactured by Apple Computer. Sharp also competes with Apple in the same markets, thus making Sharp at once a supplier and a competitor of Apple. As a result of such relationships, the fine lines between customers, competitors, and suppliers are blurring. Even the closed system of the Japanese *keiretsu* is giving way to "cross-sourcing" between competitors.

The central challenge in accessing technology, then, is not just in building effective internal R&D capabilities, but in establishing access to a supplier network around the world. Such access is critical in developing competitive advantages such as "improved time to market" and "new business development." Access to core product specialists such as Intel, Sony, and Kyocera may be as critical to competitive success as access to capital was during the earlier growth period. As a result, there is intense corporate competition to gain access to supplier networks.

The Market for Labor

To meet the new demands of global product markets and the worldwide competition for suppli-ers, corporations have also been forced to step up the intensity of their search for specialized talent. In high-technology businesses such as financial services and computing, firms have long recognized that the real currency is talent. The same is true of the emerging multi-media businesses.

There are also signs that the corporate competition for talent has become global. To offer just one example, companies such as Citicorp, DEC, Texas Instruments, and Motorola have located computer programming operations in Bangalore, India, where high-quality programmers command much lower wages than their California counterparts. As this example suggests, the market for talent is as yet relatively undeveloped; it has the most distortions—the highest transaction costs and greatest "information asymmetries" between buyers and sellers—and hence is the least "efficient" of the four markets mentioned. But, as this case also suggests, the distortions inherent in this market create opportunities for "arbitrage" by opportunistic firms.

Although such price differentials will ultimately be eliminated by companies seeking to benefit from them, much of the advantages of diversifying the corporate talent search will remain. *Competition for talent is not just about price, but about access.* A large number of high technology firms are busy setting up programs designed to gain access to highly trained people. The ability to collaborate at a distance will be a key factor in the development of a market for talent. If effective, such collaboration will represent a successful "arbitrage" of labor markets across countries.

In sum, all companies effectively compete in at least four distinct markets. Success in any one of these markets is not enough to meet the competitive demands placed on firms. Creating wealth for investors through efficient use of capital depends critically on management's ability to manage the disciplines of the product market (imposed by sophisticated customers around the world), the labor market (specialized talent), and the technology market (specialist suppliers).

DIFFERENCES IN THE ORIENTATION OF TOP MANAGERS

Over the long run, of course, the interests of each of these four corporate constituencies are united. A firm's consumers, suppliers, employees, and investors all benefit from sustained superior

Because investment in the product, technology, and talent markets requires time to generate returns, the hidden cost of the traditional modus operandi of U.S. firms will become visible only in the longer term. By continuing to treat all other markets as subordinate to capital markets, most U.S. companies are falling years behind the firms that are already attempting to balance the demands of the four markets.

performance. In the short run, however, serving all four markets simultaneously inevitably involves making some trade-offs among them. Top managers in the U.S., Europe, and Japan have traditionally shown systematic differences in making trade-offs among the four markets.

The U.S.

For example, most firms in the U.S. have responded most directly to capital market pressures while placing less emphasis on the other markets. Because this near-exclusive capital market focus reduced the competitiveness of U.S. firms during the 1970s and 1980s, many U.S. firms today are currently refocusing their energies on product markets. Without customers, they have been forced to recognize there is no business and no prospect of wealth creation. The number of corporate initiatives designed to address quality, time to market, new product development, and customer responsiveness is a sign of a fundamental change in the perspective of many U.S. top managers.

Relationships with specialist suppliers have also become a major concern of some U.S. companies. Toyota's ability to outperform the Big Three U.S. automakers throughout the 1980s had as much to do with their privileged access to suppliers (which had a vested interest in improving Toyota's quality) and new product development capability, as it did with their efficiency in employing capital. The lessons have not been completely lost on U.S. auto and other manufacturing firms.

U.S. top managers have also become more concerned today with engaging people in the tasks of competitiveness. Corporate programs for improving the quality of work life, encouraging greater employee involvement, and promoting "empowerment" have become commonplace. Such programs are part of a concerted effort by many companies to make their organizations more attractive to talented people—not only to improve their performance, but simply to retain them. Corporate accommodation of dual careers, the introduction of "flextime," and allowing greater choice of location (in part by long-distance collaboration) are all signs of a talent market that is imposing its discipline on companies.

But if recognition of the imperatives of markets other than the capital markets is gradually developing within many U.S. firms, the rhetoric and the reality do not fully match. For all the talk

about these relatively new concerns, most U.S. managers remain focused on the capital market disciplines, often to the exclusion of the demands of the other markets.

There are, of course, a number of U.S. firms that have achieved extraordinary success by managing all four markets at once—notably, Motorola, Hewlett Packard, Intel, Microsoft, Sun, and General Electric. GE, for example, has professed its commitment to creating a "boundary-less organization"—one that "stretches" its people by giving them a say in the development of the business. While this kind of rhetoric must always be discounted somewhat, it is nonetheless a far cry from the old U.S. managerial tradition of viewing people as interchangeable factors of production. It explicitly recognizes the "hard" or measurable impact on competitiveness of attending to the "soft" side of management.

But, again, firms like GE represent the exception to rule in the U.S. And because investment in the product, technology, and talent markets requires time to generate returns, the hidden cost of the traditional *modus operandi* of U.S. firms will become visible only in the medium to long term. By continuing to treat all other markets as subordinate to capital markets, most U.S. companies are falling years behind the firms that are already attempting to balance the demands of these four markets.

Japan and Europe

Japanese firms, by contrast, pay significant attention to the labor market. This is evident in their college recruiting efforts, their emphasis on internal training, and their policy of life-time employment for a selected talent pool. Japanese firms have also long cultivated strong relationships with captive "house" suppliers (in the form of keiretsus), but are now also increasingly developing supplier networks with outsiders to gain access to new technologies. These actions have allowed them to compete very effectively in the global product market, setting new world standards in product quality, customer responsiveness, and time to market. Indeed, Japanese firms across a variety of industries have succeeded in rewriting the rules of competition to their own advantage.

At the same time, however, Japanese managers have not paid sufficient attention to their investors—in large part because Japanese capital markets have long been distorted by regulatory controls and intervention.[4] The current recession, a strong yen, and competition from overseas are now forcing Japanese managers to reassess their traditional approach to the talent market. They are even reconsidering their policy of lifetime employment.[5] Until now, Japanese firms could pursue life-time employment not only because a growing economy absorbed the costs, but because of a hidden source of flexibility in the Japanese labor market: While the largest firms held onto their talented employees during hard times, employees of the suppliers and sub-contractors—as well as women and contract workers in the large firms—provided the much needed cushion (as much as 20% to 30% of the workforce).

Japanese managers are also being forced to reexamine the concept of a captive supplier base and the efficiency of long-term relationships generally. The need for privileged access to the supplier base has become more important, but sourcing only from internal house suppliers—as in the traditional keiretsu—is no longer considered essential or even valuable. Many Japanese managers are also discovering that goals such as reducing time to market, product proliferation, and increasing market share have been pursued at excessive cost to investors. With Japanese stock prices at roughly half their 1989 levels, and corporate profits sharply depressed, Japanese firms are being forced to come to a recognition that investors must be adequately compensated.

The European situation is somewhat more complex. For example, legislation requires European firms to be concerned about employment, but the competitive consequences of such legislation are unclear. On the one hand, this could make European firms more willing to invest in developing their existing talent. In practice, however, such legislative constraints on hiring and firing may well interfere with the effective development of human resources. Perhaps partly as a result, European firms have not converted this built-in protection of labor into a means of achieving greater understanding of their customers or building relationships with suppliers. Like many of their Japanese counterparts, moreover, European managers in general have not focused on providing returns to capital markets.

Such a situation could be tolerated as long as European markets remained sheltered from competition (although a completely protected economy, which creates distortions in all four markets, cannot last forever). But, now that barriers to competition are falling with the prospect of a united Europe, leading European firms are being forced to make progress along all dimensions of corporate success. They are becoming more investor-driven, more concerned with global product market competition, and more focused on gaining access to networks of suppliers. Even European governments are reexamining the wisdom of legislation that, while protecting some workers, effectively denies opportunities to others.

Convergence

Although U.S., Japanese, and European firms thus have different starting points and are traveling different roads, their paths are converging and their destination is more or less the same. Despite important differences in historical roots and institutions, corporations around the globe are all being forced to respond to the demands of the four markets.

Complicating this story are differences among nations in the stage of development, and thus in the level of efficiency, of some of these markets. U.S. capital markets, for example, exert a much more powerful (if sometimes short-sighted) discipline than do Japanese markets—although the Japanese system will change somewhat. And labor markets worldwide are clearly less efficient than product markets, at least at present. But, as firms seek to profit from such disparities and inefficiencies, the forces of global competition will reduce them.

BALANCING vs. OPTIMIZING

As top managers reflect on the wealth creation process, it will become obvious that there are important differences among the disciplines imposed by the four markets. In thinking about such differences, management must address the following issues:

Time horizon. Developing competence and access to a specialist supplier base could take as long

---

4. See Merton Miller, "Is American Corporate Governance Fatally Flawed?", *Journal of Applied Corporate Finance* (Vol. 6 No. 4), which appears immediately before this article.

5. Although lifetime employment in Japan is often described as a cultural trait, the practice is actually quite recent. It evolved around late 50s and early 60s. Given the paucity of talent at that time, it made good *economic* sense to hold onto talent. Lifetime employment was the result. Although continuous growth insulated firms from having to deal with the negative consequences of this "blanket commitment," the "real cost" of this approach is now becoming apparent.

as five to ten years. For example, if an auto supplier participates in an advanced car program, the perspective ought to be at least five to seven years. Participation in a new airframe development takes even longer; for the first three to five years of such a development program, there may in fact be no revenues at all.

Adjustments will have to be made both by the firm itself and by its first-tier suppliers as they learn to relate to each other in new ways. These relationships must be both competitive and cooperative at the same time. The same is true of key customers; it may take years to gain privileged access to customers to build up brand loyalty.

The key question here, of course, is whether the time horizons of institutional investors are sufficient to accommodate corporate investment in non-investor stakeholders. If the time horizons of capital markets are considerably shorter than the payoff period required for investments in the other three markets, are there steps managers can take to stretch them?

Transaction-Specific vs. Relationship-Specific Costs. While significant attention has been paid to transaction costs in these four markets, little attention has been paid to *relationship-specific costs*. Corporate dealings in the markets for technology, talent, and customers are often premised on not just a single transaction, but rather on an expected sequence of transactions. Repeated transactions lead to the development of a relationship, whether contractual or implicit. The goal in such cases is not just to minimize the costs of a specific transaction, but to minimize costs (or maximize total efficiency) over the entire sequence of transactions.

This has important implications for corporate policy. For example, a first-tier supplier involved in co-developing a critical sub-assembly should not be treated in the same way as another supplier selling a commodity component. And, indeed, a two-tier system now appears to be evolving in each of the four markets. Firms increasingly tend to distinguish between:

a. key suppliers and others
b. key accounts and channels and others
c. key employees and others
d. key institutional investors and others

Although near-term cost minimization is likely to be the appropriate goal in dealings with "others," the establishment of relationships with "key" stakeholders demands an investment mentality. Managers

may also find it valuable to share more information in key relationships. They will thus not be able to treat these relationships as totally competitive, but instead seek to achieve a balance between competition and cooperation. The nature of these interactions—the collective learning that takes place between the firm and its key stakeholders—is what leads to wealth creation over the long term.

Control or Value Added? The implicit assumption of financial economists in the governance debate is that investors, as owners, ought to *control* managers. Further, investors are urged to put pressure on boards to rewrite management incentive contracts so as to elicit the desired ("shareholder-wealth-maximizing") behavior. The principal problem with such a control orientation is that it discourages managers from sharing information with investors. When combined with constraints imposed by the SEC and the rest of our legal and regulatory system, a control-oriented system ensures that the information investors receive from managers will relate only to past events.

To address the heart of the U.S. corporate governance problem, this control orientation must give way to a more constructive, value-adding relationship between management and investors. In this sense, corporate relations with investors should attempt to learn from the collaborative developments now taking place between firms and their main customers and suppliers. Just as more and more firms are consulting their key customers and suppliers, outlining their strategies and inviting their counsel in shaping future directions, top managers should encourage institutional investors to become partners with management in the enterprise by sharing its strategies and its understanding of the risks underlying them.

A value-added relationship must continue to have a control component, but it must amount to something more mutually productive than an arm's length "yes or no" relationship. The process must encourage continuous informative dialogue between management and investors that aims to produce a shared understanding of the firm's strategy—of the critical assumptions underlying the strategy, the competitive challenges facing it, the yardsticks (financial as well as non-financial) by which progress toward strategic goals is evaluated, and the time period over which it is expected to play out. In short, a value-added orientation must focus on *crisis prevention rather than crisis management*.

Top managers must also recognize that the process of sustained wealth creation is a continuous act of balancing the demands of the four markets. If managers seek to optimize in any single market—be it talent, technological competence, suppliers, or investors—they are likely to fall behind in the wealth-creation process. Achieving the optimal balance among the four markets involves making the appropriate tradeoffs among them. To make the right tradeoffs (and to explain them most effectively), managers should develop communication channels and procedures that encourage active dialogue with key participants in each of the four markets—investors, suppliers, customers, and critical talent. By encouraging information-sharing, such dialogue should generate valuable longer-term commitments.

In sum, the economic and political realities of the 1990s demand the active participation of each of these four main corporate constituencies. Corporate managers are likely to be surprised by the value added that can result simply from allowing the players in these markets a greater voice in setting the broad direction of the firm.

CONCLUSION

Corporate governance is not, as capital market theory suggests, simply a matter of giving investors more control over top management. The real governance crisis in the U.S. is an *internal* crisis. It is the failure of many top managers to address simultaneously the performance, adaptability, and opportunity gaps now evident in many of our largest public companies. If our internal governance system can be strengthened, there will be much less need for intervention by capital markets.

Unfortunately, the remedies currently proposed by financial economists tend to focus on the symptoms rather than the cause of the problem. Crisis-oriented, highly selective, and sporadic intervention by shareholder activists is not the solution. Indeed, it may provide the wrong signals to the CEO. Managing the stock price in the short term is not the same as building the capacity for sustained wealth creation. To add value, top managers must consistently balance the demands of and be subject to the disciplines of four distinct markets—product markets (consumers), labor markets (specialized talent), the market for technology (suppliers), and capital markets (investors).

In the past, the orientations of top management in the U.S., Japan, and Europe toward these four markets have been quite different. Whereas U.S. management has focused primarily on meeting investor requirements, Japanese managers have devoted more attention to building relationships with employees and suppliers. In the 1990s, however, convergence among the world's best firms in their approach to these markets is inevitable, irrespective of national origin and history. For Japanese and European managers, such convergence implies greater concern for investors. For U.S. managers, it means a new, pragmatic, value-added approach—one that seeks to establish long-term relationships with investors based on mutual interest and effective sharing of information.

■ C. K. PRAHALAD

is the Harvey Fruehauf Professor of Corporate Strategy at the Graduate School of Business Administration of the University of Michigan.

GLOBAL COMPETITION IN THE '90s

BENNETT STEWART: Yesterday, we were privileged to hear C.K. Prahalad, one of the foremost corporate strategists in the country, present his vision of global competition in the 1990s. As C.K. began by noting, we have seen a remarkable power shift over the past 20 years. Once mighty industrial giants such as General Motors, RCA, Pan Am, and CBS have been humbled by upstarts like Toyota, Sony, British Airways, and CNN.

What C.K. has attempted, both in his talk yesterday and in a series of articles (with co-author Gary Hamel) published in the *Harvard Business Review* over the past few years, is to develop nothing less than a general unified theory, if you will, of corporate competitiveness. As C.K. has written in the latest issue of the *HBR*, the aim of his work is to provide answers to the following questions:

> *Why do some companies continually create new forms of competitive advantage, while others watch and follow? Why do some companies redefine the industries in which they compete, while others take the existing industry structure as a given?*

Central to C.K.'s thinking is the concept of "core competence." I will not attempt to define it here—I suspect this will be an important part of our discussion this morning. I will instead simply restate C.K.'s prescription that companies should identify their core competencies as precisely as possible, invest in the capabilities necessary to build and maintain their core competencies, and then seek to extend or "leverage" these competencies across multiple businesses.

This morning, the Continental Bank has brought together a distinguished panel of senior corporate executives who have volunteered to explore these notions of corporate strategy with C.K. They will undoubtedly reinforce many aspects of his thinking, while perhaps challenging others. I myself have a few reservations or biases—which will likely become clear later—about how these strategic concepts actually work out in practice. But, for now, let me briefly introduce all our panelists.

■ **CHARLES CLOUGH**

is the Chairman of Wyle Laboratories, a distributor of semiconductors and other computer components with approximately $530 million in sales.

■ **DENNIS ECK**

is President and Chief Operating Officer of The Vons Companies, the leading grocery retailer in Southern California, with $5 billion in sales through some 350 stores.

■ **FRANK PERNA**

is President and Chief Executive Officer of MagneTek, Inc., a $1.3 billion manufacturer of electrical equipment. The company produces such items as fluorescent lighting ballasts, transformers, motors, and controls.

■ **ROBERT PERRY**

is Chief Financial Officer of Dames & Moore, Inc., a $350 million worldwide environmental and engineering consulting services firm—and perhaps the largest of its kind.

■ **C.K. PRAHALAD**

whom I've already mentioned several times, is the Harvey Fruehauf Professor of Business Administration at the University of Michigan. Described in a recent *Washington Post* article as "the hottest strategy consultant around," C.K. has done extensive consulting for companies such as Eastman Kodak, Phillips, Motorola, and Honeywell.

■ **ED THOMPSON**

is Chief Financial Officer of the Amdahl Corporation, a company that has traditionally designed and manufactured mainframe computers, but that has also begun offering software and open systems. Amdahl is 44% owned by Fujitsu, and I look forward to hearing from Ed what it *really* is like to work with a Japanese company.

■ **LEN WILLIAMS**

is President and Chief Executive Officer of MacFrugal's, which bids well to become the McDonald's of the bargain close-out store business. They have well over 200 stores with about $550 million in sales. I note that Southeastern Asset Management owns 15% of the stock of the company. This means that my good friend Mason Hawkins, a well-known value-based investor, has confidence in Len. We'll soon see if that's justified.

Core Competence and Corporate Renewal

STEWART: I'd like to begin this discussion by asking C.K. to expand on an argument that he made yesterday—one that I endorse wholeheartedly. He said that there really is no such thing as a mature business. There are only, let's say, prematurely aged companies or aged managements. Some of our corporate clients tell me, "Bennett, this is a tough business. It's just very difficult to build value in this business. You can't expect us to thrive and grow as you would, say, in the biotechnology business."

So, C.K., do you accept the premise that there are inherently mature businesses? Or is this just an excuse for poorly motivated or unimaginative managements?

PRAHALAD: Maturity is in the way you provide a certain functionality to customers. Industrial history is full of examples. Steinway thought pianos was a mature business—and the way they serviced their customers it was indeed a very mature business. But Yamaha didn't see it the same way. True, they still make grand pianos, but they have also extracted the functionality called digital sound, and they have been able to grow that part of the business by 30% to 40% a year.

Now, there are obviously some products that become obsolete, such as the buggy-whip. But by thinking about the functionality underlying a given product or a service, and looking beyond the particular product itself, companies often discover new sources of growth and renewal.

STEWART: Well, let's take grocery retailing, which is Dennis's business at the Vons Companies. That's a fairly mature business, right? There's only so much stuff people can cram into their stomachs. How do you make a growth business out of food, Dennis?

ECK: Our industry is widely perceived to be mature. That perception is at best a half-truth. What is true is that parts of our business are intensively competitive. We respond by discovering new areas from which to grow and profit. Those areas, needless to say, are receiving most of our focus and investment.

Let me be more specific. We have what we call cross-over categories. These are products nearly all retailers now sell. Things like detergents, paper, beverages—all of these are easily available to all other retailers and discount chains to sell. We have inevitably lost market share in these categories. First, by availability and because pricing has emerged that has been very difficult for us to match with our cost structure.

What we have done in response to shrinking margins and sales in cross-overs is to think about our customer more carefully. We ask ourselves: What kinds of products can we develop that will be difficult for our competitors to duplicate? So far, we've been very successful in adding floral, bakeries, and health care. We emphasize service and services. We have tried to make ourselves the best one-stop shopping point for people who want to get efficiently through the week. This reduces our need to compete on price.

Vons' business is not mature—although if we had simply stayed with our old products, we might have been in trouble today. Vons is hoping to do $250 million in floral by the end of 1994. This is a business that in 1990 did $17 million. The great thing about floral is that it operates at times up to 70% gross margin. This also helps us to be priced more competitively in the cross-over categories.

STEWART: Let me turn now to Frank Perna at MagneTek. Frank, as in Dennis's case, I would guess you too were operating in a mature market. The electrical equipment business—things like transformers and motors and controls—does not appear to be a growth industry. Have you been able to find a way to create growth in what appears to be mature businesses?

PERNA: Many of our product lines come from businesses that we have acquired from other companies. In most cases, the sellers thought they were mature. But we bought these product lines with the idea that, no matter what happens, people still require certain types of electrical equipment. The opportunity we saw in these businesses was to build up more efficient distribution channels. And, once having established those channels for our base products, we could then use them to distribute new generations of more energy-efficient equipment. As one example, new technologies have enabled us to provide the same level of fluorescent lighting with 25% to 30% less energy.

So what we've really done is to use a distribution platform for supposedly mature products to launch new technologies and thereby generate some very exciting growth.

STEWART: Would it be fair to say that your distribution channels are the "core competence" of MagneTek?

PERNA: Yes, I think the core competence of our company is really its distribution channels—far more so than its products.

STEWART: C.K., can distribution channels be a core competence, in your scheme of things?

PRAHALAD: It can. But let me make a distinction here between what I call infrastructure and what I mean by a core competence. In many if not most cases, a distribution system is simply part of the infrastructure a company has built. It's what you do with the distribution system that has the power to turn it into a core competence.

Core competencies can, over time, become capabilities. What I mean by "capabilities" are the minimal skills that allow a company to compete. Strategy consultants these days like to talk about capability-based competition as if it were something unusual. But all competition is based on capabilities. You cannot compete if you don't have capabilities. Providing just-in-time inventory is a capability that is required today if you even want to be considered as a supplier. Capabilities are things that companies need just to play in the game.

A third distinction I want to make is between core competencies and intangible assets such as brandnames. In my articles, I define core competence as a set of multiple, harmonizable technologies and skills. My writings tend to focus on technology-based core competencies, but you can have marketing-based core competencies just as well. Things like global distribution and global brand management can also be core competencies.

For something to be a core competence, it should pass the following three tests: One, does it uniquely differentiate this company from other companies. Two, can it be leveraged to take advantage of trends in multiple businesses? And, three, is it difficult for competitors to imitate?

So, to return my earlier statement about Frank's company, distribution capabilities can become a core competence. But it all depends on what the company does with the channels.

One more comment in this context: Bennett, you asked whether the ballast business is mature or not. Just think about what would happen if people in China and India and Indonesia began buying as many bulbs per capita as we have in the U.S. This would become one of the fastest growing businesses in the world; and, as I was arguing yesterday, that is a good reason for companies like Frank's to develop a global reach. Is that a fair comment, Frank?

The opportunity we saw was to build up more efficient distribution channels and then use them to distribute new generations of more energy-efficient equipment....

So what we've really done is to use a distribution platform for supposedly mature products to launch new technologies and thereby generate some very exciting growth.

—Frank Perna—

PERNA: Yes, that's true. That's one of the reasons we have begun thinking about expanding into overseas markets in the last couple of years. A third of all the electricity consumed in the world is consumed in North America, and another third is consumed in Europe. Most of the world's population, however, is outside these two continents. As countries in Asia and elsewhere become more technically advanced, they will certainly use more electrical equipment—and the first thing is lighting. So, we expect global markets to extend the life of our products quite significantly, even those products we are currently phasing out in North America.

STEWART: C.K., to explore your concept of core competence a little further, you said companies should attempt to extend or "leverage" their core competencies across multiple businesses. But think about a company like Toyota, which has been extremely successful by focusing on just one business: automotive manufacturing. Or think about the success of Intel in microprocessors, or Dell Computer in distributing computers through mail-order catalogues. Why is it necessary for companies to have multiple businesses? Why can't they be content to dominate their customary businesses?

PRAHALAD: To describe Toyota as being only in the automotive business is inaccurate, because they're in other businesses as well. Even within the automotive business, there are many different products and markets. The markets for Cadillacs and pick-up trucks are quite different. Toyota has also moved into small earth-moving equipment, and made plans for aircraft manufacturing as well. In fact, I would argue that the long-term competition for Boeing is not only going to be Airbus, but Japanese companies like Toyota. So the critical question for management is: Can we extend our core competencies to other businesses?

Or take the case of Dell Computers, since you mentioned it. Dell has created a whole new capability in distribution—one that effectively bypasses the store-fronts controlled by companies like Compaq and IBM. It is management's job, I would argue, to look for related products that can be distributed through the same channels they've established for computers. This is what I mean by "leveraging" a core competence. For example, Dell has the necessary customer knowledge and infrastructure to become a powerhouse in software distribution. This way, software consumers would no longer have to read all the magazines to find out what software is available. Dell could effectively provide this service to its existing customer base. This would be a natural extension of its core competence—one that would transcend individual businesses.

STEWART: Okay, so you're saying that Dell's distribution expertise, its core competence, was not built up initially with the intention of selling software. But, having created that competence, management today—somewhat serendipitously—has been put in the position to expand into other products.

PRAHALAD: That's right. Companies never start out with the intention of extending a core competence across multiple products. You have to start by building a business. It's on the back of the business you build core competencies and, in so doing, you end up providing the platform for further growth.

The Benefits of Sharpening Focus: The Case of Wyle Labs

STEWART: Charlie, how would describe the core competencies of Wyle Laboratories?

CLOUGH: Well, the core competence of our business was created out of an intensely competitive situation that our company found itself in about 12 years ago. At that time, the three largest companies in the electronics distribution business controlled about 80% of the market; and there were five or six smaller firms like ours that had the rest. And these three dominant companies were large and financially strong. So, given our own modest size and limited financial resources, we decided to abandon our strategy of being a broad-line distributor of electronics and to specialize in one product: semiconductors. In so doing, we made a real break with the history of electronics distribution. We felt our best opportunity lay in concentrating our resources to build a core strength in semiconductors. We would then use this core capability to compete more effectively against all the other broad-based distributors—those companies for which semiconductors was only one of many products.

Our choice of semiconductors was based on our perception that there was a weakness in our competitors in this area that we could exploit. That weakness was lack of technical capability. The success of these large companies had been built primarily on their merchandising capabilities; indeed, their approach to electronics distribution was not much different from the approach of mass food distributors. Their strategy was to achieve scale economies by using their merchandising expertise to distribute a wide variety of products. They would inventory all the products locally, and provide very good service and low pricing. The companies were also managed by financial kinds of people with no real grasp of the technical side of the business.

In deciding to concentrate only on semiconductor products, we also chose to build a very strong technical capability by training electrical engineers to become our salesmen. And this too was a radical break with industry practice. We also used our technical salesforce to provide value-adding services that the big companies could not. For example, we used our engineering capabilities to help our corporate customers design cost-reducing semiconductor systems.

But now, a decade later, we face a new challenge. The barriers to competition we built up with our engineering expertise have been eroding as other companies have improved their technical marketing skills too. Although we probably still maintain an edge over our competitors, they have begun to go global—they have moved into Europe. And we're now pondering our strategy as to how we can supply unique services to enable us to compete and win.

STEWART: What companies do you consider to be your competitors?

CLOUGH: Arrow Electronics is one, Avnet is another.

STEWART: Have those companies maintained a broad line of electrical products, or have they chosen, like your company, to narrow their focus to semiconductors?

CLOUGH: They have maintained a broad-line national and now a global product strategy. By contrast, we have remained almost completely focused on semiconductors and have limited our marketing activity to major U.S. markets. Also, we sell only the products of U.S. semiconductor manufacturers—no Japanese or Korean lines.

STEWART: Why is that?

CLOUGH: Patriotism is part of it...

STEWART: You and Sam Walton.

CLOUGH: ...but there was also some sound business logic behind that decision. I had the conviction—even five or six years ago—that the American position in this industry was fundamentally stronger than the Japanese position, in spite of what people were saying in the popular business press and in places like the *Harvard Business Review*. The Japanese had built their capability in semiconductors around a very strong manufacturing capability that produced commodity kinds of products. But, I saw the profitable part of the semiconductor business moving away from commodities, which the Japanese companies dominated with their manufacturing skills, and toward products like microprocessors, where two American companies were emerging as the leaders. As I saw it, the microprocessor was going to become the driver of the semiconductor industry, not commodities like memory. Two companies, Motorola and Intel, would become world-wide leaders in microprocessors. And so we decided to ally ourselves very closely with those two American companies; and these alliances have proved to be very productive for us.

So our conviction proved to be right. Today, it's the microprocessor that drives electronics. The microprocessor sank IBM and revolutionized the electronics industry. What had built great companies like IBM, Unisys, and other giant computer companies was engineering, research and development, and a highly technical marketing knowledge of computer systems. Well, that all went by the board with the 386, the 486, and now the Pentium. Today, because of the microprocessor, a small company can build and sell the same system as IBM a hell of a lot cheaper and move it faster to market.

So, again, our core competence is in semiconductors. But we're now struggling with the question of whether to broaden our focus by adding other adjacent product lines around this technical capability, or by competing with our two principal competitors on a global basis. We haven't made a decision yet.

STEWART: C.K., would you be willing to offer Charlie some free consulting advice? What would you do if you were in Charlie's shoes?

PRAHALAD: If you're a reasonable consultant, the first thing you learn is *never* to give free advice.

But I will say this. What Charlie just described is an interesting way of starting to think about how companies build core competencies. There are two things he said that I think are especially important. The first is that management realized they had to think of an alternative way to compete rather than just imitating their

I had the conviction—even five or six years ago—that the microprocessor was going to become the driver of the semiconductor industry, not commodities like memory. Two American companies, Motorola and Intel, would become world-wide leaders in microprocessors. And so we decided to ally ourselves very closely with those companies; and these alliances have proved to be very productive .

—Charles Clough—

competitors. To me, that is a very critical part of the nature of competition in the '90s. That realization leads to what I like to call "competitive innovation." It is not providing different products, but rather changing the *ways* in which companies compete.

My second point is this: Although Charlie stressed the narrowing of his corporate focus, the company's core competence in semiconductor engineering has likely already provided the company with a significant new source of revenues that was not expected when the company first decided to focus only on semiconductors. Given that you now specialize in selling semiconductors, I would bet that, as a result of your technical skills, your company also does a lot of application engineering for the companies that buy your semiconductors.

CLOUGH: That's exactly right.

PRAHALAD: That application engineering represents an extension of your core competence in distributing semiconductors. As a consequence of building technical capability into your sales force, the company has now become a technical adviser of sorts, a systems developer. You are no longer just taking Product A to Location B. You have acquired a much deeper understanding of the needs of your customers. And I would argue that your ability to assist them in designing applications of the products you sell is not something other companies can easily duplicate.

Eventually, of course, other companies will. And that raises what to me is the more interesting question, the real challenge, of corporate strategy: How do you keep upgrading your competencies?

Acquire, or Build from Within?
The Case of Dames & Moore

Let me turn now to Bob Perry. Bob, could you just give us a thumbnail sketch of your company? Clearly, as an environmental consulting service, it would seem that you would have promising growth opportunities, both at home and abroad. How do you plan to grow the company?

PERRY: We started out about 54 years ago as a consulting firm specializing in "geo-technical" engineering. That's a fancy word for studying the ground on which people build refineries and power plants. We started out with one office in California, and today we have 117 offices around the world and over 3,000 employees. Roughly a third of our offices are outside the United States.

Besides expanding geographically, we have also moved into other types of engineering and environmental consulting. We have added geology, hydrology, meteorology, ecology, toxicology, and many other "ologies." We've sort of captured the market on ologies in the entire environmental framework, and we're one of the largest engineering and environmental consultants in the world today. About the same time we were expanding into the various ologies, we also initiated our move to global operations. We expanded our office network around the world to be closer to our clientele, which includes the overseas operations of most of the major American corporations as well as some foreign governments.

Our company went public about a year ago, and the issue we're facing today is how to find other avenues of growth. One possibility is to lengthen the amount of time we spend on a particular project. In other words, instead of acting just as a consultant, we're now looking to get more involved in the actual design and construction of projects of an environmental nature. We have a certain amount of that capability in-house, but the question that we face now as we try to grow is this: Should we grow slowly and patiently by just expanding in an in-house way with our own people? Or should we look more towards larger acquisitions—we have already made a number of smaller ones—to expand into design and construction in a very quick, major way?

STEWART: Bob, it strikes me that both you and Charlie seem to be struggling to define not so much a core competence, but what C.K. might call a "strategic intent"—that is, the broader mission that's going to guide your company's growth over the

longer term. Would you agree with that, C.K.?

PRAHALAD: Well, without any detailed knowledge of either of the companies, I'm uncomfortable offering any kind of analysis or prescriptions. But there are two or three issues that stand out in these two cases—and in the earlier case of ballasts and electrical equipment as well.

First, it seems clear that all these industries are going through a period of change and evolution. So the question is, How can companies create for themselves a roadmap that will help them anticipate and respond to the course this evolution eventually takes? One cannot predict exactly what the products will be even just three years down the road, much less five or ten years. But one can predict with some confidence the fundamental capabilities that will be necessary for companies in a given industry to exploit those specific commercial opportunities that actually materialize.

For example, with respect to Frank's ballast business, it seems virtually certain that miniaturization will be one of the major challenges, and thus opportunities. And so all the enabling technologies that will help the company acquire the capability to miniaturize should be explored. Do you agree, Frank?

PERNA: Yes, I do.

PRAHALAD: So, technology is not really much of a surprise at all. We can more or less say what will happen in many of the technical parameters over the next five or ten years. What is uncertain, and what is critical for businesses, is the intersection of technology and customer functionalities. The purpose of creating the roadmap—the broad strategic architecture, if you will—is to galvanize companies into preparing for the future, to set the energies of people in the right direction. This way, when the change does occur, and a new set

of consumer requirements becomes clear, companies will have built the capabilities that will enable them to respond quickly.

STEWART: What factors would you consider in choosing among different ways of achieving necessary capabilities or technology? For example, how would you choose among the alternatives of acquiring a company, licensing vendors, forming an alliance, or building capabilities from within?

PRAHALAD: First, you want to be as clear as possible about your strategic intent, and about the capabilities that will be essential to realize it. Having determined the desired capabilities, the question then becomes this: What is the lowest-cost, lowest-risk approach to getting that particular skill or capability?

Now, with regard to this second matter, I'm willing to make two broad propositions. The first is that companies that cannot grow from within will not necessarily be able to exploit collaborative arrangements. Time and again I have seen companies entering into alliances or joint ventures or undertaking acquisitions because they do not have faith in their own organizations to build a capability internally. They think that some other company's skills will substitute for their lack of ability. And such companies generally wind up being disappointed.

You may still acquire a company, it's true, but often without realizing any strategic or synergistic benefits from the acquisition. That is, acquisitions may add something to your balance sheet and P & L, but the capabilities may never be successfully developed or integrated into your own organization. Learning capabilities from an acquired company, and thus assimilating that acquisition, is quite a different task from buying the company.

So, I would argue that the ability of a company to leverage all kinds of collaborative arrangements depends heavily on its existing capacity for internal growth. In the case of hi-tech companies, moreover, acquisition is the very last thing I would consider. I'd much rather start with internal growth and, if that won't work, then consider licensing arrangements and possibly alliances. Acquisitions have a lot of toxic side-effects, especially in high-technology industries. Every hi-tech small company has a culture of its own. That is why they are hi-tech—they are all prima donnas. It's difficult to acquire such companies and make it work because you can't really *own* these kind of people.

STEWART: IBM certainly made a mess of its forays into telecommunications.

PRAHALAD: It was not only IBM. Look at GE's acquisitions of Intersil and Calma. The history of hi-tech acquisitions is littered with sad stories like these. Such acquisitions can cause problems for the acquirers, too. Acquisition-oriented companies are saying something to their own employees. How would you feel if you were a top scientist in a hi-tech company, and your management repeatedly went out and acquired another company instead of investing inside the firm?

Global Partnership:
The Case of Amdahl

STEWART: How about *partial* acquisitions? For example, Fujitsu owns 44% of Amdahl. In fact, let me now ask Ed Thompson to tell us about Amdahl. Yesterday, C.K. talked of the need for companies to achieve economies of scope by extending the corporate reach into new areas. Does Amdahl serve to extend the reach of Fujitsu? What does each party bring to the table and how does the relationship work?

THOMPSON: Well, the origins of our relationship with Fujitsu go back to 1970, when we went out and tried to

The greatest benefit we get from our relationship with Fujitsu is in technology, in the "R" part of R & D. They're awfully good in basic research in areas like semiconductor technology, optical fiber, communications, even artificial intelligence. We, conversely, are awfully good in the "D" part of R & D, in developing commercial applications for their research.

—Ed Thompson—

raise venture capital in the domestic capital markets and failed. We just didn't have the ability then to raise $50 million of five-year money to develop a large-scale processor to compete against IBM.

We did find one or two venture capitalists in the U.S., as well as a German company, willing to put up a little money. But most of the venture capital ended up coming from Fujitsu. Their investment was based on the promise of our technology and the way it could potentially complement their manufacturing op-

erations. If our technology proved to be successful, they could become a supplier of sub-assemblies and complements to us.

So Fujitsu looked at their investment in Amdahl in a way very different from that of a traditional venture capitalist. They were not looking for an immediate return on investment. In fact, to this day they've never sold a share of our stock. They viewed us as a company that had the potential to keep their factories loaded as well as a valuable source in a mutually beneficial exchange of technology. And our relationship with Fujitsu is now over 20 years old.

STEWART: So they manufacture for you?

THOMPSON: They manufacture some sub-assemblies and components. For example, they developed the bipolar ECL technology that is the chip technology in our large-scale processor. The architecture is ours. The design is ours—the micro code, the macro code, and what have you. But we selected their chip technology.

STEWART: You say you *chose* their chip technology. You really had complete freedom to make that choice?

THOMPSON: Yes, we did, at least in that particular case. And then at a point in time, we had to make some commitments on certain volumes to Fujitsu after exhausting our domestic supplier's ability to produce a high-performance bi-polar ECL chip at a competitive cost.

But let me return to the point Charlie Clough made earlier about the importance of the microprocessor, because it's also having a profound effect on our business as well. About five years ago, we too recognized the dramatically reduced cost structure inherent in that technology, and so we knew where the marketplace was going. In fact, I would say that our distinctive core competence is our knowledge of what's going on in large corporations with the largest computer installations in the world. Based on the changes we were seeing in the market, we selected Sun Microsystems and its SPARC chip for our future RISC-based processor in developing a platform using microprocessor technology. This will enable us to deliver a very attractive cost/performance processor for the large-scale open-systems marketplace. And that development is underway right now.

STEWART: But how do you benefit from being associated with Fujitsu in this way?

THOMPSON: Generalizations are always risky, but let me attempt a big one. The greatest benefit we get from our relationship with Fujitsu is in technology, in R & D. They're damned good in the "R" part of R & D. The stereotypical view of Japanese suppliers is that they are good copiers, but not good inventors. You know, they take existing technology, reverse-engineer it, and come up with a high-quality product that they then mass distribute and sell very cheaply.

But, the reality is quite the opposite in our relationship with Fujitsu. They're awfully good in basic research, in areas like semiconductor technology, optical fiber, communications, even artificial intelligence. We, conversely, are awfully good in the "D" part of R & D, in developing commercial applications for their research. And our ability in this area stems, as I said before, from our experience with and knowledge of customers that we've built up over many years. We are sometimes able to know our customers' requirements even before the customers are aware of them—although anticipating customer demands in this way can be a risky proposition.

STEWART: How does the technology transfer between the two companies actually take place? Is there a lot of interchange between your research efforts and Fujitsu's?

THOMPSON: Yes, there is a good deal of interchange. We actually make each other insiders with regard to ongoing developments in our technology. Our mutual knowledge helps both of us make better investment decisions, decisions about where they're putting in a lot of money and where we're putting in a lot of money. And, together, we do spend a lot of money on R & D. For example, Fujitsu is a $25 billion company that is spending about 11% of sales on R & D. We are a $2.5 billion company spending about 15% of our sales on R & D. So, we view our R & D as in some sense a joint effort. Both companies figure out together what it makes sense for us to develop in common, and what to develop separately.

Hi-Powered Lo-tech: The Case of MacFrugal's

STEWART: We have one more company yet to hear from. So let me turn to Len Williams, President of MacFrugal's. Len, your company is a bargain-basement, close-out firm. It seems to be at almost the opposite end of the spectrum from some of the large Japanese, hi-tech companies C.K. was describing yesterday. Do these principles of strategy really apply to a company like yours? Or is it all fairly high-falutin' stuff?

WILLIAMS: I think the same principles apply in our case. In fact, I think C.K. might find our story quite interesting. Our core competence amounts to just one thing: We believe we are the best high-gross-profit-margin buyers in the country. That is the basis of our business. And we've worked hard to maintain this core competence. We continue to be the best buyers of the kind of merchandise that we sell.

Now, it's true that, over time, we have reduced our percentage margins somewhat because of increased competition. If we had insisted on our old margins, we would have been excluded from trading in some of the best merchandise. So we've shifted one piece of our equation to become more competitive, to maintain our original core competence, if you will.

STEWART: But how does your company actually operate? How do you buy this merchandise?

WILLIAMS: We have about 20 people who buy merchandise 100% of the time, and they have lots of support staff. We buy in the U.S. and in a dozen other countries. We buy regular close-outs, we buy overproduction, we buy in virtually any situation where waste occurs in manufacturing and distributing goods. We also buy down-time in equipment.

STEWART: You buy down-time in equipment?

WILLIAMS: If we find a plastics company that has too much resin and machines aren't working, we'll bang out four or five products by the truckload. If we find a company that prints children's books and needs to flatten out their production schedule, we help them out. We buy goods any way we can. We're like old-time merchants. We buy onshore and offshore, and we're very, very flexible.

Our principal assets are money and space. We have a lot of distribution center space and lots of cash, and we can do lots of deals. One of our competitors at the moment has a cash problem, and they're going to sink like the Titanic; it's not even that big a problem, they just can't pay fast enough.

We also operate very differently from the normal retailing practice of low margins and high turnover. We don't care an awful lot about turn. What we care about is, do we have the product? We are, in fact, our own suppliers. We don't rely on suppliers to give us merchandise. We rely on ourselves to have the merchandise. For this reason, we earn high gross margins.

STEWART: How does a company like this get started?

WILLIAMS: It all started about 40 years ago with a wild entrepreneur—a man whom I've since met, talked to, and tried to understand. He began by selling some unusual products out of his station wagon. He found so much product he eventually opened a store. And now we are well on our way to having 300 stores, and the founder lives with his money in Fresno.

But I'll tell you what kind of guy he is. After I was in this business a year, and understood what I thought I could from being there, I went to see him—to see what he could teach me. And when we finished our conversation for the day, he said to me: "Do you have a strong back? Reach in my car." So I pulled out this huge African statue made out of wood. He said: "I found 400 of them. I got them all for eight bucks each."

So then I paid him $11, and later sold them for $30. It's that kind of business. So we have a different deal every day, a different way, different needs. We have a very lean management. And, as I said, we're very flexible.

STEWART: It strikes me that retailing is an industry that tends to have a geographic focus. In other words, you'll find a company like Walmart focusing largely on American markets, as opposed to going overseas. Is that because consumer tastes and customs vary so much across countries that it becomes a quantum leap to sell abroad?

WILLIAMS: I worked for an American company in Europe for four years. And we had businesses in three countries. And I've watched other American retailing businesses operating in other countries. The margins in retailing are narrow. And I've observed that the connection between success-

Our core competence amounts to just one thing: We believe we are the best high-gross-profit-margin buyers in the country. We buy regular close-outs, we buy overproduction, we buy in virtually any situation where waste occurs in manufacturing and distributing goods. We buy goods any way we can. We're like old-time merchants. We buy onshore and offshore, and we're very, very flexible.

—Len Williams—

ful retailers and their customer is often visceral; and this implies the need for geographic, local, ethnic specialization. To translate a merchandising format from country to country is very, very difficult. Marks & Spencer couldn't make it in North America. J.C. Penney, for which I once worked, couldn't make it in Europe. Sears couldn't make it in Europe. A few companies have done it, like Bennetton. But it's a very tough thing to do.

But, having said all that, I'm going to Mexico City next weekend to try to

start to learn what it takes for us to be in Mexico with free trade. Canada is easy, it's like America. I'm Canadian. You don't have to go there to figure it out. But Mexico is very different. And we're going to see if, with free trade, we can find opportunity. The population density in the cities makes it potentially attractive. And we already feel we understand Hispanic people, because they represent about 35% or 40% of our action in Southern California and the Southwest.

STEWART: Would the same thing be true of Vons, Dennis?

ECK: Pretty much. We've sent our people around the world to look for ideas and different ways of doing things. In one case, a man came back to me and said, "Dennis, you have to go to Veracy, Italy. It has the finest deli in the world." So when I next went to Europe, I rented a car and went to Veracy, Italy. And it *was* maybe the finest deli in the world.

When I returned from Europe, the man asked me, "Well, are we going to build one like that?" And I said, "No, we're not. But we're going to steal a few of his fixturing ideas, because they show product much more effectively." As I explained to him, in Veracy, Italy, you're surrounded 100% by Italians. In that setting, the product assortment, mixture, and the goods can be uniquely tailored. Therefore, the assortments can be dominant. The problem for us is we would need Italians to buy the products, and there aren't that many in a cluster in Los Angeles. (The fixtures, though, work beautifully with our Southern California assortment.)

I have a view that says when we go to borrow things from other companies, we often look at the wrong thing. We look at the superficial—in our case, at the products on display. What we should be looking for are the things that are truly transportable across markets. In this case, it was the display techniques, not the products.

STEWART: Do you carry that principle of ethnic specialization, if you will, down to the individual store, so that each store has the autonomy to merchandise and focus on its particular market, its particular neighborhood? Or do you try to get some economies of scale by standardizing things across the board?

ECK: We do both at the same time. We run three distinct formats. We have Pavilions stores, which we refer to as our "republican" format. It's a high-touch, high-feel store with expansions of product that you won't find in most supermarkets. It's meant to attract people who are really interested in food. Interestingly, there hasn't been a recession in our sales in Pavilions.

STEWART: The Clinton tax plan hasn't kicked in yet.

ECK: Well, it's what you have left over that counts.

At the other end of the spectrum, we have a group of stores we call Tianguis. They are designed for first- and second-generation Hispanic people who have immigrated to Los Angeles. In Tianguis, we try to recreate not only the products and services, but the actual "feel" of shopping they experienced in Mexico. These stores have also turned out to be very good for Asian people. They also put great emphasis on same-day freshness.

Then we have Vons, our middle group of stores. We give the managers of these stores flexibility in tailoring their product assortment and styles of service.

All three groups of stores are supplied by the same distribution channels. They are supervised by the same management and utilize all the same support systems. So, though we have three distinct operating styles, we achieve scale economies with a single support and coordination system.

STEWART: Len, tell me more about why you are looking south of the border to expand your business.

WILLIAMS: Well, you'd have to be crazy not to, because there are so many people there. As I said earlier, we feel we understand Mexican tastes because we're already dealing with Mexicans in Los Angeles and the Southwest. I would also say that some of the early alliances of American with Mexican companies have turned out quite well. Walmart, for example, went in and formed a valuable alliance.

STEWART: Dennis, it would seem to me that a company like Walmart represents a formidable competitive threat, even to innovative grocery retailers like Vons? There have long been rumors of their intent to penetrate the grocery side of the business, and there have been some false starts. But still, the company is not to be taken lightly. How do you respond to that type of threat?

ECK: Our method of responding is to continue what we're attempting to do now. We will seek out and specialize in those products and services that ordinary supermarkets cannot provide. As I mentioned earlier, we've been moving our focus away from cross-overs toward high-margin specialties like floral, delis, and bakeries. I don't believe Walmart will want to follow us there. Our current strategy is to move as far away from direct competition with Walmart as we can. This, while recognizing that we still rely on cross-over categories now at less margin. We have moved our business to a heavy emphasis on service, variety, execution, and freshness. That's the weakness of general merchandise.

But having said that, it has yet to be proved that a general merchandiser can succeed in the food business. It is rare for a food company to succeed in general merchandise. As we've al-

ready mentioned, there has not been much success by either of these industries in expanding overseas.

PRAHALAD: I think the importance of this notion of distinct national and ethnic tastes has been greatly exaggerated. As a consequence, there is more global opportunity than is commonly believed for businesses that appear very much bound to local tastes and based on one-on-one contact with consumers. For example, if you take both the merchandising and grocery retailing businesses, a significant portion of the buying already takes place overseas. So one part of the business, the supply part of the chain, has already become global.

But what about the customer interface? Are there general principles that you can transport across cultures and countries? To me the reason why large food retailers and merchandisers have not been very successful in Europe and in Asia is the domination, until quite recently, of small mom-and-pop stores. This has been embodied in the tradition of people going out and buying bread every morning at 11:00 o'clock when a fresh batch comes out. All that behavior, I would submit, is based on a certain lifestyle. It has nothing to do with an immutable national character, as people like to claim.

For example, if you went to France ten years ago and asked a Frenchman, "Would you eat frozen foods?", he would say, "Absolutely not." But, as things have turned out, a penchant for frozen foods has little to do with being French or American. It has much to do with lifestyles. If both husband and wife are working, frozen foods become an eminently respectable thing to serve. And, if you go to Paris today, I assure you you *will* find frozen foods. It's remarkable how simply increasing the number of dual income households can change what has been held to be the national character. But changes in wealth and lifestyle clearly affect consumer tastes, and in fairly predictable ways.

I would also argue that Asia—at least the large, metropolitan areas—will prove a better market for American-style food retailing than Europe. Why? Because—and you may be surprised to know this—more women work in Asia, and at better jobs, than those in the United States. And the same thing is happening within the large Indian community in London. Today, you can buy all kinds of packaged Indian food. People always tell me that Asians have this desire for freshness—and that may be true, especially if only one of the couple is working. But if both of them are working, they behave no differently from us.

ECK: Well, we actually sell to Asia. We charge a fee for busloads of Asian businessmen to tour our Pavilions stores—twenty-eight hundred bucks a bus. There is an enormous interest among Asian businessmen in our style of merchandising.

Corporate Structure: Centralized vs. Decentralized

STEWART: Let me ask a broader question. Yesterday C.K. was talking about the need for corporations to transcend their business unit mentality and encourage co-operation among different functions and businesses to exploit new growth opportunities more effectively. What are some of the remedies the companies at this table have devised to break down those organizational barriers to co-operation? How do design your measurement and reward system to encourage teamwork among different operating units?

PERRY: A few years ago, our overseas operations felt that our MIS system wasn't giving them the information they wanted quickly enough and tai-

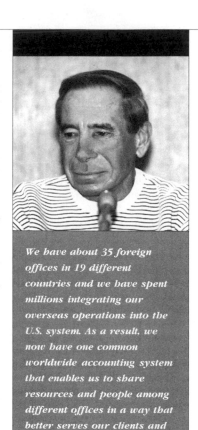

We have about 35 foreign offices in 19 different countries and we have spent millions integrating our overseas operations into the U.S. system. As a result, we now have one common worldwide accounting system that enables us to share resources and people among different offices in a way that better serves our clients and leads to the greater good of the whole company.

—Robert Perry—

lored to their specific needs. So we spent several million dollars implementing a separate MIS system for our overseas operations. But it has turned out to be a failure. So, in the last couple of years, we have spent millions more integrating our overseas operations *back* into the U.S. system. As a result, we now have one common worldwide accounting system.

What this means, for example, is that an engineer from our Paris office could spend five hours working on a project in Tokyo on a Friday afternoon, and the Tokyo project manager

would have that time recorded in his overall job costing summary on the following Monday. So our supervising managers know the time spent on their projects by all their engineers around the world, almost instantaneously. And that, of course, gives us great cost control of the projects that we perform.

We have about 35 foreign offices in 19 different countries. And there is a lot of mixing of our people working on projects. In other words, if we have a major project in France, we might bring in people from Germany and the U.K. and Italy to work on it. So our organization allows us to share resources and people among different offices—to move them to where they are most valuable—in a way that better serves our clients and leads to the greater good of the whole company.

STEWART: Bob, your company was for most of its life a partnership, and then you went public and became a C corporation. How, if at all, has this change in organizational form affected the sense of teamwork within the company?

PERRY: We were a partnership for 53 years until we went public just about a year ago. We went public for several reasons, one of which was we felt it was getting a bit unwieldy to run such a large operation as a partnership.

In the tradition of our partnership, the profits were distributed according to the profit of the *entire* firm, not the particular profitability of, say, the German or French or Australian office. All the profits were pooled and then distributed according to overall capital interests.

STEWART: And did that practice motivate people to work together more effectively?

PERRY: Yes, it did. It eliminated a great deal of provincialism.

CLOUGH: I was manager of one of Texas Instruments' European semiconductor operations for several years.

The units were organized geographically; for example, there was a TI-Deutschland, a TI-France, and a TI-Italia that all operated independently. And the conflicts, the barriers to co-operation, created by that system were difficult. The problem began with the time-honored international rivalries: the Italians didn't trust the French, the French with cause feared the Germans, the Germans looked down on the Italians. This problem was compounded by the corporate practice of driving profit measurement down to the lowest common denominator within a complex organization. Within each of these countries, we had what were called "product customer centers." These centers had the responsibility to design, manufacture, and market their product—and they were each measured individually on their profit contribution, or lack thereof. So not only did we have little incentive to coordinate our design or production activities with those of other units, but we had a duplication of functions that could have been performed in one place for all Europe.

Since then, Texas Instruments—along with many other companies, I suspect—has done away with this fragmentation of the company into hundreds of individual profit centers. All these different units have now been consolidated into six or seven operating divisions. TI has also stopped organizing according to geographical boundaries. Today, for example, they have one person who's responsible for their entire MIS capability on a worldwide basis. And the primary measure of success within the company is the profitability of the worldwide organization.

THOMPSON: Several years ago, we went to cross-functional process re-engineering teams—teams made up of engineers from the different countries, people from the different strategic business units and field business units, and some corporate people as well. Prior to forming these teams, we had operations in some 30 countries all designing, marketing, and installing systems in ways that may have been optimal from the perspective of the individual unit, but which failed to optimize the value of the entire enterprise. We found that bringing all these people together ended up providing us with a better understanding of the needs of the total corporation.

In one case, interestingly enough, our direct experience in serving clients caused us to make a change in how we were organized internally. This happened in Europe, when we were installing general ledgers and trying to figure out the optimal distribution of those systems. As a result of what we learned from that experience, we reorganized the company to reflect the new systems implementation we came up with. So, our corporate structure was changed to fit the requirements of our customers, instead of just allowing our internal structure to dictate the kind of systems we installed.

STEWART: Ed, given that the world seems to be moving away from the mainframe and toward more distributed systems, how have you addressed the need to redirect your resources and, perhaps, cannibalize your basic business? Have you made that transition? And how are you addressing that organizationally?

THOMPSON: Let me first say that we are *not* cannibalizing the mainframe business. That business is alive and well, although we have changed the name: It's now called "centralized processing." It's always going to be there.

But I agree the business is changing, and it's changing pretty dramatically. To reflect that change, we have changed the compensation plan for our sales organization to encourage them to concentrate more heavily on what we see as our growth opportunities—software and professional services, and the open systems we now offer. But, having said that, the big bucks are still in our central-processing operation.

STEWART: The big bucks in what respect—sales or gross profits?

THOMPSON: Both, although the margins are beginning to shrink, and will continue to do so over time.

STEWART: Well, what about the returns? I ask because I understand the mainframe business is being hurt by substitution in the form of distributed processing. So there must be excess capacity in mainframes relative to what was anticipated. And thus there needs to be a major withdrawal of resources, or at least a slowdown in the commitment of resources, to the mainframe business.

THOMPSON: That's certainly true, at least relative to what was anticipated. Five years ago, the large-scale processor business capacity was growing at 40% to 50% per annum. The forecasts for the next five years are only half that, about 25% per annum. And with the price competition and the commodity feature of the business, prices are going down at about that same rate.

So, the large-scale compatible processor business is a zero-growth business in terms of total industry revenues. Fortunately, though, we are in a position where we're increasing our market share. Today, we have a worldwide share that's probably in the high teens, and we expect to move rapidly into the low or mid-20s. Thus, the revenue and volume parts of it still look pretty good for us. But the margins are under a lot of pressure, and that is starting at the top and it's collapsing all the way down on the minicomputer business. In fact, the margins on all parts of the hardware side of the business are collapsing.

So, as I said, we are in the midst of a substantial transition that will move us partly into the professional services and software business, and into the open-systems licensing business over time. We will still be in the hardware business as well, but using architectures and technologies that have been optimized for cost and performance.

Changing the Management Scorecard

PRAHALAD: I would like to return to this issue of why business units don't collaborate, because I think it has a lot to do with the problems at our largest companies—the IBMs, the ITTs, the General Motors of the world. To me, the really basic issue is this: What is the scorecard for top management? What is their primary goal? Most top managements simply sidestep the question by aggregating the financial numbers of all their business units and coming up with a single financial measure for the corporation. But, as Charlie was arguing in the case of TI, this kind of divisionalized, decentralized structure forces people to think and act in very narrow ways. It breeds turf wars.

If you think about the dimensions of corporate strength in a large diversified company, it's not just a matter of expanding markets by selling in multiple countries. More fundamentally, it's a matter of leveraging commonalities among business units, or what I like to call the "white spaces" between business units. Most of the new opportunities for corporations do not exist within the box called the business unit; they tend to span those boxes, or to exist in these white spaces, if you will. People focusing only on their business units will inevitably fail to seize such opportunities.

So, given this limitation, why do managers use financial performance as their scorecard? And why do they continue to use decentralized corporate structures? Two reasons, I think:

Almost all the debate in the United States centers around stockholders. It seems to me an unexamined article of faith. I would prefer to put the issue of corporate success in different terms: How well has a company succeeded in creating wealth not only for shareholders, but for its customers and its employees? I'm concerned ultimately about the continuity of large corporations.

—*C. K. Prahalad*—

One, it makes top management's job extremely easy. What do you do if one of your business units is not performing? You change the manager. This way, you've pretended to address the problem, and you're essentially off the hook. The second reason, which I won't go into now, has to do with restrictions our governance system places on communications between management and investors—restrictions that make it difficult for companies to communicate in ways other than the language of quarterly earnings.

Now, there is no value added in that kind of relationship between top management and corporate divisions. Top managers in this decentralized system are functioning at bottom no differently than portfolio managers who trade in and out of stocks. But, if you believe you're running an operating company, then top management must take some responsibility for creating synergies, for making the value of the total corporation worth more than simply the sum of its divi-sions. Of course, management must continue to make sure that divisional managers have strong incentives to be market-focused and entrepreneurial. At the same, though, they must continually ask themselves: How do I use corporate oversight and corporate functions to leverage the different divisions, to identify and take advantage of growth opportunities that could be pursued more effectively by people from different parts of the organization acting in concert?

You cannot produce co-operative behavior unless you take a broader view of corporate performance than that provided by financial measures. You certainly will never achieve a sharing of the agenda. And that, in my opinion, is why so many of the recent corporate success stories feature Japanese instead of American companies. It's not because Japanese top managers are smarter than American managers. They have simply tried much harder to provide people throughout their organizations with a broad understanding of the corporate mission, with a vision of the corporate future. At the same time, they have continued to encourage individual entrepreneurship and accountability at the business unit level.

So we need to ask the question: To what extent can you decentralize and multiply profit centers without destroying incentives for co-operative planning and action? At what level of senior management do you begin to hold people accountable not for business unit performance, but for the success of the organization as a whole? If you look at the three levels of management below the top that characterize most American companies, each of them is typically evaluated according to the same set of numbers. The business unit managers are looking at monthly or quarterly performance, and so are the group managers and the sector managers. If all of them are marching to the same drummer, then where is the value added by the upper layers? They don't bring a different perspective to operations.

In Defense of Decentralization and Corporate Focus

STEWART: That's true enough, C.K. But let me play devil's advocate and ask the following question: What's to prevent the organization-wide pursuit of this grand co-operative vision from degenerating into an unchecked quest for growth and market share? It seems to me that this is one of the big problems faced by many Japanese companies today. In this quest for growth and continuous renewal, they have diversified well beyond their capabilities and ignored profitability altogether. So where's the accountability necessary to rein in the impulse toward excessive growth?

As you said yesterday, C.K., the best corporate system is one that achieves an ideal tension between the short term and the long term. You have to pay attention to both simultaneously; and it seems, to me at least, that too many Japanese companies have sacrificed profitability for market share. Much of this increased market share, I'm willing to bet, will never translate into profit or shareholder gains. As one observer recently put it, the Japanese economy is now "choking on an orgy of overinvestment."

One of the things I was struck with during your presentation yesterday—and in your articles as well—is this: There is not a single reference to the financial or stock market performance of any of the companies you hold up for emulation. How successful, for example, has NEC been in its financial performance relative to GTE, the American counterpart you cited? Has it earned extraordinary returns for its stockholders over this long period of time? What has been the result of NEC's being among the top five companies in market share in each of the three main areas of the computers and communications business? And isn't it in some sense misleading to compare NEC with large, diversified American companies, when the traditional format in America is not to have companies that are broad in scope, but rather to have industries made up of smaller, more focused companies?

Take the computer industry. Andrew Grove, the CEO of Intel, has stated that the American computer industry is going from being vertically integrated to "horizontal." It is moving away from dominance by companies like IBM with integrated proprietary systems that are all things to all people. IBM effectively said to its customers, "You have to take my whole product line if you want any of it." Today, of course, we have the open architecture driven by the central processing unit, and the result is that the industry has fragmented into classes of specialists—everything from Intel to Microsoft to Dell to Compaq to Apple.

So, C.K., it seems to me we should not be comparing NEC against a GTE, as you do. Rather, we should be comparing an NEC to the combination—or the sum, if you will—of an AT&T, an Intel, an Apple, a Hewlett-Packard, and a Microsoft. You see, you have to ask yourself the question: Would AT&T or GTE be more valuable and productive companies if they were all of sudden to acquire Apple and Intel and Microsoft? I very much doubt it.

THOMPSON: They couldn't afford it.

STEWART: Right, and that only goes to reinforce my point. These companies are far more valuable and efficient operating alone. I'm very skeptical about the ability of individual companies like GTE and AT&T to achieve the economies of scope you identify in NEC. Your argument seems perilously close to the fallacy that NEC is a better company than AT&T simply *because* it has a broader scope, simply because it participates in all of the C & C industries of the future? But I'm very skeptical that this is a prescription for building shareholder value, and by that I mean long-term value as well as short-term value.

CLOUGH: Bennett, let me add something to what you're saying. The same arguments apply to the electronic industry. The electronic industry isn't merely in the process of change, it is going through a revolution. We have killed our kings and queens, and now we're assassinating our presidents. The very large, historically successful companies in this industry have created enormous problems for themselves—many of which stem from sheer size—and they are now under tremendous pressure to shrink and change.

The embryonic companies of today that are going to be successful in the next ten years are companies that don't want to do it the way IBM did. For example, if you have a uniquely valuable idea for creating and marketing teleconferencing electronic equipment, you want to focus just on design and marketing. You don't want to invest in large manufacturing entities. You don't want to go out and buy the land and build on it, because you don't bring anything to the manufacturing ballgame.

Your manufacturing skills are not as good as those of people who have been honing their manufacturing skills for 20 years. And, in many cases, you may not want to market it either. Your brilliance resides in the fact that you can create this unique and better electronic equipment.

People today don't want to make investments in areas beyond their expertise. This is the new American model of enterprise—smaller companies with limited funding and resources relying on outsourcing and other forms of networking or partnerships. It's adherence to the principle of comparative advantage, focusing only on what you do best and getting other people to do the other stuff they do better. And that's really a departure from the way electronic companies operated from the late 1950s until just the last few years.

STEWART: C.K., in one of your articles, you criticized Motorola for skipping the round of 256K Dynamic Random Access Memories, or DRAMS. You argued that doing so made it very difficult for Motorola to participate in the 1-Meg stage. But, with hindsight, this seems to have been the right decision for Motorola. As Charlie said earlier, memories today are commodities. And, as a consequence, it seems clear to us now that the Japanese invested billions of dollars in building memory capacity with virtually no returns to show for it.

So, to return to my earlier question, Isn't there a possible danger in overemphasizing the need to leverage core competencies into an all-consuming quest for global leadership? Can that pursuit excuse investing billions of dollars in quest of a core competence that could become available to anybody at commodity prices?

PRAHALAD: Actually, I think you asked seven different questions. And I think it's important to unscramble them because, in any discussion of

American companies function best by putting their bets on decentralization and specialization. We're not very good at realizing economies of scope within companies, but we are unmatched at realizing economies of scope across our economy. That's my problem with C.K.'s strategic concepts—they seem to hinge on the ability of companies to realize, internally, vast economies of scope.

—Bennett Stewart—

this kind, unless you are very clear about what issue we are talking about, we can go from one to another almost seamlessly.

The first question you raised was this: Is NEC creating wealth compared to, say, GTE? It's an interesting question. If you look at profitability alone, GTE is probably more profitable than NEC. And I suspect that GTE's shareholders have done better than NEC's, at least in the last five or six years.

But if you think about what I call "wealth creation"—which is to me a much more interesting question—

then I would argue that NEC has put itself into a strategic position with much greater potential than GTE's. NEC, which started off with a much smaller endowment of capabilities and technologies and financial resources than GTE, has been creating a very different kind of wealth over the last ten years. It has achieved global leadership and significant market share in all the major C & C industries. What has GTE done during the same period? Today, they're pretty much back into the telephone operations they started with.

STEWART: Yes, but is that necessarily a bad thing? It seems, judging from GTE's stock price performance in recent years, that the market is applauding that decision to refocus and abandon their earlier diversification attempts.

PRAHALAD: Almost all the debate in the United States centers around stockholders and stockholders' returns. It seems to me an unexamined article of faith, and I'm not at all convinced that it's the only question to ask. I would prefer to put the issue of corporate success in different terms: How well has a company succeeded in creating wealth not only for shareholders, but for its customers and for its employees? Certainly shareholder interests must be served in the process. But, I believe that management's failure to consider customers, employees, and other corporate stakeholders will inevitably lead to the reduction of shareholder wealth over the long term.

In the short term, of course, management can make money simply by buying and selling companies, by functioning as opportunists moving in and out of industries at will. American managers have shown themselves to be very adept at that. But I would like to see the managements of our large companies show greater concern for *long-term* wealth creation.

Over the long term, you cannot short-change your customers and your employees and still create value. You must create a satisfying workplace—one that provides opportunities for people to grow.

So, I'm concerned ultimately about the *continuity* of large corporations—and I believe my view is shared by most societies around the world. For companies that want to survive for 50 or 100 or 200 hundred years, continuity requires a balanced view of wealth creation. If you're concerned solely with shareholders' returns, you'll never make any long-term investments in employees or in customer relations.

So, again, the fundamental issue here is coming up with the proper scorecard for evaluating top management. I'm convinced that, within the next five or ten years, there's going to be a lot of debate in this country on whether we should continue to worship only at the altar of stockholders. Is there more to running large industrial enterprises than just attending to stockholders? Is it not indeed a position of public trust?

Beyond Shareholder Value?

STEWART: Would anyone on the panel care to respond to C.K.?
WILLIAMS: I think all three groups—employees, customers, and stockholders—are critical to corporate success. But if you want to raise capital for investment in the future, you really have to satisfy the shareholders with a reasonable return. And I frankly have yet to see a business where you can satisfy shareholders without taking care of customers and employees. So I don't see the problem.
STEWART: But that still begs the question: Why should we be concerned first and foremost about shareholders?
WILLIAMS: They're the owners of the business.

STEWART: Well, yes, but I think the explanation is much broader than that. It all goes back to the fact that society's resources are limited. And when I say resources, I'm not talking about just capital or materials or equipment. I am also talking about people, human energy and brainpower—about assets of all kind, intangible as well as tangible. If we can believe Adam Smith, the way to create the greatest social wealth is to encourage every company to maximize the net present value of the enterprise. Maximizing shareholder value is important not because shareholders are especially deserving, but because it is the decision-making rule that leads to the greatest efficiency in allocating resources and, from there, to the greatest economic good for the greatest number. That's why it matters.
PRAHALAD: Okay, let me respond to that by posing an open question. The scorecard for management has always been based on its ability to marshal and allocate resources, and to maximize returns to the scarce resource. Your argument, Bennett, and most American corporate practice, is based on the assumption that capital is the scarce resource. That was true in the past. Indeed, the past success of American business was based on the ability of American managers to marshal and allocate effectively vast amounts of capital.

But, in the future, the truly scarce resource is not going to be capital, but human talent. And if that is the case, then shouldn't we now be using talent accumulation as one of our major criteria for judging corporate success?
WILLIAMS: If the accumulation of talented people were the primary measure of organizational success, then universities would win the competition hands down. But universities can't deliver the goods and services that most of us live on.

PRAHALAD: In fact, our universities may be a much better model for the next round of corporate governance than we think. Now, I know this is a very controversial issue—and I think the first part of this discussion went much too politely and quietly. But, as we enter this new world of global competition, I think we will be forced to re-examine our theory of wealth creation and its assumption of the primacy of shareholder value.

For the game has truly changed from what it was. During the industrial revolution, the accumulation of capital led to productivity increases. And that is why we won the game for the last 50 or 60 years. We were able to accumulate large stores of capital, and then use that capital stock to increase efficiency. In the next round of wealth creation—at least in knowledge-intensive businesses—human talent, or brainpower, may be a more critical resource than access to capital. That is not to say that capital is unimportant, only that it is not a uniquely differentiating factor for productivity improvement.
STEWART: I agree with your last point. But you seem to be assuming that the aim of the corporation is to maximize the *return* on capital. That is not the same thing as maximizing the *net present value* of the enterprise. I agree with you that capital is simply a commodity input to the process. It has a cost, and you have to subtract that cost along with all other expenses. What you try to maximize is what's left over after you've satisfied customers, and fully compensated employees and all the other factors in your business. That is what economists call your economic or *residual* income, that is the measure of the true profitability. What I think you're overlooking, C.K., is that such a measure considers the returns to *all* the resources employed, human as well as material, intangible as well as tangible.

The change you're describing, by the way, was what Alvin Toffler years ago called "the power shift." According to Toffler, there have been three major driving forces in history; he calls them "muscle," "money," and "mind." The Middle Ages were dominated by muscle—by violence and the threat of violence—and serfdom was the governing principle. That gave rise to the Industrial Revolution, where money became important and led to the dominance of large, centrally-directed, bureaucratic organizations. In more recent times, it was the Sears, the GMs—the mass merchandisers, mass marketers, mass manufacturers. And, today, we're going through the information revolution. Brainpower is more important today, and the marshalling of intellectual capabilities, as you said, is the right way to maximize value for companies. There's no question about that.

But, having accepted that premise, companies still have to deal with the fundamental issue of allocating the *proper* amount of resources—not too much, not too little—to any one factor, whether it be human capital or investor capital. The corporation should invest in future capabilities, of course, but only up to the point where the next dollar of investment still yields at least a dollar—adjusted for time and risk—in returns. Focusing on net present value and residual income, on what's left over after all the factors have been fully compensated, is the right way to think about the optimal allocation of resources.

I do agree with you, though, C.K., that the residual should not accrue entirely to the shareholders. A company's managers and employees should be carved into that residual, either through greater equity ownership, or in some other way that also makes them partners with shareholders in creating value.

In the long run, you end up serving your shareholders by serving your customers. In the short run, there are always conflicts between the interests of shareholders and those of customers and employees. Given limited resources, I am forced to make trade-offs among the requirements of these three groups. This, while trying to find balance between the short- and the long-term profit of the business.

—*Dennis Eck*—

Non-Financial Performance Measures and Communicating with Investors

ECK: Let me bring the discussion down a peg or two from this lofty plane. Things may be somewhat different in the hi-tech area, but in the food retailing business, it seems clear to me that, as one of the top managers of my company, my primary focus must be on my customers, their tastes and requirements.

There are not enough resources or talent—though we have a lot of both—

in our company to give our customers everything they want precisely how and when they want it. In the long run, it's true, you end up best serving your shareholders by serving your customers. In the short run, there are always conflicts between the interests of shareholders and customers. There are also conflicts between the interests of shareholders and employees. Given limited resources, I am forced to make trade-offs among the requirements of my shareholders, customers, and employees. This, while trying to find balance between the short- and the long-term profit of the business.

One of my primary responsibilities is to allocate the resources, the talent and the energy of the organization. However, we must always be pointed toward the consumer. I believe the failure of American business—where it has failed—has resulted from a failure to keep its eye on the consumer.

PRAHALAD: Dennis, it's very interesting that you should say that. For I have yet to see a company that talks about customer satisfaction or presents surveys of consumer opinion in its annual report or analyst presentations.

ECK: Then you should attend one of our analysts presentations.

PRAHALAD: Let me ask another question, then. Why don't customers evaluate the management performance of various business units? We could make customer service an integral part of the evaluation of management.

ECK: But consumers evaluate companies every day. In our business, they do it every day by their purchasing patterns. What they buy, how they buy it, and how they feel about it is a great management scorecard.

WILLIAMS: There is also a downside to using customer satisfaction and other nonfinancial considerations as criteria for evaluating management. I once worked for Federated Department Stores, and the company spent an inordinate amount of money and time trying to measure things that are basically not measurable, such as the churn of people, how many ethnic groups are you employing, and so forth. As head of a division, I was driven crazy trying to figure out just what top management wanted out of me. When they sent me my evaluation forms, the system was so complicated and had so many variables that I simply gave it back to the chairman and told him, "I can't understand this. But if I make any money based on it, just send it to me."

My job as a division manager was to make money. Just let me figure out how to do it, and all the other things will take care of themselves.

And, besides the sheer confusion and inefficiency of it all, there is another real danger to this movement to make customer and employee satisfaction an explicit part of the corporate mission: namely, that uninformed outsiders such as politicians and public interest groups become part of the debate on corporate governance. So my question is, where does this debate take place? Does it take place inside the company as part of running the business? Or does it take place in a larger format with some informed and some uninformed people? And at what cost to management time?

PRAHALAD: I agree that there is a big problem with allowing uninformed people to pass judgments on the quality of a company. But I also think that, in the U.S. system of corporate governance, investors are very underinformed about what is happening inside companies. For that reason, all they can use to evaluate your performance are the numbers you produce at the end of the quarter. And this system gives rise to two different problems. It lets subperforming managements off the hook for a long time in some cases, as in the case of GM. But, in other cases, it keeps some good, far-sighted man-

agements on too tight a rein, causing underinvestment in capabilities.

For this reason, I think we ought to spend some time asking the question: Are there alternative systems of governance that would enable us to inform our investors in more meaningful ways? In Germany, for example, the large banks that own stock in companies often have representatives that sit on corporate boards. In the Japanese keiretsus, suppliers and distributors have equity stakes and board representation in one another.

It is in the interest of American companies to provide investors with more and better information so they are not forced to make these quarter-to-quarter snap judgments about the quality of management. The result of the current system is enormous volatility, which in turn forces managers to respond in knee-jerk fashion. This is what we have gone through in this country in the last 15 years.

PERRY: Well, C.K., we've only been a public company for one year, and it is all a bit new to us, having been a partnership for over 50 years before that. But what we do each quarter is this: When we announce our earnings, we have a telephone conference with almost a hundred people on the other end. That includes all of our major shareholders and all the principal analysts around the country who follow our firm. During these teleconferences, we'll discuss major issues with them on a fairly informal basis. I was under the impression that most companies did something like this.

THOMPSON: There is a problem with that approach, though. Because of all the laws in this country restricting shareholder communication, and the general litigiousness of our society, we have been forced to filter and restrict our shareholder communications. Everything you say to shareholders becomes part of the public record. And there is a group of law

firms out there that, if you have any change in your fortunes, will immediately slap you with a law suit if they think they can make money out of it. And I have to believe that our legal rules and general litigiousness are seriously restricting the flow of communication between management and shareholders in this country.

PRAHALAD: I agree that we have big legal and regulatory problems with communications between management and investors in the U.S. For one thing, management cannot give information selectively to anybody without going to jail. Nevertheless, even within existing constraints, corporate annual reports and presentations to investors could contain a lot more information on corporate strategies than they do now.

Internal vs. External Economies of Scope

STEWART: C.K., I have what I think is a fundamental disagreement with your analysis on this point. I don't think the market fails to appreciate what management is trying to do. Rather, in many cases, it simply lacks confidence that it will accomplish it. Or, even if management does accomplish the strategic ends they hold up, they are likely to do so in a way that leaves shareholders with an inadequate return on their investment.

A perfect example of this is General Motors. For years, management lamented the level of the company's stock price, proclaiming they were investing for the long term. But, now that the long term has arrived, it turns out that shareholders' concerns were well founded. As another example, when Federal Express announced their intention to introduce Zapmail—a service that was supposed to displace FAX machines—the company's stock price dropped by $8 in a single day. And after Zapmail produced a sea of red ink, the company announced it was abandoning Zapmail, and the stock price shot up.

The academic evidence is pretty convincing in refuting this charge of stock market myopia. As all the studies show, companies that announce increases in R&D and capital expenditures experience significant stock price increases, on average, *upon the announcement.* The single major exception to this was the oil industry during the early '80s, a time of falling oil prices, when announcements of new exploration programs routinely caused sharp declines in stock prices— and rightly so, given the glut of oil that soon followed.

All this leads me, C.K., back to the point you were making about the information revolution. You have suggested that the information revolution is a force driving companies to expand their core competencies across multiple businesses. But I read its import very differently. I think it portends the worldwide breakdown of large organizations, from the overthrow of large, bureaucratic governments to the privatization of enterprises. Industries today are being steam-rolled flat. We are seeing everything from "category killers" like Walmart's taking over retailing, to the niche success of CNN against the major networks, to the flattening of the computer industry through specialization. In general, the restructuring of the 1980s not only streamlined corporate America, but moved it toward greater focus—a movement that, I would argue, has made our companies far more globally competitive than they were ten years ago.

So, it seems to me that what has made the American system work, and the way in which American companies function best, is by putting their bets on decentralization and specialization. In other words, we're not very good at realizing economies of scope *within* companies, but we are unmatched at realizing economies of scope *across our economy.* And that's where I have a fundamental problem with your strategic concepts—they all seem to hinge on the ability of companies to realize, *internally,* vast economies of scope. I just think our economy works best when those economies are realized externally.

TOM THEOBALD: I must say, Bennett, that's the first thing I've ever heard you say that I agree with.

STEWART: Well, thanks, Tom. But this may force me to rethink my position.

PRAHALAD: Bennett, I have never said that companies should do everything internally. That's not the point. In the electronics industry today, competition is in fact taking place not among individual companies, but among clusters of companies. The most successful competitors have not integrated vertically, but have developed groups of highly specialized suppliers. And these suppliers operate independently in some aspects, often supplying the competitors of their primary customer.

For example, take the case of charged coupler devices, or CCDs. Sony is one of the leaders in developing CCD technology and in manufacturing and selling CCD products. But they supply everybody, even companies that compete with their own distributors. In the case of spindle motors, 86% of them come from one highly specialized company called Nideq.

So, small companies and specialization play a major role in my view of global competition. Companies need not do everything internally, as AT&T and IBM did for a long time. What they should strive for, however, is to build and dominate a critical number of competencies that allow them, in effect, to exchange hostages with their competitors. There will

certainly be lots of corporate interrelationships in terms of the supplying of components and sub-components across competitors. But, in order to prosper, you must have something to trade that your trading partner cannot get somewhere else. If you have nothing to trade, you're in a very vulnerable situation.

STEWART: You mentioned that Canon supplies 85% of the laser printer engines for Hewlett-Packard. What does HP offer Canon in return?

PRAHALAD: That's a very interesting question. Hewlett-Packard saw their emerging vulnerability to Canon, and they were smart enough to respond by investing an enormous amount of money in laser printers. They knew they were not going to be able to compete very effectively in laser printing without the help of Canon. But instead of subcontracting the complete customer interface to Canon, they bought the engine instead. They then designed their laser printers around the Canon engine, and this enabled them to retain the direct contact with the customer.

Core Competence and the Threat of Market Power

STEWART: When you say Canon has 85% of the laser printer market, it sounds sinister. It makes Americans say, "Oh, my gosh, they're dominating markets and hollowing out our companies." But isn't the economic reality of this simply that we have a very natural and healthy process of specialization going on? HP has specialized, Canon has specialized, and now they're mutually dependent on each other. What's the matter with that? Why should we view this as a threat to American industry, as so many *Harvard Business Review* articles have done?

PRAHALAD: There is no problem with that, provided American companies have also developed some kind of specialized capabilities. The problem facing many companies, however, is that they have not made the kind of investment necessary to achieve that specialization. Therefore, they cannot enter into a partnership on an equal basis; they have nothing to trade.

For example, take the case of liquid crystal display technologies, or LCDs. In the case of active matrix LCDs, companies such as Compaq, IBM, or Apple have no other recourse but to go to Sharp and Toshiba for LCDs. Nobody makes them here. And that is where I see a problem. In other words, we can get into a very noncompetitive situation—one in which the sole suppliers of the product we manufacture or sell are also our competitors. And if we have not created enough of a specialization to trade with, we are then vulnerable.

STEWART: I don't see the problem, I really don't. Take Dell, for example. They go out and buy displays and combine them with Intel chips. Should they be concerned about their dependence upon Intel for their PC chips?

PRAHALAD: I would be extremely concerned with Intel's domination, and for the same reasons everybody is so concerned about Microsoft now. Intel does not yet compete in the PC market effectively, but they could very easily.

CLOUGH: In fact, they have a division that makes PCs.

PRAHALAD: That's right, but they don't call it PCs. They don't have the plastic around the platform. They just give it to you and say, "This is ours."

THOMPSON: Intel is also trying to get into the massively parallel processing business in the commercial marketplace. So they're also positioning themselves to try to get into our business.

PRAHALAD: I would be extremely worried about Intel if I was in this industry.

CLOUGH: Oh, absolutely. They could turn off the faucet for two days and there would be no Dell.

STEWART: But then there would be no Intel, either. Because then who else would buy from them? They would completely destroy their credibility as a supplier. You don't see the mutual dependency in all this? After all, we're not dealing with a Middle East cartel here.

PRAHALAD: The temptation to use market power once you achieve it has nothing to do with the Middle East. It's a human reaction: The Japanese do it and so will we. And that's why everybody is so concerned about Microsoft and Intel. Suppose Intel becomes big at parallel processing, and they also supply Ed at Amdahl. They don't have to say no to Ed, they can just delay shipment for six months. There are all kinds of ways to enforce a cartel. In the electronics business, if you are late by eight months, the game is over.

THOMPSON: That's right, time to market is vital.

CLOUGH: Why did Compaq cancel their agreements with AMD and go back to Intel, when they could have bought that AMD product, the 386, for a lot less? The reason was, they knew they'd no longer be a beta site for the development of next-generation processors, the 486, the 586.

STEWART: Well, let me return to my earlier question. Can the extent of Intel's domination today really be explained as the result of their ability to "leverage" its core competencies across multiple businesses? Their success—to date at least—seems to me a consequence of their choosing to focus only on microprocessors, and not allowing that focus to be diluted by pursuing other opportunities.

PRAHALAD: Bennett, I think you are misunderstanding the core competence framework. It does not say you have to be part of a very large company like NEC. I can give you 25 other companies that specialize the way Intel has, but without becoming as visibly dominant as Intel in their particular fields. In the case of LCDs, there are two or three companies that dominate that business. But we don't talk much about LCDs in this country. Every time there is a discussion here about whether we as a nation should invest in LCDs, companies talk about how critical it is, but nobody wants to make the investment.

Let me give you another example. For every hand-held device made in the world today, the critical limiting factors are battery life, size, and weight. Can you name one American company that makes miniature batteries that power your laptops and hand-held devices? It is all dominated by one group of companies that also sell the end products as well. All that I'm saying is that the temptation to play hardball in those circumstances is very great.

STEWART: Well, the Japanese companies must be earning fantastic monopoly returns from these products. But that's not what the newspapers are telling us these days. And, if they're not earning monopoly returns, what's the point of being a monopolist?

The same thing was being said about DRAMs just a few years ago. Alarmists like Charles Ferguson were saying, "We don't have an American company other than IBM that can produce DRAMs in quantity, and that's ominous." Yet, today, DRAMs are a commodity in the marketplace and, as I said earlier, the Japanese companies have ended up with enormous overinvestment.

So, my question is, Why aren't the miniature batteries going to become a commodity, too? Japanese companies compete very intensively with one another. How many competitors does it take to drive down the price of batteries until they become widely available? Again, I think we're raising all kinds of sinister flags with this focus on market share. Now, maybe the problem can exist in the product design stage, but I remain skeptical.

PRAHALAD: I'm not trying to create a sinister image. My message is basically just this: Global competition is evolving in a way that threatens U.S. companies because of their failure to invest in continually upgrading their capabilities. We can't keep assuming that companies in other countries will do all the hard work of investment while we continue to make all the money. Companies can show very good returns for a while simply by stopping investment, but that can last only so long. The day of reckoning will come.

STEWART: Well, I for one remain fairly optimistic about current trends in corporate America, and thus about our prospects. And since neither of us is likely to convince the other to change his views in the next five minutes, let's bring this to a close. I want to thank everybody who participated in this discussion. And thank you, C.K., for agreeing to be part of this. We'll see if the debate over shareholder value that you foresee actually comes to pass.

■ II. THE U.S.
CORPORATE RESTRUCTURING: THE 1980s

American business schools for the most part instruct their students that the primary aim of corporate managers *should* be to maximize the value of the organizations they run. Underlying this prescription is Adam Smith's classic formulation of the argument that the individual pursuit of self-interest ends up promoting the greatest common good. Extended to corporations, the same theory suggests the corporate pursuit of value, barring major "externalities," ends up serving the interests of all parties to the corporate contract — not only stockholders, but employees, consumers, suppliers, local communities, the IRS, and society at large. The rule for maximizing value, moreover, is quite simple: (1) take on all projects whose expected returns exceed their "cost of capital" (that is, the rate of return investors expect to earn on other, comparably risky investments) and (2) reject all others.

During the late 1960s and much of the 1970s, many of our largest public companies forgot the second part of this prescription in their desire to maintain corporate growth or increase market share—or, perhaps just as often, in desperate attempts to retain business in industries with excess capacity. The widespread pursuit of corporate growth at the expense of profitability provided the opportunities for the corporate restructuring of the 1980s. The leveraged takeovers, buyouts, and recapitalizations of the '80's helped force capital and other resources out of industries with chronic overcapacity—oil and gas, tires, paper and forest products, commodity chemicals, food processing, financial services, broadcasting, publishing, and so forth.

In *"The Corporate Restructuring of the 1980s— and Its Import for the 1990s,"* Harvard's Gordon Donaldson identifies three distinct eras of U.S. corporate management. The understanding implicit in the management philosophy of the '60s and '70s was that a company's shareholders are only one of several important corporate constituencies whose interests must be served. Top managers saw their primary task not as maximizing shareholder value, but rather as achieving the *proper balance* among the interests of shareholders and those of other "stakeholders" such as employees, suppliers, and local communities. In this view of the world, reporting steady increases in EPS was equivalent to giving shareholders their due. And, in fact, such a management approach worked reasonably well—at least as long as product markets were relatively stable, and international competitors and corporate raiders remained dormant.

In the early 1980s, however, the deficiencies of the top-down, EPS-based system began to show in several ways. Strategically diversified conglomerates such as General Mills (which proudly called itself the "all-weather growth company"), Northwest Industries, Beatrice Foods, and ITT saw their stock prices underperforming market averages even as the companies were producing steady increases in EPS. The operations of such diversified firms began to be outperformed by smaller, more specialized companies. And, as it became progressively more clear that large, centralized conglomerates were worth far less than the sum of their parts, corporate raiders launched the deconglomeration movement.

According to Donaldson, the primary accomplishment of corporate restructuring in the '80s was to expose business units once protected by the conglomerate structure and financial slack to direct product market competition, thereby forcing increases in corporate focus and efficiency. In the '90s, however, Donaldson is less optimistic about corporate management's ability to avoid the temptation to diversify. He sees the shareholder momentum behind such changes as likely to yield to demands by corporate managers and other "investors of human capital" for some measure of diversification, growth (at the expense of profitability), and financial slack (more equity)—all of which shareholders tend to view with suspicion.

In *"The Takeover Wave of the 1980s,"* Andrei Shleifer and Robert Vishny furnish evidence for Donaldson's argument that the return to specialization was highly representative—if not indeed the dominant economic motive—of the restructuring movement. For example, in their own study of hostile takeovers during the period 1984-1986, Shleifer and Vishny found that *" 72% of all assets that changed hands as a result of hostile takeovers effectively ended up being transferred to public corporations in closely related businesses within three years of the transactions."* Also noteworthy, the authors argue that popular claims that takeovers caused shortsighted cutbacks in corporate employment, capital spending, and R&D are not supported by the data.

Shleifer and Vishny's evidence is consistent, moreover, with a study by Amar Bhide (not included in this book because of space constraints) entitled "The Causes and Consequences of Hostile Takeovers" (*Journal of Applied Corporate Finance*, Summer 1989). In that study, Bhide compares the economic motives and consequences of 47 hostile takeovers of companies larger than $100 million attempted in 1985 and 1986 to those of a control group of 30 "friendly" takeovers in the same years. Whereas most of the friendly deals were designed to take advantage of vaguely defined "synergies" or to diversify the corporate "strategic" portfolio, the large majority of hostile deals were motivated by profits expected from "restructuring"—that is, from cutting overhead, improving focus by selling unrelated businesses, and ending unprofitable reinvestment of corporate profits.

The targets of hostile and friendly deals were accordingly very different. Whereas the targets of friendly mergers tended to be single-industry firms with heavy insider ownership that had performed quite well (as measured by earnings growth, ROE, and stockholder returns), the targets of hostile deals were typically low-growth, poor-performing, and often highly diversified companies in which management had a negligible equity stake. (A *Fortune* magazine poll also ranked their managements as among the worst in their industries, as judged by their management peers.)

There were also notable differences between the *consequences* of friendly and hostile deals, although some differences were not as dramatic as they have been made out to be. Contrary to the claims of takeover critics, hostile deals did not typically lead to large cutbacks in investment or blue-collar employment. And when they did—again, usually in consolidating industries with excess capacity—the cutbacks were roughly proportional to those made by other industry competitors not subjected to takeover. Those layoffs that did take place after hostile takeovers tended to be concentrated in corporate headquarters and not on the factory floor. And, as for the R & D issue, the targets of hostile takeovers didn't spend much on R & D to begin with—and this was also true of LBO firms (as we discuss later).

So, if they were not laying off rank-and-file workers and gutting investment and research programs in the drive to make a quick buck, how were corporate raiders—after paying large premiums over market and hefty fees to lawyers and investment bankers—paying the rent? The answer Bhide offers is that, besides making cutbacks in overhead and unprofitable corporate reinvestment, the raiders played a "limited, but significant arbitrage role" in buying large diversified conglomerates, dismantling them, and then selling the parts for a sum greater than the value of the conglomerate whole.

Of the 81 businesses sold by the 47 targets of hostile offers in Bhide's sample, at least 78 had been previously acquired rather than developed from within. And roughly 75% of those divested operations were sold off either to single-industry firms or to private investment groups in combination with operating management.

In "*Reversing Corporate Diversification*" (which is included in this section), Bhide extends the argument of the above study by providing a detailed comparison of diversified and single-business companies that points toward the obsolescence of the conglomerate corporate structure (at least in its current form with dispersed ownership; as we discuss below, LBO firms like KKR have shown themselves capable of managing conglomerates with much greater effectiveness). Unlike most proponents of the restructuring movement, Bhide attempts to explain not only why the market judged conglomerates so harshly in the 1980s, but why it also encouraged their formation in the 1960s.

In "*Managing for Shareholders in a Shrinking Industry*," Grumman Corporation's Chairman and CEO Renso Caporali provides a forceful statement of the U.S. shareholder-centered position as well as a nice illustration of the follies of corporate diversification. Grumman's current policy appears to be firm resistance to "*the corporate urge to waste capital by reinvesting in shrinking industries—or, even worse, by diversifying out of them.*" During the defense downturn of the '70s, as Caporali notes, "*Contractors got into subway cars, buses, watches, coffins, digital watches—any number of markets that we didn't understand. Predictably, the industry lost its collective shirt.*"

THE LBO

Contrary to popular opinion, LBOs are one of the remarkable success stories of the 1980s. So impressive were the results of the first wave of LBOs that Harvard professor Michael Jensen was moved to write an article for the *Harvard Business Review* entitled, "The Eclipse of the Public Corporation." There Jensen observed that LBO partnerships like KKR and Forstmann Little, which acquire and control companies across a broad range of industries, represent a "new form of organization"—one that competes directly with corporate conglomerates. With staffs of fewer than 50 professionals, LBO partnerships were said to provide essentially the same coordination and monitoring function performed by corporate headquarters staffs numbering, in some cases, in the thousands. As Jensen put it, "*The LBO succeeded by substituting incentives held out by compensation and ownership plans for the direct monitoring and often centralized decision-making of the typical corporate bureaucracy*." For operating managers, in short, the LBO held out a "new deal": greater decision-making autonomy and ownership incentives in return for meeting more demanding performance targets.

In a predecessor of his *HBR* article that appeared in the *Journal of Applied Corporate Finance* under the title, "*Active Investors, LBOs, and the Privatization of Bankruptcy*," Jensen argues that whereas operating managers in many large U.S. companies tend to treat investor capital as a "free" good, the primary concern of LBO firms is to produce sufficient operating cash flow to meet their high required interest and principal payments. In the average LBO of the 1980s, the debt-to-assets ratio increased from about 20% to 90%. Such heavy debt financing had the effect of making the cost of capital in LBO companies highly visible and, indeed, *contractually binding*. Failure to service debt could mean loss of operating managers' jobs (as well as their own equity investment); and it would almost certainly mean a reduction of the LBO partnership's financial (and reputational) capital.

As Jensen also demonstrates in the article, the heavy use of debt financing provides what amounts to an automatic internal monitoring-and-control system. That is, if problems were developing, top management would be forced by the pressure of the debt service to intervene quickly and decisively. By contrast, in a largely-equity-financed firm, management could allow much of the equity cushion to be eaten away before taking the necessary corrective action.

In addition to this explicit cost-of-capital target, operating managers were also provided—if not required to purchase—a significant equity stake. In the average Fortune 1000 firm, as Jensen notes, the CEO's total compensation changes by less than $3 for every $1000 change in shareholder value. By comparison, the average operating head in an LBO firm in the '80s experienced a change of roughly $64 per $1000 (and the entire operating management team owned about 20% of the equity). Moreover, the partners of the LBO

firm itself (the KKRs of this world), which is the proper equivalent of a conglomerate CEO, owned about 60% of the equity, and thus earned close to $600 per $1000 change in value.

Given such dramatic concentrations of ownership and improvements in the pay-for-performance correlation, researchers were not surprised to find major operating improvements in companies that were taken private through LBOs. There is now a large body of academic evidence on LBOs in the 1980s that attests to the following:

- shareholders earned premiums of 40% to 50% when selling their shares into LBOs;
- operating cash flow of LBOs increased by about 40%, on average, over periods ranging from two to four years after the buyout;
- there is little evidence of a decline in employment levels or average wage rates of blue-collar workers after LBOs;
- LBO firms were not doing much R & D to begin with; only about 10% of LBO firms were engaging in enough R & D before the LBO to report it separately in their financial statements;
- LBO boards, which typically have eight or fewer members, represent about 60% of the equity, on average.

In "*Lessons from A Middle Market LBO*," Professors George Baker and Karen Wruck tell the story of the O.M. Scott Company, a $200 million lawn gardening firm purchased by Clayton & Dubilier in a leveraged buyout from ITT in 1986. According to the authors, the combination of financial leverage (91% debt to capital), concentrated equity ownership (Clayton & Dubilier owned over 60% and Scott management 17.5%), and an active and financially interested board of directors led to a "fundamental change" in "both organizational structure and the management decision-making process." The details of the transformation of Scott under Clayton & Dubilier also speak volumes about what went wrong at U.S. conglomerates like ITT.

As this case also suggests, the LBO *governance* system is also fundamentally different from that of most public corporations. In fact, the structure of LBOs borrows several of the central governance features of venture capital firms. Much as in venture capital firms like Kleiner Perkins, the boards of companies owned by LBO partnerships like KKR and Clayton & Dubilier are designed in large part to overcome many of the information problems facing boards of directors in public companies. The directors of a typical LBO don't merely represent the outside shareholders, they *are* the principal shareholders. Moreover, they have become the principal owners only after having participated in an intensive "due diligence" process intended to reveal the true profit potential of the business. And, as in the case of venture capital firms, the board members in LBOs also typically handle the corporate finance function, including negotiations with lenders and the investment banking community. If operating companies get into financial or operating difficulty, the board intervenes quickly, often appointing one of its members to step in as CEO until the crisis passes. In "*The Staying Power of Leveraged Buyouts*," Steven Kaplan notes that there is a vigorous debate today among finance scholars about the "longevity" of LBOs. Do they simply provide a means for Wall Street financiers to earn paper profits by arbitraging differences between public and private markets, as LBO critics maintain? Or do they represent an inherently more efficient form of corporate organization in mature industries, as Michael Jensen and others contend? Or do they allow for a kind of corporate "shock therapy," in which ailing companies are taken private for "treatment" and then returned to public status?

The answer, it seems, is a little of each, leading Kaplan to suggest the existence of two distinct species of buyouts: (1) a "shock-therapy" variety, in which the LBO provides a vehicle for largely "one-time" increases in efficiency; and (2) a relatively permanent, "incentive-intensive" type, in which the company's investors and managers become convinced that the company is fundamentally more valuable private than public. But there is an additional piece of evidence attesting to the durability of the LBO form: Even those LBO companies that return public through IPOs retain the two distinguishing economic features of LBOs: (1) relatively high leverage (though below buyout levels) and (2) concentrated equity ownership by insiders (over 40%, on average), which of course is facilitated by high leverage.

THE CORPORATE RESTRUCTURING OF THE 1980s—AND ITS IMPORT FOR THE 1990s*

by Gordon Donaldson,
Harvard Business School

T he 1980s will be remembered in the annals of corporate America as the decade of confrontation. Managers whose claim to leadership was based on a lifetime of corporate service were under attack from external critics who asserted a widening gap between investor expectations and corporate performance. Charges of incompetence, inefficiency, indifference, wastefulness, and self-dealing were used to arouse a traditionally passive shareholder electorate to vote for new leadership. In the political vernacular of the 1990s—it was time for a change.

To those who had grown up in an era when the professionalization of business management in America had been hailed as a home-grown national treasure and a unique competitive advantage for the second half of the twentieth century, this came as a shock. The drama of a rising tide of corporate takeovers caught the public attention: corporate gladiators fighting to the death before an audience eager for the promised riches of escalating equity values. The business press seized on the excitement of the struggle for personal power and potential wealth to bring corporate affairs into the range of vision of the average citizen far beyond what had ever occurred. Hitherto unfamiliar corporate names and anonymous corporate leaders, obscure individuals suddenly appearing as sinister "raiders," and Wall Street money managers all became part of the weekly news parade of personalities involved in companies under siege.

Unfortunately, media accounts of the restructurings of the '80s have emphasized primarily the human drama of the power struggle—the personalities and the personal wealth won or lost. Even the more thoughtful academic writings, which have focused on the "market for corporate control," have tended to limit their attention to the near-term consequences for shareholder wealth. Largely missing from these analyses has been the corporate perspective: the forces driving the evolution of corporate priorities, the management process, and the operation of the traditional governance system, which continues to run the vast majority of business enterprises.

One thing is very clear. The events of the 1980s were precipitated in large measure by the common perception among investors that many of the business strategies of the 1960s and 1970s had tipped the balance of corporate priorities in favor of career employees, including professional management. As a result, the wealth of the owners was being dissipated, or so it was increasingly alleged. The phrase "management entrenchment" became popular in academic research, even in schools of business administration—a startling reminder of how far we had come from the days when the excellence of American professional management was widely proclaimed as a unique competitive advantage.

An aroused investment community sensed that there could be a payoff in the challenge initiated by a new generation of activists, outside the corporate establishment, and supported by allies on Wall Street and lending institutions looking for exceptional returns at limited risk. An increasing number of traditionally passive fund managers were no longer willing to express discontent simply by selling the stock; they began to speak out. We have seen the results.

*Excerpted and reprinted by permission of Harvard Business School Press from Chapters 1, 2, 9, 10, and 11 of the forthcoming book, *Corporate Restructuring: Managing the Change Process Within* by Gordon Donaldson. Copyright © 1994 by the President and Fellows of Harvard College; all rights reserved. To obtain copies of *Corporate Restructuring*, call 1-800-545-7685, or outside the continental U.S., 617-495-6192.

THE STRUCTURE OF THE 1970s: THE ORIGINS OF INVESTOR DISCONTENT

Why were strategies that appeared to serve these corporations so well in the 1960s and 1970s, and that were generally accepted and even applauded by investors, analysts, and the business press of the time, suddenly so radically wrong for the 1980s? Some observers believe that the answer lies in gross mismanagement by an all-powerful and self-serving group of professional managers acting with the tacit approval of a negligent board of directors.

Certainly self-interest is a part of the motivation of most, if not all, managers, as it is in other walks of life. However, the strategy and actions of large publicly owned corporations cannot be sustained merely to serve the will of incumbent chief executives. They must also serve the self-interest of some or all of the major constituencies that voluntarily cooperate to produce a profitable product or service: employees, unions, suppliers, customers, shareholders, and host communities. Thus, to understand the restructuring of the 1980s we must understand the economic rationale behind the structure of the 1960s and 1970s, which explains the motivations of managements and the interests served and why they prevailed so broadly and so long.

In the late 1960s and most of the '70s, the typical mind-set of top management can be described as follows: an introverted, corporate-centered view of the business mission focused on growth, diversification, and opportunity for the "corporate family." In the corporate rhetoric of that period, reference to the stockholder interest was strangely absent, and there was often even a renunciation of "purely economic" goals. It was a period when the social and legal climate encouraged management to adopt a pluralistic view of their responsibility to the various corporate constituencies. As career employees themselves, it was natural for management to identify with all constituents who were long-term investors in the enterprise and to view shareholders in the same light. "Loyalty" was the key word—commitment to the success of an enterprise within which each constituent found economic and social fulfillment.

But shareholders were increasingly looking beyond the individual corporate entity to find greater investment potential with the help of a new generation of fund managers who were investing in the securities of the market as a whole. New investment opportunity meant that shareholders no longer identified with individual entities but with a broad corporate portfolio. To corporate leadership, stockholders—or those who represented them—were increasingly diversified and mobile—and therefore, by definition, "disloyal"—just at the time when other constituents—notably career jobholders—were increasingly undiversified and immobile. This was significantly affected by, among other things, the two-income family anchored to a single geographic location.

Conflict over Growth, Diversification, and Financial Self-Sufficiency

Financial economists often wonder why *growth* is so central to management thinking. For the career jobholder the answer is obvious. First, growth and market share are central to most product-market strategies, keeping pace at least with the growth rate of primary demand in the industry and demonstrating competitive superiority by gaining share on one's closest rivals. Growth is also the environment that best promotes employment opportunity, improved compensation, and upward mobility. It is a more exciting environment in which to work. Finally, a growth environment is an easier setting in which to manage: more resources, more room to negotiate, easier to mask or excuse mistakes.

For the highly mobile and diversified portfolio manager, by contrast, it is the growth rate of the economy as a whole, or sectors of the economy, that is important, not that of any one company. It is the *quality* of the earnings of the individual company that matters, not quantity. If smaller means a better return on investment, then small is beautiful. If loyalty means holding resources captive to inferior rates of return, then loyalty is a bad word. There is little concern for the growth or even the survival of the individual firm. It is not surprising that the individual chief executive found this to be heresy.

There is a similar divergence of views between management and investors regarding *diversification*. At certain stages of industry and company history, diversification is essential to the preservation of management careers and to corporate survival. When product markets mature and rates of return begin to erode, it is inevitable that the corporation will search for new sources of revenue and growth potential. "Growth" and "stability" are the two words most commonly used to justify diversification. In the late 1960s, James McFarland, chief executive of

General Mills, launched an era of aggressive diversification and coined the phrase "The All-Weather Growth Company," a term designed to capture the unqualified commitment of both jobholders and stockholders.

For the jobholder it was an easier sell. One more leg on the corporate stool, as it was sometimes described, made job potential, particularly at upper levels, more secure and exciting. If the corporation was viewed as a portfolio, then growing markets could pick up the slack from mature markets in performance and resource utilization. When one market was down another would, it was hoped, be up. Thus a new base of earnings would ensure the long-term survival of the corporate entity. In keeping with the corporate portfolio concept, many corporate names were changed to a more universal image: Corn Products to CPC International, Household Finance to Household International, Armco Steel to Armco Inc., Sun Oil to the Sun Company.

At a more personal level, a motive for diversification in a company struggling to cope with the problems of corporate old age is weariness and boredom on the part of management. In private conversations, top managers admit to becoming worn down by another round with the same intractable problems. Diversification offers the prospect of new and exciting frontiers. One can only speculate as to how far personal considerations rather than corporate priorities influenced these decisions.

A third central management concern of the time, *financial self-sufficiency*, also pitted jobholder against stockholder. The men leading corporate enterprises in the 1960s and 1970s were the children of the Great Depression who, through their own experience or that of their parents, had learned to be wary of dependence on fickle capital markets and unreliable institutional relationships—to be independent, self-reliant, and self-sufficient both in personal and in corporate life. Post-war managers were thus unwilling to trust the availability of resources critical to the future of the enterprise to an unpredictable place in the queue at the capital-market window, where timing was all-important. Career jobholders particularly benefit from an internal capital market with reserves on which to draw in time of emergency, and are unaware of and unaffected by any financial sacrifice this places on equity investors.

Financial investors, on the other hand—particularly diversified ones—would prefer that the firm be dependent on explicit and regular capital-market approval for major new investment decisions. The risk that a key strategic action might be delayed or aborted by the capital-market process, which looms large to the individual CEO and the individual company, is inconsequential to the diversified portfolio holder.

Thus the central precepts that governed the corporate financial structure of the 1960s and 1970s had a clear, if unconscious, bias in favor of the investors of human capital. In defense of the managements of the time, it is not at all clear that they saw the trade-offs, so convinced were they that the corporate self-interest, and therefore the presumed self-interest of all constituencies, was being served. And, as we shall see later, the signals from the capital market regarding the strategies of the 1970s were, on the whole, supportive of management.

The Social Environment

The political, fiscal, and regulatory environment of the 1960s and 1970s represented a powerful social endorsement of the corporate strategies of the period. Most of the companies included in this study were not only large but were also market leaders. It is an axiom of competition that, as share of market increases, it becomes increasingly difficult to make further inroads on competitors' entrenched positions. Thus the rate of growth of the mature market leader tends to drift down toward the rate of growth of the industry as a whole.

In the U.S., a major factor accelerating this trend after World War II era was the active intervention of the federal government through regulation and antitrust action. It was apparent that, for these companies, further penetration into competitors' market share, particularly by acquisition, could invoke legal action that at best would involve costly delays and at worst abort the intended expansion. As a result, leading companies, particularly in mature industries, turned to unrelated diversification at home and to expansion abroad as the means of maintaining a vigorous and "hassle-free" growth environment within the company.

The pattern of funding for growth and diversification was also strongly influenced by the intended and unintended regulatory and fiscal policies of the federal government. I have already noted management's preference for financial self-sufficiency. In particular this meant the virtual exclusion of the unreliable equity markets as a source of ongoing cash requirements. This was motivated for two primary reasons. The key index of equity performance at the time was earnings per share (EPS); an increase in the number of shares, in advance of the profitable investment of the funds provided, was a sure way to slow the growth of EPS. In contrast, shares issued for the purchase of a newly acquired subsidiary or industry partner brought an immediate and usually fully offsetting increase in earnings.

The second reason to avoid new equity issues for cash was the active involvement of the government through the Securities and Exchange Commission oversight process. Designed to protect unwary investors from abuse by incompetent or unscrupulous corporate managers, it focused an uncomfortable public spotlight on a firm's investment program at a time when it might prefer anonymity. More important, the process imposed a lengthy review process of uncertain duration when timing of an issue was absolutely critical. In contrast, corporate requirements demanded access to the external equity market when the funds were needed and at a price that justified the investment. If the needed equity funds could be obtained internally, even at some delay, the planning process could be more reliable.

Happily for management, the internal equity capital market—that is, retained earnings—was encouraged and justified in shareholders' eyes by the tax policies of the federal government. The fact that most shareholders are in upper-income brackets and that tax rates favor capital gains over dividends leads to a preference for earnings retention and reinvestment over dividend distribution. One can, of course, imagine circumstances where, even with the tax differential, it might be better for shareholders to invest dividends elsewhere than to recommit earnings to perpetuate inferior returns in a weak or declining industry. Management, however, with its accustomed optimism about the latest strategic plan to rejuvenate earnings, would make no such assumption.

Overall, then, society appeared to endorse the investment and funding policies of the 1970s that were also in the corporate self-interest.

The Voice of the Capital Markets

If, as suggested previously, a management preoccupation with growth for growth's sake, unre-lated diversification, and independence from the direct discipline of the capital markets was harming investor interests during the 1970s, why was there no outcry? There were several reasons.

One was the traditional passivity of the public shareholder who, with access to a well-organized capital market, minimized the cost of real or perceived mismanagement by the quick and certain process of selling the stock rather than by the long and highly uncertain process of attempting to change management behavior. Proxy votes and the archaic ritual of the shareholders' meeting had no real power. Similarly, the growing number of potentially influential portfolio managers who were judged by year-to-year performance found selling the stock the only practical way to maximize return or to minimize the cost of investment error. There were no natural champions of the stockholder interest who would or could take on corporate leadership. The financial backing and incentive structure were not yet in place.

In the early days of these companies, there was usually a concentrated block of equity in the hands of the founders or their heirs. So a distinctive and influential equity constituency was represented. As these concentrations dispersed, management began to listen with some care to the professional security analyst and, to a lesser extent, the business press. This was particularly true of industry analysts who had built a reputation for astute interpretation of industry and company trends. Of course, management's natural tendency is to welcome favorable reports and screen out unfavorable ones, but it is hard to ignore persistent criticism from acknowledged industry experts.

But, from the viewpoint of an objective market discipline, there was a potentially fatal flaw inherent in the job analysts were assigned to do. Like individual corporate managers, they had a major long-term investment in intimate knowledge of particular industries and particular companies. A solid relationship with management was an important avenue of information. Their recommendations to buy, sell, or hold related to particular stocks of particular companies, not to portfolios. Their standard of comparison was, like management's, primarily the company's own past performance and its principal industry competitors.

In these respects, most of the companies in this study did well in the 1970s. They showed regular improvement and at least held their own in their

The basic problem of the '70s was a gradual and, at the time, imperceptible drift in the focus of the management of resources that was eroding equity returns. It was what economists would call the opportunity cost of underutilized resources— mismatched product lines lacking real synergy and critical mass, and organizational and operational slack from which constituencies other than shareholders benefited.

industry. After all, if the number of shares was not growing and total earnings were, however slowly, earnings per share would show a positive upward trend. In a generally buoyant economy, this was to be expected: a rising tide raises all boats. As a result, the firms received their fair share of positive recommendations from industry analysts. A study of analysts' reports and the business press of that time fails to reveal widespread or persistent criticism of general corporate strategy, and certainly no consensus.

The basic problem of the period was one common to most firms: a gradual and, at the time, imperceptible drift in the focus of the management of resources that was eroding equity returns. It was what economists would call the opportunity cost of underutilized resources—mismatched product lines lacking real synergy and critical mass, and organizational and operational slack from which constituencies other than shareholders largely benefited. With hindsight, the trends were strikingly clear; looking forward from the early 1970s, they were not.

THE CORPORATE RESTRUCTURING OF THE 1980s

The 1980s yielded many examples of financial restructuring under the pressure of a direct challenge to the authority of incumbent management. Under threat of a hostile bid for control, the imperative for change is obvious: do what has to be done to retain the confidence of the constituency represented by the challenger. Some of these responses were in the first instance purely defensive; but even if successful in fending off the attackers, they were usually followed by genuine restructuring designed to address lingering problems of concern to one or more constituencies whose support was essential to the long-term viability of the enterprise.

There were three distinct, but related consequences of the changes in strategy and structure widely adopted by corporate America during the 1980s. The first was the rejection of the concept of unrelated product-market diversification, the extreme form of which was the unrestrained conglomerate enterprise. In its place, the new concept was a return to the core competence of the enterprise and the shedding of all corporate activity which did not draw heavily on that core competence. In capital-market jargon, it was a return to "pure plays."

The second consequence of the 1980s was the abandonment of the concept of financial self-sufficiency—of the firm as its own internal capital market,

largely independent of the external (public) debt and equity markets for the funding of new investment. Financial self-sufficiency was a goal pursued not only through product-market diversification but also with conservative debt policy and heavy reliance on retained earnings and accumulated reserves.

The third consequence, not unique to the 1980s, was progress (or lack of it) on the persistent need for renewal of the primary source of long-term earning capacity of the enterprise. Some of the businesses discussed in this study have been locked into mature products, markets, and technologies that have persistently frustrated management's search for a secure basis for long-term growth and profitability. If the core of the enterprise has these characteristics, a return to the core has an ominous ring to it. Long-term and even short-term survival hang on the success of a renewal process, and one is struck by the sharp contrast between the restructuring of those companies in which the core remained healthy (food processing, in the case of General Mills) and those in which it was seriously impaired (steel, in the case of Armco).

As explained earlier, the corporate drive for diversification was widely and uncritically accepted in the late '60s and early '70s. Indeed, it became a central theme of the then current theory of best management practice. For example, the Boston Consulting Group's concept of the corporate product "portfolio"—as represented graphically by a two-by-two matrix of cash generation and use—called for infant market positions to be fed by mature market positions ("cash cows"). But all this was changed in the 1980s. The concept of self-sustaining growth continues to be an essential concept for small privately financed enterprise, but is now out of date for the public corporation.

What changed was the rejection of the idea that the public corporation should be insulated from the discipline of the capital markets that is imposed when the company is required to come to the equity and debt markets on a regular basis for new infusions of long-term investment capital. This discipline is reimposed when the internal capital market is broken up, peripheral business entities are sold or spun off, and the company returns to its traditional or redefined core business. We saw this when General Mills sold off its toy and fashion businesses, among others, and went back to concentrating on its historic strength in consumer foods. We also saw it when Burlington Northern split off its resources business from the railroad and when CPC divested its European corn wet-milling business.

In the process, inefficient market positions were no longer sustained indefinitely by their more successful corporate siblings but were released, either to survive independently in the marketplace or be absorbed by larger, more efficient companies in the same industry. General Mills' Kenner Parker toys division survived quite successfully for a time as an independent company, but was eventually absorbed by Tonka. An important side effect of this disaggregation process for investors was that financial information was also disaggregated and the market got a better insight into the unique financial condition of each company.

During the period when many companies were pursuing their particular conglomerate strategy, the core business was going through a transformation, surrounded and obscured by the cocoon of diversified business segments. Many of these conglomerates looked back on the 1960s and 1970s and concluded that they had "lost their way"—that is, their unique product-market identity. In this sense, the 1980s were a time for rediscovery of that identity, and to the general benefit of the economy.

In addition to the benefit from a more narrowly defined and reenergized product-market mission, the release of excess funds from overcapitalized balance sheets benefited the economy by allowing such funds to seek their most profitable use. The repurchase of stock and increased dividends were the means by which this was accomplished. While the motive in some cases may have been self-preservation—that is, by removing one of the motives for hostile takeovers—the results were nevertheless beneficial in forcing a more aggressive cash management of remaining resources.

The impact of restructuring on the mix of corporate funding between debt and equity was of more questionable benefit. One of the effects of the post-Great Depression swing to deep financial conservatism by many companies, as evidenced by triple-A bond ratings and negligible debt-equity ratios, was to reduce the influence of long-term lenders on the strategic direction of enterprise. Those of us who served on corporate boards (and I have served on several over the past 30 years) when bankers were more frequent fellow board members recall the persistent concerns of a representative of the long-term investor. With the disappearance of a dominant equity investor in the person of the

founder or his heirs—as noted in several of the companies in this study—and their replacement by anonymous, transient investment institutions, these boards lost the single-minded investor viewpoint and, perhaps, their defense against unfocused investment.

On the other hand, going from one extreme to the other is hardly the solution. The dramatic run-up of the debt-equity ratio resulting from the substitution of debt for equity as a defensive redistribution of invested capital, which we saw in cases like Martin Marietta, Safeway, and CPC, imposed an unsustainable debt-servicing burden that could be met only in the short term by asset liquidation (or, as in the case of Martin Marietta, in combination with the subsequent issuance of new preferred and common equity). The first order of business was to get the debt burden back down to levels that could be supported by continuing operations. The defensive maneuver of highly leveraged transactions can produce a level of financial risk that no management would tolerate under normal circumstances. In following that path, management is betting on the probability of a subsequent period of sustained cash flow for however many months or years it takes to return debt to normal levels. Meanwhile, myopic or dysfunctional cash management may neglect everything but the most urgent short-term expenditures. As a result, a window of strategic advantage may open to competitors if they choose to act at a moment of weakness.

Overall, however, these consequences of the restructuring of the 1980s were healthy for the economy. In recent years, much has been made of the breakdown of U.S. competitiveness in global markets, attributed, partially at least, to a preoccupation with quarter-to-quarter performance and lack of commitment to long-term investment. This study suggests an alternative explanation to that of simple investment myopia. It posits that by following a strategy of diversification and financial self-sufficiency, the corporate enterprise insulated itself from the discipline of both the product and capital markets and as a result became less sensitive to the competitive demands for long-term survival in any of its individual product-market positions. Competitive weakness in an individual product market, which would not have been tolerated in a stand-alone enterprise dependent on public capital, was often tolerated and sustained by infusions of capital from other, more successful product-market affiliates. On a stand-alone basis the unit would have found a way to succeed, have failed, or been merged with a more successful enterprise.

The primary thrust of restructuring in the 1980s was therefore to expose individual product-market positions to the competitive forces of their own product and capital markets—domestic and foreign—and in the process the fittest would survive and prosper. Viewed as a whole, the restructuring of the 1980s was a necessary adjustment to correct a fundamental divergence between corporate strategy and structure and the environment of the late twentieth-century product and capital markets. The economic pain inflicted arose primarily from the sudden imposition of long-overdue change and the shattered expectations of those who had come to rely on the strategy in place. And, as always happens, some excesses and mistakes occurred in the process.

ISSUES FOR THE 1990S

The actions of 1980s' equity investors in curtailing the scope of corporate investment, shrinking the discretionary reserves, and forcing the return of surplus funds to the direct control of the owners can be read as a vote of "no confidence" in the control exercised by professional management in the past. It is unlikely, however, that this mood of mistrust will survive a return to a healthy economy, or that the strategy and structure which the restructuring of the 1980s has produced will remain intact. After all, professional investors must in the long run place their investable funds in the custody of professional managers—they have no other choice.

In particular, the forces that have constrained investment in the 1980s with respect to diversification and growth will in the longer run be confronted with inherent organizational counterforces that cannot be suppressed indefinitely. I have pointed out that one of the primary errors committed in the 1960s and 1970s was the trend to unrelated diversification of product markets, resulting in excessive fragmentation and in the perpetuation of uneconomic entry-level product-market operations. But we clearly have not seen the end of corporate diversification, or even of completely unrelated diversification.

It is inherent in every self-perpetuating organization that it seeks to maintain a base of earnings capable of sustaining the enterprise in the long term. It is particularly true of businesses that find themselves on the downward slope of a mature

industry in which it is increasingly difficult to maintain an adequate return on investment that they will begin to probe the boundaries of investment and seek new investment opportunities with greater earnings potential.

It is difficult, however, if not impossible, to make a sudden and complete transfer of investment from one earnings base to another. Thus the typical response is to initiate diversification into a new or related product market while continuing with the old. We have seen many such examples in the case histories presented in this book. Like a person crossing a stream on stepping-stones, balance is sustained by maintaining a footing on the last stone before a confident footing is reached on the next. The trouble was that many companies, having successfully diversified into a new and more promising earnings base, never lifted their foot off the last stone. Or, having unsuccessfully probed a new product-market position, proceeded to a third and a fourth stone without conceding mistakes and abandoning the unstable footing.

There is a school of thought which says companies that find themselves in a mature and declining product-market position ought to face up to reality and go out of existence. Uneconomic enterprise ought not to be perpetuated. Liquidation or bankruptcy is the Darwinian solution for economic weakness. It is not surprising, however, that corporations (which by law have unlimited existence) and their career managers continue to explore diversification as an escape into a new and more promising environment. Efforts at diversification will continue, though it is hoped with a more focused and disciplined approach to the range of options that can be successfully exploited.

Related to the instinct for long-term survival is the organizational need for growth. It is interesting how quickly many of the businesses whose initial response to restructuring was a sharp curtailment of expansion soon followed up with a renewed growth strategy. The drive to grow is the most elemental expression of the priorities of the investors of human capital, in contrast to the desire of investors of financial capital for conservation and maximum return on investment. Surges of new investment, particularly for long-term development, inevitably undermine the ROI in the near term. This tension between the priorities of different constituent interests can be expected to persist in the large-scale publicly funded enterprise.

The Propensity to Overcapitalize

One of the consequences of the 1980s restructuring for many companies was a swing from the overcapitalization of the 1970s to undercapitalization: to a deficiency of equity funding and a just-in-time funding policy. As noted, a legitimate complaint of the earlier postwar decades was the tendency of corporations to develop a high degree of financial self-sufficiency, which meant low debt levels and substantial redundancy in asset holdings. Since funding policy is a process of anticipating uncertain future needs, and the determination of appropriate risk levels is a matter of judgment and personal risk preference, there is no scientific answer to the question of the "right" amount of redundancy to build into a financial system.

As a consequence, the tendency is for funding practice to swing, over time, from one extreme to another: from overfunding to underfunding, and back again. In all aspects of financial policy, there is a predisposition to bury one's corporate financial identity in the averages—not to appear at an extreme and thus to attract attention—to conform to the norm. Hence, there is a pendulum-like secular movement in aggregate behavior. The 1980s was a time to move in the direction of undercapitalization, lean asset structure, and excessive debt. The debt was often produced by a defensive disgorgement of excess cash, with debt-equity ratios suddenly multiplied by substituting debt for equity.

We have noted the universal tendency of companies caught in this process to then give priority to cash conservation and accelerated debt reduction. Sensing unusual vulnerability, companies moved quickly to restore normal debt levels. The extended period of recession that marked the end of the 1980s and the beginning of the 1990s has underlined the wisdom of that response for those which had time to recover their solvency. The recession, which has also served as a crash course in survival tactics for a new generation of senior managers, has undoubtedly conditioned investment and funding strategy in this decade.

Therefore, the decade of the 1990s is likely to be marked by a renewed dedication to the minimization of financial risk, the restoration of financial reserves, and perhaps a renewed interest in financial self-sufficiency. The recession of the early 1990s cannot be compared to the Great Depression of the 1930s in its impact on the management psyche, but chief executives who have been buffeted by a strained banking system and rebellious shareholders are likely to seek the comfort of deeper corporate pockets when the opportunity recurs.

The Competition for Corporate Value-Added

I have recorded how the ultimate purpose of the restructuring of the 1980s was to improve the quality of investment performance and to increase the ROE, both by reducing investment and by increasing the bottom-line return to equity holders. The cases in this book illustrate the substantial gains that were achieved in this respect. I have also noted that for there to be substantial winners—most obviously, shareholders—there had to be substantial losers—some professional managers and employees—as the corporate value-added was transferred from one constituent group to another. This trend has been reinforced by the subsequent recession.

It is impossible to predict whether the circumstances that caused power to flow into the hands of the shareholders—and in particular, into the hands of equity-oriented activists operating in the market for corporate control—will recur in the near future. The public reaction to the era of junk bonds and the tarnished reputation of Wall Street middlemen suggest that time must elapse for memories to fade before there will again be free access to the more extreme forms of financial brinksmanship. The financial institutions that provided a ready market for low-grade bonds and the bridge financing associated with takeovers have undergone a severe reexamination of their loan portfolios and are unlikely to repeat that experience anytime soon. The decade of the 1990s is likely to be an era of relative financial conservatism and caution by both borrowers and lenders.

This lessening of raw financial power in the hands of would-be corporate interventionists must be balanced against the evidence of a new and persistent mood of active oversight by some institutional equity holders which, if it continues, will keep attention focused on the stockholder interest. How successful it will be in sustaining attention to current priorities remains to be seen. Experienced managers have noted, however, that it is difficult in a large organization to maintain a high level of financial discipline continuously over long periods of time, particularly when there is a return to prosperity, profitability, and full employment. Every organiza-

> The forces that have constrained investment in the 1980s with respect to diversification and growth will in the longer run be confronted with inherent organizational counterforces that cannot be suppressed indefinitely. Efforts at diversification will continue, though it is hoped with a more focused and disciplined approach to the range of options that can be successfully exploited.

tional system works "better," from a management perspective, when there is a degree of slack in the system.

As Peter Magowan, CEO of Safeway, has said, it is difficult to wring concessions from union negotiators when you are reporting record profits. This is a reminder that prosperity and full employment strengthen the bargaining position of the investors of human capital. A return to full employment is likely to restore some or all of the give-up that occurred when equity holders had the upper hand. Thus, financial efficiency, from an equity holder perspective, is likely to be eroded at some time in the future, though perhaps not to the full extent of the 1960s and 1970s.

In summary, the several elements of financial restructuring in the 1980s were directed at the reordering of corporate priorities, which ebb and flow with the balance of power within the business organization. The interests that produced the priorities of the 1960s and 1970s are still present and will be heard from again.

The Future of Restructuring—Voluntary or Involuntary?

The principal focus of this study has been on the capacity of the modern large-scale, professionally managed business enterprise *voluntarily* to effect major structural change in a timely and efficient manner. The case studies have provided illustrations in which this complex and difficult task has been executed repeatedly and with exceptional skill. Of course, the words "timely" and "efficient" are relative terms and, with the benefit of hindsight, even management itself will conclude it could have been done better. There are also illustrations in which the system broke down and the end result was hostile external intervention. On the whole, however, were this sample assumed to be representative of the whole system, the study demonstrates a powerful instinct in modern enterprises for survival, self-renewal, and independence.

The fundamental question currently under debate concerns the extent to which professional investment managers who now dominate equity ownership should assert more direct control over the formation of strategy and structure in the companies that comprise their portfolios. Were the process of voluntary restructuring as I have defined it to continue, professional investors would refrain from intervention in direct control except as they influence the functioning of the board.

In considering possible changes in the corporate governance process, it is essential that we be informed by the experiences of the past. The observations of this study contribute important insights into the working of the system and how it is likely to perform in the future. One of these concerns the fundamental difference between the capital markets and the product markets on the dimension of efficiency and speed of response. Investors in financial assets, particularly in the United States, have become accustomed to instantaneous and frictionless reinvestment and restructuring of portfolios in response to new information or changed priorities. In contrast, investors in real assets operate in a relatively inefficient product market where a critical resource is the time necessary to effect a change in resource allocation and revenue distribution. As a result, professional investors typically lack the experience, expertise, and particularly the patience needed to manage a major corporate restructuring.

It is obvious that the resource of time is placed in the hands of one chief executive whose unique vision of the future will dominate corporate strategy as long as he or she remains in that position. Past experience suggests that the normal term of office of a new chief executive, barring ill health, obvious mismanagement, or abuse of office, is a minimum of five to ten years, during which the CEO must be allowed wide discretion—the freedom to succeed and the freedom to fail. This reality of the cycles of power in a corporation places severe constraints on the "efficiency" with which adjustment to change occurs, particularly when viewed through the eyes of the capital markets.

If used wisely, the resource of time will serve to confirm the nature of the needed change, to gain the commitment of the top management team, to carefully explore options, and, particularly, to choose the timing of change for maximum benefit or minimum loss. We have noted the time-consuming process of renegoting constituency contracts, a matter uniquely suited to career professional managers capable of delivering on those contracts. In a number of cases this entire process has taken the greater part of a decade to bring to completion, even by leaders totally dedicated to the restructuring mission.

We have observed that it is unusual for a major change in strategy and structure to be initiated and executed by the same administration responsible for the prior strategy. It is more commonly executed by a successor, with or without the intervention of the board. Hence another reason why the voluntary process takes time—the time necessary for incumbent management to recognize the need for change and step aside, or to reach normal retirement. This is the element of the process in which the voluntary system is most vulnerable since, in the absence of a vigilant and assertive board, extended delay may occur.

The advantages we have seen when the voluntary restructuring process works well are highlighted by the experience of companies in which the voluntary system has broken down and hostile external intervention has occurred. The collapse of the time frame for restructuring, which inevitably accompanies hostile intervention, necessarily restricts options, seriously weakens bargaining position, forces action regardless of the conditions of the capital and product markets, exposes the business to competitive vulnerability and excessive financial risk. By definition, restructuring, whether voluntary or involuntary, involves an element of catch-up in a deteriorating condition. However, the convulsive response to sudden external intervention imposes severe penalties that an orderly voluntary process can avoid or minimize.

Critics of voluntary restructuring under the internal governance system as practiced over recent decades will focus primarily on the "excessive" delays in response—some, but not all of which, I have described as inherent in the management of a product-market investment process. One further element of the voluntary process which we have recognized will also be a subject of debate. It is that, on the whole, restructuring voluntarily implemented by incumbent management is more "humane" than restructuring imposed by a new ownership group intent on maximizing equity values as quickly as possible. It is more humane to the extent that a deliberate objective of the restructuring process is to cushion the shock of the necessary changes on career employees, particularly those who are innocent victims of a changing corporate environment. The longer the lead time on change, the greater the opportunity.

Economists will argue that "humanity" has nothing to do with "efficiency" and that the pain inflicted by a sudden realignment of corporate goals is an inevitable consequence of an efficient market

system operating in an uncertain environment. The humane treatment of employees is, however, an important element of efficiency in practice, as an essential ingredient of trust between management and long-term contractors of human capital. "Loyalty"—two-way loyalty—is a key building block of management authority.

In summary, it is my view that the evidence of this study clearly supports the desirability of a process of voluntary restructuring as the primary means by which the private enterprise system adapts to change. However, there is a recognized cost to dependence on voluntary response, which is made most apparent when the internal governance system breaks down. Thus the potential for external intervention by capital-market agents is needed as a last resort, the threat of which helps keep management focused on action necessary to preserve its cherished independence.

PROPOSALS FOR IMPROVING BOARD OVERSIGHT

Among the companies included in this study, a significant number showed that the board of directors can play a significant role in precipitating and influencing a necessary restructuring process. This evidence is contrary to a popular impression created by critics of the current corporate governance process that boards of public companies have generally failed to exercise effective oversight on behalf of the interests of the shareholders they are elected to represent. On the other hand, there were also cases in which boards appeared to be entirely passive in the face of mounting evidence of deteriorating performance. Clearly, voluntary restructuring, particularly the board oversight function, does not work perfectly.

Looking to the 1990s, these shortfalls in the governance process cannot be ignored. The future of the internal governance process as we have known it, and of voluntary restructuring, will depend largely on our success in increasing the effectiveness of the board of directors in performing its oversight function.

Of course, no governance system that depends primarily on voluntary response to a perceived need for fundamental restructuring performs to everyone's satisfaction—or even, on some occasions, to anyone's satisfaction. Nevertheless, some individual governance processes have clearly been more responsive,

> In pursuit of a defined corporate mission, the CEO must necessarily gain and maintain the full commitment of *all* constituencies to the common objective, and in the process strike a balance among the competing interests and rewards to each constituency.

timely, and efficient than others. Thus, drawing attention to the unique characteristics of these processes provides an opportunity to make the self-governance system more efficient and less dependent on the threat of external intervention. Alertness to the opportunity for improvement is the responsibility of everyone directly or indirectly involved in the current corporate governance process.

The characteristics of a responsive system are presented as follows:

The Allocation of Accountability

Because of the common practice of vesting in one person the dual responsibilities of chief executive and chairman of the board, the important differences in responsibility and accountability of the two offices become blurred. The chief executive is, by definition, the leader of a coalition of constituencies, the most important of which are the long-term investors of human and financial capital—the primary risk takers. In pursuit of a defined corporate mission, the CEO must necessarily gain and maintain the full commitment of *all* constituencies to the common objective, and in the process strike a balance among the competing interests and rewards to each constituency.

In this regard the CEO, his or her own rhetoric to the contrary notwithstanding, cannot place the interests of one constituency always ahead of the others, particularly the interests of the shareholders. The history of corporate restructuring described in this study documents that this is, in fact, the case. The ebb and flow of priorities between investors of human capital and investors of financial capital is the primary characteristic of change from decade to decade. To use the phraseology of economic theory, the chief executive cannot be expected to place the maximization of shareholders' wealth as the number one priority at all times.

At the same time, the shareholders can be expected to press for that objective and to demand that their elected representatives, the board, do likewise. The events of the 1980s have produced a renewed sensitivity to the shareholder interest. The goal of sustained improvement in the return to investors of financial capital, which the study has documented in demonstrated results, benefits not only shareholders but, to the extent that increased profitability is retained and wisely reinvested, the long-term investors of human capital as well. Never-

theless, there is an implicit and real tension between the tests of accountability appropriate to the board and to the chief executive.

Recent efforts of some state legislatures to broaden the constituency base of boards of directors to include the interests of "investors" other than the shareholders (by means of "stakeholder statutes") may have the tendency to confuse the essential distinction between the executive and the oversight responsibility. On the one hand, it is prudent to give boards the latitude to accommodate the broader mandate of the chief executive. On the other, the primary responsibility of boards to their unique constituency remains. As Delaware Court Chancellor W.T. Allen has stated,

In most contexts, the director's responsibility runs in the first instance to the corporation as a wealth producing organization. Promotion of the long-term, wealth producing capacity of the enterprise inures ultimately to the benefit of the shareholders as the residual risk bearers of the firm, but it also benefits creditors, employees as a class, and the community generally.

When one draws the distinction between the responsibilities and accountability of the board and the chief executive, the merit of separating the office of chairman and of chief executive becomes more apparent. The call for separation, which has been receiving increasing support as a means of strengthening the oversight capacity of the board, is meeting some response in corporate practice. However, there will be strong resistance from chief executives who see the potential for mischief in divided authority. Nevertheless, the justification for a separation of accountability is clear.

An effective alternative to the preferred separation of office has been the appointment or election of a governance committee chaired by a board member other than the chief executive. Such a committee deals with the key issues of governance as they arise, and its chairman acts as board liaison with the chief executive and therefore as a shadow chairman.

Board Composition

Observation of those boards which have been most effective in influencing the course and timing of restructuring, particularly at the moment of succession to the office of CEO, suggests the need for a rethinking of the sources from which board membership is drawn. As has been noted, timely intervention, when it occurs, is never initiated by the board as a collective body, but rather by an individual board member with a unique voice of authority and the motivation and determination to act. In the individual case, this has been a former CEO, a senior lender, a founder or his descendant, or a respected senior board member.

One of the reasons for the apparent decline in board oversight and justifiable intervention is the homogenization of board membership and the disappearance of recognized "voices of authority" on the board besides the chairman. Inevitably, founding families fade away, senior lenders have been discouraged from participation on the boards of companies to which they lend—on the whole, an unfortunate development—and, for obvious reasons, former CEOs are an uncomfortable presence.

It is a common practice today for boards to be composed of a minority of inside directors and a majority of outside members, the latter drawn from the ranks of senior or chief executives of other companies, from "experts," including academics, and from political constituencies. On such boards the independent voice of authority is likely to be another chief executive who speaks from a base of experience comparable to that of the incumbent CEO—and chairman. However, as a potential voice of dissent on behalf of the stockholder interest, the outside CEO-board member has one fatal flaw. His (or her) primary allegiance is to *his* stockholder group, not to that of the company in question. He therefore has little appetite or incentive to invest precious time and attention in what will likely be an open-ended commitment, not just to start a debate on leadership but to bring it to a meaningful conclusion. There is no payoff equal to the cost.

It is no surprise, therefore, to see that it was a *retired* CEO who took on the huge personal cost and risk of confronting the incumbent chief executive of General Motors. It would be highly beneficial to the boardrooms of corporate America if greater use was made of retired CEOs as board members who would bring their experience, maturity, objectivity, *and discretionary time* to the oversight process. With careful choice, this need not create an adversarial environment and should not be threatening to a self-confident and successful chief executive.

The Function of a Strategic Audit Committee

It is common practice for boards to set aside a day or two each year for a strategic and long-range planning review. It provides an opportunity to react to the strategic plan in place and, especially, to evaluate the input from individual members of the senior management team who are potential successors to the current CEO. As is appropriate, however, the entire agenda is firmly in the control of the chief executive, who is responsible for the success of the plan. Inevitably all the focus—the specific goals and the means and time frame by which they will be achieved—is on the future.

While this exercise is always interesting and even exciting, it involves the board at the wrong end of the strategic review. To put the matter in somewhat oversimplified terms, the future is the prerogative of the incumbent chief executive, the past the unique prerogative of the board. In short, the board must make its judgments primarily on the basis of past performance, not future promise. The only real way for the board to influence the future materially is to replace the chief executive.

To draw an analogy from one of the industries included in this study—railroads—the role of the CEO in the customary strategic planning meeting is like the engineer of a train who invites the board for a brief visit to the cab of the lead engine to view with him the prospect of the elevated landscape that lies ahead. The board has no way of knowing whether the scene is reality or mirage. By definition, future plans always promise improved performance. In terms of strategic review, the proper place for the board is at the rear of the train in the caboose, in the role of brakeman, observing the slope of the terrain already traveled and whether in the longer term it has represented incline or decline. That evidence defines a credible baseline from which to judge the probability of future promise.

As a practical solution, I suggest the formation of a strategic audit committee of the board composed primarily of and chaired by outside board members. This committee would direct the gathering and presentation of the information needed to map past performance upon which informed judgments can be made. Once established, it could convene on, say, a regular three-year cycle or for a specific purpose such as the impending retirement of the CEO.

Such a committee would need modest staff support. In this respect it is important that the process

The future is the prerogative of the incumbent chief executive, the past the unique prerogative of the board. In terms of strategic review, the proper place for the board is at the rear of the train in the caboose, in the role of brakeman, observing the slope of the terrain already traveled and whether in the longer term it has represented incline or decline.

of data gathering be initiated in a period when the data are not seen as threatening to anyone. It should not be necessary, therefore, for the board to have its own analyst, but it could draw on corporate staff for this function. The role of strategic analyst is, however, a sensitive one that could at some time place the individual in the line of crossfire between management and the board.

Board Empowerment: Information

The power of a board to exercise the oversight function so as to influence the course of corporate affairs lies not in legal or organizational authority, but in access to the information that compels attention and demonstrates the need for change. If there is any one agenda item that this study lends to the governance debate more than any other, it is that:
■ in cases of major restructuring, voluntary or involuntary, the evidence of serious and persistent erosion of financial performance and structural integrity was clear and unambiguous for anyone with access to the data; and that
■ consistent tracking and regular monitoring of this information by the board is essential to potential board intervention in the strategic process, normally at times of management succession.

The case histories presented here illustrate both the nature and content of such information, which offers evidence that the corporation is substantially and persistently underperforming its competition in major respects. It is information that is clear, unambiguous, in the public domain, and therefore accessible to public investors and professional analysts. It appears in a form that uses the common language of management reporting.

As illustrated in the case histories of General Mills, Burlington Resources, and CPC presented in earlier chapters, a consistent and consecutive set of data should provide information on the record of investment and return on investment with respect to *all* of the following over the past decade or so:

(1) the company's own past performance, particularly, the long-term trends in ROE, and the market-to-book and price-earnings ratios;

(2) the performance of the company's principal competitors in the same product market and for the industry as a whole;

(3) the performance of the company's principal competitors for funds in the capital market that lie in a comparable investment-risk category; and

(4) the response of investors to this performance—particularly, shareholder returns relative to industry-average as well as S&P 500 returns—over an extended period of time.

These are the types of data and the extended time frames that should come under regular board surveillance. These are the data that no board, in company with the chief executive, could persistently ignore. For a board of directors, information is at the center of its potential power.

It may seem surprising to those unfamiliar with the internal governance process that this information is not commonly available to board members. The fact is, however, that it is unusual for consistent information to be regularly provided by management because of either benign or deliberate neglect—as much the former as the latter. "Movers and shakers" are typically singularly uninterested in the past; for them, only the future moves and shakes.

But it is also true, of course, that when the past—particularly when viewed in a comparative and competitive context—is an embarrassment, management has little interest in bringing it to anyone's attention, especially that of the board of directors. Instead, management normally prefers to emphasize plans for the future and make presentations regarding goals and implementation of strategies to achieve goals. Such forward planning, after all, is what management is all about. Goals are by definition an optimistic assertion of the upside potential designed to overcome any shortfall of the past.

It is accomplishment, then, not promise, that should be the metric of board oversight. Board time and attention to monitoring executive performance should be focused primarily on the past. Usually it is not, because adequate information is not consistently provided. *The board should insist on, and be directly involved in, determining the content of such information.*

It is curious, moreover, that in all the talk about greater involvement by professional analysts and portfolio managers, no one seems to talk about the weapon of information. If the facts of poor performance are so abundantly clear to these professionals with a stake in ownership, why do they not target individual members of the boards of offending companies and regularly confront them with the information they may be denied on the inside?

The Capacity for Intervention

Board oversight is a meaningless concept unless it includes a willingness to engage a management team in a serious dialogue on strategic direction and, if necessary, to confront an unresponsive CEO and intervene to initiate change. On the other hand, previous chapters have illustrated the fact that if product-market enterprise is to succeed, it needs extended periods of stability and continuity during which the collective investment, broadly defined, can be focused on specific economic objectives. The threat of frequent or random interruption or intervention to countermand established directives erodes morale and weakens commitment and trust. Even new CEOs, who have an implicit mandate for change, usually move cautiously in their early incumbency unless an obvious crisis is evident.

Thus the consideration of fundamental restructuring should be, and normally is, approached with proper care and caution. The essential ingredients for voluntary restructuring are convincing proof of the need for change, opportunities for near-term improvement, consensus among the board members and top management, and a visible mandate for change. Corporate activists in the field of restructuring are understandably impatient with the necessity for these conditions and despair of the time frame involved. Those accustomed to the instantaneous and continuous execution and feedback of the capital-market investment process find the product-market investment environment frustrating. This accounts for much of the persistent tension between corporate management and corporate ownership.

The issue of timing in the success of voluntary restructuring is of key importance and relates to the need for a visible mandate for change. The two most common mandates are the retirement and replacement of a chief executive and a sudden and significant deterioration in performance, particularly following a negative trend. Both pose a threat to the continuity of established initiatives and are widely apparent throughout an organization, putting it on notice of possible change. The window of opportunity is likely to open suddenly and perhaps briefly; unless the initiative is seized, the opportunity may pass. There are always those who have a strong vested interest in the status quo and actively seek to frustrate change. A second opportunity may be long in coming, as when a retiring CEO promotes a successor in his own image.

As we have seen, however, the easy cases are those in which the need for change is suddenly and dramatically apparent. The more difficult—and more common—cases are those in which there is gradual or erratic erosion over extended periods of time and no one increment of decline is an obvious mandate for board intervention into what is normally the prerogative of the chief executive and the management team.

It is therefore necessary to elevate and legitimate a periodic dialogue between the board and the chief executive on long-term strategy and structure, not about the future promise of current plans and action, but about the present and past reality of demonstrated accomplishment. The strategic audit committee can provide a mandated cycle of review that, based on consistent and objective historical evidence, invites a genuine dialogue in which, it is hoped, consensus rather than confrontation can be the outcome.

Self-Renewal and the Need for Governance Reform

Undoubtedly these suggestions for a more responsive internal governance process capable of timely and effective structural evolution will encounter the crossfire of both critics and practitioners of the established system. Critics will be skeptical of the capacity of a "failed system" to engage in a process of self-renewal. Practitioners, specifically chief executives, will be wary of changes that encourage a proactive strategic oversight process led by outside board members and a more independent boardroom relationship.

The prospect for voluntary reform of the governance process depends on the extent to which the experience of the 1980s has had a significant and lasting impact on the corporate board's sense of vulnerability to external intervention in cases of serious structural imbalance. Enough turmoil has been created to make it credible that the traditional independence of governance of the private enterprise could be lost or substantially modified by political, legal, or institutional intervention. If so, managements as well as boards may be ready for self-imposed reform that will preserve the essential managerial discretion. The price of independence is active self-discipline.

At the moment the threat of external intervention has receded. Despite its absence, the restructur-

> **In cases of major restructuring, the evidence of serious and persistent erosion of financial performance and structural integrity was clear and unambiguous for anyone with access to the data. Consistent tracking and regular monitoring of this information by the board is essential to potential board intervention in the strategic process.**

ing process continues to surface in wave after wave of downsizing as corporations reach for solid footing on which to base the next recovery. Public attention is preoccupied with the more fundamental issues of national deficits, unemployment, and foreign competition. Corporate governance reform is not just on a back burner—it is off the stove. Under the circumstances, the temptation to slip back into old and familiar patterns of governance and oversight will be strong.

Yet if history is any guide, the next period of renewed economic growth will spawn new corporate strategies and structures responsive to the new environment. In time they, too, will outlive their relevance and the old issues of restructuring will reappear, undoubtedly accompanied by a renewed debate over corporate governance. When this happens, it is to be hoped that the real lessons of the 1980s will be remembered.

This experience has provided a vivid reminder that the real discipline on those who wield corporate power, management and its governing boards, de-rives not from formal legal or organizational structures, but from the forces of the markets in which the business enterprise exists. A firm survives only if it is able to meet the competitive demands of all its principal markets: for its products or services, for capital, and for human resources. The lesson of the 1980s was that in seeking to insulate the firm from the discipline of the capital markets, through financial self-sufficiency, and from the product markets, through diversification, management's sensitivity to the needs of those two critical constituencies had been weakened or temporarily lost. In many cases, the restructuring of the 1980s was a dramatic reversal of that trend.

Reform of the governance process will function best if it does not presume to be a substitute for market discipline. By enhancing the means by which both management and the board are fully informed on the evolving market environment, the corporate governance process will offer the best assurance that enlightened and informed self-interest will produce the appropriate response.

■ GORDON DONALDSON

is the Willard Prescott Smith Professor of Corporate Finance, Emeritus, at the Harvard Business School.

THE TAKEOVER WAVE
OF THE 1980s

*by Andrei Shleifer,
Harvard Business School, and
Robert W. Vishny,
University of Chicago**

T akeovers dramatically altered the U.S. economy in the 1980s. The total value of assets changing hands in this period was $1.3 trillion. Of the 500 largest industrial corporations in the U.S. in 1980, at least 143 or 28% had been acquired by 1989. The majority of takeovers were "friendly"—that is, carried out with the consent of the management of the target firm. But there were also many "hostile" takeovers—those in which the target firm's management fought the bid. The period also saw the rise of management buyouts, in which managers used borrowed funds to buy the companies they run.

Hostile takeovers and management buyouts have sparked enormous public controversy as well as calls for and enactment of anti-takeover laws. Takeovers have been blamed for layoffs, decimation of communities, cuts in investment and R & D, short horizons of U.S. managers, increased instability resulting from higher debt, and the general decline of U.S. competitiveness. Many new state laws all but ban hostile takeovers, and Congress periodically considers federal anti-takeover legislation.

*This is a slightly revised version of an article of the same name that appeared in *Science,* Vol. 249 (August 17, 1990), pp. 745-749. Copyright © 1990 by the American Association for the Advancement of Science.

In this article, we summarize what we and others have learned about the 1980s takeover wave. The evidence suggests that takeovers in the 1980s represent a return to specialized, focused firms after years of diversification. In the 1980s, most acquirers bought other firms in their own lines of business. In addition, many diversified firms ("conglomerates") were taken over, and their various business lines were sold off to different buyers in the same line of business. Thus, to a significant extent, takeovers in the 1980s reflect the deconglomeration of American business. The hostile takeovers and leveraged buyouts that attracted so much public scrutiny facilitated this process of deconglomeration. We also show below that some of the common objections to takeovers, such as reduction of competition and cuts in employment, investment, and R & D, are not supported by the data. Although there is no long-run evidence on the post-takeover performance of the 1980s acquisitions, the past failures of conglomerates suggest that performance is likely to improve.

We begin by providing a historical perspective on the 1980s takeover wave, then address some common concerns about takeovers, and finally discuss public policy.

TAKEOVERS IN THE 1980s IN HISTORICAL PERSPECTIVE

There have been four takeover waves in the 20th century. The largest of them occurred around the turn of the century. The Sherman Antitrust Act of 1890 precluded collusive agreements between firms but allowed the creation of near monopolies with 50 to 90% market shares. In response to this law, and with the help of new stock issues during the booming market, many industries merged into near monopolies overnight.[1] The United States Steel Corporation was formed in this period and controlled 65% of steel-making capacity. American Tobacco had a 90% market share. (General Motors had the opportunity to buy Ford for $3 million, but could not find the financing!)

This wave ended in 1904 when the Northern Securities Supreme Court decision greatly expanded the interpretation of the Sherman Act. Congress firmed up this case law by prohibiting monopolization through merger in the Clayton Act of 1914.

The second merger wave came in the late 1920s, again coinciding with a buoyant stock market receptive to new securities issued to finance the takeovers. As in the first wave, most deals were mergers of firms in the same industry. At this time, although the courts no longer allowed monopoly, they still permitted the formation of oligopolies—industries dominated by a few firms.[2] Allied Chemical and Bethlehem Steel are products of this wave. This merger wave was stopped not by regulation, but by the Great Depression and the collapse of the stock market.

The third wave took the form of the conglomerate mergers of the late 1960s. Like the previous waves, it came during a stock market boom—one that enabled corporate buyers whom the stock market rewarded with high price/earnings ratios to finance their acquisitions with equity on attractive terms. Unlike those in the previous merger waves, a typical 1960s merger brought together two firms from completely different industries, leading to the formation of "conglomerates." ITT and Teledyne are famous products of this era.

The most likely reason for diversification was the antitrust policy that, after the Celler-Kefauver Act passed in 1950, turned fiercely against mergers between firms in the same industry. Unable to acquire businesses related to their own, flush with cash, and facing a favorable market for equity issues, acquirers bought companies outside their industries.

Conglomerates: Theory vs. Practice

At the time conglomerates were formed, several theories were advanced to explain how they would improve the efficiency of U.S. businesses. One idea was that control of businesses was shifted by takeovers from self-taught entrepreneurs who started their own firms to experienced professional managers of conglomerates. Another was that conglomerates were an efficient way of monitoring individual businesses by subjecting them to regular quantitative evaluations by the central office.

Perhaps the most widely accepted rationale for conglomerates, however, was the view that the central office reallocated investment funds from slowly-growing subsidiaries that generated cash, such as insurance and finance, to fast-growing, high technology businesses that required investment funds.

---

1. George S. Stigler, "Monopoly and Oligopoly by Merger," *American Economic Review*, Vol. 40 No. 23 (1950).

2. According to Judge Learned Hand's famous formulation, "Control by one firm of 64% of the industry may not be monopoly and 33% surely is not."

> The most important reason [for the failure of conglomerates] is that conglomerate builders ignored Adam Smith's principle that specialization raises productivity. In conglomerates... the crucial business decisions were made by non-specialists with only limited information who had to divide their attention and resources between multiple businesses. Some divisions were neglected; others were probably overfed.

In this way, each conglomerate created an "internal capital market" that could allocate investment funds more cheaply and efficiently than the banks or the stock and bond markets.

This alleged superior efficiency of conglomerates is probably not what brought about their existence. As in the two prior merger waves, it now seems more likely that managers simply wanted to grow their firms, and they had access to the cheap internal and external funds necessary to do so. But because of aggressive antitrust enforcement, they could not continue to grow in their own lines of business. Corporate diversification, then, should probably be viewed as a second-best alternative—at least from the point of view of growth-oriented managers.

Shareholders, however, would likely have been best served if companies had instead just paid out their 1960s profits as higher dividends. Recent evidence shows that conglomerate acquisitions typically failed. Although the buyers paid a premium to acquire the businesses, earnings of these businesses did not rise after they were acquired by conglomerates. In fact, some studies find that their earnings performance deteriorated.[3] Equally telling are the massive divestitures of assets acquired by conglomerates during the 1960s and 1970s. According to one estimate, 60% of the unrelated acquisitions between 1970 and 1982 had been divested by 1989.[4]

Why have conglomerates failed, despite all the efficiency arguments advanced in their favor? Perhaps the most important reason is that conglomerate builders ignored Adam Smith's principle that specialization raises productivity. In conglomerates, managers running central offices often knew little about the operations of the subsidiaries, and could not allocate funds nearly as well as experts could. Nor could they rely on the managers of the subsidiaries to give them honest and accurate information, since each manager lobbied for his own business and had little incentive to give up resources for the benefit of the other parts of the conglomerate.

As a result, the crucial business decisions were made by non-specialists with only limited information who had to divide their attention and resources between multiple businesses. Some divisions were neglected; others were probably overfed. For example, the Duracell battery division of Kraft is alleged to have been ignored as cheese took priority; and the cosmetics business of Revlon suffered as the company dedicated its scarce capital to expanding its healthcare subsidiaries. In addition, conglomerates lost many divisional top managers, who left to run their own shows at smaller specialized firms. The inefficiency of decision-making by non-specialists offset the potential benefits of conglomerates.

In their attempt to monitor their divisions, conglomerates developed large and expensive central offices. But these central office controls often proved much less effective than the market discipline to which stand-alone businesses are generally subjected. Such businesses face competition in product markets, competition for capital in capital markets, and managerial competition. To a large extent, divisions of conglomerates are insulated from these forces; they can afford to lose money and be subsidized by other divisions, do not have to raise external capital, and face weaker managerial competition. In some respects, conglomerates resembled state ministries in centrally planned economies, where centralized control and transfer pricing replace market forces. As this happened, many divisions of conglomerates became weaker competitors and often performed very poorly—as measured by low earnings and the high rate of divestitures. As we argue later, the takeover wave of the 1980s was to a large extent a response to a widespread disappointment with conglomerates.

The 1980s: The Sharpening of Corporate Focus

As in all past merger waves, the 1980s saw rising stock prices and rising corporate cash reserves stimulating the usual demand for expansion through acquisitions. In the 1980s, however, the Reagan Administration consciously relaxed enforcement of antitrust provisions in an effort to leave the market alone. As a consequence, intra-industry acquisitions became possible on a large scale for the first time in 30 years. The easy availability of internal and external funds for investment—coupled with the negative

---

3. For a survey of these studies, see D. C. Mueller's "The Effects of Conglomerate Mergers," *Journal of Bank Financing*, Vol. 1 (1977), p. 315. For the most recent and detailed study of conglomerate performance, see D.J. Ravenscraft and F.M. Scherer, *Mergers, Sell-Offs, and Economic Efficiency*, (Washington, D.C.: Brookings Institute, 1987).

4. See Steven N. Kaplan and Michael Weisbach, "Acquisitions and Divestitures: What is Divested and How Much Does the Market Anticipate?," University of Chicago working paper, 1990.

experience with the diversification of the 1960s and the first laissez faire antitrust policy in decades—shaped the takeover wave of the 1980s.

The return to expansion of core businesses is evident in the prevalence of two types of deals in the 1980s. In the first type, a large firm with most of its assets in a particular industry bought another large firm in the same industry. Some peripheral businesses were divested, but most of the acquired assets were kept. Such deals were common in gas pipelines, food, banking, airlines, and oil. In the second type of deal, known as a "bustup," the acquired firm was typically a conglomerate. Placing all the different kinds of assets in specialists' hands required a sale of many divisions to separate buyers.

Our own research indicates that, in 62 hostile takeover contests between 1984 and 1986, 30% of the assets were sold off on average within three years of the transaction.[5] In 17 cases of these 62 cases, more than half the assets were sold. Roughly 70% of these sell-offs were to buyers in the same line of business.

In the face of the hostile pressure to divest, some managers realized that they themselves could profit from bustups by taking their companies private and then selling peripheral business to specialized acquirers. This realization explains a significant number of leveraged buyouts of the 1980s followed by large-scale divestitures. In our own sample of LBOs executed during the period 1984-1986, sell-offs were proportionately even higher than for takeovers as a whole, amounting to 44% of total assets.

In the 1980s takeover wave, the so-called "corporate raiders" and many leveraged buyout specialists often played the critical role of brokers. They acquired conglomerates, busted them up, and sold off most business segments to large corporations in the same businesses. In a controversial *Harvard Business Review* article called "The Eclipse of the Public Corporation," Michael Jensen argued that takeovers by raiders and by leveraged buyout funds were bringing about what amounted to a "new organizational form"—one that held out the prospect of permanently delivering shareholders from the wasteful ways of public corporations largely by strengthening management incentives.[6]

The evidence, however, does not support this view. First, most takeovers do not involve raiders or LBO funds, but instead reflect the transfer of assets between two diffusely held public companies. Second, many raider and LBO-controlled firms are temporary organizations designed to last only as long as it takes to sell off the pieces of the acquired firm to other public corporations. The remaining pieces are often reoffered to the public, especially when their value has been enhanced by some operating changes.

Revlon as a Representative Case

A takeover that illustrates some of the features of the 1980s wave is the acquisition of cosmetics giant Revlon by the raider Ronald Perelman. This fiercely hostile takeover took place in 1985, at the price of $2.3 billion. Prior to the takeover, Revlon acquired many businesses outside cosmetics, particularly in the healthcare industry. The top management of Revlon thought healthcare offered better growth opportunities than cosmetics, and so reduced the investment and advertising budget of cosmetics to support the growth of healthcare.

After the takeover, Perelman sold off $2.06 billion of Revlon's healthcare and other non-cosmetics businesses. Perelman also had an offer to sell the cosmetics business for $905 million (which, combined with the $2.06 billion, shows how profitable this bustup was), but turned it down. About 60% of asset sell-offs were to other companies in the healthcare field, but some were to management buyout groups.

After the sell-offs, Revlon revamped the cosmetics business and tripled its advertising budget. Headquarters staff was also reduced, although there is no evidence of blue collar layoffs or of investment cuts. Revlon's profits increased substantially.

The Revlon sell-offs, moreover, and the eventual reallocation of those assets toward more focused companies are highly representative of takeovers in the 1980s. In our own study of the hostile takeovers of 1984-1986, we found that 72% of all assets that changed hands as a result of hostile takeovers effectively ended up being transferred to public corporations in closely related businesses within three years of the transactions. By contrast, as shown in Table 1, only 15% of the assets involved in the

---

5. Sanjai Bhagat, Andrei Shleifer, and Robert Vishny, "Hostile Takeovers in the 1980s: The Return to Corporate Specialization," *Brookings Papers on Economic Activity: Microeconomics* (1990), p. 1.

6. "The Eclipse of the Public Corporation," *Harvard Business Review*, (May-June 1989).

In our own study of the hostile takeovers of 1984-1986, we found that 72% of all assets that changed hands as a result of hostile takeovers effectively ended up being transferred to public corporations in closely related businesses within three years of the transactions.

TABLE 1
THE MOVEMENT OF
ASSETS RESULTING FROM
HOSTILE TAKEOVERS
(1984-1986)
($ IN MILLIONS)

Assets that Went to Related Corporate Buyers:	**$49,660**	**72%**
Including:		
Strategic Acquisitions Net of Sell-offs:	26,010	38%
Sell-offs to Strategic Buyers:	23,650	34%
Assets that Went to MBOs:	**10,234**	**15%**
Including:		
Direct MBOs Net of Sell-offs:	4,834	7%
Sell-offs to MBOs:	5,400	8%
Assets that Stayed with Initial Financial Bidders ("Raiders"):	**3,810**	**5.5%**
Assets that Went to Unrelated Corporate Buyers:	**3,154**	**4.5%**
Including:		
Direct Unrelated Bidders:	373	0.5%
Sell-offs to Unrelated Bidders:	2,781	4%
Sell-offs of Headquarters, Stocks, etc.	**667**	**1%**
Unidentified Sell-offs:	**1,219**	**2%**
TOTAL ASSETS THAT CHANGED HANDS:	**$68,743**	**100%**

takeovers ended up with private firms (including those formed when management and leveraged buyout specialists take divisions private). Perhaps most telling, however, only 4.5% of the assets were bought by public corporations acquiring outside of their core businesses. This last number clearly illustrates the move away from conglomerates.

Has deconglomeration and expansion in core businesses raised efficiency and U.S. competitiveness? Some economists have taken the increase in stock prices of the acquired firms—which was not nearly offset by the modest stock price declines of acquiring firms—as incontrovertible evidence that efficiency has improved. We do not take this position, since much evidence shows that the stock market can make large valuation mistakes.[7] The possibility that the stock market was overly enthusiastic about the takeovers of the 1980s should not be

dismissed. After all, the market greeted the conglomerate mergers of the 1960s with share price increases, and most of these mergers failed.[8]

Nonetheless, there are reasons to expect the takeovers of the 1980s to raise long-run efficiency. The fact that many takeovers break up conglomerates and allocate divisions to specialists creates a presumption that performance should improve. There is in fact evidence that divisions are more productive when they are part of less diversified companies, although this evidence does not focus specifically on divested divisions.[9] There is also evidence that acquired firms are less profitable than the firms buying them.[10] This suggests that more assets in an industry are being allocated to the organizations that can better manage them. Overall, then, the evidence supports cautious optimism about the efficiency of takeovers in the 1980s.

7. For a review of this evidence, see Andrei Shleifer and Lawrence Summers, "The Noise Trader Approach to Finance," *Journal of Economic Perspectives*, Volume 4, No. 19 (1991).

8. For an interesting, if not wholly convincing, explanation why the stock market may have "rationally" approved of conglomerates *at the time*, see Amar Bhide, "Reversing Corporate Diversification," *Journal of Applied Corporate Finance*, Summer 1990.

9. Frank R. Lichtenberg, "Industrial De-Diversification and Its Consequences for Productivity," Columbia University manuscript, 1990.

10. See, for example, Henri Servaes, "Tobin's Q, Agency Costs, and Corporate Control," University of Chicago manuscript, 1989.

SOME OBJECTIONS TO TAKEOVERS

The takeover wave of the 1980s aroused much public concern about reduced competition, employment cuts, and reductions in investment—especially in research and development. These concerns, however, are largely unsupported by the data.

Antitrust Concerns

Since most of the mergers in the 1980s were between firms that compete in product markets, the obvious question is whether these takeovers decreased competition and led to price increases. After all, mergers from the first two waves of this century had the explicit goal of raising prices. Some takeovers in the 1980s clearly had the potential to reduce competition and raise prices, particularly among airlines, gas pipelines and supermarkets—industries where markets are regional rather than national and thus easier to dominate. However, gaining significant market power through takeovers in the 1980s seems to have been the exception rather than the rule. First, in most cases the market share of the combined companies remained too small for effective market dominance—far smaller than that of the 1920s oligopolies, much less the turn-of-the-century trusts. Second, the share price behavior of non-merging firms in the industry suggests that large profits from decreased competition are not the driving force behind most mergers. Oligopoly theory predicts that when an anticompetitive merger takes place, all firms in the industry should experience a rise in their profits and share prices since they all benefit from industry price increases. Conversely, when an anticompetitive merger is blocked by the antitrust authorities, the share prices of all firms in the industry should decline along with those of the merging firms.

The evidence, in contrast, shows that share prices of most non-merging firms in an industry actually rise when a merger is challenged, inconsistent with the importance of decreased competition.[11] While the evidence is not conclusive, decreased competition and higher consumer prices are probably not an important consequence of takeovers in the 1980s.

Employment Consequences

The second major concern is the effect of hostile takeovers on employment. It has been argued that hostile takeovers represent a breach of employees' trust and transfer wealth from employees to shareholders through wage reductions and employment cuts.[12]

Recent research sheds substantial light on this issue. First, except in isolated episodes, there is no evidence of substantial wage cuts following hostile takeovers.[13] Second, removal of excess pension assets from pension plans did accelerate after takeovers, which probably means a reduction in expected pensions. On average, however, these removals were small.[14] Third, layoffs did rise following hostile takeovers. Among the 62 targets of hostile takeovers between 1984 and 1986, the total post-takeover layoffs were about 26,000 people, which amounts to about 2.5% of an average target firm's labor force. These layoffs, although noticeable for the target firm, are small in the context of the national economy. By comparison, General Electric cut its employment by over 100,000 between 1981 and 1987.

Post-takeover layoffs were targeted disproportionately at high-level white collar workers as hostile takeovers led to reduction of headquarters employment, consolidation of headquarters, and other corporate staff reductions.[15] The message here seems to be that, when incumbent managers are reluctant to lay off redundant headquarters employees without external pressure, hostile acquirers do the dirty job for them. It is hard to worry too much about these layoffs, since unemployment among educated white collar workers barely exists in the U.S.

In sum, transfers from employees clearly do take place after hostile takeovers, but the size of such transfers is small relative to the wealth gains of the shareholders.

11. R. Stillman, *Journal of Financial Economics*, Vol. 11 (1983), p. 225.

12. Andrei Shleifer and Lawrence H. Summers, "Breach of Trust in Hostile Takeovers," in *Corporate Takeovers: Causes and Consequences*, Alan J. Auerbach, editor, (Chicago: University of Chicago Press, 1988), pp. 33-68.

13. See Joshua G. Rosett, "Do Union Wealth Concessions Explain Takeover Premiums? The Evidence on Contract Wages," *Journal of Financial Economics*, Vol. 27, No. 1 (September 1990), pp. 263-282.

14. Jeffrey Pontiff, Andrei Shleifer, and Michael S. Weisbach, "Reversions of Excess Pension Assets after Takeovers," *Rand Journal of Economics*, Vol. 21, No. 4 (Winter 1990), pp. 600-613.

15. See Bhagat, Shleifer, and Vishny (1990), cited in note 5. See also Frank Lichtenberg and Donald Siegel, "The Effect of Ownership on the Productivity of U.S. Manufacturing Plants," *Journal of Applied Corporate Finance*, Summer 1989.

> **Post-takeover layoffs were targeted disproportionately at high-level white collar workers as hostile takeovers led to reduction of headquarters employment, consolidation of headquarters, and other corporate staff reductions.**

Effect on Corporate Investment

Perhaps the greatest public concern about takeovers is that they reduce investment in physical capital and, particularly, in R & D. Insufficient investment in physical capital and in R & D is often held responsible for declining U.S. competitiveness, as outdated products come out of outdated plants. An opposing view holds that the trouble with U.S. industry is excessive investment in businesses and technologies that should rationally be abandoned to lower-cost foreign rivals. Such investment only sucks up capital from high-tech industries and high-tech manufacturing where the U.S. should take the lead. According to this view, investment cuts in basic industries are a primary source of post-takeover efficiency gains. Takeovers are typically necessary to bring about such cuts because even managers in declining industries are reluctant to shrink operations and distribute cash to shareholders.[16]

Investment cuts following hostile takeovers have been large in some basic industries, especially the oil industry, where exploration was arguably excessive in the early and mid-1980s. One can also point to sporadic examples of investment cuts in other industries. On the other hand, our own evidence on hostile takeovers in 1984-1986 suggests that investment cuts were neither the primary reason for, nor an important consequence of, most hostile takeovers. Of the 62 takeover contests we examined, investment cuts played a major role in at most 12 cases.

Investment is more often cut in highly-leveraged acquisitions, such as leveraged buyouts. In the struggle to meet interest payments after a buyout, good projects as well as bad ones may be abandoned. But these deals represented at most 20% of the takeover activity during this period.[17] On the whole, then, with the exception of highly leveraged acquisitions, there is not much evidence that takeovers resulted in large capital spending cuts.

With respect to R & D cuts, the evidence is clear. Targets of takeovers are not R & D-intensive companies.[18] On the contrary, they tend to be companies in mature, capital-intensive industries that are perform-ing poorly and are not at the edge of technology. Because takeover targets do little R&D to begin with, there are no noticeable R&D cuts following takeovers. It is thus a mistake to believe that R&D cuts are an important motive for, or even an important consequence of, takeovers.

Takeovers and Corporate Myopia

The concern over debt and over R & D and investment cuts are part of a broader concern—one that does not pertain to takeovers alone—that managers of U.S. corporations have short planning horizons. This concern has been expressed in particular in an influential MIT study that argues that the United States economy is losing its competitiveness because the pressures of debt and of financial markets prevent managers from undertaking long-term projects.[19]

Although there may be important differences between the U.S. and Japan in terms of corporate planning horizon and willingness to invest, these differences are only marginally affected by takeovers. The differences appear to run much deeper. Part of the difference may stem from higher savings rates in Japan and more bullish stock market investors, and the rest may be due to a relatively greater emphasis by Japanese managers on growth and market share than on profitability. Takeovers are a minor factor when weighed against these other considerations.

In sum, the evidence suggests that the three common concerns about hostile takeovers—reductions in competition, employment, and corporate investment—are exaggerated. Moreover, the fact that takeovers of the 1980s have helped move assets out of conglomerates and toward more specialized users creates a presumption in their favor.

PUBLIC POLICY TOWARD TAKEOVERS

Public policy toward takeovers has taken several forms, including antitrust enforcement, state anti-takeover legislation, and changes in tax policy—particularly with respect to the tax deductibility

16. See Michael Jensen, "The Agency Costs of Free Cash Flow," *American Economic Review*, Vol. 76 (1986), p. 323. See also Jensen, "Corporate Control and the Politics of Finance," *Journal of Applied Corporate Finance*, (Vol. 4 No. 2) Summer, 1991.

17. Steven N. Kaplan, "The Effects of Management Buyouts on Operating Performance and Value," *Journal of Financial Economics*, Vol. 24 (1989), p. 217.

18. Bronwyn Hall, "The Impact of Corporate Restructuring on Industrial Research and Development," *Brookings Papers Econ. Act. Microecon.* (1990), p. 85.

19. M.L. Dertouzos, R.K. Lester, and R.M. Solow, *Made in America* (Cambridge, Mass.: MIT Press, 1989).

of interest payments on debt. We consider each of these policies briefly.

Federal antitrust policy has been quite important for takeovers. The hands-off policy in the 1980s permitted the wave of related acquisitions. In a few cases, such as airlines, enforcement should probably have been tighter. However, a return to the antitrust stringency of the 1950s and 1960s, where an acquisition which raised a firm's market share from 5% to 7% could be disallowed, would clearly be a mistake. The failed conglomerate wave was a direct consequence of this policy. In many cases, it might well be best if the firm did not make any acquisitions at all, and simply returned its excess earnings to shareholders. But, as long as corporations are committed to survival and growth, and so continue to make acquisitions, the bias toward diversification induced by aggressive antitrust is damaging. For this reason, we would like to see antitrust policy remain largely as it is.

Much more damaging interventions are currently coming from state anti-takeover laws that aim to put an end to hostile takeovers. State anti-takeover laws entrench managers and allow conglomerates to survive. The best alternative to these laws is probably a Federal law that subsumes them.

The usual justification of such state laws is that, first, they enable managers to focus on the long term without the pressure of takeovers and, second, they prevent large-scale layoffs. These arguments, while theoretically appealing, do not have a large amount of empirical support; there is certainly little support for the view that large cuts in employment result from takeovers.

The real reason for the state laws probably has little to do with these two arguments. Rather, these laws reflect the desire of target firms' managers to keep their jobs and their ability to influence legislators. The politics of the state laws are simple: managers and employees are voters as well as contributors, whereas shareholders typically reside out of state and are therefore neither.

Last, tax policy has had a large effect on takeovers. Of the many tax provisions that subsidize takeovers, the most important is the tax deductibility of interest payments. If a company pays out $1 of its profit as interest on debt, it can reduce its corporate profits tax base; whereas if it pays out the same $1 as dividends, it cannot have the deduction. This asymmetry allows firms to raise their values through increased use of debt. In this way, tax law subsidizes debt-financed acquisitions.

The extent of this subsidy is not as great as one might think, however, for several reasons. First, the target firm can itself borrow and buy back its shares and so keep the gains from increased debt from accruing to the acquirer. Presumably the acquirer can only profit to the extent that it can tolerate more debt, perhaps because it can cut some of the spending or divest divisions. Second, much of the debt is temporary, which greatly limits the value of the tax shield. As we pointed out earlier, divestitures usually lead to rapid reductions in debt.

Despite these limits on the value of the debt subsidy, there is no reason to subsidize debt at all. Limiting the tax deductibility of interest, or alternatively making dividend payments tax deductible as well, would reduce the distortion. An increase in the basic tax rate on corporate profits could keep such a reform from increasing the budget deficit.

CONCLUSION

The takeovers of the 1980s, like those of the previous merger waves, partly reflect the desired expansion of large corporations in times of easy access to funds. With the current antitrust stance, this expansion has taken place within the acquiring firms' areas of expertise and has made corporations more focused. Although the jury is still out on this takeover wave, the disappointing experience with conglomerates suggests that these takeovers are likely to raise efficiency as corporations realize the gains from specialization.

■ ANDREI SHLEIFER

is Professor of Economics at Harvard University.

■ ROBERT VISHNY

is Professor of Finance at the University of Chicago Graduate School of Business.

REVERSING CORPORATE DIVERSIFICATION

by Amar Bhide,
Harvard University

D uring the 1980s a number of corporate raiders enriched stockholders (and presumably themselves) by paying large premiums over market to acquire and then break up large conglomerates. The instinctive pronouncement of classical economists on such "bust-up" takeovers has been that if splitting up diversified companies is profitable, then it must be adding value. That is, unless buyers are systematically overpaying or target shareholders selling out at too low a price, the diversified form must be less efficient than the undiversified—at least for those companies taken over.[1]

Although its logic is compelling, the argument raises several questions. How do we know buyers and sellers are being "rational"? Why were the diversified corporations put together in the first place, and why did they survive for so long? What has changed in the meantime to make them less efficient? And, finally, is the public diversified form "wrong" only for the relatively small number of companies that are taken over, or are the divestitures by the raiders symptomatic of a more fundamental shift?

Although the possibility of irrational buyers and sellers cannot be ruled out, I shall argue that the breaking up of diversified corporations by raiders very likely has a sound economic basis. As such, it represents a significant development that all large companies will have to come to terms with. In this article, I will explore the following propositions:

The diversified conglomerate has significant economic advantages and disadvantages relative to the undiversified firm. Over time, however, the disadvantages have come to outweigh the advantages; and thus the reported shareholder gains from "bust-ups" are not simply "paper" gains, as critics of takeovers claim, but are likely to reflect real changes in operating efficiency.

It is primarily the increasing sophistication of capital markets that has eroded the advantages of the conglomerate form, making the diversified corporation a much less valuable institution than it once may have been.

Investor power, which has grown along with capital market sophistication, has reduced the ability of managers to preserve an inefficient organizational form. Therefore attacks on diversified corporations, rather than isolated instances of uneconomic behavior (or attempts to profit in the short run at the expense of the future), are likely to prove an important step in the evolution of U.S. industrial structure.

ADVANTAGES AND DISADVANTAGES OF DIVERSIFIED COMPANIES

The Two Key Differences

Although a diversified corporation typically contains units that are capable of existing as independent companies, it is more (or less!) than the sum of its parts. A $10 billion diversified corporation is different from ten $1 billion independent companies in two important respects.

One set of differences derives from the mere fact of common ownership. The dealings of stockholders, lenders, the IRS, employees, suppliers, and customers with a diversified firm are affected by the aggregated fortunes of its constituent businesses. This means for example, that the tax liability of a diversified corporation may be more or less than the sum of the liabilities of an equivalent set of independent companies. Likewise, the risks faced by suppliers in collecting their receivables or by employees in keeping their jobs may be different for a diversified corporation than for a single business entity.

---

1. Provided there are no negative externalities.

Differences also arise because of the additional administrative layer (or layers) that exists in a diversified corporation. Whereas the managers of an independent business are directly answerable to their owners, managers of the business units of a diversified corporation report to a corporate or general office. Executives and their staffs in the corporate office perform functions that would otherwise be performed by the external capital markets. Like stock analysts, they evaluate and monitor the performance of units. Like stock or bond underwriters, they evaluate funding proposals and make resource allocation decisions. Like a commercial bank, they offer cash management services. And, like the venture capitalists who sit on the boards of companies in which they invest, they offer strategic advice. As Oliver Williamson has argued, the corporate office constitutes in effect an "internal capital market."[2]

In theory, the corporate office may also try to coordinate the functional or "operating" resources of the units in order to achieve economies of scale or scope. This role, however, will not be given much consideration here for two reasons. First, as my own research has clearly demonstrated,[3] the typical targets of hostile takeovers are composed of a group of unrelated business units, most of which were previously acquired rather than developed internally. Thus, the potential for realizing operating synergies is very limited. Second, it is not clear that even companies with the potential for operating synergies among business units are very effective in realizing them. As Malcolm Salter and Wolf Weinhold have observed, while operating synergies are "widely trumpeted" as a benefit of diversification, they are rarely achieved because they require "significant changes in the company's organizational format and administrative behavior" that are difficult to come by.[4]

In fact, most large corporations have come to insist upon an arms'-length relationship between their units. They have learned that whatever benefits might be gained by coordinating the activities of multiple units (such as economies of scale in production or purchasing) are more than offset by internal bickering, delays, and the difficulty of allocating costs and revenues.

Consequently, over 80 percent of large and medium-sized companies are organized into independent strategic business units or profit centers that have limited dealings with one another. And those transactions that do take place between units are often conducted as if they were between independent firms, using market-based transfer pricing methods.[5]

Thus, when I talk about diversification and diversified companies throughout this article, I am referring only to "unrelated" diversification with little or no potential for operating synergies.

Advantages of Common Ownership

The most obvious advantage of a diversified firm is the potential for reducing corporate taxes. Owning multiple businesses allows a diversified company to transfer cash from units with excess funds to units facing cash deficits without the tax payment that might result if the transfer were to be made between two independent companies.

Diversification may also provide "insurance" benefits by pooling the fortunes of unrelated businesses and thus reducing the consolidated entity's "unsystematic risk" (or the variability of its year-to-year operating cash flow). Lower unsystematic risk may in turn lead to lower capital costs. If investors cannot easily diversify away such risks on their own, they might look to conglomerate firms for such insurance and, in return, provide equity or debt financing at a lower cost than they would for a single business firm.

Lower unsystematic risk may also help the diversified firm reduce its cost of "human capital." The assets of corporations include the skills and experience its employees develop through their continued association with the company. Some skills, moreover, are "firm-specific"—that is, they cannot be transferred readily from one employer to another. For example, IBMers knowledge of "how things get done around here" is of great value to IBM but may be of limited use to other employers.

All companies must invest, in one way or another, in their employees' acquisition of firm-specific skills.[6] Making a complete, up-front cash payment is risky

---

2. Oliver E. Williamson, *Markets and Hierachies* (New York, The Free Press, 1979).

3. See Amar Bhide, "The Causes and Consequences of Hostile Takeovers," *Journal of Applied Corporate Finance*, Vol. 2 No. 2 (Summer 1989).

4. Malcolm Salter and Wolf Weinhold, *Diversification Through Acquisition: Strategies for Creating Economic Value* (New York, The Free Press, 1979).

5. These rules of engagement are apparently taken seriously. Business folklore includes many tales of entrepreneurs profiting by "buying oil from the 18th floor of Exxon and selling it to the 33rd floor" or by "establishing a swap with Citibank New York on one side and Citibank Tokyo on the other".

6. Amar Bhide and Stevenson Howard, "Promissory and Convenience Relationships: Application to Employment Issues," Working Paper, Division of Research, Harvard Business School (1978).

because, unlike physical capital, human capital cannot be alienated; and it is difficult for corporations to ensure that employees paid to develop skills today will use those skills for the benefit of the firm in the future. Instead of such up-front payments, companies typically make a number of "implicit" commitments to reward employees as they deliver on their skills in the future.

These rewards, which might include favored promotion opportunities and job security, are vulnerable to the same accidents that can jeopardize dividend checks. Therefore, all other things being equal, employees will put greater store by the promises of firms whose fortunes are not dependent on a single business; and a diversified firm will enjoy a comparable advantage in contracting for its specific human skills.

The argument is easily extended to relationships with suppliers and customers, who may also have to make "firm-specific investments" that put them at risk. G.M.'s suppliers, for example, may have to invest in molds for stamping out parts that only G.M. will buy. Likewise Lotus' customers may invest in developing applications for its 1-2-3 software. These investments may be more readily made by the customers and suppliers of diversified firms that are perceived to be less exposed to unsystematic risk.[7]

Disadvantages of Common Ownership

One disadvantage of common ownership, however, is the "moral hazard" that attends any pooling of risks. All insurance schemes tempt individuals to take advantage of others in the group: If I buy health insurance, and if the insurance company cannot effectively discourage unnecessary visits, I have an incentive to see a doctor more often than I otherwise would. Since most other participants are faced with the same temptation, total benefits paid for doctors visits are likely to increase. And high benefits may in turn lead to higher premiums, thus inducing the healthiest participants to drop out of the scheme.

Similar problems may undermine the risk pooling arrangement provided by the diversified corporation. Consider, for example, a company whose chronic losses in the steel business are offset by the profits of its energy division. As long as the corporation as a whole is in the black, workers and managers of the steel subsidiary may be less willing to accept the painful adjustments necessary to restore profitability than if they belonged to a stand-alone enterprise.

Managers of the healthy energy division, on the other hand, will have an incentive to withhold contributions to the parent corporation—say, by hiding potential profits in organizational slack or by making investments with low expected pay-offs. Or, if they have better opportunities, managers of the profit-making entity may simply quit. To cite a much publicized case, in early 1988 Wasserstein, Perella, and others in First Boston's mergers and acquisitions department left the firm to start their own operation because they believed the profits generated by their department were being unfairly used to subsidize the trading operation.

Risk pooling also may create a conflict of interest for management. Top managers, like other stakeholders who invest in firm-specific skills, have an interest in reducing the unsystematic risks faced by their companies. They can legitimately claim that *corporate* diversification is a necessary part of their compensation package.

This self-dealing problem arises because top managers have considerable latitude in setting their own level of "diversification compensation" and because their principals, the shareholders, cannot determine whether this compensation is excessive or not. Whereas out-of-line cash compensation can be flagged by salary surveys, there are no external or market guidelines to indicate how much diversification represents fair compensation for a given level of firm-specific investment. In fact, such investment cannot even be objectively measured. Only corporate management can make the subjective judgments about the amount of insurance against unsystematic risk necessary for their companies to develop long-term relationships with suppliers, customers, and their employees. Under these circumstances, the temptation to exaggerate the value of diversification is great, especially since diversification may further other managerial goals such as corporate growth (often simply for growth's sake) and independence from shareholder interference.

Advantages of Internal Capital Markets

According to Oliver Williamson, the "internal capital markets" supplied by the corporate staff of

---

7. We should note that the advantage the diversified firm potentially enjoys in contracting with it stakeholders may not be realized if it has previously been unwilling to draw upon the resources of healthy units to meet commitments made by units in trouble. If a diversified corporation is perceived to be a loose federation of businesses committed to a policy of "each tub on its own bottom," then stakeholders are likely to deal with each business as if it were a stand-alone entity.

diversified firms have an information advantage over external capital markets. Unit managers cannot hide embarrassing facts from their bosses in the corporate office as easily as they can from outside shareholders. They are required to prepare voluminous monthly or quarterly reports, which they cannot easily doctor because unit controllers often report to the corporate offices rather than to unit managers. And if corporate executives are dissatisfied with the information they routinely receive, they have the right to demand more. By contrast, outside investors may have to file suit to force the managers to produce something as innocuous as a list of shareholders.

Internal capital markets may also be better suited to handle sensitive data. Whereas a firm cannot easily prevent information provided to outside investors from falling into the wrong hands, data provided to the corporate office can be expected to stay within the firm.

The hierarchical structure of internal capital markets may also allow management to act more effectively than outside investors on the information they possess. The executives of diversified corporations, at least in theory, possess great power: the CEO has the right to add or withhold resources from units, change their policies, or even fire their mangers. External investors are rarely organized to wield such authority. As a consequence, although they may individually know what needs to be done, outside investors may find it difficult to act collectively to bring about the necessary changes.

Superior knowledge and the power to act may also give internal capital markets an advantage in performing the following functions:

Evaluating Investments Designed to Yield "First Mover Advantages." Suppose a firm invents a widget that promises to be very profitable as long as competitors don't quickly imitate the product, allowing the inventor time to build market share. If the firm wants to raise funds from outside investors to develop the widget, such investors may demand information which, if leaked, would destroy the value of the project. But if the firm is a subsidiary of a diversified corporation, the project can be evaluated by the internal capital market without compromising its confidentiality.

On the other hand, it should be remembered that some companies are able to raise funds quite regularly for "general corporate purposes" and thus without disclosing their intended uses. This ability

suggests that, if the company has established a reputation for using capital effectively, then full disclosure may not be necessary.

Preventing a Business that Throws Off Surplus Cash from Reinvesting its Profits in Marginal Projects. Managers often have a strong preference for reinvesting cash instead of returning it to investors, even in cases where shareholders might have more attractive opportunities outside the firm. The superior monitoring and disciplinary capabilities of the top officers of a diversified corporation may give them an advantage relative to outside investors in extracting cash from constituent businesses that do not face attractive investment opportunities and thus preventing value-destroying investments.

Problem Solving. Outside investors face great handicaps in identifying and correcting problems in the companies they own. In the best of times, many managers view stockholders with suspicion and are reluctant to divulge more information than is strictly necessary. If things are going badly, they may clam up entirely. In contrast, the detailed reports that corporate executives receive may be expected to flag signs of trouble more quickly. And, as has been mentioned, the CEO of a diversified corporation can (at least in theory) intervene quickly to change personnel or policies, whereas shareholders may not be able to force change unless the problems really come to a head.

Providing Managerial Assistance. The internal capital markets may have an edge not just in times of crises, but in providing ongoing managerial assistance as well. Take the case of an exceptionally gifted manager—say, a Harold Geneen—one whose ability in cost control or consumer marketing or making astute technological bets cannot be fully used by any one firm or industry. Such an individual could be retained by investors to sit on several boards of directors, but his effectiveness as an outsider might be limited. As a CEO of a diversified corporation, however, such an individual might be better positioned to put his ideas into practice. The same argument can be extended, of course, to include a management team or function whose skills cannot be fully used by a single firm.

Advancing Short-Term Credit. It has been argued that large companies, particularly those that have diversified across unrelated business, can achieve significant savings from centralized cash management. To the extent its various operations represent different levels of production or different stages of the business cycle, the diversified corporation can perform the role of banker, channeling cash from units with excess cash to those requiring funds. In fact, such a system could conceivably eliminate the company's need to access capital from outside sources.[8]

But why should a corporate office playing banker be more efficient than the real thing? Again, the assumption must be that the corporate office has informational and disciplinary advantages over "outside" financial institutions. It can do better "credit analysis," monitor "loans" more carefully and has greater power to recover funds.

Disadvantages of Internal Markets

The advantages of internal capital markets arise, then, from the power that is concentrated in the corporate office. The underlying assumption is that the CEO's demands, whether for information or action, are more readily obeyed than similar demands made by outside shareholders.

This concentration of power comes, however, at a cost. The corporate office may suffer from several disadvantages, including:

Slow Reaction Time. The value added by corporate staffs has to be weighed against the direct and indirect costs imposed by the additional layer of management. Decisions made by unit managers that might otherwise be quickly approved by an independent firm's board (or which might not go before a board at all) may be scrutinized by several corporate employees. For example, in a diversified company, investment proposals typically have to be approved by seven levels of management.[9] The additional scrutiny may weed out poorly conceived initiatives, but may also delay projects whose success depends on quick execution.

High Overhead. Corporate second guessing can be expensive as well as slow. In 1986, for example, the average fully loaded cost of a corporate employee was estimated to be between $75,000 and $100,000 per year; and thus the total costs of a typical 400 person staff could run as high as $40 million a year.

Limited Range of Investments. Whereas the diversified company may be better than the external capital market at extracting excess cash from individual businesses, it may be at a disadvantage in reinvesting this cash. The bias towards reinvesting in existing businesses applies to diversified corporations as much as it does to focused companies—that is, corporate officers are more likely to fund investments in existing units (or make an acquisition) than to return excess funds to stockholders. And regardless of how diversified a corporation becomes, the investment opportunities available within the firm are narrower than those available in the capital markets at large. Where the resource allocators within a diversified firm may have at most several dozen business opportunities they can fund, independent investors have their pick among thousands of stocks.

Politicized Decision-Making. Since corporate officers belong to the same organization as the unit managers, they may be able to get better information than outside investors from an independent company. On the other hand, membership in the same organization may lead to less objectivity and more "politics" in resource allocation and other decisions.

Misaligned Incentives. Problems of high overhead, bureaucratic decision-making, and the like, while commonly observed in diversified corporations, are not necessarily insurmountable. Consider for example, Berkshire Hathaway, a multi-billion dollar corporation whose businesses include insurance, newspapers, confectionery, discount furniture, and children's encyclopedias. Corporate management consists of Chairman Warren Buffet, Vice Chairman Charlie Munger and five other employees (including support staff). World Headquarters (in Kiewit Plaza, Omaha) occupies less than 1500 square feet. The success of this "lean machine" is legendary.

But the average CEO of a diversified corporation usually does not have the incentives to manage like a Buffet. Rewards and punishments in the job are rarely an effective prod for superior performance. Managers of diversified corporations cannot be easily disciplined if they deliver poor performance. Size protects incumbents. The CEO of a $1 billion conglomerate is more firmly entrenched than the CEO of a $100 million dollar business—and for two reasons. First, the raiders who might be attracted

---

8. See Salter and Weinhold (1979), cited in note 4.

9. Joseph L. Bower, "Planning within the Firm," *The American Economic Review (May 1970)*, pp. 186-94.

by the turnaround opportunity that a poorly managed corporation represents will find it more difficult to raise $1 billion of takeover financing than $100 million. Second, the larger corporation is likely to have more widely dispersed shareholders, which raises the odds against a successful tender offer or proxy fight against incumbent management. And the smaller the threat of being displaced, of course, the weaker the incentives for managers to act in the best interest of shareholders.

The size of diversified companies is also an impediment to establishing appropriate financial incentives. Common sense, theoretical models, and empirical research all tell us that managers who own a lot of equity are more likely to think and behave like shareholders; whereas managers with small equity stakes are more likely to pursue private interests at the expense of their shareholders. High managerial ownership in a small single business firm is easily achieved. Quite commonly, managers are founders who retain a significant ownership stake. And if they are not, they can easily be allowed to "earn in" a reasonable share of the equity over a period of time. For example, as is common in professional partnerships, managers may be given a loan (to be repaid out of future income) to buy equity.

There are, however, a few managers of diversified corporations who do own significant stakes. To cite my earlier example, Warren Buffet and his wife own 45% of Berkshire Hathaway's stock. But Buffet is an exception. He built Berkshire Hathaway out of a small textile company; and, in contrast to the development of most conglomerates, he didn't dilute away his stake by issuing stock to acquire companies. He paid cash. Over the 25-year period (through 1989) since Buffet took control, corporate net worth has increased well over 100 times while shares outstanding have increased by less than 1%.

More generally, though, high equity ownership by managers of a diversified corporation is rare. Founding managers are less likely to be around. Diversification is typically undertaken only at an advanced stage in a corporation's "life"—that is, after growth opportunities in the original businesses have been exhausted. And even if the founders are still managing the firm, chances are that the substantial amounts of stock that are usually issued to effect diversifying acquisitions will have diluted their equity stake to an insignificant proportion.

Nor is it easy to conceive of a mechanism by which a non-founding CEO of a diversified company can be allowed to "earn in" a significant share of equity. Consider two hypothetical firms—a $100 million market value single business firm and a $1 billion conglomerate consisting of ten $100 million units—both of which have newly appointed CEOs. The small firm lends its new CEO $5 million, which allows her to purchase 5% of its outstanding stock. The CEO is expected to pay back the $5 million loan, at the rate of $500,000 a year for ten years, out of savings from an expected annual salary of $1 million. Suppose we wanted to set up a similar deal for the CEO of the diversified firm. To purchase the same 5% stake, the CEO would have to be loaned $50 million and, assuming similar tax and saving rates, be paid $10 million a year to service that debt.

But, on what grounds can we justify paying the CEO of the $1 billion firm ten times the salary of the CEO of the $100 million firm? It is not at all clear that the CEO who allocates resources and monitors the performance of ten businesses "adds more value" than the CEO who has full operational and strategic responsibility for a single business. Indeed it may be argued that the former plays a more passive, distant role and is less likely to produce bottom-line improvements than the latter.

Nor is there any evidence that higher salaries are justified by an extreme shortage of the skills required to be the CEO of a diversified corporation. Most diversified corporations have many experienced executives in their ranks. The problem in selecting a new CEO is typically one of choosing among several equally qualified candidates.

Perhaps the only serious argument for paying the CEOs of diversified corporations a premium is that they are capable of doing more harm to shareholders. And indeed, we do see in practice that CEO compensation is correlated to firm size. On average, the studies suggest, the CEO of the $1 billion corporation is likely to earn three times as much as the CEO of a $100 million firm.[10]

The Problem with Stock Options. Unable to provide their top managers with significant equity stakes, diversified firms often give them stock op-

---

10. Kevin J. Murphy, "Corporate Performance and Managerial Remuneration: An Empirical Analysis," *Journal of Accounting and Economics* 7 (1985), pp. 11-42.

tions instead. Stock options, however, are an imperfect substitute for significant equity ownership. First, stock options create an incentive for managers to maximize stock price rather than total returns. For example, because dividend payments cause share prices to be lower than they would otherwise be, managers may choose to retain cash in the firm rather than paying it out as dividends—even when attractive investment opportunities are not available.

Second, options give managers an incentive to make risky investments. Consider, for example, the CEO of a railroad who expects to retire in five years and whose stock is not expected to do much of anything during that period. Suppose it is early 1986, oil prices have fallen to $15/barrel, and an investment banker recommends the acquisition of an oil company that will look terrific if oil prices rise above $30 a barrel (but not otherwise). While shareholders might balk, the CEO's stock options will give him a strong incentive to go through with the acquisition. If oil prices do rise, so will the value of his options; if they don't, the CEO has little to lose—at worst his options will expire unexercised. In other words, incentives may get misaligned because, although shareholders can gain or lose real money, managers who own options enjoy only the upside of changes in the price of their stock.

The difficulty of setting the right incentives for the CEO of a diversified firm is similar to the problem of compensating a money manager with substantial funds under management. If a money manager has several billion dollars under management, a "performance-based" fee may induce him to invest in the riskiest stocks. This way, if the investments pay off, the manager makes a huge fortune; whereas if the value of the portfolio declines even by a small percentage, there is no way clients can make the manager share in the losses. Largely for this reason, managers of large funds are usually given an annual fee equal to about 0.6% of assets, which is paid regardless of performance. The downside, however, is that although managers are thus discouraged from excessive risk-taking, they also have little incentive to add much value. (Under this arrangement, however, clients can at least withdraw their funds when they become dissatisfied; shareholders of conglomerates are effectively denied this option.)

In small investment partnerships, by contrast, it is more common to find managers being paid an incentive fee (similar to the earn-in arrangement previously described) to motivate them to maximize returns for their investors.

THE INCREASING SOPHISTICATION OF CAPITAL MARKETS

In the previous section we established that corporate diversification amounts to much more than a simple "financial" or cosmetic rearrangement of individual enterprises. For this reason, bust-up takeovers are likely to have significant consequences for corporate operating efficiency. And the question we now turn to is whether these consequences are likely to be positive on the whole.

The answer to this question could, of course, vary from firm to firm. That is, whether any particular organization can take advantage of the benefits of diversification while minimizing its liabilities will depend, to some extent, upon the talents of the individuals who manage it and upon the history and culture of the institution. My interest here, however, is in the general case: We would like to examine why the diversified firm, which was so popular throughout the 1960s and 1970s, came under pressure during the 1980s. Is it merely a temporary shift in fashion, or has something fundamental changed that would undermine the advantages offered by the diversified firm?

Such a change, I will argue in this section, has in fact occurred. The increased sophistication and efficiency of the external capital markets have largely eliminated the advantages of the internal markets of diversified firms. Wall Street, which was once a cozy club, has been transformed. Business once conducted on the basis of connections has become much more competitive and today requires strong analytical and market-making skills. The development of these skills has in turn greatly improved the external capital market's ability to monitor corporate performance, allocate resources, and help investors diversify away unsystematic risk—all functions that were performed primarily by the managements of diversified firms in the 60s and 70s.

The Evolution of External Markets

In the heyday of the conglomerate, the internal capital markets described by Williamson may well have possessed a significant edge because the external markets were not highly developed. In those days, one's success on Wall Street reportedly depended far more heavily on personal connections than analytical prowess. But, the end of fixed stock commissions and other deregulatory changes such as the institution of shelf registration have dramatically altered the basis of Wall Street competition over the last decade or so. Investment banks and other participants in the capital markets were forced to search for the best analytical talent and to build market-making capabilities. This competitive process has resulted in a significant increase in the ability of our external capital markets to monitor corporate performance and allocate resources.

The Old Days. Two decades ago Wall Street was a sedate club. Robert Baldwin, a former chairman of Morgan Stanley, describes the work environment of the 60s as follows: "When I first came to work, every senior person left their office a little before 12:00 and came back a little after 2:00, and they all went to the Bond Club luncheons. Everybody on Wall Street did the same thing. It was a different time schedule than you have today."

Competition was less than intense. "What you got paid for in Wall Street in those days," recounts another Morgan Stanley director, "was your origination. And your origination was a relationship business. It was unconscionable for someone to buy business."

As Leon Levy of Odyssey Partners has remarked, "It was the only aristocratic business in the U.S. By that I mean the only business where a father, if he were a senior partner, could count on passing the business on to his son." Fixed commissions and issuer loyalty meant that "you didn't have to be a genius to earn a living." Investment banking fathers could therefore "pass on a franchise that was protected by 'The Club'. All the qualities for inheritance were there."[11]

By today's standards, Wall Street firms were small and thinly capitalized. In 1970, for example, Morgan Stanley, then the premier institution of the industry, had 265 employees, $7.5 million in capital, and no research department. The total capital of NYSE member firms was about $4 billion.

Deregulation. Then came "Mayday" 1975 and the end of fixed commissions. This meant that institutional customers could negotiate the fees they paid for trading and individuals could use discount brokers. The average commission paid by institutions fell from 26 cents per share in April 1975 to 7.5 cents per share in 1986. Where individuals paid 30 cents per share in commissions before Mayday, discount brokers were offering trades at 10 cents per share in 1976.[12]

Competition was further intensified with the SEC's adoption of Rule 415 in 1982, which allowed qualified companies to file a statement listing the amount of stock or bonds they expected to issue over the next two years. Whenever they believed market conditions were appropriate, these companies could quickly sell all or some portion of these securities to investors without having to prepare a new prospectus. And just as Mayday put an end to fat trading commissions, Rule 415 cut sharply into lucrative underwriting fees.

As one observer has put it, these changes "dragged the whole industry kicking and screaming into the twentieth century." Prices fell and several hundred securities firms went under. And because old established firms could no longer rely on relationships to provide underwriting or commission income, the ability to market securities became critical for survival.

The Rise of the Professional Researcher. Wall Street firms thus had to develop professional research departments to analyze the prospects of the companies whose stocks they were competing to distribute. In the mid-1970s, investment banks accordingly began to hire legions of analysts. Research methods became more sophisticated and quantitative. As one veteran analyst commented, "There used to be analysts whose spreadsheets were on the back of envelopes. But the perception was they knew what they were talking about. No one wanted to see their numbers. They moved stocks. Now I think you see a more fully rounded job. You see a demand that the analyst conduct a pretty rigorous research."[13]

Analysts also began to specialize in order to cover few companies in greater depth. "Today you have one guy doing domestic oil, another doing international oil, a third doing exploration companies, a fourth guy doing oil service," comments another experienced analyst who used to cover all these sectors *as well as* electronics companies.[14] In short, to survive in the new environment, securities firms had to develop strong analytical and monitoring skills.

Attracting customers also required firms to develop their market-making capabilities. The leading investment banks committed capital and personnel to build "block trading" desks that provided liquidity to clients who wanted to trade large blocks of stock. The stock exchanges also instituted technological changes

---

11. *Institutional Investor* (June 1987), p. 291.
12. Report of the Presidential Task Force on Market Mechanisms, pp. 11-15.

13. Bennett Kaplan, *Institutional Investor* (June 1987), p. 183.
14. Good, Barry, *Institutional Investor* (June 1987), pp. 313-318.

that, by 1986, could easily handle 200 million-share trading days. Large and small investors alike thus gained access to the liquidity that would enable them to diversify away unsystematic risk on their own at little cost.

The Consequences of Deregulation. As with many other industries that have been deregulated, total demand and revenues rose as prices and margins fell. Increased competition, and one of the greatest bull markets in history, created a stronger and more prosperous securities industry that was able to pay for the new capabilities it had to develop.

Here are a few facts attesting to this growth:[15]

From 1975 through 1986, annual trading volume rose from 4.7 to 35.7 billion shares, and commissions earned on stock trading increased from $2.9 to $13.4 billion.

Between 1980 and 1986, total revenues for the securities industry rose from $16 billion to $50.1 billion, and total profits increased from $2.3 billion to $5 billion.

From 1975 through 1986, the total capital of NYSE member firms rose from $3.6 billion to $30.1 billion. Morgan Stanley's capital, for example, increased from under $10 million to $786 million over the same period.

Increased revenues allowed securities firms to pay the higher salaries necessary to build professional research and trading staffs. In 1978, for example, there were only 41 analysts who made more than $100,000. In 1987 there were about 20 who earned more than $1 million; and compensation of between $250,000 and $400,000 was commonplace. Total employment in the securities industry grew 9.5% per year from 1980 to 1986, as compared to 1.9% in the rest of the economy. Incomes grew at an even faster rate of 21.3% as compared to 7.3% generally.[16]

With merit thus replacing birth as the primary qualification for entry and advancement, ambitious young men and women who might have previously taken up positions in large diversified companies flocked to Wall Street. In 1986, one third of Yale's graduating class reportedly applied for jobs at a single securities firm. In the same year investment banks attracted three times as many MBAs from Harvard as did industrial companies—which represents a complete reversal of the ratios that prevailed in 1979.

This shift did not mean, as some critics have claimed, that Wall Street was stealing talent away from the "real" economy. Few of the MBAs of the 1960s and 1970s were wholly devoted to getting their hands dirty on the production line. More fre-

quently, they filled positions in the internal capital market, preparing budgets and capital appropriation requests (in-house "prospectuses") or evaluating them (in-house "buy-side" research). Financial roles had been central to their careers, regardless of what their job titles implied. The principal difference in the 1980s was that they were now performing the same functions on Wall Street that they earlier would have been assigned by public conglomerates.

Furthermore, the blossoming of the external capital market was not confined to the public stock markets. Increased competition encouraged companies to seek opportunities in untraditional fields. The venture capital industry, which could fund new businesses with speed and secrecy, was one beneficiary of this process. Net new funds committed to venture capital rose from $10 million in 1975 to $4.5 billion in 1986.[17]

Entrepreneurs could approach venture capitalists with some confidence that proprietary ideas would be protected and that the venture capitalists would not behave as bureaucratically as the resource allocators of diversified companies. The venture capital industry was young; firms in the business were small and free-wheeling. In 1986, the average $30 million independent fund employed only two professionals. Whereas investments made by a diversified firm might require the "due diligence" of seven layers of management, venture capital funds could act expeditiously. And, unlike the functionaries of internal capital markets, they were prepared to bet on the visionary ideas of long-haired ex-TM instructors and to cut deals which had the potential to make the entrepreneurs whose projects they funded very rich. Thus, the external capital markets could now claim an edge even in funding information-sensitive investments—formerly a distinctive advantage of the internal market.

Rising Disclosure Requirements

Accompanying and reinforcing the financial industry's growing analytical abilities was a quiet but substantial improvement in the extent and reliability of information about companies' performance and prospects. Increasing disclosure requirements narrowed the information advantage that internal capital markets may have previously enjoyed.

As one commentator has written, accounting standards, both before and through the go-go '60s

---

15. NYSE Factbooks.
16. *BusinessWeek* (10/16/87), p. 31.

17. Venture Economics, *Venture Capital Yearbook* (1987), p. 17.

market, were "whatever you wanted them to be." Companies would "shop around for opinions"—that is, try to find pliable accounting firms that would endorse their creative book keeping. "Instant earnings" were created by the "front ending" of revenue and "rear ending of expenses."[18]

Accounting illusions, however, were exposed in the bear market and the economic contraction of the early 1970s, as several high fliers went bankrupt. The large, national CPA firms became defendants "in literally hundreds of class-action and other civil-damage suits, which took a heavy toll in the diversion of partner time, legal fees, and rapid escalation in premiums and deductibles for liability insurance."[19] Partners of big eight accounting firms were convicted of criminal fraud in the Commercial Vending and National Student Marketing cases.

In addition to shareholder suits, the accounting profession came under pressure from Congressional investigations. A Senate sub-committee produced a highly critical report called *The Accounting Establishment*. Legislation was introduced in the House proposing the creation of a federal statutory organization to regulate accountants who audited public companies.

To protect itself against lawsuits and to head off demands for more federal regulation, the profession moved for an improvement and stricter enforcement of accounting standards. Following the recommendations of the Wheat committee, the Financial Accounting Standards Board (FASB) was established in 1972. At the same time, the American Institute of Certified Public Accounts (AICPA) adopted a rule which mandated that AICPA members comply with FASB standards.

Self-regulation was further tightened in 1977, when accounting firms (rather than just individuals) first became subject to regulation. Such firms were required to have their system of quality control reviewed by a group of peers every three years. In addition firms that audited public corporations became subject to the oversight of a board composed of five prominent public members.

These changes greatly expanded the scope and reliability of the information available to the external capital markets. By the end of 1986, FASB had issued more than 80 opinions requiring public firms to disclose, among other things, information by line of business, unfunded pension liabilities, foreign currency exposures, and replacement cost accounts.

And because standards were now less flexible, outside analysts could place greater confidence in the data and more accurately compare the performance of different investment opportunities.

Increasing disclosure and the growth of the securities industry's analytical capability reinforced one another. As securities firms developed strong analytical skills, their appetite for information grew and they began to set standards for disclosure that exceeded regulatory requirements. Conversely, higher regulatory standards provided more grist for the analytical mill and enabled brokerage firms to expand their monitoring capability.

INCREASING INVESTOR POWER

The greater sophistication of external capital markets not only undermined the economic utility of diversified firms, it also eroded managers' ability to maintain a form that did not provide economic value. A sub-industry developed to take advantage of opportunities to profit from breaking up diversified firms. It included analysts who analyzed "break-up" values of diversified firms, investment bankers and lawyers with the deal-making skills needed to complete bust-up takeovers, and junk-bond financiers who provided raiders with bridge financing.

Another important trend which undermined the diversified form was a resurgence of shareholder power. Absent strong shareholders, many managers would likely have chosen to maintain a conglomerate structure—at the expense of their stockholders—in order to increase their employees' (not to mention their own) job security and to reduce their reliance on external markets for funding. But the rising power and sophistication of shareholder activists, which grew up alongside of the securities industry, made preservation of the status quo difficult and aided raiders' efforts to break up companies.

The Conglomeration of the 1960s: A Break with the Past. At the height of the conglomerate boom in the '60s, control of the large American corporation seemed to have passed permanently into the hands of managers. This was quite a switch from the early days of the modern American enterprise, when financiers wielded great influence. Although they played no part in the day-to-day management, such financiers sat on the boards of companies, had veto power over major decisions and, when the occasion demanded, changed

18. Wallace E. Olson, *The Accounting Profession*, (New York, American Institute of Certified Public Accountants, 1982).

19. Ibid.

senior executives. Bankers, for example, were instrumental in replacing Durant with Sloan at the helm of General Motors.[20]

The key to the financiers' power was that wealth was highly concentrated. In 1919, the wealthiest 1 percent of the population earned 74 percent of all dividend income; and the ownership of companies, although separated from their management, was nonetheless heavily concentrated among wealthy individuals. Such concentration conferred on the financiers the ability to bring about change.

Over time, however, the importance of the financiers has declined. Ownership by a few large shareholders has given way to ownership by many small shareholders. Why this dispersion took place is not well understood, but probable causes include the booming retail demand for stocks in the bull market of the 1920s, redistributive taxes, and the Malthusian dilution of family fortunes. (By 1948, the wealthiest 1 percent's share of dividend income had fallen to 53 percent from its 1919 level of 74 percent.) Another likely cause of this dilution of ownership were legislative acts in the 1930s and 1940s—most notably, the Glass Steagall Act—which prevented financial institutions from taking large equity ownership positions in corporations.

Yet another reason for the eclipse of the financiers, as Alfred Chandler has suggested, was that as the rapid growth of large corporations slowed, they had less need for external capital and therefore did not have to accommodate investment bankers on their boards. "Financial" capitalism, as Chandler calls it, thus gave way to "managerial" capitalism.[21]

Managers had great power under the new order. They were relatively free of the discipline of the market because the firms they managed faced a limited number of competitors, and they didn't have sharp-eyed shareholders peering over their shoulders. Consequently managers had considerable discretion in pursuing their own goals, including growth through diversifying acquisitions.

Managerial capitalism, it may be claimed in retrospect, peaked in the late 1960s. When John Kenneth Galbraith's *New Industrial State* was published in 1967, economists of Keynesian persuasion and managers of Fortune 500 companies were in charge, and all was right with the world. The economy was growing, almost without interruption: "In the two decades since World War II," noted Galbraith, "serious recessions have been avoided." Large firms enjoyed reliable profits and thus independence from meddlesome stockholders. "The big corporations," continued Galbraith, "do not lose money. In 1957, a year of mild recession in the U.S., not one of the 100 largest U.S. Corporations failed to turn a profit. Only one of the largest 200 finished the year in the red."[22]

But just when the technocracy of large corporations seemed invincible, the pendulum began to swing back in favor of stockholders. Managerial control was threatened by three trends that increased the power of the "suppliers" of capital.

First, the financial self-sufficiency of the large corporations was imperiled by changes in the general economic climate. In 1970, the U.S. faced its first recession after nearly a decade. In 1973, oil prices tripled, precipitating a severe world-wide recession in 1975. A relatively mild recession in 1980 was followed by a business downturn in 1982, which produced Depression-level unemployment in some geographic and industry sectors. In addition, U.S. firms began to face aggressive new entrants from overseas, most notably from Japan.

Large firms no longer enjoyed immunity from losses. Penn Central filed for bankruptcy; Lockheed and Chrysler were spared this fate by federal bailouts. In the 1982 recession, eight of the top 100 industrial companies and 21 of the largest 200 ended the year with a deficit. As profits declined and some firms suffered real losses, many companies lost their cherished independence from capital markets and the need for external funds became unavoidable. Corporate equity issues rose exponentially, from $16.6 billion in 1980 to $57 billion in 1986.[23] Managers could therefore no longer thumb their noses, so to speak, at investors.

Second, particularly after 1981, the federal government became an attractive alternative "customer" for capital. Large budget deficits forced the U.S. government to raise substantial funds from the capital markets, in competition with private corporations. With 14 percent annual yields and the full faith and credit of the Treasury, government bonds provided investors ("for

20. Alfred Chandler, *Strategy and Structure: Chapters in the History of American Industrial Enterprise* (Cambridge, MIT Press, 1962).

21. Alfred Chandler 1977, *The Visible Hand: The Managerial Revolution in American Business* (Cambridge, Harvard University Press, 1977).

22. John Kenneth Galbraith, *The New Industrial State*, (Boston, Houghton Mifflin, 1967).

23. *Securities Industry Trends* (March 30, 1987), p. 9.

the first time in our lives," in the words of one money manager) with a compelling alternative to stocks.

Third, and most important, stockholders became more concentrated. As managers advanced their own interests at the expense of their shareholders', they reduced the value of their company's stock. In only seven of the 40 years between 1945 and 1985 did the stocks of the 500 largest U.S. companies trade above the replacement value of their assets. With greater competition, slower economic growth, and higher bond yields, stocks took a particularly fierce drubbing after 1973. In fact, inflation-adjusted returns to stockholders were substantially negative over the 1970s. And, even after the bull market following 1982, the Dow Jones average at the end of 1987 was fully one third below its real value at the end of 1966.

Individual investors, therefore, withdrew from the stock market and put their money into housing or small entrepreneurial ventures where they could exercise more control over their investments. By 1986, stocks accounted for only 21% of individuals' financial assets compared to 43% in 1968. Individuals had been net sellers of stocks in every year since 1972. And as individual investors fled, the stockholders who remained were a relatively small number of large institutions who were potentially a more equal match for management.

Institutional ownership of stocks, which grew from 31% to 39% between 1970 and 1986, was especially pronounced in the large firms. Institutions were attracted to large companies because they could invest substantial sums in such stocks; and individuals were ready sellers as they had learned to shun companies where management did not hold a significant ownership stake. Consequently, in 1986, institutional ownership of the top 100 industrial firms was about 53%, and was roughly 50% of the next 100 firms. Institutions accounted for a majority of the ownership in nearly two thirds of the top 200 companies.

The resulting increase in shareholder power has facilitated raiders' efforts to break up diversified companies that might have been held together for purely managerial reasons. Small investors, for example, are more likely to sell their shares to a raider when they have attractive investment alternatives, such as government bonds with high real yields or stock issued reluctantly at depressed prices. Similarly, raiders stand a better chance of winning the support of a small number of professional, institutional investors who have the resources to analyze and respond to proxy solicitations rather than of many dispersed individuals.

CONCLUDING COMMENTS

On average, the unraveling of diversified companies probably makes economic sense. External capital markets have come of age, while there has been no evidence of a corresponding improvement in the functioning of internal corporate hierarchies. The diversified firm is therefore a less valuable institution than it might once have been. And, as a practical matter, because investors today are more concentrated and enjoy broader investment opportunities, they are today less tolerant of an organizational form that reflects managerial desires to perpetuate growth (often for growth's sake) and achieve financial self-sufficiency.

This is not to claim that all diversified firms destroy value or that every bust-up is guaranteed to be a financial success in the long term. Some buyers have overpaid for divested units, while following the new conventional wisdom that free-standing businesses become significantly more valuable when parted from conglomerates. Nor are all external capital markets the epitome of rationality and foresight. (In fact, I have argued elsewhere that there are serious deficiencies in our public stock market, as compared to the external markets for *private* capital.)

But it is reasonable to claim that even if *some* bust-ups prove to be mistaken (that is, end up reducing long-run value), as they almost certainly will, the general economic basis for such transactions is nonetheless sound. And although some sectors of the external capital markets have flaws, they almost certainly have an edge today over the "internal markets" of diversified companies in monitoring corporate performance and allocating capital resources.

■ AMAR BHIDE

is Assistant Professor in the general management area at the Harvard Business School. He formerly worked as both an associate for McKinsey (1980-1985) and as Vice President, Capital Markets at E.F. Hutton. Dr. Bhide also served on the Brady Commission staff, and has published a book, *Of Politics & Economic Reality* (Basic Books, 1984)

MANAGING FOR SHAREHOLDERS IN A SHRINKING INDUSTRY: THE CASE OF GRUMMAN

by Renso Caporali,
Chairman and CEO,
*Grumman Corporation**

A s you are all well aware, we in the defense industry today have fallen on hard times. Our markets are shrinking, we're faced with excess capacity, and there's a good deal of debate, particularly among politicians, about what defense companies ought to be doing to respond to such an environment. There has been a lot of talk among people in our industry about changes in defense acquisition policy, and about the need for more cooperation between industry and government. There has also been much talk about new requirements in the Middle East and analysis of a number of potential new markets.

But, as we assess the state of the industry and develop strategic plans for our companies, it seems that there is one important group that we may be overlooking—a group that has an absolute right to our attention. It's not the government, it's not the Department of Defense, it's not NASA. It's not the Navy, the Air Force, or the Army. It's not our suppliers or our communities, it's not even our employees.

It's our shareholders.

---

*The following is a speech delivered to an audience of defense company executives at the Electronic Industry Association (EIA) Annual Conference on October 12, 1993.

Now, perhaps you're saying to yourself, "Well, of course, we care about our shareholders. We do everything possible to balance their interests against those of our customers and all our other constituencies." But I would submit to you that that approach is misdirected. Management of public corporations should not be a balancing act at all. Our shareholders' interests should come first, each and every time, and in each and every decision we make.

Our primary aim must be to serve our shareholders because shareholder value provides the only reliable measure of what is in the long-term best interest of all corporate constituencies. In fact, I believe that paying attention to the interests of our shareholders is the *only* way for our companies to make it through the current round of cutbacks in the defense industry.

More than 30 years ago, James Robison, president of a textile company called Indian Head Mills, wrote his company's policy manual. Robison outlined his business vision in one, simple sentence:

The objective of our company is to increase the intrinsic value of our common stock.

Robison said the plan was not

. . . to grow bigger for the sake of size, nor to become more diversified, nor to make the most or best of anything, nor to provide jobs, have the most modern plants, the happiest customers, lead in new product development, or to achieve any other status which has no relation to the economic use of capital.

Any or all of these may be, from time to time, a means to achieving our objective, but means and ends must never be confused. We are in business solely to improve the inherent value of the common stockholders' equity in the company.

A lot of people I've talked to about this issue have reacted as though the idea is somehow extreme, a return to the days of the robber barons. In reality, every time we put the near-term economic benefit of some other corporate constituency ahead of that of the long-term interests of our shareholders, we risk damaging our companies. When we see that the workforce is bigger than the workload, but can't bring ourselves to face up to restructuring, we are not only misusing shareholder money, we're also weakening our competitive position. When we pursue unprofitable businesses because we are

fascinated by the technology or because it feeds our egos, we're mismanaging shareholder assets and weakening our companies. It is our job to make the most economic use of the capital entrusted to us—it is essential for the long-term health of our organizations.

If you can't stand the thought of that, if the idea of putting the almighty dollar ahead of everything else makes you feel like a hard-hearted, money-grubbing ogre, consider this: Without a solid financial base, we cannot create the next big technology. We cannot keep people employed, much less grow. We cannot make contributions to charities in the community if we're on the dole ourselves. In effect, then, our success in making economic use of our capital today—as reflected with more or less accuracy in our share values—is the best barometer of our ability to serve the interest of all our constituencies tomorrow.

In the current environment, the goal must be to earn a return above the cost of capital. If you can do that, you're building a strong company—one that can take advantage of business opportunities as they arise.

Now, the improved returns can go to the shareholders directly through higher dividends or other payouts of capital—which will prompt a lot of politically-motivated handwringing. Or you can take that capital and put it to work in projects where you expect to do well in the future. But that's where serious business problems can arise. The corporate urge to waste capital by reinvesting in shrinking industries—or, maybe even worse, by diversifying out of them—is hard to resist. And that's why attention to share values as a reliable means of gauging the value of various possibilities is so important. Shareholder value should be the yardstick.

In his address to this group last year, before he became deputy Secretary of Defense, Dr. Bill Perry talked about how he had looked at the five-year plans of a number of defense companies over the previous few years. "Nearly all of them," he said, "show five to ten percent a year growth. When I discuss this with them, they point out to me that they have found one of the niches in the defense budget that is still going to grow. But, in sum, these niches add up to a $500 billion budget! Clearly, that is not going to happen."

What Dr. Perry was pointing out was that, individually and as an industry, defense companies are in denial. We can't quite believe that things are

> When companies diversify, the shareholder can really get kicked around.
> Fortunately, this happens less and less these days, because we all took such a
> beating in the defense downturn of the '70s. Contractors got into subway cars,
> buses, watches, coffins, digital watches—any number of markets that we didn't
> understand. Predictably, the industry lost its collective shirt.

as bad as they seem. We have begun to believe in the infallibility of those 17-year cycles of build-up and build-down, and we have faith there will be a renewed demand for our products any day now—or at least by 1997. No matter what happens, we are sure that the other guy is in a much more desperate situation than we are. In reality, of course, we're playing musical chairs and some players will eventually have to leave.

Political events further convince us that all our companies are indispensable. At his retirement ceremony a couple of weeks ago, General Colin Powell counted off the trouble spots around the world where young Americans are on patrol: the Persian Gulf, Mogadishu, Bosnia, Korea. "America's armed forces will have a busy future," he said, "busier than in the predictable garrison days of the Cold War." And even as we take pride in the role our products play in helping to maintain world order, we tell ourselves that everything we have must be retained for that time when the world calls on us again.

We say we must maintain a strong industrial base—and that's good. But size doesn't equal strength. When we're tying up shareholder resources without reasonable hope of an appropriate return on their investment, we're doing the wrong thing. The result is a weakening, not a strengthening, of the industrial base we profess to be so concerned about.

In a sense, we have been duped by our own success, particularly in the electronic side of the defense industry. If you look at the airframe side of the defense business back in the 1950s and '60s, there were any number of new starts. A new alloy would be developed, or a new engine, and those things could yield aerodynamic advancements big enough and important enough to make a new aircraft program worthwhile. But the technology has matured sufficiently that breakthroughs now are fewer and farther between. Today new aircraft starts of a specific type (Navy attack, or Air Force fighters) are 20, 25 years apart—and the gaps are growing.

In the 1950s, there were about 18 manufacturers of tactical aircraft. Today there are five. Within 10 years, the Department of Defense predicts there will be only two. It's difficult to do an analysis that suggests the DoD is wrong.

But electronics technologies are still advancing rapidly, with new developments coming thick and fast. Improvements to electronics systems can bring new life—even new missions—to existing airframes, submarines, surveillance satellites, and other platforms. Information technologies are at the heart of advances made for tomorrow's defense. Desert Storm reinforced the need for fast, accurate information.

But electronics and information systems are the only even mildly attractive portion of a declining defense budget, and they do not offer unlimited opportunities. When I was a young engineer, we did aircraft stress and fatigue analyses using Frieden electromechanical calculators. They were about the size of a typewriter. You can buy a little hand-held scientific calculator today to do the same thing—for about twenty dollars.

Over the years, there have been breakthroughs in wind tunnel information processing, giving us mountains of reports that nobody has actually read yet. Cray has just announced that they have a new supercomputer with two hundred thousand times the power of a PC. Somewhere, we reach a limit to the usefulness of information. Sooner or later, the breakthrough developments will slow down, as will the willingness to pay for them—just as it happened with airframes. No tree grows to the sky.

We need to plan for that, before our investments get too far in front of reality: even the electronic and information side of defense will feel the effects of the classical S-shaped maturity curve. Any sensible assessment of our situation tells us that we're going to get smaller, and stay smaller. The federal "bottom-up review" defense budget calls for 60 percent cuts in modernization dollars by about 1999. Our industry has lost 900,000 jobs since 1987, and we'll lose another 700,000 by 1999.

This is bad news, and no one wants to hear it. We feel considerable pressure from our employees, our communities, and the media to do something about it. "Don't just stand there," they tell us, "diversify, build something else." But when companies diversify, the shareholder can really get kicked around. Some poor, trusting devil who has handed over his savings to a company because it has expertise in one specific area suddenly finds himself an investor in a business none of us knows very much about. He might as well have taken his money to Vegas. Ultimately, all constituencies lose.

Fortunately, this happens less and less these days, because we all took such a beating in the defense downturn of the '70s. Contractors got into subway cars, buses, watches, coffins, digital watches—any number of markets that we didn't understand. Predictably, the industry lost its collective shirt.

But the temptations are still there today, because we can see areas where defense technologies and techniques could have broad implications for improving our lives. At Grumman, for example, the same people who worked on neutral particle beams as part of the Star Wars initiative are now working with Los Alamos National Laboratories to explore ways of cleaning up radioactive waste. They've discovered that you can bombard radioactive waste from nuclear power plants with particle beams. That cuts the half life from thousands of years to a couple of decades—and so makes storage practical.

We recently submitted a proposal to build a prototype maglev—a magnetically levitated train—on a mile and a quarter test track in upstate New York at Stewart International Airport. And we're taking a careful, measured look at a number of other projects. But we're holding onto our wallets. We will expect a proper return, or we won't invest in a meaningful way. Lottery odds should tie up investments only the size of lottery tickets.

Other companies are looking at environmental cleanup work, drug interdiction, and residential security systems. As one example, Alliant Techsystems, the nation's biggest munitions maker, has proposed putting softball-sized sonar sensors on the tops of telephone poles in Washington to alert police to the sound of gunfire. There are about 450 homicides a year in Washington, and Alliant believes the technology could reduce emergency crews' response time by 85 percent. To me, this sounds like structuring a football defense around stopping extra points—but perhaps it can be of real value.

These are exciting technologies, but they're not cheap and they're financially risky. I can't think of one company in America today that could afford to go alone after maglev or crime prevention or intelligent highways or transmutation of nuclear waste. Most of these things will require massive government investment to proceed in a meaningful way—in much the same way that government invested in going to the moon a generation ago. The railroads, the airlines, and the interstate highway system, for that matter, all required the same kind of national commitment.

This is not to say that we expect government to solve all our problems—to pick winners and losers, and tell us what to do next. As Jack Welch of General Electric put it, "Governments set out to create Silicon Valley and wind up building the Motor Vehicle Department." But it is reasonable to expect government to provide some guidance about which technologies it values and will pursue. We cannot ask our shareholders to finance a technological revolution with almost no chance of a return on their investment commensurate with their risk.

We have responsibilities to each other, to our customers, to our communities, and to our employees. But we must not forget, even for a minute, whose money is at risk—because that's the only way honest assessments of probable success will be made. So after you take home all the information that unfolds over the next few days, when you sift through all the opportunities that you hear about, force yourself to ask the question: Does this really make sense? Put your ideas to the reality test of building shareholder value. The ideas that pass the test are the ones that will serve our industry well.

The economic use of capital must be the guide for every decision we make. This is how strong companies have always been built. This is how they have survived tough times such as those we face today.

LESSONS FROM A MIDDLE MARKET LBO: THE CASE OF O.M. SCOTT

*by George P. Baker and Karen H. Wruck, Harvard Business School**

n 1986 The O.M. Scott & Sons Company, the largest producer of lawn care products in the U.S., was sold by the ITT Corporation in a divisional leveraged buyout. The company was founded in Marysville, Ohio in 1870 by Orlando McLean Scott to sell farm crop seed. In 1900, the company began to sell weed-free lawn seed through the mail. In the 1920s, the company introduced the first home lawn fertilizer, the first lawn spreader, and the first patented bluegrass seed. Today, Scott is the acknowledged leader in the "do-it-yourself" lawn care market, with sales of over $300 million and over 1500 employees.

Scott remained closely held until 1971, when it was purchased by ITT. The company then became a part of the consumer products division of the huge conglomerate, and operated as a wholly-owned subsidiary for 14 years. In 1984, prompted by a decline in financial performance and rumors of takeover and liquidation, ITT began a series of divestitures. Over the next two years, total divestitures exceeded $2 billion and, after years of substandard performance, ITT's stock price significantly outperformed the market.

On November 26, 1986, in the midst of this divestiture activity, ITT announced that the manag-

ers of Scott, along with Clayton & Dubilier (C & D), a private firm specializing in leveraged buyouts, had agreed to purchase the stock of Scott and another ITT subsidiary, the W. Atlee Burpee Company. The deal closed on December 30.

Clayton & Dubilier raised roughly $211 million to finance the purchase of the two companies. Of that $211 million, almost $191 milion, or 91% of the total, was debt: bank loans, subordinated notes, and subordinated debentures. The $20 million of new equity was distributed as follows: roughly 62% of the shares were held by a C & D partnership, 21% by Scott's new subordinated debtholders, and 17.5% by Scott management and employees.

After this radical change in financial structure and concentration of equity ownership, Scott's operating performance improved dramatically. Between the end of December 1986 and the end of September 1988, sales were up 25% and earnings before interest and taxes (EBIT) increased by 56%. As shown in Table 1, this increase in operating earnings was not achieved by cutting back on marketing and distribution or R & D. In fact, spending on marketing and distribution increased by 21% and R & D spending went up by 7%. Capital spending also increased by 23%.

*This is a shorter, less technical version of "Organizational Changes and Value Creation in Leveraged Buyouts: The Case of The O.M. Scott Company," *Journal of Financial Economics,* 25 (1989).

We would like to thank everyone at The O.M. Scott & Sons Company and Clayton & Dubilier who gave generously of their time and so made this study possible: Lorel Au, Martin Dubilier, Richard Dresdale, Rich Martinez, Larry McCartney, Tadd Seitz, John Smith, Bob Stern, Homer Stewart, Hank Timnick, Ken

Tossey, John Wall, Craig Walley, and Paul Yeager. In addition, we would like to thank Ken French, Robin Cooper, Bob Eccles, Leo Herzel, Mike Jensen, Steve Kaplan, Ken Merchant, Krishna Palepu, Bill Schwert, Eric Wruck, and the participants of the Financial Decisions and Control Workshop at Harvard Business School and of the Conference on the Structure and Governance of Enterprise sponsored by the JFE for their helpful comments and suggestions. Support from the Division of Research, Harvard Business School, is gratefully acknowledged.

TABLE 1 FINANCIAL AND OPERATING DATA FOR O.M. SCOTT & SONS CO. ($ in millions)		Pre-buyout: Year ended 12/30/86	Post-buyout: Year ended 9/30/88	Percent change
	INCOME STATEMENT			
	EBIT	$18.1	$28.2	55.8%
	Sales	158.1	197.1	24.7
	Research & development	4.1	4.4	7.3
	Marketing & distribution	58.4	70.7	21.1
	BALANCE SHEET*			
	Average working capital	59.3	36.2	-39.0
	Total assets	243.6	162.0	-33.5
	Long-term debt	191.0	125.8	34.1
	Adjusted net worth	20.0	38.3	91.5
	OTHER			
	Capital expenditures	$3.0	$3.7	23.3
	Employment	868	792	-8.9

*Balance sheet figures are reported at the close of the buyout transaction. Adjusted net worth is GAAP net worth adjusted for accounting effects of the buyout under APB no. 16. In Scott's case the bulk of the adjustment is adding back the effects of an inventory write-down of $24.7 million taken immediately after the buyout.

In terms of its capital structure, managerial equity ownership, and improvement in operating performance, Scott is a highly representative LBO. Three major academic studies of LBOs have collectively concluded that following an LBO:

■ the average debt-to-capital ratio is roughly 90%;
■ managerial equity ownership stakes are typically around 17-20%;
■ operating income increases by about 40%, on average, over a period ranging from two to four years after a buyout.[1]

Such findings raise major questions about the effects of changes in organizational and financial structure on management decision-making. For example, does the combination of significant equity ownership and high debt provide management with stronger incentives to maximize value than those facing managers of public companies with broadly dispersed stockholders? Are the decentralized management systems with pay-for-performance plans that typically accompany LBOs likely to produce greater operating efficiencies than centralized structures relying largely on financial controls? Are LBO boards, characterized by controlling equity ownership, an improvement over the standard governance of public companies where directors have "fiduciary duty," but little or no equity ownership?

Although the broad evidence cited above suggests that the answer to all these questions is yes, little academic research to date has examined the changes in organizational structure and managerial decision-making that actually take place after LBOs. In 1989, we were given the opportunity to examine confidential data on the Scott buyout and to conduct extensive interviews with C & D partners and managers at all levels of the Scott organization. We found that both organizational structure and the management decision-making process changed fundamentally as a consequence of the buyout.

In the pages that follow, we attempt to explain the role of high leverage, concentrated equity ownership, and strong governance by an active board in bringing about specific operating changes within Scott. Critics of LBOs will doubtless continue to object that highly leveraged capital structures lead to an unhealthy emphasis on "short-term" results. But the changes we witnessed at Scott lend no support to this view. These changes ranged from sharply increased attention to working capital management, vendor relations, and an innovative approach to production to a much greater willingness to entertain long-range opportunities presented by new markets and strategic acquisitions. Especially in light of Scott's post-LBO performance and spending patterns, it

1. The studies are as follows: Steven Kaplan, "Management Buyouts: Evidence on Post-buyout Operating Changes," *Journal of Financial Economics*, 1991; Abbie Smith, "Corporate Ownership Structure and Performance: The Case of Management Buyouts," *Journal of Financial Economics*, 1991; and Chris Muscarella and Michael Vetsuypens, "Efficiency and Organizational Structure: A Study of Reverse LBOs," Southern Methodist University working paper, 1988.

TABLE 2
OWNERS OF COMMON
STOCK OF O.M. SCOTT &
SONS CO. AFTER THE LBO
(As of 9/30/88)

	Number of Shares	Percent of Shares
Clayton & Dubilier private limited partnership	14,900	61.4%
Subordinated debtholders	5,000	20.6
Mr. Tadd Seitz, President, CEO	1,063	4.4
Seven other top managers (250,000 shares each)	1,750	7.2
Scott profit sharing plan	750	3.1
Twenty-two other employees	687	2.8
Mr. Joseph P. Flannery, Board Member	100	0.4
Total	24,250	100.0%

All shares were purchased by owners at $1 per share. Percentages don't foot due to rounding error.

would be difficult to argue that any of these initiatives sacrificed long-term value for short-run cash flow.

CHANGES IN INCENTIVES AND COMPENSATION

Management Equity Ownership

The final distribution of equity in the post-buyout Scott organization was the product of negotiations between C & D and Scott's management—negotiations in which ITT took no part. ITT sold its entire equity interest in Scott through a sealed bid auction. Eight firms bid for Scott; although bidding was open to all types of buyers, seven bidders were buyout firms. ITT was interested primarily in obtaining the highest price for the division.

Scott managers did not participate in the buyout negotiations and thus had no opportunity to extract promises or make deals with potential purchasers prior to the sale. Scott managers had approached ITT several years earlier to discuss the possibility of a management buyout at $125 million; but at that time ITT had a no-buyout policy. The stated reason for this policy was that a management buyout posed a conflict of interest.

Each of the bidders spent about one day in Marysville and received information about the performance of the unit directly from ITT. Prior to Martin Dubilier's visit, Scott managers felt that they preferred C & D to the other potential buyers because of its reputation for working well with operating managers. The day did not go well, however, and C & D fell to the bottom of the managers' list. According to Tadd Seitz, president of Scott:

To be candid, they weren't our first choice. It wasn't a question of their acumen, we just didn't think we had the chemistry. But as we went through the controlled bid process, it was C & D that saw the greatest value in Scott.

There is no evidence that ITT deviated from its objective of obtaining the highest value for the division, or that it negotiated in any way on behalf of Scott managers during the buyout process. C & D put in the highest bid. ITT did not consider management's preferences and accepted this bid even though managers were left to work with one of their less favored buyers. Nor did ITT concern itself with the distribution of common stock after the sale.

Immediately following the closing, C & D controlled 79.4% of Scott's common stock. The remaining shares were packaged and sold with the subordinated debt. C & D was under no obligation to offer managers equity participation in Scott, and the deal clearly could be funded without any contribution by managers. But, on the basis of their experience, the C & D partners viewed management equity ownership as a way to provide managers with strong incentives to maximize firm value. Therefore, after C & D purchased Scott, it began to negotiate with managers over the amount of equity they would be given the opportunity to purchase. C & D did not sell shares to managers reluctantly; in fact, it insisted that managers buy equity and that they do so with their own, not the company's, money.

The ownership structure that resulted from the negotiations between C & D and Scott management is presented in Table 2. There are 24,250,000 shares outstanding, each of which was purchased for $1.00. As the general partner of the private limited partnership that invested $14.9 million in the Scott buyout, C & D controlled 61.4% of the common stock. The individual C & D partners responsible for overseeing Scott operations carried an ownership interest through their substantial investment in the C & D limited partnership. Subordinated debtholders owned 20.6%.

In Scott's case, high leverage combined with equity ownership provided managers
with the incentive to generate the cash required to meet the debt payments without
bleeding the company.

The remaining 17.5% of the equity was distributed among Scott's employees. Eight of the firm's top managers contributed a total of $2,812,500 to the buyout and so hold as many shares, representing 12% of the shares outstanding. Tadd Seitz, president of Scott, held the largest number of these shares (1,062,500, or 4.4% of the shares outstanding). Seven other managers purchased 250,000 shares apiece (1% each of the shares outstanding). As a group, managers borrowed $2,531,250 to finance the purchase of shares. Though the money was not borrowed from Scott, these loans were guaranteed by the company.

The purchase of equity by Scott managers represented a substantial increase in their personal risk. For example, Bob Stern, vice-president of Associate Relations,[2] recalled that his spouse sold her interest in a small catering business at the time of the buyout; they felt that the leverage associated with the purchase of Scott shares was all the risk they could afford.

Top management had some discretion over how their allotment of common shares was further distributed. Without encouragement from C & D, they chose to issue a portion of their own shares to Scott's employee profit-sharing plan and other employees of the firm. Although they allowed managers to distribute the stock more widely, C & D partners felt that the shares would have stronger incentive effects if they were held only by top managers. Craig Walley, general counsel for Scott, described the thinking behind management's decision to extend equity to additional managers and employees as follows:

We [the managers] used to get together on Saturdays during this period when we were thinking about the buyout to talk about why we wanted to do this. What was the purpose? What did we want to make Scott? One of our aims was to try to keep it independent. Another was to try to spread the ownership widely. One of the things we did was to take 3% of the common stock out of our allocation and put it into the profit-sharing plan. That took some doing and we had some legal complications, but we did it. There are now 56 people in the company who own some stock,

and that number is increasing. Compared to most LBOs that is really a lot, and Dubilier has not encouraged us in this.

A group of 11 lower-level managers bought an additional 687,500 shares (2.8% of the total) and the profit-sharing plan bought 750,000 shares (3.1%). These managers were selected not by their rank in the organization, but because they were employees who would be making decisions considered crucial to the success of the company.

The substantial equity holdings of the top management team, along with their personal liability for the debts incurred to finance their equity stakes, led them to focus on two distinct aspects of running Scott: (1) preserving their fractional equity stake by avoiding default (including technical default) on the firm's debt; and (2) increasing the value of that stake by making decisions that increased the long-run value of the firm.

If the company failed to make a payment of interest or principal, or if it violated a debt covenant, it would be "in default" and lenders would have the option to renegotiate the terms of the debt contract. If no agreement could be reached, the company could be forced to seek protection from creditors under Chapter 11. Because both private reorganizations and Chapter 11 generally involve the replacement of debt with equity claims, one likely consequence of default is a substantial dilution of the existing equity; and to the extent managers are also equityholders, such dilution reduces their wealth. But managers face other costs of default that are potentially large: they may end up surrendering control of the company to a bankruptcy court, and they could even lose their jobs.[3] In this sense, equity ownership bonds managers against taking actions that lead to a violation of the covenants.

We examined Scott's debt covenants in detail to determine what managerial actions lenders encouraged and prohibited (see Table 3 for a summary). The overall effect of these covenants is to restrict both the source of funds for scheduled interest and principal repayments and the use of funds in excess of this amount. Cash to pay debt obligations must come primarily from operations or the issuance of common

---

2. Scott refers to all of its employees as "associates." Stern's position, therefore, is equivalent to vice-president of human resources or personnel.

3. Stuart Gilson provides evidence that the managers of firms in financial distress are quite likely to lose their jobs as a part of the recovery process. See "Management Turnover and Financial Distress," *Journal of Financial Economics,* 25 (1989), pp. 241-262.

TABLE 3
SUMMARY OF DEBT COVENANTS OF SCOTT BORROWINGS TO FINANCE THE BUYOUT

	Bank Debt Restrictions	Subordinated Debt Restrictions
ECONOMIC ACTIVITIES RESTRICTED		
Sale of Assets	Only worn-out or obsolete assets with value less than $500,000 can be sold	75% of proceeds must be used to repay debt in order of priority
Capital Expenditures	Restricted to specific $ amount each year debt is outstanding	None
Changes in corporate structure control	Prohibited	Mandatory redemption if change in
		No acquisition if in default Must acquire 100% equity of target Must be able to issue $1 more debt without covenant violation after acquisition
FINANCING ACTIVITIES RESTRICTED		
Issuance of additional debt	Capitalized leases: max = $3,000,000 Unsecured credit: max = $1,000,000	Additonal senior debt: max = $15,000,000 For employee stock purchases: max = $4,250,000
	Commercial paper: max = amount available under revolving credit agreement	Pre-tax cash flow/interest expense: min = 1.0 for four quarters preceding issuance
Payment of cash dividends	Prohibited	Prohibited if in default Prohibited if adjusted net worth < $50,000,000
ACCOUNTING-BASED RESTRICTIONS		
Adjusted net worth*	Specific min at all times, min increases from $20.5 million in 1986 to $43.0 million after 1992	If adjusted net worth falls below $12.0 million then must redeem $17.0 million notes and $5.0 million debentures at 103
Interest coverage	Min 1.0 at end of each fiscal quarter	None
Current ratio	Min at end of each fiscal quarter	None
Adjusted operating profit	Min at end of each fiscal quarter, min fiscal quarter, min increases from $22.0 million in 1987 to $31.0 million after 1990	None

*Adjusted net worth and adjusted operating profit are the GAAP numbers adjusted for accounting effects of the buyout under APB no. 16. In Scott's case the bulk of the adjustment is adding back the effects of an inventory write-down of $24.7 million taken immediately after the buyout.

stock. It cannot come from asset liquidation, stock acquisition of another firm with substantial cash, or the issuance of additional debt of any kind. Excess funds can be used for capital expenditures only within prescribed limits, and cannot be used to finance acquisitions or be paid out as dividends to shareholders. Thus, once the capital expenditure limit has been reached, excess cash must be either held, spent in the course of normal operations, or used to pay down debt ahead of schedule.

A second important effect of equity ownership was to encourage managers to make decisions that increased the long-run value of the company. Because managers owned a capital value claim on the firm, they had strong incentives to meet debt obligations and avoid default in a way that increased the long-term value of the company. That is, managers

had strong incentives to resist cutbacks in brand-name advertising and plant maintenance that would increase short-run cash flow at the expense of long-run value.

As mentioned earlier, there were no cutbacks in productive capital spending at Scott. In fact, as shown in Table 1 earlier, capital spending, R&D, and marketing and promotion expenditures all increased significantly over the first two years after the buyout. Thus, in Scott's case, high leverage combined with equity ownership provided managers with the incentive to generate the cash required to meet the debt payments without bleeding the company.

The increase in capital expenditures following Scott's LBO is one way in which Scott differs from the average LBO. The large-sample studies cited earlier find that capital spending falls on average following

The large stockholder gains from the leveraged restructuring movement of the 80s
are suggestive evidence that much prior corporate "long-term" investment was little
more than a waste of stockholder funds in the name of preserving growth.

an LBO. Whether this average reduction in capital expenditures creates or destroys value is difficult to determine, because not all corporate spending cutbacks are short-sighted. To make that determination, one has to know whether LBO companies were spending too much or too little on capital expenditure prior to their LBOs. The large stockholder gains from the leveraged restructuring movement of the 1980s suggest that much prior corporate "long-term" investment was little more than a waste of stockholder funds in the name of preserving growth.

High leverage combined with leveraged equity ownership provides strong incentives for managers to evaluate long-term investments more critically, to undertake only value-increasing projects, and to return any "free cash flow"—that is, cash in excess of that required to fund all positive-NPV investments—to investors.[4] Leverage will cause managers to cut back on productive expenditures only if such cutbacks are the only way to avoid default *and* the cost to managers of default is greater than the loss in equity value from myopic decisions.

The LBO sponsor—in this case C & D—also plays an important role in guiding such investment decisions and preventing short-sighted cutbacks. Indeed, the experience and competence of the sponsor in valuing the company, evaluating the strengths of operating management, and arranging the financial structure is critical to an LBO's success.[5]

Changes in Incentive Compensation

Among the first things C & D did after the buyout was to increase salaries selectively and begin to develop a new management compensation plan. A number of managers who were not participants in the ITT bonus plan became participants under the C & D plan. The new plan substantially changed the way managers were evaluated, and increased the fraction of salary that a manager could earn as an annual bonus. While some of these data are confidential, we are able to describe many of the features of C & D's incentive compensation plan and compare it with the ITT compensation system.

Salaries. Almost immediately after the close of the sale, the base salaries of some top managers were increased. The president's salary increased by 42%, and the salaries of other top managers increased as well. Henry Timnick, a C & D partner who works closely with Scott, explains the decision to raise salaries as follows:

We increased management salaries because divisional vice presidents are not compensated at a level comparable to the CEO of a free-standing company with the same characteristics. Divisional VPs don't have all the responsibilities. In addition, the pay raise is a shot-in-the-arm psychologically for the managers. It makes them feel they will be dealt with fairly and encourages them to deal fairly with their people.

In conversations with managers and C & D partners, it became clear that C & D set higher standards for management performance than ITT. Increasing the minimum level of acceptable performance forces managers to work harder after the buyout or risk losing their jobs. Indeed, there was general agreement that the management team was putting in longer hours at the office. Several managers used the term "more focused" to described how their work habits had changed after the buyout.

The increase in compensation also served as the reward for bearing greater risk. As stated earlier, Scott managers undertook substantial borrowings to purchase the equity. Requiring managers to borrow to buy equity and adopting an aggressive incentive compensation plan greatly increases managers' exposure to Scott's fortunes. Because managers cannot diversify away this "firm-specific" risk in the same way passive investors can, they require an increase in the expected *level* of their pay to remain equally well-off.

Finally, C & D may have increased salaries because Scott managers are more valuable to C & D than they were to ITT. Consistent with this argument, managers at Scott felt ITT depended on them much less than did C & D. One Scott manager reported:

4. See Michael C. Jensen, "Agency Costs of Free Cash Flow, Corporate Finance, and Takeovers," *American Economic Review*, 76 (1986), pp. 323-329.

5. For examples of poorly structured LBOs, consider the cases of Revco, D.S. and Campeau's acquisition of Federated, both of which have been held up as representative of the problems with LBOs. A case study (by one of the present authors) reveals clearly that top management problems coupled with an inexperienced (and distracted) LBO sponsor contributed greatly to Revco's poor performance (see Karen Wruck and Michael Jensen with Adam M. Berman and Mark Wolsey-Paige, "Revco D.S., Incorporated," Harvard Business School Case 9-190-202 [1991]). In the case of Campeau's acquisition of Federated, a study by Steve Kaplan has shown that overpayment financed by leverage led to the company's default and subsequent Chapter 11 filing (see Steven Kaplan, "Campeau's Acquisition of Federated: Value Destroyed or Value Added," *Journal of Financial Economics*, 25 (1989), pp. 191-212.

"When ITT comes in and buys a company, the entire management team could quit and they wouldn't blink." As we will discuss later, ITT created a control system that allowed headquarters to manage a vast number of businesses, but did not give divisional managers the flexibility or incentives to use their specialized knowledge of the business to maximize its value.

Because C & D relied much more heavily on managers' operating knowledge, it was presumably willing to pay them more to reduce the risk of the managers quitting. At the same time, C & D was not completely dependent on incumbent managers to run Scott. Several C & D partners had extensive experience as operating managers. These partners had on several occasions stepped in to run C & D buyout firms, and they were available to run Scott if necessary. But, they clearly lacked specific knowledge of the Scott organization and were thus willing to provide financial incentives to incumbent managers to secure their participation.

Bonus. Scott's bonus plan was completely redesigned after its buyout. The number of managers who participated in the plan increased, and the factors that determined the level of bonus were changed to reflect the post-buyout objectives of the firm. In addition, both the maximum bonus allowed by the plan and the actual realizations of bonus as a percentage of salary increased by a factor of two to three.

After the buyout 21 managers were covered by the bonus plan. Only ten were eligible for bonuses under ITT. The maximum payoff under the new plan ranged from 33.5% to 100% of base salary, increasing with the manager's rank in the company. For each manager, the amount of the payoff was based on the achievement of corporate, divisional, and individual performance goals. The weights applied to corporate, divisional, and individual performance in calculating the bonus varied across managers. For division managers, bonus payoff was based 35% on overall company performance, 40% on divisional performance, and 25% on individual performance. Bonuses for corporate managers weighted corporate performance 50% and personal goals 50%.

At the beginning of each fiscal year performance targets (or goals) were set, and differences between actual and targeted performance entered directly into the computation of the bonus plan payoffs. All corporate and divisional performance measures were quantitative measures of cash generation and utiliza-

tion and were scaled from 80 to 125, with 100 representing the attainment of target. For example, corporate performance was evaluated by dividing actual EBIT by budgeted EBIT, and dividing actual average working capital (AWC) by budgeted AWC; the EBIT ratio was weighted more heavily, at 75% as compared to a 25% weight assigned the AWC ratio. The resulting number, expressed as a percentage attainment of budget, was used as a part of the bonus calculation for all managers in the bonus plan.

Thus, the bonus plan was designed such that the payoff was highly sensitive to changes in performance. This represented a significant change from the ITT bonus plan. As Bob Stern, vice-president of Associate Relations, commented:

I worked in human resources with ITT for a number of years. When I was manager of staffing of ITT Europe we evaluated the ITT bonus plan. Our conclusion was that the ITT bonus plan was viewed as nothing more than a deferred compensation arrangement: all it did was defer income from one year to the next. Bonuses varied very, very little. If you had an average year, you might get a bonus of $10,000. If you had a terrible year you might get a bonus of $8,000, and if you had a terrific year you might go all the way to $12,500. On a base salary of $70,000, that's not a lot of variation.

The following table presents actual bonus payouts for the top ten managers as a percent of salary for two years before and two years after the buyout.

Rank	Before the Buyout		After the Buyout	
	1985	1986	1987	1988
1	18.3%	26.6%	93.8%	57.7%
2	14.0	23.4	81.2	46.8
3	12.8	18.8	79.5	46.0
4	13.3	20.6	81.2	48.5
5	11.2	19.4	80.7	46.8
6	10.5	17.1	76.5	46.0
7	7.1	10.8	29.6	16.6
8	6.1	22.9	78.0	46.7
9	4.6	6.3	28.7	16.8
10	5.1	6.6	28.4	16.4
Mean	10.3%	17.3%	65.8%	38.8%

The new bonus plan gives larger payouts and appears to generate significantly more variation in bonuses than occurred under ITT. Average bonuses

The experience and competence of the [LBO] sponsor in valuing the company, evaluating the strengths of operating management, and arranging the financial structure is critical to the success of an LBO.

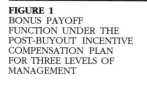

FIGURE 1
BONUS PAYOFF FUNCTION UNDER THE POST-BUYOUT INCENTIVE COMPENSATION PLAN FOR THREE LEVELS OF MANAGEMENT

■ Payoff for CEO

■ Payoff for Vice Presidents and General Manager

▨ Payoff for Other Participating Managers

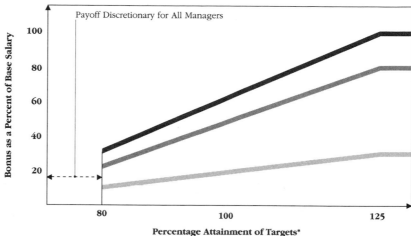

*Based on a weighted average of corporate, divisional, and individual performance.

as a percent of salary for the top ten managers increased from 10% and 17% in the two years before the buyout to 66% and 39% in the two years after, a period during which operating income increased by 42%. There also appears to be much greater variation in bonus payout across managers within a given year. In the two years prior to the buyout, bonus payout ranged from 5% to 27% of base salary, whereas over the two years following the buyout, it ranged from 16% to 94% of base salary.

In addition to measures that evaluated management performance against quantitative targets, each manager had a set of personal objectives that were tied into the bonus plan. These objectives were set by the manager and his or her superior, and their achievement was monitored by the superior. Personal objectives were generally measurable and verifiable. For instance, one objective for a personnel manager was to integrate the benefits package of a newly acquired company with that of Scott within a given period. An objective for the president of the company was to spend a fixed amount of time outside of Marysville talking to retailers and salespeople. At the end of the year, the superior evaluated whether the manager had achieved these objectives, and quantified the achievement along the same 80-

125 point range. This rating was then combined with the quantitative measures to come up with a total performance measure.

The weighted average of corporate, divisional, and personal target achievements was then used to determine total bonus payoffs. Figure 1 shows how payoffs were varied with rank and performance. If a manager achieved an 80% weighted average attainment of target goals, the payoff varied from about 30% of salary for the CEO to about 10% for lower-level managers.[6] At 125% attainment, bonuses varied from about 100% to about 30%. Between 80% and 125%, bonus payouts as a percentage of salary varied linearly with target attainment. Below 80%, payments were at the discretion of the president and the board.

The combination of equity ownership by eight top managers with a more "highly leveraged" bonus plan for thirteen others substantially changed the incentives of the managers at Scott. For those managers who held equity, the bonus plan, with its emphasis on EBIT and working capital management, served to reinforce the importance of cash generation. Those managers who were not offered equity were nevertheless provided financial incentives to make the generation of cash a primary concern.

6. For confidentiality, these numbers have been left intentionally vague.

THE MONITORING OF TOP MANAGERS

Purpose and Composition of the Board

The purpose of Scott's board of directors was to monitor, advise, and evaluate the CEO. As Henry Timnick describes it:

The purpose of the board is to make sure the company has a good strategy and to monitor the CEO. The CEO cannot be evaluated by his management staff, so we do not put the CEO's people on the board. Scott's CFO and the corporate secretary attend the meetings, but they have no vote. The outside directors are to be picked by the CEO. We will not put anyone on the board that the CEO doesn't want, but we [C & D] have to approve them. We do not view board members as extensions of ourselves, but they are not to be cronies or local friends of the CEO. We want people with expertise that the CEO doesn't have. The CEO should choose outside directors who are strong in areas in which he is weak.

At the close of the buyout Scott's board had five members. Only one, Tadd Seitz, was a manager of the firm. Of the remaining four, three were C & D partners: Martin Dubilier was the chairman of the board and voted the stock of the limited partnership, Henry Timnick was the C & D partner who worked most closely with Scott management, and Alberto Cribiore was a financing specialist. The outside director was Joe Flannery, then CEO of Uniroyal, which had been taken private by C & D in 1985. Later, Flannery left Uniroyal and became a C & D partner. He stayed on the Scott board, becoming an inside, rather than outside, director.

Over the next few years three new directors were added. One was an academic, one was a consumer products expert, and one, Don Sherman, was the president of Hyponex, a company acquired by Scott after its buyout. The academic, Jim Beard, was one of the country's leading turf researchers. Henry Timnick described the process of putting him on the board as follows:

Our objective was to find the best turf specialist and researcher in the country. We wanted someone to keep us up with the latest developments and to scrutinize the technical aspects of our product line. We found Jim Beard at Texas A&M. It took Jim a while to be enthusiastic about being on the board, and it

took Tadd a while to figure out how to get the most out of Jim. After Jim was appointed to the board, we encouraged Tadd to have Jim out on a consulting basis for a couple of days. Now Tadd is making good use of Jim.

Seitz and Timnick wanted an individual with extensive experience in consumer products businesses to be the second outside director. They chose Jack Chamberlain, who had run GE's Consumer Electronics Division as well as Lenox China and Avon Products. All board members were stockholders; upon joining the board they were each given the opportunity to purchase 50,000 shares at adjusted book value. All the directors chose to own stock.

This board structure was typical for a C & D buyout. Martin Dubilier explains:

We have tried a number of board compositions and we found this to be the most effective. If you have too many insiders the board becomes an operating committee. Outsiders fortify the growth opportunities of the firm.

The board of directors met quarterly. A subset of the board, the executive committee, met monthly. The executive committee was made up of Martin Dubilier, Tadd Seitz, and Henry Timnick. In their meetings they determined policy, discussed personnel matters, and tested Seitz's thinking on major issues facing the firm. The board meetings were more formal, usually consisting of presentations by members of the management team other than Seitz.

The Operating Partner

In each of C & D's buyouts, a partner with extensive operating experience serves as "liaison" between the firm's managers and C & D. The operating partner functions as an advisor and consultant to the CEO, not a decision maker. Henry Timnick was Scott's liaison partner. He had been CEO of a division of Mead that was purchased through a leveraged buyout, and had since worked with several of C & D's other buyout firms. Timnick spent several weeks in Marysville after the buyout closed. Following that period, he was in touch with Seitz daily by telephone and continued to visit regularly.

Timnick would advise Seitz, but felt it was important that Seitz make the decisions. When he and Seitz disagreed, Timnick told him, "If you don't believe me, go hire a consultant, then make your own decision." Initially, Seitz continued to check with Timnick, looking for an authorization for his decisions. Henry Timnick explains:

Tadd kept asking me "Can I do this? Can I do that?" I told him, "You can do whatever you want so long as it is consistent with Scott's over-all strategy."

This consultative approach to working with Scott managers was quite different from ITT's approach. Martin Dubilier explains:

ITT challenges managers not to rock the boat, to make budget. We challenge managers to improve the business. Every company takes on the personality of its CEO. Our main contribution is to improve his performance. All the rest is secondary.

Scott managers confirmed Dubilier's assessment. Meetings between ITT managers and Scott managers were large and quite formal, with as many as 40 members of ITT's staff present. Scott managers found the meetings antagonistic, with the ITT people working to find faults and problems with the operating units' reported performances. By meeting the formal goals set by ITT, Scott could largely avoid interference from headquarters. Avoiding such interference was an important objective. As Paul Yeager, CFO, describes it:

Geneen [then CEO of ITT] said in his book that the units would ask for help from headquarters; that the units came to look at headquarters staff as outside consultants who could be relied upon to help when needed. I have worked in many ITT units, and if he really thought that, then he was misled. If a division vice president went to headquarters for help, in effect he was saying, 'I can't handle it.' He wouldn't be a vice president for very long.

ORGANIZATIONAL CHANGES AND CHANGES IN DECISION MAKING

The changes in organizational structure and decision making that took place at Scott after the buyout fall broadly into two categories: improved working capital management and a new approach to product markets. These changes were not forced on managers by C & D. The buyout firm made some

suggestions, but the specific plans and their implementation were the responsibility of Scott managers. Few of the changes represent keenly innovative or fundamentally new insights into management problems. As one observer noted, "It ain't rocket science." These changes, however, led to dramatic improvements in Scott's operating performance.

Management's ability and talents did not change after the buyout, nor did the market or the assets they were managing. The only changes were those in the incentive structure described earlier and in the management control system. According to Scott managers, the biggest difference between working at Scott before and after the buyout was an increase in the extent to which they could make and implement decisions without approval from superiors.

ITT, by contrast, maintained control over its divisions through an inflexible formal planning and reporting structure. Changing a plan required approval at a number of levels from ITT headquarters, and a request for a change was likely to be denied. In addition, because ITT was shedding its consumer businesses, Scott managers found their requests for capital funds routinely denied. After the buyout, Seitz could pick up the phone and propose changes in the operating plan to Timnick. This, of course, improved the company's ability to respond quickly to changes in the marketplace.

The Working Capital Task Force

Shortly after the buyout, a task force was established to coordinate the management of working capital throughout the company. The members of the task force were drawn from every functional area. The group was charged with reducing working capital requirements by 42%, or $25 million dollars, in two years. They exceeded this goal, reducing average working capital by $37 million. The task force helped Scott managers learn to manage cash balances, production, inventories, receivables, payables, and employment levels more effectively.

Cash Management. Before the buyout, Scott's managers never had to manage cash balances. John Wall, chairman of the working capital task force, describes how cash was controlled under ITT:

Under the ITT system, we needed virtually no cash management. The ITT lock box system swept our lock boxes into Citibank of New York. Our disbursement bank would contact ITT's bank and say we need

$2 million today and it automatically went into our disbursement account.

To control cash flow in its numerous businesses, ITT established a cash control system that separated the collection of cash from cash disbursements. Receipts went into one account and were collected regularly by ITT's bank. Once deposited, these funds were not available to divisional managers. Cash to fund operations came from a different source, and through a different bank account. This system allowed ITT to centrally manage cash and control divisional spending.

When Scott was a division of ITT, cash coming into Scott bore little relation to the cash Scott was allowed to spend. After the LBO, all of Scott's cash was available to managers. They needed to establish a system to control cash so that operations were properly funded, and to meet debt service requirements. Wall describes the process as follows:

In the first six months after the LBO we had to bring in a state-of-the-art cash management system for a business of this size. We shopped a lot of treasury management systems and had almost given up on finding a system that would simply let us manage our cash. We didn't need a system that would keep track of our investment portfolios because we had $200 million borrowed. Finally, we found a product we could use. Under the LBO cash forecasting has become critical. I mean cash forecasting in the intermediate and long range. I don't mean forecasting what is going to hit the banks in the next two or three days. We could always do that, but now we track our cash flows on a weekly basis and we do modeling on balance sheets, which allows us to do cash forecasting a year out.

Production and Inventories. Between 1986 and 1988, the efforts of the task force increased the frequency with which Scott turned over its inventory from 2.08 to 3.20 times per year, or by 54%. During this period both sales and production increased. Because Scott's business is highly seasonal, inventory control had always been a management problem. Large inventories were required to meet the spring rush of orders; however, financing these inventories was a cash drain. Scott's production strategy under ITT exacerbated the inventory problem. Before the buyout, Scott produced each product once a year. Slow-moving products were produced

during the slow season so that long runs of fast-moving products could be produced during the busy season. Before the spring buying began, almost an entire year's worth of sales were in inventory.

The old production strategy took advantage of the cost savings of long production runs. But, under ITT, managers did not consider the trade-off between these cost savings and the opportunity cost of funds tied up in inventory. The cash requirements of servicing a large debt burden, the working capital-based restrictions in the debt agreements, and the inclusion of working capital objectives in the compensation system gave managers a strong incentive to consider this opportunity cost. As Wall explained,

What the plant managers had to do was to figure out how they could move the production of the slow-moving items six months forward. That way the products we used to make in May or early June would be made in November or December. Now [instead of producing long runs of a few products] production managers have to deal with setups and changeovers during the high-production period. It requires a lot more of their attention.

Managing inventories more effectively required that products be produced closer to the time of shipment. Because more setups and changeovers were necessary, the production manager's job became more complicated. Instead of producing a year's supply of one product, inventorying it, and then producing another product, managers had to produce smaller amounts of a variety of products repeatedly throughout the year.

Inventories were also reduced by changing purchasing practices and inventory management. Raw material suppliers agreed to deliver small quantities more often, reducing the levels of raw materials and finished goods inventories. By closely tracking inventory, Scott managed to reduce these levels without increasing the frequency of stock-outs of either raw materials or finished goods.

Receivables and Payables. Receivables were an important competitive factor and retailers expected generous payment terms from Scott. After the buyout, however, the timing of rebate and selling programs was carefully planned, allowing Scott to conserve working capital. Scott also negotiated with suppliers to obtain more favorable terms on prices, payment schedules, and delivery. Lorel Au, manager of Contract Operations stated,

Within two months of the LBO, the director of manufacturing and I went out to every one of our contract suppliers and went through what a leveraged buyout is, and what that means. We explained how we were going to have to manage our business. We explained our new goals and objectives. We talked about things like just-in-time inventory, talked terms, talked about scheduling. Some suppliers were more ready to work with us than others. Some said, 'OK, what can we do to help?' In some cases, a vendor said, 'I can't help you on price, I can't help you on terms, I can't help you on scheduling.' We said: 'Fine. Good-bye.' We were very serious about it. In some cases we didn't have options, but usually we did.

The company succeeded in getting suppliers to agree to extended terms of payment, and was also able to negotiate some substantial price cuts from major suppliers in return for giving the supplier a larger fraction of Scott's business.

Scott managers felt that the buyout put them in a stronger bargaining position vis-a-vis their suppliers. Wall states:

One reason we were able to convince our suppliers to give us concessions is that we no longer had the cornucopia of ITT behind us. We no longer had unlimited cash.

The suppliers understood that if they did not capitulate on terms, Scott would have to take its business elsewhere or face default.[7]

Employment. Scott had a tradition of being very paternalistic toward its employees and was a major employer and corporate citizen in the town of Marysville. Some have argued that an important source of cash and increasing equity value in buyouts is the severing of such relationships.[8] There is no evidence of this at Scott. Scott's traditional employee relations policies were maintained, and neither wages nor benefits were cut after the buyout. Scott continues to maintain a large park with swimming pool, tennis courts, playground, and other recreational facilities for the enjoyment of employees and their families. The company also continues to make its auditorium, the largest in Marysville, available for community use at no charge.

Scott did begin a program of hiring part-time employees during the busy season rather than bringing on full-time employees. This allowed the company to maintain a core of full-time, year-round employees who enjoyed the complete benefits plan of the company, while still having enough people to staff the factory during busy season. As a consequence, average annual full-time employment has dropped by about 9%, entirely through attrition, over the first two years after the buyout.

New Approaches to the Product Markets

Scott is the major brand name in the do-it-yourself lawn care market and has a reputation for high-quality products. Ed Wandtke, a lawn industry analyst, says of the company:

O.M. Scott is ultra high price, ultra high quality. They absolutely are the market leader. They have been for some time. No one else has the retail market recognition. Through its promotions, Scott has gotten its name so entrenched that the name and everything associated with it—quality, consistency, reliability—supersede the expensive price of the product.

In 1987, Scott had a 34% share of the $350 million do-it-yourself market. Industry experts report, however, that the market had been undergoing major changes since the early 1980s. Indeed, Scott's revenue fell by 23% between 1981 (the historical high at that time) and 1985. The buyout allowed Scott managers the flexibility to adapt to the changing marketplace, assuring a future for the company.

The do-it-yourself market was shrinking because an increasing number of consumers were contracting with firms to have their lawns chemically treated. Seitz had proposed that Scott enter this segment of the professional lawn-care market for years, but ITT continually vetoed this initiative. Among the first actions taken after the buyout was the creation of a group within the professional division whose focus was to sell to the commercial

7. Schelling supports the potential for an increase in bargaining power to occur as the result of a precarious financial situation. He states: "The power to constrain an adversary may depend on the power to bind oneself.... In bargaining, weakness is often strength, freedom may be freedom to capitulate, and to burn bridges behind one may suffice to undo an opponent. ... [M]ore financial resources, more physical strength, more military potency, or more ability to withstand losses...are by no means universal advantages in bargaining situations; they often have a contrary value." T. Schelling, *The Strategy of Conflict*, (Cambridge, Mass: Harvard University Press, 1960).

8. See A. Shleifer and L. Summers, "Breach of Trust in Hostile Takeovers," in A. Auerbach, ed., *Corporate Takeovers: Causes and Consequences* (University of Chicago Press, 1988).

turf maintenance market. Within two years, the segment comprised 10% of the sales of the professional division and was growing at a rate of almost 40% per year.

In response to major changes in Scott's product markets, the company also made a major acquisition less than two years after the buyout. At the time, Scott's position in the do-it yourself market was being challenged by the growth of private label brands sold at lower prices, and by a shift in volume away from Scott's traditional retailers—hardware and specialty stores—to mass merchandisers. Under ITT Scott managers did not try to develop new channels of distribution. Timnick described it as too "risky" an experiment for ITT. The acquisition of Hyponex gave Scott access to the private label market. Says Wandtke,

With Hyponex, Scott will capture a greater percentage of the home consumer market. Hyponex is a much lower priced product line. It gives them [Scott] access to private labeling, where they can produce product under another label for a lesser price. ...This will improve their hold on the retail market.

Hyponex was a company virtually the same size as Scott, with $125 million in sales and 700 employees, yet the acquisition was financed completely with bank debt. The successful renegotiation of virtually all of Scott's existing debt agreements was required to consummate the transaction. Because the new debt was senior to the existing notes and debentures, a consent payment of $887,500 was required to persuade bondholders to waive restrictive covenants. That such a large acquisition was possible so soon after the buyout demonstrates the potential flexibility of the LBO organizational form. It also demonstrates the ability of contracting parties to respond to a valuable investment opportunity in the face of restrictions that appear to forbid such action.

CONCLUSIONS

This study documents the organizational changes that took place at The O.M. Scott & Sons Company in response to its leveraged buyout. In so doing, it lends support to the findings of large-sample studies of leveraged buyouts that suggest the pressure of servicing a heavy debt load combined with management equity ownership leads to improved operating performance.

Such improvements were not the result of financial sleight of hand, but of important changes in operating strategy and management decision-making. These organizational changes came about not only because of Scott's new financial structure and equity ownership, but also as a consequence of other factors that have been largely overlooked:

■ debt covenants that restrict how the cash required for debt payments can be generated;

■ the adoption of a strong incentive compensation plan;

■ a reorganization and decentralization of decision making; and

■ the close relationship between Scott managers, the partners of C & D, and the board of directors.

We attribute the improvements in operating performance after Scott's leveraged buyout to changes in the incentive, monitoring, and governance structure of the firm. Managers were given strong incentives to generate cash and greater decision-making authority, but checks were established to guard against behavior that would be damaging to firm value. In the Scott organization, high leverage was effective in forcing managers to generate cash flow in a productive way largely because debt covenants and equity ownership countered short-sighted behavior. Value was created by decentralizing decision making largely because managers were monitored and supported by an expert board of directors who were also the controlling equityholders.

We view this study as a first step toward understanding how radical changes in financial structure, equity ownership, and compensation systems can be used as tools to improve managerial incentives and corporate performance. For companies in mature industries, the combination of high leverage and management equity ownership can provide an organizational discipline that adds value.

■ GEORGE BAKER AND KAREN WRUCK

are both Assistant Professors of Business Administration at the Harvard Business School. Dr. Baker's research explores the effects of compensation systems, performance measurement systems, and employee ownership on organizational performance. Dr. Wruck's work focuses on the organizational effects of corporate financing decisions.

THE STAYING POWER OF LEVERAGED BUYOUTS

by Steven N. Kaplan,
*University of Chicago**

I n the 1980s, an unprecedented number of public corporations and divisions of public companies went private in leveraged buyouts (LBOs). LBO activity increased from $1.4 billion in 1979 to $77 billion in 1988. Despite the large number and size of the transactions, LBOs remain poorly understood. Nevertheless, there is a healthy debate today among finance scholars about the longevity of LBO organizations and their consequences for the general economy. The answers to this debate should add to our understanding of why LBOs occur and how they add value.

In a controversial *Harvard Business Review* article published in 1989 and entitled "The Eclipse of the Public Corporation," Michael Jensen argued that the LBO could be expected to supplant the public corporation as the dominant organizational form in mature industries with excess capacity.[1] LBOs solve what Jensen calls the "free cash flow" problem confronting public companies in mature industries—namely, the tendency of management to reinvest excess capital in low-return projects (including diversifying acquisitions) instead of paying it out to investors. According to Jensen, the combination of high debt-service payments and significant managerial equity ownership in LBOs provides management with far stronger incentives to increase efficiency and pay out excess capital than those normally present in large, predominantly equity-financed, public corporations. And reinforcing these stronger incentives in many LBOs is the participation and monitoring of LBO sponsors like KKR and Clayton & Dubilier—"active investors" who structure the transaction, own the majority of the company's equity, and control the boards of directors.

If Jensen is correct that improved LBO incentives are a critical source of value, then LBOs can be expected to stay private for significant periods of time. And, even if they subsequently do go public, Jensen's view suggests that debt levels will remain high and significant equity stakes will continue to be held by managers and active investors.

Shortly after the publication of Jensen's article, the *Harvard Business Review* published a response by Alfred Rappaport called "The Staying Power of the Public Corporation."[2] Rappaport's principal objection to Jensen's argument was that high debt and concentrated ownership impose costs in the form of reduced managerial flexibility in responding to competition and change. Compounding the pressure for near-term results exerted by the heavy debt load, the typical LBO sponsor invests funds provided by outside investors who expect to be repaid in five to ten years. For these two reasons, Rappaport maintained, buyouts are inherently unstable and short-lived organizations.

There is also another important source of instability in even the most successful LBOs—one that Rappaport did not mention. As the value of the controlling investors' and managers' equity stakes increases over time, both groups bear an increasing amount of undiversified risk. One way to reduce or diversify this risk is to return the company to public ownership.

Although Rappaport does not say so explicitly, his position is consistent with a view of buyouts as a form of "shock therapy." According to this view, buyout incentives lead managers to focus directly on increasing operating cash flow, curbing unprofitable investment, and selling unproductive assets. Many of these changes are one-time events. Once they have been accomplished, the benefits of the buyout incentives become steadily less important over time. At some point, the costs arising from inflexibility, illiquidity, and excessive risk-bearing begin to out-

*This article is a shorter, less technical, and partly updated version of "The Staying Power of Leveraged Buyouts," *Journal of Financial Economics* 29 (1991), pp. 287-313.

1. "The Eclipse of the Public Corporation, *Harvard Business Review* No. 5 (1989), pp. 61-74.

2. "The Staying Power of the Public Corporation," *Harvard Business Review* No. 1 (1990), pp. 96-104.

weigh the continuing benefits of buyout incentives, thus driving LBO companies to return to public ownership.

Still another view of LBOs maintains that their primary economic function is to provide a means of breaking up large, typically conglomerate, corporations through a series of asset sales. Indeed, one study reported that 72% of the assets acquired in large hostile takeovers ended up being sold to public corporations with similar assets within three years of the takeover. For the six hostile LBOs included in this study, moreover, the percentage of assets sold off was 43%.[3]

Major asset sales to related public buyers after LBOs would not necessarily imply that ownership incentives are unimportant. But they would suggest sources of buyout gains somewhat different from those implied by the Jensen or Rappaport explanations. For example, gains from sales to related buyers could come from joint operating efficiencies between buyers and sellers, from buyers' increased market power, or even—as some observers have suggested—from "strategic" buyers' willingness to overpay for divisions.

In a recently published study of 170 large LBOs of both public companies and divisions completed between 1979 and 1986, I attempted to assess the relative "explanatory power" of each of these three competing explanations of LBOs. Briefly stated, my findings were these. As of August 1990 (the cut-off date of my study),

- 106 (or 62%) of the 170 LBO companies were still privately owned, while 41 (24%) had been purchased by publicly owned U.S. or foreign companies and 23 (14%) had become publicly owned and independent companies.

- Although 76 (or 45%) of the 170 LBO companies had returned to public status at some point after the LBO (either through an IPO or sale to a public company), 12 of these 76 had gone private again in a second LBO.

- For just those LBOs returning to public ownership, the median time spent private was just over 2 1/2 years.

- For the entire sample of LBOs, the median amount of time spent private was estimated to be 6.8 years.

- The probability of an LBO company returning to public ownership was largest and roughly constant in the second to fifth years after the LBO, and then declined somewhat thereafter.

This last finding is consistent with the existence of two distinct kinds of buyouts—a "shock-therapy" type and a longer-term incentive type. Consistent with Rappaport's argument, the large fraction of LBOs returning to public ownership suggests that the private LBO is often a transitory organizational form, bridging periods of public ownership. This seems to characterize a majority of LBOs. Nevertheless, consistent with Jensen's model and the importance of the "incentive-intensive" organization, a significant fraction of LBO assets remain private and still highly leveraged many years after the transactions. In addition, those LBOs that have returned to public ownership as independent companies now appear to be "hybrid" organizations—that is, they have concentrated equity ownership by insiders and debt ratios significantly higher than pre-buyout levels.[4]

My findings also suggest a moderate, though not primary, role for asset sales by LBO companies to public buyers in related industries. Almost 30% of the LBO companies, and over a third of the original LBO assets, ended up being owned by companies with other, mainly related operating assets. By shifting assets to related buyers, LBOs contributed to greater corporate specialization and focus.

It is also important to note that my original study excluded buyouts completed after 1986. In a more recent study of 124 large management buyouts completed between 1980-1989, Jeremy Stein and I found that later buyouts were significantly less successful than earlier ones in avoiding financial distress.[5] To examine the possibility that later buyouts were more or less likely than my sample LBOs to change organizational form, I carried out a similar analysis for 60 management buyouts of public companies completed between 1987 and 1989. As of December, 1992, 36, or exactly 60%, of the MBOs were still private—though the estimated median time spent private fell from 6.8 to 4.8 years. Although somewhat more supportive of the shock-therapy view, the updated results are generally consistent with my original conclusions.

3. Sanjay Bhagat, Andrei Shleifer, and Robert Vishny, "Hostile Takeovers in the 1980s: The Return to Corporate Specialization," *Brookings Papers on Economic Activity: Microeconomics*, 1-72 (1990).

4. The maintenance of high debt levels by private LBOs and by independent public companies is also consistent, of course, with the importance of tax benefits from debt financing. See my article, "Management Buyouts: Evidence on Taxes as a Source of Value, *Journal of Finance* 44, pp. 611-632.

5. Steven Kaplan and Jeremy Stein, "The Evolution of Buyout Pricing and Financial Structure in the 1980s," *Quarterly Journal of Economics* (Spring 1993).

SAMPLE AND DATA

My sample included all transactions identified as leveraged buyouts by either Securities Data Corporation (SDC) or Morgan Stanley & Company executed between 1979 and 1986 and with purchase prices greater than $100 million. (By excluding transactions completed after 1986, my study ensured a period of at least 3 2/3 post-buyout years in which changes in organizational form could occur.) Using the above criteria, I came up with a sample of 183 companies with a total transaction value of $83 billion when they were completed. Given that W.T. Grimm's *Mergerstat Review* reported just over $92 billion in going-private and unit management buyout transactions during the same period, my sample appears to contain about 90% of the dollar value of transactions completed between 1979 and 1986.

I obtained post-buyout information on these companies from Lotus' Datext (public and private) databases, the NEXIS database, *Wall Street Journal* articles, and, when available, financial reports filed with the Securities and Exchange Commission (SEC). Whenever possible, the corporate treasurer or controller of each sample company was called to confirm the information. The post-buyout information included, and the telephone interviews attempted to confirm, the following: (1) the date and dollar value of the original transaction; (2) whether assets had been sold since the LBO and, if so, their identity, their dollar value, the acquirer, and the organizational form of the acquirer; and (3) the current ownership status and organizational form of the company.

POST-BUYOUT STATUS—PRIVATE VS. PUBLIC

Table 1 summarizes the current status as of August 1990 of the 183 buyout companies grouped according to the year in which the LBO took place. I classified each of these companies into one of four basic categories: (1) still privately owned; (2) publicly owned; (3) liquidated; and (4) unidentified. Some post-buyout information was available for 179 of the 183 companies. The remaining four could not be identified; presumably, they had either changed their names, been sold, or gone bankrupt. There was also some uncertainty about an additional nine companies because they had either failed (and no longer existed) or had been sold in more than one transaction to both private and public buyers. For the remaining 170 companies, I was able to identify their current form as of August 1990.

As of August 1990, 106 (or 62%) of the 170 LBOs of known status were still privately owned. Of the remaining 64 (38%) that were publicly owned, 41 (or 25% of the entire sample) had been sold to other public companies and 23 (14%) had become independent public companies through IPOs. Of course, LBOs completed at the end of 1986 would have had less than four years to go public, whereas the first group of LBOs completed in 1979 would have had eleven years to change their form. If LBOs are transitory organizations with uncertain lives, one

TABLE 1
CURRENT OWNERSHIP STATUS OF PARENT COMPANY (BY YEAR OF COMPLETION)

Year	Total LBOs	Status Not Known	Liquidated	Status Known	Percent Publicly Owned Aug. 1990	Percent Privately Owned Aug. 1990
1979-1980	5	0	0	5	40.0	60.0
1981	11	0	0	11	45.5	54.5
1982	13	0	0	13	46.2	53.8
1983	16	1	1	14	64.3	35.7
1984	37	0	6	31	29.0	71.0
1985	33	1	2	30	40.0	60.0
1986	68	2	0	66	31.8	68.2
1979-1983	45	1	1	43	51.2	48.8
1984-1986	138	3	8	127	33.1	66.9
All Deals	183	4	9	170	37.6	62.4

would expect fewer of the earlier LBOs to be privately owned.

The pattern in Table 1 is roughly consistent with this expectation. Just under half of the LBOs completed by 1983 were still privately owned, whereas over two thirds of LBOs completed after 1983 remained private. But the pattern is not perfectly consistent; fewer than 36% of the LBOs completed in the year 1983 were still private, as compared to almost 55% of those completed in 1981.

Current Organizational Status—All Assets

The above findings would be misleading if many of the buyout companies made large divestitures shortly after going private and sold the divested assets to public companies. To address this possibility, I calculated the fraction of a company's assets that were private as of August 1990. For each LBO in my sample, I determined the current organizational form of all of the company's assets.

If no assets had been sold as of the cutoff date, then all of the company's assets were considered either public or private, depending on the buyout's current organizational status. For those LBOs that had sold assets, the fraction of assets still private was calculated as the value-weighted average of the public/private status of both the retained and sold assets. In the few cases in which all of the assets of the LBO company had been sold, the sale prices of the different assets were used as weights. In those cases in which some assets were not sold (and, therefore, could not be valued), accounting numbers were applied as weights to all of the buyout-company assets.[6]

As shown in Table 2, the adjustments for asset sales described above reduced the fraction of assets privately owned slightly—from 62% to 59%. The pattern of asset ownership over time was similar to that for the current organizational form of the LBOs. (The number of LBOs represented in this Table increased to 176 because I was able to trace the assets of six of the nine companies whose organizational form I was not able to determine.) The 59% result represents a lower bound on the assets remaining private because it does not reflect any post-buyout *purchases* of public assets by the private companies.

TABLE 2
OWNERSHIP STATUS OF COMPANY ASSETS
BY YEAR OF COMPLETION

Year	Number LBOs	Percent Assets Publicly Owned Aug. 1990	Percent Assets Privately Owned Aug. 1990
1979-1980	5	40.0	60.0
1981	11	42.7	57.3
1982	13	48.9	51.1
1983	14	70.0	30.0
1984	35	39.7	60.3
1985	32	43.0	57.0
1986	66	32.5	67.5
1979-1983	43	53.2	46.8
1984-1986	133	36.9	63.1
All Deals	176	40.9	59.1

Organizational Status by Year After the LBO

Instead of presenting the fraction of LBOs that are private by year of LBO completion, Table 3 presents the fraction of LBOs that were private by year after the LBO. From year 1 to year 8 after the buyout, the fraction of LBOs privately owned decreased consistently from 97% to 54%. (The fraction actually increased for years 9 and 10, but the increases are based on a small number of observations.)

TABLE 3
OWNERSHIP STATUS OF PARENT COMPANY BY LBO AGE

LBO Age	LBOs Status Known	Percent Publicly Owned	Percent Privately Owned
Year 1	179	2.8	97.2
Year 2	176	15.9	84.1
Year 3	175	25.1	74.9
Year 4	139	32.4	67.6
Year 5	93	33.3	66.7
Year 6	65	37.9	62.1
Year 7	39	43.6	56.4
Year 8	24	45.8	54.2
Year 9	7	28.6	71.4
Year 10	4	0.0	100.0

---

6. Operating incomes before interest, depreciation, and taxes of the different assets were used as weights if they could be calculated. Book assets were used if operating income results were not available, and, finally, sales, if book assets were not available. In most cases, these accounting weights are based on the accounting results for the buyout company assets in the last pre-buyout fiscal year.

Time Spent Private

Taken together, the evidence summarized in Tables 1-3 shows that LBOs return to public ownership at widely varying times. Just over 25% were publicly owned three years after the buyout, rising to almost 46% by eight years after the buyout. This pattern suggests that the typical buyout is neither permanent nor short-lived.

The percentages cited above do not distinguish between those LBOs still private from the original LBO and those that went private a second time after returning to public ownership. Table 4 presents the time relative to the year of the buyout in which LBOs returned to public ownership. Almost 45%—76 of 170—of the LBOs whose status I could identify continuously throughout the period of my study returned to public ownership at some point. Forty-two of these companies went public by issuing equity to public shareholders. The remaining 34 were purchased by publicly owned companies, both domestic and foreign. For those companies that returned to public status by either IPO or sale to a public company, the median amount of time the companies stayed private was 2.63 years.

The difference between this 45% result and the 38% cited earlier reflects the fact that 12 of the 76 companies that returned to public ownership then went private a second time. Nine of these twelve were independent public companies that chose to undertake a second LBO, suggesting that public ownership in these cases was not optimal. The remaining three LBOs had been acquired by other public companies that subsequently went private themselves.

If all the LBOs in the sample had returned to public ownership by August 1990, it would have been possible to calculate directly the "unconditional" time spent private. Because the majority of LBOs were private as of August 1990, I was forced to use a statistical procedure known as "survivor function estimation" to estimate the amount of time these still private LBOs could be expected to remain private based on past patterns of change in organizational form. Using this statistical estimation procedure, I found that the median time to public ownership for LBOs was 6.82 years. This 6.82 year period, it is worth noting, is longer than the three- to five-year period reportedly targeted by LBO associations for cashing out their initial investments.

TABLE 4 PERCENTAGE OF LBOS THAT RETURN TO PUBLIC OWNERSHIP BY LBO AGE	Year After LBO	LBOs Private at Beginning of Year i[a]	LBOs Returning to Public Ownership	LBOs Censored[b]	Cumulative Survival Rate (LBOs Private)[c]	Cumulative Failure Rate (LBOs Public)[c]
	Year 1	170	6	0	96.5	3.5
	Year 2	164	22	0	83.5	16.5
	Year 3	142	18	0	72.9	27.1
	Year 4	124	17	27	62.2	37.8
	Year 5	80	7	25	56.0	44.0
	Year 6	48	3	13	52.1	47.9
	Year 7	32	1	11	49.6	50.4
	Year 8	20	1	7	47.2	52.8
	Year 9	12	0	7	47.2	52.8
	Year 10	5	0	1	47.2	52.8
	Year 11	4	1	3	35.0	65.0

a. LBOs private at beginning of year i include those LBOs that (1) have not yet returned to some form of public ownership; and (2) were completed more than i-1 years earlier.

b. LBOs censored are LBOs that (1) were completed between i-1 and i years earlier and (2) are still private as of August 1990.

c. The cumulative survival rate, S(t), or product limit estimate equals:

$$S(t_j) = \prod_{k=1}^{j} (1 - d_k/n_k)$$

where d_k is the number of LBOs that return public at t_j and n_k is the number of LBOs that have (1) not yet returned public just prior to t_j and (2) were completed at least t_j years before. The cumulative failure rate, $1 - S(t_j)$, is the estimated fraction of LBOs that have returned to public ownership t_j years after completing an LBO. (For details of the statistical procedure, see p. 297 of my original study cited in note 1.

CURRENT LBO CHARACTERISTICS

Up to this point, I have considered only the extent to which LBOs and their assets remain privately owned. Now I turn to the following questions: Are LBO companies that return public more likely to choose an IPO and remain independent or to be acquired by other companies? And after they return to public ownership, to what extent do they retain high leverage and concentrated equity, the primary economic features of LBOs?

Independent or Strategic Assets?

As mentioned earlier, whether buyout companies remain independent or are purchased by other companies has a strong bearing on the source of value in LBOs. Although it would not imply that ownership incentives are unimportant, large and quickly executed asset sales following LBOs would suggest different sources of buyout gains from those implied by the Jensen or Rappaport explanations. Gains from asset sales to related buyers could come from joint operating efficiencies between buyers and the operations sold—or from correcting inefficiencies within the seller itself. Gains from divestitures could also conceivably come from increased market power in the case of consolidating acquisitions, or even from "strategic" buyers' willingness to overpay

for divisions. To the extent any or all of these motives are dominant, an LBO is not accomplishing a long-term change in incentives.

Table 5 classifies the companies in my sample according to their current private or public status and, within that classification, according to whether they are independent or owned by another company. As shown in the table, 49 (or almost 30%) of the 170 LBOs I could classify ended up being owned by companies (public or private) with other operating assets. Because some of the purchasers of LBO companies may have been in unrelated businesses, 30% represents an upper bound on the percentage of LBO companies sold to related buyers. Most of the companies that purchased LBOs—41 of 49—were public.

I also estimated that just over a third of all original LBO assets ended up being owned by other companies, private as well as public. The fact that less than 30% of the LBO companies, and only about 33% of the original LBO assets, ended up being owned by companies with other operating assets implies a moderate role for asset sales in LBOs. These percentages are significantly lower, for example, than the 72% reported by the study cited earlier examining a three-year period following hostile takeovers.

It is possible that asset sales were more important for LBOs motivated by hostile pressure. To test

TABLE 5
OWNERSHIP STATUS

Year	Total LBOs Status Known	Publicly Owned 8/90			Privately Owned 8/90			Percent of All LBOs Owned by Other Company
		Independent[a]	Owned by Other Company	Total	Independent	Owned by Other Company	Total	
1979-80	5	2	0	2	2	1	3	20.0%
1981	11	1	4	5	6	0	6	36.4%
1982	13	2	4	6	6	1	7	38.5%
1983	14	3	6	9	4	1	5	50.0%
1984	31	3	6	9	20	2	22	25.8%
1985	30	3	9	12	16	2	18	36.7%
1986	66	9	12	21	44	1	45	19.7%
1979-83	43	8	14	22	18	3	21	39.5%
1984-86	127	15	27	42	80	5	85	25.2%
Total	170	23	41	64	98	8	106	28.8%

a. LBO companies that are releveraged by a new LBO investor group are considered to be independently owned.

this possibility, I divided my sample into "hostile" and "friendly" LBOs. LBOs were considered hostile if: (1) the LBO received or was a response to a hostile takeover bid; (2) the LBO announcement followed the purchase of at least 5% of the LBO company equity by a hostile party in the prior six months; or (3) the LBO was a division of a company that satisfied either definitions (1) or (2).

For LBOs classified as hostile, I found that 26% of the companies and 35% of the assets ended up being owned by companies with other operating assets. For LBOs classified as friendly, the corresponding percentages were 29% and 33%. Neither of the differences between hostile and friendly LBOs was significant, and thus the extent of asset sales to strategic buyers does not appear related to the presence of hostile pressure.

Is High Leverage Maintained?

One of the distinguishing characteristics of an LBO is, of course, high leverage. My own earlier study of 76 management buyouts announced between 1979 and 1985 reported a median debt-to-total-capital ratio of 88% at the completion of the buyout.[7] This contrasts with a debt to total capital ratio of only 19% before the buyout.

LBOs that remain private need not retain their high leverage. Similarly, LBOs that return to public ownership do not necessarily eliminate their debt.

In an attempt to determine what happened to LBOs' capital structures following the transactions, I was able to collect balance sheet data as of year-end 1989 (the last fiscal year-end with such data at the time I was conducting the study) on 55 of the 121 of my sample LBOs that were still independent companies. Such balance sheet data were publicly available for 22 of the 23 LBOs that were independent public companies as of August 1990, but for only 33 of the 98 privately owned LBOs.

I measured post-buyout capital structure or leverage in three ways. The first measure was the book value of total debt (short-term and long-term) as a fraction of the book value of total capital, where total capital was the sum of total debt, preferred stock, and common equity. The second measure was the book value of total debt as a fraction of the LBO transaction value reported by SDC or Morgan Stanley.

The third measure was the ratio of interest expense to operating income before interest, depreciation, and taxes. To serve as a benchmark, I compared the first and the third measures for the LBOs with those for all non-financial public companies on COMPUSTAT with total assets of at least $100 million.

As shown in Panel A of Table 6, the 33 privately owned and independent LBOs maintained high debt levels after the buyout. At the end of fiscal year 1989, these companies had a median percentage of total debt to total capital of 98%, and total debt to the LBO transaction value of 91%. By contrast, for the control sample of all non-financial public companies, the corresponding debt-to-total-capital ratio was only 44%. The median ratio of interest expense to operating income for private LBO companies of 0.719 was also high relative to the median ratio of 0.235 for the non-financial public companies.

The 22 publicly owned and independent LBOs also maintained substantial debt, but less than the privately owned LBOs. As of fiscal year end 1989, the median percentage of total debt to total (book) capital was 72%, and total debt was 61% of the LBO transaction value. Interest expense to operating income, however, fell much more sharply than for the private LBOs. In fact, the ratio of 0.276 for the LBOs returned to independent public ownership was not much greater than the median ratio of 0.235 for the non-financial public companies.

The seeming discrepancy between the coverage and debt-ratio results was probably caused by two factors. First, book values of equity do not necessarily reflect market values, especially following a large stock market increase like that experienced in much of the 1980s. Second, interest expense to operating income will decline to the extent short-term interest rates fall—as they did from the early to the later 1980s—and operating income rises. My own study of 76 management buyouts completed between 1979 and 1985 documented increases in operating income of 15-20% in the two-year period following the transactions. Such increases in operating income would lead immediately to larger proportional increases in interest coverage ratios than in book equity.

As mentioned earlier, 49, or almost 30%, of the LBO companies in my sample had been purchased

7. Steven Kaplan, "The Effects of Management Buyouts on Operations and Value," *Journal of Financial Economics* 24 (1989), pp. 217-254.

TABLE 6
CAPITAL STRUCTURE AND
INSIDER EQUITY
OWNERSHIP AFTER LBOs

	Number of LBOs	Total Debt to Total Capital (Book Value)[a]	Total Debt to Initial Deal Value	Interest Expense to Operating Income	Inside Equity Ownership Fraction[b]
A. All Independent LBOs					
LBOs Private	33	0.978	0.910	0.719	N/A
LBOs Public	22	0.718	0.607	0.276	0.390
B. All Purchased LBOs					
Private LBO Purchasers	4	0.923	N/A	0.704	N/A
Public LBO Purchasers	31	0.481	N/A	0.248	0.066
C. Public Companies for Comparison					
		0.435	N/A	0.235	0.050

a. Total capital (book value) equals the book value of total debt, preferred stock, and common equity for fiscal year 1989.
b. Insider equity ownership is the fraction of common stock owned by managers, directors, and buyout sponsors of the independent public LBOs and by managers and directors of the public LBO purchasers.

by other companies, public or private, as of August 1990. Leverage data for the 1989 fiscal year were publicly available for 35 of these purchasers. As shown in Panel B of Table 6, the median ratios of debt to total capital and interest expense to operating income for the four private LBO purchasers were similar to those of the private and independent LBOs. By contrast, the leverage ratios for the 31 public LBO purchasers were considerably lower than those of the private purchasers, but nevertheless somewhat higher than the median leverage ratios of the non-financial public companies represented in panel C.

In sum, privately owned LBOs, both independent and purchased, maintained debt levels similar to the levels when the LBO was completed. In contrast, publicly owned LBOs, both independent and purchased, reduced their leverage ratios significantly below their initial LBO levels. Nevertheless, especially in the case of *independent* publicly owned LBOs, leverage ratios remained well above both pre-buyout levels and median public-company levels.

Does Equity Ownership Remain Concentrated?

Another distinguishing characteristic of LBOs is concentrated equity ownership. Management and the LBO promoter typically own or control 100% of the post-buyout equity. According to the Jensen view, concentrated equity ownership provides strong incentives for managers and the LBO promoter to maximize shareholder value.

By definition, LBOs that remain privately owned retain their concentrated equity ownership structure. In an attempt to test whether LBOs that return to public ownership as independent companies are still characterized by concentrated equity ownership, I was able to obtain stock ownership data for 18 of the 22 independent public LBOs for fiscal year 1989. As indicated in Panel A of Table 6, insiders (buyout sponsors and managers) held a median of 39% (and an average of 42%) of post-IPO equity in these 18 companies. By contrast, the median insider ownership of over 1,000 nonfinancial companies tracked by the Value Line Investment Survey in 1986 was reported to be 5% (with an average of 12%).

The much larger insider ownership percentages of post-IPO equity suggest that significant incentives to maximize shareholder value are still present in LBOs that return public but remain independent. This was not the case, however, for LBOs purchased by other public or private companies.

OTHER POTENTIAL INFLUENCES ON PUBLIC vs. PRIVATE

The public/private status results presented above control only for the completion date and age of the LBO. This section examines the relation between public/private status and several other variables that may affect that status.

The Importance of Size

As the market value of equity owned by undiversified LBO equity owners increases, the risk-bearing costs associated with these holdings also increase. The higher these costs, the more likely should be the LBO company's return to public ownership. If risk-bearing costs and the need ultimately to gain access to public equity markets increase with the value of the LBO transaction, larger LBOs should be more likely to be publicly owned.

To test this hypothesis, I didvided the sample into four quartiles by size and then calculated the percentage of still-private LBOs in each as of August 1990. The percentages of privately-owned buyouts from the smallest to largest quartile were 68%, 64%, 55%, and 63%. Although fewer of the larger buyouts were privately owned, the differences were not significant at conventional levels.

Surprisingly, this evidence implies at most a moderate role for the size of the LBO. One explanation is that risk-bearing costs are large in all the sample LBOs. This is possible given that the smallest LBOs in the sample are valued at $100 million.

The Importance of Active Investors

Although Jensen's arguments are relevant for all LBOs, he focuses on the role of active investors and LBO associations. The primary examples of these organizations are LBO partnerships and the merchant banking divisions of investment banks and commercial banks. Accordingly, I classified all my sample LBOs as involving one of three types of buyout investors: (1) LBO partnership, (2) merchant banking division, and (3) other.

LBO partnerships in my sample include Adler Shaykin, Clayton Dubilier, Forstmann Little, Gibbons Green, Hicks & Haas, Kelso, Kohlberg Kravis Roberts, Riordan Freeman, Thomas Lee, Warburg Pincus, and Wesray. Merchant banking divisions of investment banks are Allen & Company, Bankers Trust, Citicorp, Donaldson Lufkin Jenrette, First Boston, Merrill Lynch, and Morgan Stanley. All other sample LBOs are classified as other. These include LBOs organized entirely by management and by less well-known LBO partnerships. This classification, thus, also distinguishes between the smaller, lesser-known and the larger, better-known LBO sponsors.

I found that a lower percentage of the LBOs arranged by LBO partnerships, 54%, were private as of August 1990 than that of all LBOs arranged by merchant banks, 71%, and that of all other LBOs, 64%. (None of the differences between any two groups, however, was statistically significant.)

Divisions versus Public Companies

My sample included approximately equal numbers of LBOs of divisions and of public companies. Although it is possible that LBOs of the two groups were driven by the same causes, there are reasons divisional LBOs may be different. To a much greater extent than in divisional LBOs, managers in LBOs of public companies may have been able to use their private information to buy the company at a price below its true value. If so, the gains in such LBOs would have come from information advantages rather than from any superiority of organizational form, and public companies should have returned to public ownership more quickly than divisional LBOs.

Alternatively, one could argue that the willingness of divisional managers to do an LBO demonstrated their belief the parent corporation was managing the business incorrectly. By means of a buyout, the parent could receive a high price for the division, the managers could make the necessary changes, and then the buyout company would return to public ownership. According to this view, divisional LBOs would be more likely to return to public ownership than LBOs of public companies.

Although I found the percentage of public-company LBOs still privately owned, 66%, to be higher then the comparable percentage of divisional LBOs, 61%, the difference was not statistically significant.

UPDATING THE ORIGINAL STUDY

In part because of the risk-bearing considerations, decisions by LBO companies to stay private or go public also inevitably involve conditions in the external capital markets, particularly the IPO and junior credit markets. More restrictive credit conditions combined with a flourishing IPO market could tip the balance toward public ownership.

The study on which this article is based was written in late 1990. As a result, I imposed a cut-off date of August 1990 that excluded the active IPO market of 1991 and 1992. To address this limitation, I have extended the cut-off date to December 1992 for the original sample. As of December 1992 (and thus at least six years after the most recent LBOs in the sample), 41% of the original sample LBO companies remained privately owned (as compared to the 62% cited earlier). The estimated median time spent private dropped somewhat from 6.8 to 5.5 years (although the average dropped to only 6.6 years).

It is also important to note that my original sample excluded buyouts completed after 1986. To the extent later buyouts were different from earlier LBOs, there may also have been differences in their propensity to change organizational form. For example, in our study of 124 large management buyouts of public companies between 1981 and 1989, Jeremy Stein and I found that later buyouts were significantly less successful in meeting debt payments. (On the other hand, both our study and another[8] found that later buyouts produced similarly large increases in operating cash flow.)

To examine the possibility that later buyouts were different, I carried out a similar analysis for 60 management buyouts of public companies completed between 1987 and 1989 (a subset of the Kaplan/Stein sample just mentioned). As of December 1992, 36, or exactly 60%, of these MBO companies were still private. In the face of an active IPO market (and a weak market for LBO refinancing), the estimated median time spent private dropped to 4.8 years from the earlier estimate of 6.8 years.

These updated results are somewhat more supportive of the shock-therapy view than those in the original. Nevertheless, they are generally consistent with my original conclusions. While many LBOs—probably a majority—appear to be of the shock-therapy type and return to public ownership, a significant fraction remain private, or at least maintain the characteristics of incentive-intensive organizations after going public.

CONCLUSION

This article summarizes the findings of my study of the changes in organizational status over time of 170 large LBOs completed between 1979 and 1986. As of August 1990, 62% of these LBOs were still privately owned, 14% had become independent public companies, and 24% had been purchased by other public companies. Consistent with Rappaport's view of LBOs as inherently unstable, the percentage of LBOs returning to public ownership increased over time—especially in the second to fifth years following the transaction. After the fifth year, however, the rate falls off, providing some support for Jensen's view that the LBO is a superior organization form for companies in mature industries.

The analysis also estimated the median time an LBO remains private. In the original study, I estimated that the typical LBO stayed private for 6.8 years. When updating my findings through December 1992, I found that the median time spent private dropped somewhat to 5.5 years. Thus, while LBO organizations are not permanent, nor are they short-lived. My evidence is consistent with the existence of two distinct kinds of LBOs: those in which the process of going private functions as a kind of shock therapy for accomplishing one-time changes, and those in which the LBO is an inherently more efficient form of organization.

Furthermore, even those LBO companies that return to public ownership through IPOs typically retain the two distinguishing economic features of LBOs: highly concentrated equity ownership (management and inside investors retain over 40% ownership in the median case) and high debt levels (lower than the initial LBO levels, but higher than pre-buyout levels and median public-company levels). These results are consistent with Jensen's view of the long-term importance of incentives in increasing and maintaining corporate efficiency.

Finally, my study also finds a moderate role for LBOs in transferring assets to strategic buyers through post-LBO divestitures. Just under 30% of the LBO companies and roughly a third of the original LBO assets end up being sold to companies with other operating assets. Thus, some LBOs—but by no means the majority—appear to be motivated primarily by the opportunity to sell off unrelated operating businesses to buyers in related businesses.

---

8. See Tim C. Opler, "Operating Performance in Leveraged Buyouts: Evidence From 1985-1989, *Financial Management* (Spring 1992).

■ STEVEN KAPLAN

is Associate Professor of Finance at the University of Chicago's Graduate School of Business.

■ II. THE U.S.
RELATIONSHIP INVESTING: THE 1990s

The American corporate governance system underwent major change in the early 1990s. The process of change began in earnest in 1989, when the regulatory shutdown of takeovers and LBOs created a vacuum in corporate oversight. With the threat of takeover gone and corporate boards powerless or unwilling to act, the managements of many underperforming companies faced no serious pressure to make reforms necessary to restore profitability. As a consequence, institutional investors had no choice but to protect their investments by becoming more vocal and active. And, under the spur of institutional activists, corporate boards—witness the episodes at DEC, Sears, and GM—began to display a new forcefulness.

In *"Raiders, Targets, and Politics,"* Harvard professor John Pound provides an overview of *"The History and Future of American Corporate Control."* The central message of Pound's history lesson is that corporate America has seen much of this before. Indeed, the history of U.S. corporate governance, stretching as far back as the mid-1800s, can be viewed as a continuous "regulatory dialectic"—a process in which corporate raiders prosper, are suppressed by political reaction, and re-emerge with a new modus operandi. Viewed in this light, the junk-bond financed takeovers and LBOs of the 1980s are simply the latest manifestation of a time-honored practice in which private entrepreneurs (whether labelled "robber barons" or "corporate raiders") monitor the managements of our large, public corporations.

And thus even though the new "synthesis" in corporate control emerging in the 1990s now *looks* quite different from the furious takeover activity of the '80s, there is also likely to be much continuity in the midst of change. For example, Pound argues that tender offers "will become rehabilitated." But, at the same time, such transactions

will shift dramatically to become political rather than financial devices, used as an alternative form of voting referendum. Instead of seeking to take down offers quickly and coercively, acquirers will leave offers open and let shares accumulate, using their record to demonstrate the correctness of their position.

In this new "political" approach to corporate control envisioned by Pound, institutional investors will be forced to assume the position of referee, moderating between the claims of management and dissident investors. As such, institutions will find it in their own interest to discourage "excessively hostile and manipulative dissident initiatives" while at the same time providing management with "carrot-and-stick incentives to seek active feedback from shareholders on corporate policy."

In *"Institutional Investors and Corporate Governance,"* Columbia Law School's Bernard Black reinforces and extends Pound's argument by making the case for greater institutional voice. Institutional *voice*, which Professor Black takes pains to distinguish from institutional *control*, is defined as a state of affairs in which institutional investors can easily

■ own 5% to 10% equity stakes (but not much more) in particular companies;

■ select a minority (but not a majority) of a company's board of directors;

■ talk to each other, and *collectively* (but not individually) influence major corporate actions (but without interfering in day-to-day operations).

Greater institutional voice can be expected to benefit shareholders in a number of ways: by prodding reluctant corporate boards into decisive action; by discouraging empire-building through acquisitions and thus sharpening corporate focus; by persuading management to pay out excess capital and dismantle value-reducing barriers to takeover; and by encouraging management to take a longer view of the corporate future. When set against these expected benefits, according to Black, the potential costs of institutional voice, which have long been exaggerated, pale into insignificance.

In *"Mutual Funds in the Boardroom,"* Mark Roe argues that mutual funds may be the best suited of all U.S. institutional investors for playing an active role in corporate governance. He accordingly recommends modifying the subchapter M tax rules and certain provisions of the Investment Company Act of 1940—notably, those forcing mutual funds into their current "hyperdiversification"—that now discourage mutual funds from taking large positions in individual companies.

One major controversy in the U.S. corporate governance debate concerns the one-share, one-vote rule. In *"Regulating the Equity Component of Capital Structure: The SEC's Response to the One-Share, One-Vote Controversy,"* Ronald Gilson commends the SEC's Rule 19c-4, which preserved companies' ability to have dual-class voting structures while banning the potentially coercive exchange offers (or "dual-class recapitalizations") sometimes used to achieve them.

In "*Building Relationships with Major Share-holders: A Case Study of Lockheed*," Lockheed's VP-Treasurer Walter Skowronski collaborates with John Pound in describing the company's greatly revised and expanded investor relations program, together with its new procedure for giving major investors a say in the selection of new directors.

The section ends with the "*Stern Stewart Roundtable on Relationship Investing and Share-holder Communication*," in which Joel Stern and Bennett Stewart discuss the opportunities and challenges held out by this new shareholder activism with a group of corporate CFOs, representatives of institutional investors, investor relations specialists, and academic accountants.

Why academic accountants, you might ask? Relationship investing is in part a response to an "information gap" between management and investors about corporate prospects. This information disadvantage of investors—which almost certainly causes the share values of some companies to be lower (and others higher) than they should be—is made worse by the failure of accounting statements to reflect long-run corporate profitability. Some panelists accordingly argue that more realistic accounting conventions could stimulate relationship investing by providing a "new language" for companies to use in communicating their long-term prospects to investors. (A vigorous dissenter from this line is the University of Rochester's Jerold Zimmerman, who argues that accounting information was never intended to help outside investors value companies—nor can it be expected to do so, given the liabilities now facing Big Six accounting firms.)

Other panelists—including former New York State Controller Edward Regan—discuss the promise held out by *nonfinancial* corporate performance measures. And still others, particularly the corporate investor relations specialists, discuss new trends in shareholder communication that concentrate on appealing directly to the "buyside"—that is, on achieving direct contact and continuous dialogue with institutional shareholders. Once viewed as a form of Madison Avenue PR, investor relations is increasingly being run by corporate finance people who aim to talk the language of sophisticated investors. Moreover, corporations are "targeting" institutional investors they feel would make ideal long-term partners and, in some cases, even compensating corporate IR people according to their ability to persuade such institutions to invest.

But better information is, of course, only part of the story. Besides better channels of information, institutional investors are also seeking more of a voice in major corporate decisions. Exemplifying this trend, the LENS Fund's Nell Minow describes the role of institutional investors in bringing about change at Eastman Kodak.

RAIDERS, TARGETS, AND POLITICS: THE HISTORY AND FUTURE OF AMERICAN CORPORATE CONTROL

*by John Pound,
Harvard University**

I n the collective consciousness, the active market for corporate control of the 1980s stands discredited. Takeovers, LBOs, and the associated flotsam and jetsam have disappeared. The financing market has collapsed, along with the leading investment bank that aided corporate raiders. Proxy contests at large companies often appear to be ineffective. Institutional shareholders have become organized and sometimes vocal, but have been subjected to increasing criticism and political pressure. Overleveraged companies—the apparent victims of the 1980s—search for new equity funding. *Fortune Magazine* asked recently: "Was the sound and fury worth it?" Their answer was a resolute "No."

The collapse of the takeover movement of the 1980s, and indeed the broad political backlash that it has provoked, appear to place American corporate governance at a crossroads. The tactics of the past are no longer workable; yet there are as yet no clear signs of a viable alternative. There are many calls for wide-ranging reform, and there are many predictions about what kind of oversight process should and will arise, virtually all of which postulate some kind of permanent, radical change. Many economists argue that without changes in the laws to permit the re-emergence of takeovers, effective corporate oversight is doomed. By contrast, would-be reformers like Michael Porter are calling for a wholly new system of corporate governance—one in which centralized oversight and sweeping legal changes would replace the contentious takeover tactics of the past two decades.

Given these forces, it may seem to fly in the face of political and economic reality to suggest that the death of the market for corporate control has been greatly exaggerated. But the history of American corporate governance suggests just this conclusion. History shows that there have been many periods of transition in governance similar to the one we are now experiencing. Many times before, corporate "raiding" has given rise to political backlash, new laws, and regulations—and there has resulted a temporary suspension of the oversight process. The ultimate result is never revolution, but rather evolution. After a brief respite, market participants devise new tactics that reflect changes in the legal, political, and economic environment, and a vital free market in oversight reasserts itself.

*This interpretative essay draws on accumulated work on corporate governance and corporate control contained in both the legal and financial literature, as well as my own research on the history of the market for corporate control. It also draws on my experience as an adviser to institutional investors and a participant in proxy activity.

147
A COMPARISON OF THE U.S., JAPAN, AND EUROPE

The revived market for corporate control of the 1990s will be governed by the same underlying dynamics as its 1980s predecessor. At its core will be a new class of active, entrepreneurial investors. As in the '80s, such investors will buy stakes in publicly-held corporations and bargain with management to bring about productive change and thereby realize a profit on their investment. The tactics of such entrepreneurs, however, will be markedly different from those employed by "raiders" during the 1980s. They will be less overtly hostile and less often aimed at achieving quick and complete control. Entrepreneurs will run independent directors for corporate boards, form committees to examine corporate policy, make proposals for specific changes in corporate strategy, make new "patient" equity investments in return for board representation, and make acquisitions through carefully orchestrated negotiations with target corporations and their major investors.

I call this new model of corporate oversight a "political" approach. This is because the new process reflects the rules and values that guide oversight of elected representatives in the public sector. The political model is based on substantive debate about the corporate agenda, limited suggestions for corporate change, negotiation, and compromise. Through the critical examination of current corporate strategies, the articulation of alternative corporate plans, and the mounting of limited voting challenges, the political model allows investors to address corporate shortcomings and solve problems.

This new dynamic is already apparent in the corporate governance arena. In 1992 alone, a significant number of companies have responded to pressures from investors that, while quite unlike the takeover pressures of the '80s, have increasingly proven effective in bringing about change. The names include a roster of companies with clear problems that the takeover mechanism did not and could not resolve, such as General Motors, Sears, Control Data, Hartmax, and Chrysler.

The political model is arising as a consequence of two major factors unique to the current transformation in the corporate governance arena. The first important change is the increased ownership concentration among institutional owners, which creates a more informed, more sophisticated, and more readily reachable audience for initiatives to change corporate policies. The second major development is the sweeping set of deterrents to control changes

and financial transactions encoded in corporate charters and state laws over the past decade. These changes have greatly diminished the economic benefits from the tactics of the takeover era, and tilted incentives toward the use of the political model.

To those steeped in the take-no-prisoner takeover battles of the past decade, political corporate governance initiatives may seem like pale ghosts in comparison. But the reality may well prove very different. The political model offers important benefits over the tactics of the takeover decade, including principally the ability to bring about major corporate change without the costs and disruption of an acquisition or change of control. At the same time, the political model is more sustainable in the broad view of public policy, because it reflects American traditions in the governance of all major institutions, public and private. The political model thus offers the prospect of a more sustainable governance process than did the one prevailing a few short years ago. If current trends continue and solidify, the result could be a sustainable, effective, and uniquely American process of corporate control. It would be a system based on substantive debate and expert oversight by active investors working in conjunction with—and kept honest by—major institutional investors.

THE AMERICAN ENTREPRENEURIAL OVERSIGHT SYSTEM

Unlike the corporate governance systems in other major industrialized countries—including those in Germany, France, Japan, and to a lesser degree Britain—the American system of governance has never relied on a stable set of close relationships between large financial institutions and major corporations. Rather, it has relied upon no one and everyone—upon the actions of uncounted numbers of individual, corporate, and institutional investors, operating within a deep, liquid, and anonymous securities market. Within that market, investors search for evidence of significant management mistakes—mistakes that can be reversed, and whose reversal means higher profits and an increase in share values. Investors finding mismanaged companies can then use the anonymity and liquidity offered by our stock market to secretly amass a position at current prices. Having built this position, they can then use the voting power associated with those shares, along with the voting power of other shareholders with similar beliefs, to bring about change. If they are successful, and their views are correct, corporate performance improves and share prices rise—and they profit from their undertaking. It is the potential for such profits that motivates a very large number of American financial market participants to consider, plan, and actively pursue entrepreneurial oversight activity.

Oversight by entrepreneurial insurgent investors has been generated by two central (and related) features of U.S. capital markets: their fragmentation and their openness to innovation. The fragmentation of our capital markets can be attributed in large part to a strong populist political undercurrent that pits Main Street against Wall Street. This has resulted in legal and regulatory constraints that have prevented the rise of an entrenched set of financial intermediaries with broad oversight authority, as has occurred in Germany and Japan. The absence of large institutional monitors, in turn, has created a vacuum that individual entrepreneur-monitors have found ways to fill. The opportunity for innovation has stemmed from the market's lack of entry barriers, depth, liquidity, and anonymity. These features have created the opportunity and incentive for specialized entrepreneur-monitors to arise, even if their objective pertains to only one company.

Entrepreneurial initiatives have historically been pursued through two broad strategies. One is direct acquisition of a controlling interest in the target company; the other is use of a relatively small amount of voting power to bargain, usually through public suasion. In simplistic terms, these two approaches are epitomized by the acquisition and the proxy contest. These tactics may be combined, however, and indeed they really reside along a continuum. The more voting control the entrepreneur acquires directly, the less is the need for bargaining with management or exhorting outside investors. Viewed on a broader canvas, there are virtually endless ways entrepreneurs can combine share ownership with suasion so as to exert influence on management. Tactics may be friendly or hostile, and can range from subtle negotiation to brute exertions of financial force. The entrepreneur, seeking maximum profits, chooses those tactics that combine acquisition and suasion so as to exert the critical degree of influence over management *at minimum cost*.

Having attained influence over or control of a target corporation, entrepreneurial investors can employ a variety of different organizational and incentive devices to change corporate strategy and structure. Some entrepreneurs may seek a quick one-time strategy shift, such as sale of a division, and thereafter end their relationship with the corporation. Others, with different skills and interests, may choose to run the corporation over the long term. To do so, they may take control of the board but otherwise leave the organizational structure of the firm intact. Or they may form a buyout group and take the corporation private. Or they may increase their investment through a preferred stock purchase—an arrangement that entitles them to board representation but also provides a guarantee that they may expand their influence should corporate performance fall off. These and other diverse oversight mechanisms all accomplish broadly similar goals, permitting entrepreneurs to gain influence over the management of corporate assets and impose a new organizational structure that leads to more efficient use of resources. There is nothing magic or optimal about any particular system or device. Indeed it is not the system itself that is important, but rather the entrepreneur's expertise, and the availability of some vehicle through which his or her ideas and influence can be brought to bear.

Literally millions of investors follow the approximately 20,000 nationally-traded public corporations in the U.S. Over the course of time, many become—sometimes inadvertently—entrepreneurial monitors. Any shareholder who reads a proxy statement, becomes alarmed at a management proposal, and takes action is serving the functions of an entrepreneur. In each generation of corporate history, however, there has also been a class of *professional* entrepreneurial monitors—people who devote their careers to seeking gains from undertaking insurgent initiatives. The most successful have become national figures, amassing huge amounts of wealth and power through a seemingly quick and effortless series of financial plays. The pattern is similar whether the entrepreneur is Robert Young in 1955 or Carl Icahn in 1985.

Six primary characteristics distinguish entrepreneurial investors from other market participants who also sometimes undertake corporate control initiatives. First, entrepreneurs are typically self-made individuals, unaligned with establishment corporate and financial power structures. This independence enables them to undertake truly insurgent initiatives without fear of economic reprisal. (In personality, many are indeed anti-establishment: 1960s raider Victor Muscat named his investment company Defiance Industries.) Second, raiders typically operate through small and short-lived economic organizations, such as investment partnerships; this once again minimizes both the economic costs and political visibility they risk from their actions. Third, true entrepreneurs are principals, not agents, risking their own wealth and reputations on the success of their ventures. Fourth, entrepreneurs are typically underdiversified investors; as such, they signal their credibility and "bond" their commitment to other shareholders by risking a relatively large proportion of their own wealth on individual ventures. Fifth, entrepreneurs are risk-seekers, free from legal and personal impediments that would prevent their pursuing highly aggressive investing strategies. And finally, entrepreneurs are individuals who have acquired the ability to identify corporations in need of major change and then devise effective, sometimes confrontational, means for bringing about such change.

The decentralized, market-based monitoring performed by such entrepreneurs has several important advantages over the centralized systems of Germany or Japan. There is greater specialization of labor. Oversight is not forced upon organizations whose main expertise is in other areas, such as fiduciary investment management, but rather is pursued by individuals and organizations dedicated to the monitoring purpose. There is greater freedom from conflicts of interest because the monitoring function does not have to be performed by institutions with long-term business ties to corporations. There is a far larger number of individuals devoting time to searching out company problems, and thus a greater likelihood that problems will be quickly caught and corrected. And, because of the wide audience of potential entrepreneurs demanding and producing such information, there is more information produced and disseminated about public corporations in the U.S. than in Japan or Germany.

But entrepreneurial monitoring also has two broad shortcomings. One is the potential for self-dealing. Because entrepreneurs are not long-term, visible players, there is more room for insincere entrepreneurs to bluff their way into power in order to steal assets than exists in a centralized monitoring system. Much of the early evolution of U.S. corporate law can be viewed as a game of "catch-up" aimed at warding off abuses by entrepreneurial investors as

well as by managements. The potential for self-dealing remains, however, particularly at smaller companies where entrepreneurs are accorded less political and public scrutiny.

The second broad shortcoming with the entrepreneurial system is that it can solve only a limited class of structural corporate problems. Because entrepreneurs must rely on outside information to analyze target companies, and because they take such large risks in order to signal their credibility and press for change, they cannot undertake initiatives at troubled companies with complex problems that have no readily apparent solution. Insurgents are thus attracted by simple and obvious problems such as an underperforming division, low payouts, or poor use of cash flows; they are not attracted by problems such as insufficient innovation or changing consumer preferences.

Overall, the vast amount of entrepreneurial activity in the American corporate arena, its varied forms, and the broad record of economic change that has resulted suggest that the entrepreneurial system of monitoring is robust and effective. It mimics the American democratic traditions of public-sector governance, eschewing any mandated or centralized solution to oversight, and instead relying on a decentralized system whose very eclecticism renders it resilient to changes in politics, economics, and the identity of the central players.

A BRIEF HISTORY OF CORPORATE RAIDING

By the mid-1800s, decentralized monitoring by entrepreneurial investors was widespread in U.S. markets. Monitoring tactics ran the gamut from informal suasion to hostile takeovers. At the more informal end of the spectrum, shareholders formed committees to investigate management practices, made proposals about specific corporate policies, opposed management initiatives, and pressed for enhanced disclosure. In 1885, for example, dissatisfied stockholders formed a committee to demand more information from the Broadway and Seventh-Avenue Railroad Company. "Their curiosity seems reasonable," noted the *New York Times*. "They have an inkling that their company has issued $500,000 of bonds of its own and guaranteed $1,125,000 for the Broadway surface road, but they do not know by what authority or for what purpose."

Full proxy contests for control were also widespread. Reporting on a dissident victory in one such contest in 1860, the *New York Times* said that "it was believed that the progress of financial disembarrassment under the late Board, a majority of whom held but a very small share of Stock interest, has been too slow for a property of such important productive capabilities."

Hostile takeovers became common by the late 1860s, and a first set of famous takeover artists arose, including the infamous Jay Gould and Jim Fiske. Early takeover entrepreneurs sought to acquire blocks of stock from families, founders, and institutional investors that would give them working control, or allow them enough leverage to wage a successful proxy contest. In some cases where a few big blockholders were willing and able to sell full control, entrepreneurs could accomplish takeovers in complete secrecy, without any public notice that ownership of a major corporate entity had changed hands.

Early in the 20th century, entrepreneurial oversight came to include a new, larger-scale, and more formal kind of proxy contest—one in which dissidents and management campaigned for support coast-to-coast among tens of thousands of dispersed individual shareholders. In 1915, W.C. Durant captured control of General Motors through a nationwide campaign. In 1929, John D. Rockefeller, holder of 15% of Standard Oil, mounted a campaign to oust the chairman and his board. In 1932, A.P. Giannini, founder of Transamerica Corporation, came out of retirement to re-claim control of an empire that he had come to believe was poorly managed by its current officers.

Also common in this era were proxy solicitations over specific aspects of corporate policy. In 1903, Talbot Taylor and Company solicited stockholders of the Southern Pacific Company, arguing that the directors were administering company affairs so as to favor the Union Pacific Railway, a large holder with representation on the Southern Pacific Board. In 1930, the *New York Times* noted that ten proxy contests were currently underway, only two of which were aimed at achieving control of the target company's board. At Freeport Texas Company, a stockholders' committee sought to impose more extensive disclosure requirements on management. At Youngstown Sheet and Tube, a stockholders' committee was trying to thwart a merger with Bethlehem Steel. At the Chicago, Rock Island, and Pacific Railway, stockholders opposed a new bond issue. Two contests involved competing reorganiza-

tion plans for troubled companies. In summing up this activity, *The Times* reported, "Opinion on Wall Street is that the livelier interest which stockholders are taking in their companies as exhibited by these disagreements is a good omen as to the progress of business."

In the years immediately following World War II, proxy contests grew and came to include secret attempts to amass larger and larger blocks of voting shares, presaging the rise of the modern hostile tender offer. Beginning with the period of unprecedented economic prosperity in the late 1940s, a new generation of professional entrepreneurial investors arose—one unmatched since the "robber barons" of the 1870s and 1880s.

Norton Simon was one typical example of the new breed of entrepreneur. In 1943, Simon took over the ailing Hunt Packing Company. In the ensuing years he rebuilt it into one of the largest and most profitable food corporations in the nation, whose flagship product was Hunt Catsup. In 1946, he approached Ohio Match Company, announced that he owned a substantial stake in that firm, and asked for a seat on the board. Through the mid-1950s he continued to build a far-flung empire that included Wesson Oil, Harbor Plywood, McCall's Publishing, the Saturday Review, Wheeling Steel, the Northern Pacific Railway, and American Broadcasting-Paramount Theaters. Commenting on Simon's activities in 1955, *Time Magazine* observed, "In each case, he calls his operations 'a technical service to management,' and rarely fights for complete control unless the company scorns his ideas."

By 1955, a series of entrepreneurial giants had emerged, undertaking initiatives at some of the largest corporations in the United States. The largest and most famous were Robert Young's successful bid to oust management at the New York Central Railroad in 1954 and Louis Wolfson's unsuccessful quest for control of Montgomery Ward in 1955. Commenting on the trend, *Time Magazine* noted:

An old phrase is gathering new meaning among U.S. businessmen. The phrase is "company raiding." Today, some businessmen use the phrase to describe shrewd investors who snap up an undervalued company with the idea of liquidating it for a quick profit; others apply it to investors who take over such firms and ram through drastic changes to improve the properties and turn in bigger profits. The phrase has been applied to Robert R. Young, Louis Wolfson,

Patrick McGinnis—to anyone, in fact, who starts a proxy fight, whether for good or ill, or who takes over a company. ...

By any name, company raiding or company revitalizing, Chicago's Pat Lannan thinks that his operations—and those of many other raiders—are good for U.S. business. ... Executives who are attuned to stockholder desires are faster to expand into promising new fields, and less likely to hoard capital against some distant and unlikely rainy day. Says raider Lannan: "'Raider' is a term coined by frightened managers. For every Robert Young-New York Central Contest and every Wolfson-Montgomery Ward fight there are thousands of management changes going on today. Every management change sets off the reorganization of still other companies. This is a rebellion of the owners."

In the late 1950s, a new entrepreneurial device began to appear in the corporate governance arena: the cash interfirm tender offer. The primary advantage of the tender offer over the proxy contest, according to both observers and principals of the day, was lower costs. In a tender offer, the entrepreneurial investor had only to name a price at which he was willing to buy a large block of shares, and then wait to see whether sufficient shares were tendered. There was no coast-to-coast campaign, no stream of communication and analysis, and no need to convince relatively uninformed investors of the correctness of the insurgent's cause. As Victor Muscat, a well-known entrepreneur, put it, "[Proxy fights] aren't worth the trouble. Tender offers are easier. At least the money is going into stock and not such things as proxy solicitations and court suits."

Tender offers grew in frequency and size throughout the 1960s, serving as the vehicle for a new series of corporate entrepreneurs. The increased size of tender offer targets was made possible by increased financing availability. Banks had begun by the early 1960s to compete for the right to finance bids. Such financing was "contingent"—that is, linked to the ability of the bidder to attract a sufficient number of shares—and therefore virtually costless for the entrepreneur to secure. Contingent financing meant that entrepreneurs with reputations could make bids for companies much larger than their own.

In the early 1980s, hostile takeover bids began to be financed by contingent commitments to issue high-yield publicly-traded bonds. This innovation, spearheaded mainly by the upstart investment bank Drexel Burnham, expanded by a quantum leap the scope of activities available to entrepreneurs. It enabled them to undertake initiatives at the largest corporations if their reputations were sufficiently good to support the financial commitment. In addition, Drexel came increasingly to serve as the focal point of ongoing investment "pools." Such pools, which closely resembled those common in the late 1800s, allowed a group of related individuals and organizations to continually draw upon one another for capital to fund a variety of corporate initiatives.

Also rising to prominence in the 1980s were investment partnerships, which were used by entrepreneurs to assemble financing to undertake initiatives at large corporations. The rise of investment partnerships was spurred by the emergence of institutional investors and particularly public pension funds, which made it possible to raise very large amounts of money from a few major investors. Concurrent with the rise of investment partnerships was the rise of one specific form of partnership transaction—the leveraged buyout. Large LBOs made use of the joint innovations of the investment partnership and the broad new market for public debt. The partnership provided a pool of equity capital through which the partners acquired stock ownership. At the same time, the large public debt market provided the means to raise money to buy out pre-existing public investors.

RAIDERS, LAWS, AND POLITICS: THE EVOLUTIONARY CYCLE OF ENTREPRENEURIAL INVESTING

While corporate raiding has been a constant in American capital markets since the early 1800s, there have been dramatic shifts over time in the intensity and scope of corporate raiders' activities. In active times, the frequency of initiatives has increased along with the size of target companies. In each new period of raiding, moreover, the tactics and rhetoric used by entrepreneurs have differed markedly from that which came before.

Cycles of decline and rebirth in entrepreneurial activity have been driven by three factors. One is changing economic circumstances. As broad economic conditions shift, and with them the average economic conditions of major corporations, entrepreneurial initiatives as a whole become more or less profitable. Times of economic expansion and prosperity create the best opportunities for corporate raiders; prosperous times give rise to resource-rich companies making easily-corrected mistakes, such as over-conservatism or poor acquisitions. Lean times, in contrast, give rise to resource-poor corporations living on the edge, where there is little to gain from immediate and simple changes in corporate strategy, and hence little incentive for entrepreneurs to risk their wealth in pressing for change.

The second cause of the broad cycles in corporate raiding is the cycle of creation and destruction in entrepreneurial tactics. Each new period of entrepreneurial activity is accompanied by a new set of tactics, which allows the new generation of raiders to influence corporate management and decision-making subject to the laws and regulations of the time. Defending companies and the intermediaries that advise them seek to invent strategies that make the new offensive tactics strategically ineffective or too costly. Ultimately, at the end of each entrepreneurial era, effective defensive strategies that are readily available at low cost create a temporary shutdown in entrepreneurial activity, rendering obsolete an entire generation of entrepreneurs expert in a particular, well-established set of tactics.

The march of defensive tactics is apparent in each major period of corporate raiding. In the late 1800s, corporations defeated shareholder proposals and proxy initiatives by moving meetings and changing the bylaws without notice. They defeated takeovers by issuing new stock to managers in order to lock up ownership. In the 1910s and 1920s, corporations responded to heightened proxy activity by adopting dual-class recapitalization schemes, until they were prevented from doing so by an edict from the New York Stock Exchange. In the 1950s, corporations by the hundreds eliminated cumulative voting and classified their boards of directors to escape proxy contests by corporate raiders. They waged counter-fights for control of their assailants and sold their most valuable assets to third parties. In the 1960s and 1970s, corporations adopted another wave of classified boards and supermajority amendments, and engaged in "pac-man" counter-takeovers, attempting to buy the companies that were trying to buy them. In the 1980s, corporations adopted a panoply of new takeover protections. They introduced "stakeholder" amendments and poison pill plans; sold friendly blocks to white squires and ESOP plans; changed their charters to

require lengthy pre-notification of proxy initiatives; continued to engage in "scorched earth" defenses; executed defensive recapitalizations; and sought once again to issue dual-class stock, until deterred by an SEC ruling.

The third broad influence on corporate raiding is politics. Throughout American history, there has been a widespread and profound political distrust of financial entrepreneurs and financial markets. Corporate raiders in particular have drawn suspicion and anger due to their vivid and predatory gambits to acquire companies, amass quick and spectacular profits, and buy and sell assets with vast symbolic importance to thousands of individuals. Popular sentiment about raiders can be seen as early as 1868, when the *New York Times* said that

[Recent revelations] bring to light the rottenness which underlies great speculative movements on the stock exchange. They demonstrate the manner in which truth, fair dealing, and all characteristics of a credible business relationship are trampled on Wall Street. They prove what manner of men they are who take the lead in colossal transactions, who command unlimited banking facilities, who force prices up or down at will, who damage or improve public credit and inflict distress upon the multitudes.

The deepest political ire is reserved for entrepreneurial tactics that are purely financial—that is, predicated solely on buying and selling, preferably with speed and secrecy. Such tactics arouse Americans' populist distrust of the riskiness, complexity, and apparent unaccountability inherent in large financial market transactions. Perhaps more important, they appear to reflect contempt for the American "due process" model of both public- and private-sector governance—a model predicated on open, substantive debate and a rigorously observed process that ensures full participation by all constituents.

The American political suspicion of financial schemers combines with the incentives guiding entrepreneurs to create a vicious cycle of invention and destruction in corporate raiding. Entrepreneurs seek to invent strategies that minimize costs and maximize profits. Such strategies naturally emphasize speed, secrecy, direct purchases of shares, and other tactics whose very purpose is to circumvent the costly and cumbersome trappings of the public-sector due process model of governance. As purely financial tactics become more successful, they are

As institutional ownership continues to grow and becomes more long-term—both
inevitable trends in the next 20 years—institutions will become virtually compelled
to engage in active oversight, risking both economic and legal reprisals if they ignore
their often unwanted role as swing voters.

directed at ever-larger corporations. Then comes the inevitable reaction, driven by public suspicion of financiers and their tactics, which in turn leads ultimately to sweeping new regulations. The managements of large corporations, with the resources to organize politically, often become the most effective promoters of new regulation, stirring populist fears of financial manipulators and deploring violations of corporate due process. In 1954, for example, the American Institute of Management decried

adventurers who do not hesitate to promise the impossible to stockholders distressed at the turn of events and bewildered as to what to do. They seek out situations of partial failure, not because they are imbued with a desire to institute reforms which objective analysis shows to be needed, but because only circumstances of distress can stampede the uninitiated stockholder into surrendering himself into their hands... Their purpose is self-enrichment and the enlargement of personal power.

The resulting march of regulations over time makes for a vivid chronicle. In the early 1900s, the antitrust laws were enacted in part due to the vast suspicion caused by corporate raiders of the late 1800s. In the 1910s and 1920s, a broad reform of state corporate laws occurred, prompted in part once again by popular suspicion of financiers including corporate raiders. In the 1930s, new financial regulations were laid down based on populist suspicions of unstable financial markets and unscrupulous financiers; regulations aimed at raiders included the SEC's proxy rules, the banking laws, and the Bankruptcy and Reorganization Act of 1936. In the 1940s and 1950s, significant revisions of the proxy rules occurred with the aim of constraining raiders, until, by 1956, the rules imposed significant new costs on large-scale proxy contests. The tender offer era provoked new regulations including the Federal Williams Act, new state laws governing voting rights and hostile control transactions, and alterations in the Federal Reserve's margin requirements making contingent financing more expensive and difficult to use to fund hostile offers.

THE FORCES SHAPING THE NEXT ERA OF ENTREPRENEURIAL OVERSIGHT

The early 1990s have seen a sharp decline in the activity of corporate raiders. That decline can be attributed to the three factors just described. The recession drained corporate resources and, hence, has dramatically reduced the number of targets of potential corporate raids. New defenses, particularly poison pills, have made hostile cash tender offers difficult if not impossible, and much more risky and expensive. And the political backlash against the raiders of the '80s has both provoked widespread new regulations and created significant informal costs for anyone undertaking hostile initiatives.

The current constriction of entrepreneurial activity has led many observers to argue that the corporate control and corporate governance process as we know it have essentially been eliminated, wiped out by both changing ownership structure and the march of takeover regulation. In fact, of course, the historical record rejects this viewpoint, and suggests that the current lull in corporate raiding is temporary. The underlying incentives for entrepreneurial initiatives—the potential profits from revising inefficient corporate policies—remain unchanged. When the current macroeconomic recession ends and corporations emerge resource-rich once again, entrepreneurial activities will reappear.

The next era of corporate governance will be shaped by two broad forces: (1) the legal restrictions and political backlash against overtly hostile, financial corporate control initiatives, and (2) the new importance of large institutional investors in the structure of share ownership. Together, these forces will create a significantly changed dynamic in the governance arena.

The intensity of the political backlash against entrepreneurs that currently permeates the corporate control arena is remarkable. In no other era except perhaps the late 1800s have entrepreneurial initiatives provoked such a powerful reaction. The main source of provocation was, of course, the dominance of tender offers, and their effects on the rhetoric and politics of corporate governance during the 1980s.

Tender offers were a remarkably cheap, direct, and effective means for pursuing entrepreneurial initiatives. But they circumvented the "democratic," or "due process," approach to corporate governance to an unprecedented degree. They reduced the entire substantive debate over corporate policy to a matter of price per share—a salutary development for shareholders, but a disastrous one from the viewpoint of the broad political dialogue. In the tender offer era, raiders did not have to inform shareholders and the public about their substantive concerns with corporate policy; their entire purpose appeared to be financial manipulation with the aim of quick profit. And they were tremendously, and unprecedentedly, effective. The result was widespread suspicion of entrepreneurial tactics, coupled with a dramatic decline in public understanding of entrepreneurs' motives and objectives, even as entrepreneurial initiatives grew to began to challenge the very largest American companies.

Then came the large LBOs of the late 1980s, which represented perhaps a still greater affront to the political process. Like tender offers, they substituted an acquisition price for all substantive debate about the target corporation. But, unlike tender offers, they also removed the firm from the public arena and, thus, from any semblance of political accountability. To those steeped in a populist tradition that demands openness and democratic structure as remedies for the abuse of power, the LBO constitutes the ultimate manifestation of the arrogance of financial entrepreneurs.

The backlash that arose as a consequence of these transactions was remarkable by historical standards. A broad political persecution was ultimately aimed at the linchpins of the debt market—Drexel Burnham in particular—in which virtually every arm of the Federal Securities laws was used as a lever to constrain entrepreneurial financing. By 1990, as a consequence, raiders were in retreat, some were even in prison, and the financial market that spawned the booming entrepreneurial market of the 1980s lay in shambles.

As dramatic as the backlash against hostile transactions has been, it will be temporary in its effects. Similar backlashes have occurred before. They last only until memories dim and a new class of entrepreneurs arrive. In contrast, the second broad force affecting the evolution of corporate governance—the increased concentration in institutional ownership—is permanent. It will affect the dynamics of the market throughout the next generation of oversight activity.

Increased ownership concentration among major fiduciary investors, together with indexation, constitutes the most significant and dramatic transformation in equity markets to occur in the past half-century. Ownership is fast becoming more concentrated than at any period since the late 1800s. This is conferring upon major institutions both an unprecedented degree of voting power and the incentive to

invest resources in making informed oversight decisions. As ownership continues to grow and becomes more long-term—both inevitable trends in the next 20 years—institutions will become virtually compelled to engage in active oversight, risking both economic and legal reprisals if they ignore their often unwanted role as swing voters.

The calculus of institutional monitoring is vivid. Consider, for example, an institution owning 1% of the Mobil Oil Corporation. The market value of this position is approximately $250 million. Now suppose that there is a proposed corporate event that has the potential to cause a 5% reduction in the value of Mobil's stock. The institution has an incentive to spend up to $12.5 million to research or act so as to prevent this event, no matter how diversified its portfolio. For an indexed fund, the calculus is straightforward; it cannot sell. But even for a non-indexed fund that could "churn" its Mobil holding in response to bad news, the economics are equally compelling. A decision to sell a block that large would ultimately give rise to transaction costs of at least 1% of the value, or $2.5 million. Thus, a fund dissatisfied with Mobil's performance would be better off spending hundreds of thousands—even millions—of dollars to create a change in policy than simply selling its stock.

Despite this compelling calculus, the growth in institutional ownership will not result in the transformation of governance to a centralized process, as many have predicted, in which institutions monitor public corporations in a manner similar to that found in countries like Germany and Japan. Such a transformation would be inconsistent with the broad American populist political sentiment that has always precluded the rise of a stable financial elite. It would also violate the American premise that governance of public and private institutions should remain an open and inclusive process predicated on decentralized power. The rules and regulations governing institutions already make such a process virtually impossible, by creating broad legal liabilities for active involvement with specific portfolio corporations. Should such a centralized process begin to emerge, moreover, it is likely that it would itself provoke a political reaction and more regulation—just as the current regulations were provoked by active institutional monitoring in earlier eras. The emergence of a centralized monitoring process has been predicted by reformers for over 100 years, but it has never come to pass.

[In the new "political" approach], institutional investors would deter excessively
hostile and manipulative dissident initiatives; but, at the same time, they would
provide management with carrot-and-stick incentives to seek active feedback from
shareholders on corporate policy.

It is equally unlikely that institutions will often take the lead as activists in a decentralized, entrepreneurial monitoring, playing the role of active insurgents aimed at displacing a specific corporate management or reversing a specific corporation's policies. Four broad forces will constrain most large institutions from acting as insurgents. The first is once again the regulatory structure, which creates potential liabilities for fiduciaries if they pursue risky, confrontational activity at portfolio corporations. Second, as large financial players with significant political visibility and ties to the establishment, institutions face significant potential for political backlash from taking a leadership position in governance. At the least, they could lose valuable corporate clients by appearing to become raiders; at the worst, their actions could provoke sweeping new regulations aimed at constraining their activities. Third, most institutions do not have the relative expertise in the area of active entrepreneurship. Their focus is passive, risk-averse management of diversified portfolios, which is very different from the active, risk-seeking, underdiversified activities pursued by entrepreneurs. Fourth, and perhaps most important, institutions do not have the economic incentive to risk financial, political, or reputational resources on active monitoring. Faced with pressure to maximize returns, fiduciaries might undertake entrepreneurial activities if there were no alternative—that is, if no other market participants were willing to take the lead in instigating oversight activity. But the reality is precisely the opposite. The specialization fostered by the low costs, liquidity, and ease of entry in American financial markets guarantees that a class of entrepreneurs will arise to take those risks instead. This allows institutions to assume the role of referee rather than protagonist, facilitating active oversight while not risking retribution.

The tension between the incentive to become involved and protect value, and the broad political and legal costs of such active involvement, will thus lead institutions to become more active but adopt a wide variety of compromises. The precise compromise adopted by each institution will depend on its size, client and beneficiary base, governance structure, and the preferences and expertise of its own managers. Some institutions will be content to remain entirely passive, sitting on the sidelines and voting on entrepreneurs' initiatives. Others will engage in quiet behind-the-scenes negotiations with management while avoiding the limelight. A few will undertake full-fledged entrepreneurial initiatives at specific corporations. These will typically be smaller, less-diversified, "value" investors, whose organizational structure more closely resembles that of raiders than that of large private and public pension funds. Indeed, two major proxy contests of the past two years—those at Cleveland Cliffs and XTRA—were undertaken by aggressive, less-diversified institutions.

Underlying these diverse strategic responses will be one almost universal organizational change. Large fiduciaries will take steps to ensure that, when necessary, they can engage in expert analysis and monitoring of specific corporations. Some institutions will develop the necessary expertise internally; others will seek and retain outside experts who can supply the needed expertise on a case-by-case basis. Either way, the legal and economic consequences of their ownership positions will leave institutions with little choice but to adapt their organizations so as to become expert voters and monitors. With increasingly significant ownership stakes, individual institutions will find themselves in the (often unwelcome) position of swing voter. The resulting legal, regulatory, political, and economic pressure will spur the development of new institutional capabilities and expertise.

VICIOUS CYCLE OR SUSTAINABLE PROCESS?

In the next few years, as entrepreneurs invent and apply new tactics, oversight activity will gain momentum once more. Insurgency will proliferate, begin to be aimed at larger corporations, and steadily become more confrontational and less friendly, just as has occurred in previous eras. Managements will then begin to perceive a new threat, and intermediaries will begin to invent new defensive tactics. At this stage—one which is really already underway—there will be a significant fork in the road. Two very different evolutionary paths will open up.

The first path is the same, well-trodden one of previous eras: increasingly extreme raider tactics, management opposition, political backlash, and new regulation. This is the outcome predicted by the broad history of corporate control. The themes underlying management response and political backlash are already evident. The first is suspicion of the power and goals of institutional investors, who, in the grand populist tradition, will be cast as manipulative, secretive, short-term, and seeking differential advantage over small stockholders. The second is interference in corporate affairs. Managements will argue that the new, incremental attempts to generate debate about corporate policy constitute meddling that distracts corporate executives from their day-to-day responsibilities and lessens efficiency.

The second path is different. It is a unique potential outgrowth of the current politics, laws, and ownership structure in the governance arena. That path is compromise and moderation, based on a "bargain" between management, insurgent investors, and institutions. Such a politically-sensitive, but still fundamentally market-based, solution could ultimately result in a sustainable, moderate, but effective process of corporate control. I call the resulting process "political" not just because it involves negotiation and compromise, but also because the oversight dynamic would more closely parallel that in the public-sector arena.

The political approach to corporate control would have three elements. Insurgents would undertake more moderate initiatives, aimed at securing board representation or changes in specific corporate policies rather than sudden shifts in ownership or control. Managements would respond by opening up their governance structure in incremental ways to solicit feedback from large, long-term institutional holders and thereby make the corporation more responsive to signals from capital markets. Institutional investors would act to enforce both sides of the bargain through their voting decisions and active participation in the policy arena. They would deter excessively hostile and manipulative dissident initiatives; but, at the same time, they would provide management with carrot-and-stick incentives to seek active feedback from shareholders on corporate policy.

In the short term, such a set of compromises is likely to obtain by default, simply because of the current political and legal environment in the corporate control arena, which militates strongly against any form of full-force hostile initiative. In the longer term, its enforcement will depend upon the active efforts of institutional investors.

It might seem that active work to enforce a political process of corporate control would amount to pure altruism on the part of institutions who would be better off spending their time and resources elsewhere. But, in fact, the opposite is true: enforcement of the bargain is perfectly in keeping with institutional incentives. Enforcement requires no more

than that institutions make informed voting decisions—something they must do in any event. Moreover, adopting voting policies consistent with the political approach is in the best interest of institutions caught between maximizing portfolio returns and minimizing political backlash from sup-porting raiders. By supporting measured oversight, institutions can capture the benefits of entrepreneur-ial initiatives, while escaping the backlash that will occur if corporate governance activity once again turns contentious and extreme.

As in all compromises, none of the direct protagonists in the corporate control arena will entirely like this bargain. Many dissidents will welcome institutional support on incremental initiatives, but be frustrated at not being able to mount full-scale contests for complete control of targets. Similarly, many corporate managements would prefer a system with no feedback—no discomfiting questions or activities by shareholders—to one that encourages that activity so long as it is not extreme. Each side will exhort institutions to abandon the compromise and throw their support wholly behind that side's cause.

Over time, however, both entrepreneurial investors and management as a class will be helped by the emergence of a political approach to governance. Entrepreneurs who focus on influencing corporate policy and securing incremental change will less often be annihilated by legal and political backlash, and indeed will also less often be wiped out economically by betting it all on the wrong company. Similarly, managements who open up corporate governance structures to allow investor input will gain an early warning system—one that alerts management to problems before raiders appear. In so doing, managements will increase their ongoing political capital with major investors and thus maximize shareholder support for existing policies.

ENTREPRENEURIAL TACTICS UNDER THE POLITICAL MODEL

A clear evolutionary path exists for the tactics of active corporate oversight, if they are to be effective yet also escape the political backlash of previous eras. In the short term, this evolution will begin simply because the current atmosphere demands a more measured approach. In the long term, the evolution will be sustained only if such an approach is actively supported by both institutions and corporations.

At the broadest level, the new approach to entrepreneurial oversight must be premised on an explicit rejection of traditional, hostile tactics. Initiatives can be contentious in the political sense—involving active disagreement—but cannot appear predatory, manipulative, or coercive. Initiatives must also be based on substantive debate, inclusion, and respect for due process to escape the broad suspi-cion of purely financial plays. They must seek to downplay or even avoid publicity, so as to limit the potential for the appearance of conflict. They will less often seek to secure quick and full acquisition or control of targets.

A first broad tactical arena where new tactics can and will emerge is the proxy contest. Under the political model, proxy contests will shift toward serious debate of substantive corporate policies. They will be longer than the contests of the past decade, because the smaller stakes of entrepreneurs and the more highly politicized atmosphere of institutional decision-making will lead entrepreneurs to devote more time and care to building their own reputations and image in the public arena. Contests will also become more informationally sophisticated, so as to facilitate real debate rather than hostile name-calling. Protagonists will borrow overtly political tactics from the public-sector voting arena. Dissidents will seek to build their own stature by enlisting reputable third parties in support of their cause, seeking public endorsements, and nominating independent director candidates of national stature. In all of these varied respects, proxy contests will become more like those of the 1950s—the pre-tender-offer era—which resembled national election campaigns in their scope, strategy, and tactics.

A second broad arena where new tactics will emerge is acquisitions. In pursuing takeover bids, entrepreneurs will attempt to pursue good-faith "negotiated" acquisitions that are premised on sensible and convincing substantive reasons for effecting the combination. Entrepreneurs will develop, and make active efforts to publicize, a well-articulated strategic plan for the corporation, and then use the plan to generate political support. When launching their bids, they will take their case to major institutions to emphasize their own legitimacy and accountability, and to allow institutions to escape the charge that they tender their shares mechanically for short-term gains. Tender offers will become rehabili-

tated, but will shift dramatically to become political rather than financial devices, used as an alternative form of voting referendum. Instead of seeking to take down offers quickly and coercively, acquirers will leave offers open and let shares accumulate, using their record to demonstrate the correctness of their position. This political use of the tender offer mechanism, so different from its original tactical use as a quick and semi-coercive way to acquire shares, was on prominent display in the AT&T-NCR battle earlier this year.

In addition to traditional takeovers and proxy contests, a new kind of entrepreneurial activity could arise in the governance arena as a consequence of heightened institutional ownership. Entrepreneurs can undertake initiatives aimed purely at exerting pressure for specific changes in corporate policy. In the new era, with its highly concentrated ownership and highly sensitized corporate politics, it will in many cases be sufficient just to provide information about inadequate corporate policies and thus spur debate. This will provoke change because corporations, seeking to raise capital from major institutions and always cognizant of the possibility of a voting or acquisition threat, will have to refute insurgents' arguments or eventually make the proposed changes.

Entrepreneurs could also potentially designand employ a wide variety of informal tactics to build support for corporate change, borrowing once again from the public voting arena. For example, they could revive the age-old concept of the shareholder committee in updated form, appointing a group of independent experts to study and report on corporate policy. Such a committee can function much like a shadow cabinet in a parliamentary system, issuing reports, speaking with shareholders, and generating a well-articulated alternative platform for corporate policy. This may prove to be a more effective way of promoting change than representation on the corporate board, because outside committees would be free to communicate their views and ideas, while board members immediately face constraints due to their position as corporate insiders. Late in 1990, Carl Icahn formed such a committee at USX Corporation. Three months later, the result was a significant restructuring—a result Icahn had sought unsuccessfully through other, traditional corporate control tactics for almost five years.

Even more informal and low-cost non-voting possibilities exist. Entrepreneurs can distribute reports to shareholders. They can hold extensive conversations and seek to get their message out through the press. They can submit director nominations to the corporate nominating committee—as did activist Robert Monks at Sears in 1991—and place pressure on the corporation to respond by offering shareholders the chance to vote on the proposed nominees. They can hire an industry expert to meet with shareholders and offer the expert's services to the corporation. Each of these actions is very inexpensive compared to the traditional proxy contest of the past. But each, like good political tactics, can mobilize support, put pressure on management, and thereby begin to generate momentum for change.

A shift away from voting contests to year-round monitoring where entrepreneurs continually raise questions about corporate strategy could ultimately constitute the most profound change in entrepreneurial oversight to materialize in the next decade. Much as American politics has changed in the past 30 years, revolving less around formal election contests and more around constant interaction with well-financed and active interest groups, the new corporate governance environment could give rise to a class of insurgent investors who act as lobbyists rather than opposition candidates. They could make proposals, communicate with investors and analysts, meet with management, and eventually bring about change—all without ever filing a proxy statement, making a shareholder proposal, or nominating a director candidate. Such initiatives will also have strong political appeal, creating an even more substance-and-debate-based oversight process, and further distancing entrepreneurs from the financially-based, gain-control-by-force tactics of the past two decades.

Ultimately, corporations will respond to these changes by themselves adopting significant shifts in their strategy for dealing with large investors. Rather than seeking to erect new barricades, corporations will begin to build new bridges to the institutional investment community, changing their investor relations process so as to create a more direct link between financial market concerns and internal corporate decision-making. Most institutions will welcome these overtures, because their underlying political sensitivity will lead them to prefer compromise with corporations over sponsorship and support of insurgents, if such compromise is offered. A few maverick CEOs have already begun to take this approach. At Lockheed Daniel Tellep has put in place an ambitious program to reach out to institutional investors. At Ceridian Corporation (the restructured Control Data Corp), the board has invited its top ten institutional holders to attend one of its regular meetings. In the coming decade, the more far-sighted executives will begin to embrace the opportunities inherent in this approach without the prodding of a dissident initiative.

As yet, it is not clear that these kinds of non-confrontational, compromise trends will turn out to be the new equilibrium in the market for corporate control of the 1990s. There is a natural tendency for both entrepreneurs and corporations to press for maximum advantage. If this happens, a renewed cycle of entrepreneurial offensives and corporate defenses will build through the decade. But if these moderate trends do indeed prevail, a unique opportunity looms to build a more sustainable process of corporate oversight, marked by more measured tactics, less political backlash, and, ultimately, greater long-term economic effectiveness. The emergence of such a political model would truly constitute a significant and salutary change in the American entrepreneurial oversight system.

■ JOHN POUND

is Associate Professor of Public Policy and Director of the Corporate Voting Research Project at the Kennedy School of Government, Harvard University.

INSTITUTIONAL INVESTORS AND CORPORATE GOVERNANCE: THE CASE FOR INSTITUTIONAL VOICE

*by Bernard S. Black,
Columbia Law School**

C orporate governance is on the national agenda. The press bemoans the competitive failures of American firms, including stagnant productivity in the service sector where most Americans work. Could our corporate governance system be part of the problem?

Scholars point to Germany, with its strong universal banks, and Japan, with its main bank/keiretsu system, as offering different and perhaps better corporate governance models.[1] The Securities and Exchange Commission, responding to institutional pressure, reforms its proxy rules and sponsors a roundtable on Corporate Governance and American Economic Competitiveness. Institutional investors press corporate boards to address management weakness and some boards respond.

More broadly, new academic research calls into question the belief that the separation of ownership and control in many American public companies is an inevitable result of the scale of modern industrial enterprise. Shareholders, including institutional investors, are still mostly weak and passive. Even the few "activist" institutions do very little compared to their counterparts in other countries. What has changed is our understanding of *why* American institutions are so passive.

In the conventional view, shareholder passivity is inescapable. Modern firms have grown so large that they must rely on many shareholders for capital. The shareholders then face severe "collective action" problems in monitoring the managers' actions. Each shareholder owns a small fraction of a company's stock, and thus receives only a fraction of the benefits of monitoring, but must bear the full cost of its own monitoring efforts. Thus, passivity serves each shareholder's self-interest, even if monitoring promises gains to shareholders as a group.

According to the new "political" theory, institutional investors *could* overcome the incentives for passivity that arise because each holds a fraction of the shares in any one firm. They *could* become influential shareholders and monitor corporate managers. A large bank, insurer, mutual fund, or pension fund *could* hold sizeable stakes in very large companies, and still be reasonably diversified. About 95% of the risk reduction benefits of diversification are captured if an investor owns 20 stocks; about 99% of the benefits are captured if the investor owns 100 stocks. The institutions don't need to hyperdiversify—to hold a thousand or more "names" in their portfolios—as many do today.

*This article is adapted from several of my academic articles: "Agents Watching Agents: The Promise of Institutional Investor Voice," 39 *UCLA Law Review* 811 (1992); "The Value of Institutional Investor Monitoring: The Empirical Evidence," 39 *UCLA Law Review* 895 (1992); and "Securities Regulation and Corporate Governance: Adapting Old Rules to a New Paradigm" (work in progress). Full citations to the academic literature can be found in my prior work.

1. See, for example, Michael T. Jacobs, *Short-Term America: The Causes and Cures of our Business Myopia* (Harvard Business School Press, 1991); W. Carl Kester, *Japanese Takeovers: The Global Contest for Corporate Control* (Harvard Business School Press, 1991); Michael Porter, "Capital Choices: Changing the Way America Invests in Industry," *Journal of Applied Corporate Finance* (Summer 1992); Mark Roe, "Differences in Corporate Governance in Germany, Japan and America," (Columbia Law School Center for Law and Economic Studies working paper No. 86, 1992); Lester Thurow, *Head to Head: The Coming Economic Battle Among Japan, Europe and America* (1992).

American institutions, though, are kept passive by a complex web of federal and state rules. Legal rules keep financial institutions smaller than they would otherwise be, and discourage the institutions from acting together. Legal rules push institutions to hold debt instead of equity. Legal rules push each institution to hold small percentage stakes in a huge number of companies, instead of large stakes in a limited number of companies. Legal rules make it especially dangerous for shareholders to intervene in companies in financial trouble, where the need for intervention is greatest; make it especially difficult to enter the boardroom, where oversight might be most effective; and let corporate managers largely control the shareholder voting agenda.

In contrast, rules that encourage shareholder oversight of corporate managers are few and weak. Money manager cultural norms and conflicts of interest reinforce the legal disincentives for oversight; legal rules don't do much to control the conflicts. In a different legal environment, financial intermediaries could monitor the actions of corporate managers. In other countries, they do.[2]

The political explanation for shareholder passivity suggests that managers *could* be more accountable to shareholders. That ought to be good news. Accountability is central to efficiency for any large organization, be it a government, a university, or a corporation. The other forces that tend to keep corporate managers from wasting the shareholders' money, including financial incentives and product market competition, are often weak or come into play only after much damage has been done. The challenge is to fix what ails General Motors in *1982*, when its problems were already obvious to outsiders, instead of in *1992*, after $100 billion or so had been wasted. Strong shareholders *might* have intervened—or elected a board that would intervene—before GM became everyone's favorite example of the problems with inbred corporate management.[3]

Accountability, though, is never pleasant to those being held accountable. It's no surprise that the Business Roundtable is trying hard to keep the obstructive laws in place. The Roundtable's principal complaints are that legal reform will let institutions become too powerful, and that the benefits of shareholder oversight haven't been proven.

The argument that institutions will become too powerful is a red herring. One can imagine a world where financial institutions are strong and managers of operating companies are weak. But the U.S. is not remotely close to such a world today. Nor can it become so without massive legal reform—on a scale that few support and that is implausible in light of the political forces that brought us to where we are today. The moderate reform I advocate here is better described as requiring corporate managers to *share* some of the power they now have.

It is true that that the benefits of increased oversight by institutional investors are unproven. The benefits of oversight can't be proven—*or disproven*—as long as the laws that discourage oversight remain in place. Would American companies be better off if we ask one set of agents—the money managers who run our financial institutions—to watch another set of agents—the corporate managers who run our large corporations? We can't know for sure.

We can, though, make an educated guess. We can look for evidence of systematic shortfalls in corporate performance that institutional investors *could* remedy. We can assess whether institutional money managers have incentives to act in ways that increase corporate value. We can evaluate the downside risk from reform: Are the *possible* problems with institutional oversight more serious than the *known* problems we face today?

This article begins by reviewing the political model of American corporate governance, including the principal legal rules that help to keep financial institutions passive. I then collect the evidence on systematic shortfalls in corporate performance, including the malfunctioning of corporate boards, corporate diversification strategies, takeover decisions by both bidders (who often pursue bad acquisitions) and targets (who often resist value-increasing combinations), governance rules that heavily entrench corporate managers, corporate

---

2. The political explanation for institutional investor passivity is developed most fully in Bernard Black, "Shareholder Passivity Reexamined," 89 *Michigan Law Review* 520 (1990); and Mark Roe, "A Political Theory of American Corporate Finance," 91 *Columbia Law Review* 10 (1991). See also Alfred Conard, "Beyond Managerialism: Investor Capitalism?," 22 *University of Michigan Journal of Law Reform* 117 (1988); Joseph Grundfest, "The Subordination of American Capital," 27 *Journal of Financial Economics* 89 (1990); John Pound, "Proxy Voting and the SEC: Democratic Ideals Versus Market Efficiency," 29 *Journal of Financial Economics* 241 (1991).

3. In this article, I will use General Motors as an example of the benefits that might come from greater shareholder oversight. General Motors is hardly the only case where shareholder intervention was long needed, but it has the advantage, for present purposes, of having massive problems that were long obvious to the outside world and long ignored by management.

Institutional voice involves *sharing* of power, both between managers and
institutional shareholders and among institutional shareholders. It lets money
managers watch each other at the same time they are watching corporate
managers, and corporate managers are watching them.

tendencies to retain and squander excess cash, and manager compensation. Unshackled institutions *could* take steps to remedy these problems.

I then argue that in a regime of *institutional voice*, money managers will have incentives to take those steps, and for the most part *only* those steps, that increase the value of the companies they own. I also explain why the downside risk from institutional voice is modest compared to the potential gains. By *institutional voice*, I mean a world in which
■ institutions can easily own 5-10% stakes in particular companies, but can't easily own much more than 10%;
■ institutions can easily talk to each other and select a minority of a company's board of directors, but can't easily exercise day-to-day control or select a majority of the board;
■ a half-dozen institutions can *collectively* influence major corporate actions, often indirectly through the board of directors, but any one institution can't do much on its own.

Institutional voice can be seen as occupying a middle range along a continuum with passivity at one extreme and *institutional control*—control of particular firms by particular institutions—at the other extreme. Institutional voice involves *sharing* of power, both between managers and institutional shareholders and among institutional shareholders. It lets money managers watch each other at the same time they are watching corporate managers, and corporate managers are watching them.

The case for reform to facilitate institutional voice is that the potential benefits are substantial, while the downside is small. Thus, the *expected* gains outweigh the *expected* costs. Moreover, if the benefits prove to be small, that will probably be because money managers do little monitoring (as some skeptics predict[4]). But then little will have been lost.

In contrast, I see greater risks in the wholesale reform, advocated by Michael Porter and others, that would let financial institutions control particular companies in the way that Deutsche Bank controls Daimler-Benz. Advocates of drastic reform argue that tinkering with the current system won't produce the oversight we need. Other governance models, though, have problems as well. The approach advocated here is to tinker first, and see if tinkering works.

THE POLITICAL MODEL OF AMERICAN CORPORATE GOVERNANCE

A description of the political model of American corporate governance most sensibly begins with the passivity model that it challenges. In the passivity model, each shareholder owns a small fraction of a company's stock. This creates severe collective action problems. Suppose, for example, that shareholder *A* owns 1% of firm *X* and is deciding whether to wage a proxy campaign to convince other shareholders to support a voting proposal. Shareholder *A* must bear the cost of that effort, but will receive only 1% of the gains from success, while other shareholders can free ride on her efforts. Moreover, any one shareholder's vote is unlikely to affect whether a proposal passes. Many shareholders therefore choose *rational apathy*; they don't vote at all, or adopt a crude rule of thumb like "vote with management." This makes *A*'s proposal less likely to succeed, which further reduces the incentive to make a proposal in the first place.

The political model begins by observing that passivity is not graven in stone. Shareholders will often remain passive when a sole owner would monitor. But they will still act when their private gain from monitoring exceeds their private cost. Moreover, legal rules affect the incentives to stay passive. A shareholder who owns a large percentage stake in a company will do more monitoring than a shareholder who owns a small stake. Thus, legal rules that prevent shareholders from owning large stakes, prevent shareholders from acting jointly, or increase monitoring costs all reduce oversight. Conversely, rules that reduce costs or facilitate cost-sharing among shareholders would encourage oversight.

Apathy may also be less rational than the passivity story suggests. Both a shareholder's gains from the preferred voting outcome, and the likelihood that her vote will be decisive, increase in proportion to the number of shares owned. A shareholder who owns 1,000 shares is 1,000 times more likely to cast a decisive vote than a shareholder who owns a single share, *and* realizes 1,000 times the gain if her vote is decisive. Thus, when the voting outcome is in doubt, the incentive to cast an informed vote increases *exponentially* as

---

4. See, for example, John Coffee, "Liquidity Versus Control: The Institutional Investor as Corporate Monitor," 91 *Columbia Law Review* 1277 (1991); Louis Lowenstein, *Sense and Nonsense in Corporate Finance* (1991); Edward Rock, "The Logic and (Uncertain) Significance of Institutional Shareholder Activism," 79 *Georgetown Law Review* 445 (1991).

shareholdings grow. A holder of 1,000 shares has 1,000,000 times more incentive to cast an informed vote than a shareholder who owns a single share!

The passivity story also ignores the incentives created by diversification. Large institutions typically own stock in many firms. This creates the potential for economies of scale in monitoring. Many governance issues arise in similar form at many companies. A shareholder who offers the same voting proposal at a number of companies can sharply reduce her per-company solicitation cost, yet obtain the same per-company benefit from a successful campaign. Similarly, a shareholder who votes on the same proposal many times has an incentive to vote more carefully.[5]

The first element of the political model, then, is the claim that collective action problems are manageable. Institutional investors have incentives to do *some* monitoring. The incentive to remain totally apathetic when voting decreases *exponentially* with size of holding. Diversification further increases incentives for some forms of monitoring.

The second principal element of the political model is a factual claim about institutional size. Many financial institutions are large enough to be reasonably diversified and still own 5-10% stakes in all but a handful of the very largest firms. If monitoring is valuable, large institutions have incentives to hold such stakes, and to use the influence those stakes convey. Yet few institutions hold such 5% stakes, almost none hold 10% stakes, and very few try to influence corporate actions. The central question is: *Why* do American financial institutions hold only small stakes? *Why* do they do so little monitoring of corporate managers?

Much of the reason, the political model suggests, lies in legal rules. A broad array of state and federal rules raises the cost and legal risk of a proxy campaign or other forms of monitoring, and makes it hard for a single shareholder to own a large stake in a single company, or for a group of shareholders to act together. Some of the legal barriers are intentional. We made political choices to keep banks, insurers, and mutual funds out of corporate boardrooms.[6]

To summarize: Banks, insurers, and mutual funds face legal limits on their ability to hold large percentage stakes; banks and insurers are limited in their ability to own equity at all; banks are kept small by interstate banking restrictions; pension funds are encouraged by law to take diversification to ridiculous extremes. Active 5% shareholders must file a disclosure form under section 13(d) of the Securities Exchange Act. A 10% shareholder is subject to short-swing profit forfeiture under Exchange Act section 16(b). An influential shareholder may be considered a control person, with severe consequences under securities, bankruptcy, and other laws. No shareholder can cross the trigger percentage for a firm's poison pill, often only 10-15%, without manager approval. Most of these rules apply to shareholder groups as well as individual shareholders.

The list goes on. Tax rules discourage corporate crossholdings; accounting rules disfavor crossholdings under 20%; active shareholders risk antitrust entanglements. Under some state antitakeover statutes, shareholders who wage a voting campaign can lose their voting power, or become obliged to offer to buy everyone else's stock at a premium to market! Legal obstacles are especially great if shareholders want to choose even a minority of directors, instead of rubberstamping the incumbents' choices. In many areas, the law is uncertain. That creates legal risk, which discourages oversight by institutional fiduciaries, who face personal risk on the downside while their beneficiaries get most of the upside. State corporate law lets managers exert substantial control over the shareholder voting agenda. Managers can control the voting of some shares they don't own. For example, they can park stock in friendly hands, even in the middle of a proxy contest.

What the rules don't do is as important as what they do. Legal rules *could* help shareholders overcome collective action problems. Legal rules *could* reduce monitoring costs. They *could* shift some costs to the company where they will be borne pro rata by all shareholders. They *could* limit managers' ability to use corporate funds to oppose monitoring efforts, and limit managers' power to stuff the ballot box in

---

5. Diversification can increase incentives to monitor even for company-specific issues. Diversified shareholders may take action at firm *X* partly because doing so can deter firm *Y*'s managers, who want to avoid similar attention. Also, action at a number of troubled firms can contribute to a change in boardroom culture that benefits one's whole portfolio. For example, the recent shake-up at GM will encourage greater activism by the boards of many other companies.

6. On the political history of some of the principal rules, see Roe (1991), cited in note 2; Mark Roe, "Political Elements in the Creation of a Mutual Fund Industry," 139 *U. Pa. Law Review* 1469 (1991); and Pound (1991), cited in note 2.

a proxy campaign. Yet few oversight-facilitating rules exist.[7]

Regulation is pervasive. It not only governs what the institutions can do, it also *defines*, in important ways, what the institutions are and establishes boundaries between them. Banks, insurers, mutual funds, and pension funds could each be defined differently than they are now, if we so chose. We have nothing like the German universal bank; Germany has nothing like our mutual funds; Japan has no analogue to our pension funds. Regulatory detail matters.

The third and defining element of the political model, then, is the impact of politics on corporate governance. A web of legal rules defines our financial institutions, limits institutional size and influence, and obstructs oversight of corporate managers, while relatively few rules encourage oversight. No single rule prevents shareholder action, but their cumulative effect is often enough to make passivity the preferred course.

A fourth element of the model is money manager conflicts of interest. Many money managers may remain passive and support corporate manager proposals on controversial issues, because antimanager votes or other monitoring efforts can cost them corporate business. Corporate pension plans, the largest category of institutional investor, are controlled by corporate managers.

Legal rules keep financial institutions weak. Conflicts then make already weak institutions even weaker. In contrast, if institutions were strong, they might use conflicts of interest to strengthen their monitoring efforts. For example, a weak bank will hesitate to oppose actions by a major client. But if the bank had a large stake, the client's managers would hesitate to take actions that the bank might oppose. Conflicts could make strong institutions *more* likely to hold large, influential stakes. Those conflicts would then be a price we must pay for oversight, instead of a barrier to oversight.

Legal rules and conflicts of interest are interwoven. Our rules limit some conflicts and ignore others. We tightly control institutional power and the conflicts it might bring. We could, but do not, prevent

corporate managers from coopting financial intermediaries. Instead, we let corporate managers act as trustees for corporate pension plans and let a corporate pension plan own and vote the sponsoring firm's stock. Tax rules encourage corporate managers to give chunks of the company's stock for free to friendly voters through employee stock ownership plans; corporate law lets managers sell stock and control how some shareholders vote through "standstill" agreements; strongly conflicted stockbrokers can *often*, and banks can *always*, vote shares held in street name when the client doesn't give voting instructions. Conflict of interest rules for corporate pension plans exist, but aren't very actively enforced.

Cultural factors matter too. For example, for half of this century, insurers could not own stock. Insurers can own some stock today, but they own relatively little and remain mostly passive. That may reflect the combined impact of the remaining rules, of conflicts of interest, and of insurer fear that power, if used, would provoke a legislative response. But continued passivity could also result from culture lagging behind legal change. Certainly, money manager culture today encourages money managers to try to out-trade their competitors, rather than joining with them to monitor corporate managers. If legal rules change, culture might follow, but surely with a lag.

Lastly, the sequence of historical developments may be important. For example, deposit insurance made high bank leverage possible. Competition from levered banks then made high leverage a necessity for all banks. As a result, bank equity as a percentage of assets is far lower today than when deposit insurance was introduced in the 1930s. The desire to hold risky stock positions *might* have provided a reason for banks to keep a stronger equity base, but banks and bank holding companies aren't permitted to hold much voting stock, nor to do much with the stock they own. Today, with their equity capital eroded, banks couldn't hold large stock positions even if the legal barriers disappeared.

Will financial institutions hold large stakes and become active monitors if legal rules permit them to?

---

7. In some areas of law, a baseline—the absence of relevant regulation—is easy to construct. We can then conclude that Rule *X* discourages oversight, or Rule *Y* would facilitate oversight. In other cases, there is no obvious baseline. Does state corporate law, which lets managers issue stock to friendly shareholders, even at a discount to fair market value, *discourage* oversight? Or, since corporate law is necessary to the existence of corporations, should we take this power as a baseline,

and object that other legal rules do not *facilitate* oversight by limiting stock sales that are intended to frustrate oversight? The more general claim of the political model is that the rules we have produce very little shareholder oversight of corporate managers, and that a plausible alternative set of legal rules *could* produce substantial institutional oversight.

Comparative analysis provides some clues. Banks are powerful in Japan and Germany; insurers are influential in Great Britain. Polish privatization is being designed to foster bank and mutual fund oversight of corporate managers. American insurers and banks were once powerful, before politicians clipped their wings.

Moreover, institutions own over half of the equity in American public companies—a percentage that continues to grow.[8] It's common for a company's 15 largest institutional shareholders to have voting power over 20% or so of its stock, despite the rules that create incentives for the institutions to limit their stakes in any one company. That is already enough to create some incentives to monitor. If legal restrictions were loosened, the percentage stakes held by the largest institutions would likely grow, and monitoring incentives would be correspondingly stronger. The institutions would surely do *more* monitoring if legal rules changed; perhaps they would do much more.

EVIDENCE ON THE POTENTIAL VALUE OF SHAREHOLDER OVERSIGHT

The political model makes the *positive* claim that financial institutions *could* play an important role in monitoring corporate managers. It does not answer the *normative* question: What role *should* financial institutions play in corporate governance? While we don't know how valuable institutional oversight of corporate managers will be, there is ample evidence of systematic shortfalls in corporate performance that institutional oversight *could* remedy, often indirectly through stronger boards of directors.

First, boards with a majority of independent directors—even the imperfectly independent directors we have today—perform better, on average, than other boards; yet only a minority of public companies have such boards. Second, conglomerates are less efficient than more focused companies, yet many firms are widely diversified and unrelated acquisitions remain common. Third, many takeovers

are mistakes. The bidder, and often the bidder and target together, lose market value. Conversely, target managers resist many value-increasing combinations. Fourth, manager-entrenching governance rules reduce a firm's market value, on average. Fifth, many mature firms retain excess cash and then spend the cash unwisely. Sixth, CEO compensation has escalated in recent years, is far higher than in other countries, and bears little relationship to long-run firm performance. These six areas illustrate, but in all likelihood don't exhaust, the places where institutional oversight can add value. These areas combine clear, well documented problems with reasonably straightforward solutions. Future research may well uncover other problem areas.[9]

Independent Directors

Too many outside directors still see no problems, ask no tough questions, owe their loyalty to the CEO who chose them instead of the shareholders, have conflicts of interest because of business ties to the company, or simply don't work very hard. Some recent quantitative studies, though, provide evidence that even the imperfectly independent directors we have today do a better job than non-independent directors. Truly independent directors might do better still.

The board's single most important task is replacing the CEO when necessary. Boards with at least 60% independent directors (outside directors without close ties to the company) are more likely than other boards to fire a poorly performing CEO. Since boards are generally slow to fire CEOs, these firings are likely to increase company value, and the stock market so interprets them. Stock prices also increase, on average, when companies appoint additional outside directors.[10]

Independent directors also seem to be less willing to let managers overpay to acquire another company. John Byrd and Kent Hickman report that tender offer bidders with majority-independent boards earn roughly zero returns from acquisitions, while bidders without a majority of independent directors

8. Carolyn Brancato & Patrick Gaughan, *Institutional Investors and Capital Markets: 1991 Update* (Columbia Law School Institutional Investor Project, 1991), report that institutional investors owned 53% of the equity in American public companies, up from 45% in 1986 and 38% in 1981.

9. I have tried to be conservative in interpreting the empirical literature. Often, my conclusions are more cautious than those that the authors draw from their own work. Unless otherwise specified, all results cited are reported by the authors to

be statistically significant at the 95% confidence level or better. References in this article to stock price returns are to returns adjusted for risk and for general market movements, often called "abnormal" returns.

10. See Robert Weisbach, "Outside Directors and CEO Turnover," 20 *Journal of Financial Economics* 431 (1988); Stuart Rosenstein & Jeffrey Wyatt, "Outside Directors, Board Independence, and Shareholder Wealth," 26 *Journal of Financial Economics* 175 (1990).

The board's single most important task is replacing the CEO when necessary. Boards with at least 60% independent directors (outside directors without close ties to the company) are more likely than other boards to fire a poorly performing CEO. Since boards are generally slow to fire CEOs, these firings are likely to increase company value, and the stock market so interprets them.

suffer losses. Bidders with majority-independent boards also offer lower takeover premiums. Moreover, companies with majority-independent boards realize stock price increases when they adopt poison pills, while other companies experience stock price declines. This suggests that investors believe that majority-independent boards are more likely to use the poison pill to obtain a higher premium rather than to block all bids.[11]

Stock ownership may also affect how directors act. For example, independent directors of companies that become hostile takeover targets, suggesting breakdown in normal governance mechanisms, own less stock than directors of nontargets.[12]

There is some weak evidence that the actions of independent directors may improve corporate profitability. Barry Baysinger and Henry Butler report that the proportion of independent directors in 1970 correlates with 1980 return on equity, relative to industry norms. The direction of causation seems to run from more independent directors to higher performance rather than the other way around. On the other hand, researchers have not found a significant *same year* correlation between the proportion of independent directors and various measures of corporate performance.[13]

We need more research on what makes for a good board, but the available evidence suggests that director independence is valuable. If so, institutions can increase company value by pressing portfolio companies to appoint a solid majority of independent directors, insisting that directors own significant equity stakes, installing nominating committees composed of independent directors, and perhaps selecting some directors themselves.

Shareholder attention to board composition and structure can invigorate the standard model of corporate governance, in which shareholders rely on directors to undertake the detailed, company-specific oversight that the shareholders can't easily do themselves. Shareholder oversight can potentially change cultural norms for board structure and

how directors are expected to act. Some of this is happening already. Once controversial issues—like boards having a majority of independent directors—increasingly reflect the status quo. Many directors and boards are still co-opted or asleep, but directors are more willing than they were in, say, 1970 to question or replace a CEO or other corporate officers. When the Chrysler board responds to institutional pressure and forces Lee Iacocca to step down as CEO, other directors notice. When the General Motors board wakes up, replaces the CEO and chief operating officer, and installs an independent chairman, everyone notices.

Corporate Diversification

Institutional oversight can also add value by discouraging corporate diversification. The evidence that corporate diversification reduces company value is consistent and collectively damning. Stock price reactions to unrelated acquisitions during the 1980s were negative and lower than returns to related acquisitions.[14] And stock prices often jump when a conglomerateur retires or dies unexpectedly. For example, Allied-Signal's stock rose 13% when CEO Ed Hennessy was forced out last year, and Gulf & Western's stock jumped 40% in one week when CEO Charles Bluhdorn died.

The accounting data is consistent with the stock price evidence. The profitability of unrelated acquired units either declines after an acquisition or shows no significant change, when large gains are needed to justify typical takeover premia.[15] Many unrelated acquired units are later divested. This suggests—and accounting evidence confirms—that most of these acquisitions were mistakes.

The evidence on conglomerate acquisitions is consistent with studies that relate corporate performance to diversification, without regard to whether the diversification resulted from an acquisition or from internal growth. For example, Richard Caves and David Barton report that diversification is "seri-

11. See John Byrd and Kent Hickman, "Do Outside Directors Monitor Managers?: Evidence from Tender Offer Bids," *Journal of Financial Economics* (forthcoming 1992); James Brickley, Jeffrey Coles & Rory Terry, "The Board of Directors and the Enactment of Poison Pills" (working paper 1992). Byrd and Hickman review their own and other studies of the value of independent directors in "The Case for Independent Outside Directors," in this issue.

12. See Anil Shivdasani, "Board Composition, Ownership Structure, and Hostile Takeovers," 15 *Journal of Accounting & Economics* (forthcoming 1992).

13. See Barry Baysinger & Henry Butler, "Corporate Governance and the Board of Directors: Performance Effects of Changes in Board Compostion," 1 *Journal of Law, Economics & Organization* 101 (1985)

14. Overall bidder returns during the 1980s were negative, and returns were lower for unrelated than for related acquisitions. See, for example, Kevin Scanlon, Jack Trifts & Richard Pettway, "Impacts of Relative Size and Industrial Relatedness on Returns to Shareholders of Acquiring Firms," 12 *Journal of Financial Research* 103 (1989); Neil Sicherman & Richard Pettway, "Acquisition of Divested Assets and Shareholders' Wealth," 42 *Journal of Finance* 1261 (1987).

15. See David Ravenscraft & F.M. Scherer, *Mergers, Sell-offs and Economic Efficiency* ch. 4 (1987); Paul Healy, Krishna Palepu & Richard Ruback, "Does Corporate Performance Improve After Mergers?," 31 *Journal of Financial Economics* 135 (1992).

ously hostile" to manufacturing efficiency.[16] The number of industries in which a company operates correlates with lower Tobin's q (the ratio of market capitalization to replacement value of a company's tangible assets, which is often used as a rough measure of performance), less R&D, lower stock price, and lower return on equity. Conversely, an increase in focus correlates with stock price gains.[17]

We also know that, on average, the lower the managers' stake in a company, the more industries the company operates in and the more unrelated acquisitions it makes, after controlling for firm size.[18] This suggests that diversification is undertaken because it's good for empire-building or risk-averse managers, not because it's good for shareholders. Institutional investors, who are already diversified across companies, are ideally situated to discourage conglomerate acquisitions and to urge companies to divest unrelated businesses. Indeed, institutional pressure may partly explain the trend in the 1980s toward greater corporate focus.

Good and Bad Takeovers

The evidence strongly suggests that unrelated acquisitions degrade corporate performance. More generally, takeover bidders suffered stock price declines, on average, in the 1980s.[19] Overpayment is common in unrelated acquisitions, but other factors also predict negative bidder returns. Suspect characteristics include: paying with stock instead of cash; purchase of a fast-growing or well-run target, as measured by Tobin's q; preexisting weak management of the acquirer; competing against another bidder for the target, especially as a "white knight"; low management stock ownership in the acquiring firm; and high level of free cash flow.[20]

Acquirers can suffer large percentage stock price losses for large acquisitions or transactions that combine more than one suspect characteristic. In one recent study, acquirers suffered a 4.8% price drop when they announced large, unrelated takeovers; in another, tender offer bidders that had both low Tobin's q and high free cash flow suffered average losses of 5.9%, even though an average bidder had four times the market capitalization of its target; in a third, acquirers lost 11% of the target's pretakeover market value.[21] Moreover, actual acquirer losses are probably higher than the stock price data show, because investors already expect some companies to make overpriced acquisitions.

The stock price evidence is consistent with other evidence of acquisition success or failure. Low bidder returns predict greater likelihood of future divestiture, greater likelihood that a subsequent divestiture will be preceded by poor performance at the divested unit, and greater likelihood that the bad bidder will become someone else's target.[22] Moreover, manager-controlled companies make more acquisitions than shareholder-controlled companies, and companies with low management stock ownership make worse acquisitions, which suggests that some acquisitions benefit growth-minded managers at the expense of shareholders.[23]

16. Richard Caves & David Barton, *Efficiency in U.S. Manufacturing Industries* 7 (1990); see also Frank Lichtenberg, "Industrial De-Diversification and Its Consequences for Productivity," 18 *Journal of Economic Behavior & Organization* 427 (1992).

17. See Birger Wernerfelt & Cynthia Montgomery, "Tobin's q and the Importance of Focus in Firm Performance," 78 *American Economic Review* 246 (1988) (Tobin's q); David Ravenscraft & Curtis Wagner, "The Role of the FTC's Line of Business Data in Testing and Expanding the Theory of the Firm," 34 *Journal of Law & Economics* 703, 721-22 (1991) (R&D); Dean LeBaron & Lawrence Speidell, "Why Are the Parts Worth More than the Sum?: 'Chop Shop,' A Corporate Valuation Model," in *The Merger Boom* 78 (Lynn Browne & Eric Rosengren eds. 1987) (stock price); Winson Lee & Elizabeth Cooperman, "Conglomerates in the 1980s: A Performance Appraisal," *Financial Management* 45 (Spr. 1989) (return on equity); Robert Comment & Gregg Jarrell, "Corporate Focus and Stock Returns" (Univ. of Rochester Working Paper MR 91-01, 1991) (correlation between focus and stock returns).

18. See Yakov Amihud & Baruch Lev, "Risk Reduction as a Managerial Motive for Conglomerate Mergers," 12 *Bell Journal of Economics* 605 (1981); William Lloyd, John Hand & Naval Modani, "The Effect of the Degree of Ownership Control on Firm Diversification, Market Value, and Merger Activity," 15 *Journal of Business Research* 303 (1987).

19. See Bernard Black, "Bidder Overpayment in Takeovers," 41 *Stanford Law Review* 597, 603-04 (1989) (collecting studies). More recent studies include Byrd & Hickman (1992), cited in note 11; Henri Servaes, "Tobin's q and the Gains from Takeovers," 46 *Journal of Finance* 409 (1991).

20. I collect studies on the factors that affect bidder returns in Black (1989), cited in note 19. More recent studies include Servaes (1991), cited in note 19 (cash versus stock; target's Tobin's q); Yakov Amihud, Baruch Lev & Nikolaos Travlos, "Corporate Control and the Choice of Investment Financing: The Case of Corporate Acquisitions," 45 *Journal of Finance* 603 (1990) (cash versus stock); Larry Lang, Rene Stulz & Ralph Walkling, "A Test of the Free Cash Flow Hypothesis: The Case of Bidder Returns," 29 *Journal of Financial Economics* 315 (1991) (target's Tobin's q, relative bidder versus target q); Larry Lang, Rene Stulz & Ralph Walkling, "Managerial Performance, Tobin's q, and the Gains from Successful Tender Offers," 24 *Journal of Financial Economics* 137 (1989) (relative bidder versus target q); Randall Morck, Andrei Shleifer & Robert Vishny (1990), "Do Managerial Objectives Drive Bad Acquisitions?," 45 *Journal of Finance* 31 (1990) (acquirer quality).

21. See Scanlon, Trifts & Pettway (1989), cited in note 14; Lang, Stulz & Walkling (1991), cited in note 20; Steven Kaplan & Michael Weisbach, "The Success of Acquisitions: Evidence from Divestitures," 47 *Journal of Finance* 107 (1992).

22. See Kaplan & Weisbach (1992), cited in note 21; Mark Mitchell & Kenneth Lehn, "Do Bad Bidders Become Good Targets?," 98 *Journal of Political Economy* 372 (1990).

23. See Lloyd, Hand & Modani (1987), cited in note 18; Amihud, Lev & Travlos (1990), cited in note 20; Wilbur Lewellen, Claudio Loderer & Ahron Rosenfeld, "Merger Decisions and Executive Stock Ownership in Acquiring Firms," 7 *Journal of Accounting & Economics* 209 (1985); Victor You, Richard Caves, Michael Smith & James Henry, "Mergers and Bidders' Wealth: Managerial and Strategic Factors," in *The Economics of Strategic Planning: Essays in Honor of Joel Dean* 201 (Lacy Thomas ed. 1986).

There is some evidence that the institutions can discriminate between good and bad takeovers. In Britain, which has few legal impediments to collective shareholder action, the major institutions often refuse a takeover bid, despite the resulting decline in the target's stock price.

In some cases, to be sure, the target's gains may exceed the acquirer's losses. But one-fourth to one-third of acquisitions involve bidder dollar losses that exceed target gains. These percentages are higher for classes of takeovers that involve one or more of the suspect characteristics noted above. For example, purchase of a target with high industry-adjusted Tobin's q by a low-q bidder produces negative combined bidder and target returns on average, and stock-for-stock mergers produce combined returns that aren't significantly different from zero.[24] Moreover, if investors expect some acquirers to overpay, the stock price data will understate the number of takeovers with combined bidder and target losses.

Influential shareholders could study closely acquisitions that have suspect characteristics, and object where appropriate. They might even object *per se* to a sufficiently suspect class of acquisitions, such as unrelated acquisitions by poorly performing bidders. Given the large transaction costs of takeovers, an ounce of prevention might be better than a pound of the cure that's now often dispensed—subsequent divestiture, either voluntarily or after the errant bidder has become someone else's takeover target.

Conversely, there are many takeovers—especially related takeovers, takeovers by well-run bidders, and takeovers of poorly-performing targets—that are likely to increase the combined value of bidder and target. For example, a high Tobin's q bidder acquiring a low-q target produces strong combined bidder and target returns.[25] When combined value gains are likely, shareholders can press the target's managers to negotiate a deal that makes sense for both sides.

A key factor in how much value institutional oversight can add in the takeover arena is whether the institutions can distinguish between good and bad takeovers, because there are many of both. If the institutions—or stronger boards of directors—can distinguish good deals from bad, then oversight can add substantial value. If the institutions instead act as if all takeovers are good and the more the better, much potential value will be left on the table.

There is some evidence that the institutions can discriminate between good and bad takeovers. In Britain, which has few legal impediments to collective shareholder action, the major institutions often refuse a takeover bid, despite the resulting decline in the target's stock price. And in the recent AT&T bid for NCR, many institutions opposed AT&T's bid because they thought AT&T's losses would exceed NCR's gains, though others saw only the quick dollars on the NCR side of the ledger.

Manager-Entrenching Governance Rules

A fourth systematic shortfall involves governance rules that discourage takeovers or proxy contests, or otherwise strengthen the position of incumbent managers. Adopting blank check preferred stock, a staggered board, a supermajority vote to approve a merger, or a poison pill, or eliminating cumulative voting, reduces stock prices by a percentage point or two, on average.[26] Dual-class recapitalizations by large New York Stock Exchange companies in the mid-1980s caused an average stock price loss of about 2%, even though most firms that adopted dual-class structures already had strong insider control.[27] Influential shareholders may be able to roll back proincumbent rules and recapture some of the losses, or at least prevent the spread of such rules. For governance rules that require a shareholder vote, institutional opposition is already strong enough to prevent most companies that lack these rules from adopting them.

State "antitakeover" laws also depress stock prices by 1% to 5% depending on the strictness of the law.[28] Institutional lobbying can limit the legislative damage, as it already has in some cases. The institutions can also push companies to opt out of coverage, or to reincorporate in states with less restrictive laws. Many large companies, under institutional pressure, did opt out of the extreme Pennsylvania law.

24. See Servaes (1991), cited in note 19; Kaplan & Weisbach (1992), cited in note 21.

25. See Lang, Stulz & Walkling (1989), cited in note 20; Servaes (1991), cited in note 19.

26. See, for example, Sanjai Bhagat & James Brickley, "Cumulative Voting: The Value of Minority Shareholder Voting Rights," 27 *Journal of Law & Economics* 339 (1984); Sanjai Bhagat & Richard Jefferis, "Voting Power in the Proxy Process: The Case of Antitakeover Charter Amendment," 30 *Journal of Financial Economics* 193 (1992); Gregg Jarrell & Annette Poulsen, "Shark Repellents and Stock Prices: The Effects of Antitakeover Amendments Since 1980," 19 *Journal of Financial Economics* 127 (1987); Robert Bruner, *The Poison Pill Anti-takeover Defense: The Price of Strategic Deterrence* (Institute of Chartered Financial Analysts 1991).

27. See Gregg Jarrell & Annette Poulsen, "Dual-Class Recapitalizations as Antitakeover Mechanisms: The Recent Evidence," 20 *Journal of Financial Economics* 129 (1988).

28. See, for example, Jonathan Karpoff & Paul Malatesta, "The Wealth Effects of Second Generation State Takeover Legislation," 25 *Journal of Financial Economics* 291 (1989).

We can't simply add the stock price impact for each proincumbent rule to estimate the overall impact of a number of such rules at a single company. At some point, managers may be so entrenched that further proincumbent changes will have only modest effects. For example, only firms with weak takeover defenses show significant negative stock price reactions to antitakeover laws. Still, the consistent sign of the stock price reactions to various proincumbent rules suggests that an optimal set of governance rules could increase a typical company's stock price by several percentage points.

Moreover, if strong defenses are good for some firms but bad for others, perhaps because takeovers that still occur will tend to produce higher premiums, the *average* stock price losses understate the potential gains if shareholders can approve proincumbent governance rules at firms where the rules are desirable, and reject proincumbent rules at other firms. Consistent with investors' ability to distinguish between firms, James Brickley, Jeffrey Coles, and Rory Terry report that poison pill adoptions by firms with majority-independent boards produce stock price increases, while adoptions by other firms produce stock price losses.[29]

Stock price losses from proincumbent governance rules *suggest* that such rules decrease corporate performance, but accounting studies are less clearcut. *Good* performers are slightly *less* likely than average performers to have strong proincumbent rules. This could merely mean, though, that good performers feel less need for takeover protection.[30] The greater noise in accounting data may explain why the stock price evidence is stronger than the accounting evidence.

Corporate Cash Retention

There is substantial evidence that many managers hoard excess cash and then spend the cash unwisely. Baumol, Heim, Malkiel & Quandt report that companies earned dismal returns of between 3% and 4.6% on retained earnings over various time periods between 1949 and 1959. Michael Jensen collects more recent evidence that firms with free cash flow (cash flow in excess of that needed to fund the firm's positive net present value projects) often waste that cash flow on unprofitable growth.[31] Leverage-increasing transactions, which decrease manager access to cash, generally increase share prices, while leverage-decreasing transactions generally decrease share prices. Leveraged bidders also make better acquisitions, while bidders with low Tobin's q (suggesting weak management, limited reinvestment opportunities, or both) and high cash flow make especially poor acquirers. Sooner or later, excess cash seems to burn holes in managers' pockets.[32]

If cash wasting is common, shares of companies that are expected to waste cash should trade at a discount to the firm's asset value. There is some evidence consistent with this. Mark Mitchell and Ken Lehn report that bidders who realize negative returns in acquisitions, suggesting overpayment, often make attractive targets for someone else. And leveraged buyout premiums correlate with undistributed cash flow for companies with low management holdings, where waste is most likely.[33]

Jensen's solution—very high leverage—gives too little weight to bankruptcy and workout costs. Companies need some borrowing capacity and cash reserves for bad times or new opportunities. High leverage also leads some companies to reduce R&D spending and capital investments.[34] An unfettered takeover market also offers no clean solution. The threat of takeover can discipline some cash-rich companies, but it lets other firms spend their cash on unwise acquisitions.

Institutional oversight, directly or through the board of directors, may discourage overspending

---

29. Brickley, Coles & Terry (1992), cited in note 11.

30. See Lilli Gordon & John Pound, "Governance Matters: An Empirical Study of the Relationship Between Corporate Governance and Corporate Performance" (Kennedy School of Government working paper, 1991). Gordon and Pound's explanation—that proincumbent rules lead to poor performance—implies that *poor* performers should be *more* likely than average performers to have such rules, which they don't observe.

31. William Baumol, Peggy Heim, Burton Malkiel & Richard Quandt, "Earnings Retention, New Capital and the Growth of the Firm," 52 *Review of Economics & Statistics* 345 (1970); Baumol, Heim, Malkiel & Quandt, "Efficiency of Corporate Investment: Reply," 55 *Review of Economics & Statistics* 128 (1973); Michael Jensen, "The Takeover Controversy: Analysis and Evidence," in *Knights, Raiders & Targets: The Impact of the Hostile Takeover* 314 (John Coffee, Louis Lowenstein & Susan Rose-Ackerman eds. 1988).

32. See Lang, Stulz & Walkling (1991), cited in note 20; Clifford Smith, "Investment Banking and the Capital Acquisition Process," 15 *Journal of Financial Economics* 3 (1986).

33. See Mitchell & Lehn (1990), cited in note 22; Kenneth Lehn & Annette Poulsen, "Free Cash Flow and Stockholder Gains in Going Private Transactions," 44 *Journal of Finance* 771 (1989). I collect additional evidence consistent with rational discounting in Black (1989), cited in note 19.

34. See Bronwyn Hall, "Corporate Restructuring and Investment Horizons," (National Bureau of Economic Research Working Paper No. 3794, 1991). Louis Lowenstein, *Sense and Nonsense in Corporate Finance* ch. 2 (1991), develops a case study of the business costs of high leverage in the department store industry.

> *Institutional oversight may discourage overspending more effectively than the crude correctives of takeovers and high leverage. The institutions can encourage companies to limit themselves to a reasonable cushion for hard times and unforeseen opportunities, and return the excess to shareholders through dividends or stock repurchases.*

more effectively than the crude correctives of takeovers and high leverage. The institutions can encourage companies to limit themselves to a reasonable cushion for hard times and unforeseen opportunities, and return the excess to shareholders through dividends or stock repurchases. Oversight can reduce the likelihood that managers will fritter away the cushion on misguided expansion. Ongoing oversight could also make institutions more willing to provide capital to firms in financial distress, and thus reduce the cushion needed in ordinary times. That, in turn, would limit the inevitable temptations of surplus cash.

Manager Compensation

CEO compensation has tripled in real terms over the last 15 years, while the inflation-adjusted compensation of line employees has declined and profits have been lackluster. American CEOs make far more than their counterparts in other countries, both in absolute dollars and as a multiple of average employee pay. At the upper reaches of the compensation sweepstakes, "mega-grants" of stock and options have become outlandish, sometimes approaching $100 million in value. This has led to widespread criticism of the ways in which corporate executives are compensated.[35]

The problem has several aspects. First, compensation levels correlate weakly with performance. Even so-called "bonuses" are often earned in bad times as well as good. Some top managers own enough stock so that stock price changes significantly affect their net worth, but many do not.[36] Fluctuating earnings often lead to escalating pay, as up years get rewarded while down years go unpunished.

Second, the huge gap between CEO and line employee pay may erode worker morale. It's hard to pinch pennies when the CEO is raking in millions. It's hard for workers who remain after a layoff to shoulder extra work when the CEO is richly rewarded for his "tough" (on someone else) policies.

Publicity about fat-cat CEOs getting rich while they lay off workers may also affect the political climate for business generally. And even the raw dollars have become a significant fraction of corporate profits, given that the pay of other senior executives generally rises with CEO pay.

What to do is less clear. We don't know the right level of pay. Tying compensation to long-term performance is attractive in theory, but there is little evidence that this improves performance. Many CEOs are already wealthy enough that more wealth may be a limited incentive, though if so, one wonders why they are paid so much. Conversely, CEOs whose pay is too performance-sensitive may be more risk-averse than diversified shareholders would want.

At the least, though, the process by which CEO pay is determined needs change. Today, the CEO hires a compensation consultant to suggest the CEO's pay to a compensation committee consisting mostly of other CEOs. Few CEOs are happy with below-average pay, and few boards are willing to admit that their CEO is below average. That produces a ratcheting effect as everyone tries to equal or better the average. Institutional investors could insist on a more arm's-length process.

THE RISKS FROM INSTITUTIONAL VOICE

I have explored reasons to believe that the *potential* benefits of institutional oversight are significant. But what are the risks? Could institutional oversight prove to be counterproductive? The possibility exists, but the downside risk from a regime of institutional *voice* (as opposed to institutional *control*) is modest.

Money managers, like corporate managers, are agents who act on behalf of others—beneficial owners, their own firms, their own shareholders. Like any agents, their interests can diverge from those of their principals. Nonetheless, for the most part, money managers benefit by monitoring when—and only when—doing so increases company value. They will surely make mistakes, but their incentives are in the right place. And monitoring is easier than managing. Investors don't need to be able to run an auto company to know that General Motors and American Express have been mismanaged, nor do they need special skill to realize that Mobil had no business buying Montgomery Ward.

Money managers have some incentives to divert income to themselves at the expense of their beneficiaries or other shareholders. But most money managers have much less ability than corporate

---

35. See, for example, Graef Crystal, *In Search of Excess: The Over-Compensation of American Executives* (1991).

36. See Michael Jensen & Kevin Murphy, "Performance Pay and Top-Management Incentives," 98 *Journal of Political Economy* 225 (1990).

managers to divert corporate income to themselves, even if they wanted to. They can't come close to matching the centimillion dollar pay of Steve Ross at Time-Warner, or Roberto Goizueta at Coca-Cola.

Money managers' incentives to *try* to divert corporate income to themselves are also limited. First, as long as money managers must cooperate to influence corporate actions, they can watch each other. The same institutions will interact repeatedly, across companies and across time. Moreover, one-time gains won't have much effect on the value of a diversified portfolio. This makes reputation an important constraint on money manager actions. Money managers who cheat once haven't gained much. Money managers who cheat repeatedly are likely to get caught, lose the cooperation of other money managers, and thus lose their influence.

Reputation is also important in the political arena. Corporate managers are politically powerful and eager to clip the money managers' wings. American politics has a long history of limiting the power of financial institutions. Real or perceived abuses can lead to a political response, and money managers know it. This further limits their incentives to cheat.

In addition, money managers have strong incentives not to breach fiduciary duties or other legal rules *because* they are agents and will lose much more if they're caught than they will gain if they succeed. Typically, their principals will reap most of the gain from diversion of corporate income, insider trading, antitrust violations, or other misdeeds. Yet the money manager faces severe personal liability if caught. Thus, the money manager's cost-benefit calculus overwhelmingly favors staying well within the applicable legal rules.

Institutional voice won't merely recreate the same agency problems at a different level. Money managers have less opportunity—and because of stronger fiduciary duties, less incentive—to divert income to themselves than corporate managers. Moreover, money managers will be more closely watched in their role *as monitors* than corporate managers are today. The institutions can watch each

other in a way that corporate managers cannot. Moreover, financial institutions face political constraints that corporate managers do not. Stronger oversight of public companies will also mean stronger oversight of publicly held financial institutions. Lastly, it's easier for investors to watch money managers, because money manager performance is more readily quantifiable and because investors, acting *individually*, can withdraw funds from money managers but can't withdraw funds from companies.

An oft-heard claim is that institutional investors are myopic, and will force corporate managers to run their businesses for short-term profit. The short answer is that the claim is false. All available evidence shows that institutional investors are *not* systematically myopic. R&D, for example, is the quintessential long-term investment, yet (1) stock prices react favorably, on average, to increased R&D spending; (2) if investors undervalue R&D, R&D-intensive firms firms should be more vulnerable to takeovers, but R&D-intensive firms are *less* likely to be acquired than other firms; and (3) if institutional investors are more myopic than other investors, they should own lower percentages of R&D-intensive firms, but institutions hold *higher* stakes in such firms.[37] Similarly, stock prices react favorably to increased capital expenditures, and institutions are heavy owners of firms with high Tobin's q's, which tend to be high-growth, low-dividend firms where the investment payoff is far in the future.[38]

In addition, if *some* money managers are short-sighted (as anecdotal evidence suggests), those money managers won't do much monitoring, because the payoff for monitoring is only over the long run. Pension funds, which have been the most active institutions to date, should be especially long-term oriented. That's where their liabilities are. The big institutions certainly claim to be long-term investors. Many are heavily indexed, which is consistent with a long-term horizon.

Moreover, greater institutional voice may *reduce* any myopia that now exists. Greater voice should improve information flow, and thus let shareholders rely less on short-term earnings as a

37. See Su Chan, John Martin & John Kensinger, "Corporate Research and Development Expenditures and Share Value," 26 *Journal of Financial Economics* 255 (1990); Gregg Jarrell, Kenneth Lehn & Wayne Marr, "Institutional Ownership, Tender Offers, and Long-Term Investments" (Securities & Exchange Commission, Office of Economic Analysis, 1985); J. Randall Woolridge, "Competitive Decline and Corporate Restructuring: Is a Myopic Stock Market to Blame?," *Journal of Applied Corporate Finance* 26 (Spring 1988); Jonathan Jones, Kenneth Lehn & Harold Mulherin, "Institutional Ownership of Equity: Effects on Stock Market

Liquidity and Corporate Long-Term Investments," in *Institutional Investing: Challenges and Responsibilities of the 21st Century* 115 (Arnold Sametz & James Bicksler eds. 1991).

38. See John McConnell & Chris Muscarella, "Corporate Capital Expenditure Decisions and the Market Value of the Firm," 14 *Journal of Financial Economics* 399 (1985); Woolridge (1988), cited in note 48; Comment & Jarrell (1991), cited in note 17; John McConnell & Henri Servaes, "Additional Evidence on Equity Ownership and Corporate Value," 27 *Journal of Financial Economics* 595 (1990).

signal of long-term value. Greater ability to monitor may also make institutions more willing to make long-term investments. One does not, after all, hear complaints that Japanese and German banks, who can exercise effective voice, do so myopically. Voice can be an alternative to a quick exit.

CONCLUSION

The central problem of corporate law in this century has been who, if anyone, will watch the managers who run our large public corporations. Oversight by institutional shareholders can't solve that problem by itself. But institutional oversight, through a mixture of formal voting initiatives and informal persuasion, can serve as one strand in a web of imperfect constraints on managerial discretion. Other constraints include the product, capital, and labor markets, corporate takeovers, management incentive compensation arrangements, creditor oversight, bankruptcy risk, fiduciary duty, and cultural norms.

Institutional oversight can sometimes complement, sometimes replace, and sometimes strengthen other constraints. Consider, for example, the interplay between institutional oversight and takeovers. Institutional oversight can *complement* takeovers by permitting a change of *management*, or closer oversight of the current managers, without the need for a costly and disruptive change of *ownership*. Oversight can partly *replace* takeovers by reducing the number of firms that are managed badly enough to justify a takeover at a typical 50% premium to market. Oversight can also *strengthen* the takeover constraint by limiting defensive tactics and discouraging misguided acquisitions, so that the takeover mechanism operates more smoothly.

The test for the desirability of reform is not whether institutional oversight is free from risk, nor whether institutional oversight is ideal. Institutional shareholders are imperfect monitors. But they're the only monitors we've got, and there is much that they *could* do. The policy question is whether oversight by institutional shareholders is better than no shareholder oversight. Should we rely exclusively on the other imperfect constraints on corporate managers? Or should we add one more imperfect constraint to the mix?

Some risk of institutional abuse of power exists. But we need to balance the *risk* of such abuses against the potential monitoring gains, and against

the *certainty* of continued abuses by corporate managers under the current system. The goal should be to find a rough optimum in which there is some institutional oversight, some risk of institutional abuse of power, and some continued corporate manager abuse of discretion. The claim here is that the risks from a regime of institutional voice are modest, and likely to be outweighed by the expected benefits.

Ultimately, the case for reform is: Let's try it and see if it helps. If the institutions become active monitors, benefits are likely to exceed costs. The institutions have incentives to monitor only if they believe that the gains outweigh the associated costs. Indeed, because of collective action problems, the institutions will monitor only if they believe that the gains are a *multiple* of the related costs. If the institutions don't become active monitors, both benefits and costs should be small.

The case for reform is strengthened because reform needn't be permanent. If unexpected problems arise, legal rules can again restrict institutional power. History tells us that power-limiting rules are politically feasible, if they are needed. Moreover, legal reform is likely to take place at a measured pace. Early reforms, such as the SEC's recent proxy rule changes, will let us learn more about institutional oversight, and the potential gains and risks from institutional voice. There will be time enough to stop, in the unlikely event that institutional abuse of power becomes prevalent.

Reform, though, should emphasize the *process* of shareholder voting, not substantive governance rules. Should the CEO also chair the board of directors? Should CEO compensation be heavily stock-based? Should large shareholders select some board members? We simply don't know whether these and other changes will help corporate performance, nor whether the answers vary across firms. Lawmakers shouldn't guess at the answers. Instead, they should empower shareholders to make their own decisions about when monitoring is valuable. Shareholders ought, on average, to make better choices than lawmakers. Shareholders are also better able than lawmakers to correct their mistakes, and have stronger incentives to do so.

An assessment of what institutional shareholders *can* do must be tempered by recognition of what they *can't* do. The institutions have neither skill nor time nor incentives to question ordinary business decisions. This is probably just as well, because corporate managers need freedom to take risks and make mistakes. We can, though, expect that large shareholders can structure the managers' incentives to be more congruent with shareholder incentives, discourage actions such as diversification that benefit managers but not shareholders, and step in when the managers, having been given enough rope to hang themselves, do so repeatedly. We can hope that the average quality of management improves, even if many weak managers remain.

To move toward a world of institutional voice, we partly need to reduce the legal obstacles that now exist. But we also need to affirmatively encourage voice. We need not just to *deregulate*, but to regulate *differently*. We need to redefine the role of institutional shareholders so that the institutions *will* monitor if monitoring is valuable.

For example, part of working together will often be cost-sharing, which reduces collective action barriers to oversight. We can reduce regulatory barriers to cost-sharing by *not* applying rules that govern individual shareholders of a specified size to a loose cost-sharing group that isn't trying to exercise control. But we can also take positive steps to shift some costs of shareholder action to the firm—for example, by changing the rules to allow investor access to the company proxy statement. We also need to limit corporate managers' control over the shareholder voting agenda, their ability to stuff the ballot box, and their efforts to exploit money manager conflicts of interest.

In addition to facilitating cost-sharing and cost-shifting, we need to reduce the costs that active shareholders incur in the first place, and the procedural hurdles they must surmount. Examples include easy access to the shareholder list that the company already has, which reduces shareholder cost at trivial cost to the company; deregulating institutional proxy solicitation; and letting shareholders respond to a manager proposal in the company proxy statement.

The focus of reform must be on invigorating *institutional* oversight of corporate managers. There is no hope, now or ever, of sustained oversight of corporate managers by individual investors. Individual investors are too small; collective action problems are overwhelming. But if institutional oversight increases company value, small shareholders will benefit too. Small shareholders are at risk only if the institutions use their influence to transfer corporate wealth to themselves at the expense of other shareholders, in amounts that *exceed* the monitoring gains. But it is precisely this danger that reform *limited to institutional voice* is intended to avert.

Eventually, we will have to face the question of the stopping place. Where do we draw the rough line between institutional *voice* and institutional *control?* How do we discourage control without unduly chilling voice? But for now, and for some time to come, the regulatory task is easy. Legal rules keep institutions far toward the passivity extreme of a continuum running from passivity to control. We ought to move toward the middle of the continuum—toward the world that I have called institutional voice. This article has documented the substantial upside from such changes, and explored why the downside risk is limited. That makes reform a good, though not a certain, bet.

■ BERNARD BLACK

is Professor of Law at Columbia University School of Law. He has written extensively on corporate governance issues, including "Agents Watching Agents: The Promise of Institutional Investor Voice," 39 *UCLA Law Review* 895 (1992), and "Shareholder Passivity Reexamined," 89 *Michigan Law Review* 520 (1990).

MUTUAL FUNDS IN THE BOARDROOM

by Mark J. Roe,
Columbia Law School*

T he primary mission of mutual fund regulation has been to protect the small investor. While this goal should remain primary, we need to add the goal of improving corporate governance. Mutual funds could be more useful in corporate boardrooms. But do the Investment Company Act of 1940 and subchapter M's tax rules make a useful role more difficult than it has to be?

Adolf Berle and Gardiner Means articulated the dominant paradigm for understanding the large public firm, just prior to passage of the 1933 Act and the founding of the SEC. Huge capital needs dictated by technology required that large enterprise raise money from far-flung investors who, with their own diversification needs, took small bits of a company's equity. This atomization of shareholding shifted power from shareholders to managers. The securities laws mitigate many problems arising from that shift by facilitating and mandating information flow from inside the firm to outside. Because this shift of power from shareholders to managers has, until recently, been seen as inevitable, we could pursue goals such as protecting the small investor and fostering corporate democracy without wondering if protective rules also facilitated a shift in power to managers. If the shift was inevitable, a rule that encouraged the shift just hastened or intensified the inevitable.

A closer reading of history, however, and a quick look at other nations suggests that there's more to the story than technology and scale economies dictating an inevitable shift from shareholders to managers. Firms could instead have raised capital from far-flung investors *through* large, powerful financial intermediaries. The intermediaries could then have sat in corporate boardrooms and balanced authority with the CEO. Moreover, if there's a short-term bias in the stock market, intermediaries with big blocks could help remedy the problem. Soft and proprietary information does not flow easily to securities traders. It would flow better to big stable blockholders who sit in the boardroom.

For better or worse, Germany and Japan have had financial institutions—usually banks or insurers—with a big role in firm governance. We could not, even if we wanted to, replicate the foreign systems here, if only because American banks and most insurers are not now strong enough. Bank regulation and extensive deposit insurance also make the task too risky.

If there is a value to institutions with big blocks sitting in the boardroom, mutual funds are a good place to start, because for them the costs of error are low. If an experiment with mutual funds fails, the errant mutual funds are easily disbanded or reconstructed. Failed banks with deposit insurance cannot so easily be changed.

Mutual funds rarely participate in corporate governance. They are intermediaries that channel funds from disparate individuals into investments. They gather and process information about industrial investments that their owners cannot easily gather and process. They do the paperwork that individuals begrudge. Yet they are not usually intermediaries in the sense that they take the funds of disparate investors, invest them in concentrated holdings in America's largest companies, and then enter the corporate boardroom to represent their shareholder beneficiaries.

*This article is based on my previously published articles, "Political Elements in the Creation of a Mutual Fund Industry," 139 *University of Pennsylvania Law* *Review* 1469 (1991), and "A Political Theory of American Corporate Finance," 91 *Columbia Law Review* 10 (1991).

In the 1930s some mutual funds began to act as monitoring intermediaries. They underwrote securities, became active players in bankruptcy reorganizations, and participated in management.[1] The 1936 tax act, followed up by the 1940 Investment Company Act, induced them to stop and become more passive. Passivity rules were not unintended. The Administration and Congress *wanted* to eliminate mutual fund (and other banker) control of industrial companies. Explanations for the severance can be seen in (1) popular opinion that mistrusted large financial institutions, (2) public-spirited rules intended to foster stable mutual funds for the average investor, (3) the accidents of tax doctrine, and (4) a glimmer of an interest group story as some political actors decided to favor local managers over Wall Street.

In 1937, while chair of the SEC, William O. Douglas told a stunned audience that included nearly every important Wall Street investment banker:

[T]he banker [should and will be] restricted to...underwriting or selling. Insofar as management [and] formulation of industrial policies...the banker will be superseded. The financial power which he has exercised in the past over such processes will pass into other hands.[2]

THE 1940 ACT RESTRICTIONS

When Congress passed the 1940 Act, cognoscenti recognized that the mutual fund offered a third function, beyond diversification and expert management: "[the investor] may be able to join in the purchase of control of one or more other corporations."[3] But Congress disliked mutual funds with control. Only unscrupulous financiers mixed investment with control: "The investment company [has] become the instrumentality of financiers and industrialists to facilitate acquisition of concentrated control of the wealth and industries of the country." Congress must "prevent the diversion of these [investment] trusts from their normal channels of diversified investment to the *abnormal* avenues of control of industry..." Congress might have "to completely divorce investment trusts from investment banking..." Congress thereafter directed the SEC to draft legislation.

The SEC declared in its proposed bill that "the national public interest...is adversely affected...when investment companies [have] great size [and] have excessive influence on the national economy." A good many of the 1940 Act rules (and perhaps other early SEC rules) should be seen as coming out of this now-forgotten goal. In 1935, 56 investment companies had controlling interests in 187 portfolio companies.[4] The SEC thought that little good could come out of investment company control over portfolio companies. The investment company might fail, due to the lack of diversification. It might pump money into the portfolio company to protect a large position. It might unwisely change the financial policy or capital structure of the portfolio company; it might force dividends out at too high a rate. Finally, it might force a merger on terms disadvantageous to minority interests in the controlled company.[5]

The SEC conceded that mutual fund control could help resolve the informational and organizational problems of scattered shareholders; as sophisticated investors with specialized personnel, the investment company would have expertise, the motivation to improve managerial performance, and the financial clout to see their views implemented.[6] Nevertheless, the disadvantages of investment companies with the power to control outweighed the advantages. The SEC wanted mutual fund directors and employees off the boards of all portfolio companies; they wanted a Glass-Steagall-type severance. Eventually the SEC had to compromise with the mutual fund industry, but it still achieved a great deal of severance.

Diversification. A mutual fund cannot advertise itself as diversified if it owns in the regulated part of its portfolio more than 10% of the stock of any

1. Several 1930s congressional and administrative documents are the source for the analysis here: Stock Exchange Practices: Report of the Comm. on Currency and Banking, S. Rep. No. 1455, 73d Cong., 2d Sess. 333-34, 363, 381-2, 393 (1934) [sometimes known as the Pecora Report, in reference to its final chief counsel]; SEC, Report on the Study of Investment Trusts and Investment Companies 8, 22, 370-721, 2624 (1939-1942); SEC, Abuses and Deficiencies in the Organization and Operation of Investment Trusts and Investment Companies, Pt. III, H.R. Doc. No. 270, 76th Cong., 1st Sess. 2501 (1939); Hearings on S. 3580 Before Subcomm. of the Sen. Comm. on Banking and Currency, Investment Trusts, and Investment Companies, Pt. I, 76th Cong., 3d Sess. 36, 131-32, 206-07,

216-20, 807 (1940). The reader can find details on the cited materials in the articles I referred to in footnote 1.

2. William O. Douglas, *Democracy and Finance* 32, 41 (1940).

3. See Alfred Jaretzki, The Investment Company Act of 1940, 26 Wash. U.L.Q. 303, 305 (1941) (Jaretzki represented a group of investment companies at congressional 1940 Act hearings).

4. Wharton School of Finance and Commerce, A Study Prepared for the SEC, H.Rep. No. 2274, 87th Cong., 2d Sess. 399 (1962).

5. Ibid., at 400.

6. Ibid., at 400.

company. Three-quarters of the portfolio is subject to this fragmentation rule, *even if* that influential block of stock is a small portion of the fund's portfolio.

The disclosure elements makes sense. The 10% limit does not. A mutual fund might be diversified, yet hold a big percentage of a firm, with that block still a small percentage of the fund's portfolio. The hidden goal was to reduce control, not to promote diversification. (The big block might raise liquidity disclosure problems, to be discussed below. But this is a different problem.)

Networks and affiliates. The 1940 Act leaves a quarter of the portfolio free from the fragmentation rules; and theoretically the fund could choose not to call itself diversified and then not be subject to the fragmentation rules. (I say theoretically because as the next section shows, penalty tax rules track the 1940 Act rules.)

For the part that could be concentrated, other restrictions apply. True, the 1940 Act does not expressly prohibit a mutual fund or its employees from sitting on the board of a portfolio firm. But if a fund owned 5% of a portfolio firm's stock, or sat on its board, the firm would become a statutory affiliate of the fund *and* others owning 5% of the portfolio firm.[7] Various recapitalizations could not then go forward without SEC exemption. The SEC's blanket exemptions seem not to apply if anyone involved, such as a deputized director, gets incentive compensation.[8] SEC rules also prohibit joint affiliate action without SEC exemption; again, current blanket exemptions may not cover what could be typical efforts at joint influence.[9] Yet, to be effective in the boardroom, mutual funds might ally with others. Moreover, the statute and the SEC's Section 17 rules here are unusually opaque.[10] While joint action has the potential for abuse, blanket rules similar to those promulgated in the 1980s, but improved, might exempt those settings where abuse is unlikely.

Interplay with 16B and 13(d) is a problem. If a director's seat is attributed to the fund, the fund must return any "short-swing" trading profits. This poses a problem because open-end mutual funds cannot help but engage in some trading, because of their own shareholders' redemptions and purchases. Mutual funds should rightfully fear that application of a deputization doctrine—that a portfolio firm's director who is close to the mutual funds will be seen as the funds' agent—will trigger unwanted legal obligations, irrespective of the size of the mutual funds' ownership of the portfolio firm. If groups of funds joined together to send in a director, they too would have reason to be wary of application of a deputization doctrine. Moreover, group action triggers filing requirements, if 16(a) tracks 13(d), meaning that the funds must constantly file and re-file and worry that others in the group might forget a timely filing.

Subchapter M of the Internal Revenue Code. The mutual fund that would control would be taxed unfavorably on its *entire* portfolio, since the tax code allows only *diversified* mutual funds to pass income through to shareholders, without levying taxes on the conduit mutual fund. The 1936 Revenue Act provided a notion of diversification that was repeated in the 1940 Act (and one that is not found in any modern textbook on corporate finance): mutual funds had to have their investments in companies constituting no more than 5% of the portfolio *and* constituting no more than 10% of the *portfolio company's* outstanding stock. Later, in 1942 the tax code was amended to allow half of the portfolio to be more concentrated; but, no more than 50% of that concentrated half, or 25% of the fund's assets, can go into a single company's stock.[11]

A mutual fund needs pass-through tax status. If a mutual fund wished to sell services as an intermediary/monitor, dividing its portfolio into four or five stocks, it could not get that pass-through tax advantage. And no mutual fund could *ever* threaten a portfolio company that it would devote more than a quarter of its assets to obtain a majority of the portfolio company's stock and oust management. That threat, and the influence it would yield, is *always* prohibited for a subchapter M mutual fund.

Investment trusts: carrying on a business? In the 1930s, mutual funds' pass-through status as

---

7. Investment Company Act of 1940, 2(a)(3); 15 U.S.C. 80a-2(a)(2) (1988); 17 C.F.R. 17a-6 (1990).

8. 17 C.F.R. 270.17a-6(a)(5), (b)(1)(iii); Ronald Gilson and Reinier Kraakman, "Investment Companies as Guardian Shareholders: The Place of the MSIC in the Corporate Governance Debate," *Stanford Law Review* (1993, forthcoming).

9. 17 C.F.R. 270.17d-1.

10. Id.; 17 C.R.F. 270.17d-1(d)(5)(i). See also R. James Gormley, "On the Same Side of the Table: Is Investment Company Act Rule 17d-1 Partly Invalid?," 20

Securities Regulation Law Journal 115, 117-18 (1992) (Section 17d rules are "a morass of unascertainable depth," SEC acknowledges 17d as "uncertain"; plausible legal advice when a 17d question arises is "prayer consistently applied.")

11. I.R.C. 851(b)(4). Venture capital firms, which would provide monitoring for *small* firms, not the large firms that are our subject, are partially exempt from the no-control provision. I.R.C. 851(e).

untaxed vehicles was challenged. The key issue was whether the trust carried on a separate business. If it controlled an operating company and affected its policies, then it was carrying on a business of managing companies. Trusts in the 1930s said that when they only assembled a passive portfolio, they were not carrying on a business, and weren't taxable. But then the IRS said that even managing a diversified portfolio was itself a business and, in 1935, the Supreme Court agreed.[12]

Only the unit investment trust was left insulated from corporate taxation, because it ordinarily does not buy or sell securities, once *someone else* assembles the trust. The trustee passively collects and distributes income.

Liberalization in the 1936 Code. The 1936 tax code "liberalized" these tax results by expanding pass-through status to funds that fragmented and took no positions greater than 10%, positions large enough that they were thought likely to yield influence. Yes, such funds were carrying on a business. But it wasn't a "real" business. It was the business of picking stocks and bonds, not of making operating decisions.

Legal change. The fragmentation rules in the 1940 Act and the tax code should be dropped. In the modern securities market, the central protection to buyers of the fund is adequate disclosure of the structure of the fund's portfolio.

The basic concept of diversification in the two acts is well-meaning but antiquated. The laws' notion of diversification—no more than 5% of a single issuer—offers little in the way of investor protection; the mutual fund could put all of its monies into a single industry, making the fund ridiculously undiversified in a financial sense, although still able to satisfy *legal* requirements for diversification.

Protecting unsophisticated investors. Congress feared unsophisticated investors would invest in mutual funds expecting diversification but be unable to evaluate the portfolio. The SEC testified that a mutual fund's *only* positive function was to provide diversification; any extension risked thievery. Keeping mutual fund managers out of controlling positions kept them free from conflicts of interests. The

fund's investment adviser, an investment bank, could use the control exerted by the mutual fund to obtain securities underwriting business from the controlled portfolio company. Or the investment vehicle that controlled industry could be used to unload unwholesome securities onto a gullible public. These are serious problems, but they can be addressed without a blanket prohibition on influence.

Deregulation could be coupled to a back-scratching prohibition: no ownership stakes greater than 5% if the fund, or an affiliated group, sells pension services to the company in question. Moreover, the owner of a mutual fund has more power to deal with conflicts of interest of *mutual fund* managers than she does to deal with conflicts of interest of *corporate* managers. To sever her ties with conflicted or underperforming *corporate* managers, the shareholder must overcome a severe collective action problem. She must mount a takeover or proxy contest to get rid of the offending managers. True, she can sell her shares to someone else. But that someone else is inextricably bound to the offending managers, unless *he* can overcome the collective action's problems. Since he will be so bound, he will pay her only for the value of the package: a pro rata interest in the firm *with these managers*.

By contrast, the owner of the typical open-end fund can *redeem* her shares. She can send the shares back to the fund, *and get her money back from the investment company*. The offending managers could quickly find themselves with no assets to manage. Redemption is a serious risk for sub-par mutual fund managers.

"Interval" funds. Regulation forces an extreme trade-off for investors that might make "big block" funds difficult to use. Highly liquid open-end funds that redeem overnight provide excellent discipline to fund managers: Make a big error and the fund will find itself with no assets.

As noted above, the interplay of boardroom seats with 16B is a problem for mutual funds that must stand ready to redeem. Closed-end funds are an alternative, but they do not discipline fund managers as well as the open-end structure, because the assets cannot move out easily. And persistent discounts make the structure unpopular.[13]

---

12. *Morrissey v. Commissioner of Internal Revenue*, 296 U.S. 344 (1935).
13. Reinier Kraakman, "Taking Discounts Seriously: The Implications of "Discounted" Share Prices as an Acquisition Motive," 88 *Columbia Law Review* 891, 902-05 (1988).

Business entails trade-offs. But the 1940 Act doesn't allow a trade-off here. It doesn't allow the investor to buy a vehicle where the fund would take big illiquid blocks and the investors could redeem only on, say, three-months' notice. Such vehicles would be particularly useful for retirement money, for which the investor has a long horizon and expects not to spend for decades.

The SEC staff's recent proposals to permit interval funds[14] are good ones. If put in tandem with portfolio rule changes, general joint action exemptions and coordination with 16B to allow funds to take big blocks and ally with other institutions to put agents into the boardroom, the proposals could help improve corporate governance and informational flow. Such changes should help facilitate more and better relational investing between financiers and corporate managers.

Anti-cartel theory. In 1942, Congress slightly liberalized the portfolio fragmentation requirements, at the behest of the mutual fund industry. But it said no more than 25% could go into the stock of two or more controlled companies "engaged in the same or similar trades or businesses or related trades or businesses."[15] Owning 20% of the stock of a portfolio company gave the mutual fund control for purposes of the fragmentation requirement. The legislative history shows an example:

Investment company W...has its assets invested as follows: ...10 percent [of its assets] in corporation B, 25 percent in corporation C. ...Investment company W owns more than 20 percent of the voting power of corporations B and C. Corporation B manufactures radios and corporation C acts as its distributor and also distributes radios for other companies. Investment company W fails to meet the requirements of section 361(b)(4) since it has 35 percent of its assets invested in the securities of two issuers which it controls and which are engaged in related trades or businesses.[16]

Boardroom presence might require industry knowledge. If the fund cannot concentrate its influential blocks in a single industry, or its vertically related parts, assembling a staff would be difficult or impossible. There's some reason to think that foreign financial institutions link customers and suppliers in productive relationships.[17] Subchapter M raises the costs of such linkages in the U.S. True, the 20% limit is high enough that it is a small barrier. But (1) it is an unnecessary cost. Antitrust should be the standard to judge such linkages; subchapter M is overkill. And (2) it illustrates some of the general thinking behind subchapter M and the 1940 Act: Industrial linkages with mutual funds were discouraged because they were thought to accomplish no good. The evidence from abroad today seems to indicate finance can help link industry.

Subchapter M produces odd results. If the mutual fund keeps its entire portfolio fragmented, it can put its entire portfolio into a single industry. A few mutual funds do this, giving their shareholders little diversification. But the fund managers cannot put more than 25% of its assets into control blocks in a single industry; the fund *cannot concentrate* investments in a single industry without tax penalty. No diversification *and* no influence.

Why not to the limits of subchapter M? The SEC might view reform as unnecessary, if the institutions do not ask for relief. There's much to be said for not fixing it until someone in the industry tells the SEC it's broken. But any gains from shareholder blocks and boardroom representation are shared by all shareholders, and to some extent by employees and customers of the firm. The blockholder can only capture part of these gains. The cost of getting out front, of paying to petition the SEC for what might only be a small part of your business, may be a sufficient deterrent. Yet any gains accrue not just to the mutual fund beneficiaries, but to other shareholders, employees, and those that deal with the portfolio firm. Currently successful fund managers might not like to open up new areas for competition where they may be less successful. They may fear even minor risks that the mutual fund industry would be viewed as a riskier place for investors to put their savings.

True, mutual funds do not use what leeway they have to take big blocks. But, subchapter M requires that a fund seeking big blocks simultaneously be a fragmented fund (for half its portfolio) and a big-

---

14. Division of Investment Management, Securities and Exchange Commission, "Protecting Investors: A Half Century of Investment Company Regulation" 425, 442 (May 1992).

15. Revenue Act of 1942, 170(a), Pub. L. No. 77-753, 56 Stat. 798, 878 (1942), codified at I.R.C. 851(b)(4)(B).

16. Revenue Revision of 1942: Hearings Before the Comm. on Ways and Means, 77th Cong., 2d Sess. 122 (1942).

17. Ronald J. Gilson and Mark J. Roe, "Understanding the Japanese Keiretsu: Overlaps Between Corporate Governance and Industrial Organization," 102 *Yale Law Journal* 871 (1993).

Mutual fund control could help resolve the informational and organizational problems of scattered shareholders; as sophisticated investors with specialized personnel, the investment company would have expertise, the motivation to improve managerial performance, and the financial clout to see their views implemented.

block fund (for the other half). Because subchapter M's portfolio rules require that the fund have the mandated portfolio at the end of each quarter—it's a quarterly maintenance test, not an "incurrence" test—a fund at the law's limit that receives an untimely stock dividend, buy-back offer, or redemption order could find itself in violation. And joint action limits (under 13(d), 16(a), and the 1940 Act's Rule 17) and interplay with 16B raise the cost of bulking up of votes. Finally, with the stark choice between closed and open end, trade-offs cannot be made between liquidity and easy fund accountability (by investor ability to redeem).

With other larger American financial institutions—banks, for example—largely precluded from action, perhaps for good reason, mutual funds may need more leeway to be effective. Moreover, there's reason to believe that institutional investor voice works if—and perhaps only if—there are *multiple* big blocks.[18] But with banks and insurers out of the picture, and with investor communication historically costly (partly because of the 13(d) rules, recently sensibly reformed), multiple blocks just have not been there. This problem will continue for banks and insurers. Mutual funds are a good place to start.

CONCLUSION

Just after Berle and Means announced the emergence of the public corporation with uncontrolled managers at the helm, Congress raised the cost of mutual fund influence in industry. The restrictions in the 1936 tax code and the 1940 Act make it impossible to deploy a majority of the fund's portfolio in control blocks. The 1940 Act raises the cost of control for the unregulated part of the portfolio by regulating or prohibiting activities with affiliates.

In other countries, powerful financial institutions have been influencing firms with big blocks of stock. America, with a much more highly developed mutual fund industry, may have a chance to leapfrog some foreign nations in corporate governance. Fractional reserve banks are inherently unstable, and not well-suited to owning big blocks of stock. Mutual funds, properly regulated, may give us some of the benefits of big blocks, without some of the institutional costs that arise when banks hold large blocks.

---

18. See Mark J. Roe, "Some Differences in Corporate Structure in Germany, Japan, and America," 102 *Yale Law Journal* (1993) (forthcoming).

■ MARK ROE

is Professor of Law at Columbia Law School. He is at work on a book, from which this article is adapted, about the legal restraints—and their underlying legal, political, and economic features—on corporate ownership, structure, and goverance.

REGULATING THE EQUITY COMPONENT OF CAPITAL STRUCTURE: THE SEC'S RESPONSE TO THE ONE-SHARE, ONE-VOTE CONTROVERSY

*by Ronald J. Gilson,
Stanford University and
Columbia University*

O ver the years, capital structure regulation and research has been consumed with the search for the optimal capital structure—more specifically, for the right debt-equity ratio. A number of regulatory regimes were premised on the belief that one could identify the "right" amount of debt. Until 1979, the Securities and Exchange Commission rendered advisory reports concerning the feasibility of a plan of reorganization under Chapter X of the Bankruptcy Act. Feasibility meant "that the proposed capital structure should be sound."[1] The Public Utility Holding Company Act of 1935 required the SEC to disapprove the issuance of securities by utility holding companies if the security was "not reasonably adapted to the [company's] security structure." In both cases, the focus was on the level of debt. Section 18(a) of the Investment Company Act of 1940 is more direct; it prohibits an investment company from issuing debt securities unless after the issuance "it will have an asset coverage of at least 300 per centum."

Nor did this fixation on debt levels change with the 1958 publication of Modigliani and Miller's irrelevance propositions.[2] Rather than putting aside questions of debt levels as irrelevant, financial economists spent the next 30 years rising to the challenge: How could the presence of debt in the capital structure alter a corporation's return stream, or the market's expectation of that return stream, so that the level of debt would once again matter?[3]

During this same period, the role of equity in the corporate capital structure was largely ignored. As Holstrom and Tirole recently put it, "the finance literature has traditionally ignored the fact that a share does not merely confer a right to a residual return stream. It also gives a vote."[4]

The 1980s changed that. With the rise of hostile takeovers, control of a corporation—and, hence, the voting characteristics of equity—became a central focus of analysis, and both academics and regulators took notice. Most significantly, in July, 1988 the Securities and Exchange Commission undertook a bold regulatory initiative—the adoption of Rule 19c-4—whose goal was to influence, although not to specify, the make-up of the equity component of the capital structure. The initiative proved unavailing, as a Federal Court of Appeals promptly concluded that the SEC lacked the statutory authority to pursue it.[5]

But while the court's action swept away the SEC's response, the problem remained and has again been brought to a head by the efforts of one securities exchange to change its rules concerning voting rights. Because the SEC must approve or reject this proposed rule change, the Commission is back to where it stood in 1987, before Rule 19c-4's adoption. In this essay, I recount the SEC's efforts at regulating the equity component of capital structure and then suggest that the odyssey continue but with a change in venue: to Congress.

1. In re Broadway-Exchange Corp., 15 S.E.C. 256, 267 (1944).
2. Franco Modigliani & Merton Miller, "The Costs of Capital, Corporation Finance, and the Theory of Investment," 48 *Am. Econ. Rev.* 261 (1958).
3. See, e.g., Merton H. Miller, "The Modigliani-Miller Propositions After Thirty Years," 2 *J. Econ. Perspec.* 99 (1988); Sudipto Bhattacharya, "Corporate Finance and the Legacy of Miller and Modigliani," 2 *J. Econ. Perspec.* 135 (1988).

4. Bengt R. Holstrom & Jean Tirole, "The Theory of the Firm," in *Handbook of Industrial Organization* 63, 85 (R. Schmalensee & R. Willig eds., 1989).
5. See *The Business Roundtable v. Securities and Exchange Commission*, 905 F. 2d 406 (D.C. Cir., 1990).

BACKGROUND: ONE SHARE, ONE VOTE AND DUAL CLASS RECAPITALIZATIONS

Financial economists' general lack of interest in the terms of the equity contract is understandable. For most of the 20th century, common stock appeared to have unchanging and uncontroversial attributes: the residual profits interest and one vote for each share. Beginning in 1926, the New York Stock Exchange (NYSE) prohibited the listing of nonvoting common stock as well as the common stock of companies with multiple classes of voting stock whose votes were not proportionate to their equity. The American Stock Exchange (AMEX) also prohibited nonvoting stock, but was more lenient with respect to multiple classes of voting stock.[6] None of this seemed to matter very much, because very few companies showed any interest in varying the familiar characteristics of the equity component of the capital structure. Between 1940 and 1978, only 30 issuers of non-voting or multiple voting common stock were the subject of secondary trading; in no single year did the number of such issuers exceed eleven.[7]

The advent of hostile takeovers in the 1980s made the terms of the equity contract a matter of intense concern. Between 1976 and 1979, only four firms recapitalized to change the equity component of their capital structure from a single class of common stock with each share having one vote, to two classes of common stock with disparate voting rights. Between 1980 and 1987, 93 firms recapitalized in this fashion, with 43 dual class recapitalizations occurring in 1986 and 1987 alone.[8] And while these recapitalizations could be accomplished in a number of ways, the outcome was always the same. The transaction resulted in management or a dominant shareholder group holding shares of high-voting rights stock and the public shareholders holding shares with reduced voting rights.[9]

At this point, listing requirements governing voting rights became a subject of competition between the exchanges, and the more lenient AMEX standards were seen by the NYSE as conveying an advantage. In September, 1986, the NYSE responded by announcing the abandonment of its 60-year commitment to one share-one vote. The exchange proposed to amend its listing requirements to allow the creation of a class of limited voting right common stock by reducing the voting rights of existing common holders, provided that a majority of independent directors and public shareholders approved.

Because the NYSE is a self-regulatory agency under Section 19 of the Securities Exchange Act of 1934, the proposed change in its rules required SEC approval. The Commission's initial strategy was to defer action on the NYSE's proposal while it urged the NYSE, AMEX, and NASDAQ to negotiate among themselves a common position that could be jointly presented for approval. When these negotiations failed, the SEC began the process of formulating its own rule.

SEC RULE 19c-4: FORCING A SEPARATION OF A POOLING EQUILIBRIUM

The NYSE's proposed rule posed a real quandary for the Commission: Was there any reason to interfere in the competition among the exchanges over listing standards concerning the terms of the equity contract? Certainly, the SEC had no reason to enshrine a particular kind of equity structure as optimal; thus, there was little to commend Commission action to assure continued prohibition of the original issuance of common stock with low or no voting rights.[10] However, the competition between exchanges did not really concern new issuances of low-voting stock. The conflict was over dual class recapitalizations by which a publicly held company changed the equity component of its capital structure to replace a single class of voting stock with two classes, one of which—given to management or an existing shareholder group—has voting power substantially greater than its interest in equity.

The stated justification for such a recapitalization is that centralizing control in those receiving the superior voting rights stock will increase the value

6. Joel Seligman, "Equal Protection in Shareholder Voting Rights: The One Common Share, One Vote Controversy," 54 *Geo. Wash. L. Rev.* 687 (1986), carefully sets out the history of the voting rights standards of the stock exchanges.

7. Ronald Lease, John McConnell & Wayne Mikkelson, "The Market Value of Control In Publicly-Traded Corporations," 11 *J. Fin. Econ.* 439, 450-52 (1983).

8. Kenneth Lehn, Jeffry Netter & Annette Poulson, "Consolidating Corporate Control: Dual Class Recapitalizations versus Leveraged Buyouts," 27 *J. Fin. Econ.* 557, 570 (1990)(Table 1).

9. See Ronald J. Gilson, "Evaluating Dual Class Common Stock: The Relevance of Substitutes," 73 *Va. L. Rev.* 807 (1987).

10. Some academic support remained for prohibiting dual class common stock structures. See Louis Lowenstein, "Shareholder Voting Rights: A Response to SEC Rule 19c-4 and to Professor Gilson," 89 *Col. L. Rev.* 979 (1989).

> Giving management of a company with substantial free cash flow more voting control than residual equity would serve only to strengthen management's incentive and ability to favor itself through the corporation's capital budgeting decisions. No gain would result in which public shareholders could participate.

of the corporation and, it follows, the value of the limited voting rights shares. However, the substance of the dual class recapitalization transaction is identical to an alternative transaction form: a leveraged buyout that also shifts control to a participating management or an existing shareholder group. In a dual class recapitalization, shareholders whose voting rights are reduced typically receive nothing more for the transfer of control than a small dividend increase. In contrast, shareholders of companies subject to an LBO typically receive a very substantial premium. From this perspective, dual class recapitalizations hardly seemed worthy of encouragement.[11]

In favor of approving the NYSE proposal to extend listing to companies that undertake a dual class recapitalization—and thereby allowing competition to take its course—was the equity version of the Miller-Modigliani irrelevance propositions. In a perfect capital market, the arbitrage mechanism that drives the Miller-Modigliani result would also cause dual class recapitalizations and LBOs to have the same impact on firm value. The relative prices of the two classes of common stock following the dual class transaction would reflect the same sharing of the gains from shifting control that is reflected in the premium shareholders receive in an LBO.

Suppose the transaction is cast as a dual class recapitalization in which public shareholders receive an increase in future dividends as compensation for reduced voting rights. If a shareholder prefers cash, as would have been received for his voting rights in an LBO, the shareholder can sell the limited voting rights stock at a price that reflects the present value of the increased dividend. The difference in market price between shares of the single class of common stock before the recapitalization and shares with lower voting rights but a higher dividend after the recapitalization reflects the portion of the gain from centralizing control that accrues to the shareholder receiving lower voting stock.

In a perfect market, selling limited voting shares after a recapitalization should yield the same amount of cash as the shareholder would have received if the transaction originally had been structured as an LBO. In both cases, the increase in value results from

fixing control in a particular group, and the size of the premium and its sharing among those who give up and get control should be the same, whether reflected as an increase in a stream of dividends, as in a recapitalization, or as a premium over market as in an LBO. Put differently, the increase in value of the non-controlling shares following a recapitalization transaction should be the same as the premium paid in an LBO, and non-controlling shareholders should be indifferent. If equivalence did not hold, then arbitrage would correct the imbalance.[12]

The regulatory implication of perfect market equivalence is to stay out of the way; there is no reason to prefer any particular equity structure, nor any reason to prefer one means of getting there. The problem, of course, is that markets are not perfect. In fact, the impact on the value of non-controlling shares differs substantially when control is centralized through a leveraged buyout and when it is centralized through a dual class recapitalization. In an LBO, public shareholders earn very substantial premiums, on the order of 30 to 40%. In a dual class recapitalization, shareholders at best get no gain at all.[13] Just as the regularity of observed capital structure suggested that information and incentive effects resulting from market imperfections may explain why capital structure is not irrelevant,[14] the regularity of the differential experience of shareholders depending on the method of consolidating control suggests that information and incentive effects resulting from market imperfections may explain why the difference between an LBO and a dual class recapitalization is not irrelevant. And if that is the case, then the difference may have regulatory implications. If the empirical patterns simply represent an efficient market response to the presence of transaction costs, no case for regulation exists and the Commission has no reason to interfere with competition between the exchanges. Alternatively, if the empirical patterns provide evidence of coercion of public shareholders by inside shareholder groups taking advantage of the fact that LBOs are mediated through a market while dual class recapitalizations are mediated through the corporate proxy process controlled by the inside group, then regulation may be necessary to avoid a race to the bottom.[15]

---

11. See Gilson, cited in note 9, at 816-20.

12. The transactions should be identical from the perspective of those acquiring control as well. If the transaction is initially cast as an LBO, the same result as a recapitalization can be achieved by a subsequent public offering.

13. See Gilson, cite in note 9, at 816-820; see also Lehn, Netter & Poulsen, cited in note 8.

14. See, e.g., Holstrom & Tirole, cited in note 4, at 78-86.

15. The coercion explanation for dual class recapitalizations is developed in Jeffrey Gordon, "Ties That Bond: Dual Class Common Stock and the Problem of Shareholder Choice," 76 *Cal. L. Rev.* 3 (1988); Richard S. Ruback, "Coercive Dual Class Exchange Offers," 20 *J. Fin. Econ.* 153 (1988).

The difficulty confronting the SEC was that the existing data were consistent with both efficient self-selection and shareholder coercion. The more benign explanation for the different patterns contemplates two types of companies that stand to benefit in very different ways from fixing control in the hands of inside shareholders. The first consists of stable, successful firms with high market share in slow-growing, mature industries. Their market share and the absence of market growth generate substantial amounts of "free cash flow"—that is, operating cash flow that cannot be profitably reinvested in the firm's core business. Centralizing control over these companies eliminates the agency problem Michael Jensen has identified as the "waste" of free cash flow.[16] An LBO is the appropriate mechanism in such cases because the monitoring and incentive features of debt serve to increase firm value by eliminating free cash flow. And the operation of the market for corporate control—through the potential for competitive bidding—ensures that public shareholders will participate meaningfully in the gains from the transaction.

A dual class recapitalization could not achieve the same benefits for this type of company. Giving management of a company with substantial free cash flow more voting control than residual equity would serve only to strengthen management's incentive and ability to favor itself through the corporation's capital budgeting decisions. No gain would result in which public shareholders could participate.

The second type of company that might stand to gain from fixing control in an inside group is quite different. These companies suffer not from free cash flow, or an excess of capital, but from a capital shortage. They are in an earlier stage of development, both in terms of the market in which they operate and in their own organization. Entrepreneurial company founders remain in a dominant position and face a dilemma when they seek to finance growth. Sale of new equity will dilute their control; but if they avoid dilution by purchasing a proportionate amount of the new shares, the cost is an uncompensated increase in the unsystematic risk associated with already undiversified portfolios. For

these companies, a dual class recapitalization positions the company to secure capital for positive net present value projects without forcing the dominant shareholder group either to dilute their control or bear a disproportionate amount of the cost.

The empirical evidence is consistent with this explanation of the type of firms that centralize control through dual class recapitalizations rather than leveraged buyouts. A study by Megan Partch found that companies that effected dual class transactions were relatively young—half had been publicly traded for less than ten years and 27% for less than five years. Virtually all companies in her sample stated that a main purpose for the transaction was to allow additional capital to be raised without diluting a dominant group's control. And that justification was more than just boilerplate; in the two years following the dual class transaction, almost 40% of the sample companies made public offerings of limited voting rights securities.[17] Another study found that companies effecting dual class recapitalization were very likely to issue new lower-voting equity after the transaction, and to have significantly higher growth of sales and number of employees, higher ratios of research and development and advertising to sales, and lower rates of undistributed free cash flow than firms that consolidate control through an LBO.[18] Finally, my own study presents evidence suggesting that firms engaging in dual class transactions are in markets with relatively high growth rates.[19]

From this perspective, the empirical pattern of transaction forms that develops when transaction costs are introduced provides no justification for regulatory action by the Commission. The manner by which consolidation of control occurs depends on the presence or absence of an otherwise unconstrained agency conflict between management and shareholders: Control is consolidated through a market by means of an LBO when agency costs are significant, and through a corporate election by means of a dual class recapitalization when, because of the discipline of competition in a fast-growing product market, agency costs are insignificant.

This efficient self-selection story has an appealingly happy ending: the presence of transaction

---

16. Michael Jensen, "Agency Costs of Free Cash Flow, Corporate Finance, and Takeovers," 76 *Am. Econ. Rev.* (Papers & Proc.) 323 (1986).

17. Megan Partch, "The Creation of a Class of Limited Voting Common Stock and Shareholders' Wealth," 18 *J. Fin. Econ.* 313 (1987).

18. Lehn, Netter & Poulsen, cited in note 8.

19. See Gilson, cited in note 9, at 832n. 66.

> A successful regulatory effort had to operate as a kind of forcing contract, requiring companies to reveal their true characteristics through the transaction form they chose. That is, a rule should differentiate between those companies for which a dual class recapitalization reflected efficient self-selection and those for which it reflected only coercion.

costs simply leads companies to select the most appropriate transaction form. But it is not the only story that is consistent with the observed transaction patterns; there is also a dark side to the data. Here the critical distinction is not the economic characteristics of the firm, but the presence of a pre-transaction dominant shareholder group. The story is one of coercion. A dual class recapitalization will be selected when, because of an existing control group, public shareholders would have difficulty resisting the transaction. This explanation for dual class transactions focuses on public choice defects in the corporate electoral process that prevent shareholders from protecting themselves.

From this perspective, a justification for regulation appears. As with efficient self-selection, the move from a perfect to an imperfect market results in a systematic pattern of transaction forms. But in this darker view, the pattern reflects not efficiency, but coercion: if a dominant shareholder group exists, it uses its position to exploit public shareholders by a dual class recapitalization. In the absence of recourse to coercion, control can only be consolidated by paying for it through a market transaction like an LBO.[20]

The presence of conflicting explanations for the transactional regularities associated with dual class recapitalizations and LBOs presented a serious problem when the SEC took up the question of whether to regulate the equity component of the capital structure. Based on the empirical evidence, one cannot confidently determine whether the observed choice of transaction form reflects efficient self-selection based largely on whether the product market—quickly expanding or mature—in which the particular company participates adequately constrains agency costs, or whether the chosen transaction form instead reflects inefficient self-selection based on the pre-transaction distribution of shareholdings: when a dominant shareholder group exists, public shareholders are coerced. A successful regulatory effort had to operate as a kind of forcing contract, requiring companies to reveal their true characteristics through the transaction form they chose. That is, a rule should differentiate between those companies for which a dual class recapitalization reflected efficient self-selection and those for which it reflected only coercion.

This was the clever twist that shaped Rule 19c-4—the Commission's regulatory response to dual class recapitalizations. The key to the efficient self-selection explanation for dual class recapitalizations is the firm's ability to raise equity for positive net present value projects without forcing the dominant shareholders to bear a disproportionate amount of the cost either through a dilution of their position or, if dilution is avoided by additional investment, through an uncompensated increase in their unsystematic risk. In turn, the key to the coercion story is a dominant shareholder group's ability to force public shareholders into further strengthening the dominant shareholders' position by reducing the public shareholders' voting power.

So put, it is apparent that the efficient self-selection explanation requires only that new equity can be raised without diluting the dominant group's position; their control need not be strengthened. In contrast, coercion can operate only if the dominant group's position is strengthened at the expense of existing public shareholders. A rule that allowed the public offering of a new class of low- or non-voting common stock would allow new equity to be raised without dilution. Yet, because such a public offering would not affect the voting rights of existing public shareholders, the offering could not be coercive. Thus, prohibiting the alteration of the voting rights of existing public shareholders, but not the sale of a second class of limited or nonvoting common stock, precisely threads the needle between efficient self-selection and coercion.

The Commission took just this tack in Rule 19c-4. New issues of low- or non-voting common stock were allowed. Transactions that reduced the voting rights of existing common shareholders were prohibited. The result was a quite limited incursion into the realm of capital structure regulation. The Commission's rule made no effort to identify an optimal equity contract; it recognized that in some circumstances two classes of common stock with differential voting might be efficient, while in others a single class was the best result. Rather, it regulated only the governance process to force a separation between companies motivated by efficient self-selection and companies motivated by coercion.

---

20. Gilson, cited in note 9, at 833-39, discusses the empirical support for the coercion explanation of the incidence of dual class recapitalizations.

THE EXCHANGES' PUZZLING RESPONSE TO THE JUDICIAL INVALIDATION OF RULE 19c-4

The court's decision in *Business Roundtable*[21] should have been a non-event. The court did not hold that the exchanges and NASDAQ were prohibited from adopting listing standards that reflected Rule 19c-4. The decision concluded only that the Commission lacked the power under the Securities Exchange Act of 1934 to force the rule's adoption. Thus, a fitting end to the story might have been that the exchanges and NASDAQ adopted the substance of Rule 19c-4 voluntarily. The Commission had always preferred a cooperative solution reflecting an agreement among the NYSE, AMEX, and NASDAQ, undertaking the rule-making process in the first place only after the three parties were unable to agree on a common position.

For a time, it seemed that a cooperative solution would prevail. Because the NYSE had modified Section 313 of its Listed Company Manual to conform to Rule 19c-4, the court's decision did not alter the voting rights standards applicable to NYSE companies (although *Business Roundtable* left the exchange free to modify those standards). At least at the outset, the NYSE remained committed to the substance of Rule 19c-4. The NASD followed a similar course. While the immediate effect of the decision was to leave NASDAQ without a voting rights standard, the NASD then elected to adopt a 19c-4 type rule.

That left only the AMEX. Because it had never adopted Rule 19c-4, *Business Roundtable*'s invalidation of Rule 19c-4 reinstated the previous AMEX rule that allowed dual class recapitalizations subject to specified director and shareholder approval. The AMEX then created a special committee to study the matter. Based on that committee's recommendation,

the AMEX adopted a voting rights standard that was filed with the SEC for its approval in June, 1991.[22] The Commission has yet to act on that proposal.

The AMEX proposal takes a very different tack than Rule 19c-4. Rather than prohibiting dual class recapitalizations, the AMEX's proposed standard sets certain shareholder approval requirements for transactions that reduce the voting power of existing public shareholders. Specifically, a disenfranchising transaction requires the approval of either two-thirds of the outstanding shares including the votes of the dominant shareholder group, or a majority of the shares not held by interested shareholders.[23]

After the AMEX proposal, the NYSE gave up the fight—although, to be fair, the approach ultimately proposed by the NYSE was more restrictive than that of the AMEX. Growing out of a series of symposia on corporate governance, the NYSE proposed to allow disenfranchising transactions subject to approval by a majority of a committee of independent directors, a majority of the full board of directors, and a majority of the shareholders who are not interested in the transaction.[24]

The puzzle is why the NYSE backed away from its support for prohibiting dual class recapitalizations and joined the AMEX in allowing such transactions to go forward provided that public shareholders have a "sufficient" say in their approval. Interestingly, both exchanges offered the same explanation for rejection of the Rule 19c-4 approach, a cryptic reference to the same perceived flaw in the Rule: "It did not afford corporations sufficient flexibility to meet their needs."[25] As used, however, the term flexibility seems to be a euphemism.[26] The concern could not be over flexibility in adopting an optimal equity contract; Rule 19c-4 did not restrict the substance of the capital structure a

---

21. *The Business Roundtable v. Securities and Exchange Commission*, 905 F. 2d 406 (D.C. Cir., 1990).

22. American Stock Exchange, Rule 19c-4: Proposed Rule Change by American Stock Exchange, Inc., File no. SR-Amex-91-13 (June 11, 1991)(amending Section 122 of the AMEX Company Manual).

23. This requirement sounds more restrictive than it is. If a dominant group already owns 30% of the outstanding stock, then it needs the votes of only 51% of the public shareholders to meet the test. If the group held 40%, then only 44.5% of public shares need be voted in favor of the transaction. The AMEX considered but rejected a rule that would require a majority of the unaffiliated shares because that would "impose a 'tyranny of the minority.'" AMEX proposal, cited in note 21, at 9.

24. New York Stock Exchange, Inc. Symposium on Corporate Governance, "One Share-One Vote" Summary, Discussion Draft (May 29, 1992). Note that the NYSE proposal is more restrictive than that of the Amex in two important respects. First, the NYSE required a majority of the unaffiliated shares, thereby rejecting the AMEX's concern with "a tyranny of the minority." Second, the NYSE required approval by a committee of independent directors. In contrast to the backing away

from Rule 19c-4 by the NYSE and AMEX, the NASD continues to support its own 19c-4 type rule. See Report, New York Stock Exchange, Inc. Symposium on Corporate Governance 7-8 (March 29, 1992).

25. New York Stock Exchange, Discussion Draft, cited in note 23, at 2. In rejecting the substance of Rule 19c-4, the AMEX spoke in terms of "the desirability of flexibility in creating capital structures." AMEX proposal, cited in note 21, at 22-3.

26. In the edited transcript of the proceedings of the NYSE Symposium on Corporate Governance, Stephen Friedman, the chair of the AMEX committee, expanded somewhat on the flexibility concept. He expressed concern that Rule 19c-4 would lead to a situation where "some companies could have multiple class capital structures and others could not." In his view, the AMEX proposal reflected the benefit that there was "a fair way to convert an existing publicly-held company from a single class to a multiple class structure." Yet Rule 19c-4 allowed any company to adopt a multiple class structure by a perfectly fair means: the issuance of new stock in a market-mediated transaction. Something other than flexibility was of concern.

> Rule 19c-4 represented a clever, narrowly focused regulatory initiative. [B]y prohibiting... only the disenfranchisement of existing common stockholders, the Commission forced a separation between companies seeking a more efficient capital structure and companies seeking to coerce shareholders into giving up voting rights.

company selects. Rather, the rule restricted only the *process* by which multiple-class capital structures could be adopted—by market-mediated sales of new shares, not electoral-mediated disenfranchisement of existing shares. But this restriction was central to the SEC's concept of a forcing regulation—one that separates transactions involving efficient self-selection from those involving coercion. Under the Commission's approach, reducing the voting rights of existing shareholders, as opposed to issuing a new class of low- or non-voting stock, served no special efficiency purpose; all efficiency goals could be achieved by new issuances that did not serve to increase the control of a dominant shareholder group. The distinction has nothing to do with flexibility of capital structure; it has to do with shifting control.

So what "flexibility" did Rule 19c-4 deny companies? The answer reflects the same phenomenon that first initiated the interest in the equity component of the capital structure: the fear of hostile takeovers. A dual class recapitalization is a foolproof defensive tactic. Once a dominant group has absolute voting control, the company cannot be taken over without the group's approval. But Rule 19c-4 essentially eliminated dual class recapitalizations as a defensive tactic. Dual class *capital structures* remained viable, but dual class *recapitalizations* were prohibited. The difference, of course, is that issuing a new class of low- or non-voting stock is not a defensive tactic at all; issuing new securities allows new capital to be raised without diluting the existing dominant shareholder group, but it does not allow the dominant group to *increase* its control at the expense of other shareholders. If the dominant shareholder group wants to increase its level of voting control, Rule 19c-4 required that it be paid for.

Thus, the SEC is really back to where it started concerning dual class recapitalizations. The issue is not specifying the optimal capital structure—what the terms of the equity contract should be. Nor is it protecting capital structure flexibility. Neither the AMEX proposal nor the NYSE discussion draft explains what flexibility in choosing a capital structure Rule 19c-4 restricted. Reading between the lines, however,

leaves the unmistakable impression of entrenchment at work. The issue seems to be whether management can insulate itself from takeovers by acquiring control without paying for the privilege. Both the new NYSE and the AMEX proposals contemplate that shareholders can be coerced into agreeing to reduce or give up their voting rights. Rule 19c-4 had largely eliminated that possibility.

CONCLUSION: WHERE DOES THE SEC GO FROM HERE?

Rule 19c-4 represented a clever, narrowly focused regulatory initiative. By eschewing any interest in regulating the substance of the equity contract, the Commission left the market to determine what equity terms best fit particular corporations. And by prohibiting not the issuance of new low-voting or non-voting common stock, but only the disenfranchisement of existing common stockholders, the Commission forced a separation between companies seeking a more efficient capital structure and companies seeking to coerce shareholders into giving up voting rights in favor of an existing group. Rule 19c-4 restricted only the companies with coercion on their minds.

Thus, despite the NYSE and AMEX bemoaning the loss of "flexibility" to build defenses, Rule 19c-4 remains the right approach. The question is only where the SEC goes from here: How should the Commission respond to the court of appeals' holding in *Business Roundtable* that the SEC lacked the statutory authority to impose Rule 19c-4 on the exchanges and NASDAQ?

The obvious next step is for the SEC to request new legislation from Congress. But the framing and orchestration of that request is a sensitive task. What the SEC does not need is a congressionally-mandated one-share, one-vote rule. That would put Congress in the role that the Commission has declined for itself: defining the optimal equity component of the capital structure. The Commission needs only the authority to impose Rule 19c-4, an approach that facilitates, rather than displaces, market determination of efficient capital structure.

■ RONALD GILSON

is the Charles J. Meyers Professor of Law and Business at Stanford University and Professor of Law at Columbia University's Law School.

BUILDING RELATIONSHIPS WITH MAJOR SHAREHOLDERS: A CASE STUDY OF LOCKHEED

by Walter Skowronski,
Lockheed Corporation, and
John Pound,
Harvard University

C orporations are increasingly coming under scrutiny for their responsiveness to the concerns of their major institutional investors. Adapting to this challenge is proving a dramatic and sometimes dizzying shift for management and directors.

Just a few years ago, the responsiveness of managements and boards to investors was generally not an issue unless and until a takeover threat materialized. Likewise, shareholders typically saw little need to provide feedback to corporate managements. Today, however, there is increasing pressure for a new kind of ongoing accountability. Companies are increasingly being encouraged to redesign their policies and procedures so as to build long-term relationships with their shareholders.

In the past year, these pressures have been directed primarily at two areas. One is ongoing shareholder relations, including direct communication between large institutional holders and top management. Many public and private pension funds have recently sought meetings with senior executives, directors, and other corporate officials to discuss performance and express their concerns as investors. The second is director selection. Institutional shareholders have become increasingly focused on the role that boards of directors play in effective corporate governance. As a result, a number of large, long-term oriented institutions have turned to the board of director selection process as a focal point to ensure that board candidates adequately represent the interests and address the concerns of all shareholders.

In theory, this broad shift in focus—and the processes that can potentially result from it—can be beneficial to both corporations and investors. A system that not only allows but actively seeks out shareholder feedback can ensure that corporations are continually apprised of the perspectives and concerns of their holders. It should also allow for complex corporate strategies and goals to be communicated effectively to a company's major investors.

Over the past three years, Lockheed Corporation has materially changed the way it communicates with its shareholders. Lockheed's new programs have facilitated significant high-level dialogue between major institutional shareholders and management, thus allowing management decision-making to incorporate relevant inputs of its investors. Lockheed was also the first large public corporation to take an approach to the selection of new directors that directly involves the input of major institutional shareholders in the nomination process—an approach now being imitated by other large companies.

Lockheed's new programs did not arise in a vacuum. They were developed partly in response to an outside initiative by Harold Simmons, a large active investor who had accumulated a 20% stake in the company and was attempting to gain control. Faced with that challenge, Lockheed developed new programs and policies to certify to its shareholder base and the financial community its commitment to gaining their confidence and ongoing support. In this article, we provide a history of the development of Lockheed's new programs and procedures along with an overview of their current status.

THE SETTING: A MOVE TO
DIRECT COMMUNICATION

Lockheed's 1990 annual meeting took place under a good deal of pressure from outside shareholders. Harold Simmons, who had announced a proxy challenge against the company a few weeks earlier, had found considerable support among Lockheed's major institutional holders. The defense industry was in the midst of a major structural change driven by declining defense budgets—a change which had adversely affected overall investor interest and the valuations of all the companies in the industry.

At this time, Lockheed's investor communications had been focused on the research side of the financial community, and not directly on shareholders. This practice was then the prevailing corporate approach to investor relations; and, in fact, Lockheed's IR activities had long been perceived very favorably by the financial community. Unfortunately for Lockheed, its message was not being effectively relayed to investors—in part because analysts were placing excessive weight on large write-offs that obscured the company's prospective earnings power. As a consequence, there was a significant lack of understanding in the investor community about Lockheed's business strategy, market position, and financial prospects.

The net result was significant support for Simmons among investors, including some of the leading active institutions. Although not sufficient to give Simmons a victory, in the closing days of the campaign it created a significant impetus for the company to examine what it could do to correct investor misperceptions and address shareholder concerns.

The campaign itself had provoked Lockheed into a much more substantive and direct series of communications with its major investors. In the face of the challenge, it quickly became evident that the company's reliance on research analysts to communicate its message was not an effective way of dealing with the existing situation; it was failing to reassure a number of large shareholders dissatisfied with the company's financial performance that management was taking appropriate corrective action. Simmons represented for them an alternative, or at least a catalyst for change. And Simmons' initiatives in turn led to a series of pointed, often jarring, face-to-face meetings between members of

management and major investors. The question that naturally arose from these meetings was: what would follow the proxy challenge?

The natural tendency in proxy challenges had been to declare the situation over and finished once the campaign had been won. Communication, to the extent that it occurred at all, was usually tactical. But the sentiment among Lockheed senior managers and the board was that much could be learned from the experience; and, indeed, the aggressive and direct communication of the proxy contest eventually became the model for the company's new ongoing investor relations program.

Such an approach represented the "right thing to do" not just in the aftermath of the first proxy campaign but, more important, in terms of communicating effectively and on a timely basis to investors. Equally important—and most pertinent to the then still unresolved Simmons situation—Lockheed management was convinced that a new approach to communicating with investors would also serve as the best tactical response to the threat of a second proxy challenge. To deal effectively with such a challenge, it was imperative that the company's message be clearly communicated and that investor misperceptions be remedied and their concerns addressed.

At its 1990 annual meeting, Lockheed made a series of pledges to make policy changes over the coming year. Several involved corporate governance changes in response to clearly expressed shareholder preferences. The most significant pledge, however, pertained to the board of directors. Lockheed promised to add between one and three new outside directors and to accomplish this through a process involving its institutional shareholders. (In later making good on this pledge, Lockheed became the first publicly held company to establish a formal procedure involving major institutional investors in the director selection process.) A second significant pledge was to structure an ongoing process, as part of a comprehensive, two-way investor relations program, that elicited shareholder input on major corporate issues.

These pledges had themselves been derived from the input received during meetings with major investors prior to the annual meeting vote. In these meetings, Lockheed officials had asked investors for their frank opinions about the company's performance as well as their views on selected corporate governance issues. In response, many investors

Over the past three years, Lockheed Corporation has materially changed the way it communicates with its shareholders. Lockheed's new programs have facilitated significant high-level dialogue between major institutional shareholders and management, thereby allowing management decision-making to incorporate relevant inputs of its investors.

emphasized the lack of communication; some stressed concerns with the board's composition and independence; and others had very definite positions on a wide spectrum of specific corporate governance topics. Many shareholders expressed concerns with certain corporate strategies, with a number offering specific suggestions for change.

Taken as a whole, Lockheed's actions in response to these meetings have ended up achieving both near-term and longer-run objectives. To be sure, these actions were not sufficient to dissuade Simmons from mounting a second proxy challenge in 1991. But, in the midst of Simmons' second proxy challenge, management received nearly unanimous support from other major shareholders, thus leading to the sale by Simmons of almost all of his Lockheed stock. In terms of longer-run goals, the company has now developed a well-informed, involved, and supportive shareholder base whose investment objectives are consistent with and serve to reinforce the company's strategies and prospects.

THE DIRECTOR NOMINATION PROCESS

Starting the Process

There was no model and, indeed, no accumulated wisdom about how to involve outside shareholders in the director search process. About the only received wisdom on the subject was "don't do it"; the near-universal feeling was that to do so could result in a process that might move beyond the control of the company and lead to undesirable results.

With that backdrop of uncertainty, management began to develop a process immediately after the 1990 annual meeting. There was no master plan laid out beforehand; rather, steps were taken that seemed reasonable at the time. At each juncture the goals were relatively straightforward and sensible: to maintain control of the process; to be responsive in spirit and in fact to the institutions that had supported Lockheed's board and given it a chance to carry out its pledge; and to institute a genuinely participative process that seemed likely to result in an excellent set of directors.

In the first step of this process, Lockheed's Chairman and CEO Daniel Tellep sent a note to over 50 major institutional shareholders of the company. Broadly speaking, these were the company's largest shareholders and the ones with whom Lockheed

senior management had held the most intensive meetings during the proxy initiatives. The note indicated that, as promised, Lockheed was pursuing an effort to appoint new independent directors using input from shareholders, and it asked each institution for any thoughts or guidance on how to structure such a process.

The responses contained a plethora of views, ranging across a wide spectrum of issues. Some pertained to the broad structure of the board and involved reforms that were not part of the game plan contemplated by Lockheed's board. One, for example, suggested the establishment of an advisory committee made up of institutional investors and board members. Another proposed minimum stock ownership for board members. A variety of other suggestions dealt with other kinds of corporate governance issues and went beyond the charge of finding new directors.

Many other institutions did not respond. They indicated that they felt it was not their role to become involved in the selection of directors. Others commented it was the company's responsibility to elect directors, but that those elected should represent all shareholders, not specific groups or individuals.

A series of specific suggestions were made, however, about how to recruit good new candidates. Several institutions suggested that a process be initiated in which institutions were canvassed for names and then consulted again on a prospective list of nominees. Several institutions also suggested that Lockheed hire a seasoned executive recruiting firm and give it the unusual charge of developing a broad-ranging list of new director candidates—broader than that usually contemplated by companies who pursue director search through their own network of contacts. Others also suggested that Lockheed begin the process by reviewing its criteria for board members and circulating those criteria to investors for comment. Those suggestions all became part of—and, indeed, provided the basis for—the process that was to follow.

It should be immediately apparent that the fears of some who have advocated resistance to these kinds of consultative processes were realized in this first canvassing of shareholders. Suggestions were all over the map, and many were wholly impracticable. According to conventional wisdom, this should have put the company in a bind—that is, in the uncomfortable position of declining the requests of certain shareholders after having solicited them. But in fact this was not the case. Precisely because the process was open and involved suggestions from many shareholders, no shareholder was unreasonable when informed that a process was taking shape that did not directly incorporate a specific suggestion. The key, as common sense would suggest, was to respond to each suggestion and ensure that people felt that their suggestions had been received and considered. That process, together with the sensible plan that eventually came out of it, was enough to elicit positive feelings from those who had taken the time to respond.

It is also interesting to note that financial institutions responded differently by class. The response of many money managers to the initial inquiry was that choosing Lockheed's directors was the company's responsibility and thus a process they were not inclined to participate in. In contrast, a broad and diverse set of responses was received from the public pension funds, many of whom were clearly enthusiastic about the opportunity to become involved in such a process. Indeed, an even broader trend among the responses was to accord Lockheed considerable respect and flexibility. Most respondents, even while making specific suggestions, noted that they believed that Lockheed should do what it felt to be best and most prudent as it pursued its search process.

The result of this phase was the rough outline of a plan for proceeding. That plan involved further refinement of Lockheed's director criteria, retention of a good executive search firm, the development of broad lists from which to draw directors, and the commitment to involve shareholders as the process moved forward.

Generating Names

Processing responses to the first note and developing a rough plan of action took approximately three to four weeks. While the basic plan was taking shape, a second note went out to the institutional holders who had received the first. This note indicated that Lockheed was now seeking specific suggestions for individuals whom they believed would make good directors of the company.

The second note also contained the company's newly-revised criteria for directors—criteria that reflected a generic updating as well as inputs from major institutional investors. The mandatory retirement age, for example, was dropped from 72 to 70.

Stock ownership was required. The importance of independence was reaffirmed and recodified with more explicit language and definitions. These revised criteria were intended to signal Lockheed's concern about the integrity of the process and to discourage respondents from suggesting names that would clearly not fit with the company's needs.

Again, a reasonable number of institutions responded. Many of the respondents this time were the same, but some new ones emerged and some old ones remained silent. There was more representation by money managers at this stage and less by the public funds; the latter were more vocal about process but less so about the specific people who should be brought onto the board.

There were also some concerns expressed by selected institutions who had been hoping to see a different sort of process emerge from the first round. The company's response to these institutions was to contact them and ask for their patience in awaiting the rest of the process and the results. Company officials acknowledged that, as carefully structured as the process was, it could not possibly completely satisfy all the interested participants. But again, the intrinsic pluralism of the process was a significant benefit. Had only a few institutions been involved at this stage, it would have been more difficult to ask any one institution to subordinate its own concerns to the benefit of the broader process.

About 50 names of potential directors were forwarded to the company by the institutions responding to this request. This is clearly a significant number, and it was clear that some institutions had gone to some effort to identify suitable names. Most of the responses were thoughtful and contained clearly plausible suggestions.

This institutionally-generated list was then complemented by two additional lists. One was prepared by Korn/Ferry, the executive recruiting firm retained by Lockheed. This list, which had approximately 90 names, resulted from a search for individuals, primarily in Lockheed's core and related industries, with appropriate credentials and talents. The other list was an internally-generated list that contained the names of individuals known to and suggested by present members of the board and senior management. This list comprised approximately 20 names.

All told, then, the input phase resulted in over 150 names that needed to be screened and evaluated. Clearly, relative to most director searches, a remarkably different path had been followed already. Instead of a few names of close contacts, the company now had a large number of qualified individuals—most of whose names had arrived through truly independent channels.

Evaluation and Winnowing

At this point, the people managing the director recruitment process faced a challenge quite unlike the one usually posed by the process of nominating corporate directors. Typically, a small number of likely candidates are found and informal, low-key interviews conducted with the chairman and members of the board. Lockheed's situation differed dramatically. The name-generation process had resulted in over 150 possible candidates with tremendously diverse backgrounds. Again, critics of a more open corporate process might have argued that their worst fears had been realized. The traditional view would have been that this exercise in pluralism had resulted in a landslide of names and a situation bordering on chaos.

In fact, however, all that was necessary once again was an incremental approach to change. Lockheed personnel together with members of the Korn/Ferry director search team set up a process to sort through the names. The screening process was structured to involve several stages at which obviously poor fits could be eliminated. Incrementally tighter criteria were imposed at each stage, resulting in a step-by-step winnowing process that isolated the most desirable set of individuals.

The first screen applied to all the names on the list was one suggested earlier in the process by one institutional investor. In response to our first letter, that institution had suggested refining the criteria for directors and applying them rigorously to the new pool of director candidates. Among these criteria were experience relevant to Lockheed's business operations and adequate time availability to make a dedicated commitment. To ensure that directors were selected who were not spread too thin, individuals that served on too many boards were weeded out. The exact number allowed varied by specific situation, but generally it meant no more than one or two other outside boards. This was once again the result of an earlier institutional suggestion.

This first pass through the list reduced the number of names from 150 to about 80. The 80 "survivors" were then transferred to Korn/Ferry for the next stage of screening. This stage involved

calling all 80 prospective candidates to determine their interest in the position. Prospective candidates were told that their names had been suggested as director candidates for a large West-Coast high-technology company. Specific information was also provided on the duties associated with service on Lockheed's board, which involved ten regular meetings per year, additional committee meetings, and the possibility of additional special meetings to deal with various strategic issues.

This round of calls, which took most of the summer, once again produced a surprising winnowing of the list: from about 80 names, it dropped to less than 50. Almost half of the respondents indicated they were not interested in the position. For most, the reason was the West-Coast location, which would have meant travelling across the country at least once per month for the foreseeable future. Several others also indicated that they did not wish to serve on additional boards.

At this point, the list was once again reviewed for any individuals who might be inappropriate, incorporating inputs from the Company's external legal and financial advisors. Korn/Ferry then went back and recontacted the 50-odd remaining individuals. This time, the call was to say that the company in question was Lockheed and to determine whether this changed anyone's interest. The result was the loss of approximately ten more people. Of those that dropped out, several had conflicts with a Lockheed board position, such as a relationship with a Lockheed buyer or supplier.

The by-now 40-person list was then reviewed by the nominating committee. These individuals had met a series of important threshold tests established by Lockheed's broad criteria for directors: they were interested and available; they were willing to devote the necessary time and effort and held no more than two other outside board positions; they had relevant expertise; and they had no apparent conflicts. At this stage, the nominating committee took the process the next step by going through the list carefully with an eye to isolating its preferred candidates. The result of the nominating committee's work was to reduce the list of names to the low 20s.

Institutional Consultation and Selection

Up to this point, the process had taken almost six months. It had begun with a broad outreach and the generation of a huge number of names. The result was slightly more than 20 individuals whom the nominating committee felt comfortable considering as nominees to the Lockheed board.

The final phase of the process was then begun. The first part of this phase was to share the screened candidate list with selected institutional investors, asking them for their comments on the candidates. Once again, for those schooled to distrust open communications with institutions, to embark on this effort would be seen as risky and bordering on insane. The result could have been an irrational free-for-all that tarnished names and negated months of work. But involving major shareholders was also fundamental to Lockheed's pledge at the outset of the process, and without it the process would not have been truly participative. So the contacts were set in motion, once again with no prior experience on which to base expectations.

Contact was made with the largest institutions who had been active in making suggestions in the early rounds of the process. The contact was simple and straightforward. Calls were placed by Korn Ferry, who reviewed the candidate list with each shareholder and solicited its views on the candidates. The calls were purposefully low-key; they neither implied that the institutions should have comments nor did they state what would be done with those comments that were received. The institutions were also requested to treat the information confidentially.

The result was a series of diverse responses. Several identified candidates on the list that they considered unacceptable or inappropriate for one reason or another. Several also indicated particular enthusiasm for some of the named candidates. Along with comments about various potential directors came considerable positive feedback about the process and the consultation itself.

The obvious question was what to do with the negative feedback on some candidates. Lockheed chose to treat it as tantamount to a veto. The reasoning was simple: With over 20 available candidates, there was considerable flexibility and thus no reason to jeopardize this participative process by choosing a candidate unpalatable to one or more of Lockheed's major investors. The result of this procedure was to drop a few more candidates off the list, thus reducing the remaining pool to just under 20.

The remaining list then went back to the nominating committee, which attempted to rank the candidates by preference. Each of the candidates

were interviewed by Lockheed Chairman, Dan Tellep, to assess the candidate's interest, commitment, and, quite important, personality compatibilities. At this point, it became very clear that Lockheed had indeed screened down to a group of highly qualified candidates.

Further working down of the "final" list resulted ultimately in the selection of four new candidates— one more than the maximum number that Lockheed had contemplated appointing when the process began. This reflected the high quality of the individuals identified by the process, and the enthusiasm that had been generated among the members of the nominating committee, the board as a whole, and management. It was viewed as an opportunity to add an usually diverse and talented set of new directors to the company.

The four new director appointees also represented clearly the influence of institutions and the structure of the search process. Of the four, two had come originally from the Korn/Ferry list, one from Lockheed's internal list, and one from institutional suggestions. One was a defense industry expert; one was a CEO with experience in a clearly relevant and related industry; and two were members of the financial community. Of the latter two, one was the vice chair of a major insurance company with extensive equity investment experience; the other was chairman of a highly respected West-Coast money management firm with several billion dollars under management.

The reaction to the nominees by the financial community was unambiguously favorable. The outstanding credentials of the new directors, their overall stature,and the financial community's representation were all viewed as very positive for Lockheed.

Pursuing the Process Over the Long Term

The director selection process and aggressive communication program held by Lockheed during the year after the proxy challenges created heightened support among institutional investors. Again, those viewing this kind of effort as one aimed solely at defending against outside attacks would have counseled that the process now be abandoned. It had served its purpose and now a more normal approach to director selection could be re-established.

But Lockheed's view was different. In the view of senior management and the board, the experience had been tremendously beneficial and resulted in a more informed and remarkably successful director selection process. In addition, it had involved Lockheed's major institutional investors in a meaningful way, while not imposing any obvious costs on the company save the devotion of time and resources to the director search process. That was not viewed as a negative. From the perspective of shareholders and management, it was felt, what better place to expend incremental resources than on ensuring that the people who oversee the company are chosen in a manner that reflects input from its shareholder base.

A commitment was thus made to employ a similar, but scaled-down process for future director selections, one which screens off of a broad candidate list and reflects inputs from major investors. To date, it has been employed in the search for two additional directors.

DEVELOPING AN OPEN COMMUNICATIONS PROCESS

The second broad task faced by Lockheed after the initial proxy challenge was to develop a more systematic and open series of general communications with institutional investors. It had become evident during the first proxy contest that Lockheed had not provided major institutions with the kind of open communication channel they desired; indeed, many had not heard from the company for years prior to the onset of the proxy contest.

But Lockheed was not out of step with corporate America—it was out of step with a changing investor environment. Up to that point, Lockheed had previously focused its investor relations activities on the research side of the financial community, assuming that analysts' subsequent communications with investors would prove a satisfactory shareholder link. As mentioned earlier, this was the established practice among corporations at the time. Unfortunately, institutional investor requirements were changing; institutions were becoming more active and seeking greater inputs *directly* from corporations.

Lockheed once again committed to developing a process that would address these problems in a permanent, ongoing manner. The idea was not to engage in a one-time, proxy-driven propaganda campaign and then retreat; it was rather to establish regular, long-term lines of communication with all

shareholders, especially major institutional investors. The aim was not just to communicate to shareholders, but also to listen to and make use of important and relevant feedback.

The crux of the new process was a thoroughly restructured approach to investor relations—one that involved significant executive management support and participation. Investor relations had always commanded a high profile within Lockheed, but now the function assumed greater urgency.

The center of the expanded program was an on-going series of individual meetings with major shareholders throughout the year. In addition, regular quarterly review meetings were held in New York and Boston for shareholders, analysts, and investors. These typically aimed to provide the following: (1) a brief review of the company's operating and financial performance for the most recent quarter; (2) a discussion of major developments and emerging issues, and (3) a detailed business presentation by the president of one of Lockheed's four major operating groups.

Lockheed also created a new series of newsletters tailored specifically to the information needs of the financial community. These covered a wide range of topics, including corporate performance, program wins, strategic market developments, and corporate governance. Other special publications were developed to summarize the company's markets, operations, performance, opportunities, and investment merits. Internal communications were also expanded through regular memoranda and presentations providing key Lockheed managers with current updates on market performance and perspectives, as well as the valuation of Lockheed and its "peer" stocks. Selected independent surveys were used to provide valuable feedback to complement that being received by executive management through the ongoing investor relations program. Lockheed's board was also briefed regularly on the company's absolute and relative market performance and on current investor perspectives and concerns relating to the industry and the company.

For outside investors, this was a signal that their concerns would be taken seriously and incorporated when appropriate into policy-making. The fundamental concept was expert, structured, two-way communication that would help Lockheed stay abreast of investor concerns and perspectives.

In addition to the continuing communications provided by the company's enhanced investor relations function, Lockheed CEO Daniel Tellep made a personal commitment to be integrally involved in regular meetings with the largest and most active Lockheed shareholders. In so doing, he ensured that the senior manager in the firm would be directly available to shareholders—to receive their views and positions as well as to clearly communicate Lockheed's message.

During the year between the two proxy challenges, these meetings proved valuable forums for ascertaining investors' broad perceptions of the company; for describing in detail the company's direction and operations; and for addressing major strategic and corporate governance issues raised in the first proxy challenge. In the longer run, however, they have become an important and useful forum for discussing strategies, major corporate programs and policies, and significant investor issues. Overall, they have clearly provided feedback important for both Lockheed management and the board.

The feedback has also pertained to decisions both micro and macro in context. For example, direct shareholder feedback precipitated a proposal in the second proxy challenge to eliminate expensive media advertising. The proposal was accepted by the challenger, resulting in millions of dollars in savings. In addition, shareholder feedback provided valuable inputs for Lockheed's decisions on dividends and the structuring of a major share repurchase program. Many of the company's corporate governance actions reflected relevant investor perspectives on such issues as poison pills, minority representation, termination benefit agreements, and cumulative voting.

Shareholder involvement has also led to a better understanding of the company's strategic direction and a supportive posture for major corporate developments. Late last year, for example, Lockheed purchased the Fort Worth fighter division of General Dynamics in a large, debt-financed transaction—an acquisition that could easily have been negatively received by investors due to the significant leverage involved and to material misperceptions in the analyst community about the division's operating cash flows. Instead, effective communications ensured that it was reasonably understood and favorably received. Since the transaction's announcement, Lockheed's stock has increased over 40 percent.

The long-term importance of the communications link that has been established would be difficult to overstate. Lockheed has developed good working relationships with its major institutions that serve as a source of important shareholder support and continuing feedback.

CONCLUSIONS AND IMPLICATIONS FOR THE GOVERNANCE PROCESS

Lockheed has gone from being a company out of touch with its major investors to one in close communication with them. Last year it was honored by the California Public Employees Retirement System—one of its leading opponents in the 1990 proxy contest—for its positive response to that fund's concerns and for its more general changes in corporate governance. Moreover, the process at Lockheed and its outcome have several important implications for other corporations now wrestling with how to react to pressures from the market on broad issues of corporate performance and governance.

The first lesson is that to respond, and respond positively, to these pressures yields significant benefits. Generalized capital market dissatisfaction cannot be willed away and usually stems from well-defined causes. Many companies ignore it; others attempt to respond in ways that are either designed to shut out the market or provide a window-dressing cure. Lockheed's experience suggests the benefits from re-examining policy and making genuine changes in response to capital market concerns. Indeed, our experience demonstrates that the resulting policy changes at Lockheed have significantly strengthened the company.

A second broad message is that extensive consultation with responsive institutional investors can be made to work. Lockheed's director selection process would have been viewed by many managements as an unacceptable gamble that involved abdicating power and allowing institutions undue influence. That is not what happened. Instead, at every juncture, rational and commonsense approaches by Lockheed met with reasoned and sensible responses from investors; the process was self-reinforcing over time.

A third broad message is that companies need not be afraid of disagreements that can arise from these kinds of consultations and processes. Relating to investors in the modern capital market is, not surprisingly, like practicing good politics. Investors care greatly about whether the company is making

The trends place corporations in an uncomfortable position and have in the past few years generated significant negative reaction from many corporate managements. They effectively force companies to invent communications and governance processes significantly different from those that have gone before.

a genuine and committed effort to respond to their concerns. If the answer is yes, they can and often will agree to waive (or suspend) specific objections to help move the broader process forward. Involvement in real conversations provides sufficient general affirmation for investors to be able to engage in such give-and-take—and everyone benefits.

A fourth very important message is that communication and genuine openness to the market is far more important than specific bureaucratic solutions that focus on structure and specific processes. Lockheed's new director selection process illustrates this point most vividly. It is important to recognize that much of this process was managed in a manner that was nominally inconsistent with the growing institutional focus on *independent* nominating committees (in fact, Lockheed's nominating committee consists entirely of independent outside directors). The legwork in the early stages of Lockheed's process was undertaken by members of its senior management team. Much communication was directly with Lockheed's CEO. The nominating committee was closely involved and very important, but did not micro-manage every aspect of the process.

Clearly this hardly mattered. Indeed, in many ways, it was better this way—because there was no one better to involve in close conversations with both directors and institutional investors than the CEO. This illustrates how important it is that investors be flexible and that the ultimate focus be on communication and direct interaction between the company and the financial community. The Lockheed process could have been derailed early had investors insisted on one bureaucratic solution—for example, complete control of the director search process by the nominating committee. Precisely because the focus was on ensuring an open and effective process rather

than on any particular structure, Lockheed's senior management was allowed to fashion an effective program in direct consultation with investors.

The changes at Lockheed are, of course, part of a more general movement. For all their commonsense appeal, these trends place corporations in an uncomfortable position and have in the past few years generated significant negative reaction from many corporate managements. First, they effectively force companies to invent communications and governance processes significantly different from those that have gone before. This alone creates a great deal of pressure in the corporate organization. It is one thing to ask corporations to alter their practices incrementally and within a well-defined framework; it is quite another to ask them to design wholly new structures and processes from scratch. Second, they create a real concern among management and the board of directors about losing control of the agenda.

The Lockheed experience provides a blueprint for other companies considering restructuring their nominating process or their approach to ongoing communication with investors. But its most important messages are broader than this. Investors should seek, and companies should provide, open communications. Those communications may in turn result in any number of different specific solutions and new processes. What matters is not so much the exact protocol followed, but rather the commitment on the part of the company to becoming responsive to capital markets.

At its 1991 annual meeting, Lockheed's motto was "promises made, promises kept." It was an appropriate motto given the events of the prior year—one that many public companies may soon find themselves seeking to live up to through improved communication and governance processes.

■ WALTER SKOWRONSKI

is Vice President and Treasurer, Lockheed Corporation.

■ JOHN POUND

is Associate Professor of Public Policy, Kennedy School of Government, Harvard University.

RELATIONSHIP INVESTING AND SHAREHOLDER COMMUNICATION

JOEL STERN: Good morning, and welcome to this discussion of relationship investing and shareholder communication. The general purpose of the Roundtable will be to consider the recent rise of institutional investor activism and the opportunities it holds for corporate management to increase their share values by cultivating relationships with "longer-term" investors.

Some finance and legal scholars have proposed that companies give institutional investors greater voice in corporate strategic decisions, perhaps by inviting them into the boardroom. But another possibility—probably somewhat less troubling to management—is to improve the quality of their communication to investors by providing information that goes beyond what is provided by conventional accounting statements. Thus, one of the major themes in the discussion will be the limitations of current financial reporting. We would like to consider ways to improve the quality of corporate shareholder communications by devising new financial measures, or perhaps non-financial measures, that would give a more realistic picture of long-run corporate profitability.

■ In fact, there are no fewer than five major issues that we would like to address this morning. **First** is the longstanding controversy about the relationship between market efficiency and accounting disclosures. As most of you are aware, Chicago-school financial economists tend to think that by the time the information is released by the auditors, investors have already found alternative sources for that information. According to this view, most accounting information is already reflected in stock prices when disclosed, and thus there's not much point in improving accounting if nobody pays much attention to it. So we want to start by exploring what role, if any, more realistic accounting could play in improving the efficiency of capital markets.

■ The **second** major subject is a very intriguing one called "relationship investing." Stated in brief, the underlying proposition is that publicly traded companies can increase their share values by targeting a particular group of "patient" (or, as I prefer to call them, "value-based") investors. We at Stern Stewart have long argued that there are "lead steers" who effectively dominate the pricing process on Wall Street. Some obvious names that come to mind are Warren Buffett and Peter Lynch, but there are many others. And it may well be worth a considerable corporate effort to enlist such investors among the firm's major shareholders.

■ The **third** issue is whether and how we can improve existing financial measures of performance. The current search for relationship investors may reflect in large part the inadequacy of the accounting information that is regularly disclosed by companies to sellside analysts—the largely meaningless quarterly compilation and reporting of earnings per share. To the extent this is so, better financial measures could help stimulate relationship investing. Such measures could become a new language, in effect, for communicating with and thus attracting sophisticated investors.

■ **Fourth**, corporate IR efforts may also want to make use of *non-financial* performance measures—of things like product quality, and customer and employee satisfaction—that could help investors better evaluate future corporate performance. Ned Regan, who has been kind enough to join us this morning, is leading a research effort in that direction, and I'm confident he will tell us about the promise these kinds of measures hold out for improving the dialogue between management and shareholders.

■ **Fifth** and last is the broader issue of corporate governance and board supervision, and how it interacts will all these other issues I've just mentioned.

■

To discuss these timely and provocative matters, we have assembled a very distinguished group of participants, and I will mention them now in alphabetical order:

BASIL ANDERSON is the Chief Financial Officer of Scott Paper Co. Basil has just succeeded in instituting at Scott a major change in the financial measures that guide the company's investment planning, periodic performance evaluation, and executive compensation decisions.

CAROLYN BRANCATO is executive director of the Columbia Institutional Investor Project at Columbia Law School. Carolyn, who runs her own economic consulting firm called Riverside Economic Research, also recently completed work as staff director of the Competitiveness Policy Council's study of corporate governance and financial markets.

GEOFFREY COLVIN is Assistant Managing Editor of *Fortune*, and a member of the magazine's Board of Editors.

JUDITH DOBRZYNSKI is a senior writer at *Business Week*. Judy wrote the magazine's recent cover story on "Relationship Investing" and, some time before that, the cover story on "Corporate Governance."

ALEX LEHMANN was formerly Vice President of investor relations at Whitman Corporation, and now is a consultant specializing in valuation issues. While at Whitman, Alex developed a very proactive approach to corporate IR—one that I think you'll find quite interesting.

NELL MINOW is one of the principals (another is Robert Monks) of the Lens Fund, a highly-publicized active investor that takes large positions in underperforming companies. Their role in spurring the break-up of Sears is probably their major accomplishment to date, but they are also hard at work at American Express, Kodak, and Westinghouse.

KRISHNA PALEPU is Professor of Accounting and Finance at the Harvard Business School. Krishna, along with Harvard colleague Robert Kaplan, is in the process of putting together a symposium on non-financial measures of corporate performance.

EDWARD REGAN has been New York State Controller for the past 14 years—and a remarkably effective one, judging from the performance of the State's pension fund over that period. Starting midnight tomorrow, however, Ned will cease to be a politician and will become President of the Jerome Levy Institute, an economics thinktank at Bard College. There he will lead a research project on corporate governance.

JOSEPH SHENTON is President of OLC Corporation, a corporate investor relations consulting firm that studies the behavior of institutional investors and now has close to 150 corporate clients. Joe is in the business of trying to help corporations choose the appropriate investor clienteles and then help ensure that such clienteles are heavily represented in the shareholder base.

DEREK SMITH is Executive Vice President of Equifax Inc. in charge of insurance information services. Besides adopting a new internal financial measurement system, Equifax recently announced a leveraged Dutch auction share repurchase that was widely applauded by Wall Street. It should be interesting to hear the thinking behind that *financial* strategy—and the message Derek thinks it has sent to the company's investors.

EUGENE VESELL is Senior Vice President of Oppenheimer Capital. Gene and his colleagues, who have about $25 billion under management, have been practicing relationship investing long before anyone thought to give it a name. They have $18 billion invested in the equities of some 65 companies, giving Oppenheimer Capital an average position of about $250 million, and a 10% or greater ownership stake in about half their portfolio companies.

JEROLD ZIMMERMAN is Professor of Accounting at the University of Rochester's Simon School of Business. He is also the founding co-editor of the *Journal of Accounting and Economics*, a distinguished publication produced at the University of Rochester. Jerry has been among the four or five superstars in accounting research over the last 15 to 20 years. Last but not least are my Stern Stewart colleagues, **BENNETT STEWART**, who will serve as my co-moderator in this discussion, and **DON CHEW**, a founding partner of Stern Stewart and Editor of the Continental Bank *Journal of Applied Corporate Finance*. With that introduction, let me turn the floor over to Bennett Stewart.

What Accounting Was Never Meant to Be

STEWART: Thanks, Joel. Well, as you can see, we've been remarkably successful in narrowing the focus of this discussion.

Let's begin with this issue of the accounting framework that seems to underlie a lot of the concern expressed about the "short termism" of corporate America. Accounting conventions require corporations to expense much of their long-term investment, their R&D, their outlays for employee training, software investments, and so forth. The concern expressed by corporate managers is that investors focus myopically on near-term accounting results, thus placing an excessive discount on payoffs expected from promising long-run investment. Such allegedly systematic undervaluation of corporate investment then forces corporate managers to underinvest in the corporate future, or at least to invest in the wrong projects.

Let me begin by asking Professor Jerry Zimmerman to give us an academic perspective on these issues. Jerry, how is it that we have ended up with the current accounting system? And has it accomplished what it was really intended to do, or is it failing us in some important sense?

ZIMMERMAN: In the interest of full disclosure, let me preface my remarks with a disclaimer. The view I am about to offer is not widely held among my accounting colleagues, many of whom would likely argue that my views are speculative—that is, not sufficiently backed up by the existing body of accounting research. But, in fact, there is quite a bit of evidence that supports what I'm about to say.

Bennett Stewart has written an article called "Market Myths" in the *Journal of Applied Corporate Finance*

that does a wonderful job of summarizing the ways in which accounting conventions fail to measure economic reality. I agree with almost everything Bennett has to say in that article, but I think he's left out probably the most important market myth of them all—namely, the notion that accounting numbers were ever demanded, or *intended* for use, by shareholders for the purpose of valuing companies. Although accounting numbers do provide some information to investors, they are not a primary source of information for our capital markets. And, as long as institutions like the SEC and FASB continue to regulate disclosure, I suspect reported accounting numbers will never be very useful for investors in setting stock values.

The accounting systems that we have today—the historical-cost-based numbers that we all love to hate—have developed over hundreds of years. They can be traced back to the first "joint stock" or publicly owned companies of the 14th Century and even earlier. The problem that the accounting and auditing systems were originally designed to solve was the very basic problem of stewardship. Take the case of the East India Trading Company, which was an early joint stock company. Let's say they had a manager 4000 miles away running a trading post, and they shipped that person a boatload of goods. The purpose of accounting was to ensure that the manager used those goods to serve the company's interests and not just his own.

Another important function of accounting—one that developed somewhat later with the rise of public debt markets—was to control conflicts of interest between a company's bondholders and its shareholders. The problem was this: How could managers, as representatives of the shareholders, make credible promises to the bondholders that they would not

pay out excessively high dividends or invest in excessively risky projects? To reduce these conflicts, companies contracted privately with their bondholders to hire reputable, third-party accounting firms to gather and report certain kinds of information that would be useful in monitoring management's compliance with debt covenants. This was all done privately; there was no SEC, no public regulatory body, to demand that this information be provided. And the system worked.

STEWART: At this point, though, Jerry, the companies were closely held, right? The owners were not widely dispersed as they are today?

ZIMMERMAN: No, these joint stock companies had lots of owners. The East India Company had hundreds of shareholders.

Today, of course, the SEC would have us believe—and this is another part of that same market myth your article fails to mention—that the 1929 stock market crash was caused by inadequate financial disclosure and that the existence of the SEC now somehow protects us from further stock market crashes. But, having recently experienced the Crash of 1987, we now know that the SEC and mandated financial disclosure do not prevent stock market declines.

So, the *primary* function of the financial accounting system was never—and nor is it today—to provide information for valuation decisions. It was designed to provide *internal* measures of performance to serve as guides in running companies, and to protect outside investors from opportunistic managers. It's basically an auditing function: Count the cash and make sure the inventories are what they're supposed to be. It's a basic control system. It is not *primarily* a system for shareholder valuation of companies as going concerns.

Of course, many people still believe the primary function of these systems is to provide information for valuation, but this expectation has created an enormous problem for the public accounting profession. Those who bought into this accounting myth 50 years ago are now in a Catch 22: The partners of what used to be the Big Eight firms (it's now down to the Big Six, of course) are saying to themselves today: "Yes, we can provide this information for valuation. But every time the stock market crashes, we get sued for poor financial disclosure. We are being litigated out of existence."

Today, the legal costs of Big Six firms are running at about 10 to 15% of their total revenue. Because they can't get insurance any more, they're self-insuring. If we have a few more big lawsuits, we will no longer have a Big Six audit industry. In that event, the SEC may eventually end up requiring American corporations to be audited by a government body like the GAO.

STERN: Jerry, you mentioned that one objective of accounting statements was to provide information for lenders to the company. If this information helps lenders make better judgments about credit risk, why wouldn't that kind of information also be useful to shareholders?

ZIMMERMAN: For one thing, lenders are really insiders in a way that, at least in the U.S., outside shareholders can never be. As part of their credit evaluation, lenders routinely ask corporate borrowers to provide extensive financial disclosures that they then keep privately. That kind of confidential exchange of private information is not permissible between management and shareholders in the U.S. This private exchange of information can be valuable because there is often important strategic information that companies don't want to disclose to their competitors, but only to certain investors.

Although accounting numbers do provide some information to investors, they are not a primary source of information for our capital markets. And, as long as institutions like the SEC and FASB continue to regulate disclosure, I suspect reported accounting numbers will never be very useful for outside investors in setting stock values.

—*Jerold Zimmerman*

Another important difference between lenders and shareholders is that lenders care primarily only about downside risk. Lenders are much less interested than shareholders in going concern values, and much more concerned about liquidation values. They want to know what the assets will be worth if the company can't meet its interest payments.

STEWART: But, Jerry, isn't it possible that a perception could become a reality? You're saying that the accounting system was never *intended* to be a system for measuring value by the stock market. But isn't it conceivable that, through the efforts of the SEC, it could have become one. After all, the research you have published in your own *Journal of Accounting and Economics* has shown that stock prices respond in fairly predictable ways to earnings "surprises." Doesn't that partly contradict your position?

ZIMMERMAN: No. Going back to the seminal research of Ray Ball and Phil Brown in 1968, the stock market anticipates *most* of the news in accounting earnings by the time the numbers are released. The market has more timely sources of information than accounting numbers, including voluntary management disclosures and financial analysts' reports. Joel described the importance of "lead steers" in the pricing process. I doubt these people use accounting earnings as their primary source of information about companies' future cash flows.

Keeping Three Sets of Books: The Case of Scott Paper

STEWART: Let me turn now to Basil Anderson. Basil, as CFO of Scott Paper, would you say that Jerry's view of the "irrelevance" of accounting to the stock market valuation process is one that is shared by your senior manage-

At Scott, we have developed an information system and financial performance measures that we feel are appropriate across a range of corporate decisions: capital budgeting, evaluation of divisional performance, management compensation awards, and so forth. And the financial measures we use to guide those decisions are quite different from what we're required to report to the SEC.

—Basil Anderson

ment colleagues at Scott? And what do you find when you talk to your investors? Are they greatly interested in your quarterly financial results?

ANDERSON: One of the big challenges for us as a company is trying to reconcile the internal management information we need to run our business with the kind of information we *think* is required by investors on the outside. Of course, what we think investors want is to some extent dictated by SEC disclosure requirements. But, if we can believe people like Joel Stern and Bennett Stewart, there may well be kinds of information required by investors that are different from what is required by the SEC. To the extent this is true, companies could end up seeing a need to keep three different sets of books. And keeping three sets of books is not only costly and time-consuming, it can create lots of internal confusion about what the company is trying to achieve.

At Scott, we have developed an information system and financial per-

formance measures that we feel are appropriate across a range of corporate decisions: capital budgeting, evaluation of divisional performance, management compensation awards, and so forth. And the financial measures we use to guide those decisions are quite different from what we're required to report to the SEC.

Communicating with investors, however, continues to pose the greatest challenge for us. Although the securities analysts and other representatives of the investment community I interact with tend to ask questions very much consistent with what the SEC and the accounting profession requires, these numbers have very little to do with how we manage and evaluate our own performance internally. Without any definite sense of the kind of information investors want from us, we simply try to do the best we can to respond.

STEWART: Basil, let's suppose you are rolling out a major new product line in Europe, and the costs associ-

ated with that investment will be expensed for two or three years before any benefits begin to show up in your financial statements. According to accounting conventions, much of that investment must be treated as an expense that reduces reported earnings. Yet, viewed from the perspective of a business person or an owner, it really represents an investment in the future.

How do you reconcile those two perspectives? How do you prevent yourself from underinvesting?

ANDERSON: Our own history of investment and capital spending would show that the perceived short-term focus of Wall Street has not prevented us from embarking on big expansion projects with longer-term payoffs. We do the best we can to inform Wall Street about the expected payoffs from our investment. But, as I said earlier, the disparity between how public accountants treat this investment and how we regard it internally creates a challenge for us in communicating with investors.

ALEX LEHMANN: Communicating effectively with investors is indeed a challenge. But it also represents a continuous opportunity to provide the kinds of information investors need to value a company. Basil referred to the expected payoffs from Scott's capital projects. Clearly that is what investor relations is all about: helping investors get a feel for the expected payoffs from both existing and new investment, and creating realistic expectations about the level of future cash flow and the investment necessary to provide that growth.

The Case for Accounting Reform

STEWART: Let me turn now to Krishna Palepu of the Harvard Business School. Krishna, you have a perspective on this issue that is somewhat different from Jerry Zimmerman's.

PALEPU: I would say my view of the world complements more than it contradicts Jerry's view, but I strongly disagree with part of his opening statement. The original intent of the accounting system may well have been the internal control and monitoring functions that Jerry described, but the limitation of this kind of historical analysis is that it may obscure important evolutionary change. In 1993, it may not be all that useful to be looking at the East India Company. The world economy has changed significantly over the past 300 years, and it's not implausible to me that the basic function of the accounting system could have evolved along with it. Part of the job of academic accountants like Jerry and me is of course to *describe* the past, and to explain why the existing accounting system looks the way it does. But another role for us academics is to suggest the possibility for change, to take a role in *prescribing* changes in the accounting system that would make accounting information more useful to investors.

For this reason, I welcome the SEC's challenge to the accounting profession to provide better measures of performance, non-financial as well as financial. Such measures ought to be designed to help investors monitor the value of their investments and keep track of how well management is using the capital they have committed. In fact, I believe the FASB has explicitly adopted this aim as their top priority in their ongoing redesign of the accounting system.

But despite the FASB's professed aim of facilitating communications between managers and investors—and here I'm about to agree with Jerry—the great majority of the FASB's actual rulings are really done with the mentality of a traffic cop: They just want the road to be clear; they don't seem to care as much whether any-

Even if the market is pretty good in valuing companies in the aggregate, individual companies may well be either overvalued or undervalued because of "information asymmetries" between managers and outside shareholders. If I were the CFO of an undervalued company, one of my principal responsibilities would be to figure out a way to get my story out. And one way to accomplish that would be to devise useful leading indicators and then make them the centerpiece in the voluntary or non-SEC part of my investor communications program.

—Krishna Palepu

body drives on it or not. For this reason, the FASB basically doesn't want to play an active role in addressing a problem like the one Bennett is talking about—that is, the treatment of long-term investment and R&D. If you look at the items on the FASB agenda at any point in time, there will always be a lot more items that relate to either expenses or liabilities, and a lot fewer to revenues and assets.

So there's a definite bias in terms of what the FASB is trying to do. As Jerry suggested, the accounting standards are designed more to protect the interests of creditors than to shed light on the going-concern value that accrues largely to shareholders. Creditors are interested primarily in the downside, but shareholders are interested in the upside as well. Shareholders are interested in assets as well as liabilities, future revenues as well as current expenses. So I think we need to move toward an accounting

system that aims to tell more of the complete story—while still keeping in mind, of course, who is telling the story and their incentives to get the story right.

STEWART: But, it seems to me that accounting still has one necessary and inescapable limitation. It is based upon historical results, it is a recording of past events. Since investors are by their nature forward looking, I don't see how we can expect any accounting-based system to play a major role in the dialogue that needs to take place between management and investors.

PALEPU: I disagree. In many cases, a company's recent history may well be the most reliable guide to the future and, hence, to its going concern value. At the same time, you could supplement these historical disclosures with some leading indicators that might actually tell investors where the company is going.

STEWART: Would you give us some examples of what you mean by leading indicators?

PALEPU: Well, suppose a company is making an investment in the design and marketing of a new product. When evaluating the progress of that investment for internal purposes, management will generally have a set of intermediate goals or milestones they use to assess whether they are on track. Companies could disclose some of these internal goals to the investment community without giving away the store.

Now, it's true some managers are worried that disclosure of strategic information could undermine their firms' competitive position. But while such concerns are valid, they are probably overstated—because competitors typically cannot replicate a really innovative strategy just by reading about it. For example, take the case of Walmart. Its strategy has become a matter of public knowledge, but very few competitors have been able to replicate it.

Indeed, I would argue that if a company's strategy can be readily replicated by another company, then it is not a source of sustainable competitive advantage. Much of the value of corporate strategy, I suspect, comes not from strategy *per se*, but rather from how effectively the strategy is implemented.

STEWART: Krishna, that reminds me of the message of your Harvard colleague Amar Bhide, who wrote a great *Harvard Business Review* article called "Hustle as Strategy." Amar's argument is that strategic brilliance is becoming less important to corporate success than execution and efficiency.

For example, I recently read in *Business Week* that whereas it took Chrysler two and a half years and $1.7 billion to come up with a new compact model, it took General Motors five or six years and some $3 billion

to develop its own compact, the Saturn. It's not hard to see from these two numbers why GM is having such problems. But what really struck me about this story is that I was learning about these time-to-market and investment cost measures—things that are really critical to evaluating the operating efficiency of auto manufacturers—*not* from the company's annual or quarterly reports, but from reading *Business Week*. This is precisely the kind of information investors need to know to gain a competitive edge.

So, it's no wonder investors don't expect to learn much from reading a company's annual report. Even if companies did disclose such information in their quarterly or annual reports—which they typically don't, unless it puts them in a consistently favorable light—it's already stale information by the time it comes out.

PALEPU: But there are many ways of communicating with shareholders that can be far more effective than the annual report. The annual report is simply the culmination of the financial reporting process; it's often more a ceremonial event than a source of information. Some companies use quarterly reports to provide management discussions of capital spending and progress toward meeting stated corporate goals. For example, if your internal corporate objectives include an increase in customer service and a decrease in new product cycle times, then it makes a lot of sense for management to tell the investment community about these goals, and about its progress in meeting them. It makes sense to give investors a roadmap, if you will, and then promise that you will faithfully chart your progress in bad times as well as good.

Credibility is, of course, a very important part of this whole disclosure process. To the extent you succeed in establishing credibility with

the investment community, a corporate IR program may have far more ability to supplement its financial disclosures with information about some of the nonfinancial leading indicators I mentioned earlier.

STERN: Krishna, let me present an alternative hypothesis, perhaps in a somewhat extreme form. Let's assume that all this accounting information is of absolutely no value to investors at all; it plays no role in determining the price of a company's shares. Assume further that you know the management of a poorly performing company was about to be replaced by a management team with a reputation for delivering results. Would that alone be sufficient basis for committing investment funds to such a company?

PALEPU: Management reputation certainly plays a major role. But if I were putting $100 million into a company, I would also like to know something about the new management's plan for reforming the business, for creating new growth, and for funding that growth. For example, if I were going to invest in IBM, I would need to know more than just that Lou Gerstner was coming in to run IBM and that he had a lot of stock options.

STERN: I would argue that top management's reputation represents a very important part of this market valuation process. Take the case of Eastman Kodak reported in today's *Wall Street Journal*. The article announced that Chris Steffen, the CFO hired a few months ago to push forward the restructuring of the company, is now leaving. There was a 15% drop in the price of Kodak's shares as soon as the announcement was made. When it was first announced he was coming on board, there was an almost identically large *increase* in the price of the shares.

I would argue that Steffen's reputation for doing what needs to be done significantly altered investors' expectations of future performance at Kodak. No accounting system that measured historical performance would have helped investors make the decision to buy when Steffen came on or to sell when he left. All you needed to know was whether he was coming or going.

NED REGAN: I think the shares would have dropped even if Steffen hadn't resigned. Yesterday's *Wall Street Journal* showed clearly that two people were trying to run the same company. I read that story and said to myself: "Goodbye Kay or goodbye Steffen."

Old-Fashioned Relationship Investing: The Case of Oppenheimer Capital

STERN: Well, I suspect we will come back to Kodak later in this discussion. But now let me turn to Eugene Vesell of Oppenheimer Capital. As I said earlier, Gene started practicing a kind of relationship investing long before anybody thought to give it a name.

Gene, would you tell us about Oppenheimer Capital and how it works? For example, do you use accounting-based information in evaluating investment candidates, or do you place more emphasis on other non-financial, perhaps more forward-looking, indicators?

VESELL: Joel, before I answer your last question, let me respond to the point you just made about reputation. You suggested that all you need to know about a company is management's reputation. Well, I essentially agree with that statement, but I would add that there's one other important consideration: the extent to which management's compensation is tied to shareholder value.

We at Oppenheimer have about $26 billion in assets under management. Our total equity investments are in the $17-$18 billion range. So we're fairly large, but not one of the

We like companies that are run as if they were private; maximization of cash flow and minimization of taxable reported earnings are the goals we want management to pursue. The fact that the company is run to maximize cash flow, not earnings, sends a very powerful signal to us that they are managing like owners. Our own firm, Oppenheimer Capital, is owner-managed; we're a publicly traded MLP with significant management ownership. And we look for other companies that are owner-managed...We want managers to be owners with us.

—Eugene Vesell

giants. And, unlike the giants, we tend to take very concentrated positions. As you mentioned earlier, we have about 65 positions (though a typical account will own only 35-40 stocks). Hence, an average position is about $250 million. However, we do have a dozen holdings over $400 million.

STEWART: What percentage of the stock does that typically represent?

VESELL: We often own 10% or more of a company's shares. In our larger companies, that obviously tends to be a little smaller; for example, we own only about 5-6% of Sprint. But, in our smaller companies, our stakes are quite large. We own 20% of Dole, over 15% of Sundstrand, 14% of Transamerica, and over 15% of Freeport McMoran.

STEWART: Let me stop you with Freeport McMoran. That's a very difficult company to analyze from the outside because of the depletion allowances and the diverse kinds of assets. How do you evaluate a company like that? Their accounting statements are virtually meaningless.

VESELL: I couldn't agree more. Well, as Joel was suggesting, it's the reputation and the incentive compensation of the top management that were perhaps the most important factors driving our investment decision. The quality of the board of directors was also important.

With respect to the assets themselves, the best we could do was to assess their value using very imprecise, essentially qualitative judgments—although we did have some hard numbers on "proven reserves." The company's principal asset is a copper and gold mine in New Guinea, and we used those estimates of reserves to make a present value calculation of the value of those assets. And after making some back-of-the-envelope adjustments for their other assets and liabilities, we said to ourselves:

"Gee, what you can touch here is worth 50% to 75% above the current stock price."

But, once more, what we were really banking on was the reputation and incentives of management. In the case of Freeport McMoran, management had a record for both finding new assets and then, once they found them, of managing those assets very efficiently.

STEWART: But how would you know they were managing assets efficiently if you couldn't make sense of the financial statements?

VESELL: Well, as you say, historical accounting numbers were not much of a guide. The company has dual incorporation in Indonesia and Delaware, which even complicates the accounting more, because Indonesian tax laws allow you to write off a fair amount of the capital spending. And let me stop here and point out that we *want* our companies to write off their investment as quickly as possible. We like companies that are run as if they were private; maximization of cash flow and minimization of *taxable* reported earnings are the goals we want management to pursue.

So, in this case, we were able to look through the accounting statements to find the cash flows generated by the mining operations. And the fact that the company is run to maximize cash flow, not earnings, sends a very powerful signal to us that they are managing like owners. We also used the very solid stock price performance following the merger of McMoran Oil and Freeport Sulphur as another useful indicator of their ability to manage assets.

STEWART: I understand that, although the company is very adept at finding mineral reserves, they don't insist on taking them out of the ground.

VESELL: That's right. Unlike many natural resource companies, they have specialized in doing only what they do best. If they find new mineral reserves, they're not committed to developing them. They will sell the reserves if they can find a buyer willing to pay a high price for those reserves, presumably because the buyer brings more value added to the mining process. As managers, their aim is not to maximize assets under control, as so many American companies have done, but rather to maximize rates of return on capital and thus shareholder value. They really know how to manage investor capital.

And, as I mentioned earlier, we invest in companies where there's clearly a strong bond of common interest between management and the shareholders. Our own firm, Oppenheimer Capital, is owner-managed; we're a publicly traded MLP with significant management ownership. And we look for other companies that are owner-managed, either directly or through incentive compensation schemes like Stern Stewart's leveraged stock purchase plan. We want managers to be owners with us.

STERN: Gene, would it also make a difference if boards of directors had significant stock ownership?

VESELL: It may make a difference in some cases, but I'm not as convinced. Because of our large positions, I'm often asked the question, "Do you like inside or outside boards?" My answer is always, "A plague on both their houses." I know a lot of CEOs who serve as directors on other companies' boards. When I have asked them about their role on these other boards, they tell me quite candidly: "We don't have the information and the time to be very useful."

STERN: But, perhaps the reason they don't have time is that they don't have much of a personal stake in the outcome. They simply receives the fees and the reputational enhancement of sitting on another company's board.

But what if you could get board members to invest their annual directors' fees in, say, slightly out-of-the-money options that are taxless to them until exercise, and on the same basis as the managers? Would that make you feel better about their level of commitment to shareholders?

VESELL: It would, but I'm not sure it's practical from a time point of view. I'm on the board of a private company, and I've got 30,000 options. We had a board meeting in which we were contemplating an acquisition, and the material we were asked to review in preparation for the meeting was several inches think. I just don't have time to do this. So I agree with Jack Welch's position at GE; he sits on no boards other than GE's.

But I agree with you 100% in principle. If you could get people who would serve as full-time, professional directors—people who really have something to offer—then your board incentive system could become very important.

STEWART: So, Gene, what you seem to be saying is that the corporate governance issue we've heard so much about is a phoney.

VESELL: Totally. The real issue is getting the managers inside the company to run the company in the interests of shareholders. You've got to provide *management* with the right incentives to add value.

GEOFF COLVIN: I couldn't agree more that the key is to provide management with the right incentives. But who is going to provide those incentives? Only one body: the board. And since these incentives almost always increase the risk of management's pay package, imposing them may be a disagreeable task. I would argue that, for obvious reasons, outside directors have a somewhat better shot at doing this than insiders—and for this reason, the outsiders versus insiders debate is important.

Back to Accounting

STERN: Jerry, what's your response to the suggestion that we can improve our accounting system?

ZIMMERMAN: In the enthusiasm to improve financial disclosures, there's something important that's being left out of this discussion. We have a set of institutions in place in this country that have a good deal of control over these disclosures. We can sit around this table and dream up the world's best financial disclosures, but the critical question is: "What will the SEC do? What will the FASB do? And what will the plaintiff bar do?"

In Bennett's article called "Market Myths," he shows quite clearly that accounting numbers do not reflect economic reality, and that sophisticated investors—the people who dominate the price-setting process at the margin—quite sensibly pay little attention to accounting numbers. At the very least, our capital markets are quite capable of correcting the distortions built into our accounting framework.

In place of conventional accounting numbers, Bennett proposes making several modifications of accounting conventions to arrive at a financial measure he calls "economic value added," or EVA. Now, how does he do it?

STEWART: Actually, Jerry, in fairness to Joel, I should confess here that most of these ideas were originally his.

ZIMMERMAN: Okay, how do *they* do it? Well, they capitalize corporate R&D instead of expensing it all immediately; they use the full-cost accounting method rather than the successful efforts method; and they add back non-cash expenses like deferred taxes and amortized goodwill to the income statement.

But what are they really doing in the process? Where did these numbers originally come from? They came from the SEC and FASB. It is these same institutions, and the incentives of the people running them, that are at the heart of the problem. They are not really interested in becoming part of the solution. So why do we think that, if Krishna and his colleagues derive better accounting numbers, the SEC and FASB will sanction them? It's these very same institutions that for 60 years now have been mandating accounting disclosures that Joel Stern and Bennett Stewart then have to undo.

STEWART: I too have little hope for acceptance of these measures by the SEC and the FASB. In fact, an endorsement by the SEC would almost necessarily limit their usefulness to the most sophisticated investors—the kind most companies ought to be attempting to reach. In my experience, the most effective shareholder communications are those that focus on performance measures that companies have devised for their own *internal* purposes and to fit their own special circumstances. And when management volunteers to tell the market about those customized measures—especially when such a communication strategy is combined with significant management stock ownership—then I can see investors responding very strongly to such disclosures. But, again, I don't think it's either necessary for, or realistic to expect, the SEC to endorse these more customized kinds of performance measures.

PALEPU: Well, I think the SEC and the FASB can play a positive role in this process. I recently attended a conference on "Financial Reporting in the 21st Century" that had as its declared goal a fundamental rethinking of the U.S. financial reporting system. That conference, I would also point out, was sponsored by one of the Big Six accounting firms and had the blessing of the FASB.

ZIMMERMAN: That may be so, Krish. But I think the overriding concern of professional accountants today is to change the financial reporting system in ways that will reduce their exposure to lawsuits. That's the main thing public accountants are thinking about right now, not improved numbers for valuation purposes.

PALEPU: Well, I agree that we also need to revise auditors' legal liabilities and the excessive litigation our system invites. But that doesn't preclude the possibility of changing accounting measures for the better. We could solve the legal problem in part by restricting private rights of action to only the most minimal set of disclosures. And, by so doing, we could then provide corporate managers with much more freedom to customize their disclosures in a way that sheds light on the value added by their own activities.

Now, of course, you could still object that there's little need for better accounting if the market is already efficient. But I disagree. My view of market efficiency is that, on average, the value of the market portfolio consisting of all companies is probably priced correctly. But even if the market is pretty good in valuing companies in the aggregate, individual companies may well be either overvalued or undervalued for long periods of time because of what academics refer to as "information asymmetries" between managers and outside shareholders. So although a *portfolio* might be correctly valued, many of the individual stocks that make up their value could be significantly undervalued. Because managers could know more about their firm's prospects than outsiders, the market will automatically discount the value of those shares to reflect their informational disadvantage.

So, if I were the CFO of an undervalued company, I think one of my principal responsibilities would be to figure out a way to get my story out. And one way to accomplish that, as I suggested earlier, would be to devise useful leading indicators and then make them the centerpiece in the voluntary or non-SEC part of my investor communications program.

DON CHEW: Krishna, Joel was suggesting earlier that the most effective shareholder communication is the kind targeted for a small, highly sophisticated group of investors—the lead steers, if you will. But there are major regulatory barriers to sharing information privately with only certain investors. Have you thought of a way of getting around these SEC barriers to talking privately to a small group of investors? Or should companies instead design all-purpose communications that seek to reach all investors at their own levels of sophistication?

PALEPU: Well, I agree there are legal barriers, not to mention competitive risks, to sharing certain kinds of information with outside investors. But I think such risks have been greatly exaggerated. Even within the current institutional framework, there is much that could be done. In fact, I have done a number of case studies describing innovative disclosures some American companies have recently devised. For example, Home Depot, a retailer with an innovative strategy, discloses in its annual report a lot of data about the way its stores are managed. And Comdisco, the world's largest computer leasing company, provides detailed information on how it assesses and manages the residual values of its leased computer equipment. In both these cases, the information disclosed is critical for investors in assessing management performance and estimating share values.

STEWART: I too think the competitive risks of sharing strategic information have been overstated. As you said earlier, Krishna, strategy itself has been devalued by technological advances in information and the increasing pace of change; and, as a consequence, execution and flexibility are becoming the keys to success.

What really matters to investors today is not corporate strategy, but the management *process* and the incentives that go along with them. For this reason, I think companies could benefit greatly just by focusing their disclosures on how they manage, what their goals are, how they monitor their progress in meeting those goals, and what their incentives are to bring it all off. So, it's not the specifics of strategy that are important—indeed, in some sense, a company's strategy is changing everyday—but rather the corporate process that would give investors a sense of management's alertness and incentives to respond to continuous change.

Abolish the SEC?

VESELL: As a long-time value-based investor, I was delighted to hear Professor Zimmerman's view about the irrelevance of accounting for stock market investors. I don't mean to suggest that accounting is completely useless. Accounting is sort of the language that you have to learn to get started. But then, as an outsider, you have to learn to translate those numbers in a way that allows you to get a sense of what's going on inside the company.

ZIMMERMAN: That's right. We know that investors are always looking for profits in undervalued or overvalued stocks. And we also know that accounting numbers do have some information content. When they're announced, whether it's in Jakarta or elsewhere, the stock market reacts. But that isn't what accounting numbers were designed to do.

The fundamental difference between Krishna and me is that he has a lot more faith in the SEC than I do. My view is that if I've gone to the same witch doctor for the last 60 years and he's killed off every one of my relatives, I think it's time to shoot the witch doctor. If you want to have improved financial disclosures in this country, the best way is to abolish these blocking institutions and let the companies innovate and invent disclosures that make sense.

STEWART: You think we should abolish the SEC...entirely?

VESELL: I would agree with that.

STEWART: So what you're advocating is essentially a free-market, voluntary, unregulated system of disclosure?

ZIMMERMAN: That's right. And I would also eliminate the insider trading laws. You really can't communicate effectively with the lead steers under the existing insider trading laws. Even if Basil at Scott Paper has the world's best story, he can't whisper it to somebody like Gene Vesell.

STERN: Ned, as New York State Controller until midnight tomorrow, what do you think about these outrageous statements from Professor Zimmerman that we don't need any regulation of disclosure at all?

REGAN: Well, it's less outrageous than having Congress appoint the GAO to audit Scott Paper. But that's about all I can say for the proposal. I can't go along with the idea of an unregulated, completely voluntary market in corporate disclosure. It seems obvious to me we need regulation of disclosure.

ZIMMERMAN: Capital markets worked fine before 1933. Stocks were bought and sold...

REGAN: And a lot of little people were left with worthless paper.

ZIMMERMAN: A lot of people were left with significantly less valuable paper in 1987, too. Stock markets go up and down, despite the best intentions and efforts of auditors and regulators.

Prior to the founding of the SEC in 1933, most NYSE companies issued audited financial statements. Firms have an incentive to do that without the SEC. But look at what the SEC and the FASB have done to our accounting systems. It's because the accounting numbers do not reflect economic reality that people like Joel Stern and Bennett Stewart can make a living advising companies how to undo the harmful effects that come from using those numbers to make decisions.

REGAN: But the SEC doesn't prevent a company from disclosing its strategy, from disclosing its level of customer satisfaction, and the quality of its goods and services relative to that of its peers. They could do all that today, but they don't. The CEO of Scott talks about all these things with his division chiefs, but he doesn't talk about them with his board and with his shareholders. There's nothing in the world to prevent all of this from being discussed in the boardroom and communicated to investors in language they can understand.

So, you can still have your regulatory framework to provide a minimum amount and type of disclosure. But management can exceed that minimum whenever they wish. If they don't, at some point, some Scott shareholders are going to file a resolution to demand to see how the company judges the quality of its product as compared to its competitors. Shareholders know that that issue is discussed everyday on the shop floor at Scott Paper and they would like to know that information.

The Promise of Nonfinancial Measures

STERN: Ned, you are directing a taskforce of sorts to develop nonfinancial performance measures. Would you share with us some of your findings and recommendations?

The SEC doesn't prevent companies from disclosing their strategies, from disclosing their levels of customer satisfaction, and the quality of their goods and services relative to that of their peers. They could do all that today, but they don't. There's nothing in the world to prevent all of this from being discussed in the boardroom and communicated to investors in language they can understand.

—Edward Regan

REGAN: There is a lot of work going on today on nonfinancial measures of corporate performance. There is a study being conducted by an AICPA group headed by Ed Jenkins, the Chicago partner of Arthur Anderson. Another is a group led by Bob Eccles and Jim McGee in Cambridge that is being sponsored by Ernst and Young and the FEI, the Financial Executives Institute. A third study is being done in Toronto by a group of former business people and scholars to assess how these nonfinancial factors—including, interestingly, the corporation's social reputation—correlate with financial results and stock market performance. And Bob Reich at the Labor Department has started a fourth study that will attempt to measure employee satisfaction and involvement and correlate those measures with stock price. So that's at least four groups, and there are probably others doing it.

The AICPA study, like the FEI study, is looking to develop nonfinancial measures such as the ones I've just mentioned—quality of goods and services, employee satisfaction, and customer satisfaction; there are at least a dozen items on the agenda at the moment. Essentially what they are trying to do is to develop industry standards and norms for, say, the paper industry. (And, Basil, I'm making things up here a little bit, but I'm still a politician until midnight.) For example, there might be a measurable standard for customer satisfaction in the paper products industry that could be compiled and reported to investors like the New York State pension system.

And I think it's important to note that this study is being sponsored by the official institution of CPAs and undertaken by some of its members. Some of these CPAs have declared, at least in private to me, that their primary motive for conducting the study is their level of dissatisfaction with existing financial measures as indicators of future performance and value. They have told me that the current financial reporting system doesn't work—and that's, of course, exactly what we're hearing now from people around the table who are far better versed than I on this subject.

Now, I'm not saying this dissatisfaction with current accounting measures is the *prevailing* view among CPAs. Ed Jenkins doesn't necessarily have smooth sailing among his colleagues in conducting this study.

STEWART: So we all agree, then, that quarterly reports don't mean very much to investors?

REGAN: That's right. And, frankly, few people in the public pension system industry are even capable of understanding such reports. You're wrong if you think politicians who run public pension funds are capable of understanding this stuff.

STEWART: Well, why couldn't public pension funds retain investment advisers like Institutional Shareholders Services to do the research for them?

REGAN: They can't pay what somebody would pay a Morgan Stanley or Oppenheimer Capital to do due diligence on a company. And that's one reason I think this research on nonfinancial measures is important. These measures could be especially valuable to public institutional investors, to institutions like us that can't afford to have financial experts on their payroll and who don't relate well—and I put myself at the head of this list—to narrowly focused financial information. This is private-sector-oriented information, but public pension funds are run by public-sector, civil-service-oriented individuals. And it seems to me that a promising way to enhance the ability of what I refer to as the "new" or "reawakened" public-sector shareholder is to give

the people that run those institutions a corporate performance report on something to which they can relate.

Marty Lipton recently proposed the idea of an internal business audit; it's really a revival of something Peter Drucker has been proposing for years. It would not be a financial audit, but a business audit. My guess is that, if the companies themselves began to experiment with the disclosure of these kinds of nonfinancial performance measures, such disclosures would be widely accepted and encouraged by the investment community.

More on Non-Financial Measures

STERN: Let me turn to Carolyn Brancato, who is staff director of this project with Ned Regan. Carolyn, would you summarize the major findings and proposals of this work to date?

BRANCATO: I want to add a couple of observations to Ned's comments.

One of the key nonfinancial measures of performance whose development we hope to encourage is some method of assessing how much, and how effectively, companies are spending to reposition themselves strategically to compete in world markets. As in the Scott Paper example mentioned earlier, I'm thinking of capital expenditures with longer-term payoffs, not something that will show up immediately in the bottom-line EPS.

Why do I think there's a need or demand for such measures? Let me explain by offering a brief recent history of Wall Street. I started my career in 1967 as a securities analyst. In those days we used slide rules, we read Graham & Dodd, and we were fundamentalists. In the late '60s, the institutional investors as we now know them—the pension funds, the mutual funds, and so on—accounted for only about 28% of the equity holdings in the country. (They now account for

upwards of 55%.) Most of the money that was managed came through large investment banking and brokerage houses, and it was managed for large individual accounts. Even the retail money was sort of herded together, and so there was a group of houses that engaged in quite a lot of fundamental analysis.

Brokerage commissions at that time were fixed, not negotiated as they are today. The move to floating commissions in the early 1970s led to a major change in the way Wall Street did business. Many of the big research houses phased out much of their fundamental research activities.

But, as fundamental analysts in the late '60s, we routinely attempted to look through accounting statements to get at normalized, cash-flow-based measures of corporate performance. We never simply took the income statement and the balance sheet at face value. We started with reported accounting numbers, then examined the footnotes, and ended up adding our own layers of information—some of which we got from talking directly to company CFOs. There was also, of course, a whole cadre of technical analysts—the "head and shoulders" people, if you will—but we sort of looked down our noses at them and said, "No, we're fundamentalists and we really know the company."

But today things are different on Wall Street. Consider the consequences of the tremendous flows of money into institutional investors. The large pension funds simply don't have the ability to make these fundamental decisions; in fact, their portfolios are indexed as often as not. In short, the money has moved away from these fundamental-oriented houses that were dominant in the late '60s.

So, largely as a result of these changes, we are now looking to groups like Oppenheimer Capital and the Lens Fund to reinvigorate the old-fashioned kind of fundamental analysis we once practiced. At the same time, as Ned just mentioned, we're also looking for new, particularly nonfinancial, measures of corporate performance. Such measures will help those kinds of investors who can't do the sophisticated financial analysis themselves. For example, we're looking for new ways to reflect R&D, and worker training and education—and for proxies for employee and customer satisfaction—that tend to correlate strongly with current and future corporate performance.

STERN: Are you arguing, then, that the shift from fixed to floating commissions and the increasing flow of funds to institutional investors was a bad thing?

BRANCATO: The consequences have been mixed, good and bad. On the one hand, the growth of pension funds means that our economy has become more effective in distributing wealth throughout the system. On the other hand, there are many companies that feel very constrained by having their shares in the hands of large institutions. They don't know quite how to deal with some of these large pension funds that are sitting on huge piles of money, but whom they believe lack the financial sophistication to understand their financial reporting. Twenty-five years ago, companies felt they could sit down with a relatively small group of analysts and tell their story to a receptive, fundamentally-oriented audience. That's no longer true today.

LEHMANN: I would like to add a different perspective here. On the domestic equity side, only about 10% of all tax-exempt funds managed are indexed. In my experience as a director of corporate IR, index managers typically do not have the need to talk to corporate IR people. But I have found many more fundamental managers who are quite receptive to di-

We are now looking for new, particularly nonfinancial, measures of corporate performance to help those investors who can't do the sophisticated financial analysis themselves. For example, we're looking for new ways to reflect R&D, and worker training and education—and for proxies for employee and customer satisfaction—that tend to correlate strongly with current and future corporate performance. Such measures, by closing the information gap between the lead steers and more passive indexed investors, can serve to extend the informational basis for relationship investing to a much broader base of investors.

—Carolyn Brancato

rect contact with the corporations they invest in. I would also point out that the active buyside manager is way ahead of all but a handful of sellside analysts when it comes to valuing businesses. And corporate IR practices have adapted to this reality by seeking much more direct contact with the buyside than when I entered the field ten years ago.

In Search of The Lead Steers

STERN: Let's turn now to Joe Shenton, who is an adviser to corporations on targeting investor clienteles. Joe, what do you think about what Carolyn just told us about Wall Street?

SHENTON: We have studied the effects of changing the commission structure on Wall Street, and our basic conclusion is that the market was much more efficient with respect to information flows in 1967 than it is today—and precisely for the reason Carolyn just mentioned: without fixed commissions, many brokerage houses

lost their financial incentive to do fundamental research. In 1967 brokers earned 35 to 50 cent commissions for moving a share of stock. Today they earn only four to six cents a share.

For this reason, the quality of sellside research has fallen off dramatically over the past 25 years; indeed, the sellside has become essentially irrelevant to the major lead steer investors—to people like Gene Vesell, for example.

VESELL: I was one of those brokers in the 1970s. And there was a very good economic reason for allowing the brokerage commissions to float. In the old days, investors were being forced by regulation to subsidize the research activities of my brokerage firm and others. I think we're far better off with market-based commissions. This way, investors who are willing to pay their broker for fundamental research can volunteer to pay them directly, without having it built into the commission schedule.

SHENTON: I don't dispute that floating commissions are a better deal for investors. But it has affected corporate disclosure and investor relations in some sense for the worse. If I were a company in the late '60s or early '70s and I wanted to communicate effectively to the investment community, I would visit the ten to twelve sellside analysts that covered my industry, tell them my story, and they in turn would spread the word for me. They had every incentive to do so in those days.

Take Otis Bradley, who was a very well-known and widely-followed analyst of computer stocks in the '60s. When Otis announced a buy recommendation, that company's stock would go flying off the charts. Bradley was the epitome of a lead steer investor—and he was a sellside analyst! When an Otis Bradley research report came out, the information would be all over Wall Street and reflected in the stock price within minutes.

Today, by contrast, the best research is clearly being done by people far removed from the sellside. I was very interested in hearing Gene Vesell's account of how he gets his information. As Gene just told us, it has almost nothing to with the quarterly reports required by the SEC. The issue here is not who's mandating the information, it's who's smart enough to supplement the publicly available information with other, more reliable and useful kinds of information. In my experience, the smartest investors tend to find alternative, often nonfinancial, kinds of information—and they use that information to earn higher rates of return.

STERN: Where do they get the information from?

SHENTON: They dig it. And they get some of it from management.

STERN: If that is so, then why are you maintaining that markets are less efficient today than they were in 1967?

SHENTON: Because the best research is not shared, it is not spread around Wall Street the way it once was.

STERN: Why would that make any difference? I thought stock prices were set at the margin.

CHEW: In fact, a recent study—by Jeremy Stein of MIT and Ken Froot and Andrei Shleifer of Harvard—shows that stock prices now respond far more quickly to corporate news than they did in the '60s and '70s. And, given the advances in information technology, it would be very surprising to find that markets were less efficient today than 25 years ago.

SHENTON: Well, I agree with you both that the information is reflected quickly in the price of the stock. But I'm not talking about prices here, but about information flows. The information flows between companies and the investment community are not nearly as direct as they once were. As I said, a corporate IR director can no longer send his message to ten or twelve sellside analysts and be confident that the market is getting the word. And, deprived of these customary channels, many companies today just choose not to make the effort to tell their story. Instead, they fall back on the SEC safe harbor and disclose just the bare minimum.

But let me also say this. Before I started my consulting firm, I worked in corporate investor relations for 17 years; and, in spite of what you may be reading in the press, there's nothing new about relationship investing. John Neff was giving me heartaches in 1973, when I was director of IR at Northwest Industries. He was the most active investor I have ever seen. Relationship investing has been around in the same way venture capital has been around. It's the same model of corporate governance that is also used in LBOs, which of course came out of the venture capital industry. It's simply the model of highly sophisticated

investors buying large stakes in companies and then having very good channels of communication (often including board seats) and very strong incentives to get information.

STEWART: So, even if the brokerage firms no longer have a strong interest in doing fundamental research today, the high rates of return promised by relationship investing have provided a new incentive for gathering fundamental information.

SHENTON: I agree. But, as I said earlier, there's nothing new about relationship investing; it's been there all the time. The brightest investors have always found ways to get information that give them a real competitive edge.

And for those companies worried about legal liability from providing unorthodox types of disclosure, I have another message: You don't need written disclosures to communicate with lead steer investors. There are lots of other ways to do so that don't violate the securities laws.

But, to reach lead steers, the first thing you have to do is to find out who they are. As Joel suggested earlier, there may be 50 investors who really determine the stock price of Scott Paper at the margin. These are the people who buy or sell in large quantities when the price falls too low or rises too high. All the other 5,000 investors may increase your trading volume, but they don't have any material effect on the stock price.

STEWART: But doesn't this sort of contradict Ned's point about the importance of this passively managed money sitting in public pension funds?

SHENTON: Yes, it does. I'm saying that the corporate IR strategy ought to aim for the highest common denominator. If you aim your financial communications for the most sophisticated investors, they will take care of the share price. Don't worry about the mass of investors. Instead seek out the 50 investors that are going to make a difference to your stock and communicate with them.

STEWART: That's part of the reason why I am very uncomfortable about *mandating* the use of nonfinancial information. I'm not saying that nonfinancial information is unimportant. It's clearly very important for *internal* management purposes.

Three years ago I was doing some work with Whirlpool on performance measurement, and they had put together a very sophisticated system for measuring customer satisfaction, product quality, employee commitment, degree of innovation—and it was all summarized on a single page. It was spontaneously developed by the company for their internal purposes. That makes all the sense in the world; and it may even make sense to share some of this information with outside investors. But to standardize these measures across all companies and then *mandate* their disclosure to investors seems pointless.

BRANCATO: Our commission has never suggested that such disclosures be mandated. We recommended that they be developed to close this information gap between the small groups of very sophisticated investors doing fundamental analysis and the large pension funds indexing huge blocks of money. As Ned said, these funds simply don't have the resources to do sophisticated financial analysis. And the nonfinancial measures we're now experimenting with—even if the most sophisticated investors do not need them to value the shares—could provide useful information to guide the investment decisions of the less sophisticated investors.

STEWART: But that's precisely my point. If investors are unwilling to pay for the information in the form of a higher stock price, then why do it? I just don't see how disclosure of these *standardized* nonfinancial measures

can help companies increase their stock prices—which, to me, is the true test of effective disclosure.

BRANCATO: My point is this: These nonfinancial measures of performance, by closing the information gap between the fundamentalist lead steers and more passive indexed investors, can serve to extend this informational basis for relationship investing in a way that involves a much broader base of investors.

VESELL: I should point out, however, that we at Oppenheimer manage a lot of public pension money, including some of New York State's. We're talking about $5 or $6 billion of public money that we're delighted to manage. So this information gap may not be as large as we are making it out to be.

STERN: So, even though commissions have disappeared, it would seem from Gene's comment that we have evolved into a system where 50 to 100 lead steers now do the work that some 1,000 security analysts were doing 25 years ago. And this system seems to work quite well—so much so that Oppenheimer Capital is winning over the business of public pension funds because of its ability to generate superior returns.

A Corporate IR Perspective

ALEX LEHMANN: There is another kind of information gap that divides even the fundamentalists. As I said earlier, there is a tremendous divergence between most brokerage or sellside research—which is based on the accounting model and geared toward predicting next quarter's EPS—and the approach of sophisticated buyside institutional investors, as represented by somebody like Gene Vesell.

I represented Whitman Corporation for about eight years starting in 1983. It's a fairly complex company, a

conglomerate. At that time, the company was comprised of six independent, freestanding businesses. My job was first and foremost to communicate one on one with the buyside. I set myself the task of identifying our 50 largest shareholders, getting to know them, and maintaining an ongoing dialogue with them. We discussed the company's goals and strategies—typically in terms of cash flows rather than conventional EPS. And, in the course of many discussions, it was always my aim to clarify any corporate actions or decisions that might have led to misunderstanding or uncertainty.

Put a little differently, our purpose was to create an appropriate or realistic set of investor expectations. The key was to establish and then maintain credibility and, by so doing, to try to make a complex company as simple as possible for investors to understand. As I said, most of our communications effort was directed at the buyside investment community, the people who owned our stock. The sellside analysts came in later in the process and proved very useful in leveraging our buyside efforts.

I discovered a few things along the way. First, to communicate effectively, you have to value the company's businesses regularly; such regular exercises in valuation give you the ammunition for productive discussions with investors. Then you have to be timely and consistent. Maintaining a sense of continuity is key, for example, when there is a change at the top. I served three CEOs during my eight years and, as you would expect, they each had different views about what the company should be or become. Also, maintaining reasonable expectations is difficult when management deviates from a carefully explained strategy or when it makes overly optimistic earnings predictions. The result is a credibility gap.

The active buyside manager is way ahead of all but a handful of sellside analysts when it comes to valuing businesses. Corporate IR practices have adapted to this reality by seeking much more direct contact with the buyside than when I entered the field ten years ago.

My job was first and foremost to communicate one on one with the buyside. I set myself the task of identifying our 50 largest shareholders, getting to know them, and maintaining an ongoing dialogue with them. The sellside analysts came in later in the process and proved very useful in leveraging our buyside efforts.

—Alex Lehmann

When you look at the portfolio turnover of different institutional investors, you will find that there are many who are interested in little more than higher EPS next quarter. Knowing my lead-steer investors, I had to decide how much time I wanted to spend with each of them. Most important, though, 35 of the 50 largest holders in 1983 were still with us when I left the company in 1991. Investors like nothing better than holding on, provided management performs and creates value.

STERN: Judy, from your vantage point at *Business Week*, what do you make of Alex Lehmann's approach to corporate investor relations at the Whitman Corporation? Is it something that many other companies might be able to borrow?

DOBRZYNSKI: I find the approach very interesting. In my experience, companies pay far too much attention to the sellside analysts. And I think it's the companies themselves that are inviting the investment community to focus on the quarterly numbers. If companies want the analysts to focus on longer-term performance measures, they ought to start talking to the buyside people—and perhaps they could even attempt to educate the sellside in the process. Maybe the sellside isn't as limited as we're all making it out to be.

So, in an important sense, then, companies are really getting the kinds of investors they deserve. If you appeal to the lowest common denominator, that's what you'll wind up getting—at least that's the message that Alex and Joe Shenton seem to be giving us.

The Case of Equifax

STEWART: Derek, as the former CFO of Equifax, and now an Executive Vice President running one of its major business lines, you have faced this kind of issue of being evaluated periodically on an EPS basis. Your company now seems to be undergoing a transformation of sorts, a significant change in both its internal management process and in its disclosures to the investment community. Could you tell us a little about what prompted these changes?

SMITH: Let me start by saying that much of U.S. accounting and regulatory process is counterproductive and archaic. As a consequence, it is reducing the competitiveness of U.S. companies in the global marketplace. Many poor management decisions are made in order to make public companies look good in terms of improved financial results. Fortunately, some companies such as Scott and Equifax are trying to manage *value* by creating new performance measures, a "second set of books." But I contend that too many important business decisions of U.S. companies continue to be driven by short-term accounting results—by management's belief that the investment community forces them to maximize reported earnings—and by executive compensation systems that reward management according to EPS instead of long-term value.

The issue I've heard everyone discuss is how we ought to *measure* value. But, frankly, I'm not as interested in measuring value as I am in how we're going to *create* value. It's this focus on creating value, and our level of dissatisfaction with the effectiveness of conventional measurement systems in driving value, that prompted Equifax to implement a new financial framework. We wanted to redirect our overall process toward the pursuit of value—or, more precisely, to minimize any temptation provided by our accounting system to interfere with rather than encourage the creation of value.

VESELL: Could you say a little more about the difference between creating value and measuring value?

SMITH: The accounting system reflects historical performance. But, given the pace of change today and the power of on-line information technologies, these accounting *statistics* have minimal value as real-time decision tools. As CFO, I couldn't wait for reported financial results. By the time those numbers were calculated and consolidated, new market developments, competitive events, and changing conditions usually had made them obsolete.

Management at Equifax has determined that there are two critical success factors in creating value—possibly the two most important—that traditional reporting methods ignore. The first is people. We must have superior people focused on the right issues, and we must be able to monitor their performance in meeting our most critical goals. The second is the business, or management, processes Bennett mentioned earlier.

This second critical factor made us face the realities of the problems created by the accounting systems. There are simply too many ways to produce better accounting results by making business decisions that fail to add value or, even worse, reduce value. Our old system was not encouraging the kind of value-creating behavior in our operating executives that we wanted.

But, try as we might to free ourselves from the traditional system and decision rules, traditional methods and habits of behavior die hard. For every relationship investor that really will give you a long enough time horizon, there are a whole slew of conventional EPS investors who, even if they don't ultimately set your price, can certainly divert your attention.

Accounting for Marketing: The Case of CUC International

STEWART: Well, let me give you an example I came across recently where this kind of conflict between account-ing and economics comes into play. Take the case of a cellular phone business that pays Radio Shack $500 for each new cellular subscriber it signs up. The $500 amounts to a finder's fee, a marketing outlay that will take the company about two years to recoup.

Now, because of this heavy initial outlay, which the accounting system forces you to expense entirely in the year incurred, fourth-quarter earnings would be significantly reduced by a sharp growth in new sign-ups in that quarter. And what tends to happen, I'm told, is that in the fourth quarter of every year, sales come to a standstill because people are beginning to look at the year-end earnings figures that drive their bonuses. So here's an example where an accounting policy and incentives tied to the earnings are clearly having a material adverse impact on the business.

PALEPU: But, in fact, Bennett, companies can and do capitalize some of their marketing expenditures. Paul Healy at MIT and I just finished writing a case about a company with an accounting problem very similar to the one you just described. The company, which is called CUC International, is also in an annual subscription kind of business. It's also the kind of business where you spend a lot of money signing up somebody; and then if they stay with you, you make a lot of money because the service itself doesn't cost much to deliver.

Therefore, to the extent you can retain your subscribers, you have what amounts to an annuity for a significant period of time. The problem faced by CUC's management was finding a way to communicate to the market that its marketing outlays had a promising payoff down the road.

The way CUC initially chose to communicate its prospects was to capitalize a significant portion of their marketing outlays. But when they did so, a number of highly vocal sellside analysts criticized the accounting practice as too aggressive. So the company was faced with the choice of flouting the accounting norms endorsed by the analysts or finding some alternative method of convincing the investment community it was really creating value through these marketing outlays.

STEWART: But if they're using more conservative accounting methods, and everybody knows that, then shouldn't the higher "quality" of earnings be acknowledged by the market in the form of a higher P/E ratio? Isn't that what the theory says should happen?

PALEPU: Well, there are two reasons why that might not happen in this case. For one thing, CUC is a somewhat smaller company; and, at the time it was facing this problem, it had a relatively limited institutional following. And I happen to believe that such companies still operate in what I would call "pockets" of market inefficiency—in less efficient segments of the market.

My second point is that the problem is not just one caused by accounting distortions. There is a real economic uncertainty surrounding the payoff from these marketing outlays. That is, when you sign up new subscribers, there is no guarantee they are going to stay with you beyond a quarter or two. CUC's managers have a better handle on this than outsiders, but it is difficult to communicate this kind of information effectively.

So, to overcome this communication problem, CUC went back to conservative accounting and then undertook a very bold change in the *financial* structure of the company. They went out and borrowed a lot of money to pay a special dividend and repurchase their shares in the open market. And although this dramatic recapitalization did not lead to an immediate increase in its share value—

> *We used a major change in financial structure, including a significant repurchase of our stock, to accomplish two important value creation initiatives internally and to communicate that information to investors.*
>
> *One, we were reducing our cost of capital through increased financial leverage. Two, we were indicating our internal commitment to increasing the capital efficiency of our ongoing businesses.*
>
> —*Derek Smith*

this took place over the next year or so—it did achieve one very notable change: It led to a very sharp increase in institutional ownership of CUC's shares, from 5% to 88%. And, interestingly, more active and sophisticated institutions like Tiger Management and Fidelity began reporting purchases of very large stakes.

So I would describe this as using financial change to "signal" management's confidence in the firm's prospects. And, over the two years following the recap, the value of the shares—including the large cash distribution—rose by some 96%.

BRANCATO: That story illustrates perfectly the existence of the information gap between sophisticated, fundamentals-driven investors and more passive institutions. If CUC had been able to devise an effective measure of its subscribers' satisfaction, it might not have had to resort to such a financial solution—and it might have retained its less sophisticated investor clientele in the process.

The Equifax Recap: Signalling Through Capital Structure

STERN: Derek, while you were still CFO at Equifax, the company did a somewhat similar financial recapitalization—a Dutch auction share repurchase—that was very well received by the market. What were you thinking when you did that, and what message did that send to your shareholders?

SMITH: That decision was part of a comprehensive change in the financial philosophy and measurement systems that guide our corporate decision processes at Equifax. We needed to find a way to communicate the value implications of these changes, and so our new financial structure was intended to be a powerful signal of these changes in the operating approach of the company. In effect, we used a major change in financial structure, including a significant repurchase of our stock, to accomplish two important value creation initia-

tives internally and to communicate that information to investors.

One, we were reducing our cost of capital through increased financial leverage. Two, we were indicating our internal commitment to increasing the capital efficiency of our ongoing businesses.

The *internal* message sent by our leveraged recapitalization was probably even more important than the external one. I was more concerned about signalling to our own management team the importance of making management decisions consistent with increasing value for our shareholders. I believe that if we do the right things internally, the market will figure out what we're doing, even it does take some time to get the point across.

STERN: Well, it didn't take much time for the market to react. My understanding is that your shares went up by some 20% within a month or two of the announcement.

VESELL: How did you decide on your capital structure? Were you driven by the rating agencies or by the economics of the business?

SMITH: We wanted to maintain a prudently leveraged capital structure—one that would enable us to command an investment-grade rating. The second part of your question is more difficult to answer. I hesitate to say that our leverage ratio was dictated entirely by the economics of the business because the rating agency decisions are driven only partly by pure economics or cash flows. As you know, there are some rating agency criteria that don't seem completely consistent with the economics of an information technology business.

To illustrate my point, a lot of Equifax's market assets are not on our books. We're in the financial and insurance information reporting business. The value of these businesses is not driven by hard assets, but by databases and information gateways that don't show up on the balance sheet. If you were using only the traditional financial ratios to assess our credit risk, none of our important assets would show up in the analysis.

STERN: If you can't kick it, how can you borrow against it?

SMITH: That's certainly the old formula. So, to keep our rating consistent with our true risk profile, we had to communicate to the agencies the unique nature of Equifax. We proved to be successful in telling our story, in part because there is a somewhat new appreciation of the ability of certain intangible assets to generate cash flow to service debt over the long term. To make your case with the rating agencies, you really have to take the initiative to educate them. But, if you take the time and do the job well, they are an intelligent and responsive audience.

VESELL: I'm frankly surprised you've succeeded in doing that; the rating agencies have a strong conservative bias.

SMITH: It wasn't easy, but we achieved a mutual understanding.

STERN: Well, Derek, if you were as persuasive with the rating agencies as you were in making the case in your most recent annual report, I can see why you were able to succeed. Equifax's new annual report provides very effective discussions of the company's new financing policy and financial measurement system.

Clientele Effects

STEWART: Joe, how would you expect the market to react to that kind of fundamental change communicated by Equifax? Would the investor base change? And what has your research shown about how different kinds of investment clienteles affect share prices?

SHENTON: Let me start by responding to the last question first. As you

There may be 50 investors who really determine the stock price of Scott Paper at the margin. These are the people who buy or sell in large quantities when the price falls too low or rises too high. Corporate IR strategy ought to aim for those 50 investors. If you aim your financial communications for the most sophisticated investors, they will take care of the share price.

—Joseph Shenton

know, Bennett, we at OLC have done some research demonstrating not only the existence of very different investor clienteles, but also that different kinds of investors tend to seek out different kinds of companies to invest in.

We started by taking ten of the most popular investment approaches and then assigned each of some 5,000 institutional investors to one of those ten categories. At one end of the spectrum is the Miller and Modigliani discounted cash flow approach that Stern Stewart has transformed into its EVA corporate performance measure—the kind that LBO investors were presumably using throughout the '80s. At the other extreme are technical analysis, indexation, and other purely computer-driven methods of trading. Between these extremes, and ranging from active to passive, are strategies like earnings momentum models, sector rotation models, and a variety of others.

Our next step was then to attempt to determine whether these different investor clienteles were attracted to different kinds of companies. For example, we used your Stern Stewart performance 1,000 rankings to come up with the following insight: As companies move up in your ranking system—thus becoming more profitable and more valuable in the view of the stock market—the more active, value-based investors increase their percentage holdings. And when companies move down in your MVA ranking system, the value-based investors bail out and the passive investors come in and take their place. (And, incidentally, I should point out that when we tried to find these clientele effects using other ranking systems like *Fortune*'s or *Business Week*'s—ranking systems that essentially measure size rather than profitability or value added, the clientele effects disappeared.)

Now, what are these clientele effects I'm talking about? Well, think about the story Derek just told us about Equifax. That story, quite frankly, wouldn't mean much to the average sellside analyst. Of course, you can talk to sellside analysts and try to educate them that the company is moving to manage for long-term economic value, but you won't get much of a response. The sellside has a vested interest in stimulating a lot of short-term trading, not in encouraging long-term investing. Consequently, their principal interest is in forecasting next quarter's EPS. To make an effect on sellside people, you really have to talk in standard EPS terms.

Early in the process of contemplating this fundamental change in its financial measurement system, Equifax decided that they were going to appeal to a fairly small group of investors—say, the 50 most sophisticated institutions out of a potential 5,000. They targeted their presentations to that group of 50, and half of those investors eventually became investors in Equifax. And this was certainly not a serendipitous event; these were the lead steer investors.

Now, what did Equifax accomplish by this? Well, what they really did was to shorten the time it took the market to place the proper value on the firm's shares. Without such a targeted IR program, it probably would have happened naturally anyway. But it would have taken much more time, and there likely would have been a lot more volatility in getting there.

The fact of the matter is, the market's ability to value shares properly depends greatly on the quality of the information management is providing. If you do a poor job of communicating with investors, you're much more likely to be undervalued at any given time. But if you instead design your communication to appeal to the people who are going to set the

price—and you can figure out who they are—then you can influence the valuation of your shares.

STERN: But what about the other investors? Do you make any attempt to court them?

SHENTON: I have nothing against passive investors, but they're just not equipped to respond to fundamental issues. And it's far more cost-effective to devote a company's IR budget to influencing the views of the most sophisticated, value-based investors—most of whom, in my experience, tend to be long-term investors. In fact, such investors make their money by taking advantage of some of the short-term "noise" trading, by profiting from the fluctuations caused by less sophisticated investors' trading on the last quarter's earnings.

So, when Equifax set about communicating its story, it chose 50 investors from the active investor categories. In helping companies choose their investors, we look for investors that have taken similar risks, but without a large concentration in the given industry. For example, I would examine Gene's portfolio at Oppenheimer to evaluate whether Equifax represents a good fit. And if there were few other information services companies in the portfolio, and Oppenheimer had showed a willingness to take on companies with a moderate degree of financial risk—or, more pointedly, it had shown itself to be attracted to companies volunteering to increase their financial leverage—then we might have a nice fit.

STEWART: Joe, are you saying that relationship investors by and large fall into this top category of value-based, sophisticated, fundamentals-oriented investors?

SHENTON: Absolutely. Gene Vesell is clearly a value-based, fundamental investor. So is Warren Buffett. When I was at Northwest Industries in the

'70s, Buffett was a 5% holder and that was relationship investing.

And let me make one very critical point about shareholder communications. Disclosure is not a one-way communication; it's really about establishing a two-way channel. Effective corporate IR means seeking out and listening to influential investors. This can help management design the performance measures that investors find useful. It's this kind of two-way communication and beneficial exchange that is the ultimate goal of relationship investing.

STEWART: If a company finds that it has an inordinately high proportion of passive investors, does that tell you anything?

SHENTON: If you have mostly passive or short-term investors—and a lot of companies do—it's either because your company is reasonably well run and has taken the attitude the market will take care of itself, or it is poorly run and value-based investors have bailed out. One thing our research has disclosed is that a "passive neglect" approach to corporate IR—as reflected by an increasing proportion of passive, short-term investors—is associated with an *increase* in a company's beta. That's very clear from our data. On the other hand, having lots of value investors can be bad news as well as good. A sharp increase in value investors could mean they sense a change of management control in the offing.

But, in general, it's good to have value-based investors. For example, look at what is happening in healthcare today. The most sophisticated investors are seizing profit opportunities created by the general devastation of healthcare stocks. These investors were not short-term earnings momentum or sector types; they were long-term investors taking advantage of the opportunities created by such short-term trading strategies.

STEWART: Does having more active, sophisticated investors typically lead to a better dialogue with management, and thus to better corporate governance?

SHENTON: Well, that's likely to be true if management's primary objective is to maximize the value of the company's shares. If your interests as a manager are identical with those of investors, then you clearly want to communicate regularly and clearly with investors. They should be viewed as your partners in the enterprise.

But if management is not completely committed to maximizing value, then they're not likely to want to get too close to investors. In such cases, the long-term, sophisticated investors are not likely to hold your shares. And the short-term, passive types that will hold your shares will effectively keep the firm on a very tight tether, responding to every blip in quarterly earnings.

Superactive Investors: The Case of the Lens Fund

STEWART: Let's now turn to Nell Minow, who, together with Bob Monks, recently launched the Lens Fund. Nell, how would you characterize the Lens Fund? Are you just an ordinary active investor, or does your style take you off the charts?

MINOW: We're very much off the charts. Normally, when you talk about active versus passive investors, you're really just talking about whether they're buying or selling. We are in the business of active management of the ownership rights conferred by common stock. Most money managers buy stock that they hope will go up. We buy stock and then we try to make it go up ourselves by exercising the rights that come with share ownership.

Our first case study was at Sears, where we used our initial purchase of

Relationship investing is not something new; it's been with us since the days of the joint stock companies and Adam Smith. Whether we're talking about venture capital for start-ups, LBOs for mature companies, or the management of large public companies, the essence of relationship investing is the same: it's having large-stake investors, and supplying them with information about and some measure of influence over corporate strategic decisions.

—Nell Minow

100 shares to initiate a process that led eventually to the break-up of a company that had become too large and lost its focus. By the time that break-up took place, we had accumulated enough shares to make up all of our costs (including a full page ad in *The Wall Street Journal* that called the board of directors a "nonperforming asset") and then some.

I would like to comment on a couple of the things that have been said. I was especially interested in Professor Zimmerman's opening point that the fundamental purpose of accounting was to monitor the stewardship function of corporate management. It seems to me that the real issue underlying this discussion is that of stewardship: Are managers doing the best possible job for the shareholders whom they supposedly represent, or are there signficant agency costs arising from conflicts of interest between management and shareholders?

Now, in order to answer this question, investors need good information. When I'm looking for information, I want the kind of information that will best help me to evaluate what the CEO and directors are doing. I don't need to hear everything that they hear in the boardroom; my agenda as a shareholder is limited, which is one consequence of my limited liability. But, as Bob Monks and I said in our book *Power and Accountability*, there is a reason accounting principles are called "generally accepted" and not "certifiably accurate." The best you can say is that they provide some consistency. You may be comparing apples and apples, but that does not answer your question about tomatoes. For this reason, Bennett, I think you are wrong to dismiss the relevance of nonfinancial measures for shareholders—I think that Carolyn Brancato and Ned Regan are on to something potentially quite valuable.

I also have another major objection to something I heard earlier. In communicating with investors, companies should not underestimate the importance of index investors. Information is not just about buying and selling, gentlemen. Information is about how you behave as an owner. And index investors can become very active as owners. Certainly that's been true of CALPERS, Wells Fargo, and a number of institutions I've worked with. And let me tell you that these institutions, even the indexers, want all the information they can get. If institutional investors didn't want information and influence, Bob Monks and I would not have started the Lens Fund.

What kinds of information do they want? Well, one thing they clearly value is all the information they can get about executive compensation plans. One piece of information that is not currently required, but one I find immensely useful, is the dilution impact of stock option plans. And my old firm, Institutional Shareholder Services, helps a lot of institutional investors by providing them with this information.

Now, I agree with Joe Shenton that relationship investing is not something new; it's been with us since the days of the joint stock companies and Adam Smith. Relationship investing has in fact been crucial to economic development (if it had not taken hold, we would be living in a socialist society today). As an entrepreneur myself, when I go to seek venture capital, the first thing the venture capitalist asks me is, how many seats can he have on the board? And this is the essence of relationship investing, whether we're talking about venture capital for start-ups, LBOs for mature companies, or the management of large public companies. It's having large-stake investors, and supplying them with information about and some

measure of influence over corporate strategic decisions.

In the case of Eastman Kodak, we intend to stay with Kodak to see through some major changes. We put our money where our mouth is. And if you get our money, you're going to get our mouth. And Joe Shenton is quite right, by the way, in saying that the best corporate executives will want to listen to what we have to say.

STERN: How long have you been in Kodak?

MINOW: Since the fund began—that is, about a year ago.

STERN: Why did you get into Kodak in the first place? Or, more generally, how do you choose to make your investments?

MINOW: We have invested in four companies to date. It's our intention to be substantial investors in no more than four companies at any given time, so that we can pay very careful attention to each of them.

One of our investment criteria is significantly substandard rates of return over several time horizons: one-year, three-year, and five-year periods. We work with Batterymarch, which provides all kinds of numbers for us on strategic momentum. We want to know if they're drifting downward or if they've already started to go back up.

We also do things like NEXIS searches on management to see whether we can isolate management as the variable that is depressing the stock. We're looking for companies where there's the largest possible gap between the value that could be there and the value that the market is showing. And it has to be a gap that we can influence. If it's a company that has industry-wide problems, if it's in a heavily regulated industry, or if management has a substantial number of shares, then we're not going to get into it. It has to be something where we can affect the outcome by acting

as shareholders, within the authority and by using the rights that accompany stock ownership.

STERN: How do you decide when it's time to get out? Kodak, for example, recently took a very positive step by encouraging its managers to buy stock in the company.

MINOW: Yes, we were thrilled about it.

STERN: And the stock price has since gone up by more than 25%. What else do you think they might do to enhance its value?

MINOW: We continue to believe that Kodak is highly susceptible to change if pushed. The imaging technology in their business is changing very dramatically and they have invested heavily in it. But their efforts to diversify have been disastrous, and we think that there's money to be made by reversing the process.

STEWART: I think there's two major changes Kodak can make. One, as you suggest, they can unwind the diversification. They have a very large chemical company, they have imaging, they have photography, and they have the pharmaceuticals company. Simply splitting the company into pieces—whether as independent companies through spin-offs to shareholders or by selling some of the businesses to other companies—should create considerable value.

The second thing you could do would be to stop using the huge gross profit margins on film to subsidize other businesses. As in so many conglomerates I've observed, the cash flows from the profitable businesses end up being wasted on organizational inefficiencies; they never make it down to the bottom line. Kodak has a huge management infrastructure that is crying out to be rationalized by going through the kind of core process redesign that has been laying off middle managers across America. Either Kodak's top management just can't make the hard decisions, or they've lost sight of the fact that it's execution that matters. It's not grandiose strategic thinking, but process redesign that makes the difference these days.

MINOW: That's right. And results are what the compensation scheme has to be designed to promote. And that's what the board has to be designed to promote.

STERN: Nell, are there certain kinds of nonfinancial measures you have asked Kodak to provide?

MINOW: We wrote Kodak a 22-page letter filled with questions about options we wanted them to consider. All but one page described strategic and financial initiatives; one page related to governance issues, focusing on the relationship between shareholders and directors. We did not say we wanted them to make those changes immediately. Rather, we said we were intelligent people with a significant financial investment at stake. And that, given the limits of *publicly available information*, we had certain questions that we wanted to explore with management. We met with Whitmore and Steffen several times, and we continue to be in close contact with the company.

PALEPU: Would you make public the brief that you wrote Kodak?

MINOW: It's not public at the moment, and won't be unless our communication with management breaks down.

PALEPU: But, if you're convinced your analysis is correct, why not make the document public and rally the support of other investors? This may give you even more leverage with management than you have now.

MINOW: True, but until we feel that leverage is needed, our approach is less confrontational. First we go to the CEO. If that works, fine; then we don't need to go farther. If that doesn't work, then we go to the board of

directors. And if that doesn't work, and only then, do we go to the shareholders, and the press.

VESELL: What is your exit strategy?

MINOW: We have an exit price in mind when we go in—although that is subject to continuous revision. In fact, we have already taken some gains in Kodak because the price run-up made it more than 25% of our portfolio. We are designed to be an enhancement to an indexed portfolio. At the moment, it's all our own money, but we hope to change that fairly soon.

VESELL: How do you determine the price at which you're going to sell?

MINOW: Based on a sort of a traditional investment-banker, break-up-value analysis. This is not going to continue to be our strategy forever, but all the companies in our portfolio at the moment are there because they are conglomerates. That's one thing shareholders really have the information and the power to change in underperforming companies; they get to decide whether this should really be one big, diversified company or three separate companies. That's where there's the biggest opportunity to add value.

STEWART: Nell, what you are saying is that the '80s ended too soon. The deconglomeration wave reached as far as R.J. Reynolds; but, when it receded, we still had companies like Procter & Gamble and Sears and GM that needed to be restructured back into their basic parts. So, what you and Bob Monks are really now doing is the unfinished work of the restructuring of the '80s.

MINOW: Well, I think of what we're doing as a refinement of the takeover era. The takeover era brought some very important corrections, but it did so in a brutal and scattershot way. I think that we can do it in a more humane and, ultimately, more efficient way.

STERN: Four at a time? It may take forever at that rate. I would hope that just the threat of the Lens Fund owning stock would prompt many underperforming companies to reform from within—even if you never arrive. That would be a true sign of your effectiveness.

MINOW: I agree. In fact, I think the most telling measure of our success will be when the announcement of our investment becomes itself a buy signal to the general market. And I think that will happen. When Steffen's departure was announced yesterday, we got about a dozen phone calls from institutional investors with substantial stakes in Kodak asking us what we were going to do and if we wanted their help.

VESELL: What have been the results of your approach to date?

MINOW: As we near the end of the first year, we have substantially outperformed the S&P index with a 20.5% return. It would be about twice that if Westinghouse hadn't continued to be so recalcitrant. But keep your eyes on Westinghouse.

Incentive Compensation as a Substitute for Takeovers

STEWART: In 1985, CEOs or CFOs would likely have been concerned about their stock prices in large part because of the threat of hostile takeover. That threat seems to have all but disappeared. Basil, are you still concerned about Scott Paper's stock price? And are you more or less concerned than, say, back in the mid-1980s?

ANDERSON: In fact, I would argue that, because of fairly recent changes in our incentive compensation plan, the management and employees of Scott Paper are probably *more* concerned about our stock price today than they were five or ten years ago. In the past, our company's compensation philosophy was to pay higher-than-average salaries and modest bonuses. Today, our salaries are set at roughly the median level for large companies, but there is lots more incentive-based pay and stock options. So my own personal compensation, as well as that of most of our top executives, now depends significantly on how the stock performs.

STEWART: Nell, do you find now that the new SEC disclosures on management compensation are helpful to you as an investor? Do you think that's a productive change?

MINOW: Yes, I'm absolutely delighted about it. In fact, I think the disclosures provided by the compensation committee are the most important ones of all for investors. I want to know what companies are trying to achieve with the compensation plan. It's not how much the CEO gets paid, but the goals the company is setting for him. Are they trying to maximize earnings per share or long-term economic value? I like to see these goals spelled out clearly. But if I instead see just a lot of boilerplate in the compensation report, then I become very suspicious.

STEWART: Then you would agree with Michael Jensen that it's not how much we pay our CEOs that really matters, but rather how they are paid?

MINOW: Very much so. I want to see that the interests of the shareholders and the managers are closely aligned. If that's the case, then I'm delighted if the CEO makes a bundle.

But, at the same time, let me repeat a recent remark by Bud Crystal that really struck me. He said that if you go short on every company that gives restrictive stock grants to the CEO, you're going to make out like crazy. Why? Because that company is effectively saying, "We don't think the stock's going to go up, but we want the CEO to get something anyway." It reminds me of Sears' grant to Mr. Martinez of yet another "guaranteed bonus." A guaranteed bonus—which,

incidentally, is my favorite oxymoron—really tells you something about whether the man is willing to bet on himself or not.

CHEW: The same thing seems to hold for relationship investors. There's a study that demonstrates that when Warren Buffett and other relationship investors buy common stock, then that's a buy signal for the other stockholders—the stock will outperform market averages over the next few years. But if Buffett takes a convertible preferred instead of the common, then that's a sell signal. The signal, as you suggest, Nell, is in the structure of the contract.

MINOW: Yes, and that's the reason that the compensation committee report is going to be tremendously important.

As for other potentially valuable nonfinancial disclosures, I was very much influenced by Dick Crawford's book about human capital. I'd like to know from companies how much money they're spending on training and their employee turnover rate. I also look at the quality of the products and the extent to which there is a commitment to total quality management. If somebody gets the Baldridge Award, I think that's very useful information.

I also love to see disclosures about the governance component of the company. I want to make sure that they have a governance system that encourages listening. This includes having a majority of independent directors, an independent nominating committee, and, perhaps most important, regular private meetings of the independent directors without the CEO or other company employees. And I look to see the level of activism in the company. If I bought every company that CALPERs targeted, I would be making terrific returns. Last year, on an investment of $500,000, CALPERS made $137 mil-

lion in extraordinary returns in their shareholder initiative program. And I would defy anybody in the room to find another investment that made that kind of return.

Investing for the Long Run

STEWART: Gene, how do you contrast your approach in investing with that of the Lens Fund? It seems there's some similarities in that you both take major stakes—but you're not quite as provocative.

VESELL: Well, I'd say we're not quite as *vocal*. We may in fact be equally provocative.

STEWART: Do you make recommendations to companies that they make certain changes?

VESELL: We certainly do. We are not at all hesitant to talk about things that we think we know something about. Such things would generally be financial rather than operational, often involving management compensation.

But incentive compensation is by no means a panacea. We've found, to paraphrase Buffett, that if you have good assets but you're not in bed with good people, the people will win out. It's very hard to make money if you've got a really bad management. Most of the scars I have acquired during my years in this business have come from situations where we attempted to combine good assets and bad people.

STEWART: But you don't have an investment in Kodak or Sears. Why is that?

VESELL: It's not our cup of java. We try, in general, to invest in good businesses; and, in some instances, the businesses are better than the accounting results would suggest. We know Chris Steffen very well because we own about 10% of Honeywell, and we're very familiar with what he did there. We're just not knowledgeable enough about Kodak. We don't swing at every pitch.

DOBRZYNSKI: Do you have a predetermined exit point? How and when do you decide to get out and take a gain?

VESELL: When we go into a company, we establish what we think is the rational economic value of the enterprise; and we buy if that value is significantly higher than the current stock price. But once we buy a company, our time horizon—as Buffett said when he bought his stake in Coca Cola—is forever. We don't want to sell.

In fact what we want to achieve is the continuous value creation, if you will, that can be achieved by a management intent on maximizing cash flow over the long haul. If the assets are managed correctly, and if the free cash is either reinvested in projects above the cost of capital or returned to shareholders (if there are no promising projects), then management can achieve continuous value creation. And's that the process we try to foster at Oppenheimer-owned companies. But, when we live with our investments for a long time, we constantly monitor the price/value relationships of our companies very carefully.

STEWART: Gene, you heard Derek Smith talk about share repurchase earlier, and you just mentioned it now. How do you look at dividends, which are just another way of distributing cash to investors? Does dividend yield or dividend payout enter into your valuation method?

VESELL: No, not really. Dividends are just one of several ways you can return your excess capital to investors—and we prefer stock repurchase.

STEWART: Do you typically tender your shares into repurchase offers?

VESELL: Only if the offer is made at a large premium over the stock price. Otherwise, and provided we feel it's a company in which want to increase our investment, we almost always choose to increase our proportional ownership instead of tendering our shares.

STERN: Gene, are there big risks to you from having to pay a huge premium to take a large equity position to get in, or from having to take a huge discount to get out?

VESELL: Not if we're correct in our buying or selling decisions. Because we're typically buying things that are out of favor and other people are selling, it's surprisingly easy to buy them. And if the company does well, then it should be relatively easy to get out.

Let me give you an example. At one time we owned as much as 25% of Fruit of the Loom. We started buying it at $12 or $13, and then it went down to six or seven. So we had no trouble buying all we wanted. We own somewhere between 5% and 10% of the company now. We started selling it in the high 30s and then sold more in the high 40s. There was no problem selling it at that point in time.

So if you're right, there's no problem. And even if you're wrong—we have owned a lot of American Express and haven't done very well with it—there can still be plenty of liquidity.

Indexed Activists: The Case of New York State

STERN: Let me turn back to Ned Regan, who, as I mentioned earlier, is now serving out his next to last day as a public servant. Ned, Joe Shenton has sort of suggested that it may not be worth companies' spending much time with indexers like your New York State fund. Yet you've defied his expectations in a way by becoming an active investor in a number of cases. Would you tell us why you've chosen this unusual blend of activeness and passivity?

REGAN: Well, it's not just New York State. There are other pension funds getting involved in corporate governance on a selective basis. This involves hundreds of billions of dollars of assets, and it's growing.

Our own system for investing is quite different from what we've heard described today. We don't look at compensation and most other governance issues. I don't care about inside boards or outside boards. In fact, there are just two important considerations for us—and what I'm about to say is probably true of many of the large public pension funds. First, we are virtually permanent owners; we don't sell—and so we are concerned only about the long-term performance *prospects* of corporations. Second, we try to identify chronic underperformers. Having done so, we then attempt to determine if and how their strategy, their culture, and ultimately their performance can be improved—and, most important, whether the board understands this. After we identify these companies, we don't play the chase-the-headlines-and-gang-up-on-them game, provided they understand what needs to be done.

STEWART: Is that because you're convinced that these more forceful actions would not work?

REGAN: It's because we are permanent owners and have a fiduciary duty to do something constructive about the egregious underperformers in the portfolio.

STERN: Isn't it true, though, Ned, that your forebearance could partly reflect something else? It may be dictated in part by the fact that your own personal net worth is not affected by the potential increases in the value of the portfolio if you became even more active? You don't get paid based on the performance of the portfolio.

REGAN: Of course not. But I do get elected based on it. The taxpayers contribute next to nothing to our pension fund, and they like that. I could get re-elected on that alone.

STERN: Well, let me put it this way. Let's say you knew that if the value of the New York State portfolio went up by 20% during your tenure, you would have a very strong assurance of being re-elected. Now, the question I'm asking is this: What if you could double that amount to 40% by becoming even more activist than you are now? Would you consider doing it? Or would you acquire a reputation as a trouble maker among your political colleagues?

REGAN: Well, these are not matters that I really think about much. Again, our approach is very simple: We're permanent owners (and, as I said, there are hundreds of billions managed by funds like ours). And we have a fiduciary duty to do something about the clearly identified underperformers in the permanent portfolio.

We have developed our own system for picking the underperformers. And, on the basis of that system, we recently identified National Medical Enterprises and A&P. In the case of National Medical Enterprises, we had become quite involved with the company well before its problems made the headlines. And we're now in the midst of discussions with A&P as to whether we will solicit votes against their board. We also came across A&P before *Forbes* or anyone else ran stories on them.

Of course, two swallows a spring don't make, but we think we're on the right track. And, from my vantage point, it appears that some of the large public pension funds are headed in a very similar direction—and for the very simple reason I just mentioned: If you're not going to sell that underperforming stock, what are you going to do about it?

STERN: Why don't you sell it?

REGAN: Because we're indexed, we're permanent owners. There are probably no more than 200 people in the country who understand the biggest investment movement in the country—and thousands of well-informed people who don't. I am continually amazed by the level of ignorance about the large public institutional investors in this country. We've been indexed, permanent owners for twelve years, it's no secret. Ten or eleven years ago we were the largest indexer in the country. We had more assets indexed than all the rest combined. But all that's changed. Now there's some $300 or $400 billion being indexed in this way.

But, to come back to your original question, Joel, we don't sell stocks because we are civil-servant oriented; we're a long way from being professional stock pickers. And, as you know, over the long run, indexed funds outperform 75 or 80% of all professional money managers.

I would also tell you that, when running an indexed fund, it is very important to maintain the discipline of the index—in our case, we index against the S&P 500 and 400 and the Russell 2000. By selling just one stock, I would be undermining the discipline of the index. In fact I once discovered that, when I turned my back, my staff at the other end of the hall just couldn't resist doing the same thing—deviating from the index. They wanted to create their own "enhanced" S&P 500 in the worst way, but I quickly stopped that.

So we rode IBM down but we rode everything else up. And, as most of you probably know, New York State has been very well served by just matching billions of dollars against the S&P 500. We pay about $20,000 a year to manage the $20 billion we have in indexed equities—and we have simply ridden the market up over the past 12 years. If we hadn't been indexing, our asset management fees would have run $30-40 million per year.

So, we don't deviate from the index. Adhering to the discipline is essential. And I think my staff's the best in the country.

STERN: But what does that mean when you say they're the best in the country? They're the best at earning the market rate of return?

REGAN: We have the lowest transaction costs of any of the pension funds. The annual costs of running our $60 billion fund are well below a million dollars. As a consequence, New York taxpayers have gotten what amounts to a free ride on the stock market boom of the last 12 years.

STEWART: Ned, could you tell us more how you would go about energizing poorly performing companies?

REGAN: It's a fairly deliberate process. In the case of National Medical Enterprises, we filed a resolution with the company just last week—but this was after lengthy analysis that revealed to us that the company is in trouble. Similarly, in the case of A&P, we started to analyze their problems at least six months ago.

STEWART: So, although you can't pick stocks that are undervalued in the classic Graham and Dodd fundamental sense, you can pick stocks that have underperformed. And then you can use the voting power that comes with your shares, together with the voting power of the other funds, to bring management to the table. Like Nell Minow, you serve as catalyst investors to bring about dramatic change in those companies.

REGAN: But many large public investors do this, although we don't make a lot of noise about it. In fact, we deliberately avoid publicity when doing this. When I told the *Wall Street Journal* and the *New York Times* about A&P, they ran awful stories saying that I was waging a "proxy war." As a consequence, I didn't say a word to them about National Medical Enterprises.

VESELL: I know something about A&P. We used to own 10% of the shares. A German family owns 51% of it.

REGAN: That's right. We think that family has one idea in mind, and it is not the minority shareholders. So, we are planning to mount a solicitation of the 50 largest minority shareholders to withhold the vote from the board of directors.

STEWART: Is this Joe Grundfest's "just vote no" approach?

REGAN: That's right. We've done some very elaborate analysis of the company, which we have shared with the company and will share with the other shareholders. And we'll probably do something similar with National Medical Enterprises when their shareholder's meeting comes around, which is not for another six months or so.

So what is our motivation here for doing all this? I get satisfaction—and there are dozens of public pension fund trustees like myself—just from my sense of doing my job correctly. It has nothing to do with money. When we saw the problem at National Medical Enterprises, we acted to uphold our fiduciary duty to our beneficiaries to maximize the return to the fund. And you're going to see a lot more public pension funds doing the same thing in the next few years. I don't know what name you people will give that kind of investing, but that's what's coming.

STEWART: Ned, it seems to me that your two levers to promote change are the vote and the publicity that comes with public office.

REGAN: But I have never sought public attention for this activity; in fact, I've discouraged it.

STEWART: But, without some kind of a threat, aren't you just a paper tiger?

BRANCATO: I don't see how you could view somebody with $60 billion under management as a paper tiger.

REGAN: Our approach is to influence companies through relatively private dialogue, at least initially. What we are doing is to file resolutions with individual companies asking for changes in the corporate by-laws that would require the proxy to be opened to long-term shareholders to put in a couple of hundred words analyzing the performance of the company. The independent directors would then have the right to counter with their own couple of hundred words. By putting this dialogue in the corporate proxy, we could limit the excesses of the media that I prefer to avoid. Of course, we need some media exposure, but this would enable us to contain the excesses that come with a telephone call or a press release.

STEWART: Forgive me for pressing this point, but I just don't see how such indirect means can force really recalcitrant managements to move.

REGAN: Well, let me put it this way. We do a report showing chronic underperformance, and then we share that with management and the board. If they don't respond, then we send this report to other fiduciaries with a cover letter that says: "We have determined that you hold this stock in your portfolio. Here's a 20-page study that shows that this company is underperforming and, most important, has no interest in reforming. You, as a fiduciary, should withhold your vote from this board. If you don't, you are breaching your duty because the value of your portfolio is going to remain unnecessarily low unless you help us initiate change." So hopefully they vote with us and we end up with, say, a 35% vote against the board.

STEWART: Fantastic. That's just what I wanted to hear you say.

STERN: Well, this is a most fortunate ending to this discussion—because I really wanted to give Ned Regan the last word before going off to his new assignment. It also gives us the opportunity to salute him for a job well done.

REGAN: Joel, you may take this as my last word as a public official.

■ III. JAPAN (AND GERMANY)

There are remarkable similarities between the Japanese and German corporate ownership and governance systems. As relationship-based rather than market-based systems, both are characterized by extensive participation by financial institutions (in Japan they are called "main banks" and in Germany "universal banks") and widespread corporate cross-holdings. And, until quite recently, both nations had been among the world's most rapidly growing economies in the post-War era.

In *"Governance, Contracting, and Investment Horizons: A Look at Japan and Germany,"* Carl Kester makes the case for the superiority of at least certain aspects of the Japanese and German governance systems. In particular, Kester cites the strong, but flexible, ties between manufacturers and suppliers (reinforced in part by intercorporate ownership of shares) for their ability to encourage highly specialized, long-term investment—the kind of investment that is likely to be neglected in the purely arm's-length, contractual relationships between U.S. manufacturers and their suppliers. As Kester summarizes his case,

"The 1980s have seen the emergence of a kind of Darwinistic competition among systems of contractual governance for global dominance. Judging from the remarkable contemporary successes of German and Japanese companies, and recent innovations [in the U.S.] that embody components of governance commonly found in Germany and Japan, it is by no means clear that classic Anglo-American governance standards will be the winner in this competition. This is not to suggest that the German and Japanese systems are ideal, simply that they may be more efficient than the Anglo-American systems in coping with hazards posed by risky investment in new environments."

In *"To Whom Does the Company Belong? A New Management Mission for the Information Era,"* Toshiba Chairman Aoi offers an attractive vision of a new "information age" in which the critical determinants of corporate success are continuous technological advance supported by an unwavering commitment to human resource development. In support of these goals, Mr. Aoi also calls for a "new metric" of corporate performance—one that, unlike standard financial measures, attempts to weigh the entire range of social benefits (not just profits or shareholder returns) from corporate activity against all their social costs.

In *"Corporate Governance and Corporate Performance: A Comparison of Germany, Japan, and the U.S.,"* Steven Kaplan furnishes evidence that each of these three national governance systems appear to be reasonably effective in disciplining inefficient managers. After observing that German and Japanese companies have responded in "American" ways to their more recent economic difficulties and strong currencies, Kaplan concludes that there are no "clear differences" among the three nations "in managerial incentives to manage for the short term or the long term."

Kaplan does concede, however, that the U.S. system is likely to have one important advantage over the Japanese and German systems—namely, its ability to exert control over large, mature companies with limited growth opportunities in their core businesses. One source of that advantage is the fact that U.S. managers hold much larger equity positions than managers in Japan and Germany. Because they own more shares, U.S. managers are less tempted to overinvest and more likely to take corrective action such as necessary downsizing. And, combined with the greater equity ownership of U.S. managers, it is much easier for U.S. than Japanese companies to return cash to shareholders. Until 1995, it was illegal for a Japanese company to repurchase its stock, and such repurchases are still greatly restricted.

In *"The Hidden Costs of Japanese Success,"* Carl Kester reinforces Kaplan's argument by observing that, in the late '80s, Japanese companies in mature industries were sitting on large amounts of cash that could not be profitably reinvested. Instead of returning that capital to stockholders, as American companies were forced to do by the restructurings of the '80s, Japanese managers were using their excess cash to fund two highly questionable strategies: (1) diversifying into unrelated businesses (every one of 10 companies in "sunset" industries studied by Kester was making a large investment in biotechnology!); and (2) setting up securities trading operations to offset declining earnings in their basic businesses.

In *"Redressing Structural Imbalances in Japanese Corporate Governance,"* Howard Sherman and Bruce Andrew Babcock of Institutional Shareholder Services argue that "structural change in Japanese corporate governance is overdue and is, in fact, under way." As international capital markets have begun to replace bank financing as the primary source of capital in Japan, both the power of the lead banks and the government's ability to direct corporate behavior through credit control have been diminished.

Moreover, the current recession in Japan—the worst since World War II—has placed the system under such strain that change seems unavoidable. With the stock market still down almost 50% from its 1989 high, pressure from dissatisfied shareholders is mounting, and the practice of corporate cross-shareholdings has come under attack. As a consequence of these developments, the authors argue, *"Japanese business leaders are open as never before to considering other models of corporate governance, including the U.S. model."*

In their list of closing recommendations for structural change, the authors urge Japanese companies to consider changes that preserve the benefits of its old system—particularly the freedom to pursue long-term growth—while accommodating international institutional investors by incorporating new and better methods of ensuring management accountability. More specifically, the authors suggest that Japanese boards and shareholders pay more attention to shareholder returns and ROE along with other performance goals, and that they implement institutional shareholder communication programs at the board level. Further, they suggest that boards include fewer members in total, but more independent outsiders. They also propose greater stock ownership by management and an end to the "interlocks" between parent and subsidiaries that allow profits to be shifted between them. Finally, they call for improvements in the Japanese proxy voting system—an archaic, corporate-dominated system that makes even the cumbersome U.S. proxy system appear friendly to shareholders.

At the same time, the authors also suggest that U.S. shareholders attempt to meet Japanese corporate boards "at least half way" by respecting differences in culture and business practices in Japan and by making greater efforts to understand the nature of the businesses they invest in as well as the corporate groups affiliated with their portfolio companies.

GOVERNANCE, CONTRACTING, AND INVESTMENT HORIZONS: A LOOK AT JAPAN AND GERMANY

by W. Carl Kester,
Harvard Business School*

Businesses operate within a network of commercial interdependencies. Some companies are more self-contained than others in the extent to which transactions are carried out in-house. But few, if any, are so vertically and horizontally integrated as to be entirely self-sufficient in the sourcing of factors of production and the delivery of finished goods to end users everywhere. All businesses exist within the context of contractual relations with others that purchase or supply goods, services, and capital.

How these contractual relationships are managed can influence the amount, type, and timing of a company's investment decisions. This is especially true for investments involving assets dedicated to support transactions with one or a few particular customers, dependent on unique inputs obtained from a few specialized suppliers, fixed locationally, or otherwise difficult to redeploy in other productive activities.[1] Such specialized investments often convey the advantage of greater operating efficiencies in their specific uses relative to general purpose assets. They are also risky, however. Once put in place, their specificity exposes owners to potentially steep declines in value if the transactions being supported by the assets suddenly shrink in volume (for example, due to defection from the trading relationship by a major counterparty) or if important counterparties attempt to exploit the assets' low value in alternative uses by demanding new terms of trade in their favor.

In general, when companies can build and maintain strong, enduring commercial relationships, they will be more favorably disposed to investment in specialized assets. Conversely, where relationships are weak and ephemeral, companies may invest less or elect to invest in assets of a more general purpose nature. They might rationally forgo operating efficiencies that may be associated with specialized assets in order to avoid the risks of dependency on a weak, short-term relationship.

Differences in investment patterns associated with the duration of transacting relationships may contribute to the perception that some firms are far-sighted in their planning while others are myopic. To the extent the ability to maintain stable business relationships varies systematically across nations, so too may investment patterns and the perceived extent of managerial time horizons in different countries. Thus, Japanese management may be credited with acute long-term vision in part because of the enduring business relationships characteristic of Japanese industrial groups, or *keiretsu*. American managers, on the other hand, might be accused of short-sightedness in their planning and investment partly because of the shorter-term, arm's-length contracting milieu in which they typically operate.

*The author is grateful for valuable research assistance provided by Robert Lightfoot. Additional support provided by Kim Clark, Noriko Kameda, Jay Lorsch, Elizabeth MacIver, and Malcolm Salter is also gratefully acknowledged. This paper has been prepared for the conference, *Capital Choices*, a joint project of the Council on Competitiveness and Harvard Business School. It has benefitted substantially from comments by conference participants.

1. See Oliver E. Williamson, *The Economic Institutions of Capitalism: Firms, Markets, Relational Contracting*. New York: Free Press, 1985, particularly pp. 43 to 102, for an illuminating discussion of asset specificity, ownership, and the governance of contractual relationships.

This paper surveys the governance of business relationships or, more accurately, "contracts" in Germany and Japan—two nations whose manufacturing sectors are highly competitive with that of the United States. The primary purpose of the comparison is threefold: to identify important differences in the contractual governance systems of these nations, to provide economic rationales for these differences, and to develop insights concerning the potential effects of such differences on the investment decisions of corporations domiciled in these countries.

Briefly, this study finds that Japan and Germany rely upon a number of non-contractual safeguards against the hazards of self-interested opportunism to promote the building and maintenance of long-term business relationships. Chief among these are close relationships with large financial institutions that are major equity owners as well as lenders, and that are able to exert considerable influence through board representation and, at times, direct intervention into operating management. This is a significant institutional difference with governance in the United States. Cross-shareholding arrangements, extensive information-sharing, and reliable personal trust relationships are also important.

The effectiveness of the German and Japanese contractual governance systems in sustaining stable but flexible business relationships also helps explain the lower frequency of large-scale takeovers in those nations relative to the United States. In meeting competitive threats posed by German and Japanese corporations, the United States should consider relaxing constraints on the formation of close vertical relationships among corporations, particularly those separating banking from commerce and those inhibiting active board-level involvement by other large financial institutions in those industrial companies in which they own stock.

CONTRACTING AND INVESTMENT

Investment is at least partly a contracting problem. It is not uncommon, for instance, to observe corporate capital appropriations committees requiring that sponsors of large-scale investment projects reduce the uncertainty surrounding their proposals by obtaining long-term purchase or supply agreements, comfort letters, or some other explicit expression of advance commitment from customers and suppliers critical to the success of the project. Lenders may also require such commitments as a condition of their loan. The absence of such commitments can result in deferred, reduced, or even no investment whatsoever.

This aspect of investment decisions has long been recognized in both the agency-theory and transaction-cost economics literature. The latter strain of literature—most commonly associated today with Oliver Williamson and, before him, Ronald Coase[2]—has sought to answer the question of whether a company should own assets outright, thus internalizing certain transactions and subjecting them to hierarchical control, or simply procure its needs on the open market. It deals with optimal organization of exchange and the problem of determining the optimal boundary between the administrative hierarchy of the firm and the markets in which it transacts.

Reliance on arm's-length transactions in the market allows for greater specialization in production activities and the realization of scale economies. At the same time, it also poses risks associated with self-interested opportunism. After a company invests in some expensive and highly specialized assets dedicated to supporting a stream of transactions with a particular customer or supplier, for example, that party could threaten to abandon its relationship with the investing company if terms of trade are not shifted in its favor. Legal adjudication of such disputes may be too slow, costly, and cumbersome to be relied upon constantly as a means of handling such problems.

Absorbing key suppliers, customers, or subcontractors (that is, integrating vertically) may afford greater control and relieve some of the hazards of self-interested opportunism, but often at the expense of efficiency. The high-powered incentives the market provides can be difficult to replicate and manage inside a large, vertically integrated organization. Moreover, other conditions that Oliver Williamson labels "bureaucratic disabilities" (such as overextension of managerial capabilities and the internal politicization of decision-making) often

---

2. See Oliver E. Williamson, *The Economic Institutions of Capitalism: Firms, Markets, Relational Contracting.* New York: Free Press, 1985; and Ronald H. Coase, "The Nature of the Firms," *Economica* N.S. 4 (1937) pp. 386-405.

American manufacturing corporations have tended to address the hazards of investment in specialized assets by achieving comparatively high degrees of integration; relying heavily on formal contracts enforced by courts; and relying on arm's-length, bid-priced transactions with a large number of competitive suppliers, customers, and subcontractors.

plague such organizations. The problem is to devise a system of governing business relations that optimally balances the economies and hazards of transacting in the market with those of administratively controlling the same activities within a hierarchical organization.

In contrast, the agency cost literature—most commonly associated today with Michael Jensen and William Meckling, and before them, Adolph Berle and Gardiner Means[3]—focuses more on the problems associated with the separation of ownership and control in the modern corporation. Again, for reasons of self-interested opportunism, hired agents such as corporate managers cannot always be counted on to act in the best interests of the principals (the shareholders) who engaged them. Within the context of modern stock corporations, considerable shareholder value may be dissipated by managers whose interests are not closely aligned with those of investors. Rational investors will recognize this possibility in advance and reflect expectations of self-interested actions by managers in the prices paid for the corporation's securities.

The central problem, then, is the creation of cost-effective monitoring, bonding, and incentive systems that will reduce the losses associated with the separation of ownership from control. When prevailing systems prove inadequate, the market for corporate control is depended upon to concentrate ownership, thereby enabling owners to improve the company's patterns of investment, alter poorly designed contracts, end other value-reducing policies, and, if necessary, change management itself.

Despite some formal differences in these theories, both may be viewed as branches of a broader stream of literature concerned with the economics of contracting. Both take up the universal problem of coping efficiently with the hazards of dependence on self-interested second or third parties to accomplish some economic aims. And both are essential to an appreciation of the economic purpose served by various elements (for example, as we shall see, cross-shareholding arrangements and concentrated ownership by large financial institutions) of a given national system of corporate governance, many of which are too frequently dismissed as mere cultural artifacts or blatant attempts simply to restrain trade without offsetting efficiency gains.

NATIONAL DIFFERENCES IN CONTRACTUAL GOVERNANCE

The plethora of different organizational forms populating capitalist economies are evidence of the wide breadth of responses to problems of governance of which such economies are capable. The diversity within even a single country's borders can be staggering, making it problematic to define any one system of governance as prototypical of an entire nation. Nevertheless, broad differences do appear to separate the systems most commonly found among large corporations headquartered in different countries such as Germany, Japan, and the United States. Moreover, they differ broadly in ways that are likely to contribute to differences in investment patterns, particularly with respect to investment in specialized assets.

By and large, American manufacturing corporations have tended to address the hazards of investment in specialized assets by achieving comparatively high degrees of integration; relying heavily on formal contracts enforced by courts; and relying on arm's-length, bid-priced transactions with a large number of competitive suppliers, customers, subcontractors, and so forth. In the automotive industry, for example, General Motors and Ford tend to be more vertically integrated than most of their major Japanese and German counterparts, and yet rely on *five to ten times* as many suppliers. Sharply defined lines tend to delineate one stakeholder group from another in the typical American corporation, and there are reasonably clear boundaries separating a firm from the factor and product markets in which it transacts. German and Japanese companies govern relationships rather differently, relying more extensively on implicit, relational contracting and on somewhat different safeguards and dispute resolution processes to enforce adherence to formal contracts.

The auto industry offers a particularly good setting for observing alternative contractual governance systems. Even the most vertically integrated assembler must still source thousands of parts from outside suppliers; hence, supplier-assembler relations are especially important. Also, many assets used in support of automobile production have high degrees of specificity. Some equipment and tools,

---

3. See Adolph A. Berle, and G. C. Means. *The Modern Corporation and Private Property.* (New York; MacMillan, 1932); and Michael C. Jensen and William Meckling, "Theory of the Firm: Managerial Behavior Agency Costs, and Capital Structure," *Journal of Financial Economics* 3 (October 1976), pp. 305-360.

for example, are unique to a particular car model; supplier factories built close to an assembly plant (to support just-in-time parts delivery), for instance, tend to be highly location specific. The scale of investment can also be large relative to internally generated cash flow, requiring frequent sourcing of funds from external creditors and shareholders; hence, the importance of financial contracting and investor relations. Finally, the governance system displayed by each country's participants in the automotive industry is also reasonably typical of that found elsewhere in the country in question, although restriction of the sample necessarily limits the generality of the conclusions.[4]

Japanese Contractual Governance

From a Western perspective, many Japanese business practices seem so idiosyncratic as to defy complete comprehension by non-Japanese. Indeed, some common practices (for example, reciprocal trade, reciprocal equity ownership, lifetime employment) are frequently dismissed by Americans as being little more than subtle mechanisms for restricting trade and competition, or as efforts by a managerial elite to entrench themselves in positions of power.

An alternative view presented here is that many of the apparent idiosyncrasies of Japanese management should instead be considered as elements of well-integrated corporate and contractual governance systems that function effectively to foster transactional efficiencies by making it easier to build and maintain long-term business relationships. Whatever the original motivation behind their implementation, their roles have evolved such that today they constitute a set of economically rational responses to the hazards posed by investment.

Autonomy vs. Control. Japanese corporations are well known for their tendency to engage in tight, long-term vertical relationships. Such relationships are made most manifest in so-called *keiretsu*—complex groups of companies federated around a major bank, trading company, or large industrial

firm. Virtually all Japanese auto manufacturers may be identified with such industrial groups. Mitsubishi Motors, for example, is a member of the Mitsubishi keiretsu, the modern descendant of the pre-World War II Mitsubishi zaibatsu (a much more tightly knit group of related companies formerly controlled by a holding company). Likewise, Toyota and Nissan lie at the center of reasonably well-defined industrial groups made up of suppliers, dealers, insurers, other types of service companies, and so forth.[5]

Japanese keiretsu tend to be characterized by a great deal of stability in group affiliation and loyalty as far as the preferred status group members give each other in their business dealings. Slowing growth and the liberalization of financial markets have imposed some stress on these relationships.[6] Still, if a Japanese OEM can source parts and equipment within its own group, it is highly likely to do so, though rarely ever on an exclusive basis. Furthermore, intragroup trade will tend to be reciprocal to the extent practical. Thus, Mitsubishi Motors is sure to be sourcing some of its steel requirements from Mitsubishi Steel and some of its equipment from Mitsubishi Heavy Industries. They, in turn, will be sure to include Mitsubishi Motors's autos and trucks in their vehicle fleets.

It is important to recognize, however, that this stability and loyalty to the group is not simply a cultural artifact that can be counted upon to yield high levels of performance. The same sort of hazards associated with self-interested opportunism that exist elsewhere in the world reside within keiretsu as well. Longevity of business relationships could lead to complacency and loss of efficiency if, for example, a group member begins to take its business with others for granted. Sustaining a complex network of business relations within the group may also require a narrowing of the scope for independent action and the occasional subordination of individual corporate interests to that of the group at large. There can be no assurance that this will take place voluntarily if all group members are left to their own devices. Thus, intragroup commercial relationships are never exclusive. Even *within*

4. The companies included in this study's field sample are as follows: For Germany, BMW, Daimler-Benz, Porsche, Volkswagen, and Robert Bosch (a major German auto parts supplier); for Japan, Honda Motor, Mitsubishi Motors, Nissan Motor, Toyota Motor, and Calsonic Corp. (a major Japanese auto parts supplier). The executives interviewed within this sample were those responsible (at various ranks up to and inclusive of managing directors and members of management boards) for managing purchase and supply contracts, and external corporate funding. All interviews were carried out in the second half of 1990.

5. Honda is different in that it is not considered to be a core company of such a group (its main bank, in fact, is the Mitsubishi Bank). Nevertheless, like most other large Japanese companies, it does maintain steady, close vertical relationships with a network of suppliers, dealers, and providers of capital.

6. For further discussion of these effects, see David Scharfstein, "U.S.-Japanese Corporate Finance, *NBER Reporter* (Cambridge, MA: National Bureau of Economic Research, Fall 1990), pp. 5-8; and W. Carl Kester, *Japanese Takeovers: The Global Contest for Corporate Control* (Boston, MA: Harvard Business School Press, 1991).

> Many of the apparent idiosyncracies of Japanese management should instead be
> considered as elements of well-integrated corporate and contractual governance
> systems that function effectively to foster transactional efficiencies by making it
> easier to build and maintain long-term business relationships.

TABLE 1 GOVERNANCE, CONTRACTING, AND INVESTMENT TIME HORIZONS: INTRAGROUP SALES AND PROCUREMENT IN MAJOR JAPANESE KEIRETSU, 1981	Six Major Keiretsu	Original Zaibatsu Groups[b]	Modern Groups[c]
Average Intragroup Sales[a]			
Presidents Council Members	10.8%	13.4%	8.6%
All Group Industrial Companies	20.4	29.0	14.9
Average Intragroup Procurement[a]			
Presidents Council Members	11.7%	14.8%	9.1%
All Group Industrial Companies	12.4	18.6	8.2

Source: Kigyo Shudan no Jittai ni tsuite, June 21, 1983.
a. Statistics are exclusive of group financial institutions.
b. The Mitsubishi, Mitsui, and Sumitomo groups.
c. The Fuyo, DKB, and Sanwa groups.

keiretsu, the power of competition is respected for its ability to generate low costs, high quality, and attention to customers' demands. Notice, for example, that intragroup sales and procurement shown in Table 1 varies between 8% and 30%, indicating extensive dependence on non-group business as well.

Japanese auto assemblers struggle constantly with the trade-off between the adaptive efficiencies associated with having high degrees of control over their suppliers and the operating efficiencies derived from the application of high-powered market incentives. This trade-off is fine-tuned continuously through frequent discussions among managers of suppliers and those of OEM's. The assemblers strive to walk a fine line between reaffirming their commitment to long-term relationships and granting outright guarantees of business—the latter, clearly to be avoided.

Strongly influencing this routine management of business relationships at the level of the individual manager is a larger governance machinery that has evolved in Japan to attenuate the hazards of long-term dependence on a few autonomous parties while simultaneously preserving many of the advantages. This machinery has five major components: relational contracting; management transfers and lifetime employment; extensive intragroup information-sharing; reciprocal equity ownership; and selective intervention by core shareholders to force adjustments.

Implicit, Relational Contracting. Although formal contracts among parties in a long-term relationship do exist in Japan, they bear little resemblance to the sort of classical written contracts more likely to be used in Anglo-American business environments. In the automotive industry, a typical contract between an assembler and a group supplier consists of two parts: a so-called "basic agreement" and a "claims compensation agreement." The latter is essentially a contingent claims contract that delimits liability in the event that a part's failure results in damages.

The basic agreement, in contrast, is a written declaration of both parties' intentions to engage in a mutually beneficial exchange relationship. While the agreement usually contains language pertaining to confidentiality with respect to the use of new technologies, executives responsible for managing the supply relationship doubt that even these provisions are legally binding. Indeed, few articles, if any, in the basic agreement bind the buyer and seller to rules and procedures. A typical basic agreement essentially states that, "The buyer and seller will operate on a basis of mutual respect for each other's autonomy and undertake to establish and maintain an atmosphere of mutual trust in business dealings."[7] Although basic agreements nominally have life spans of one year, there is a

---

7. Ballon and Tomita (1988, p. 54) claim more generally that a typical Japanese contract does not even state definitely the transactions at stake so as not to restrict the flexibility considered necessary for good performance. They also quote a typical final clause as reading, "Concerning matters not stipulated herein or any doubt about the stipulation both parties shall settle them upon deliberation." Still other common language will declare that, "Should a disagreement arise, the parties

will settle it amicably by consultation." Both clauses would seem to undermine the very purpose of entering into a contract in the first place, at least from a traditional Anglo-American legal perspective. Resort to court enforcement would seem to be ruled out by the very contracts themselves!

See Robert J.Ballon and Iwao Tomita, *The Financial Behavior of Japanese Corporations* (Tokyo: Kodansha International, 1988).

strong presumption of continual renewal throughout a model's life span.

The importance attached to this seemingly innocuous basic agreement reflects a fundamental difference between the Japanese and Anglo-American business environments in the governance of contractual relationships. The latter tends to be highly discrete in that the scope of the agreement is carefully defined as are exact terms of exchange, performance specifications, specific duties under relevant future contingencies, and, at times, formal procedures to be followed (for example, third-party arbitration) to settle disputes arising from contingencies not otherwise explicitly provided for. To the extent possible, conditions defining non-performance are stated and the potential consequences of the same are relatively predictable. At all points during the life of the agreement, whether it be in its execution, adjustment, or in the adjudication of a dispute, the point of reference is the formal contract itself.

In Japan, the signing of basic agreement (or the equivalent) is tantamount to the initiation of a long-term relationship. And for most Japanese companies, particularly those engaged in intragroup trade, the reference point for all future discussions regarding the transaction in question tends to be the entire business relationship itself, not merely the formal contract. Consider this response from a senior Japanese automotive executive when asked to explain the lack of precision and even enforceability (for example, with respect to preserving confidentiality) of most of the articles in the basic agreement:

In America, you have many rules [to govern business transactions]. Here in Japan, everything is very fluid. There may be rules, but they are constantly changing to suit the environment....The overall benefits of an ongoing relationship is what really matters.

Put differently, the execution and adaptation of business agreements in Japan are made primarily by reference to an internal set of norms and expectations built up over a long history of transacting. In this sense it may be said that Japanese contractual governance is of a more relational, continuously negotiated nature and relies less extensively on legal rules, third-party assistance to effect change, or litigation as a means of resolving disputes.[8]

Managerial Interactions and Lifetime Employment. The ongoing negotiated character of Japanese contractual governance places a heavy burden on communication between the transacting organizations. Transfers of management, one of the more prominent Japanese business practices, provides much of the infrastructure for bearing this burden. Management transfers from assembler to supplier were reported "to happen all the time," according to one Japanese executive. Mid-career managers and engineers are frequently temporarily transferred from assemblers to suppliers to help out with specific problems or to represent the assembler in some collaborative effort with the supplier. "Retiring" assembler executives are also often placed permanently with supplier as directors or in other senior management positions. Thus, for example, the president of Calsonic Corp., a major supplier of heat-related auto parts and a member of the Nissan Motor group, is a former Nissan executive. Similarly, former Toyota executives sit on the board of Nippondenso, another major parts supplier in the Toyota group.

Whatever the proximate cause for these transfers, one of the important side effects is the creation of an extensive web of enduring personal relationships among individual managers in each of the transacting companies. These are crucial to the efficacy of relational contracting in Japan, for the terms of such agreements are held more between individual managers interacting at the trading interface than between the companies per se. It is at this individual managerial level that mutual obligations are formed and bonds of trust are hammered out.

Once created, the Japanese practice (primarily among large companies) of "lifetime" employment functions to preserve these personal relationships for many years. It also raises the cost to individual managers of untrustworthy, opportunistic behavior. In short, a Japanese manager's effectiveness, and thus his value, depends quite heavily on his reputation for trustworthiness and his ability to contract implicitly with counterparts in other companies. This gives the individual manager as well as the company a stake in the ongoing transacting relationship.

---

8. This Japanese attitude toward contractual governance is made manifest in a number of ways. Ballon and Tomita (1988, p. 55), cited in the previous note, point out that Japan counts only about 12,000 practicing lawyers, very few of which are employed by corporations. The legal departments of most large companies are euphemistically called "archive sections" and are staffed by approximately ten or so regular employees who typically receive their legal training through experience in the company. Their primary mission is to resolve disputes, not to manage litigations.

Even *within* keiretsu, the power of competition is respected for its ability to generate low costs, high quality, and attention to customers' demands.

Monitoring and Information Sharing. The maintenance of long-term relationships is not left entirely to trust and forbearance on the part of individual managers, however. Extensive monitoring by main banks—that is, traditional lead lenders that usually also own stock in their client company—and various associations of group member companies is also a common Japanese practice. Such monitoring diminishes the amount of hidden information and reduces the scope for undertaking hidden action. Indeed, a second important by-product of managerial transfers and placement of alumni officers with key suppliers or customers is the creation of an information sharing network.

Sometimes augmenting this informal network is an institutionalized one made up of senior company officers. The president of Mitsubishi Motors Corp., for example, is a member of the *Kinyo-kai*, a council of presidents of 28 major Mitsubishi group companies that meets monthly to "promote friendship" and exchange views on a wide array of business and economic matters. Included in the council are presidents of companies such as Mitsubishi Heavy Industries (a key supplier to, former parent of, and still a major shareholder in Mitsubishi Motors), Mitsubishi Bank (Mitsubishi Motors' main bank), Mitsubishi Electric (a supplier of electronic parts and audio equipment), Mitsubishi Steel Manufacturing, and other Mitsubishi companies with which Mitsubishi Motors has business dealings. Similarly, Toyota Motor is a member of the *Wakabu-kai* (presidents' council) of the Tokai group and has "observer" status in the *Nimoku-kai* of the Mitsui group. Nissan Motor is also a member of the *Fuyo-kai* of the Fuyo group.

Suppliers to the large assemblers also have their associations. Toyota's 175 primary suppliers are organized into a group known as the *Kyoho-kai* (roughly, "a club for co-prospering with Toyota").[9] Nissan's 162 primary suppliers are organized into the *Takara-kai*; and Mitsubishi Motors', into the *Kashiwa-kai* (Honda's primary suppliers are not organized into an explicit association as such).

Among their several purposes, these clubs and councils serve as important safeguards in the Japanese machinery for governing relationships. They do so as collectors and disseminators of information about members' experiences with each other or, in the case of the supplier organizations, with a common purchaser. The reputation effects of various decisions are thereby magnified. By reducing the potential for abuse of long-standing business relationships, their longevity is increased.

Gilson and Roe also identify the very production process itself as a source of considerable information and mutual monitoring by Japanese companies doing business with each other.[10] With production less vertically integrated under a single administrative hierarchy, and yet organized in such a way as to depend heavily on reliable, just-in-time delivery of high quality parts and components, even modest variations in timeliness and rejection rates yields daily measures of how other factor providers are performing. High levels of relationship-specific investment, coupled with intense product market rivalry among vertically cooperative groups, provides substantial incentives for factor providers cooperating in a joint production process to monitor each other closely and intervene to correct problems as needed.

Reciprocal Equity Ownership. Often paralleling implicit reciprocal trade agreements among Japanese companies are cross-shareholding arrangements. For example, in 1990 Mitsubishi Corporation owned 1.6% of Mitsubishi Heavy Industries, which, in turn, owned 3.2% of Mitsubishi Corporation. Although these cross holdings are usually small on a bilateral basis, between 10% and 25% of all the outstanding shares of group members are generally held within the keiretsu itself.[11] If share ownership by non-group financial institutions and other industrial corporations with important business ties to a group's members are added to these figures, the fraction of shares held by key corporate stakeholders generally more than doubles. Indeed, as shown in Table 2, 70% of the outstanding equity of publicly listed Japanese companies are owned by financial institutions and other corporations. Accompanying many (though not all) of these holding by the financial and corporate sectors are implicit but widely understood and rigorously observed agreements not to sell shares held in connec-

9. Dodwell Marketing Consultants, *The Structure of the Japanese Auto Parts Industry*, 4th edition, Tokyo: 1990, p. 36.

10. Ronald J. Gilson and Mark J. Roe, "Comparative Corporate Governance: Focusing the United States Inquiry" (New York: Columbia Law School, 1992). Unpublished working paper.

11. Intragroup shareholdings of some of the major keiretsu in 1990 were as follows: the Mitsubishi group, 25.3%; the Sumitomo group, 24.5%; the Fuyo group, 18.2%; the Mitsui group, 18.0%; the DKB group, 14.6%; and the Sanwa group, 10.9%.

TABLE 2
COMPARATIVE
CORPORATE OWNERSHIP
STRUCTURES, 1990-1991

	Germany	Japan	United Kingdom	United States
Financial Sector				
Banks[a]	8.9	25.2	0.9	0.3
Insurance Companies	10.6	17.3	18.4	5.2
Pension Funds[b]	—	0.9	30.4	24.8
Investment Companies and Other	—	3.6	11.1	9.5
Total	19.5	47.0	60.8	39.8
Non-Financial Sector				
Non-Financial Businesses	39.2	25.1	3.6	N/A
Household	16.8	23.1	21.3	53.5
Government	6.8	0.6	2.0	—
Foreign	17.7	4.2	12.3	6.7

Sources: Deutsche Bundesbank, Tokyo Stock Exchange, ProShare, and Federal Reserve Board "Flow of Funds".
a. All types, including bank holding companies.
b. Public and private.

tion with on-going business relationships. A decision to sell equity held under these arrangements would be viewed as a clear repudiation of the relationship.

However, cross shareholdings among Japanese companies play a larger role in the governance process than as merely a signal of commitment to a long-term relationship. They also have the effect of creating a complex blend of claims held by two companies against one another. This is clearest in the case of lender-borrow relationships, for a Japanese company's major lenders usually also rank among its major shareholders. In the case of Nissan Motor, for example, six of the firm's major lenders in 1990 accounted for ¥192.1 billion ($1.4 billion) of Nissan's then total outstanding borrowings of ¥579.5 billion ($4.4 billion). At the time same time, these six lenders also held shares in Nissan worth approximately ¥558 billion ($4.3 billion). These financial institutions were neither pure debt nor pure equity holders. Their overall investment in Nissan was akin to owning a "strip" of Nissan's capital base. To the extent that, say, a major trading company associated with a keiretsu simultaneously has a supply agreement with a customer, extends trade credit to that customer, purchases output from the same company, and owns equity in it, the co-mingling of claims becomes even more pronounced.

One important benefit derived from this tendency to hold a blend of different financial and other contractual claims against a company is to reduce the frictions that might normally arise among various stakeholder groups owning separate and distinct claims. The incentives to breach contracts with suppliers and customers in the interests of transferring value to shareholders, or to borrow money and then take extraordinary risks that might benefit shareholders at the expense of lenders, are reduced when the injured stakeholders are the company's own principal shareholders. Helping troubled companies work out temporary financial problems will also be easier when the principal providers of capital hold roughly comparable bundles of senior and junior, short-term and long-term claims against the company; conflicts of interest and free-riding problems will be minimized.

Selective Intervention. Perhaps the most powerful safeguard in the Japanese contractual governance system is the ability of one or more equity-owning stakeholders to intervene directly and explicitly from time to time in the affairs of another company when necessary to correct a problem. This is by no means a routine or highly frequent occurrence, but it is common—indeed, expected—under certain circumstances.

Typically, such intervention is undertaken by a company's main bank, usually to remedy nonperformance in the face of impending financial distress. This "responsibility" generally falls to the troubled company's main bank because it is usually the largest single supplier of capital and has quicker access to more information than most other equity-owning stakeholders. It also typically holds both debt and equity claims against companies for which it acts as main bank. Whereas fear of triggering so-called "equitable subordination" of their loans keeps most American lenders on the sidelines until a loan agreement is formally breached, and even then restrains their degree of intervention, Japanese main banks effectively assume such subordination from the outset and take far-reaching, early steps to limit the damage. For example, the Dai-Ichi Kangyo Bank, main bank for the Kojin Corporation, voluntarily repaid all of Kojin's debts to other banks when Kojin failed. DKB then assumed sole responsibility for recovering loans from Kojin.

Main bank intervention may also occur for reasons other than financial distress. Dispute resolution and sheer dealmaking (though seldom on a fee basis) by banks among client companies also take place. For example, a Tokai Bank executive assumed the presidency of a client company, Okuma Machinery Works, in order to resolve a bitter dispute between labor and management over who was to succeed the company's founder-president. In another case, the Sumitomo Bank's financing of companies such as Nissan, Mazda, and Matsushita Electric allowed it to act as a go-between in arranging sheet-metal supply contracts with these companies for Sumitomo Metal Industries, one of its group clients.[12]

Such intervention, however, is by no means limited to banks. Although less common, major industrial stakeholders will take decisive steps to supplant an important supplier's or customer's autonomy with temporary de facto administrative control when nonperformance becomes imminent. Mitsubishi Electric, for instance, has taken leadership in the restructuring of Akai Electric, a major supplier and purchaser of electronic parts and equipment within the Mitsubishi group.[13] More recently, Nissan Motor has assumed effective operating control of Fuji Heavy Industries, the maker of Subaru automobiles. Although Nissan owns only 4% of Fuji's stock, it has consistently sent executives to become directors of Fuji, relies on Fuji to produce Nissan brand passenger cars, and collaborates with Fuji in the manufacture of aerospace and marine products. The de facto "takeover" has occurred without the restructuring of any debt or a single share of stock changing hands among Fuji's major equity-owning stakeholders.

German Contractual Governance

The German automotive companies studied in this survey stand between the Japanese and the Americans with respect to supplier relationships. They are more vertically integrated than the Japanese, but less than the Americans. Likewise, they rely on two to three times as many primary parts suppliers as the Japanese, but considerably less than half those of the Americans.

This relative position in supplier relationships is consistent with the principal features of German corporate contractual governance. As shown below, it is quite similar to Japanese governance in a number of ways, particularly with respect to company-bank relationships. On the whole, however, safeguards against opportunism are not quite as strong in Germany as in Japan, particularly with respect to vertical relationships in product markets. Automotive suppliers in Germany enjoy much greater autonomy than do those in Japan. Predictably, therefore, we observe a somewhat greater reliance on formal rather than implicit, relational contracting and a higher degree of vertical integration in Germany.

German Corporate Ownership Structure. Because shares of most German corporations are held in bearer form, it is extremely difficult to document the ownership structure of German corporations. But the available evidence suggests that, as a group, large German companies engage in fairly extensive cross-shareholdings. According to reports of a study by the German Monopolies Commission, there were 88 cross-shareholdings among Germany's largest 100 corporations in 1984.[14] Financial institutions are especially large holders of equity in German companies, second only to other business corporations. Deutsche Bank, for example, owns 28.1% of Daimler-

---

12. For an account, see Michael Gerlach, "Business Alliances and the Strategy of the Japanese Firms," *California Management Review* (Fall 1987), pp. 126-142.
13. See Kester, (1991), pp. 70-73, for a detailed discussion of this involvement.

14. David Shirreff, "Bankers as Moral Monopolists," *Euromoney*, March 1987, p. 71.

Benz's stock, although this is an unusually large stake among the German auto producers. More broadly, German banks as a group own nearly 9% of all domestically listed shares of German companies, and own more than 25% of at least 33 major industrial corporations.[15] Insurance companies owned closer to 11% of such shares (see Table 2).

In addition to direct share ownership, German banks also act as depositories for stock owned by other classes of shareholders. At the end of 1988, DM411.5 billion shares, or approximately 40% of the total market value of outstanding domestic German shares, were deposited in German banks. When added to their own share ownership, nearly 50% of listed German corporate shares are directly or indirectly under their stewardship.

This role as a share depository has been quite important to German corporate governance because of what is known as the *Vollmachtstimmrecht*— the ability of banks to vote shares held in deposit on behalf of the depositor. For many years this right of proxy was virtually automatic, indefinite in duration, and did not require instructions from the true shareholder. It was a condition of the deposit itself known as the *Depotstimmrecht*. Today it is restricted insofar as the right of proxy must be renewed every 15 months and banks must solicit voting instructions from shareholders. Nevertheless, as a practical matter, banks continue to obtain wide latitude in the voting of shares held on deposit, giving them considerable effective voting power.

As with Japanese company-bank relationships, shares of stock owned by banks are traded infrequently, if at all. In most cases, the equity-owning bank of a large industrial corporation will be one of its *Hausbanks* (comparable to Japanese main banks) with which it has a long history of banking business. Deutsche Bank is considered Daimler-Benz's Hausbank, and has been so since it engineered the merger of the Mercedes and Benz automobile companies when they encountered financial distress following the deaths of their founders. Since then, Deutsche Bank has maintained a substantial equity ownership in Daimler-Benz, and the chairman of the latter's "supervisory board" (described below) has traditionally come from Deutsche Bank.

Board Composition. The influence of large German shareholders is exercised largely through a body known as the *Aufsichtsrat*, or supervisory board. It is one of the more important safeguards embodied in the German system of corporate governance. Briefly, German commercial law provides for two forms of limited liability stock companies: the *Gesellschaft mit beschränkten Haftung* (GmbH); and the *Aktiengesellschaft* (AG). The former is privately owned and unlisted, the latter publicly owned and listed on a German stock exchange.

By law, AGs have two-tiered boards. The *Vorstand*, or management board, has day-to-day executive authority over the company and is the real decision-making body on most matters. Typically, it has between five and fifteen members who are full-time salaried executives of the company, each of whom is responsible for a "portfolio" of businesses or administrative functions.[16] Members of the Vorstand are appointed by the Aufsichtsrat for terms usually lasting three to five years.[17] The Vorstand must report to the Aufsichtsrat (which usually meets quarterly) and gain its consent for major financial and investment decisions.

The Aufsichtsrat, in contrast, is a true supervisory board, not an executive one. It is usually composed of 9 to 22 members. As a consequence of the Co-determination Act of 1976, half of these are required to be elected worker representatives (at least one of which, however, must be a member of the company's management). The other half of the board is elected by shareholders and consists entirely of members who are *not* full-time employees of the company.[18]

In effect, the shareholder-elected half of the German Aufsichtsrat is equivalent to the "outside" directors of an American corporation, or the "non-executive" directors of a British corporation. An important difference, however, is that these German "outside" directors are more commonly drawn from the executive ranks of other major corporations or financial institutions that have a major stake of some sort in the company in question. That stake may be a substantial equity investment, a long-standing lending relationship, a vertical purchase or supply arrangement, or, as in Japan, some combination of these various types of claims. Alternatively, they may

---

15. *Ibid.*, p. 71.

16. GmbH's with employment of more than 500 persons must also have a two-tiered board. Instead of a Vorstand, however, GmbH's have a much smaller *Geschäftsführung* (Executive Committee) made up of a chairman, a sales director, and a third director responsible for nearly everything else.

17. Reappointment is generally anticipated unless nonperformance or other imperatives mitigate such action.

18. It is not uncommon, however, to have retired company executives elected to the Aufsichtsrat. In fact, the chairman of the Aufsichtsrat is quite often the most recently retired chairman of the Vorstand.

German "outside" directors are commonly drawn from the executive ranks of other major corporations or financial institutions that have a major stake in the company. What they typically are *not* are disinterested experts appointed to give their presumably objective points of view, or sheer status lenders such as are sometimes observed on American and British boards.

be representatives of wealthy families or family foundations that are large stock owners. What they typically are *not* are strictly disinterested experts in some field appointed to give their presumably objective points of view, or sheer status lenders such as are sometimes observed on American and British boards.[19] Instead, as a group, these directors tend to mirror the company's most important investor and business relationships. They also can and, from time to time, will exercise considerable influence in the shaping of corporate strategy through the composition of the Vorstand.[20]

Although legally responsible for representing shareholder interests at large, German Aufsichtsrat members are also able to act as de facto representatives of, and monitors for, other stakeholder interests. Bank executives on the boards of industrial corporations are especially well positioned to act in this capacity.[21] To the extent their banks lend to the corporation in question, the interests of creditors as well as shareholders are directly represented. By virtue of banks' extensive lending business and large equity stakes in the German *Mittelstand* (middle market), bank executives may also indirectly reflect the interests of smaller suppliers, customers, and subcontractors that service the needs of the larger industrial corporations.

Small Numbers and Reputation Effects. Given the wide decision-making latitude afforded top management of large corporations virtually everywhere, voluntary forbearance from opportunism on their part is expected—indeed, depended upon—for purposes of efficient corporate and contractual governance, particularly so when implicit contracting is widely prevalent, as in Germany and Japan. Obviously, such forbearance is not always a reliable safeguard against abuse.

But neither is widespread reliance on such a safeguard as naive as may first be supposed. The successful preservation of trust relationships and the implicit contracts they support is at least partly the consequence of the severe adverse reputation effects that would ensue a major breach of trust.

While such effects can be anticipated in any business environment, they tend to be magnified in Germany by the relatively small circle of companies and executives that dominate big business there.[22] In 1984, the supervisory boards of 79 of Germany's 100 largest companies had at least one member who was on the management board of another company in the top 100. Within this 100, 20 companies each had between 17 and 36 executives sitting on supervisory boards of other top-100 firms. Just 8 large banks and insurance companies collectively accounted for more than 45% of the total number of board-level management links within the top 100. In 1987, 12 management board members of Deutsche Bank participated on the supervisory boards of 150 AGs, and 200 other management and corporate advisory committees.[23]

German automotive executives consistently underscored the high level of confidentiality that Aufsichtsrat members maintained with respect to the information they were given at board meetings. Even so, it is difficult not to imagine this relatively small circle of German executives sitting on interlocking boards as an effective, even if informal, information-sharing network. At the very least, the *potential* for sharing information that would have significant reputation effects must be seen to exist. This alone should serve to limit abuses of trust relationships, thereby promoting efficient implicit contracting.

Comparison and Summary

For all its subtleties and apparent idiosyncrasies, contractual governance in Japan can ultimately be

19. See Peter Lawrence, *Managers and Management in West Germany* (New York: St. Martins Press, 1980), p. 36.

20. For example, Alfred Herrhausen, co-chairman of Deutsche Bank and chairman of Daimler-Benz's Aufsichtsrat, was instrumental in collaborating with Edzard Reuter, former deputy chairman of Daimler-Benz's Vorstand, to shape and implement Daimler-Benz's ambitious diversification into high-technology businesses in 1985 and 1986. It reportedly was also Herrhausen's influence that helped push through a major restructuring of Daimler-Benz's Vorstand in 1986 that created five separate divisions and added three new members favoring diversification.

21. In an intricate study of board-level linkages among German industrial and financial corporations Ziegler, Bender, and Biehler (1985) identified 453 primary and 1175 secondary (i.e., directors of two companies working with each other on the board of a third company) "interlocks" among directors sitting on supervisory boards of Germany's 325 largest corporations. These were classified into 20 clusters and subclusters of directors' networks. In general, German banks displayed the greatest number of linkages. Deutsche Bank had by far the largest network of interlocks, reaching 239 other companies through primary and secondary linkages. Overall, however, they conclude that German board linkages represent, ". . . a coalescence of major interests from both the financial and non-financial sectors. Banks act more like integrators cross-connecting industrials from various economic sectors and other fractional interests." See Rolf Ziegler, Donald Bender, and Hermann Biehler, "Industry and Banking in the German Corporate Network," in *Networks of Corporate Power: A Comparative Analysis of Ten Countries.* Frans N. Stokman, Rolf Ziegler, and John Scott, eds. Cambridge, U.K.: Polity Press, 1985, pp. 91-111.

22. *Ziegler et al.* (1985), cited in the previous note, document the tightness of this network within their sample of 325 major German corporations.

23. Shirreff (1987), pp. 71-72. One bank executive, Manfred Meier-Preschany, reportedly sat on 42 different supervisory boards during his fifteen-year tenure as a member of Dresdner Bank's management committee. It should be noted that German law prohibits one person from being a director in more than ten different companies except under special circumstances such as one or more companies being a subsidiary of another on whose board the individual is a member. Under such special conditions, the maximum number of directorships is fifteen.

viewed as a rational attempt to secure the best of two worlds as far as investment is concerned. By tying themselves to one another in groups, yet eschewing outright majority ownership and control, Japanese corporations strive to exploit high-powered market incentives that derive from independent asset ownership and exposure to product-market discipline. At the same time, reliance on close monitoring and selective intervention by key stakeholders allows them to adapt terms of trade as needed in response to changing circumstances. In lieu of arm's-length transactions among many strictly autonomous market participants, or extensive integration of asset ownership under large administrative hierarchies, Japanese corporations transact on a middle ground characterized by implicit contracting, close personal-trust relationships among managers, and extensive information sharing. Abuse of such business relationships is mitigated, and their longevity fostered, by the spreading of large *minority* equity claims among major stakeholders such as key lenders, customers, suppliers, subcontractors, and so forth. By enhancing adverse reputation effects associated with opportunistic behavior, lifetime employment also helps mitigate moral hazards and preserve long-term business relationships.

This system of governance is not without its faults, of course. Excess manpower, excessive product proliferation, *over*-investment in declining businesses, unrelated diversification beyond organizational capabilities, and mismanagement of huge corporate excess cash balances are relatively commonly observed inefficiencies in Japanese business.[24] But these problems notwithstanding, the over-arching effect of the Japanese contractual governance system has been to foster considerable transactional efficiencies among Japanese companies doing business with each other, which, in turn, has promoted investment and global competitive success.

German contractual governance bears many similarities to the Japanese system, particularly with respect to the maintenance of long-term lender-borrower relationships and bank ownership of equity. In at least one important respect—the composition of corporate boards of directors—German governance provides a somewhat stronger safeguard against moral hazards associated with information asymmetries than does the Japanese system. Japanese boards tend to be heavily dominated by strictly inside managing directors. Retired executives of important equity-owning stakeholders join these directors as "alumni" representatives of their former employers. German supervisory boards, in contrast, are at least 50% composed of salaried executives of the corporation's major shareholders and/or other important stakeholders.

In a number of other respects, however, German contractual governance provides somewhat weaker safeguards as far as the preservation of long-term relationships is concerned. Although supervisory board representation is concentrated among a relatively small number of executives that sit on many different boards, the sort of temporary personnel transfers at lower levels of management that is so common in Japan are not so in Germany. Information sharing is less institutionalized in Germany than it is in Japan, which uses presidents' councils and, in the automotive industry, assembler-affiliated supplier associations. Although cross-shareholdings in Germany are quite extensive relative to U.S. experience, it does not appear as widespread a practice as in Japan. Banks, for example, own only about 9% of listed shares in Germany, but closer to 22% in Japan.

These differences in safeguards appear to be associated with differences in contracting norms and the extent to which companies in each country rely upon external procurement versus in-house production. Evidence from the automotive industry indicates that German companies depend more heavily upon formal contracting and less on relational contracting, rely upon a greater number of external suppliers, and are more vertically integrated than their Japanese counterparts.

Differences between Germany and Japan are more matters of degree than of kind, however, especially in comparison to common practice in the United States. By and large, both nations have evolved highly effective systems of contractual governance as far as the promotion of long-term relationships and corporate investment is concerned.

---

24. See Kester (1991), cited in note 5, pp. 219 to 235, for further discussion of these inefficiencies.

25. Germany saw a surge of acquisitions in the late 1980s. It was stimulated by an increase in the capital gains tax scheduled to take place in 1990. Sellers were primarily retiring founder-managers of medium-sized companies who faced succession and/or personal liquidity problems.

> *Germany and Japan have not needed active takeover markets because of the efficiency with which their traditional corporate and contractual governance systems have dealt with hazards associated with information asymmetries, investment in specialized assets, and the agency problems of large organizations.*

Both have also had remarkably quiescent markets for corporate control, at least as far as large-scale takeovers are concerned.[25] Hostile takeovers are virtually unheard of in both countries. These facts contrast sharply with the U.S. and U.K. experiences. The reason for the contrast has relatively little to do with the law. Legal restrictions on combinations in Japan, in fact, are remarkably lax compared to the present body of Federal and state statutes controlling mergers and acquisitions in the United States. Cultural differences among these nations may contribute to the contrast, but there is no need to assign them dominance as a determinant of national differences in the market for corporate control.

Germany and Japan have not had active markets for corporate control largely because they have not needed them, not because they did not want them or could not tolerate them. They have not needed active takeover markets because of the efficiency with which their traditional corporate and contractual governance systems have dealt with hazards associated with information asymmetries, investment in specialized assets, and the agency problems of large organizations. This efficiency has reduced the need to integrate vertically in order to secure upstream sources of supply or downstream markets. It has also blunted the need to exercise outright voting control in order to effect change in corporate strategies and policies detrimental to the welfare of the company's owners.

REFLECTIONS ON ANGLO-AMERICAN CONTRACTUAL GOVERNANCE

From the perspective of many American managers today, reconciling the competing aims of various corporate stakeholders seems an ever more challenging task. Judging from public statements by many executives, providing adequate financial returns while investing to ensure long-run competitive strength is perceived to be a particularly vexing problem. American managers of publicly-held industrial corporations increasingly view many important shareholders not as owners with a genuine interest in the corporation as an enduring enterprise, but as a cadre of distant, often indifferent professional money managers uninterested in the responsibilities of corporate ownership and quick to dump the company on anticipation of a single poor quarterly earnings report. Similar, albeit less frequent, complaints can be heard about other stakeholders that may seem to have thrown over any concept of loyalty to the company in favor of the immediate private gains to be had by switching allegiances.

This managerial malaise raises several important questions. Why have corporate stakeholder relationships with the firm, particularly those of equity owners, evolved to this state? Does the Anglo-American system of corporate governance need a complete overhaul or is it, in fact, an imperfect but still superior (compared to that of other nations) system? If it does need fixing, how so? What vision should guide us in making our reforms?

Vertical Anti-Trust versus Efficiency in Exchange

The German and Japanese experiences provide two perspectives to help in addressing these issues. In the late nineteenth and early twentieth centuries, some features of their modern contractual governance systems could have been observed in American commerce and finance as well. The United States did not, of course, have mammoth industrial zaibatsu or German-style combines dominating its economic landscape. But like their German and Japanese counterparts, large American banks owned equity in, as well as provided loans to, and underwrote the bonds of, their major industrial clients. The fortunes of these financial institutions became intimately linked to those of their major customers, resulting in close monitoring and coordination of their activities. Reciprocal trading agreements among companies were common, as were various forms of discriminatory pricing and subsidization among companies having trading relationships and common suppliers of capital. Tie-ins, resale price maintenance, territorial restrictions, outlet restrictions and the like formed *vertical* contractual restrictions where outright vertical integration was absent.

As these relationships and restrictions became more prominent in the modern industrial firm, the three nations evidently studied these arrangements through different lenses. Germany and Japan chose the lens of exchange efficiency, magnifying the role of these arrangements as individual elements of a broad system of contractual governance. Those systems were seen as highly effective in securing long-term, vertical trading relationships. Confidence in these relationships was central to the encouragement of investment in specialized assets which, if managed otherwise in an unrestricted market setting, would provide the basis for substantial trading hazards to the investing and transacting firms. Concern for adverse side effects from restraint of vertical trade was dominated by concern for effectiveness in contractual governance.

In contrast, the United States tended to view similar arrangements individually through the lens of anti-trust. Market power and restraint-of-trade effects were magnified relative to others. Where Germany and Japan saw efficiency and sought to preserve it, the United States saw abuse and sought to remedy it.

At inception, U.S. anti-trust legislation was an appropriate response to the monopoly power created by large *horizontal* mergers. Later, a theoretical economic preoccupation with entry barriers contributed to interpretations of anti-trust laws that created an inhospitable legal environment for virtually *any* type of non-standard contractual restraints, vertical, as well as horizontal, exchange efficiencies notwithstanding. By the 1960s, nearly any action or agreement that restricted the actions of transacting parties relative to what would otherwise transpire in a perfectly competitive market characterized by standard price-quantity transactions was construed as anti-competitive per se.[26] Meanwhile, banking and securities legislation (the Glass-Steagall Act of 1933, the Securities and Exchange Act of 1934, the Investment Company Act of 1940, the Bank Holding Company Act of 1956, and the Employee Retirement Income Security Act of 1974) and tax laws pertaining to mutual funds constrained the degree to which banks and other large "inside" investors could involve themselves in corporate supervision.[27]

This public policy posture made difficult and costly, if not actually impossible, many of the institutional arrangements used in Germany and Japan for contractual governance purposes. In contrast to the blended claims and stable long-term relationships promoted by their tolerance for restrictive contracting, U.S. intolerance of the same fostered a kind of "stakeholder pluralism"—a proliferation of separate and narrowly focused claimants that function effectively as special interests within the corporate body. The different claims of American corporate stakeholders became more explicit, more sharply differentiated, and less customized in ways designed to preserve long-term continuity in the pairwise identity of transacting parties. Much implicit, idiosyncratic contracting was replaced with standardized contracting wherein market participants bought and sold in arm's-length transactions at uniform prices with comparatively few bilateral restrictions.

In short, many of the building blocks of corporate and contractual governance that were considered so important in Germany and Japan for purposes of joining together the interests of diverse stakeholder groups were cast aside in the United States. A different system evolved accompanied by greater divisiveness among stakeholders motivated by private gain. As diversification and greater internal cash-flow generation provided relief from product and capital market tests in the 1960s and 1970s, returns that might otherwise have accrued to equity investors were diverted to other corporate stakeholders. Dispersed and separated from management, shareholders had only weak, indirect control over the companies they owned through their election of directors. In lieu of selective intervention by equity-owning banks such as has evolved in Germany and Japan, the United States, with its bias for market-ordered solutions to trading hazards, developed an active market for corporate control as a mechanism for integrating control over specialized assets and for effecting substantial change when shareholder interests were being abused.

The Market for Corporate Control

The desirability of corporate takeover activity in the United States has been the subject of much debate and even Congressional inquiry. Proponents point to evidence of greater operating efficiencies and the creation of tremendous shareholder value to support arguments that an active market for corporate control is both necessary and beneficial.[28] On the

---

26. See Oliver E. Williamson, "Antitrust Enforcement: Where it has been; where it is going." In John Craven, ed., *Industrial Organization, Antitrust, and Public Policy.* Boston: Kluwer-Nijhoff Publishing, pp. 41-68.

27. See Franklin Edwards and Robert Eisenbeis, "Financial Institutions and Corporate Myopia: An International Perspective." (New York: Columbia University; and Chapel Hill, N.C.: University of North Carolina; December 7, 1990). Unpublished working paper.

28. Michael Jensen (1988), for example, notes that in the ten year period between 1977 and 1986, mergers and acquisitions produced gains for selling-firm shareholders aggregating $346 billion (in 1986 dollars). (See Michael C. Jensen, "The Eclipse of the Public Corporations," *Harvard Business Review*, September-October, 1989, pp. 61-74.)

other side of this debate are many professional managers who believe hostile takeovers sap the vitality of American business by diverting management's time and foreshortening the execution of good long-run strategies.

Between these two poles of the debate is a middle ground. An active market for corporate control may be both necessary and desirable within the context of the Anglo-American style of corporate and contractual governance. Nevertheless, that *system* itself may be only second best in reconciling shareholder-value maximization with the priorities of other stakeholders. Researchers are probably right in concluding that, under the *prevailing* Anglo-American system of governance, considerable shareholder value would be forgone if there were not a free and active market for corporate control. But this conclusion should not obscure the warnings of experienced managers on the firing line that the system itself may be hamstringing their ability to compete successfully with world-class competitors in new global markets.

Reforming Anglo-American Contractual Governance

Anglo-American contractual governance is by no means static. As stiffer competition from Germany and Japan is encountered, so too are some of the limitations of the Anglo-American system. This, in turn, stimulates evolutionary change. As we undergo this process, we could do worse than experiment with some of the building blocks of governance that have been used to good effect in Germany, Japan, and elsewhere. Indeed, such experimentation can already be observed among the American auto assemblers. All three are striving to source more parts externally from fewer suppliers with whom they are striving to build closer, longer-term, and more flexible contracting relationships.

However, this is not to suggest that the governance systems of corporations of other nations can simply be transported. Many nations may not prefer the particular tradeoff between efficiency in governance and restraint of trade that has been struck in Japan, for example. Nor is it clear that industrial keiretsu could be replicated in other parts of the world. Established patterns of business and contractual governance found in the many parts of the West today may simply be too far removed from those of Germany and Japan to expect a transformation to that extent.

But there may be exchange efficiencies to be gained by enabling the development of more tightly knit networks of companies with more stable long-term trading relationships. A concentration of ownership within such networks, a spreading of residual claims (equity) among other classes of corporate stakeholders, and close monitoring and control by a few sophisticated institutional suppliers of capital capable of early intervention are key attributes of the German and Japanese systems that are also worthy of emulation elsewhere.

It should be emphasized again that the success of contractual governance as practiced in Germany and Japan is not culture bound. It does not depend upon any special sense of corporate loyalty, work ethic, willingness to submerge private interests to those of a group, or propensity to seek consensus. These attributes may exist in abundance in Germany and Japan, and may contribute to the success of their systems. But the systems themselves are fundamentally engineered to prevent the sort of investment hazards that arise from self-interested opportunism—hazards faced by companies the world over. That is, they have the clear-cut *economic* purpose of promoting transactional efficiency and investment in specialized assets. Hence, barring explicit legal restrictions, their better attributes should be portable across national borders.

Consider some of the deals and trends observed in other parts of the world. When Italy set out to implement its five-year plan to modernize its telecommunications system, it elected to do so by means of a collaborative arrangement between American Telephone and Telegraph and Italtel, the state-owned Italian telecommunications equipment maker. The agreement with AT&T was sealed in 1989 by an exchange of 20% equity stakes between Italtel and AT&T-Network Systems International, a joint venture between AT&T and Philips. Similarly, Istituto San Paolo di Torino, one of Italy's major banks, entered into a 5% cross-shareholding arrangement with Salomon Brothers, a leading U.S. investment bank, when the two institutions struck an agreement to cooperate in the areas of corporate finance, asset securitization, and securities distribution. Other such cross-shareholding arrangements were also set up between San Paolo and Compagnie Financiere de Suez of France, and with Hambros of the U.K.

Under the Chirac privatization program, France deliberately sought to nurture at least some aspects of German and Japanese corporate governance among

French corporations. At the time of the public offerings of stock in the large banks and industrial companies being privatized, roughly 20% of the stock would be placed in the hands of *noyaux durs*—a group of roughly 15 to 20 banks, insurance companies (predominantly French, but interestingly also including some Japanese institutions), and industrial corporations that were to function as a hard core of stable shareholders. These were provided equity in privatized companies under the restriction that they keep 80% of the shares allocated to them for at least two years and thereafter provide the issuing corporation with a three-year pre-emptive right to repurchase up to 80% of any stable shares offered for resale.

Japanese corporations themselves have demonstrated the transportability of their own style of governance. Japanese-affiliated automakers in the United States have successfully entered into supply contracts with American auto-parts producers that are patterned after their relationships with suppliers at home. Typically, these involve heavier reliance on suppliers in the initial design and development of some parts and subassemblies, close coordination of production to take advantage of just-in-time delivery systems, rapid responses to needed product changes, and extensive monitoring and even occasional intrusion by the assembler into the operations of the supplier. Long-term relationships with a few suppliers, sometimes accompanied by minority equity stakes in them, are also used in the United States in lieu of the more common American practice of entering into one-year, bid-priced contracts with many suppliers. However foreign this method of doing business may seem at first, American suppliers that have successfully won the business of a Japanese-affiliated producer claim they have been positively affected. Higher production efficiency, better quality, and lower costs are the benefits most com-monly reported. Some American suppliers are even extending similar practices to their own upstream suppliers. So too are American automobile assemblers in managing their own supplier relationships.

The goals of achieving stability in the corporate stakeholder coalition, particularly with respect to ownership, while simultaneously controlling opportunism by individual members, will be fostered not so much by regulating and limiting the market for corporate control as by the reshaping of corporate and contractual governance in the West. Enacting legislation making it more difficult or costly to take over a company is merely treating the symptom of a larger governance problem and not the root causes. Artificially locking shareholders into corporate ownership through tax carrots and sticks is no solution either if the moral hazards and other agency problems associated with investments are not efficiently controlled.

What is required instead is greater flexibility and wider scope in the range of contracting arrangements available for use by transacting companies. The governance advantages of closer lender-borrow relationships and the onslaught of foreign competitors benefitting from such relationships suggests a need to reconsider those legal constraints that restrict equity ownership and active board participation by banks and other large financial institutions. Obviously, changes such as these carry potential costs and hazards as well as benefits. But the nation would do better to focus its debate about the conduct of business on the issue of how much liberty to grant companies in the development and maintenance of long-term vertical relationships rather than, say, the benefits and costs of an active market for corporate control.

The 1980s have seen emerge a kind of Darwinistic "competition" among systems of contractual governance for global dominance. Judging from the remarkable contemporary successes of German and Japanese companies, and recent innovations that embody components of governance commonly found in Germany and Japan, it is by no means clear that classic Anglo-American governance standards will be the winner of this competition. This is not to suggest that the German and Japanese systems are ideal, simply that they may be more efficient than the Anglo-American system in coping with hazards posed by risky investment in new environments. The United States would do well to recognize this as it strives to contend with the relatively new competitive challenges posed by its major economic competitors.

■ CARL KESTER

is Professor of Business Administration at the Harvard Business School and author of *Japanese Takeovers: The Global Contest for Corporate Control* (Harvard Business School Press, 1991). His recent research has focused on financial sources of international competitive advantage.

SELECTIONS FROM

CORPORATE GOVERNANCE IN JAPAN AND THE UNITED STATES

THE SECOND INTERNATIONAL SYMPOSIUM ON

GLOBAL FINANCIAL MARKETS SPONSORED BY

THE MITSUI LIFE FINANCIAL RESEARCH CENTER

AT THE UNIVERSITY OF MICHIGAN

KEIDANREN KAIKAN, TOKYO

MAY 11, 1993

Joseph White, Dean of the

Michigan Business School, opened

the symposium by extending a welcome to an

audience of 600 business leaders, regulators,

and academics who filled the main auditorium

of the Keidanren Kaikan.

Koshiro Sakata, President of the Mitsui Life

Insurance Company, followed with

congratulatory remarks directed to the

organizers of the conference. Following the

principal presentations, three of which are

printed below, the symposium concluded

with a summary and closing remarks by

Professors E. Han Kim of the

Michigan Business School, and

Takaagi Wakasugi of Tokyo University,

the co-directors of the Mitsui Life Center.

Koshiro Sakata

Joichi Aoi

Merton Miller

C. K. Prahalad

TO WHOM DOES THE COMPANY BELONG?: A NEW MANAGEMENT MISSION FOR THE INFORMATION AGE

by Joichi Aoi,
Chairman of the Board,
Toshiba Corporation

L et me begin by congratulating Mitsui Life on sponsoring this second international symposium with the University of Michigan's Graduate School of Business. I am pleased to see that the event is being held in such a grand manner, and feel honored to be given the opportunity to speak to you today.

The subject of today's symposium is the governance of corporations in Japan and the United States. There has been a lively debate on corporate governance here in Japan, in the U.S., and in a number of European countries as well. I would like to share with you some of my personal views on the subject. In so doing, I will also discuss what I believe to be the most important considerations for corporate management in leading their companies into a new era of technology-based competition.

The basic issue underlying the corporate governance debate can be stated very simply: To whom does the company belong? That is, should corporate managers view themselves primarily as stewards of their investors' capital and so aim to maximize shareholder value? Or should they view themselves instead as custodians of their companies' "human capital," and thus concentrate more on protecting the interests and developing the knowledge and skills of their employees.

Over the long run, of course, these two perspectives need not be mutually exclusive. Both capital and people are essential to corporate success, and the requirements of both investors and employees must eventually be met. But, as I will argue later, in a world characterized by increasingly global and technology-based competition, the development of human resources has become a much more important corporate function than it was in the past. In the last analysis, moreover, corporate success will depend on management's ability to satisfy not just its investors and employees, but the entire range of interests that make up our society.

THE GOVERNANCE DEBATE IN THE U.S.

The U.S. corporate governance debate was fueled by the stockholder activism of the 1980s. During this period, U.S. institutional investors such as pension funds became more financially sophisticated and used their expertise to exert more influence on the managements of the companies in which they had invested. The participation of institutional investors also helped make possible the wave of hostile takeovers that forced the top managers of many U.S. companies out of their jobs. As a result of this takeover activity, the corporate governance issue in the U.S. has been broadly characterized as a "contest for control" between management and shareholders.

Today, there is a widespread perception that the corporate restructuring of the '80s—and the adversarial relationship between management and investors underlying it—was leading to the industrial decline of the U.S. In the '80s, American companies across a broad range of industries lost market share to global competitors. The rigid shareholder-based controls exerted by the U.S. governance system have been blamed for enforcing a short-term profit mentality on U.S. companies—a mentality that impaired their ability to compete with their more far-sighted German and Japanese competitors.

In the 1990s, however, the U.S. governance system has undergone significant changes. Although by no means eliminated, the problem of shortsightedness in many U.S. companies has been mitigated in a number of ways: most notably, by encouraging more active participation by outside directors and establishing longer-term relationships with institutional investors. Some U.S. companies have also made the attempt to build stronger relationships with other important corporate "stakeholders" such as customers, employees, suppliers, financial institutions, and the local communities in which they do business.

Thus, the perspective of U.S. managers on corporate governance has broadened considerably in the '90s from its near-exclusive preoccupation with shareholders during the '80s. Nevertheless, the primary focus of the U.S. governance debate remains the balance of power between managers and shareholders; and thus proposed solutions to the U.S. governance problem focus on means of increasing the effectiveness of corporate boards in transmitting shareholder influence and enforcing shareholder control. They reflect an *external* approach to the problem, as opposed to the *internal* one I will propose.

THE GOVERNANCE DEBATE IN JAPAN

Unlike the U.S. experience, the corporate governance debate in Japan did not get underway until the 1990s. In this country, the governance discussion has clearly come in response to economic adversity. Since the bursting of its stock market "bubble," Japan has experienced a sharp and sustained downturn of its economy during the past three years. Corporate earnings, investment, and stock prices have all declined significantly, and we are now in the midst of a period of harsh correction and adjustment.

One of the leading participants in the Japanese corporate governance debate has been the Nomura Research Institute, or NRI. NRI recently published a report that came to the following major conclusions:
- First, the declines in corporate earnings and share prices have by far exceeded those that would have been expected in a purely "cyclical" downturn, and NRI has attributed the severity of such declines to a "structural" overcapacity stemming from lax investment criteria employed by Japanese companies.
- Second, the practice of cross-holdings of shares among Japanese firms has prevented shareholders from exerting sufficient influence on management, with negative consequences for efficiency.
- Third, in addition to denying shareholders any means of effective oversight or control over their investment policies, Japanese companies also tend to compound the problem by retaining excess capital rather than returning it to shareholders in the form of higher dividends or share repurchases. Failure to pay out excess capital leads to inefficiency.

As you can see from these conclusions, although there are some differences in focus between the U.S. and Japanese governance debates, there is also a common set of concerns. In both countries, there is a perception that corporate management is not sufficiently accountable to outside constituencies, and that something must be done about it.

But, in order to evaluate the nature and extent of this problem, we need to examine a few basic questions first: What are corporations in the first place, and how did they originate and develop? And how have their organizational structures and activities changed over the years? Are corporations today doing the right things to prepare for a modern environment that includes intense global competition, often based on technological superiority? These are the basic issues that confront corporations around the world as they approach the 21st century.

A BRIEF LOOK BACK

The notion that business is conducted primarily by corporations dates back to the 1600s, when the East India Company was established in Great Britain and when similar companies were established in the Netherlands and France. Prior to the formation of these companies, spices produced in Asia were transported overland. The East India Company revolutionized world trade by transporting spices and other exotic goods overseas by ship, which led in turn to the establishment of plantations and further developments. It was the *form* of the "joint stock" corporation—in which hundreds of outside investors could each buy fractional ownership interests in a single entity—that allowed such large and risky ventures to obtain the necessary capital.

Between the 1600s and the beginning of the 20th century, corporations were responsible for technological innovations—particularly during the Industrial Revolution of the 19th century—leading to greater productivity and higher standards of living throughout the industrialized world. But there was one important difference between those companies and their modern-day counterparts. Although the East India Company had hundreds of shareholders, most corporations in the late 19th and early 20th century were closely held. Even in the world's largest corporations, there was a heavy concentration of ownership and owner-managers were the rule rather than the exception.

But, as a result of the rapid growth of U.S. financial and securities markets in the first decades of this century, the ownership structure of U.S. corporations changed dramatically. In fact, a survey conducted as early as 1932 revealed that, in 85% of the largest 200 U.S. public companies, no single stockholder owned more than 10 percent of the shares. Thus, even in 1932, the separation of ownership from control that U.S. corporate governance critics complain about today was already well advanced. Even then, shareholders had effectively delegated the function of corporate management to a relatively new class of "professional" managers—that is, managers who were not also major stockholders.

In the second half of the 20th century, this proliferation and dispersion of shareholders spread to all the industrialized countries—and Japan was no exception. Professional managers everywhere competed by means not of their own accumulated capital, but on the basis of their knowledge and ability.

This worldwide development of professional managers in turn enabled corporations to enlarge their operations and achieve significant economies of scale and scope. The result was further increases in productivity and standards of living worldwide.

In recent years, however, the nature of corporate competition has changed fundamentally. Indeed, I would say that we have entered a "new era" of management. But before describing this new age of competition and the ways companies are adapting to it, let me first offer a brief definition of the corporation—one that will allow us to recognize what remains the same in corporations even as they are going through continuous change.

In my view, the corporation is an organization of people and resources whose basic purpose is to add value by transforming technological innovation into goods and services demanded by the society. In the process of converting new technology into valued goods and services, corporations bring together different kinds of resources—notably, capital, labor, management skills—and then attempt to organize themselves in the way that leads to the most productive use of all the resources. And let me elaborate on a few key terms. My definition of "technology" is meant to be comprehensive, encompassing innovations not only in products, but in the way services are provided. By "value-added" I mean the sum total of the benefits deriving from corporate activities that support the upgrading of our society as a whole.

So, the fundamental aim of corporate activity is to promote technological innovation that leads in turn to value-adding products and services. To the extent such products and services are valued by society, society rewards the corporation—or all its different contributing groups. Consumers receive valuable products and services, shareholders earn higher returns on their capital, employees receive higher wages and benefits, and local communities prosper. In this sense, the corporate mission is tied firmly to advancement of the social interest. The productive efficiency achieved by corporations in competition with each other yields collective benefits to all.

PEOPLE VS. CAPITAL IN THE NEW INFORMATION AGE

This brings me back to my initial statement of the fundamental question of corporate governance: To whom does the company belong? The two most popular approaches to this issue can be summarized very succinctly: Proponents of one view hold that companies are consolidations primarily of *capital*; proponents of the other that companies are primarily consolidations of *people*.

Both of these viewpoints, I hasten to say, contain an important element of truth and yet both are incomplete. The relative weight that can be assigned to each can also change over time.

Until fairly recently, for example, corporate success throughout the world was based on achieving scale economies from mass production intended for mass consumers. That was the model of industrial society that prevailed throughout the late 19th century and the first half of the 20th. The primary economic interest of society lay in the efficient production of homogeneous products in large enough quantities to achieve significant reductions in prices to consumers. And the principal means of achieving such efficiencies was large-scale investment in plant and equipment financed by large amounts of investor capital. The ability to raise and redeploy capital, then, was the primary ingredient in corporate success; people were secondary, interchangeable factors of production.

Today, however, we are in the midst of a transformation from an industrialized to an information-oriented society—a shift that can be expected to continue well into the next century. Increasingly, information networks are being established that will give people everywhere inexpensive access to huge stores of information housed in all variety of databases. For corporations, perhaps the most important consequence of this information revolution is the resulting diversification of consumer tastes and preferences. The increased sophistication of consumers has led to rising demand for both higher-quality and more specialized products. And this fragmentation of mass markets has in turn required important changes in production such as flexible manufacturing and better inventory controls.

There has also been a major shift in the way information flows. In the past, information was transmitted for the most part in one direction—primarily from large corporations to their consumers, suppliers, and distributors. Today we are seeing a two-way street for information between corporations and their major customers and suppliers. Developing such channels of information is critical for corporations attempting to keep up with continuous changes in consumer demand.

Greater demand for customized products also means a larger role for employee initiative and creativity. When we speak of employee "creativity," we are referring in part to their ability to anticipate consumer demands. All companies have employees with highly subjective tastes, idiosyncratic ways of thinking, and distinctive kinds of know-how. Corporations should be organized so as to identify and encourage the development of these human "assets" in such a way that each individual feels challenged and committed to contribute to the company's success.

And this is perhaps even more true of service industries, where corporate success has always depended heavily on the performance of employees. Because service businesses in all industrialized nations are expanding far more rapidly than manufacturing, the importance of employees' contribution to corporate success is growing.

In sum, the information revolution has elevated the importance of development of human resources relative to capital management. The companies that succeed in the information age will be those organizations best able to integrate people, goods, and capital. Those companies that fail to stimulate and harness the creative potential of their employees will be shaken out in the new competitive environment.

A NEW METRIC OF CORPORATE SUCCESS

But having said this, let me return once again to my original question: To whom does the company belong?

As I suggested earlier, it belongs in part to its shareholders, and it belongs in increasing part to its employees. But neither of these is a complete answer. In my view, the complete answer is that the corporation belongs to society. As the economic priorities of society change, so too must corporate priorities. And as a better informed society leads to further diversification of the tastes and values of its citizens, corporations must place increasing emphasis on investing in and getting the most from their employees.

This view of the corporation as accountable to a broad range of social interests also leads to a different way of evaluating corporate performance. In the past, it has been customary to focus on the profits earned by a particular company. But there is another measure of corporate success that may be more relevant: namely, the total social benefits derived from a corporation's activity net of any social disadvan-

We are in the midst of a transformation from an industrialized to an information-oriented society. For corporations, perhaps the most important consequence of this information revolution is the resulting diversification of consumer tastes and preferences. The increased sophistication of consumers has led to rising demand for both higher-quality and more specialized products.

tages. For example, in developing *internal* measures of performance, corporations may choose increasingly to capitalize rather than expense their outlays on training, software, and R & D. Such outlays represent investments in the corporate future, and corporate *internal* accounting (and perhaps external accounting, too) should recognize these realities of the new management era.

As another example, measures to reduce the emission of chloro-fluoro carbons, or CFCs, may impose significant costs on individual companies. By volunteering to bear their fair share of these costs, however, corporations will be contributing to the social welfare. And in the kind of social cost-benefit analysis by which companies will inevitably come to evaluate their performance, corporate contributions to social problems will increasingly be viewed as "investments" in a firm's social standing.

Such investments are important because more extreme critics of corporations—those who subscribe to the "born-evil" theory of corporations—are convinced that *all* profit-seeking activities are, by their very nature, harmful to the social interest. All countries have such people, and they tend to have political influence out of all proportion to their numbers. To combat such misguided criticism, corporations in all nations will have to devote more resources not only to social causes like public health and the environment, but also to educating the public about the social benefits of corporate activities.

Another issue that arises regularly in Japanese discussions of corporate governance concerns the negative consequences of the widespread *cross-holding* of shares. Such cross-holdings reinforce the natural tendency of managers to insulate their companies against pressure from "outsiders," which include shareholders as well as representatives of other social interests. Proposals for reform typically include the appointment of outside directors and improvements of the auditing system.

I personally believe that outside directors could do much to help companies recognize and respond to the interests of society as a whole. Accordingly, several years ago we at Toshiba set up an advisory board composed entirely of outsiders. The purpose of the board, which meets about twice a year, is to advise top management on broader social as well as economic issues that are typically outside the scope of normal business issues. And my understanding is that many of the largest companies in Japan have introduced similar systems on a voluntary basis.

The information revolution I mentioned earlier makes the function of such a board all the more valuable. With greater access to information, outsiders can more easily monitor the activities of companies—and the companies themselves can more readily see the interests of those outside the company. As I stated earlier, companies can no longer afford to remain indifferent to the interests of those outside the company. As part of a complex social fabric with conflicting as well as common interests, corporations must seek to win and retain the trust of all the various segments and strata of society.

"QUALITATIVE" GROWTH: THE CHALLENGE OF THE NEW MANAGEMENT ERA

Further complicating the challenge of the new, more competitive global environment are radical changes in political economy now taking place. After half a century of the Cold War, the world is seeking to create a new order.

Today, we are at a critical turning point in that process. In the 1980s, the world economy experienced rapid economic growth, but the 1990s are proving very different. The United States is faced with twin deficits in its fiscal and trade sectors. Attempts to integrate the European Community are being frustrated by conflicts of interest among various EC member nations. And, in the former Eastern European nations as well as Russia and the new CIS, there is complete economic disarray. At the same time, some lesser developed countries are saddled with heavy debt burdens, while issues of environmental conservation appear to be pitting the economic interests of LDCs against the social concerns of industrialized nations.

And, as I mentioned earlier, the Japanese economy is now in the midst of a severe adjustment phase. Most Japanese companies, representing virtually all industrial sectors of our economy, are moving ahead with severe restructuring efforts aimed at producing "qualitative" growth in the new era, as opposed to the "quantitative" growth and expansion that characterized the '80s and earlier. By "qualitative" growth, I mean the formidable task of producing higher-quality, often more specialized, products in lower volumes for more demanding consumers while still economizing on capital, labor, and other social resources.

In confronting this new challenge, we are faced with the necessity of re-examining all aspects of

Japanese-style management—a management style that, until recently, was regularly cited as a major contributor to the competitive successes of our companies. As I stated earlier, the corporate *raison d'etre* is the same; it remains the creation of value-added products and services through technological innovation. What demands a radical shift in management perspective, however, is the growing diversification of tastes and values of consumers (and, as I discuss later, of employees). With the advancement of the new information society, companies must invest more heavily in their human resources and place greater emphasis on giving full play to human intellectual creativity within the organization. The competition for technological innovation, productive efficiency, and more sophisticated consumers demands it.

TECHNOLOGY, HUMAN CAPITAL, AND INDIVIDUALISM (WITH AN ASIDE ON INVENTORY MANAGEMENT)

Let me say a bit more about technology and human development in corporations, because it's something that has been much on my mind lately. I have always felt that technological innovation is the most important factor in corporate success. It's true, of course, that technology *per se* may be more important in manufacturing than in service businesses. And, as I noted earlier, the growth of the world economy is increasingly moving away from manufacturing and toward services. But regardless of whether a company belongs to the manufacturing or the service sector, continuous innovation—be it new developments in technology, or valuable changes in organizational structure and processes—must always be critical to competitive success.

During the past two decades, the world has witnessed a transition from an industrial to an information-oriented society. During this time, semiconductors, computers, office automation, and innovations in communication, image, and information technology have all played a central role in economic growth. But the real force underlying all this change and technological innovation is the human mind—human brainpower, if you will. Technological innovation is linked inextricably with changes in the mindset of people—changes which have also expressed themselves in the remarkable proliferation of new consumer tastes and values.

Underlying this diversification of consumer tastes and values is the natural human urge for self-realiza-tion, which means in part differentiating oneself from others. Technological innovation has allowed fuller expression of this urge and, in so doing, has further increased the "demand" for diversity *within the corporate environment*. This means that unless corporations are able to satisfy employee demands for greater opportunity for self-realization, they will find themselves lagging in the competition for technology. And if this happens, their products and services will eventually fail to attract consumers, and the organization will lose its justification for being.

Along with this urge toward self-expression has come increased popular demand for "consumer sovereignty" as a national economic goal. In the past, Japanese companies were remarkably successful in transforming Japan into an economic superpower. This was an appropriate social goal for an industrial society. These days, however, we hear much talk about the need for a better quality of life for the Japanese people. Japan, many observers have suggested, ought to seek to become a "lifestyle" superpower as well as an economic superpower.

Such a change in economic goals may require a redefinition of the Japanese concept of "social wealth." I believe that a society is wealthy only to the extent that it satisfies the demands of its citizens. In the new information age, such demands are shifting from simple material satisfactions to a desire for more sophisticated and higher-quality goods. Social wealth is thus reflected not in the abundance of physical assets such as oil and land, but rather in the quality of life of its people. A lifestyle superpower is a nation that secures a better quality of life for its citizens.

Corporations must contribute to social wealth by changing their objectives in a way that better meets the demands of consumers. Technological innovation is the key to improving quality of life, in large part because consumer demand is undergoing continous change. Staying on the cutting edge of technology allows companies to anticipate changes in consumer needs—and, in some cases, even to create them—rather than responding after the fact.

At the same time, of course, the successful commercialization of technology also requires continuous attention to current consumer demands. For example, our basic challenge at Toshiba is to develop products that harmonize our technological advantages with consumer demands and the capabilities of our manufacturing system. The ideal toward which we are striving is a completely flexible manufacturing system in which we can produce a

> Our basic challenge at Toshiba is to develop products that harmonize our technological advantages with consumer demands and the capabilities of our manufacturing system. The ideal toward which we are striving is a completely flexible manufacturing system in which we can produce a large variety of products in ever smaller quantities, thereby eliminating the need to carry inventory.

large variety of products in ever smaller quantities. To the extent we can achieve this ideal—and we have made considerable progress toward it in recent years—while also improving our distribution systems, we could conceivably eliminate the need to carry inventory altogether.

Why is inventory management so important? There are directly measurable costs, of course, associated with warehousing inventory. And, in our present recessionary phase, we often hear about the need to reduce such costs by making inventory adjustments that anticipate the future strength of the economy. But I think that inventory management has a much greater significance than direct costs. Indeed, I would submit that relying on inventory is the *greatest* source of inefficiency in business. Stocks of inventory effectively block the flow of information between consumers and producers. Such information in turn provides the basis for other important decisions throughout the organization—in strategy and planning, research & development, and marketing, as well as production. And, as we progress further into the new information era, I predict that the ideal of the "stockless" corporation will become a new model for management.

THE FUTURE

In the past two decades, the Japanese economy has weathered two major oil crises as well as the competitive problems stemming from the appreciation of the yen. In each case, we have overcome these problems by giving full play to the creativity of our people in confronting technological challenges. I am confident that technological advance also holds the solution to our current problems. To remain competitive, companies in all nations must continue to develop their technological capabilities.

The key to developing such capabilities lies in developing and making the best use of corporate human resources. In the new "intelligent information-oriented society," as we refer to it at Toshiba, it is human capital—intellectual value-added, if you will—that will increasingly differentiate successful from unsuccessful companies. The slowing of worldwide economic growth rates combined with the diversification of values of the various segments of the society is now forcing companies to draw upon and give full expression to their intellectual resources.

And just as diverging consumer tastes are forcing companies to differentiate themselves by pro-ducing goods and services with more originality, employees are also changing their views of the companies. Unlike the past, Japanese employees are no longer married to their companies; they view their jobs as only a part of their lives. Moreover, they are seeking workplaces in which they are able to develop their talents and perform work they find challenging and worthwhile. In meeting such new demands from employees, Japanese companies will benefit from encouraging greater individual initiative and entrepreneurial spirit.

To achieve this goal of greater employee self-realization, however, reform of the present Japanese education system is essential. While our companies are seeking people with varied skills and interests, our education system continues its attempt to produce only "genius people" by emphasizing test scores and instilling uniformity of approach. For this reason, our school system is failing to prepare our young people to help Japanese corporations compete in the new world economy.

In closing, let me state once more my conviction that there are two critical requirements for corporate success in the 1990s and beyond: continous technological innovation and a firm commitment to development of human resources. We have entered into a new era in corporate management—one that is being driven fundamentally by advances in information technology. Largely as a result of cheap access to information of all kinds, consumer tastes have become much more diverse, specialized, and sophisticated. To compete effectively, companies must not simply respond to changes in consumer demand; they must also anticipate and even "create" them through imaginative product innovation.

In responding successfully to such change, companies perform an important social mission by contributing to the vitality and growth of all aspects of society. Through their ability to create products and services valued by global consumers, companies enrich not only their shareholders and employees, but an entire network of corporate constituencies that includes suppliers, local communities, and government. Nations around the world today are faced with formidable challenges: the global environment, conservation, industrial waste, the aging of society, expanding the role of women in the workforce, and addressing the shortage of skilled labor. As important members of society, corporations must participate in devising solutions to these problems.

CORPORATE GOVERNANCE AND CORPORATE PERFORMANCE: A COMPARISON OF GERMANY, JAPAN AND THE U.S.

by Steven N. Kaplan[1]

C orporate governance systems have received an increasing amount of attention from academics, government, the popular press, and businesses themselves. Much of this attention has focused on differences between the U.S. system and those of its two strongest industrial competitors, Germany and Japan.

The U.S. corporate governance system is generally characterized as a "market-based" system. U.S. capital markets are liquid and company ownership is relatively unconcentrated. Managers are supposedly monitored by an external market for corporate control and by boards of directors that are usually dominated by outsiders. The German and Japanese governance systems, by contrast, are characterized as "relationship-oriented" systems. Ownership in Germany and Japan is concentrated and capital markets are relatively illiquid. Managers in those countries is allegedly monitored by a combination of banks, large corporate shareholders, and other intercorporate relationships that are maintained over long periods. An external market for corporate control is small, if not altogether absent.

1. This paper forms the basis for a talk presented at the conference on "Corporate Governance—Structural Reforms in the American and German Corporation Law," in Heidelberg, July 1, 1995. This research was supported by the Lynde and Harry Bradley Foundation, the Olin Foundation and the Center for Research in Security Prices.

TABLE 1
A COMPARISON OF
GERMAN, JAPANESE, AND
U.S. GOVERNANCE
SYSTEMS

	Germany	Japan	U.S.
EXECUTIVE COMPENSATION	Moderate	Low	High
BOARD OF DIRECTORS	Management/ Supervisory	Primarily Insiders	Primarily Outsiders
OWNERSHIP	Concentrated: High Family/ Corporate/ Bank	Less Concentrated: High Bank/High Corporate/Low Management	Diffuse Non- corporate/
CAPITAL MARKETS	Relatively Illiquid	Somewhat Liquid	Very Liquid
TAKEOVER/CONTROL MARKET	Minor	Minor	Major
BANKING SYSTEM	Universal Banking	Main Bank System	

These differences in governance systems (which are summarized in Table 1) are generally in turn associated with differences in managerial behavior and firm objectives. One view, probably the majority one, argues that the close financial ties and relationships in Germany and Japan "reduce agency costs and allow investors to monitor managers more effectively than in the U.S."[2] According to this view, there are lower costs to changing poorly performing management because banks and large shareholders have the power to make needed changes. Costly hostile takeovers or proxy fights are avoided.

This view is also associated with claims that German and Japanese firms are less concerned with or affected by short-term earnings, and are therefore better able than U.S. firms to manage for the long term—that is, invest in projects with long-term pay-offs. This view assumes that current stock prices can diverge significantly from long-term shareholder values. Because banks and large shareholders have both better information and more power to use that information than the widely dispersed shareholders of the typical U.S. company, financing is said to be more readily available for value-increasing long-term projects in Germany and Japan. The supposed monitoring and information advantages have led some to call for the U.S. corporate governance system to imitate aspects of the German and Japanese systems.[3]

Others argue, however, that the German and Japanese systems entrench managers and employees at the expense of shareholders. Banks, allied with incumbent managers, may receive abnormally high fees or interest rates in exchange for agreeing to bail out managers (and their companies) in cases of poor performance and financial distress, even when it is not efficient to do so.[4]

As suggested above, many observers have been quick to distinguish the U.S. system from those of Japan and Germany, and to draw conclusions about the nature of those differences. Most of these distinctions, however, are based on anecdotes, cases, and surveys. In contrast, three of my own studies (including one with Bernadette Minton) provide some of the first systematic evidence on how the German and Japanese systems operate and how they differ from the U.S. system.[5] The results are not always in agreement with the anecdotes.

In this essay, I summarize and discuss the implications of the results of these three studies. Executive turnover in all three countries increases significantly with poor stock performance and earnings losses. Executive compensation in both Japan and the U.S. is also related to stock returns and earnings losses. The effects in all three countries are generally economically and statistically similar. The fortunes of German and Japanese top executives, therefore, like those of

---

2. Grundfest (1990), p. 98. See also Aoki et al. (1994), Hoshi et al. (1990 and 1991), Lipton and Rosenblum (1991), Porter (1992), and Prowse (1990).

3. In particular, see Porter (1992) who argues that the U.S. system leads to underinvestment.

4. See Abegglen and Stalk (1985), Baums (1992 and 1993), and Coffee (1991) for a discussion of these views. Milgrom and Roberts (1992) and Roe (1993) are also sympathetic to this conclusion.

5. Kaplan (1994a and 1994b) and Kaplan and Minton (1994).

their U.S. counterparts, are strongly affected by stock performance and current cash flows. Sales growth, a measure of market share, plays a smaller role.

In sum, there is no evidence that U.S. managers have any more incentive to be short-term oriented than their German and Japanese counterparts. Managers in all three countries appear to be affected by similar forces to roughly the same extent. At the end of the paper, I offer an explanation for these similarities and some conjectures about the relative advantages and disadvantages of the three governance systems.

WHAT INCENTIVES DO CORPORATE GOVERNANCE SYSTEMS PROVIDE?

As noted above, most discussions of managerial motivations in Germany, Japan, and the U.S. are based on anecdotes or surveys. In my research, I decided to test the anecdotes by asking one simple question: What incentives do the different corporate governance systems really offer to top managers? Specifically, by understanding why top managers are fired and why they are paid more, one can infer what incentives they actually have.

The Relation Between Managerial Rewards and Punishments and Firm Performance

Two of my studies cited earlier examine corporate governance in the largest companies in the three countries—42 firms in Germany, 119 in Japan, and 146 in the U.S.—from 1980 to 1988. Both studies focus on the top group of managers or operating executives in each firm in these countries. These executives are management board members in Germany, representative directors in Japan, and executive directors in the U.S. In the next several paragraphs, I describe the management and board structures in the three countries in more detail.

In Germany, the management board—the *Vorstand*—is comprised of the seven or eight top managers. They include the Chairman, who is the equivalent of the CEO. German firms also have a supervisory board—the *Aufsichtsrat*—which is the equivalent of an outside board in the United States. Under the German "co-determination" system, the supervisory board includes both shareholder and labor representatives. In larger public companies, the supervisory board will typically have 19 members.

In Japan, the typical board has 21 members, almost all of whom are insiders. The president is the chief executive officer or CEO. In each company, three or four directors, including the president, are given special rights to represent the company. These are known as the representative directors.

Finally, in the U.S., the firm is governed by a board of directors of typically 13 or 14 members. Approximately one-third of them are insiders and two-thirds are outsiders. The CEO is the most powerful of the managers and directors. My research focuses on executive directors, those operating managers who are also on the board of directors. This group typically includes four or five members, and it always includes the CEO.

The first question I asked was this: What kind of performance causes the top operating managers in these firms to lose their jobs? In technical terms, this involved estimating the following regression:

Probability of losing job = a + ß × Performance + e

I used four measures of firm performance: (1) company stock returns; (2) sales growth; (3) change in pre-tax income as a fraction of total assets; (4) and a dummy variable equal to one if pre-tax income was negative. Sales growth was meant to be a measure of market share, and, presumably, a measure of "long-term" managerial success. The dummy variable for negative pre-tax income was perhaps the most short-term measure of performance.

The turnover results are presented in Figures 1, 2, and 3. In all three countries, managers are more likely to lose their jobs when their company's stock performs poorly (Figure 1). In all three countries, managers are more likely to lose their jobs when their company experiences an earnings loss (Figure 2). In fact, Japanese and German managers are approximately twice as likely to lose their jobs in a year with a loss than in a year with positive earnings. Interestingly, the sensitivities or relations in the three countries are not different from one another in a statistical sense.

Finally, managers are more likely to lose their jobs in Japan and the U.S. when sales growth is poor (Figure 3). Surprisingly, German managers appear to be unaffected by poor sales performance. Furthermore, sales growth is less important in Japan than earnings and stock performance.

The second set of tests considers top management compensation and its relation to firm performance in Japan and the U.S. It is true, as is commonly

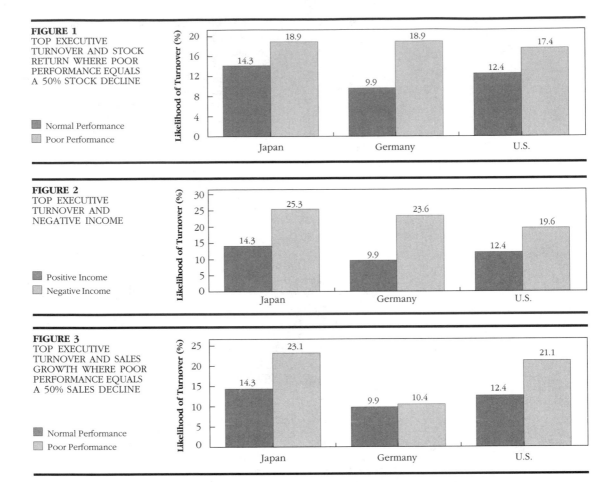

FIGURE 1
TOP EXECUTIVE TURNOVER AND STOCK RETURN WHERE POOR PERFORMANCE EQUALS A 50% STOCK DECLINE

■ Normal Performance
□ Poor Performance

Likelihood of Turnover (%)

Japan: 14.3, 18.9
Germany: 9.9, 18.9
U.S.: 12.4, 17.4

FIGURE 2
TOP EXECUTIVE TURNOVER AND NEGATIVE INCOME

■ Positive Income
□ Negative Income

Likelihood of Turnover (%)

Japan: 14.3, 25.3
Germany: 9.9, 23.6
U.S.: 12.4, 19.6

FIGURE 3
TOP EXECUTIVE TURNOVER AND SALES GROWTH WHERE POOR PERFORMANCE EQUALS A 50% SALES DECLINE

■ Normal Performance
□ Poor Performance

Likelihood of Turnover (%)

Japan: 14.3, 23.1
Germany: 9.9, 10.4
U.S.: 12.4, 21.1

believed, that Japanese executives do earn lower levels of cash compensation than U.S. executives.[6] The important question for incentives, however, is *when* are the top managers in those two countries paid more?

To answer this, as with turnover, I estimated a simple regression:

$$\text{Percentage change in compensation} = a + \text{ß} \times \text{Performance} + e$$

using the same four measures of performance. The results are presented in Figures 4 and 5.

Just as we saw with top executive turnover, Japanese management compensation is strongly related to earnings, stock, and sales performance. And, again, the sensitivities in Japan and the U.S. are virtually identical: a two standard deviation change in stock returns leads to a roughly 8% increase in compensation in both Japan and the U.S. An earnings loss leads to a 13% pay cut in Japan and a (statistically indistinguishable) pay cut of 18% in the U.S.

What do these results for turnover and compensation mean? Three very different systems generate very similar outcomes. The fortunes of both German and Japanese managers, like those of U.S. managers,

---

6. These data were unavailable for German executives.

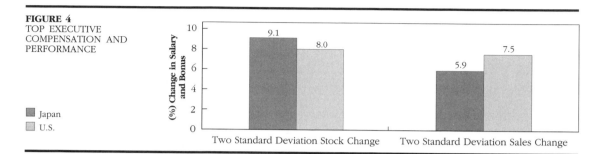

FIGURE 4
TOP EXECUTIVE
COMPENSATION AND
PERFORMANCE

■ Japan
□ U.S.

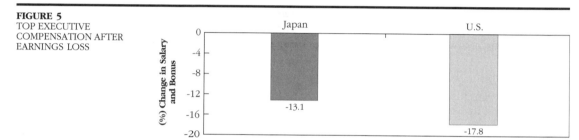

FIGURE 5
TOP EXECUTIVE
COMPENSATION AFTER
EARNINGS LOSS

are apparently tied to stock performance and current cash flows—measures that some would refer to as "short-term." Furthermore, the punishments and rewards for German and Japanese managers are not more sensitive to sales growth—a measure some would refer to as "long-term"—than those of the U.S. If anything, they are less sensitive. It is difficult, therefore, to reconcile these findings with the view that German and Japanese managers are more "patient"—i.e., can ignore current cash flows to pursue increases in market share or sales growth. Finally, it is also difficult to reconcile these results with the view that the U.S. system is more short-term.

These results, in turn, suggest two broader conclusions. First, successful corporate governance systems respond to current measures of performance such as earnings and stock prices. Second, the current stock price is likely to be a reliable indicator of a firm's current and future health.

The Impact of Banks, Corporate Shareholders, and Relationships

The results for top executive punishments and rewards relative to stock and earnings performance in Germany and Japan cannot be driven by an external

market for corporate control because such a market does not exist in either country. This section considers possible explanations for or sources of the turnover-performance and compensation-performance results summarized above. As noted earlier, the most likely forces behind those results are banks, large corporate shareholders, and other intercorporate relationships.

Two of the three studies cited above present evidence on the importance of those forces in Germany and Japan, respectively. The first question the two papers ask is this: When do banks or large shareholders take an active interest in the sample companies? The papers measure such an interest as reflected in particular types of board appointments. In Germany, I studied new appointments to the supervisory board. In Japan, Bernadette Minton and I examined appointments of "outsiders" to the board, where outsiders were individuals who are not lifetime firm employees, but have previous work experience at a bank or large shareholder.[7]

Both supervisory board appointments in Germany and outside appointments in Japan were found to increase with deteriorating stock performance. These results are consistent with the governance relationships in Germany and Japan playing a monitoring and disciplinary role.

---

7. Kaplan (1994a) and Kaplan and Minton (1994)

TABLE 2		Competitive Markets	Uncompetitive Markets
WHEN DO GOVERNANCE DIFFERENCES MATTER?	GROWING/CHANGING	Least	Somewhat
	MATURE	Somewhat	Most

Bernadette Minton and I also undertook a more detailed comparison of outside appointments in Japan. We found that appointments of bank directors in Japan—outsiders affiliated with banks—increased with earnings losses, as well as with poor stock performance. Appointments of outsiders in Japan also increased with measures of the intensity of the relationships. For example, appointments of bank directors increased with the amount of a firm's borrowings from banks; and appointments of corporate directors increased with shareholder concentration and with corporate group affiliation.

While these results are consistent with governance relationships in Germany and Japan playing a monitoring and disciplinary role, they are also consistent with an "insurance" interpretation in which the presence of an outsider signals to suppliers, customers, or others that the bank or the affiliated corporation will support —that is, bail out and hence insure—the appointing firm. Minton and I attempted to distinguish between these two interpretations by considering the relation between outside director appointments and top executive turnover. We found that turnover increased substantially in periods when outsiders were appointed, even when controlling for firm performance. We interpreted this result as evidence that banks and corporate shareholders play an important monitoring and disciplinary role in Japan.

Overall, therefore, the results indicate that the bank and intercorporate relationships in Germany and Japan play a monitoring and disciplinary role. In this sense, the relationships do appear to substitute (at least in part) for the more market-oriented U.S. control mechanisms.

Why Are the Results So Similar?

The bottom line of the three studies is that very different corporate governance systems in Germany, Japan, and the U.S. generate very similar outcomes. The key similarity is that all three countries have successful market economies. In this section, I discuss why I think the results have to be similar.

To understand this, it helps to look at two dimensions (summarized in Table 2). First, governance differences should be less important when firms cannot survive if they don't maximize their value. That will be true when product markets are competitive, government subsidies are small, and few (economic) rents are available. In those circumstances, managers face two basic choices: maximize or fail. Managers who do not maximize, and often their firms, will not survive.

Second, governance differences become less important as firms require more capital. When industries are growing or changing and firms need capital, it is difficult to obtain financing to pursue excessive or unprofitable growth. In other words, if a firm's corporate governance structure allows its managers to waste resources, that firm will not be able to obtain financing. Given that competitive product markets and competitive capital markets dominate most capitalist economies, the great similarity in the German, Japanese, and U.S. results should not be particularly surprising.

Governance, in a real sense, takes care of itself when industries are growing and changing, and when industries are competitive. For this reason, differences in governance are likely to matter most in companies operating in mature industries or in noncompetitive industries where firms can survive for substantial periods without maximizing, and waste substantial resources in the process. Michael Jensen has described such firms and industries as being susceptible to large "agency costs of free cash flow"—that is, a tendency to invest surplus operating cash or capital in negative-NPV projects (notably, diversifying acquisitions).[8] U.S. oil companies in the early 1980s, and many Japanese firms in the late 1980s, fit this description.

Which System Is Best?

The final and most interesting question to be addressed is which governance system, if any, is best?

Along the dimensions I studied in my research, the three systems are similar. There is no clear

---

8. Michael Jensen (1986). See also Jensen's article at the beginning of this book.

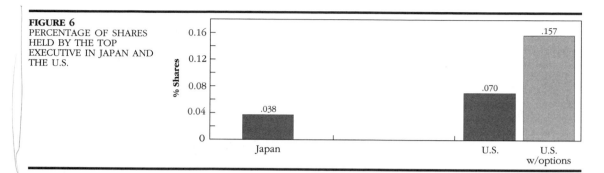

FIGURE 6
PERCENTAGE OF SHARES HELD BY THE TOP EXECUTIVE IN JAPAN AND THE U.S.

difference between the three governance systems in responding to poor stock and earnings performance. This result has been confirmed, moreover, by the recent responses of German companies to competitive difficulties and exchange rate movements. Japanese companies also have responded in "American" ways to its recession and strong yen. There also do not appear to be clear differences in incentives to manage for the short term or the long term.

As I argued in the previous section, there are good reasons to believe that the similarities are the inevitable product of successful market economies. In other words, as long as an economy is competitive or market based, governance systems will be pushed by the market to become relatively efficient. For this reason, different systems will generate satisfactory outcomes.

While the three systems are similar in many respects, there are two respects in which the U.S. system has important advantages, particularly over the Japanese system. First, the U.S. system provides better incentives to firms that are already performing well. Such firms will include those in mature industries or in industries that are not perfectly competitive. The better incentives come from the fact that U.S. managers hold much larger equity positions than managers in Japan (see Figure 6) and, probably, managers in Germany. Because they own more shares, it is arguably less tempting for U.S. managers to overinvest or waste the extra cash that a successful firm generates. If anything, these incentives have

become stronger since 1992, when the U.S. Securities and Exchange Commission (SEC) both imposed stricter reporting requirements on executive compensation and gave shareholders greater ability to communicate with each other and, ultimately, with management.

Second, it is relatively easier for companies to return cash to shareholders in the U.S. (and German) systems. U.S. companies pay dividends and are allowed to repurchase stock (which are tax advantaged). Furthermore, U.S. companies also pay out large amounts of cash when they purchase other companies (for cash). In Germany, although share repurchases are illegal, dividend payments are tax advantaged.

In contrast, it is very difficult for companies to return cash to shareholders in Japan. Until 1995, it was illegal for a Japanese company to repurchase its stock. Such repurchases are still greatly restricted. Dividend payments in Japan are also problematic because so many shares are held by other companies. Under the Japanese tax code, dividend payments to other corporations are tax disadvantaged. Furthermore, the substantial cross-holdings mean that only a fraction of dividend payments will actually leave the corporate sector and go to noncorporate investors.

Overall, then, the three governance systems generate similar outcomes for companies that perform poorly. Nevertheless, the U.S. system is arguably more effective than Germany's and, particularly, Japan's, in discouraging successful companies from overinvesting.

■ STEVEN KAPLAN

is Professor of Finance at the Graduate School of Business, University of Chicago and a research fellow of the NBER.

REFERENCES

Abegglen, James, and George Stalk. *Kaisha: The Japanese Corporation.* New York: Basic Books, 1985.

Aoki, Masahiko. "Towards an Economic Model of the Japanese Firm." *Journal of Economic Literature* 28 (March 1990): 1-27.

Aoki, Masahiko, Hugh Patrick, and Paul Sheard. "The Japanese main bank system: An Introductory Overview." In Masahiko Aoki and Hugh Patrick (eds.), *The Japanese Main Bank System: Its Relevancy for Developing and Transforming Economies.* Oxford: Oxford University Press, 1994.

Baums, Theodore. "Corporate Governance in Germany: The Role of the Banks." *The American Journal of Comparative Law* 40 (1992): 503-526.

Baums, Theodore. "The German Banking System and Its Impacts on Corporate Finance and Governance." Working paper, Institut fur Handels- und Wirtschaftsrecht, Osnabruck, Germany (1993).

Coffee, John. "Liquidity versus Control: The Institutional Investor as Corporate Monitor." *Columbia Law Review* 6 (1991): 1277-1368.

Hoshi, Takeo, Anil Kashyap, and David Scharfstein. "The Role of Banks in Reducing the Costs of Financial Distress in Japan." *Journal of Financial Economics* 27 (September 1990): 67-88.

Hoshi, Takeo, Anil Kashyap, and David Scharfstein. "Corporate Structure Liquidity and Investment: Evidence from Japanese Panel Data." *Quarterly Journal of Economics* 106 (February 1991): 33-60.

Kaplan, Steven N. "Top Executives, Turnover, and Firm Performance in Germany." *Journal of Law, Economics, & Organization* 10, No. 1 (April, 1994a): 142-159.

Kaplan, Steven N. "Top Executive Rewards and Firm Performance: A Comparison of Japan and the U.S." *Journal of Political Economy* (June, 1994b).

Kaplan, Steven N., and Bernadette Minton. "Appointments of Outsiders to Japanese Boards: Determinants and Implications for Managers." *Journal of Financial Economics* (1994).

Kester, W. Carl. *Japanese Takeovers: The Global Contest for Corporate Control.* Boston: Harvard Business School Press, 1991.

Lipton, Martin, and Steven Rosenblum. "A New System of Corporate Governance: The Quinquennial Election of Directors." *University of Chicago Law Review* 58 (1991): 187-253.

Milgrom, Paul, and J. Roberts. *Economics, Organizations and Management.* Englewood Cliffs, N.J.: Prentice Hall, 1992.

Porter, Michael. "Capital Disadvantage: America's Failing Capital Investment System." *Harvard Business Review* (Sept.- Oct. 1992): 65-83.

Prowse, Stephen. "Institutional Investment Patterns and Corporate Financial Behavior in the U.S. and Japan." *Journal of Financial Economics* 27 (September 1990): 43-66.

Roe, Mark. "Some Differences in Corporate Structure in Germany, Japan, and the United States." *Yale Law Journal* 102 (1993): 44-67.

THE HIDDEN COSTS OF JAPANESE SUCCESS

by W. Carl Kester,
Harvard Business School*

T he stage is being set in Japan for overt conflicts among corporate stakeholders and the emergence of struggles for corporate control. Managers in sunset industries are pushing to restructure corporate strategies, particularly in the direction of greater product market diversification. Upholding implicit promises of lifetime employment and maintaining the growth of their enterprises are prominent motives. This restructuring is being undertaken with less bank oversight than ever before and in the face of ever-mounting demands from these important shareholders for better financial returns.

As these trends continue, the bone of contention among Japanese corporate stakeholders will be the use of the excess cash building up on corporate balance sheets. Excess cash tends to be a lightning rod for conflict among corporate stakeholders the world over. Cash is a highly visible asset; its value is easily measured and the amounts available can be quickly ascertained. More important, cash is the most liquid and fungible of all assets. Hence it is the easiest to deploy in the interest of particular stakeholders. Not surprisingly, therefore, decisions about how to allocate cash bring into sharp relief disagreements among stakeholders about the future direction of the firm. In the West, chronic failure to deploy cash in the interest of shareholders has led to an active and sometimes hostile market for corporate control. Through the functioning of this market, corporate ownership is concentrated, management replaced, and cash returned to suppliers of capital.

Shareholder welfare is enhanced when cash is deployed in those activities promising at least as much value in terms of discounted future cash flows as the amount expended in the present. Other stakeholders might prefer to see cash deployed differently. Employees would presumably prefer richer compensation and greater job security. Upstream suppliers might want to see production capacity expanded. Downstream customers might be expected to favor investments that lead to better quality, lower costs, and more reliable delivery whether or not shareholder value is increased.

Needless to say, such diverse interests need not be mutually exclusive. Many investments will simultaneously expand capacity, provide jobs, and lower production costs, as well as create value for shareholders. Such uses of cash will naturally entail little or no conflict among stakeholders. When internally generated capital is scarce relative to available uses, conflicts over the use of cash are more likely to be resolved in favor of shareholders and/or other suppliers of capital to the firm. The scarcity of internal funds will drive managers to source funds externally, thereby exposing their decisions and plans to the scrutiny of the suppliers of capital. Generally, new capital will be forthcoming only if investors are confident that their interests will be protected and their welfare advanced.

*From W. Carl Kester, *Japanese Takeovers: The Global Contest for Corporate Control.* Boston: Harvard Business School Press, 1991. Copyright © 1991 by the President and Fellows of Harvard College. Reprinted by permission.

In the West, chronic failure to deploy cash in the best interest of shareholders has led to an active and sometimes openly hostile market for corporate control. Through the functioning of this market, corporate ownership is concentrated, management replaced, and cash returned to suppliers of capital.

Even if managers elect not to seek external capital, thus avoiding capital market tests of the perceived efficacy of planned investments, product market tests may apply. Rivalry among competitors in the company's product markets will exert a disciplinary force driving managers to seek sustainable competitive advantage, which is the very foundation of value creation for shareholders. The company's internal control systems and incentive compensation schemes tied to equity interests may further constrain the scope of managerial discretion in the use of cash when capital is scarce.

Stakeholder conflict about the use of cash tends to be greatest when internally generated cash is abundant relative to investment requirements. Under these conditions, managers enjoy greater latitude in its deployment. A surplus of cash relative to value-creating investments allows managers to minimize capital market oversight. The imperatives of product market competition can be satisfied without precluding the ability to pursue other stakeholder priorities. Internal monitoring and control may also be less strictly executed when cash is liberally available. Management's incentive alignment with equity may be too weak to overcome its desires to act in its own interests or that of other stakeholders demanding a greater share of the firm's economic rents. The result often is the investment of excess cash at rates of return below the cost of capital.[1] If such investment becomes chronic, conflicts among shareholders, managers or other corporate stakeholders will eventually emerge. They will be costly to the extent that corporate resources must be devoted to resolving the dispute, valuable commercial relationships are ruptured, or corporate performance suffers in the course of the dispute.

MODERN USES OF CASH

The upshot of a decade of adjustment following the first oil shock is the emergence in Japan of a manufacturing sector that has substantial cash flow relative to its needs and much reduced monitoring of its entrenched managers. Except for the possibility of voluntary forbearance on the part of these managers, it seems all but inevitable that cash will

begin to be deployed in ways that have little bearing on the achievement of product market competitiveness or parity growth in the value of stakeholder claims. Under present circumstances, cash can be more easily devoted to the pursuit of individual stakeholder goals. Recent evidence suggests that not only *can* excess cash be appropriated by stakeholders other than the true residual claimants (equity), but it actually is being so appropriated. The clearest manifestations of such uses of cash can be seen in the unrelated diversification plans being pursued by many major Japanese corporations today and even in the management of cash itself.

UNRELATED DIVERSIFICATION

Compared to their American counterparts, Japanese industrial corporations have consistently maintained a higher proportion (about 10% more) of their total assets as cash and marketable securities.[2] Historically, and even for some firms today, three primary considerations may explain the difference. First, cash and deposits were kept relatively high during the rapid growth period in part because of the high degree of bank borrowing and the common use of compensating balances in conjunction with such loans. Sufficiently large amounts of cash were tied up in compensating balances (up to 70% of nominal amount of the loan in come cases) to elevate effective borrowing costs to levels that exceeded the 15% interest rate ceiling established in the Interest Rate Control Law for loans of more than ¥1 million. The practice was sufficiently widespread and frequent that it elicited periodic reprimands from the Ministry of Finance.[3]

A second motive for maintaining relatively large cash balances and less debt than might otherwise be optimal was a preference shared by managers worldwide for using internally generated or privately procured funds to support capital investments whenever possible. Owing to the asymmetry of information that commonly exists between a corporation and its public capital markets, issuing risky securities such as equity in order to raise new funds is often greeted skeptically by potential investors. Is the issuing corporation raising new funds because it

1. For a further discussion of such agency costs, see Michael C. Jensen, "Agency Costs of Free Cash Flow, Corporate Finance, and Takeovers," *American Economic Association Papers and Proceedings* (May 1986), pp. 323-329.

2. W. Carl Kester, "Capital Ownership Structure: A Comparison of United States and Japanese Manufacturing Corporations," *Financial Management* (Spring 1986), pp. 5-16.

3. Stephen Bronte, *Japanese Finances, Markets, and Institutions* (London: Euromoney Publications, 1982), p. 17.

Stakeholder conflict about the use of cash tends to be greatest when internally generated cash is abundant relative to investment requirements. A surplus of cash relative to available value-creating investments allows managers to minimize capital market oversight.

possesses great new investment opportunities, or is it merely timing the market—issuing stock today while its price is relatively high rather than later when it may be lower? To the extent that investors cannot be sure and the company is unable or unwilling to communicate credibly the superiority of its investment opportunities, investors confronted with this sort of moral hazard will hedge their bets. They will buy the new securities at a price that reflects the *average* worth of new projects undertaken by the company rather than the project's true value. From the company's point of view, this may mean selling the securities at an unfairly low price. If the price is too low, the company may even prefer to cancel the project rather than "give away" too much of its value.

One way to avoid this outcome is to maintain financial slack on one's balance sheet and/or preserve access to creditors who can accurately assess the value of the investment opportunities facing the company. For many large Japanese companies, close bank relationships were the solution to such a problem. Most of the companies in my field sample, for instance, did not feel that they were especially capital constrained during the high-growth period, primarily because of the commitment their main banks displayed.

Not all Japanese industrial corporations have identically close relationships with banks, however. For those that do not, maintaining higher degrees of financial slack on the balance sheet may be important. One would expect this to be all the more imperative before financial liberalization made possible the issuance of a wide array of securities in highly liquid capital markets. The empirical evidence supports this hypothesis. During the 1977-1982 period, investment by Japanese companies with close bank affiliations was unaffected by fluctuations in financial liquidity. For a sample of "independent" companies without close bank ties, however, investment was strongly influenced by their levels of liquidity.[4] Thus, for the latter type of Japanese manufacturer, maintaining some financial slack in the form of excess cash may be a rational adaptation to the information asymmetries and moral hazard dilemmas that inevitably plague large, impersonal capital markets.

Finally, maintaining substantial cash balances may have been a means of making credible a company's commitment to implicit contracts with some of its major stakeholders. The promises of lifetime employment and future retirement benefits are good examples. When queried about why so much cash and marketable securities were being held, managers in the field sample most frequently cited labor considerations. As one manager put it, "If we began paying out the cash as dividends, the employees would probably become angry and frightened. 'You are spending our future,' they would say. 'Why are you draining the company of funds rather than keeping it inside and securing our welfare?' I am sure their concerns would ultimately prevent us from giving the cash to shareholders."

These concerns are not unfounded. The promise of lifetime employment is an implicit contract with employees, not a written guarantee that could or would be enforced by Japanese courts or regulators. The company must be alive and solvent in the long run if this promise is to be kept. Promised retirement benefits are of a more explicitly contractual nature, having been formally agreed to through collective bargaining. But until very recently, such benefits were not paid as an annuity from a pension fund. Rather, retiring employees would usually receive a lump-sum settlement on separation from the firm, the amount paid depending on the seniority of the employee and salary history with the company. Companies usually set up accounting reserves related to this liability, but are not required to earmark funds specifically for it.[5] Thus, for all practical purposes, retirement benefits in Japan have been unfunded. It is only natural, therefore, that labor should look to the company's liquidity to gauge its ability to maintain employment through adversity and to make good on future retirement settlements.

The deployment of excess cash by some Japanese companies in the post-1985 period can be construed as an attempt to dip into this nest egg for purposes of making good on implicit promises of lifetime employment to labor and management. As we saw earlier, Japanese companies trapped in sunset industries maintained higher levels of employment in their existing businesses in the 1980s

---

4. Takeo Hoshi, Anil Kashyap, and David Scharfstein, "Corporate Structure, Liquidity, and Investment: Evidence from Japanese Industrial Groups," *Quarterly Journal of Economics*, forthcoming.

5. The maximum permissible size of the reserve is equivalent to 40% of the liability that would be incurred if all employees voluntarily separated at the rate of the balance sheet.

than could be justified on the basis of either their near- or long-term outlook. At the same time, they are spending or planning to spend their cash to enter new businesses in order to maintain job continuity for current workers and managers. This reduces current profitability and likely represents a transfer of value from shareholders to employees.

Take the case of Nippon Steel. Only time will tell how successful Nippon Steel's diversification will be, but there are good reason to view at least some of its new ventures—the most unrelated businesses such as biotechnology and communications systems—with skepticism. For many companies, unrelated diversification strategies have proved to be of dubious value. Alfred Chandler's study of the evolution of modern industrial enterprises in Germany, the United Kingdom, and the United States finds that the most successful large enterprises were those that developed and nurtured what he calls "organizational capabilities": unique managerial skills and organizational hierarchies to govern technically sophisticated production facilities and distribution networks. The application of these organizational capabilities to an ever-larger market in a company's existing line of business or in new markets for closely related products (e.g., branded food products) allowed them to achieve very large scale and eventually market dominance. By contrast, companies that pursued unrelated diversification into businesses in which they had no such organizational capabilities foundered or even failed.[6]

Michael Porter's conclusions in a study of diversification strategies of 33 major U.S. corporations pursued between 1950 and 1986 are consistent with Chandler's.[7] In Porter's sample, the most successful strategies were pursued by companies like Procter & Gamble and IBM. Such companies diversified primarily into closely related fields, and even they did poorly when they dabbled in unrelated areas. The worst performers—CBS, RCA, Gulf & Western, and Westinghouse—pursued aggressive diversification strategies into unrelated businesses. For these companies, Porter concludes that "corporate [unrelated diversification] strategies...dissipated instead of created shareholder value." For many of them, pressure to perform in the 1980s has meant dozens of divestitures that have effectively undone the strategies followed in the prior decades. Indeed,

the American M&A boom of the 1980s is widely viewed as a "supply-driven" wave. The market for corporate control forced underperforming corporate giants to regurgitate poorly fitting businesses, which were ultimately sold to companies with the organizational capabilities needed to manage them effectively.

Even Japan does not lack such examples of severe underperformance due to unrelated diversification. Under its domineering former president, Shinzo Ohya, the Teijin Corporation undertook a far-reaching, American-style diversification strategy starting in 1965. The oldest and once largest textile company in Japan, Teijin entered such new businesses as cosmetics, automobile sales, oil exploration in Nigeria and Iran, large-scale farming in Brazil, and restaurants in England. Deeply entrenched at the center of this far-flung corporate empire was Ohya himself. He became virtually the only person in this functionally organized, highly centralized company that understood its complexity and could administer it. The tenuousness of his grasp was revealed, however, when sharply rising oil prices drastically reduced the profitability of Teijin's core business, synthetic fibers. In the absence of this business's contribution to the consolidated profits, the weak performances of the company's many other smaller businesses became evident. Dramatic restructuring began in 1978, but not until Ohya's death in 1980 did withdrawal from businesses other than fibers, textiles, and chemicals begin. Company insiders estimated that Ohya's diversification strategy cost the company at least ¥30 billion in after-tax profits (between 35% and 40% of the equity's market value in the late 1970s), not to mention the expenditure of immense amounts of management's time and energy trying to turn the company around.

However well intentioned their plans, a number of other large, cash-rich companies in Japan appear to be running a similar risk of diversifying beyond the reach of their existing organizational capabilities. Of the ten companies in my field sample with threatened or slowly growing core businesses (primarily steel and metal products, chemicals, textiles, fibers, and branded consumer products), three were entering or renewing emphasis on engineering and construction activities, three were developing advanced materials of various sorts, and five were

---

6. Alfred Chandler, *Scale and Scope* (Cambridge, MA: Harvard University Press, 1990).

7. Michael Porter, "From Competitive Advantage to Corporate Strategy," *Harvard Business Review* (May-June 1987), pp. 43-59.

Japanese companies trapped in sunset industries maintained higher levels of
employment in their existing businesses in the 1980s than could be justified on the
basis of either their near- or long-term outlook. At the same time, they are spending
or planning to spend their cash to enter new businesses in order to maintain job
continuity for current workers and managers.

entering some segment of the information processing or telecommunications systems markets. And *all*
were seeking commercial applications of in-house
biotechnology research.

For some, the new fields represent natural
extensions of their existing businesses. The commercial application of biotechnological research, for
example, may be quite appropriate for a chemical
or food products company. But computer electronics,
software engineering, real estate development, and
chains of health clubs appear much less so. Naturally, rationalizations for entering these largely unrelated businesses are readily available, but they tend
to beg credulity. One manager in the field sample
claimed that sometimes there was no clear rationale
for entering a new business other than that a
provocative opportunity presented itself. "Often, we
buy an interesting new venture first and then think
up a strategic reason later," he frankly admitted.

Perhaps new organizational capabilities will
eventually be developed to handle these unrelated
businesses. The tendency of Japanese companies to
manage many of the new businesses through joint
ventures with partners that have managerial as well
as technical competence in the fields is evidence
that diversifying parents frequently recognize their organizational limitations and act sensibly in light of
that fact. Moreover, it must be noted that the new
businesses typically account for less than 10% of the
parents' total revenues and costs.

However, most hope to see these businesses
account for one-third or more of total revenues by
some point in the mid-1990s. Given the scope of the
diversification efforts being undertaken, it is by no
means obvious that successful organizational and
managerial adaptation will take place within the
planned time frame. Some undoubtedly will succeed. But the past unrelated diversification experiences of industrial enterprises worldwide make it
difficult to be sanguine about the prognosis.

THE TREASURY AS PROFIT CENTER

Japanese corporate financial managers are using their new freedom in global capital markets to
experiment and innovate as never before. This
might be nothing more than what one would expect.
Lowering the cost of capital is at least desirable if not
actually necessary to survival in a world where one's
competitors are also assiduously procuring low-cost
funds. But coming as it does during a cash glut and

a period of competitive dominance enjoyed by
many Japanese corporations, the exercise of this
new-found financial freedom is unlikely to be checked
by the rigors normally imposed by the competition
for funds in capital markets or the competition for
profits in product markets. The result has been the
uncoupling of financial policies and financial execution decisions from overall corporate strategy. For a
number of prominent Japanese corporations today,
the purpose of corporate finance has gone beyond
merely enabling operating managers to carry out
their plans. Making money through the treasury
function has become an end in itself.

This phenomenon is at once sufficiently new
yet sufficiently widespread in Japan that it has been
dubbed with the journalistic appellation, "*zaiteku*"
(perhaps best interpreted in its common usage as
"financial technology" or "financial engineering").
The scope of the term is quite wide referring to
virtually any profit-seeking financial activity: stock
market speculation, arbitrage, foreign exchange
speculation, or the lending of funds at some positive
spread. *Zaiteku* transactions can be as simple as
borrowing funds in the commercial paper market
and depositing them at higher interest rates, or as
complicated as the execution of a long chain of
transactions that begins with non-yen Euromarket
financings and concludes with the purchase of yen
bond futures in Tokyo. As an example of a simple
transaction, Toshiba claimed an ability in 1988 to
issue commercial paper at a 4.0% cost to it while
depositing those same funds at a 4.5% rate. Hitachi
made a similar claim with respect to funds borrowed
directly from banks. For an example of complexity,
Sumitomo Corporation uses at least four offshore
subsidiaries in London, Luxembourg, the Cayman
Islands, and Panama to execute hundreds of millions
of dollars of Eurobond transactions accompanied by
currency and interest rate swaps, which are then
invested in yen bonds or other Euro-instruments
denominated in several different currencies.

One of the most common *zaiteku* maneuvers
entails the issuance of low-coupon convertible bonds
or bond-warrant units, often denominated in foreign
currencies but swapped into yen. The proceeds are
then invested in *tokkin* funds that facilitate tax-
favored speculation in stocks. An important advantage of trading through *tokkin* funds is anonymity.
When its shares are being bought and sold by
another, a company can determine only that a *tokkin*
investor is doing the trading; it is unable to identify

the specific investor. Although accurate data about *tokkin* funds are difficult to obtain, *Euromoney* reported in a special survey that as of the first quarter of 1987, about ¥30 trillion had been invested in such accounts, which were expanding at the rate of ¥1 trillion a month. About 35% was said to be invested in equities.[8]

What is motivating Japanese industrial corporations to become so proactive in their management of excess cash? Historically, they had relegated finance to a backseat enabling function and "stuck to their knitting" as far as operations were concerned. Why, for that matter, is there so much financial slack today on Japanese corporate balance sheets?

One argument may be that corporations in Japan have access to unique financial arbitrage opportunities or information that make them distinctly better managers of cash than their shareholders. *Zaiteku* might be viewed as simply another perfectly valid means of creating value for the firm's many stakeholders.

This is a tenuous explanation at best. Corporate treasurers may face unique investment opportunities or have better information than individual shareholders in Japan, but the same can hardly be said for the banks, insurance companies, and other corporate stakeholders making up the bulk of the typical large corporation's ownership. In fact, if anything, treasurers of manufacturing corporations and their brokers/advisers may be less well situated to assess the risks of their financial positions and discern whether or not a *zaiteku* transaction is creating value for the corporation in the true sense of the word.

Consider those who claim to be earning positive spreads on funds borrowed in the commercial paper market or from banks. These spreads are achieved only by mismatching the maturities of the paired assets and liabilities. The borrowing is done on a relatively short-term basis, while the deposits are committed for a longer period such as a year or more. The company taking such a position generally counts on rolling over its short-term debt on a favorable basis and inevitably takes an interest rate risk in the process. Those who relend low-cost capital at a positive spread are also taking on credit

risk, something banks are skilled at evaluating but most manufacturers are not. In both instances, the positive spreads being earned may be barely adequate, and quite possibly inadequate, compensation for the risks involved.

There also seems to be widespread misunderstanding among many corporate treasurers about the gains to be had from *zaiteku* operations involving the issuance of low-coupon convertible bonds and bond-warrant units. Nearly all financial managers in my field sample considered such securities to represent very low-cost funds because of the 3%, 2%, and even 1.5% coupons attached to them. Some treasurers even claimed to have obtained a *negative* all-in cost of financing with such securities when issuing in a foreign currency and swapping into yen! However, these conclusions involve a numerical sleight-of-hand: the value or the option to convert, or the value of the warrant component of a unit, is left out of the analysis. The funds are "cheap" only if these options are mispriced in the company's favor when the security is sold. This reality was either missed or brushed aside by many of the financial managers who were interviewed. They generally replied that any equity issued on conversion of the bonds or exercise of the warrants was still quite cheap in view of the very slight dividend yields paid on the stock (generally substantially less than 1% of the market value of the stock). Perhaps because of the more passive role stable shareholders have played in recent years, there was limited appreciation at best for the generally high implicit costs associated with new equity in the form of investors' expected returns from capital gains.[9]

A prominent, albeit extreme, example of miscalculated financial risk taking is that of Tateho Chemical Industries. A regional supplier of electro-fused magnesium for steelmaking, Tateho went public in 1978 with sales of ¥3.4 billion, capital of ¥4.7 billion, and no bank debt. With new access to public capital markets, Tateho began raising funds in the Swiss franc and Eurodollar markets starting in 1983; it also borrowed heavily from local financial institutions. Virtually all of these newly raised funds were devoted to *zaiteku* operations, resulting in a

8. "Zaiteku Sends Stocks and Tokkin Soaring," *Euromoney: Special Survey*, April 1987, pp. 130-131.

9. Corporate financial managers may still have been right about the cost of their company's equity, but for the wrong reason. When queried about whether or not the Tokyo Stock Exchange was properly valuing their company's stock, many responded that their stock was overvalued. Were that true and if a correction

in price was expected soon, then issuing equity-linked securities may indeed have been a way of raising "cheap" capital from the point of view of the pre-existing shareholders. However, to the extent these securities flow back into the hands of existing shareholders before a correction occurs, even this rationale for why equity-linked securities were a source of cheap capital fails to make sense.

substantial ¥800 million nonoperating profit in fiscal 1984, 80% of reported total pretax profits for that year. The following year, it began investing in the Japanese government bond futures market, which was opened in October 1985, borrowing still more to increase its capital committed to *zaiteku*. By the end of fiscal 1987, Tateho had built its annual securities trading gains to ¥2.2 billion and was confident enough to publish *forecasted* securities gains for fiscal 1988 of ¥23.0 billion!

Unfortunately, the government bond market failed to perform as anticipated. Both the cash and futures markets for government bonds collapsed during May-July 1987 (the benchmark 5.1% Japanese government bond Number 89, due in 1996, lost about 15% of its value during this 90-day period). In mid-May, Tateho owned ¥20 billion of futures contracts to purchase government bonds for which only 3% margin had to be committed. Perhaps because of his success in riding out a short bear market for government bonds in 1986, Takaki Kobayashi, a managing director and chief treasurer for Tateho, plunged more deeply into the futures market in early June, building Tateho's position to possibly as much a ¥200 billion at one point during the slide. The bear market failed to turn around, however. By August, Tateho had incurred losses in the futures market estimated at ¥28 billion, an amount exceeding the book value of its net total assets. By September, it sought and received the support of its main bank, Taiyo Kobe, and seven other lenders, who agreed to postpone repayment of ¥20 billion so that Tateho could cover payments in the futures market.

Although uncharacteristic of the Japanese financial community, it was perhaps predictable that such a dramatic incident would be followed by a round of finger pointing. Japanese banks have roundly criticized the securities industry, which they claim encourages unsound speculation by pushing convertible or bond-warrant underwritings tied to *zaiteku* investments and failing to make margin calls according to regulation. For its part, Taiyo Kobe bank was charged with laxness in the monitoring of its client; apparently, it was not until August that the bank learned the true depth of Tateho's losses.

Both bankers and brokers questioned the understanding of the bond market held by Kobayashi, the chief engineer of Tateho's *zaiteku* operations.[10] Naturally, the rest of Tateho's top management has also been severely criticized for exerting inadequate control over Kobayashi and allowing such an exposure to develop in the first place. At a September 1987 news conference, Tateho's chairman, Tadashi Kawabe, and its president, Shigeru Senzaki, were unable to distinguish between the cash and futures markets for government bonds. They lamely explained, "Because they were called government bond, we thought they were safe instruments."[11] While some managers in Japan view the Tateho *zaiteku* incident as an isolated case not likely to be repeated, many see it as but the tip of an iceberg. In any event, as one banker put it, "The case is a very good illustration of the problems embraced by the main bank amid the financial liberalization under which its client business corporations are shunning bank loans and are free to raise funds from the world's capital markets."[12]

If sheer ignorance and folly were what ultimately ensnared Tateho, it was the prospects of offsetting declining operating performance with easy *zaiteku* gains that lured it into the trap. As Japanese steel output declined with the rise of the yen in 1985 and 1986, so did Tateho's profits. In its fiscal year ending in March 1987, operating profits fell by 64%. Yet Tateho's total pretax profit actually rose by 45%, having been buoyed by its ¥2.2 billion securities trading gain for that year. Tateho was not alone in its heavy reliance on *zaiteku* profits to shore up the bottom line. As shown in Table 1, net nonoperating earnings (a proxy for *zaiteku* profits) were a large fraction of total pretax earnings for many of Japan's largest and best-known companies. In fact, were it not for such earnings, 47 of Japan's 250 largest corporations would have shown no profit at all in 1987! Thus *zaiteku* has helped many Japanese companies mask eroding earnings from operations, but often at the expense of assuming risks that they are poorly equipped to handle.

A DISCIPLINARY VOID

Tremendous success in product markets around the world, the retention of much of their cash flow, and fewer good investment opportunities in core

---

10. Kathryn Graven, "Japanese Executive, Bosses and Broker Dispute Responsibility for Huge Losses," *The Wall Street Journal*, September 28, 1987, p. 28.

11. Yoko Shibata, "The MD Might Have Gone Mad," *Euromoney* (October 1987), pp. 63-73.
12. Ibid., p. 69.

While some managers in Japan view the Tateho *zaiteku* incident as an isolated case not likely to be repeated, many see it as but the tip of an iceberg....*Zaiteku* has helped many Japanese companies mask eroding earnings from operations, but often at the expense of assuming risks that they are poorly equipped to handle.

TABLE 1
NET NONOPERATING INCOME OF MAJOR JAPANESE CORPORATIONS, 1987

Company	Amount (¥ billion)	Percentage of Pretax Income
Toyota Motor	149,644	37.6
Nissan Motor	127,004	107.1
Mitsubishi Corp.	46,329	58.3
Matsushita Electric	40,536	79.8
Sharp	30,917	81.7
Sumitomo Corp.	21,646	47.0
Nippon Oil	21,044	106.7
Sony	19,823	150.2
Victor Company of Japan	17,118	132.4
Nissho Iwai	15,021	50.5
Aginomoto	12,503	40.8
Hanwa	11,446	65.0
Murata Mfg.	10,279	50.3
Fujisawa Pharmaceutical	10,079	53.4
Mitsui O.S.K. Lines	9,253	295.9
Settsu	8,715	66.3
Marubeni	7,916	25.6
Kyocera	7,408	21.6
Toyo Engineering	6,880	271.4
Nissin Food Products	6,289	33.7

Source: NEEDS: Nikkei Financials (magnetic tape). Nihon Keizai Shimbun, Inc. Data-bank Bureau Information Service Department, Tokyo, 1987.

businesses have produced considerable financial slack for Japanese corporations. Coupled with freer access to global capital markets, this has led to a distancing of Japanese industrial corporations from their owner/lender banks, a widening of managerial discretion over the allocation of resources, and a drive to escape dependence on a single industry.

The evidence presented here suggests that freedom from product and capital market discipline is prompting Japanese managers to deploy cash in ways more likely to benefit themselves and other employees of the firm by preserving jobs than to benefit other stakeholders, suppliers of capital in particular. The risky, probably uneconomic use of excess cash to speculate in financial markets and plunge into strategies of unrelated diversification are two major deployments in this vein.

In this regard, the remarkable success of Japanese companies in the postwar period has revealed

a hidden and potentially debilitating cost. The managerial discretion afforded by excess cash has given rise to the expression of latent self-interests that were successfully contained during Japan's high-growth period. Today, some Japanese stakeholders appear to be gaining at the expense of others without any immediate prospects of recontracting. With their diminished control over the supply of capital, and being largely owned by their industrial clients, the ability of lending- and share-owning financial institutions to undertake corrective action is greatly reduced. It is the removal of this vital safeguard in the Japanese corporate governance system that will lead to a different Japanese market for corporate control—one that will be more active and more frequently punctuated with bids by investors hostile to incumbent management. Recent struggles for corporate control in Japan signal the advent of this new market.

■ CARL KESTER

is Associate Professor of Business at the Harvard Business School. He has published widely on Japanese corporate finance and strategic resource allocation.

REDRESSING STRUCTURAL IMBALANCES IN JAPANESE CORPORATE GOVERNANCE

by Howard D. Sherman and Bruce Andrew Babcock, Institutional Shareholder Services, Inc.[1]

For most of the post-war period, Japan's economic system has worked so well that it has been cited as a model for reform elsewhere. U.S. policy experts, for example, have pointed to the results of the Japanese system in advocating an end to the legal prohibition against U.S. banks holding shares in U.S. corporations (a dominant feature in Germany as well), in encouraging long-term "relationship investing," and in calling for a national industrial policy.

But the balance of power in Japanese corporations is shifting. As equity and internal financing replace bank financing as the primary source of capital in Japan, the power of the lead banks and the government's ability to direct corporate behavior through credit control are waning. As the economy continues to suffer, the protective impact of cross-shareholdings is under increasing stress. As a result, the potential power of outside institutional shareholders is rising.

Today Japanese business leaders are open as never before to considering other models of corporate governance, including the U.S. model. Before examining the implications of this model for Japanese corporations, however, a close look at the current structure of the Japanese corporate governance system is in order.

LEAD BANKS AND CROSS-SHAREHOLDINGS

In the Japanese corporate system, the distinction between inside and outside shareholders is far more important than in the U.S. or the U.K. In Japan, inside shareholders have power, outside shareholders do not. By the same token, inside directors have power, outside directors do not—indeed, there are none there to wield it.

The dominant feature of the Japanese corporate governance system is cross-shareholdings by affiliated companies—often corporate groups and their lead banks. Members of these companies hold key positions in each other's stock. For example, a lead bank often holds stock in and lends to all other members of the corporate group, intervening in their operations when necessary.[2] These groupings include both the formal *keiretsu* and other, less formal, corporate groups. Other influential forces in corporate governance in Japan include the government and a preponderance of industry associations such as the Keidanren.[3]

In contrast to the United States, friendly acquisitions play only a minor role in Japanese governance (in 1991, for example, there were only 18), and hostile takeovers play no role, despite relatively low levels of insider ownership.[4] Shareholder lawsuits are unheard of. The Japanese proxy voting system is skewed

---

1. This article consists of excerpts from a much longer report on the Japanese, U.S., and U.K. corporate governance systems that was published by Institutional Shareholder Services in May, 1993.

2. This situation parallels to some extent the German economy, which is dominated by its three largest banks.

3. The Keidanren is similar in function to the Business Roundtable in the United States, but it has far more influence in government as well as authority over its members. There are also many industry- and product-specific associations that are influential in their respective industries and as lobby groups for member interests.

4. Six percent versus 10.6% for a sample of *Fortune* 500 companies (Lichtenberg and Pushner 1992, 8).

5. These are the Coordination Division, Capital Market Division, Corporate Finance Division, Trading Market Division, Securities Business Division, and Inspection Division (Japan Securities Research Institute 1992).

sharply in favor of management, weakening the prospects for such Western-style reforms as board independence, strong audit committees and internal auditing, and shareholder rights. As a result, outside shareholders of Japanese corporations—both the Japanese and the foreign investors who are not part of the cross-holding group—have few avenues of influence.

REGULATION

Equity markets in Japan are governed under the Japanese Securities and Exchange Law, which went into effect on May 7, 1948. The biggest revision since then occurred in 1971, when new rules governing corporate disclosure were enacted in response to the first wave of foreign investment in Japan.

The primary regulatory body in Japan is the Securities Bureau of the Ministry of Finance (MOF). Until July 1992, this bureau monitored Japan's securities markets through six separate divisions.[5] On July 20, 1992, in the wake of a spate of Japanese stock market scandals and resulting criticism of the MOF, an additional body, the Securities Exchange Surveillance Committee (SESC), was established under the wing of the Securities Bureau.

The SESC, which is nominally independent, is charged primarily with monitoring corporate compliance with existing securities laws and with investigating breaches of these laws. The chief officers of the SESC are appointed by the MOF and approved by Japan's main legislative body, the Diet. There was an attempt by Japan's Ministry of International Trade and Industry (MITI) to have the new body established outside the MOF, along the lines of the U.S. Securities and Exchange Commission (SEC), but the MOF argued successfully that this would lead to a duplication of authority with existing MOF divisions.

Regulatory authority in Japan is fragmented among government bureaucracies that exercise partial control over companies in their respective industries.[6] This has led to many gray areas of regulatory control where responsibilities are not clearly defined. The broad aspects of Japan's industrial policies are determined by the MOF and the MITI, which are often in conflict with each other over priorities.

As traditional industrial policy-making methods have weakened, a shift toward more Western methods of fiscal and monetary controls has developed. This has given rise to a new power center in Japan, the Bank of Japan (BOJ). Nominally under the control of the MOF, the BOJ appears to have at least some small measure of independence, judging from reported policy conflicts (whether real or imagined) between the two.

The rivalry between the MOF and the MITI runs deep and has been a feature of bureaucratic Japan for several decades. The MOF is the clear superior in this relationship, but the MITI often plays the role of the dissenting voice on policy issues and is usually more open to change than the MOF. The MITI is generally charged with managing structural changes such as winding down the shipbuilding industry or slimming down the steel industry. This gives it valuable influence with many companies, and it is an important body in all central regulatory decisions in Japan.

Gyosei Shido

Bureaucratic control, generally through the MOF, has worked through the well-known system of *gyosei shido*, or "administrative guidance." Through this system, bureaucratic authority is asserted through several layers of action, each with increasing severity.

■ The first layer of control is regulation. Products or processes are simply not approved or are delayed interminably if the MOF or some other concerned bureaucracy does not support the request.

■ The second layer of control is group pressure. The MOF applies pressure on related companies, suppliers, acquaintances, and others to get them to explain their dislike of corporate plans. Pressure through other *keiretsu* companies is naturally more effective than if a company is unaffiliated.

The last and most effective control is the control of credit. By tightly controlling the banks in Japan, the MOF can force a cut-off of credit to a company or its group if it insists on a nonsanctioned course of action.[7]

---

6. For example, construction companies are monitored in some activities by the Construction Ministry, and telephone and telecommunications companies are monitored by the Postal Ministry, which also regulates the vast funds on deposit in post office accounts.

7. One example of this came in the mid-1980s, when a major company tried to import gasoline from Singapore for sale in the retail market. This was not technically illegal, but the bureaucracy had not officially sanctioned a liberalization of retail gas outlets at that time. Banks were forced to cut off credit to this corporation. The solution to this stand-off speaks volumes about Japanese corporate governance and bureaucratic control. The corporation concerned had contracted to buy gasoline from a Singapore company. In order to honor its obligations, the corporation arranged for this gasoline to be sold to an approved dealer in Japan and then bought it from that dealer—at a higher price. The Japanese distribution system had worked its magic.

Liberalization of Japanese financial markets and internationalization of its corporations have weakened, if not mortally damaged, *gyosei shido*. The growth of outside financing sources (see below) has not only diminished bank influence over corporations but also loosened the banks' bureaucratic stranglehold on corporations through credit controls. At the same time, persistent financial scandals in the last few years involving leading corporate, political, and bureaucratic figures have undermined the authority of all the players and called many of the old "management" tools into question.

CORPORATE FINANCING

Like every established market, Japan has evolved to the point that equity financing, especially from public investors, is now the critical component of sustained economic growth. Here are some leading indicators of change in Japanese corporate finance:

■ In 1980, equity represented 12% of corporate financing in Japan. In the early 1990s, that figure was close to 30%, according to one source (Japan Securities Research Institute 1992), and between 30% and 40%, according to another (Watanabe and Yamamoto 1992, 37).[8]

■ In the manufacturing sector, equity-related capital (including retained earnings, convertible bonds, and warrants) represents nearly 80% of typical capitalization (Watanabe and Yamamoto 1992, 37).

■ In 1975, fully 72% of equity capital was raised from existing shareholders. In 1989, the peak year for equity financing, Japanese corporations offered 83% of new equity issues to the general public (Watanabe and Yamamoto 1992, 35).

■ Cross-holdings represent the biggest single type of owner. Generally, 20% to 30% of a subsidiary's shares are held directly by the parent company, with another substantial portion of shares spread throughout group companies, usually giving the group a majority control.

■ Japanese life insurance companies have become an important source of new funds, and now own between 2% and 5% of shares in most major companies. They have become both major shareholders (often

bigger than the company's main bank) and important creditors to corporate Japan. As a result, they have begun to seek a larger role in corporate governance, to a certain extent trying to replace the banks.

■ By law, banks are not allowed to own more than 5% of shares in any single nonaffiliated company. Thus, within a corporate group, a company's main bank usually will own 4.9%, with secondary banks owning another 2% to 3%.[9]

■ Dependence on bank financing is no longer accepted willingly by major Japanese corporations—if it ever was.[10] Even when desired by management, relying on main bank financing in an economic downturn is not as readily available as it once was. Bad debts, shrinking assets, and expensive rescue operations for the most distressed group members limit the ability of banks to lend both within and outside the group.

The implications of these shifts are clear. As the importance of outside equity capital grows, Japanese corporations will feel an increased need to strengthen their relations with nonaffiliated shareholders.

RECENT SIGNS OF TROUBLE

In the 1990s, Japanese businesses have begun to face growing demands by previously "passive" shareholders for greater returns on their investments. These demands were misinterpreted and even ignored during the go-go, high-liquidity days of the late 1980s,[11] but the seemingly never-ending scandals and financial losses now resulting from that period have brought the deep flaws in the corporate governance system to light. As one senior Bank of Japan official put it in an interview with the *Financial Times* (January 11, 1993), "I was going to call 1992 our *annus horribilis,* but I think we had better reserve that term for 1993."

In the first two years of the financial contraction in Japan (1990 and 1991), the MOF and the BOJ repeatedly insisted that the industrial sector of the economy would not be too adversely affected by the problems of the financial sector. The belief that the economy could be rescued by traditional methods continued into 1992, when the BOJ began to loosen

---

8. S. Watanabe and I. Yamamoto, 1992 "Corporate Governance in Japan: Ways to Improve Low Profitability," *NRI Quarterly* 1 (3) (Winter 1992): 28-45.

9. The legal limit was 10 % until the mid-1980s, when regulators cut this in half.

10. According to James Abbegglen and George Stalk in *Kaisha: The Japanese Corporation* (1985), "The conclusion is that dependence on a bank is no more to the liking of Japanese management than management in other countries, and for leading Japanese companies is no longer a significant issue."

11. *Financial Times,* February 5, 1993, 11.

its monetary policy. Interest rates were steadily lowered throughout 1992, and a large fiscal stimulus package was announced in the summer. But, despite these actions and much fanfare by the government and press (an effective tool in the past), the economy has showed little signs of responding. The old tools have not been working as expected.

Evidence is mounting that Japan's economic slowdown in the '90s is not just a run-of-the-mill slowdown, but one of Japan's worst and potentially longest-lasting recessions in the post-war era. However, the debate on the exact nature of the current economic malaise continues to rage in Japan. The official government position is that this remains a normal slowdown, but a growing number of economists and ex-government officials argue that structural change is under way. As Naohiro Amaya, former vice minister at the MITI, expressed it,

Japan is particularly susceptible to the Peter Pan syndrome. Even though the economy is now adult, many people behave as if we are a child.[12]

Amaya, one of the architects of Japan's success, believes that the Japanese economy is beginning a long period of adjustment during which it will grow only slowly, a period that could last until the late 1990s.[13] Most economic indicators are at extreme levels seen only twice since the end of World War II, with no clear signs of bottoming out. And these poor economic indicators are accompanied by an unprecedented level of crisis in the financial system, limiting the ability of the government and *keiretsu* to mount traditional rescue operations.

The Japanese economy went into recession by all but some technical measures. Slow growth in the third quarter of 1992 forced the Japanese government to face reality, and it more than halved its official growth forecast for the financial year ending March 31, 1993, dropping it to 1.6%. Moreover, virtually every sector of the economy is experiencing money problems. Real money supply growth is close to zero. Bank lending has become anemic (except for costly rescue operations) despite record low interest rates, yet these show little sign of stimulating the economy or supporting the stock market. Commercial real estate prices have fallen at least 40% from their highs. In February 1993, the stock market, despite artificial support by the government, was 55% below its 1989 high.

Corporate profits for the year ending March 31, 1993, were headed down for the third straight year, with bank profits dropping for the fourth straight year. This made the earnings drought for Japanese companies the longest since the early 1950s. Bankruptcies were pushed to record levels, both in number and in value (*Financial Times*, February 5, 1993).

The only bright spot in 1992 was a massive trade surplus of over $120 billion. Yet this was more of an embarrassment than a blessing for the Japanese government, which even then was seeking to improve its relations with its major trading partners. It also perversely affects corporate planning, as Japanese corporations expect greater foreign protectionism to result from the surpluses.

In 1992, moreover, a wide range of research institutions, both Japanese and foreign, conducted serious, in-depth analyses of the business practices of Japanese corporations in order to identify the reasons for the unexpectedly severe drop in corporate earnings in the country. These new studies brought to light a number of major misconceptions about Japanese corporate performance in the last decade. *Probably the most widespread misconception has been the myth of high profitability of corporate Japan. In fact, the opposite has been true.*

In its *Special Report #224, Fiscal 1991 Financial Statements Analysis*, the BOJ found that most of the restructuring undertaken by Japanese manufacturers in the 1980s, though widely admired and emulated by their U.S. and European competitors, failed to improve Japanese corporate profitability. Much of the apparent improvement in Japanese companies' financial performance in the last decade was a reflection of inexpensive capital rather than improved efficiency. Among its other findings, the BOJ reported that

As well as these cyclical cost-cutting efforts... moves to review, reevaluate, and partially restructure medium term strategies and project development plans are intensifying.... Also, moves towards adding value and diversified small-lot production are also being reviewed where they are considered to have been pursued to an extreme, and initiatives to address improvements in production efficiency...are spreading.

---

12. *Ibid.*

The BOJ concluded that Japanese corporations made excessive use of capital in the late 1980s, failing to take into account the long-term demand for many of their investments. Essentially, Japanese corporations were making low-return, long-term capital investment commitments based on short- and medium-term capital costs. The medium term has arrived, and many of those investments are no longer profitable at current financing costs.

LABOR CHALLENGES

The collapse in corporate profitability is forcing previously unthinkable changes in Japan's vaunted lifetime employment system, which in reality never applied to more than half of the labor force in the first place. In the first two poor earnings years (1990 and 1991), corporations followed the traditional labor-related cost-cutting measures of overtime cutbacks and bonus reductions. At first, these changes had no noticeable effects. The labor market in the early 1990s appeared to be unusually robust despite dropping corporate profits, even when compared with the mild economic slowdown of 1982.

But these appearances belied a very different economic reality. In fact, companies were holding on to workers they did not really need in response to government predictions of a looming labor shortage. More recently, there has been a sharp drop in job offers and a jump in the national unemployment rate. Though this rate is still low, the rise indicates that firms are belatedly making adjustments to their labor forces.

According to articles appearing on January 1993 in the *Financial Times*, labor accounted for 43% of fixed costs for the average Japanese company, and a recent survey of corporations by the Japanese Ministry of Labor indicated that most companies felt that they were significantly overstaffed. Nikko Securities estimates that in the July-September quarter of 1992, 900,000 workers in the manufacturing sector, or 6% of that sector's workforce, were "unemployed within their companies." (That is, they were still on the payroll but had little or nothing to do.) Another new aspect of this recession, documented in an article appearing in *The Economist* (February 13, 1993, 67), was that, as in the United States, many of the surplus workers are white collar, traditionally the least productive of all Japan's workers.

Pioneer Corporaion's attempt to force early retirement on 35 senior but unnecessary managers, widely publicized in Japan for being the first attempt

of its kind, was an indication that Japanese companies wcre becoming less willing to bear the costs of the lifetime employment system. Pioneer later backed down somewhat, insisting that it hadn't really set a deadline for the managers' dismissal. However, the company also said at the time that the purpose of the move, to shock and stimulate the workforce, had been accomplished.

The government and business are at odds on what to do about these problems. The government has urged restraint on hard-pressed businesses. The government clearly fears that the cracks in the Japanese labor market will widen rapidly in the near future. The Labor Ministry recently met with a number of large employers and insisted that they use all measures to maintain employment (*Washington Post*, March 3, 1993). Kunihiko Saito, chief of the Labor Ministry's Employment Security Bureau, asked a meeting of business leaders to refrain from canceling plans to employ new graduates and retire older workers (*Financial Times*, February 19, 1993). However, business is beginning to resist such directions, as the cost of following these directives starts to rise. "Restructuring based on squeezing or reducing personnel costs is an urgent priority. In some cases survival is at stake," declared the Japan Research Institute, a private sector research group (*Financial Times*, February 5, 1993).

Business managers are now questioning the ability—if not the right—of the bureaucracy to mandate actions by corporations. Furthermore, they are banding together to see what they themselves can do to address Japan's economic malaise. This points the finger squarely at the corporate decision-making process and, more broadly, at the general corporate business philosophy of "growth over all else." Although defended as long-term planning, such a philosophy was in fact driven largely by short-term considerations. In the easy-money environment of the late 1980s, Japanese corporate managers could look forward to an immediate impact on sales and asset growth of large-scale investment plans, ignoring the longer-term dangers to corporate profitability and, ultimately, to shareholder returns.

One potential conclusion to be drawn here is that Japanese corporations need to focus more on shareholder value. This notion, however, faces natural obstacles in the Japanese business culture. There are numerous reasons for Japanese corporations to continuously expand, the first and foremost being the dominant philosophy in Japan of growth over all else. This stems from several areas, including pressures to "keep up with the Joneses" (corporate prestige and image), the goal of maintaining the labor force, and the natural tendency of bureaucracies to grow.

The current campaign for *kyosei* by the Keidanren at least pays lip service to improving profitability rather than increasing sales. This debate was initially brought into the public arena by Akio Morita, chairman of Sony Corp. At the time, he was severely criticized within Japan for making his calls for change, but as the economy worsened and the trade surplus began to balloon, Morita's calls for change were publicly adopted by the Keidanren. However, there is much debate in Japan about what exactly the new word actually means for Japanese corporations; and its late adoption by the Keidanren raises doubts, particularly overseas, about whether this is a true change or just another tactical move by Japanese business to blunt criticism of rising trade surpluses.

SYSTEM STRENGTHS

Japan's history of economic growth would seem to validate its time-honored system of cross-shareholdings, tight-knit corporate groups, informal affiliations, and strong governmental coordination, unchecked by intervention from outside shareholders or a market for corporate control. Moreover, this system has an intuitive logic. It turns the management (agents) of one member of a corporate group into partial owners (principals) of the corporate group, or "family," as a whole, presumably reducing agency costs. The classic theory is that continual monitoring and occasional intervention by a company's lead bank prevent the most extreme mistakes in corporate strategy, leading to greater corporate efficiency and diminishing the need for an active market for corporate control to correct these mistakes. The accepted rationale is that because most banks hold both equity and debt in their portfolio, they have a strong financial incentive to monitor corporate performance and intervene when necessary. Even more important, they also have the standing to intervene in Japan through laws that allow financial institution equity ownership and also through the board seats held by these institutions.

Many observers, both within Japan and around the world, argue that this Japanese system is so strong that no other means of checking management behavior is necessary—i.e., that no corporate governance modifications are required. But the system is under such strain that change seems unavoidable. As noted above, public shareholder interests are not being satisfied with a system that places group objectives over corporate performance. And, perhaps most surprising, evidence is mounting that corporate cross-shareholdings have lessened, not improved, corporate efficiency.

THE EMPIRICAL RECORD

Three important private-sector studies challenging the status quo have appeared in recent years.

LIA-Japan Study.[14] The Life Insurance Association of Japan published a study in December 1992 that documents a poor year for Japanese corporations in FY 1991. It finds low yields and payout ratios for dividends, low return on equity, and high share premium reserves.

Lichtenberg and Pushner Study.[15] In their 1992 study of cross-shareholdings by banks, *Ownership Structure and Corporate Performance in Japan*, Frank R. Lichtenberg and George M. Pushner find that equity ownership by Japanese financial institutions, which assume an oversight role, "may effectively substitute for the missing external takeover market." On the other hand, Lichtenberg and Pushner also find evidence that "high levels of intercorporate shareholding insulate firms from their own problems, at the expense of firm performance. Further, we find a notable positive influence of insider ownership."

Testing the impact of financial institutions on Japanese corporate performance, Lichtenberg and Pushner focus on "the lower tail of productivity and profit distributions" and find "almost a truncation of these poor states in firms with a large ownership share by financial institutions." They conclude that "financial institutions exert a positive influence in line with their larger role of monitoring and occasional intervention" (2, 19), a finding supported by a number of other recent studies.

On the other hand, Lichtenberg and Pushner also state:

---

13. *Ibid.*

14. Life Insurance Association of Japan, *The Status of Efforts to Return Profits to Shareholders Report*, (December 18, 1992).

15. F. R. Lichtenberg and G. M. Pushner, "Ownership Structure and Corporate

Despite the positive influence of financial institutions, our evidence does not imply that the financial business group effectively replaces Japan's missing takeover market in all cases. For keiretsu-affiliated firms with high corporate ownership and low institutional ownership, the absence of takeovers or substitute mechanisms is reflected here by relatively poor performance. (25)

Lichtenberg and Pushner find that corporate cross-shareholdings "appear to insulate the firm from outside interference, but at the expense of profit and productivity. While it is argued that this stable intercorporate shareholding frees managers to pursue long-term strategies without worrying about short-term profits, our results linking corporate ownership levels with reduced profit and productivity imply that this insulation adversely affects both near and long term performance" (25).

Watanabe and Yamamoto Study.[16] In their above-cited salvo for change, Watanabe and Yamamoto (1992) take a critical look at the historic role of banks and other financial institutions in Japanese corporate governance. They begin by noting Japan's status as a governance example.

In the United States, the argument is gaining credence that stable shareholding, combined with "keiretsu" alliances among companies, has contributed much to Japan's economic development by making long-term investments possible, leading to increases in the international competitiveness of Japanese corporations. Some even argue that the United States should adopt a system similar to the stock cross-holding in Japan or the stable ownership of stocks seen in Germany. (30)

They find, however, an element of classical economic (self-interested) behavior by banks.

In most cases, rather than simply monitor the credit quality of their existing loans, the banks became involved with the management of the companies they were lending to in their group, with a view towards assisting their growth. This was because, in a financial system in which the main bank was the dominant intermediary, growth achieved by companies in the main bank's group always resulted

in increased lending to these companies and greater profits for the bank. (34)

They also find that the chief goal of the typical lead bank in Japan is to expand deposits and the revenue stream from the group companies, not to maximize corporate performance, efficiency, or firm value.

[B]ecause of the controls in place on the development of financial products and on interest-rate competition among banks, the primary objective of banks was to pursue quantitative expansion of their deposit and loan base. (33)

To compound the problems, Watanabe and Yamamoto find that these relationships have been strained during the last decade.

Japan's major manufacturing corporations are experiencing a substantial downtrend in profitability that has pushed returns on investment—including returns on equity—to their lowest levels in the postwar era. One cause of the profitability decline can be found in the maladjustment of the basic framework of corporate management—the structure of corporate governance—because of changes in the business environment since the 1980s. In this sense, the current economic recession gripping Japan can be called a "governance recession." (28)

Over the past decade or so, major corporations have significantly reduced their dependence on bank financing by improving their cash flows—to the extent that the basic elements of corporate governance have gradually been lost, including the supervisory role of banks and the burden of interest payments [emphasis ours]. The core strategy of many corporations is simply to increase recurring profits, without giving proper consideration to the interests of shareholders. Thus, in the name of "long-term" growth, companies have continued to make investments that earn low returns, creating a situation in which surplus assets earning low returns can easily build up in the balance sheets of companies. (28)

Now that companies are no longer subject, at least not nearly to the same extent as before, to the

---

Performance in Japan," working paper no. 4092, National Bureau of Economic *internal discipline and external oversight from a bank, we believe the lack of an effective mechanism of corporate governance—one that seeks to insure that investments are undertaken with expected rate-of-return goals that are appropriate in relation to the cost of capital—will prove detrimental to the interests of shareholders in the long run and depress stock prices. Furthermore, we believe it will prove detrimental to the national economy, contributing to wasteful uses of capital and distortions in the allocation of resources. (37)*

Watanabe and Yamamoto test the "common wisdom" that defends Japan's cross-shareholdings by noting the past four decades' decline in average return on equity (ROE) for 245 manufacturing companies in the Nomura Research Institute 400. This stood at 5.6% at the end of fiscal year 1991, the lowest level in 40 years. The authors reject one possible explanation, that the decline is attributable to a decrease in the use of borrowed funds for financing and greater use of retained earnings and paid-in capital (decreases in leverage often lower ROE). Instead, the authors find that the major cause for the decline in the average ROE of major Japanese manufacturers can be attributed not to changes in the debt/equity structure but rather to a decline in the rate of return on total capital employed.

We suspect that changes in the framework of corporate governance—which structurally made for lax investment decision-making by companies—were at work. If so, the deterioration of corporate earnings in the current recessionary environment ... can be viewed as a consequence of inadequacies in the structure of corporate management, and the current recession can be called a "corporate governance recession." (32-33)

They go on to say:

One might say the crux of the problem of corporate governance in Japan is also a lack of "responsible" shareholders, as well as the fact that the stable cross-holding of shares isolates corporate managers

from the discipline of a speculative stock market, depriving managers of an effective system for checking against the accumulation of surplus assets. Stable cross-holding of stocks insulates managers from speculative investors, thereby enabling managers to carry out long-term investments without having to first answer some hard questions. In short, the cross-holding of shares leads to a lack of close external monitoring on management, leaving it up to managers to discipline themselves. Japanese managers have considerable freedom to run companies as they see fit. (43)

Watanabe and Yamamoto provide a closer look at Japanese decision making and profit goals.

Why do Japanese companies place such great emphasis on showing an increase in annual recurring profits, even by realizing hidden profit through selling and buying back long-held cross-holding stocks, resulting in accounting profit but unnecessary tax burdens? Is it not because society considers recurring profits all important and expects to see higher recurring profits each year? (45)

To shift from recurring profits to required rates of return as the yardstick for investment decision-making will, above all, require the strong commitment of top management. Not a few Japanese companies today are starting to introduce such American investment management concepts as "internal rate of return" and "net present value." However, the managers who use these tools do not seem to take them seriously enough. Even if a hurdle rate is determined for investments, project plans are usually prepared so as to exceed that rate on paper, so that the attempt to screen out inappropriate investments by evaluating them against hurdle rates can become for all practical purposes meaningless. (44)

Kaplan Study. [17] In a recent paper, Steven N. Kaplan (1992) studies top management turnover and compensation and their relation to firm performance in the United States and Japan. The general thrust of the results is that the relations between managerial rewards and performance are surpris-

Research, Inc., June, 1992.
   16. S. Watanabe I. Yamamoto, cited earlier.
   17. S. N. Kaplan "Top Executive Rewards and Firm Performance: A Compari-

son of Japan and the U.S.," working paper no. 4065, National Bureau of Economic Research, Inc., May, 1992. See also by Kaplan, "Ownership Structure and Corporate Performance in Japan," working paper no. 4092, National Bureau of Economic Research, Inc., June, 1992.

ingly similar in Japan and the United States. Top executive turnover is negatively related to all three types of financial performance—stock, sales, and earnings—in both countries.

These basic results suggest that Japanese managers are motivated by factors that affect stock price. And they are motivated to roughly the same extent as U.S. managers.

Although the reward-performance relations are generally similar, one difference emerges. Turnover and compensation in Japan are most sensitive to low or negative earnings — and more so than in the United States.

However, conditional on generating a positive level of earnings [his emphasis], the Japanese managers seem to have a great deal of freedom. In particular, this implies that Japanese may be able to invest in new projects that do not pay off in the short-run as long as past projects are profitable enough to generate positive income. It does not, however, necessarily imply that such investments will increase a firm's (stock) value. (4)

This research may never point to a neat conclusion, as it offers compelling evidence both for and against Japan's traditional corporate governance system. Japan's corporate cross-shareholdings clearly have contributed to the competitiveness of the economy as a whole, and clearly allowed for long-term planning. These advantages should not be lost in the new balance. But common sense says that it is equally true that stable cross-shareholdings do not always lead to maximum efficiency. Without a real threat of change, managements of individual companies have little incentive to worry about maximizing efficiency or profits.

FINANCIAL GOALS

Before we can embark on a discussion of corporate governance reform, we have to understand the monetary goals of any reform. What should the financial goals of Japanese corporations and investors be? What are the appropriate performance measures by which a corporate governance system should be judged? What is the appropriate time frame?

Growth in market share and *continued employment* clearly have been two of the dominant corporate goals in Japan for most of the post-war period. A more difficult item to assess is what performance measures are typically used by Japanese corporations. As suggested by the studies reviewed below, annual profitability is considered an important financial goal, whether it is attaining an *increase in annual profits* or *achieving enough profits to satisfy lead bank requirements*. Generating *adequate cash flow* to cover debt charges is also a high priority for Japanese managers. Japanese managers also pay attention to *stock prices* as a measure of the overall value of the firm.

What seems to be missing, however, is a systematic effort to link management decisions with *total shareholder returns—stock price plus dividends*. Japanese managers do not appear to consistently manage their earnings stream, cash flow, or debt/equity mix or use standard return on investment (ROI) and net present value (NPV) project analysis with an eye towards maximizing shareholder value. Although the evidence is mixed, the hierarchy of Japanese corporate financial performance goals appears to be as follows:

- Sales growth: HIGH priority
- Lifetime employment: HIGH priority
- Cash flow: HIGH priority
- Profitability: HIGH priority
- Stock price/firm value: MIXED priority
- Total shareholder returns: LOW priority

A key question for corporate governance in Japan is whether Japanese corporations should place more emphasis on total shareholder returns. If so, a number of related issues must be dealt with as well:
- How should this goal be balanced against other financial goals?
- When should this shift take place (now or after the economy has recovered)?
- Are reserve allocations used appropriately?
- Is Japan's dividend policy serving shareholder interests anymore?
- Does the current prohibition [relaxed in 1995] against stock repurchases serve shareholder interests?

The argument in support of a focus on total shareholder returns is strong. The chief responsibility of the board of directors of any corporation—whatever its nationality—is to maximize shareholder wealth, and there is no better bottom-line measure of how shareholders' investments in the enterprise are faring than total returns.

Nevertheless, as with accounting measures, executives can take actions that can significantly boost shareholder returns in the short term but harm long-term performance. It has been forcefully asserted that many U.S. companies have followed unwise business and financial strategies that increased short-term shareholder wealth at the expense of long-term corporate performance. It is difficult to argue that such strategies are not in the best interests of long-term investors. But over the long haul, increasing shareholder returns must be the ultimate objective of the corporation if it wants to retain equity financing.

Therefore, shareholders ideally would evaluate their returns over a long enough period of time, such as five years, to factor out any short-term aberrations. Moreover, this measure should be viewed in conjunction with other performance measures. For these reasons, many Japanese investors and even some prominent Japanese managers are looking to different models of corporate governance.

RECOMMENDATIONS FOR REFORM

Structural change in Japanese corporate governance is overdue in Japan, and is, in fact, under way. And it is taking place whether the bureaucracy or the government recognizes it or not.
■ The bureaucracy's ability to manage the economy through traditional methods has been severely eroded by the financial liberation of large Japanese corporations, which can no longer be pressured to do whatever the bureaucracy asks.
■ Corporations and banks in Japan are under extreme financial pressure, and although the Japanese government allowed publicly held corporations to delay reporting their stock losses until March 1993 and eased disclosure requirements for the March 1993 period as well, the situation remains bleak. Without additional government intervention, the systemic problems could progress through a series of domino-like stock sales and a frightening stock market crash.
■ The financial liberation of the large Japanese corporation led to a period of excessive over-investment by a broad range of companies in Japan, large and small. Lacking proper oversight, many major corporate projects began on a weak footing and now face—or are now experiencing—severe financial stress.

This danger was partially created by the government itself, but many of the changes made are now beyond government control, being part of broader international trends and Japanese corporations' reactions to them. These problems even more clearly highlight the bureaucracies' waning influence. The most significant changes are in the area of new accounting and financial disclosure standards, heightened capital adequacy requirements for banks, and broad financial reform. The negative effects of these changes, heightened by deflation of corporate assets, have made the holding of underperforming assets more unattractive than ever.

As these changes occur, Japan must move in new directions yet retain the benefits of its old system—generally the license to pursue long-term growth—as it accommodates the new players. The positive influence of financial institutions on Japanese corporate governance was a good, but never a perfect, substitute for other means of management accountability. As their positive impact diminishes, and as the government stretches even further to impose artificial control over an increasingly free-market system, Japan must look to new modes of governance.

Japanese managers, directors, and shareholders—as well as policymakers—can all play a role in bringing about productive change. Japan should note that independent directors and their second-cousin, monitoring by non-affiliated institutional shareholders, have been shown to add value to firms in the United States. Though the Japanese governance system may not be ready yet for such innovations, it is in the companies' long-term interest to work toward them.

Our more specific recommendations are listed below:
BOARDS AND SHAREHOLDERS
■ Pay more attention to shareholder returns and ROE along with other performance goals.
■ Implement institutional shareholder communication programs at the board level. This could be done by creating a new board committee to address outside shareholders, or by using the new audit/financial target committee.
BOARDS AND MANAGEMENT
■ Reduce the number of directors on boards whose size has made them unwieldy.
■ Name outside directors and provide them with statutory powers and use of corporate funds.
■ Promote greater use and rotation of independent auditors. The new audit regulations under consideration are a positive first step in this direction. A positive and forthright application of the new regulations by companies will do much to enhance their image in investors' eyes.
■ End interlocks of parent and subsidiaries, which enable shifting of corporate profits.
■ Encourage more stock ownership by management.

PROXY VOTING SYSTEM

- Improve proxy disclosure on director nominees by providing clear and detailed explanations of their corporate affiliations.
- Simplify the share registration and voting process. Companies can facilitate single account registration through JASDEC or other means, such as an industry facility. Companies can also facilitate issuance of single proxy cards for nonresident shareholders.
- Spread out the timing of shareholder meetings and release proxy material earlier and, for corporations with a large American shareholder base, in English. By improving the timeliness and accessibility of their communications to shareholders, companies will inspire greater confidence and trust—which could translate into larger and longer-term holdings.
- Encourage development of independent Japanese shareholder research and proxy voting organizations and associations. The United States offers several successful models for such organizations.

As in the United States, with its strong laws governing pension fund investments and corporate disclosure, regulatory change may be required in a number of areas if Japan wants to promote change. Because the power is so heavily centralized in the MOF and the MITI, that is where, along with the Bank of Japan and Tokyo Stock Exchange, most change is likely to occur and where this report's message is directed.

To meet Japanese corporate boards at least half way, U.S. shareholders also must take certain steps.
- First, U.S. institutions voting their Japanese proxies must respect the different culture and business practices in Japan and adopt voting policies that reflect these differences.
- In particular, they need to understand fully the nature of the businesses they invest in as well as the corporate groups affiliated with their portfolio companies. This requirement parallels efforts in the United States to promote more "relational investing." Outside shareholders can convert potential hostility to hospitality if they take the time to learn the lay of the land—and their place in it.
- Obviously, U.S. institutions must go through the proper channels, requesting voting assistance through their global custodian, which in turn will request assistance from their Japanese subcustodian.
- If relationships with companies prove difficult, U.S. investors should realize that they may appeal to regulatory authorities. The Group of Thirty, the MOF, the MITI, and the SII, discussed above, are open to U.S. as well as Japanese investors. Also, the International Organization of Securities Commissioners (IOSCO), based in Toronto, can hear appeals from global investors in all countries.

These suggestions are only a beginning for all concerned.

- HOWARD SHERMAN AND BRUCE BABCOCK

are, respectively, Senior Vice President and Senior Analyst of Institutional Shareholder Services, Inc., a Washington, D.C.-based advisor to institutional investors.

■ IV. EUROPE AND (AND SOUTH AFRICA)

As in Japan, corporations in continental Europe have traditionally subordinated shareholder interests to those of employees and other corporate stakeholders. But, with the "Eurosclerosis" of the '80s and '90s becoming progressively worse, calls for change in European corporate governance have become more insistent.

In the summer of 1995, the Centre for European Policy Studies, a research organization that makes recommendations to the governing body of the European Union, issued a new set of guidelines for corporate governance standards in the EU. Among the principal recommendations were (1) one-share, one-vote (unless shareholders approve a dual class structure); (2) an expansion of shareholder voting rights, including the right to vote on election of directors, dividends, capital authorizations, and company by-laws; (3) fair treatment of minority shareholders in takeovers; and (4) greater use of outside directors capable of exercising independent oversight.

The growing presence of American institutional investors in Europe is one of the forces propelling such inititatives. But, as much as European policymakers might want to encourage infusions of foreign capital, they are also facing powerful resistance from economic and political groups favored by the status quo—entrenched management, labor unions, and their political allies.

In "*Corporate Ownership and Control in the U.K., Germany, and France,*" Julian Franks and Colin Mayer observe that there is a fundamental difference between the French and German "insider systems" of corporate ownership and control and the "outsider systems" that prevail in the U.K. and the U.S. On the issue of the relative superiority of the two systems, however, the authors remain uncommitted. They argue, on the one hand, that the concentrated ownership and limited takeover activity of the continental European system would seem to be more conducive to longer-term relationships between the company and its investors. Nevertheless, such concentrated insider ownership can also lead to costly delays in undertaking necessary corrective action (including downsizing and asset sales), particularly if the owners receive non-monetary benefits from owning and running a business. The authors conclude by saying that although none of the existing theories of corporate governance offers a completely satisfying explanation of the differences between the two systems, the "durability" of both suggests that each has "devised

effective ways of disciplining poor managers and otherwise promoting efficiency."

In our second article, Brian Kantor, Jos Gerson, and Graham Barr provide an economic justification of South Africa's somewhat unusual corporate ownership structure (unusual at least to those accustomed to the U.S./U.K. tradition of one share-one vote). Six very large South African pyramid companies, commonly referred to as "groups," exercise effective control over companies representing 70% of the Johannesburg Stock Exchange (and four of the six groups are controlled by single founders or their families). Although it has come under attack for a variety of reasons (by critics ranging from the ANC to U.S. Trade Representative Mickey Kantor), the authors defend the group system as an efficient outcome of a largely voluntary process in which South African owner-managers compete for capital supplied by South African institutional investors. "*In the U.S.,*" as the authors note, "*LBO partnerships such as KKR have achieved, with limited equity, similarly concentrated control over a diverse group of companies by virtue of their ability to raise substantial debt funding from institutional investors.*" And, to back up their claims, the authors provide some interesting market-based evidence that the top management of the groups add value to individual companies at the base of the pyramid.

Kantor et al. also consider the possibility, however, that exchange controls that have for some time prevented South African investors from diversifying internationally may have provided "artificial" support to the system, driving up the values of those groups with significant overseas holdings. When exchange controls are fully dismantled, such investors may choose to transfer part of their capital from the groups to more direct investments in overseas companies or mutual funds. This development could in turn lead the groups to shed (or "unbundle") some of their diversified domestic asset holdings. On the other hand, as the authors suggest, it may simply prompt the largest groups to become even larger by pursuing more international diversification through their own expanded opportunities for direct foreign investment. In this view, the "voteless majority" of South African institutional investors—those who have been rewarded in the past for entrusting their funds to the groups—may choose to continue to leave much of their international diversification to the groups rather than pursuing it on their own.

The next two articles discuss European parallels to corporate restructuring in the U.S. In the first, Professors Mike Wright and Ken Robbie of the University of Nottingham, and Steve Thompson of the University of Manchester, provide a broad overview of European restructuring activity based on their own research findings. The U.K., for example, saw a wave of management buy-outs during the 1980s that produced significant gains in operating productivity. The size of such gains, moreover, was found to be strongly correlated with management's percentage of equity stake.

The article that follows consists of interviews with four European executives whose companies have adopted "American-style" strategies emphasizing strengthened management incentives combined, where appropriate, with financial leverage. Under CEO Christopher Bland, London Weekend Television undertook the first "public LBO" in Britain. Manfred Klein has helped guide the German company Benckiser through a series of divestitures of unrelated businesses followed by leveraged acquisitions in consumer products. And Co-Directors Henri Blanchet and Christian Moretti have created in Dynaction a highly successful French conglomerate that bears a striking resemblance to KKR.

In *The Economic Import of Europe 1992,"* Professor Alan Shapiro uses lessons from the U.S. experience with deregulation and restructuring in the 1980s to speculate about the consequences of an integrated pan-European market. After expressing skepticism about the ability of EC member countries to resolve major remaining conflicts, Shapiro goes on to predict that much as U.S. corporate restructuring served to undo the effects of poorly planned mergers and acquisitions, many overseas corporate investments justified by expectations of scale economies from new markets will prove disappointing. Rather than size or market share, Shapiro argues, the keys to success are likely to be *"discriminating cost cutting and market segmentation based on a clear view of the company's competitive strengths, while firmly resisting the inefficiencies that tend to breed in large, especially diversified organizations."*

In *"Corporate Governance Changes Make Inroads in Europe,"* Howard Sherman argues that new codes of best practice for boards of directors, executive compensation, and takeovers released in the summer of 1995 represent a "significant turning point in European corporate governance." Although the specifics of each code reflect compromise based on national and EU business practices and political pressures, they together represent *"a marked move towards greater transparency, shareholder empowerment, and director oversight—the basic tenets of U.S.- and U.K.-style corporate governance."* As Sherman also observes, *"These trends are likely to take hold over the next few years as privatization programs lure more U.S. and U.K. investors into continental Europe and as competition for listings among stock exchanges worldwide forces European companies to adopt more transparent disclosure standards and raise oversight standards for boards of directors."*

CORPORATE OWNERSHIP AND CONTROL IN THE U.K., GERMANY, AND FRANCE

by Julian Franks,
London Business School, and
Colin Mayer,
Oxford University

Differences among national financial systems have been a subject of continuing debate for well over a century. The primary distinction drawn by economists has been that between "bank-based" and "market-based" systems.[1] In the stylized description of bank-based systems, companies raise most of their external finance from banks that have close, long-term relationships with their corporate customers. By contrast, the market-based systems of the U.K. and the U.S. are characterized by arm's-length relationships between corporations and investors, who are said to be concerned primarily about short-term returns.

While these distinctions cannot be dismissed, they have proved to be difficult to formulate with much precision. Empirical evidence does not provide grounds for the sharp distinction that would have been expected if there were fundamental differences in the structure and operation of national economies. Nevertheless, there is one area in which there are clear differences in the structure and conduct of economies that are deep-rooted and open to quite precise quantification. These differences concern the ownership and control of corporations.

In their 1932 classic, *The Modern Corporation and Private Property*, Adolph Berle and Gardiner Means warned that the growing dispersion of ownership of U.S. stocks was giving rise to a potentially value-reducing separation of ownership and control.[2] In 1976, the general argument of Berle and Means was given a more rigorous formulation by Michael Jensen and William Meckling in their theory of "agency costs."[3] Agency costs, loosely speaking, are reductions in value resulting from the separation of ownership from control in public corporations. Pointing to a roughly tenfold decline in the percentage of managerial stock ownership of large U.S. public companies between the 1930s and the 1980s, Jensen argued that dispersed ownership was leading to major inefficiencies in U.S. companies, particularly in the form of widespread conglomeration. In this view, the rise of hostile takeovers and LBOs in the 1980s was a value-increasing response by U.S. capital markets—one that reduced agency costs by removing inefficient managers and, especially in the case of LBOs, concentrating corporate ownership.[4]

More recently, however, a study by Harold Demsetz and Kenneth Lehn has argued that concentrated ownership is likely to have had significant costs as well as benefits.[5] That is, besides providing stronger incentives to maximize value, concentrated ownership can impose costs in two ways: (1) by forcing managers and other inside shareholders to bear excessive company-specific risks—risks that could be borne at lower cost by well-diversified

* This paper is a revised version of a paper entitled "Ownership and Control" that was written for the International Workshop at the Kiel Institute on "Trends in Business Organization: Increasing Competitiveness by Participation and Cooperation," June 13 and 14, 1994. It is based on an inaugural lecture that was given by Colin Mayer at the University of Warwick on February 1, 1993. It is part of a project funded by the ESRC (no. W102251003) on "Capital Markets, Corporate Governance and the Market for Corporate Control." We are grateful to participants at the workshop for helpful comments and in particular to our discussant, Martin Hellwig. We are also grateful to Marc Goergen and Luis Correia da Silva for research assistance on the project.

1. For recent interesting examples of this, see F. Allen and D. Gale, "A Welfare Comparison of the German and US Financial Systems," CEPR-Fundacion BBV

Conference, April 1994; and J. Edwards and K. Fischer, *Banks, Finance and Investment in Germany* (Cambridge: Cambridge University Press, 1994).

2. A. Berle and G. Means, *The Modern Corporation and Private Property* (New York: MacMillan, 1932).

3. For the original formulation of agency theory, see M. Jensen and W. Meckling, "Theory of the Firm: Managerial Behavior, Agency Costs and Ownership Structure," *Journal of Financial Economics*, No. 3 (1976).

4. See M. Jensen, "The Agency Costs of Free Cash Flow: Corporate Finance and Takeovers," *American Economic Review* 76 (May, 1986); and M. Jensen, "The Eclipse of the Public Corporation," *Harvard Business Review* (1989).

5. H. Demsetz and K. Lehn, "The Structure of Corporate Ownership: Causes and Consequences," *Journal of Political Economy*, 93 (1985), 1155-77.

outside stockholders; and (2) by allowing inside owners to capture private benefits at the expense of minority or outside owners. In the view of Demsetz and Lehn, ownership patterns should reflect a trade-off between the incentive benefits of concentrated ownership and the expected costs arising from excessive concentration of risk and the potential for expropriating minority holders.

In this paper, after a brief summary of existing theories of corporate ownership and control, we describe patterns of ownership in France, Germany, and the U.K. We also review the evidence (much of it our own) on the operation of the market for corporate control in the U.K. and Germany. As we conclude, none of the existing theories offers a completely satisfying explanation of the differences between the *insider* ownership systems of Germany and France, on the one hand, and the *outsider* systems of the U.S. and the U.K. on the other. Nevertheless, given the durability of the two systems, both appear to have devised effective ways of disciplining poor managers and otherwise promoting efficiency.

THEORIES OF OWNERSHIP AND CONTROL

There are two strands of literature that are relevant to this discussion. The first concerns the determinants of corporate ownership, and the second focuses on the operation of the market for corporate control.

With regard to ownership there are three classes of models. The first is the industrial economics literature on vertical relationships—for example, those between manufacturers and their suppliers. This class of models seeks to explain the tendency of upstream and downstream firms to own each other (or to remain independent companies) in terms of the "externalities" that may exist between the parties.[6] For example, upstream firms will not always take full account of the interests of downstream firms in the prices that they charge and the way in which they treat their purchas-

ers. In such a case, joint ownership may be required to "internalize this externality" in the absence of suitable contractual alternatives.

A second, related, class of literature on ownership argues that transaction costs may make transactions through markets more costly than internal activities within the firm.[7] It may be difficult or costly to write the contracts necessary to undertake transactions between firms through the marketplace. Discouraging "opportunistic" breaches of implicit contracts may be accomplished more effectively inside the firm than through the marketplace.

A third literature on ownership is concerned with the effect of incomplete contracts on the incentives that firms have to make long-term, highly specialized investments— the kind of investments that would have little value if transferred beyond the context of the particular firm.[8] Joint or vertical ownership is viewed as a means of encouraging such "firm-specific" investments by guaranteeing that important parties will honor their implicit commitments to projects involving joint effort (for example, those involving suppliers and manufacturers).

According to this theory, one would expect to see joint ownership where (1) it is difficult to use contracts to avoid expropriation of subsequent returns; (2) there is a high degree of "complementarity" between the assets of the two firms; and (3) one of the assets or one of the owners of the assets is particularly important to the other party and should therefore become the owner of both the assets. These theories suggest that we would expect patterns of ownership to reflect complementarities in production.

The second major strand of literature is concerned with corporate control. Separation of ownership and control in outsider systems like the U.S. and the U.K. have prompted the rise and refinement of a number of mechanisms designed to limit the agency problems with dispersed ownership.[9] Such mechanisms include monitoring and control by non-executive (or "outside") directors, pay-for-performance management incentive systems, and a market for corporate control.

6. See, for example, A. Dixit, "Vertical Integration in a Monopolistically Competitive Industry," *International Journal of Industrial Organization*, 1 (1983), 63-78; M. Salinger, "Vertical Merger and Market Foreclosure," *Quarterly Journal of Economics*, 103 (1988), 345-56; and W. Waterson, "Vertical Integration, Variable Proportions and Oligopoly," *Economic Journal*, 92 (1982), 129-44.

7. See, for example, R. Coase, "The Nature of the Firm," *Economica*, 4 (1937), 386-405; O. Williamson, *Markets and Hierarchies: Analysis and Anti-Trust Implications* (New York: Free Press, 1975); O. Williamson, *The Economic Institutions of Capitalism* (New York: Free Press, 1985); and M. Aoki, B. Gustafsson, and O. Williamson, *The Firm as a Nexus of Treaties* (London: European Sage, 1988).

8. See, for example, B. Klein, R. Crawford, and A. Alchian, "Vertical Integration, Appropriable Rents and the Competitive Contracting Process," *Journal of Law and Economics*, 21 (1978), 297-326; S. Grossman and O. Hart, "The Cost and Benefits of Ownership: A Theory of Vertical and Lateral Integration," *Journal of Political Economy*, 94 (1986), 691-719.; O. Hart and J. Moore, "Property Rights and the Nature of the Firm," *Journal of Political Economy*, 98 (1990), 1119-58.

9. See H. Manne, "Mergers and the Market for Corporate Control," *Journal of Political Economy* (1965), 110-20; and A. Alchian and H. Demsetz, "Production, Information Costs and Economic Organization," *American Economic Review*, 62 (1972), 777-95; and E. Fama and M. Jensen, "Separation of Ownership and Control," *Journal of Law and Economics*, No. 26 (1983).

Most financial economists' attention to date has focused on the operation of the corporate control market or, in popular parlance, the takeover market. In the standard conception of this market, corporate raiders identify companies that are not being managed so as to maximize shareholder value. Raiders launch bids for controlling ownership that, if successful, give them the right to bring about value-increasing changes in strategy and, in many cases, top management.

PATTERNS OF OWNERSHIP IN FRANCE, GERMANY, AND THE U.K.

The stereotypical description of the structure of corporate sectors runs as follows: There are a large number of small companies that are privately owned by individuals, families, and partners; and there are a much smaller number of large companies that are quoted (or "publicly traded") on the stock market and owned by a large number of individual shareholders. Complicating this pattern somewhat, a significant fraction of the shares of quoted companies are owned by institutional investors—in particular, pension funds, life insurance firms, and mutual funds.

Corporate Ownership in the U.K.

The above description fits the U.K. reasonably well. There are over 2,000 U.K. companies quoted on the stock market out of a total population of around 500,000 firms. Almost 80% of the largest 700 companies are quoted on the stock market, and the value of companies quoted on the stock market is around 81% of the GDP. Approximately two-thirds of the equity of quoted U.K. companies is held by institutions.

But this pattern of ownership is by no means universal; on the contrary, it appears to be the exception rather than the rule. Although the U.S. has more quoted companies than the U.K., in most other countries the number of quoted companies is far lower. In Germany, for example, there are fewer than 700 quoted companies and in France less than 500 (see Figure 1). In both countries, the value of quoted companies amounts to only 25% of GDP (Figure 2). In short, quoted companies in Germany and France

account for a much smaller fraction of total national corporate activity than those in the U.K. and the U.S.

In the U.K. and the U.S., moreover, ownership is widely dispersed among a large number of institutions or individuals. Most of the equity of quoted U.K. companies is held by institutions, but no one institution owns very much of any one company. In the U.S., the largest category of shareholders is individuals.

In most of continental Europe, however, ownership is much more concentrated. Consider the ownership pattern revealed in Figure 3, which shows the percentage of (approximately) the largest 170 quoted companies in France, Germany, and the U.K with a single large (at least 25%) shareholder. In only 16% of the U.K. companies did a single shareholder own more than 25% of the shares. By contrast, in nearly 85% of the German firms there was at least one shareholder owning more than 25%; and almost 80% of the French companies had at least one shareholder with more than 25% ownership. In short, concentration of ownership is much greater in corporations based outside the U.K. and the U.S.[10]

Corporate Ownership in Germany and France

In France and Germany, by far the single largest group of shareholders is the corporate sector itself. Figure 4 breaks down large share stakes in 171 large quoted German companies by different groups of investors—banks, investment institutions, companies, government, and so forth. It reveals that a majority of the large share stakes are held by companies. The next largest group is families, followed by trusts, institutional investors, and foreign companies.

Although there is a commonly held view that banks control corporate Germany, banks actually come far down the list of large stakeholders. Nevertheless, the control exerted by banks is significantly greater than their direct equity holdings would suggest. As holders of the bearer shares owned by their customers, they are able to exercise proxy votes on behalf of dispersed shareholders. (And, since all the companies studied here are quoted, at least a portion of the shares are widely held.)

---

10. For a comparison of ownership in Japan and the U.S. that makes a similar observation, see S. Prowse, "The Structure of Corporate Ownership in Japan," *Journal of Finance*, 47 (1992), 1121-40. In the case of Japan, the largest group of shareholders is financial institutions.

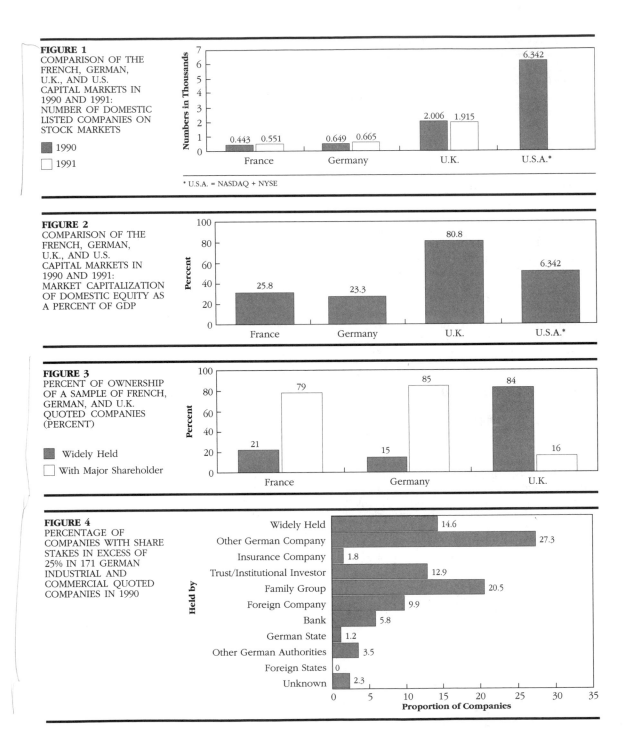

FIGURE 1
COMPARISON OF THE FRENCH, GERMAN, U.K., AND U.S. CAPITAL MARKETS IN 1990 AND 1991: NUMBER OF DOMESTIC LISTED COMPANIES ON STOCK MARKETS

■ 1990
□ 1991

Numbers in Thousands

France: 0.443 / 0.551
Germany: 0.649 / 0.665
U.K.: 2.006 / 1.915
U.S.A.*: 6.342

* U.S.A. = NASDAQ + NYSE

FIGURE 2
COMPARISON OF THE FRENCH, GERMAN, U.K., AND U.S. CAPITAL MARKETS IN 1990 AND 1991: MARKET CAPITALIZATION OF DOMESTIC EQUITY AS A PERCENT OF GDP

Percent

France: 25.8
Germany: 23.3
U.K.: 80.8
U.S.A.*: 6.342

FIGURE 3
PERCENT OF OWNERSHIP OF A SAMPLE OF FRENCH, GERMAN, AND U.K. QUOTED COMPANIES (PERCENT)

■ Widely Held
□ With Major Shareholder

Percent

France: 21 / 79
Germany: 15 / 85
U.K.: 84 / 16

FIGURE 4
PERCENTAGE OF COMPANIES WITH SHARE STAKES IN EXCESS OF 25% IN 171 GERMAN INDUSTRIAL AND COMMERCIAL QUOTED COMPANIES IN 1990

Held by

Widely Held: 14.6
Other German Company: 27.3
Insurance Company: 1.8
Trust/Institutional Investor: 12.9
Family Group: 20.5
Foreign Company: 9.9
Bank: 5.8
German State: 1.2
Other German Authorities: 3.5
Foreign States: 0
Unknown: 2.3

Proportion of Companies

FIGURE 5
PROPORTION OF
DISCLOSED STAKES BY
SIZE OF STAKES IN 171
GERMAN INDUSTRIAL
AND COMMERCIAL
QUOTED COMPANIES
IN 1990

PANEL A. HELD BY TRUSTS/INSTITUTIONAL INVESTORS (NO. OF STAKES = 54)

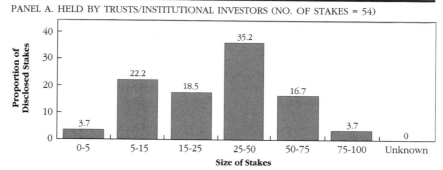

PANEL B. HELD BY BANKS (NO. OF STAKES = 39)

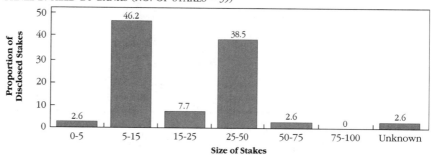

PANEL C. HELD BY FAMILY GROUPS (NO. OF STAKES = 58)

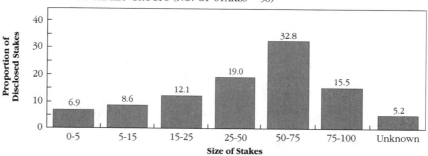

PANEL D. HELD BY OTHER GERMAN COMPANIES (NO. OF STAKES = 80)

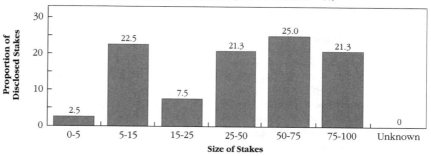

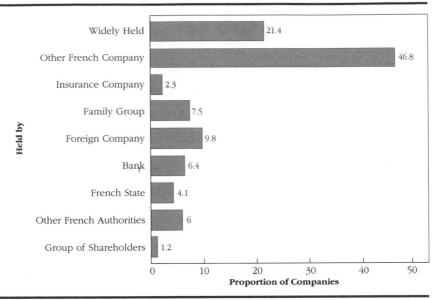

FIGURE 6
SHARE STAKES IN EXCESS
OF 25% IN 155 FRENCH
INDUSTRIAL AND
COMMERCIAL QUOTED
COMPANIES IN 1990

Figure 5 provides more detail on the ownership of the 171 large German companies analyzed in Figure 4. As shown in Figure 5A, trusts and institutional investors are sometimes large shareholders in German companies. However, their share stakes are rarely majority holdings. The same holds for banks (Figure 5B): there are some large share stakes but rarely majority holdings. This contrasts with the pattern of family ownership. In almost one-third of the cases, families appear to be majority holders of German companies (Figure 5C).

In examining these figures, one should keep in mind that they refer to the *largest* German companies. Thus, in contrast to our earlier description of the U.K. ownership structure, large-block family ownership is a highly representative feature of the largest enterprises in Germany. This raises the interesting question (to which we return later) of how and why German (and French) families play a much more significant role in corporate ownership than, say, their U.K. counterparts.

The other group that emerges as having majority shareholdings in Germany is the German corporate sector (Figure 5D). Not only do German companies have many and large stakeholdings in other German firms, but also these intercorporate shareholdings are often majority ones. What makes such corporate equity stakes in other firms especially

noteworthy is that these are all quoted companies, not just subsidiaries of other companies.

In sum, then, while German banks do have quite large share stakes, they are rarely majority shareholders. The pattern for insurance companies, trust, and institutional investors is very similar—some large but rarely majority shareholdings. The two dominant investor groups in German companies are families and other German firms.

A remarkably similar pattern emerges for France. First, as noted above, the proportion of large stakeholdings in total is about the same as in Germany. Figure 6 summarizes the ownership distribution for 155 large quoted French companies. As in the case of Germany, a majority of these stakes are held by other companies. Other large stakeholders in French firms are foreign companies, families, and banks.

Further detail on the ownership of these 155 French companies is provided in Figure 7. As we saw in the case of Germany, there are some large stakes held by insurance companies but these are rarely majority holdings (Figure 7A). Banks have some large minority shareholdings, often in excess of 25% (Figure 7B). But, as in Germany, it is French families (Figure 7C) and other French companies that have the largest proportion of majority shareholdings (Figures 7C and 7D).

FIGURE 7
STAKES HELD IN 155
FRENCH INDUSTRIAL
AND COMMERCIAL
QUOTED COMPANIES
IN 1990

PANEL A. HELD BY INSURANCE COMPANIES (NO. OF STAKES = 27)

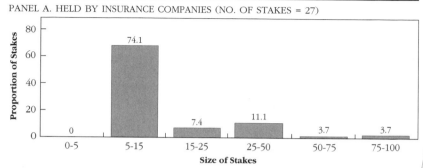

PANEL B. HELD BY BANKS (NO. OF STAKES = 21)

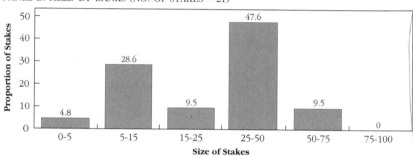

PANEL C. HELD BY FAMILY GROUPS (NO. OF STAKES = 33)

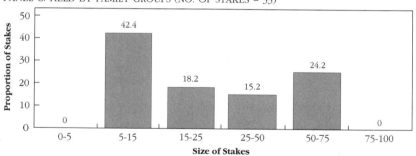

PANEL D. HELD BY OTHER FRENCH COMPANIES (NO. OF STAKES = 149)

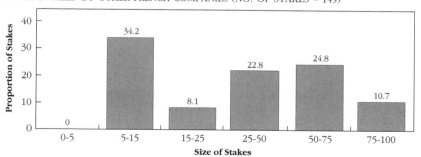

forward contracts should be adequate.

Though falling in the same second-generation category, the exchange-traded currency futures and options have substantially smaller percentages of adoption than swaps and OTC options. The greater use of over-the-counter products is

FIGURE 8
PROPORTION OF DISCLOSED STAKES HELD BY THE STATE IN GERMANY[1] AND FRANCE[2]

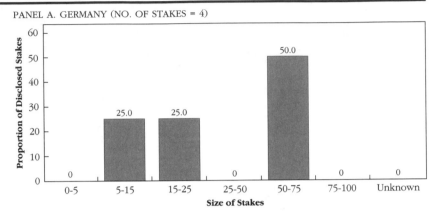

PANEL A. GERMANY (NO. OF STAKES = 4)

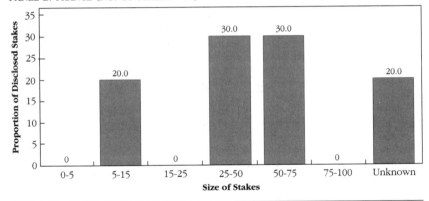

PANEL B. FRANCE (NO. OF STAKES = 10)

1. In 171 German industrial and commercial quoted companies.
2. In 155 French industrial and commercial quoted companies.

There is, however, one notable difference between France and Germany, and that is the comparative importance of state ownership of large companies. As shown in Figure 8, share stakes by the state are more prevalent and tend to be larger in France than in Germany.

Four Cases of German and French Corporate Structure

The ownership patterns of individual firms reveal a number of characteristics that are hidden in the aggregate data. Figures 9, 10, and 11 show the ownership structures of three prominent and representative German companies—Renk AG, Kromschroder AG, and Metallgesellschaft AG. Fig-

ure 12 describes the ownership of the French water company, Degremont.

What can we learn from these exhibits?

■ First, they show the extent of equity holdings of corporations in each other's shares. These investments are frequently in quoted companies and are often by firms in a related or the same industry. Figure 9, for example, shows a large holding by MAN AG, a large German engineering company that produces buses, lorries, and machines, in Renk AG, another mechanical engineering company. Ruhrgas (shown in Figure 10) is a gas company that owns Elster, another gas company.

■ Second, the other corporate owners are frequently *not* trading partners. For example, the

FIGURE 9

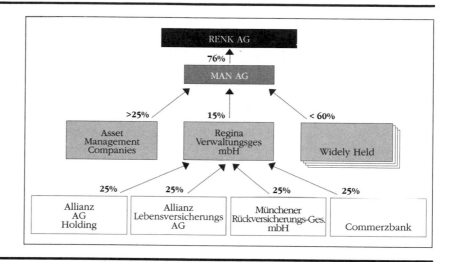

FIGURE 10

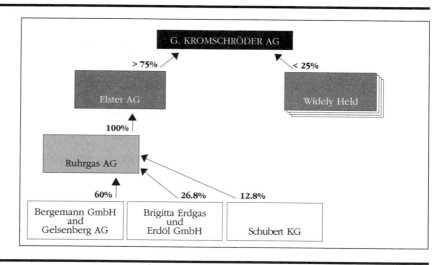

gas company Elster holds Kromschroder, a precision mechanics and optics company.

■ Third, banks and insurance companies often emerge higher up in the ownership tree. For example, partnerships between Allianz, which is a German insurance company, and German banks show up in a number of large corporations. Allianz and Deutsche Bank between them have a controlling interest in the holding company of Metallgesellschaft (Figure 11). Allianz, Allianz's life insurance company, and Commerzbank have a controlling interest in a holding company that has a large stake in MAN. And, as shown in Figure 12, Compagnie Financiere de Suez, Credit Lyonnaise, and UAP all have significant holdings in Société Lyonnaise des Eaux-Dumex, which in turn owns Degremont.

Thus, institutional owners play a prominent role in all three countries. But, whereas institutional ownership is highly dispersed in the U.K., it is highly concentrated in France and Germany. And, as the above illustrations further suggest, the corpo-

FIGURE 11

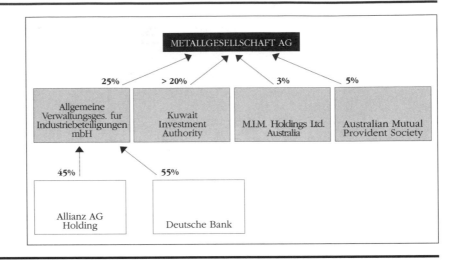

FIGURE 12

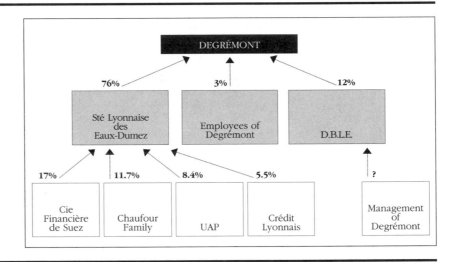

rate governance role of outside shareholders in France and Germany is even less significant than the small number of quoted companies in these countries would suggest. For, even in those cases in which companies are quoted on the stock market, controlling shareholdings often reside with other companies.

Therefore, as we noted earlier, the German and French corporate governance systems are perhaps best described as *insider* systems (see Figure 13). Insider systems are those in which the corporate sector has controlling interests in itself and in which outside investors, while participating in equity returns through the stock market, are not able to exert much control. By contrast, the U.K. and the U.S. are *outsider* systems of corporate control, in which there are few controlling shareholdings (what controlling blocks do exist are rarely associated with the corporate sector itself). And, as we discuss below, these differences in ownership systems give rise to very different forms of corporate control.

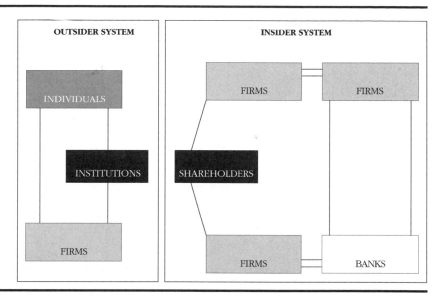

FIGURE 13
CORPORATE CONTROL
SYSTEMS

OUTSIDER SYSTEM

INDIVIDUALS

INSTITUTIONS

FIRMS

INSIDER SYSTEM

FIRMS

FIRMS

SHAREHOLDERS

FIRMS

BANKS

THE MARKET FOR CORPORATE CONTROL IN THE U.K.

The takeover market is active in the U.K. During the merger waves at the beginning of the 1970s and the end of the 1980s, as much as 4% of the total U.K. capital stock was acquired by takeover (or merger) in one year.[11] Furthermore, it has been estimated that about 25% of takeovers in the 1980s were "hostile" in the sense of being rejected initially by the incumbent management.[12] Of those bids that were hostile in nature, approximately one-half were successfully completed.

There are two empirical studies of takeovers that have attempted to distinguish takeovers designed to correct past managerial failure from those that were not. In a 1991 study of the U.S. market, Kenneth Martin and John McConnell investigated the disciplinary role of corporate takeovers in the U.S. over the period 1958 to 1984, using a sample of 253 successful tender offers. They classified a takeover as "disciplinary" if there was any change in the CEO of the target firm. Their study, somewhat surprisingly, reported no difference in bid premiums associated with disciplinary and non-disciplinary takeovers and only moderate evidence of

differences in the share price performance of targets of disciplinary and non-disciplinary bids prior to takeover.

In a study published in 1995, we reported similar results for a sample of 80 contested bids in the U.K. in 1985 and 1986.[13] We found that for a range of financial variables, including share price returns, dividends, and cash flow rates of return, the performance of targets of hostile bids in the six years prior to a bid was not statistically distinguishable from that of samples of either accepted bids or non-merging firms. In fact, the dividend performance of targets of both friendly and hostile bids was *appreciably better than* that of firms in the lowest deciles of share performance. Whereas poorly performing firms frequently reduced their dividends, targets of hostile and friendly bids rarely reduced their dividends in the two years prior to a bid.[14]

We also repeated our analysis of U.K. firms using Martin and McConnell's definition of managerial failure as replacement of top management. But, again, we found found little evidence that managerial control changes in takeovers were a response to poor financial performance. The past performance

11. See our article, "Corporate Ownership and Corporate Control: A Study of France, Germany and the UK," *Economic Policy* (1990).
12. T. Jenkinson and C. Mayer, *Hostile Takeovers* (London: MacMillan, 1994).
13. J. Franks and C. Mayer, "Hostile Takeovers and the Correction of Managerial Failure," *Journal of Financial Economics* 40, (1996), 162-81.

14. Although it appears inconsistent with standard explanations of the control market, such a finding is consistent with Jensen's free cash flow theory of takeovers, in which companies with excess capital tend to overinvest. See Jensen (1986), cited earlier.

of acquired firms where managers were replaced was not significantly worse than the performance of those targets in which top managers were retained.

All these results question the common association of markets for corporate control with the correction of managerial failure. Nevertheless, even in the absence of poor pre-merger performance, we did find evidence of considerable restructuring after takeovers. More precisely, we found that levels of asset disposals and restructurings were significantly higher in cases where bids were either hostile or followed by managerial control changes. Furthermore, we found that managerial dismissals were much higher in hostile than in friendly bids. Indeed, nearly 80% of executive directors either resigned or were dismissed within two years of a successful hostile bid.

In sum, then, while the market for corporate control does not appear to be associated with the correction of managerial failure as measured by past corporate performance (which we henceforth refer to as *ex post failure*), it does give rise to substantial corporate restructurings in the form of asset disposals and executive dismissals (*ex ante failure*). One possible interpretation of these results is that hostile bids can occur, even in the absence of any evidence of poor past performance, in the expectation that the acquiring firm will implement a new and more valuable policy in the future (an explanation that would fall under the classification of *ex ante failure*). In support of this argument, we found in the previously mentioned study of takeovers that hostile bidders paid much larger premiums over market than friendly acquirers, which is consistent with higher expected benefits from the planned restructurings of targets of hostile bids.[15]

THE MARKET FOR CORPORATE CONTROL IN GERMANY

In a recently published study, we found that during the 1980s the total number of mergers in Germany was only about one-half of those in the U.K.[16] More significantly, in contrast to the active market in corporate control in the U.K., there have been just four recorded cases of hostile takeovers in Germany since World War II, and three of those four have occurred within the last six years.

Several explanations have been suggested for the low level of hostile takeovers in Germany. The first focuses on the dominant position of banks resulting from owning corporate equity and sitting on the supervisory boards of many quoted German companies. As noted earlier, German banks' holdings of equity are a quite modest proportion of the total, but they exercise considerable control by virtue of their ability to vote in proxy contests the bearer shares they hold in custody for customers.

The second explanation is that voting right limitations prevent predators from acquiring controlling interests in firms. German companies frequently pass resolutions at shareholders' meetings limiting the voting right of any one shareholder to a maximum of 5%, 10%, or 15% of total votes, irrespective of the size of the shareholding. The justification for such voting restrictions is that, in the absence of a U.K.-style takeover code, they protect minority shareholders from predators who, after acquiring a controlling interest, attempt to dilute the value of the minority's investments.

The third explanation is that it may prove difficult to remove members of the supervisory board and thereby gain control of a company, even when a majority of the shares are tendered. The supervisory board comprises representatives of employees as well as shareholders. For an AG (public limited company), 50% of the board is composed of employee representatives, who by tradition vote with the incumbent management.

Case studies of hostile takeovers in Germany provide evidence of the effectiveness of these institutional features as barriers to takeover.[17] The unwelcome bid by Pirelli for Continental, Germany's largest tire manufacturer, was launched in September 1990. During the course of the bid, substantial share stakes were acquired by allies of the two parties: Italmobiliare, Mediobanca, and Sopaf in the Pirelli camp; BMW, Daimler-Benz, and Volkswagen in the Continental camp. These share stakes were in large part acquired from individual investors and investment institutions.

At the time of the Pirelli bid, there was a 5% limitation on the voting rights that could be exercised by any one shareholder. Prior to launching the bid, Pirelli attempted to have the 5% limitation removed so as not to dilute the voting rights of its own (and its partners') holdings. A motion for removal of

15. J. Franks and C. Mayer, "Corporate Control: A Synthesis of the International Evidence," mimeo.

16. J. Franks and C. Mayer, see [13].

17. Ibid.

the restriction was passed at a shareholders' meeting in March 1991, thereby paving the way for Pirelli to launch a tender bid for Continental. Nevertheless, the removal was delayed (and never implemented) due to a court action by shareholders objecting to rule violations of minority interests.

The Continental case illustrates that voting right restrictions can introduce a two-stage procedure into German takeovers. In the first stage, predators solicit the support of small shareholders to have voting right limitations removed. In the second stage, a normal tender can be launched. The Continental case suggests that the first stage can represent a significant, though not necessarily insurmountable, barrier to takeover.

Although the management board of Continental was resolutely opposed to the merger, the supervisory board showed itself more willing to explore merger possibilities with Pirelli. This difference in approach resulted in the dismissal of the chairman of the management board in May 1991. He was replaced by a chairman who was more sympathetic to merger discussions.

The Continental case suggests that neither proxy votes nor voting right restrictions are absolute defences against hostile takeovers, though the latter certainly slows down the process. Furthermore, the supervisory board may remove members of the management board, though this is less easy to achieve than in the U.K.

The main impediment, however, to an Anglo-American market for corporate control is the ownership structure of German companies. In the Continental case, there was no major shareholder who owned a stake of 25% or more, thus allowing Pirelli and its partners to build large holdings. Two other hostile takeovers in Germany—that of Feldmühle Nobel and the bid by Krupp for Hoesch—were also for firms in the small set of German companies with dispersed shareholdings. In the latter case, Krupp was able to amass a stake of 24.9% without the knowledge of Hoesch or the investment banking community. The purchase of this stake took more than five months to complete, involved purchases on the German, London, and Swiss stock exchanges, and was a crucial tactic in gaining control. Without such a stake, a merger would have proved unlikely or impossible, since all previous attempts at friendly mergers in the industry had failed.

Where ownership is concentrated, direct control is effectively exercised by boards. This is reflected in a close association between ownership and represen-tation on supervisory boards, in particular in the all-important position of chairman. In the small proportion of companies where ownership is dispersed, bank representation on supervisory boards is more in evidence. This suggests that, in widely held companies, proxy votes and voting restrictions together permit banks to exercise effective control through board representation.

A DISCUSSION OF THE EVIDENCE

The evidence presented above on national differences between corporate ownership and control can be summarized by the following observations:

1. There are marked differences in the ownership structures of similar companies in different countries.

2. Intercorporate holdings of companies are very significant in some countries but not others.

3. Large shareholdings by families are of much greater importance in some countries than others.

4. Markets for corporate control are little in evidence in countries with concentrated ownership.

5. Even where companies are widely held, markets for corporate control are seriously restricted in some countries.

6. Bank control is associated primarily with widely held companies where the market for corporate control is restricted.

7. There is little association of the market for corporate control with poor past performance (or *ex post failure*).

8. Corporate control transactions such as take-overs lead to substantial restructuring and management changes (which can be interpreted as evidence of *ex ante failure*).

How well do the theories of ownership and the market for corporate control square with these observations? The answer is not well at all; they leave a large number of unresolved issues.

First, it would not be expected that the broadly similar production technologies that are employed in different countries would give rise to the marked variations in ownership patterns recorded in this paper. Moreover, it is difficult to imagine that there are sufficient differences in production complementarities across countries to explain much larger intercorporate holdings in some countries than in others.

Second, the large family holdings in France and Germany suggest that families in those countries either (1) possess greater managerial skills or (2) derive larger "private" benefits from control (larger at least in relation to the value they could realize by selling their controlling interest) than their English and American counterparts. It is possible that regulation may create greater private benefits in some countries, for example, by being more permissive towards insider trading or providing less protection of minority interests.[18] In this respect, regulation may have important consequences for the structure of corporate organization.

Third, if markets for corporate control improve corporate efficiency, why are they largely absent in some countries? For example, it is very difficult to understand why markets for corporate control in Germany are restricted by bank intermediation *even* in cases of widely held companies where there are weak incentives for shareholders to exert control directly themselves.

On the other hand, if the market for corporate control really does work to correct managerial failure, the puzzle posed by the U.K. is why there is so little evidence of poor pre-bid performance. And, in the absence of poor pre-bid performance, why is there so much restructuring after the takeover?

In this sense, then, current theories of ownership and control fail to provide adequate explanations for the ownership structure and operation of either U.K. or Continental European capital markets. For example, there is clearly more to the determination of ownership in the U.K., Germany, and France than complementarity in production. Moreover, the market for corporate control does not appear to perform its assumed function of correcting managerial failure—or not at least the kind of failure that manifests itself in substandard operating and shareholder returns.

One might suggest that dispersed public ownership, because of its efficiencies in risk-bearing and the liquidity of public markets, is better suited to providing capital for large-scale corporate expansions. But this ignores the reality that even companies with concentrated share ownership can raise external equity while retaining control through either the issuance of dual class shares or the "pyramiding" of intercorporate holdings (as illustrated earlier in the case of several German and French companies).[19] It also ignores the

fact that active secondary markets can be (and are) organized in shares other than those that are part of the controlling block.[20]

Concentrated ownership, as suggested by Demsetz and Lehn, is likely to occur for one or both of the following reasons: (1) the greater potential for owners to exercise control over managers increases the value of the enterprise (relative to the value it would command under dispersed ownership), or (2) there are "private" benefits to owners of exercising control—that is, benefits that do not accrue to (and may even come at the expense of) minority stockholders. Both of these factors are likely to explain the extent of family ownership in Germany and France. Concentrated ownership allows investors to exert *direct* control, which is presumably much less costly than the indirect control exerted by takeover markets (especially given restrictions on takeovers in Continental markets). And the private, perhaps even non-monetary, benefits of owning a large enterprise (which may include greater powers to keep minority shareholders at bay) may well be larger in France and Germany than in the U.S. or the U.K.

Nevertheless, the differences in the extent of family ownership of public corporations among these nations remain a puzzle. Unless the relative costs of direct and indirect control can be shown to vary greatly among countries, or unless families in different countries attach very different values to private benefits, the diverse forms of ownership cannot be readily explained.

The hypothesis we offer is that the different patterns of ownership across countries are associated with different forms of corporate control that allow for different kinds of correction. Large share stakes and concentrated ownership are likely to be more effective in responding to *ex post* managerial failures (poor past performance), in large part (as we will argue below) because of the "information and agency costs" that confront dispersed shareholders. And there is at least one piece of supporting evidence for this argument: In a recent study (with a colleague), we found that those companies in the bottom decile of corporate performance were

---

18. And differences in estate taxes may lead to differences in ownership; for example, many large family interests in U.S. companies are reportedly sold to pay estate taxes.

19. For a defense of the economic efficiency of the pyramid ownership structure, see the article (immediately following this one) by Brian Kantor, "Shareholders as Agents and Principals: The Case for South Africa's Corporate Governance System."

20. For a paper arguing that this may be an important source of information for structuring incentives for management, see B. Holmstrom and J. Tirole, "Market Liquidity and Performance Monitoring," *Journal of Political Economy*, 101 (1993), 678-709.

far more likely to replace their managers than those with dispersed ownership.[21] By contrast, dispersed ownership seems to be more effective in correcting *ex ante failure*—that is, in bringing about valuable restructuring and management changes in cases where financial performance has been adequate, but managers have failed to maximize value.

At first sight, this argument would appear to suggest that national systems with dispersed ownership will tend to achieve more efficient resource allocations than those with concentrated ownership. Nevertheless, there is a problem presented by dispersed ownership—namely, the inability of a large number of small shareholders to make "commitments" to other key corporate stakeholders such as employees and suppliers.

A simple example illustrates the point. Consider a company with 100,000 shareholders each owning one share in a firm. An alternative prospect, for example, a proposed acquisition emerges. A sale of a majority of shares results in a change in corporate policy to the detriment of existing stakeholders (suppliers, purchasers, and employees). Individually, shareholders base their decision to sell purely on the price which they are offered since the action of any one shareholder has no effect on policy. In addition, the loss sustained by stakeholders in the event of a change in policy cannot be attributed to the actions of any one shareholder. In contrast, large shareholders know that if they sell their shares, they will affect corporate policy to the detriment of stakeholders. Their decisions will be affected by the loss of their reputation as well as the price for their shares

According to this description the key distinction between corporate systems concerns the degree of anonymity of shareholders. To a much greater extent than in the U.S. or the U.K., the Continental system allows a large number of small investors to buy and sell shares without having any effect on control. At the same time, large investors such as families or other companies—those who are likely to have the best information about the firm's long-run prospects—effectively guarantee the ability of the firm to make good on strategic commitments.

On the other hand, the advantage of dispersed ownership is that outside shareholders who are not bound by prior commitments are more likely to seek the highest value control group *at any point in time*. Thus, dispersed share ownership achieves value maximization, at least over the short run, although possibly at the expense of valuable long-term relationships with other stakeholders.[22]

It is in this sense, then, that the U.K. and the U.S. financial markets may be considered "short-term." Dispersed shareholders cannot commit to the same extent as concentrated owners and cannot therefore sustain the same set of prior relations. This kind of short termism thus does not represent a mispricing of securities or excessive trading of shares, but is rather a direct result of the structure of ownership. And if the short-term orientation of dispersed shareholders limits their ability to commit to key corporate stakeholders, it also provides a potentially valuable flexibility (an ability to reduce operating leverage, if you will, by converting fixed into variable costs). For this reason, in cases where little investment is required of other stakeholders, or relationships can be sustained through explicit contracting, dispersed share ownership may well lead to more efficient allocation of resources than a concentrated ownership burdened by commitments.[23]

Moreover, while it is possible to provide a rationale for high levels of concentration of ownership, majority (or large minority) intercorporate ownership remains very hard to explain. Indeed, the main puzzle presented by the Continental ownership structure is this: Where control is retained within the corporate sector through large corporate shareholdings and corporate representatives who serve on supervisory boards, management is likely to enjoy a high degree of protection from external influences. Managerial failure will not be corrected, either directly by large outside shareholders such as families or indirectly by takeovers, as in economies with dispersed shareownership. Thus, one plausible view of the insider system holds that the complex web of intercorporate holdings in France and Germany is designed, not to promote efficiency, but to perpetuate control within the corporate sector itself.

21. J. Franks, C. Mayer, and C. Renneboog, "The Ownership and Control of Poorly Performing Companies in the U.K.," working paper (1995).

22. This provides the basis for the Shleifer and Summers assertion that shareholders are unable to make commitments to other stakeholders and employ managers to do this on their behalf. The observation here is that through concentrated ownership some financial systems permit investors to make commitments. (See A. Shleifer and L. Summers, "Breaches of Trust in Hostile Takeovers," in *Corporate Takeovers: Causes and Consequences*, ed. Alan Auerbach (University of Chicago Press for National Bureau of Economic Research, 1988).)

23. Franks and Mayer (1996), cited above, emphasize another distinguishing feature of insider and outsider systems and that is the importance of committees. Control in insider systems is exercised by committees that can reflect the interests of parties who, for credit constraint reasons, are underrepresented in ownership stakes. In Germany, stakeholder representation on boards is in part dictated by legal considerations.

CONCLUSIONS

There are pronounced differences in the ownership patterns of corporate sectors across countries. The U.K. and the U.S. have large quoted sectors with share ownership dispersed across a large number of investors. (In the U.K. the dominant shareholding group is institutional investors, in the U.S. it is individual investors.)

In contrast, France and Germany have small quoted sectors. Perhaps more significant, even the largest quoted companies in France and Germany typically have at least one shareholder owning more than 25% of the equity and, in many cases, even a majority shareholding. Such large shareholdings tend to be held either by the founding family or by other corporations. In this sense, both France and Germany can be seen as having "insider systems" of corporate ownership, as contrasted with the "outsider systems" of the U.K. and the U.S.

The different ownership systems are associated with very different forms of corporate control. There is an active market for corporate control in the U.K. and the U.S., but very little in the way of a market for corporate control in France and Germany. In the case of Germany, even in the comparatively small widely held component of the quoted sector, the market for corporate control is impeded by proxy votes and voting right restrictions that effectively confer more power on banks than on the concentrated ownership segment.

Some economists have suggested that complementarities in production can make vertical relationships (including intercorporate block holdings) a cost-effective way of reducing transaction costs or "completing" incomplete contracts. Nevertheless, the patterns of intercorporate ownership we observe in France and Germany do not appear to be particularly closely associated with trading relationships. And, in further contradiction of this theory, similar companies have quite different ownership structures in the U.K., on the one hand, and France and Germany on the other.

In theory, the market for corporate control should be closely associated with the correction of managerial failure. In practice, however, there is very little evidence of a relation between the incidence of hostile takeovers and poor corporate performance. The performance of targets of hostile takeovers in the U.K. is close to that of the average quoted company. At the same time, however, hostile takeovers do result in considerable restructuring and managerial turnover. This can be construed as evidence that targets, while performing up to averages, were failing to *maximize* shareholder value.

The different patterns of ownership in the U.K. and in France and Germany create different incentives and corporate control mechanisms. Concentrated ownership would seem to encourage longer-term relationships between the company and its investors. But, while perhaps better suited to some corporate activities with longer-term payoffs, concentrated ownership could also lead to costly delays in undertaking necessary corrective action, particularly if the owners receive non-monetary benefits from owning and running a business. And although widely dispersed ownership may increase the likelihood that corrective action will be sought prematurely (that is, in cases where the firm is suffering a temporary downturn and outsiders rush to sell their shares), the presence of well-diversified public owners may also be more appropriate for riskier ventures requiring large amounts of new capital investment.

In short, different forms of ownership would appear to be suited to promoting different types of activity. Concentrated ownership may be necessary where investment by other stakeholders is important and cannot be promoted contractually, but dispersed ownership will be advantageous where little investment is required by non-investor stakeholders or where adequate contracts can be written that protect their interests. What is finally very hard to explain, however, is the high level of intercorporate holdings in the French and particularly the German systems. Such holdings, while possibly achieving some coordination benefits, are also likely to create insider systems that are largely immune to necessary corrective intervention by outside investors.

■ JULIAN FRANKS AND COLIN MAYER

are Professors of Finance at the London Business School and Oxford University, respectively.

SHAREHOLDERS AS AGENTS AND PRINCIPALS: THE CASE FOR SOUTH AFRICA'S CORPORATE GOVERNANCE SYSTEM

*by Graham Barr,
Jos Gerson, and
Brian Kantor,
University of Cape Town**

T he Johannesburg Stock Exchange (JSE) is dominated by a small set of very large companies whose principal assets are shares in other listed subsidiary and associate companies. These alliances of industrial, commercial, mining, and financial service companies are commonly referred to as "groups." Ownership in the principal companies of the groups and their major operating subsidiaries is widely diffused, although South African institutional investors are typically well represented (as they are in the U.S.) among the shareholders. Management *control* of the groups, however, is highly concentrated, typically in the hands of the founder or his family.

Such concentration of control has been accomplished by the use of tiers of holding companies, best described by the term "pyramid companies." A pyramid company is one whose major or only asset consists of a controlling (that is, more than 50%) shareholding in another company. Although ownership of the ultimate holding company at the top of the structure is highly concentrated, ownership of the group parent company and its subsidiary companies becomes progressively more diffused among outside shareholders as one moves closer to the operating base of the groups. By means of such pyramid holding companies—and also by way of cross shareholdings and voting trusts—founders or their families retain control over vast assets with ownership claims on them that can be less than 10%.

The companies comprising the six largest groups on the JSE presently account for over 70% of the value of all the shares quoted on the exchange.[1] The market capitalisation of the largest of the groups, the Anglo American-De Beers Group (hereafter referred to as "Anglo"), amounted to 38% of the JSE in June 1993. And the Anglo-American Corporation itself, which is the most important company in the Anglo group, estimated in its 1994 annual report that the companies controlled by it produce about 7% of South Africa's GDP.

In addition to their size, another distinguishing feature of the groups is the diversity of their holdings. For example, although Anglo-American is known as a "mining house" (to reflect the fact that a majority of its assets are in the mining sector—primarily in gold, diamonds, coal, and platinum), almost half the company's assets are in sectors outside of mining, such as banking, insurance, and widely diversified industry. Or consider the Rembrandt group, the second largest in South Africa, with effective control of over 14% of the JSE. Besides Rembrandt's two core interests, cigarettes and banking, the group also has an important investment in mining in the form of a controlling stake in the mining house, Goldfields Ltd. (Anglo also, incidentally, has a 26% (non-controlling) shareholding in Goldfields.)

The next two largest groups are those associated with South Africa's two largest life insurance companies, Sanlam and Old Mutual, which account for 11% and 12% of the JSE, respectively. Both are mutual organisations, and thus they are owned not by shareholders, but by the holders of their insurance policies. In addition to its interests in insurance and financial services, the Sanlam group owns a large stake in the mining house Gencor Ltd. The Old Mutual is the most important shareholder in some

*The paper draws heavily on the ongoing research programme at the University of Cape Town on Corporate Structure and Control. The research is supported by the Chairmans Fund of the Anglo-American and De Beers Corporation for whose support we are most grateful but who bear absolutely no responsibility for the analysis or conclusions reached. The authors would also like to thank the editor for many excellent suggestions and probing questions that have improved the text a great deal.

1. See R. McGregor, *McGregor's Who Owns Whom: The Investors Handbook*, 10th Edition (Johannesburg: Juta & Co, 1991).

important industrial companies, including the conglomerate Barlows (which was recently broken up).

Another important grouping, valued at about 5% of the JSE, is that of Liberty Life Insurance Company, South Africa's third largest life insurer. Liberty Life has strategic, though not full controlling, interests in Standard Bank (until recently, South Africa's largest bank), in South African Breweries (SAB), widely regarded as South Africa's most successful industrial enterprise, and in the Premier group of industrial companies. SAB is controlled by another holding company, Bevcon, in which Liberty has a large shareholding. But, reflecting the extent of cross-ownership in South Africa, ultimate control over SAB rests with Anglo-American (by virtue of one of its holding companies' interests in Bevcon).

The smallest of the six large South African groups is Anglovaal. Anglovaal is also listed as a mining house, even though a majority of the assets of the group are in diversified industry. In addition to the six large groups, the JSE lists a numerous smaller groups. Indeed, new groups are continuously emerging from successful, usually family-controlled, operating companies, most of which are already listed.[2]

In sum, the corporate ownership structure that has come to dominate South Africa is quite different from the proportional ownership (or "one-share, one-vote") arrangements that prevail in other national economies such as the U.S. and the U.K. In this paper, we explain not only why the group structure has arisen in South Africa, but also why it may represent an efficient solution to a problem encountered by all national economies—namely, how to enable controllers of an enterprise to finance new growth without surrendering control. In the U.S., for example, the opportunity to issue low- or non-voting shares (which has been strongly discouraged in South Africa) provides founders with such opportunities. And LBO partnerships such as KKR have achieved, with limited equity, similarly concentrated control over a diverse group of companies by virtue of their ability to raise substantial debt funding from institutional investors. Toward the end of the paper, we also present some evidence from South African stock returns to support our argument that the pyramid structure may well be an economically efficient system of corporate governance—one that serves the interests of *all* shareholders.

SEPARATION OF CONTROL AND OWNERSHIP

As noted, there are two key features of the South African groups that dominate the listings on the JSE. First, the shareholders in the parent company of the group have a stake in a diversified portfolio of operating companies. Second, the ownership and control of the group's parent companies and its principal operating companies are separate in the sense that control rests with a very small minority of shareholders. The vast majority of shareholders in the group operating subsidiaries, although owners, are thus non-controlling shareholders. That is, although each listed subsidiary or associated company of the group has its own independent set of shareholders, control is exercised by those shareholders who control the parent company and its principal operating companies.

In most large groups, moreover, the controlling shareholders are still members of the family that founded the enterprise that constitutes the operating core of the group. They have used the methods just described to accomplish their goal of diversifying their own wealth across different sectors of the economy (and in many cases around the world), while maintaining control over the group. Thus, the Oppenheimers continue to control the Anglo group, the Ruperts control the Rembrandt group, Donald Gordon controls the Liberty alliance with Standard Bank, and the Menells and Hersovs control Anglovaal. Such families control their respective groups with relatively small percentage ownership claims—generally less than 10% of the underlying assets and, hence, less than a 10% claim on the dividends generated by their groups.[3]

The two other large groups—those controlled by the Old Mutual and Sanlam—are different in character. In their case, there is no founding family interest and the sheer size of the funds under their management enables them to achieve the benefits of diversification and control without the same dilution of ownership. They typically exercise shareholder control with significantly larger stakes in the operating companies associated with their groups than is either possible or desirable for the family-controlled groups. Old Mutual and Sanlam in fact tend to control group companies by the conventional method of owning close to 50% of the shares. Their sheer

2. Ibid.

3. Ibid.

financial muscle enables them to control companies; by contrast, the group families must rely on layers of holding companies if they wish to diversify and yet retain control.[4]

Institutional shareholdings in South Africa, of which the Old Mutual and Sanlam comprise the largest part (with about 50% of all institutional assets between them), have become the overwhelmingly dominant shareholding in South Africa.[5] Paradoxically, were it not for the holding companies and pyramid structures that allow tight control by the groups, the large institutions would be effective owners and controllers of much more of the South African economy. It is the voluntary participation of the institutions in a corporate governance system of control without concomitant majority ownership that is the distinctive feature of the South African corporate landscape. No important capital-raising exercise by South African corporations can hope to succeed without institutional support, even though such capital contributions rarely confer institutional control.

ESTABLISHING SOME GENERAL PRINCIPLES

Some Essential Trade-offs

There are two obvious reasons why the founding owner and manager of a firm may want to share the rewards and risks of the enterprise with outside partners or shareholders. The first is that, by attracting outside capital, the firm can expand more rapidly than otherwise. If economies of scale are realised, the enterprise will be larger and more profitable than in the absence of outside funding, and the founder's return on investment and wealth will be greater.

The second, less widely recognised, reason for founders to sell additional shares and reduce their original stake in the enterprise is to diversify their portfolios of holdings. The proceeds of the sales of shares in the firm can be used to reduce the debt of the firm or to finance investments in activities unrelated to the core business of the firm. Acquisition of a business that is not closely associated with the core business will clearly create a less specialised

enterprise and hence a more diversified shareholding for the founder.

Thus, diversification by the founder might be pursued either inside or outside the firm, depending on the preferences of the founder and the constraints that will be revealed in the terms obtained for the newly issued or exchanged shares. In the U.S. and the U.K., of course, corporate diversification has come under strong attack from shareholder activists and corporate raiders. And the fact that any diversification strategy pursued by a company, while still under the effective control of the founding owner, may reduce the returns available to the non-controlling (or "outside") shareholders is one of the risks of investing in such companies. To the extent the outside shareholders already have well-diversificd portfolios of their own, *they* are likely to prefer, all other things equal, that the firm remain highly specialised. But the founder may prefer otherwise; and if the capital required for expansion is to be raised, some compromise or trade-off between the insiders and outsiders will have to be reached.

Of course, there is a great variety of other ways that an owner-manager and controlling shareholder can disappoint outside shareholders. Potential conflicts of interest abound, not least of which relate to the benefits in cash and kind that the controlling shareholder may be awarded for management services. Another conflict may occur over the issue of who is to succeed the founder as ultimate controller. The possibility of such conflicts will be recognised by potential outside investors; indeed, the probability of such conflicts arising, and the expected costs associated with resolving them, will partly determine the price at which outside capital is obtained.

Thus, the mere possibility that the controlling shareholder and owner-manager will act against the interests of non-controlling suppliers of capital inevitably forces the owner to make some compromises or trade-offs for absolute power in exchange for capital. Minority shareholders usually have some protective rights written into company law; and providers of debt finance, who are particularly vulnerable to exploitation by shareholders, typically use debt covenants to achieve some control over

4. The structure of corporate ownership and control in South Africa has been most carefully analyzed by Jos Gerson in "The Determinants of Corporate Ownership and Control in South Africa," University of California, Los Angeles, unpublished Ph.D. thesis (1992).

5. The reason for such institutional dominance has everything to do with the highly favorable tax treatment of designated contributions to retirement funds

managed by institutional asset managers. See Graham Barr and Brian Kantor, "The Changing Pattern of Savings in South Africa 1970-1991," *Studies in Economics and Econometrics*, 18 (1994a), 3:59-76.

how their money is used. Debtholders also often attempt to secure their loans. And some debtholders—notably, the very large German banks and Japanese "main" banks, and the limited partners in U.S. LBO partnerships such as KKR and Forstmann Little—seek the additional protection that comes with having equity as well as debt claims. Such "hybrid" investing techniques give outsiders the legal authority to watch over their capital more effectively.[6]

Most businesses that remain small and owner-managed choose to do so for reasons other than the lack of entrepreneurial skills of their founders. A more serious limiting factor is often their inability to raise extra outside capital on favorable terms because they are unable to inspire the required trust in potential outside suppliers of capital. In economists' language, the "agency costs" and "information costs" of raising outside capital are simply too high for most owner-managed businesses.

Diluting Voting Powers

The power to manage the affairs of a company in a way that any individual shareholder or group of shareholders might wish clearly increases with the percentage of votes commanded. But, in most countries, the power to cast 50% or more of the votes at the important meetings of the company will mean effective control. Effective control may be defined as the legal power to appoint the board of directors, who in turn appoint the senior management to run the company in some agreed-upon fashion. A 50% majority is usually more than sufficient for this purpose; and, depending on the cohesion of the other voters, a smaller share of the votes cast may be enough in most circumstances to control appointments to the board of directors and hence crucial business decisions.

The standard presumption in the U.S. and U.K corporate governance systems is that ownership entitles the shareholder to proportional representation.[7] This presumption reflects the reality that, in the vast majority of American and English companies, one share commands one vote. But one share does not always and everywhere translate directly into one vote. An entitlement to a proportion of the cash distributed by the company may not mean the same proportion of votes; and, in this sense, ownership may not confer control. If regulations do not prohibit such arrangements, shares may command less than one vote or no vote at all.

Thus, while more or less appropriate for the U.S., Britain, and Australia, the rule of one share-one vote does not apply to a number of other national economies where small groups of shareholders with relatively low-percentage (though large-dollar) claims to ownership often exercise effective control. Such powers are typically gained through the issuance of low-voting or non-voting stock. Low-voting shares are widely used in countries such as Sweden, Denmark, Finland, and Switzerland. Some use of limited voting shares is also made in the U.S., but their use (as we discuss below) has long been viewed with suspicion and therefore been constrained by law and regulation.

The Economic Equivalence of Pyramid Companies and Limited Voting Stock. In South Africa, laws prohibit the issuance of non-voting shares and, until quite recently, JSE regulations strongly discouraged the issue of *low*-voting shares.[8] But where the law forbids such arrangements, the same end can be achieved with legal devices such as holding companies or pyramids. Such arrangements are commonplace not only in South Africa, but also in Belgium, France, Italy, Hong Kong, Canada, and Korea (and they were popular in pre-War Japan). In some cases, notably Sweden, both holding companies and low-voting shares are permitted.[9]

A holding company is one whose assets *include* shares in another company. A pyramid company may be defined as one whose *only* asset is shares in another company for the purposes of exercising control. If the holding company owns 50% or more of this other company, it can exercise full control over its subsidiary company. Thus, a shareholder with 50% of the votes in a holding company that owns 50% of another company has effective control of both. Control of the second, or subsidiary, firm can

6. For an account of the financial structure of LBO partnerships, and their similarity to Japanese "main" banks, see Michael Jensen, "LBOs, Active Investors, and the Privatization of Bankruptcy," *Journal of Applied Corporate Finance*, Vol. 2 No. 1 (Spring 1989).

7. As exemplified by Harold Demsetz and Kenneth Lehn, "The Structure of Corporate Ownership: Causes And Consequences," *Journal of Political Economy*, 93 (December, 1985), 1155-1177.

8. Such policies were changed in 1995 and new shares of low-voting or so-called "N" shares are now being listed.

9. See C. Bergstrom and K. Rydqvist, "The Determinants of Corporate Ownership: an Empirical Study on Swedish Data," *Journal Of Banking and Finance*, 14 (August, 1990), 255-269.

be exercised with 50% of 50%, or just 25%, of the claims to the cash distributed by the subsidiary.

This process by which ownership is separated from control can technically be repeated many times, with a large number of layers of holding companies formed specifically for the purposes of maintaining control while reducing the claims to ownership. The end result could be made identical to the outcome had the controllers of the parent company instead been able to raise extra capital by issuing additional low-voting or non-voting shares.

Besides limited voting shares and pyramid companies, there are other alternatives for effecting control without proportional ownership. In Germany, the large clearing banks are said to play a key corporate monitoring role as suppliers of equity as well as debt capital, and as trustees for many other shareholders. Japanese "main banks" appear to play a similar corporate surveillance role over group-like structures called keiretsu.[10] And, in the U.S., as noted, LBO partnerships like KKR and Forstmann Little control large asset holdings across a wide range of industries by using large amounts of debt supplied by institutional investors. Or, for an even more recent example, consider the Spielberg Katzenberg Dreamworld venture, in which the founders have succeeded in attracting broad institutional investor participation while retaining a controlling minority equity stake.

Law Not Economics

Given, then, the advantages in some cases of allowing founders of enterprises to retain control (together with their often strong preference to do so), one can argue that the forces that encourage such founders to cede control when they raise capital from outsiders are not necessarily economic, but rather legal or regulatory ones. It is important to recognise, for example, that the present system of corporate governance in the U.S., Britain, and Australia has been deeply influenced by longstanding policies that have promoted the principle of one share-one vote.[11] In 1926, the New York Stock Exchange prohibited the issue of dual-class common stock with different voting rights—a policy that was not relaxed until 1986. The American Stock Exchange appeared to be more sympathetic to firms with multiple classes of voting stock, though use of such provisions was fairly limited until 1980.[12] Pyramid holding companies, which were once prominent in the American utilities industry,[13] were outlawed by the Public Utility Holding Company Act of 1935. In addition, the taxation of dividend flows between legally separate companies in the U.S. has largely prevented the formation of holding companies. In Britain, the issuance of non-voting shares was prohibited in 1948 by an amendment of the Companies Act, and the London Stock Exchange refuses to list holding companies whose main assets are a controlling shareholding in another listed company.

More recently, however, the U.S. attitude toward limited voting shares appears to have shifted toward greater tolerance. In the early 1980s, there was extraordinary growth in the number of dual-class shares trading on the American Stock Exchange—a development that can be explained largely as a defensive response by top managements threatened by the prospect of takeover.[14] The New York Stock Exchange responded to this new form of competition by abandoning the one-share, one-vote rule it established in 1926. Such a change, however, required SEC approval. And, after much debate, the SEC finally proposed a rule (Rule 19c-4) that allows *the issuance* of new low-voting or non-voting stock, but prohibits *exchange offers* to replace outstanding voting shares with limited voting shares (because such offers are felt to be potentially "coercive").[15]

The SEC's ruling is of interest here because it recognises that there are legitimate reasons for

10. See A.Horiuchi, F. Packer, and S. Fukuda, "What Role Has the "Main Bank" Played in Japan?" *Journal of International and Japanese Economies*, 2 (1988), 160-180.

11. As Bernard Black has commented, *"Scholars increasingly recognise that the large American public corporation, with its strong managers and weak, dispersed shareholders, may have evolved not because it is efficient, but in response to this web of state and federal rules that constrains institutional investors. In other countries institutional investors face fewer obstacles to oversight and are far more active than they are here."* (Bernard Black, "Next Steps in Corporate Governance Reform: 13(d) Rules and Control Person Liability," *Journal of Applied Corporate Finance*, Vol. 5 No. 4 (1993):49-55.)

12. See Ronald J. Gilson, "The SEC's Response to the One-Share One-Vote Controversy," *Journal of Applied Corporate Finance*, Vol. 5, No. 4 (1993): 37-43.

13. See A. Berle and G. Means, *The Modern Corporation and Private Property* (New York: Commerce Clearing House, 1932.)

14. The ban on exchange offers is based on the SEC's concern about biases in the shareholder voting process—particularly, the pressures on large institutional funds to vote with management on proposals. There is no such concern for investors when companies issue new low-voting shares. For an explanation and defense of this ruling, see Gilson (1993), cited earlier.

15. The New York Stock Exchange, however (with some prodding from the Business Roundtable), opposed the SEC's ruling. And the NYSE's opposition was reinforced by a Federal Court of Appeals' ruling that the SEC lacked the statutory authority to impose Rule 19c-4. See Gilson (1993),cited earlier.

Given the advantages in some cases of allowing founders of enterprises to retain control, one can argue that the forces that encourage such founders to cede control when they raise capital from outsiders are not necessarily economic, but rather legal or regulatory ones.

issuing low-voting shares. The ban on exchange offers reflects the SEC's concern that low-voting shares can be used by incumbent management to disenfranchise shareholders by blocking value-adding changes in control. At the same time, the SEC ruling acknowledges the economic reality that controlling shareholders of a company typically *issue* low-voting shares to finance a worthwhile expansion without diluting their own control, and that they are able to do so *with the full agreement of the non-controlling shareholders*.

Reinforcing this argument, many countries have no restrictions on issuing low- or non-voting shares; and, in such cases, differential voting shares tend to be widely used. Moreover, countries *with* restrictions on low-voting shares seldom have restrictions on the exercise of controlling power through holding companies. And, provided inter-company dividend flows are not subject to taxation, large diversified companies may well prefer to work partly through legally separate, wholly- or partly-owned subsidiaries, rather than through divisions of a larger conglomerate. Even in countries with listing restrictions on both non-voting shares and holding companies (such as the U.S. and U.K.), firms can circumvent such constraints simply by choosing not to list. As noted earlier, the highly successful LBO partnerships like KKR represent a form of corporate organisation that is strikingly similar to that of the South African groups.[16]

In sum, a 50% voting rule for control purposes is not the barrier to maintaining absolute control it may appear to be. Control can be maintained by a small minority of shareholders and separated from ownership, *provided the suppliers of capital are willing to buy what are implicitly or explicitly non-voting or low-voting shares*. Outside investors are clearly prepared, at a price, to trust and in fact to encourage the minority controllers to exercise control on behalf of all shareholders.

BACK TO SOUTH AFRICA: FIRST SIGNS OF "UNBUNDLING"?

In South Africa, there have been important preliminary moves toward deconglomeration by the Old Mutual and Sanlam and, more recently still, by

JCI. For example, Gencor, the mining house controlled by Sanlam, recently spun off some of its industrial subsidiaries to its shareholders to become a much more highly specialised mining house. In the process, a number of the holding companies that were formed to help Sanlam secure control of Gencor were eliminated. At roughly the same time, the Old Mutual announced its decision to split up the conglomerate Barlows into three constituent parts, of which the original but reduced Barlows remains one. (Even with such "unbundling," however, Sanlam continues to be by far the largest individual shareholder in both Gencor and its unbundled parts, with a holding of around 30%. And the Old Mutual remains in effective control of Barlows and the two new independent companies, with about a 30% direct shareholding in each.)

But, at the same time these two large mutuals were unbundling, Liberty Life took a step in precisely the opposite direction. Liberty recently created a new subsidiary, Libsil, which represents the insertion of yet another layer between the shareholders who control Liberty Life through the holding companies Libhold and Libvest, and the operating companies controlled by the latter companies. Prospective shareholders in the new Libsil were offered a share in a combination of operating companies that have little in common other than their connection with Liberty Life. The formation of Libsil was designed to enable the controlling shareholder, Donald Gordon, the founder of Liberty Life, to reduce his stake in these operating companies without reducing his controlling position in them.

The initial offering by Liberty Life, both to its own and to outside shareholders, was for a 20% stake in Libsil. It is instructive to note that the initial stake in Libsil was offered, first to general shareholders of Liberty Life, and then to other outsiders, at a discount of 10% to the underlying value of the assets to be owned by Libsil. Selling shares at such a discount is clearly part of the price Donald Gordon is prepared to pay for implementing a financial structure that furthers his goal of control with increased diversification.

In the future, the 80% Liberty Life stake in Libsil will almost certainly be reduced further until the crucial 50% level is approached. At this point, no

---

16. The U.S. LBO market is an extension of the U.S. venture capital market. The functions performed by the leading group controllers in South Africa seem to parallel closely the role of the leaders in the venture capital market. See Michael Jensen, "LBOs, Active Investors, and the Privatization of Bankruptcy," *Journal of Applied Corporate Finance* (1989), cited earlier.

doubt, consideration will be given to establishing yet another holding company for the purposes of maintaining Liberty Life's control over Libsil while further reducing Liberty Life's ownership of the operating companies. In this fashion, layer upon layer is added to the pyramid; at each stage control is maintained but percentage ownership of the operating companies is decreased and hence diversification increased.

The Trade-off Examined More Closely

The essence of this process of concentrating control while diffusing ownership claims is that the founding entrepreneurs are able to attract outside share capital, on favorable enough terms to themselves and their partners, without conceding control. What made this arrangement attractive to Liberty Life shareholders in the Libsil case was the 10% discount to the underlying value of the assets. For outside shareholders—those investors who come over time to supply the great bulk of group equity capital by volunteering their own funds—this means entering into a one-share, one-vote relationship only in the most narrow legal sense. They do so, however, at a price acceptable both to them and to their controlling partners who end up with a reduced stake in the enterprises.

Rather than merely acquiescing in what is not a one-share, one-vote equal relationship, outside shareholders may in fact be enthusiastic about the benefits they expect to receive from the controls that will continue to be exercised by the founding owners over the managers of the various operating companies. The opportunity to ride along with the founder comes with a price, however. The price is that the diversification strategy will be designed primarily to satisfy the controlling interests and not the interests of the majority of shareholders.

In effect, the near-silent majority of shareholders trade off their power to control the structure of the companies they own for the benefits of the controls and entrepreneurship that they believe will

continue to be exercised on behalf of all shareholders by the controllers. The ordinary non-controlling shareholder is generally able to diversify quite adequately through the share market. In choosing to go with the portfolio of a minority controlled group, outside shareholders may well be regarding the ability of the founding fathers to create value for them as adequate compensation for what might be regarded by some investors as needless duplication of their own ability to diversify.

MEASURING THE PERFORMANCE OF THE SOUTH AFRICAN MINING HOUSES

There are two principal objections raised against the South African group structure. First is what may be described as the *anti-trust* case; namely, the charge that the groups represent an unhealthy concentration of economic power and that the existence of large groups reduces competition in the market for goods and factors of production. The second thrust of the criticism is against the *conglomerate* nature of the groups which, it is argued, reduces their value to shareholders.[17]

In the remainder of this paper, we confine ourselves mainly to responding to the second objection: namely, the tendency of conglomerates (at least in the U.S. and elsewhere outside South Africa) to produce substandard performance. Because advocates of unbundling have directed so much of their criticism at the South African "mining finance houses,"[18] we began by examining the long-run stock price performance of the five largest South African mining houses: Anglo-American, JCI (owned and controlled by Anglo-American); Gencor (part of the Sanlam group); Goldfields (with Rembrandt its most important shareholder); and Anglovaal (which, as in the case of Anglo-American, is both a mining house and the parent company of its group). Each of these mining houses are group-like structures in and of themselves; and, through their diversified holdings, they in turn exercise control

---

17. It is important to recognize that while the parent company holds a conglomeration of different interests on behalf of its shareholders, other companies in the group will have a different though sometimes common set of shareholders. Some of these allied companies will be conglomerates in their own right. A conglomerate is perhaps most accurately defined as a company with diversified operations and a common group of shareholders. A group therefore is not strictly speaking a conglomerate.

18. Such criticism can be traced, in large part, to the fact that the mining houses, alone among the South African parent companies, publish periodic estimates of their own Net Asset Values and that the market values of the mining houses

generally trade at significant discounts to these NAVs. Although advocates of unbundling interpret such discounts as indications of the potential gains from unbundling, the discounts themselves are misleading because the NAVs include not only the market value of the listed investments held by the house, but the director's updated valuation of the unlisted investments held by the house. In short, the critics' use of such NAVs involves a comparison of apples and oranges.

For an explanation of these NAVs and their misinterpretation by advocates of unbundling, see Graham Barr and Brian Kantor, "The Discount to Net Asset Value, Unbundling and Shareholder Interests," *De Ratione*, 8 (1994b), 1: 44-59

Over the period January 1989 to June 1993, the mining houses appear to have
created significant shareholder value over and above the values of their
listed holdings.

TABLE 1 AVERAGE RETURN AND VARIABILITY FROM VARIOUS JSE INDICES JANUARY 1971-DECEMBER 1992	Jan71-Dec80		Jan81-Dec92	
	Average	St.Dev.	Average	St.Dev.
Returns from All Share Index	19.31	25.05	18.75	24.42
Returns from Mining Finance Index	19.15	33.24	17.93	29.63
Returns from Industrial Index	16.91	24.56	21.18	20.29
Returns from Mining House Index	16.98	32.84	18.81	31.43
Returns from All Gold	27.84	38.08	10.84	33.87
Banker's Acceptance Rate	7.69	2.13	14.95	3.60
RSA Long Term Rate (15yr+)	9.44	1.09	15.34	1.62
Consumer Price Index	10.04	2.63	13.40	2.12

*Annualized percentage basis. Returns on the indices are calculated as ex-post Log returns i.e. RX = 100*Log(X/X(–12))
+ DYX, where: X is the index, X(–12) is the index lagged 12 months, DYX the dividend yield on the Index; RX is then
the ex-post Total Return.

over smaller groups of allied firms, each with its own set of shareholders.

As shown in Table 1, Anglo-American and the other four leading mining houses have in fact served their shareholders exceptionally well over the past 20 years. For example, over the period 1971 through 1980, shareholders in the mining houses earned an average return of 17% per annum (which, although some 230 basis points lower than the All Share Index, was about 700 basis points higher than the average annual increase in the South African CPI over the same period). During the period 1981 through 1992, the average return was almost 19% (slightly higher than that of the All Share Index and about 550 basis points higher than the average rate of inflation).

These returns to shareholders of the mining houses, being diversified to the degree they are, are largely representative of the share market as a whole. Nevertheless, as the standard deviations of the returns suggest, mining house shares are more risky than industrial and financial shares (though less risky than a portfolio of gold shares). When real gold and commodity prices have moved in their favor, the mining houses—as one would expect—have provided higher returns than industrial shares or the market as a whole. But, when the commodity price trends have moved against mining houses, the returns have fallen below those of the broad market. This, of course, is the meaning of higher risk.[19]

MEASURING THE PERFORMANCE OF THE LISTED PORTFOLIOS OF MINING HOUSES

We next compared the returns to shareholders of the mining house to the returns available to an individual investor who held all the same underlying listed shares in the same proportions as the mining house. The issue tested here is whether shareholders, acting on their own and forming the equivalent of an investment trust with the similar proportions of listed assets, would have done better without the parent company. The difference between the returns from such a simulated investment trust and the returns from an investment in the parent mining finance house can be viewed as the contribution to shareholders by the head office.

As shown in Table 2, over the period January 1989 to June 1993, the houses without exception provided significantly higher returns—though with somewhat higher risk—when compared to the returns available to an individual investor holding the exactly the same listed investments in the same proportions, independently of the controlling house.[20] During the periods examined, the houses appear to have created significant shareholder value over and above the values of their listed holdings. Viewed in light of this evidence, the houses seem not to have been a burden to their shareholders, and thus the case for unbundling the mining houses

19. Whether the returns of the mining houses reported in Table 1 were sufficient to compensate investors for the added risk of the shares is another question—one that cannot be answered just from these 20 years of data.

20. The portfolios of the respective houses are as indicated in "The Mining Finance, Earnings & N.A.V Review," first compiled by William Bowler for Fergusson Bros., Hall,Stewart & Co.Inc., in October 1988. Thus the returns from

an investor in Anglo American are compared to the returns from a portfolio that combined De Beers (with a weighting of 19%) Minorco (18%) Amgold (18%) Other Gold, as represented by the All Gold Index (22%), JCI (8%), Amic (8%), and Rustenburg (7%). These listed assets accounted for 73% of the Anglo portfolio of the time and so the weights for the simulation exercise were scaled up proportionately to the levels indicated in the table.

TABLE 2	Mining House		Portfolio of Listed Assets	
COMPARISON OF MINING HOUSE RETURN WITH THE RETURN OF A PORTFOLIO	Avg. Ret.(%)	Std.Dev.(%)	Avg. Ret.(%)	Std.Dev. (%)
OF ITS COMPONENT SHARES IN THE — Anglo	14.85	31.50	6.02	25.00
PROPORTIONS HELD AT — AngloVaal	22.32	23.70	15.54	16.70
JANUARY 1989 — Gencor	10.20	25.64	1.78	20.22
JANUARY 1989-JUNE 1993 — GFSA	5.46	30.24	−0.17	27.52
— JCI	19.62	27.37	8.31	26.11

in the interests of its shareholders is not at all apparent.[21]

THE PRINCIPAL-AGENT PROBLEM AND THE CONSTRAINTS ON THE CONTROLLING SHAREHOLDER: ESTABLISHING SOME TESTABLE HYPOTHESES

Where the controllers of a corporation have succeeded in retaining a majority of the votes despite having less than a simple majority of the ownership claims, there is no possibility of separate control by managers. The managers may of course have all the appearance of independence, and wide powers may be delegated to them; and if the corporation performs up to expectations, there would be no need for the controlling shareholders to interfere. It is when the management fails to live up to expectations that the ultimate authority of the controlling shareholders will be exercised. Within a South African group, the removal from office of an unsatisfactory chief operating officer and team is a simple task; there are no proxy or takeover battles required.

The hostile takeover, however, is also rendered impossible in the South African corporate governance system, and thus one set of potential principal-agent problems is substituted for another. While controlling shareholders have the absolute power to appoint and dismiss managers and to hold them accountable, there is no guarantee that the controlling shareholders will not abuse their power to promote their own interests at the expense of the majority of non-controlling shareholders. Thus, in order to dilute their ownership claims by issuing

shares at all levels of the group structure and still retain control, the controllers have to be able to satisfy prospective investors that they are unlikely to abuse the powers vested in them.

To devise tests of these arguments, we began by identifying a number of key variables that determine the attractiveness of group companies to voteless outside investors, and we then found empirical "proxies" for these variables in the South African context. After so doing, we next attempted to measure the explanatory power of each of these variables in determining the percentage ownership (i.e., claims to dividends) of the controller for a large representative sample of South African listed industrial corporations.[22] The less attractive a company's shares to outsiders, we reasoned, the larger percentage ownership the controller would be forced to retain.

The key variables we identified were as follows:

Reputation. The controlling shareholder must enjoy a reputation for integrity as well as management competence.[23] Such a reputation will be revealed by the track record of the controller. We predict therefore that, in an environment where holding companies are not discouraged or differential voting shares are permitted, *the greater the reputation of the controlling shareholder, the lower will be the observed percentage claim to dividends from the operating companies under control.*

Since reputation cannot be observed directly, we selected two proxies for it. The first was the controlling shareholder's wealth as listed on the JSE. (The wealth of the controller would have been a better proxy, but that, of course, is unknown, except perhaps to the tax authorities.) Our second proxy for

---

21. A full analysis of the mining finance house and the discounts to net asset value under which they trade has been presented by Barr and Kantor (1994b), cited earlier.

22. Establishing the ownership claims of the controlling shareholder for each company (in many cases one or other of the leading groups discussed above) meant a careful dissection of the patterns of holding companies and cross holdings. See Gerson (1992), cited earlier.

23. We have been struck by the importance of reputation effects in the U.S. venture capital market. The role of the leaders in the venture capital market seems to parallel closely the functions performed by the leading group controllers in South Africa. See C.B. Barry, C.J. Muscarella, J.W. Peavy, and M.R. Vetsuypens, "The Role of Venture Capital in the Creation of Public Companies: Evidence from the Going-public Process," *Journal of Financial Economics,* 27 (1990):447-472.

To dilute their ownership claims by issuing shares at all levels of the group structure and still retain control, the controlling shareholders have to be able to satisfy prospective investors that they are unlikely to abuse the powers vested in them.

reputation was the price/earnings multiples of the companies under control. Our hypothesis is that, *the higher the observed average P/E ratios of the companies under control, the lower the ownership claims of the controlling shareholder.*

Exposure. The amount of the controllers' personal wealth actually invested in the companies under control also reveals the exposure of the controller to the risks of failure of the companies under control. Obviously from the outside shareholders' perspective, the more the controller has to lose, the better the protection provided against poor management or decisions biased in favor of the controller.

Relative Income. To resolve any agency conflicts, it is clear that the controller's equity should dwarf any remuneration received as a director or manager. This helps to align the controller's incentives with those of the outside shareholders. Since CEO compensation in South Africa tends to reach a maximum limit of less than $1 million (which is quite low by U.S. standards), whereas income from shares is simply proportional to the value of the shareholding and thus has no limit, the value of the controller's shareholding (in other words, his listed wealth) can be used as a proxy for the fulfilment of the "relative income" condition. To meet this condition, the controller requires a very substantial equity stake. Only the wealthiest families are likely to possess the requisite wealth; professional managers, by contrast, are unlikely to possess such a stake in the company.

Wealth. Besides the three variables cited above, group wealth was also included as a key independent variable because it was considered to be both a proxy for the controlling group's past reputation and for its ratio of share income to managerial income. Wealth was calculated as the value of all JSE shares owned by each dominant shareholder group. Unlisted assets (those that were not even indirectly reflected in the value of listed shares) were ignored and it was assumed that wealth reflected on the Exchange would be a satisfactory proxy for total wealth. We hypothesised that the *greater is the wealth of the controlling group, the lower would be its percentage claim on dividends.*

Group P/E. The price/earnings ratio of the group ("Group P/E"), the average share price to historical earnings ratio of the companies in the sample under the control of each controlling shareholder, was included as an independent variable to serve as a proxy for its current reputation. It was hypothesized that *the higher the PE-ratio, the lower would be the percentage claim to dividends held by the controlling shareholder.*

Firm Size and Firm-Specific Risk. The other variables that were thought to be of significance in determining the stake of the controlling shareholder are firm size and firm-specific risk. Research has shown that firm size is an important determinant of the degree of concentration of ownership, with larger firms having less concentrated ownership.[24] Thus, we predicted that *for any risk averse shareholder of given personal wealth, the larger the size of the firm, the smaller the desired equity stake of the controlling shareholder.*

At the same time, however, the potential for greater control could, under certain circumstances, encourage concentration of ownership. Specifically, if a given company's earnings are characterised by a high degree of firm-specific risk, the shareholders would likely find it worthwhile to monitor management more closely.[25] In such cases, the largest single shareholder, or alliance of shareholders, would typically hold an above-average share in order to maintain tighter control over management.

Such considerations, however, apply only in a one-share, one-vote environment. If tight control can be achieved without a large stake, then the controller would, all other things being equal, want to hold a smaller stake in a more risky company. Thus, the influence of "firm-specific risk" (as measured by the variability of that part of the return from the individual company not explained by the returns from the market as a whole) on the controller's equity share is not obvious from an *a priori* standpoint.

The Findings

These various hypotheses were tested using a cross-sectional regression model for a sample of 235 majority-controlled companies from a total of 437 companies listed on the Industrial Board of the JSE. Financial data were taken from financial statements presented by these companies for fiscal years ending in either 1989 or 1990.

---

24. See Demsetz and Lehn (1985), cited earlier.   25. Ibid.

The results provided strong support for our hypothesized theories. We were able to explain about 38% of the variation in the ownership stakes of the absolute controllers (as measured by the adjusted R^2 of the regression). Such ownership stakes varied between less than 5% for the controllers of Anglo-Vaal to well over 50% for some of the typically much smaller, owner-managed corporations listed on the JSE. The coefficients for the variables *wealth, group P/E* (the controlling group's average P/E ratio) and *firm size* all proved significant with the expected sign. But the influence of *firm risk* was insignificant, which is consistent with our prior assumption of an indeterminate sign.

Foreign-owned companies typically hold a larger direct stake for control purposes, which has the effect of raising the average ownership stake. It was not considered useful to follow the chain of control offshore, and so a dummy variable was used to allow for this effect. A second dummy variable was used to allow for the influence of the two large mutual companies. Not surprisingly, when mutuals were included, their role as controllers had the statistically significant effect of increasing ownership claims.

When the foreign and mutual influences were excluded altogether, the overall adjusted R^2 declined to 0.34 without affecting the statistical significance of the other variables. Such results may be regarded as very satisfactory in themselves and broadly supportive of the underlying thesis. Nevertheless, the limitations inherent in the statistical analysis should be recognised. The regression equation captures a pattern of ownership and control that is the result of a dynamic process. The full characteristics of such a system cannot be captured with a point-in-time cross-sectional study.[26]

A CAVEAT

Some observers skeptical of the efficiency of the group system argue that capital controls have artificially inflated the stock prices of all South African companies and so contributed to the perpetuation of the current group-dominated system. When such controls are ultimately lifted, this argument runs, share prices will fall generally and increased activ-

ism by institutional shareholders will force the unbundling of the groups, much as they have helped bring about the break-up of conglomerates in the U.S. Moreover, in response to stock price evidence of the kind we have just presented, such skeptics would point to the case of Japan, where stock prices have fallen by over 50% since 1990, and where the entire corporate governance system is now being re-examined.

In response to such speculation, our discussion of corporate governance in the South African context has produced evidence of the superior *relative* performance of the parent companies of some of the groups. Indeed, we have attempted to explain the ability of some of the controllers of the groups to reduce their ownership stakes, while retaining control, *precisely as a consequence of* their superior results for shareholders. Clearly, in any long-run view, it is relative performance that must determine the structures of governance (regulations permitting).

Exchange control, to the extent it succeeds in its aim of preventing net capital outflows, would by definition mean greater demand for domestically issued securities, whether denominated in either the local or other currencies.[27] Such favorable price effects would, however, be general to all securities and not be confined in any obvious way to any one class of securities issued, for example, by the major groups. In other words, exchange control does not necessarily influence relative performance.

Before considering the possible relative security price effects of exchange control, it is useful to question the effectiveness of exchange control in South Africa or elsewhere. It is an empirical issue whether exchange control actually succeeds in its purpose of increasing the available supply of capital over time and so increasing net demands for the protected currency and for securities issued in the protected domestic capital market. Clearly, the effectiveness of exchange control cannot be taken for granted in South Africa or elsewhere.

Often what may be gained by exchange control in prohibiting certain defined and easily monitored transactions is lost in others less easily controlled. Aside from the more obvious forms of corruption, in a country as open to trade as South Africa has been

---

26. For a full explanation of the regression procedures, see Gerson (1992).

27. South Africa has applied its own version of exchange control regulations since 1961. The initial reason for these controls, which has remained their justification, was to protect the currency against capital flight encouraged by political uncertainty. The stated intention of the new government of South Africa

is gradually to remove these controls. In March 1995, as a first step, they removed the controls that had prevented non-residents from buying and selling Rand-denominated securities directly from each other. This meant the unification of what had been a dual currency system, with a commercial and financial rand trading side by side.

(where foreign trade accounts for more than 50% of GDP), there are countless opportunities to disguise capital movements as foreign trade items. Under- or over-invoicing, transfer pricing between branches, substituting dividend or interest payments for capital repayments are all means of moving savings across frontiers. The more one class of transactions is constrained, the more others are encouraged.

There is also the effect over time on the net flows of foreign investment. Exchange control may, more or less effectively, lock in an existing stock of foreign investment. But while this keeps capital from leaving, it largely prevents additional capital from coming in. Over time these net effects are likely to harm more than they help domestic security markets.

South Africa provides lots of evidence for the view that what may be gained on the swings of exchange control is lost by others on the roundabouts of exchange control evasion. After 1970, the pattern of household savings changed dramatically in favour of pension and retirement funds managed by institutions and away from banks.[28] Increases in inflation, working together with the tax code, accounted for part of this shift away from banks and mutual funds. But an additional explanation of the practical disappearance of what might be described as "discretionary" household savings were the efforts made to avoid exchange controls. Such discretionary savings were being placed with foreign banks, trusts, and mutual funds.

The South African institutions managing domestic savings enjoyed no relief from exchange control, which effectively forced them to hold only securities issued in South Africa and denominated in Rands. There was no direct way they could hedge their portfolios against currency or country risk.

South African corporations, however, were not so tightly bound by exchange control. Some had made significant foreign investments before exchange control. Many others received permission to make additional investments offshore. Such authority usually required evidence of satisfactory payback in the form of dividends received and the like. In addition, the many South African corporations that export precious metals and commodities (whose prices are denominated in dollars) were effectively protected against currency risk.

Institutional investors therefore had the opportunity to hedge their currency and country exposures by making investments on the JSE that acted as proxies for direct investments in foreign currencies or markets. The so-called pure rand hedges—companies quoted on the JSE whose assets and earnings all came from outside South Africa—found particular favor in times of political and currency uncertainty. Therefore, because of the lack of opportunity to make portfolio investments offshore, exchange control influenced relative share and other market values by encouraging demands for domestic securities that had a rand hedge quality. By the same logic, when exchange control is removed, any premium paid for rand hedges must fall away.

The issue for us is whether the exchange control system gave particular advantages to the groups themselves as compared to their more focused rivals. All the groups have significant off-shore holdings, some of which predate exchange control. For example, the offshore diamond production and distribution interests of De Beers and the 61% holding of Richemont in Rothmans, the international tobacco company, have clearly been of advantage to them. Besides its over 30% stake in the De Beers mining company, Anglo also has a major stake in Minorca, a London-based international mining house that currently generates about 10% of Anglo's reported earnings. Richemont is a Swiss-registered company that receives all of its income offshore. Barlows, Liberty, and Gencor have all built up significant offshore holdings in recent years.

The ability of South African companies generally to make successful overseas investments and manage exchange risk has represented part of the value created for their shareholders. It has also, however, been an essential component of doing business in South Africa. Thus it is difficult to see why an end to the need to manage exchange control, or exchange rate risk itself, should either harm or help group-like structures. Good shareholder control is presumably as valuable when firms are subject to exchange control as when they are free of it.

When South Africa companies and investors are freed of exchange control, domestic residents and institutional investors will have direct alternatives to the rand hedges found on the JSE and any rand hedge premium that now exists will fall away.

---

28. Barr and Kantor (1994a), cited earlier.

The South African institutional asset manager may also become less important as foreign investors are attracted to the market and South African wealth is repatriated. These investors will tend to seek what South African-domiciled savers will try and avoid—namely, South African-specific risk. The net weight exercised by the different investor constituencies will in turn influence relative values on the capital market. South African entrepreneurs and managers will be required to respond to such shifts in values in ways that serve the interests of their shareholders. How well they do so will depend on their capabilities as managers and as the controllers of managers.

All South African corporations, including the groups, will have more freedom to diversify internationally in the absence of exchange control. The opportunity to diversify internationally is likely to encourage a more focused, less conglomerate structure for large South African corporations, including those under close control. For controlling shareholders, reducing their country risk may become a higher priority than reducing their industry-specific risk. Non-controlling shareholders may well benefit from such tendencies; that is, the trade-off of diversification they have generally been required to make in the past for participation of the controlling shareholder may turn out to be a smaller one in the future. The advantages of good control for all shareholders can certainly be exercised within a less diversified structure.

HISTORY REPEATING ITSELF

The group system in South Africa, which has its origins in the development of the South African gold fields at the turn of the century, is perhaps the central feature of South African capitalism.[29] It has survived apartheid and appears to be capable of surviving in the democratic, post-apartheid era. There was a time when Afrikaans nationalism regarded the groups with enormous hostility as rival and unfriendly sources of power that threatened the Afrikaner and his state.[30] The Afrikaner learned to live with the groups and even formed at least two powerful groups strongly identified with Afrikaners.

It now looks very much as if history is being allowed to repeat itself. A few black-African controlled groups have already made their appearance on the JSE with the encouragement of established interests. New African Investment Limited (NAIL) provides a good example. NAIL is controlled by a consortium of well-known black-African business personalities, including Dr. Nthtato Motlana (who is also a director of Anglo-American). NAIL acquired from Sanlam and others a number of somewhat diverse and listed operating companies, the most significant of which was a 30% holding in a listed life assurance company, Metlife. The finance to pay for these acquisitions was raised from the established groups and banks through share and debt issues.

Control of NAIL has been secured by means of a listed pyramided holding company, Corporate Africa Limited (Corpaf). The controlling interest in Corpaf is in turn held by an unlisted company CAI, which owns 63% of Corpaf, which holds 51% of NAIL. CAH, another unlisted company, in turn holds 79% of CAI. The major shareholder in CAH, with a 40% shareholding, is N H Motlana and Sons (Proprietary) Limited. The unlisted N H Motlana and Sons is reported as being controlled by Dr. Motlana with a 60% interest. In this way, the ultimate controller of NAIL, Dr. Motlana, exercises control over NAIL with just a 6.1% claim on the dividends.[31] This clearly is a potent form of black-African empowerment.[32] The progress of this group, and the quality of control exercised on its behalf, will be watched with great interest by the non-controlling institutional investors.

A potentially more important development has occurred very recently, with the unbundling into three parts of JCI, the mining house controlled by Anglo-American. The intention to unbundle JCI and to invite black participation was announced in March 1994. Special enabling tax legislation was passed by the South African parliament in November 1994, with the final details announced in February 1995. The three groups to be spun off from JCI are, first, Anglo American Platinum Company (Amplats), which will hold platinum and unlisted diamond interests; Amplats will continue to be controlled by Anglo-American. The second company will be a new JCI Limited; this company will hold what were the old JCI's interests

29. See T. Gregory, *Ernest Oppenheimer and the Economic Development of Southern Africa* (Oxford University Press, Cape Town, 1962).

30. See H.F. Kenney, *Power Pride and Prejudice: The Years of Afrikaner Nationalist Rule in South Africa* (Jonathan Ball, 1991).

31. $6.09\% = (.60 * .40 * .79 * .63 * .51)/100.$

32. The details of NAIL and its structure are to be found in the pre-listing prospectus issued by the holding company CAF. This may be found in Business Day, 11th October 1994.

> The opportunity to diversify internationally is likely to encourage a more focused, less conglomerate structure for large South African corporations, including those under close control. For controlling shareholders, reducing their country risk may become a higher priority than reducing their industry-specific risk.

in gold, coal, ferrochrome, and base metals, as well as 10% of Johnson Matthey PLC, a 10% holding in Amplats, and an unspecified interest in De Beers Diamond Mining Company. Black participation in this large new company with a projected net asset value of R6,4bn. ($1.8 billion) is being actively sought, and Anglo-American intends to give up its control of this company. The third company to be spun off from the original JCI, for which black control is being sought, has been named Johnnies Industrial Corporation Limited. It will hold what were JCI's interests in property, media, motor, food, beverages (including what is an effective controlling interest in SAB), and other unspecified industrial interests. This company had a net asset value of R6,9bn. (about $2 billion) at the beginning of 1995.[33]

Clearly, interest in the group structure—and more particularly in close control—will no longer be one identified only with South African whites. It is also becoming clear that, as the opportunities that such a system provides for the ANC's constituency have become apparent, its previous hostility to the group system has begun to moderate.[34]

CONCLUSION

A central problem of modern capitalism is the potential loss of control over managers and the resulting sub-optimal use of resources that can occur when the rights of ownership are widely dispersed among shareholders who lack either the knowledge or the incentive to discipline management. As we argue in this paper, concentrating

control with an influential minority of shareholders may be an answer to this problem. Nevertheless, such arrangements introduce their own kinds of agent-principal problems—problems that have to be addressed if systems of concentrated shareholder control are to survive.

It would seem that in countries where barriers to group formation are not erected by governments, such groups, or group-like structures, play an important role in the economy. The group system in South Africa that at once allows control to be concentrated and wealth to be diversified is in large measure an outcome of the competition for capital and managers. The process of group creation and development should therefore generally be tolerated rather than threatened by hostile regulation. The appropriate threats to established interests and institutional arrangements in South Africa and elsewhere should be allowed to come from financial innovations that are neither restrained nor aided by financial regulations. In practice, such interventionist regulatory initiatives tend to have some predetermined, usually politically-motivated, sense of an appropriate structure for governing corporations.

Conglomerates and groups may work for some wealth owners in some settings at some points in time. There should be no predisposition in favor or against them. The best governed corporations are those that by definition survive the "market test." The best policy is to ensure that the barriers to competition—including competition among different corporate structures and governance systems—are kept at a low level.

---

33. Details of these arrangements may be found in a statement published by JCI in the the Cape Times, February 27th, 1995.

34. To quote the ANC Economic Policy Guidelines published in 1992, "...The concentration of economic power in the hands of a few conglomerates has been detrimental to balanced economic development in South Africa. The ANC is not opposed to large firms as such. However the ANC will introduce anti-monopoly, antitrust and mergers policies in accordance with international norms and practices, to curb monopolies, continued domination of the economy by a minority within the white minority and promote greater efficiency in the private sector..." (African National Congress, Ready to Govern, Economic Policy Guidelines, Johannesburg (1992)).

■ GRAHAM BARR

is an Associate Professor with a joint post in the Departments of Economics and Statistical Science at the University of Cape Town.

■ JOS GERSON

is the Senior Economist for Davis Borkum Hare & Co. Inc., a South African stockbroker.

■ BRIAN KANTOR

is Professor of Economics at the University of Cape Town.

CORPORATE RESTRUCTURING, BUY-OUTS, AND MANAGERIAL EQUITY: THE EUROPEAN DIMENSION

*by Mike Wright and Ken Robbie,
University of Nottingham, and
Steve Thompson,
University of Manchester**

C orporate restructuring has emerged over the past decade or so as a worldwide phenomenon involving the following related elements: (1) a reconcentration of equity ownership in the hands of insiders, either managers themselves or inside investors well-placed to monitor the efforts of managers; (2) a substitution of debt for equity in the capital structure of the new entity, thus facilitating the reunification of (equity) ownership and control and imposing a binding requirement for debt servicing in lieu of the looser, more comfortable, obligation to outside stockholders; and (3) a redefinition of the organisation's boundaries, usually in the direction of greater specialization, accomplished through the voluntary divestiture of non-core activities by means of spin-offs, sales to third parties, or management buy-outs.

While some restructuring transactions have undoubtedly involved excesses—particularly those completed in the last years of the 1980s—the U.S. evidence is, on balance, highly favourable.[1] Corporate restructuring deals have created significant shareholder value, with the initial acquisition premiums typically being vindicated by subsequent improvements in performance and asset utilization. Indeed, as Michael Jensen has argued, it has been the very success of the earlier LBO deals—which in turn allowed the dealmakers to arrange transactions without committing their own capital—that encouraged overpayment in the later ones.[2]

The purpose of this article is to review the spread of corporate restructuring throughout Europe. We argue here that, although the underlying rationale for buy-outs is fundamentally the same in Europe as in the U.S., the markets for management buy-outs and associated transactions vary considerably across European economies. Such differences in turn stem from differences in the organisation of national capital markets and in the financing of industry in general. For example, the U.K. has an active market for corporate control that most closely resembles the takeover market in the U.S.; and it should thus come as no surprise that the U.K. has the highest level of MBO and takeover activity among European countries. By the same logic, buy-out activity appears at its lowest in those continental European countries where stock market control is poorly developed. These countries are also experiencing increases in the number of buy-outs, but such buy-outs are typically used to effect changes in control in family-dominated and other closely-owned private corporations.

*The authors would like to acknowledge generous financial support for the Centre for Management Buy-out Research from Barclays Development Capital Ltd and Touche Ross Corporate Finance.

1. G. Yago, "Corporate Restructuring in the US," chapter 2 in B. de Caires, M. Wright, and S. Thompson (eds.), *Corporate Restructuring, Euromoney,* 1990.

2. See Jensen's contribution (especially pp. 8-9) to "The Economic Consequences of High Leverage and Stock Market Pressures on Corporate Management: A Roundtable Discussion," *Journal of Applied Corporate Finance,* Vol. 3, No. 2, Summer, 1990, pp. 6-37.

After examining the recent development of both the U.K. and European buy-out markets, we then go on to discuss the following:
■ the contrast between the U.S. and European experiences with takeovers and MBOs of publicly traded companies;
■ the development of mezzanine finance in the U.K. and continental Europe;
■ the exit routes chosen by buy-out investors; and
■ the importance of managerial equity stakes and other control devices in improving the performance of newly bought-out companies.

MANAGEMENT BUY-OUTS IN EUROPE: VARIETY AND COMPLEXITY

The European buy-out market scarcely existed until the 1980s, and in some countries has only begun to develop in the past few years. In order to create a national market in buy-out and restructuring transactions, three main conditions must be met. First, of course, there must be sufficient buy-out opportunities, which in turn implies a supply of companies willing to sell and manager-investors willing to buy. Second, there must be a development capital and financial infrastructure capable of funding the transactions, including a legal and taxation environment that facilitates debt-financed changes in control. And third, there must be suitable exit routes for buy-out investors to "cash out" and realise their gains.

Although we take up each of these conditions later, we will simply note here that, at present, only the U.K., Ireland, France, Sweden, and the Netherlands can be considered to have reasonably well-developed markets for buy-out transactions. Some buy-out activity has also been observed in Denmark, Italy, Switzerland, Germany, Belgium and Finland, but elsewhere in Europe corporate restructuring activity is virtually unknown.[3]

According to data we have collected and analyzed at our Centre for Management Buy-out Re-search (CMBOR), the European buy-out and take-over market has been dominated by the U.K., which has experienced more restructuring activity (both in terms of numbers and value of transactions) than all other European countries combined. In 1989 (as shown in Table 1), there were 503 U.K. buy-outs and buy-ins with a total value of £7.5 billion ($15 billion). In the same year, we estimate the total comparable activity elsewhere in Europe to have been 369 transactions with a value equivalent to £3.23 billion ($6.4 billion).[4]

As shown in Figure 1, moreover, the U.K. combined buy-out and buy-in market grew throughout the 1980s. At the same time, the proportion of "buy-ins"—those transactions where the CEO of the new company is not part of the incumbent management team—relative to buy-outs rose steadily. In 1990, however, although the volume of transactions appears to have held up, the average value of the transactions—as in the U.S.—has fallen sharply, with very few deals larger than £25 million ($50 million).

Corporate Divestitures

The European markets vary not only in size, but also in the principal sources of their restructuring opportunities (see Table 2). In the U.K., for example, by far the largest proportion of deals arises from the voluntary divestiture of divisions or subsidiaries by domestic or, in a few cases, foreign-owned companies. Such divestitures in turn reflect the reality that the U.K. has long had an active takeover market that has facilitated the creation of diversified companies. The majority of divestments by such companies involve the separation of underperforming or strategically unwanted subsidiaries that have resulted from earlier merger activity.[5]

Like the U.K., the Netherlands and Sweden have many large, highly-diversified, publicly traded companies; and their corporate sectors have also exhibited high levels of divestment activity.[6] In France, Germany and Italy, by contrast, the market

3. Detailed expositions of the differences between European buyout markets are contained in B. Chiplin et al, "Management Buy-outs: The Prospects in Europe: A Ten Country Study," 3i Occasional Paper, July 1988; Initiative Europe/CMBOR, *Europe Buy-out Review*, Initiative Europe, July 1990; M. Wright, S. Thompson, B. Chiplin and K. Robbie, *Buy-outs and Buy-ins: New Strategies in Corporate Management*, Graham & Trotman, 1991.

4. For a detailed analysis of trends, see B. Chiplin, M. Wright and K. Robbie, "Management Buy-outs in 1990—Annual Review from the Centre for Management Buy-out Research," CMBOR, Nottingham, 1990.

5. In part, divestitures seem an inevitable consequence of conglomerate mergers—that is, some of the acquired businesses will prove unnecessary—but

it also reflects a more recent recognition of the difficulties of administering diversified companies. For more commentary on this point, see S. Thompson and M. Wright (eds.), *Internal Organisation, Efficiency and Profit*, Oxford, 1988. For an exposition of the similar arguments in respect of the U.S., see, for example, J. W. Kensinger and J. D. Martin, "The Quiet Restructuring," *Journal of Applied Corporate Finance*, Vol. 1, No. 1, pp. 16-25, 1988, and Amar Bhide, "Reversing Corporate Diversification," *Journal of Applied Corporate Finance*, Vol. 3, No. 2, Summer, 1990, pp. 70-81.

6. In continental Europe, unlike the U.K., the difficulties in obtaining comprehensive transaction information made it impossible to distinguish between management buy-outs and management buy-ins.

TABLE 1 ESTIMATED NUMBER OF BUY-OUTS AND BUY-INS IN EUROPE TO THE END OF 1989	Country	1987	1988	1989	Total 1980-1989
	Austria	3	5	5	15
	Belgium	4	10	12	52
	Denmark	5	20	31	63
	Finland	5	14	16	40
	France	50	100	130	430
	Germany	8	36	25	111
	Ireland	21	14	12	131
	Italy	3	10	21	52
	Netherlands	30	30	41	245
	Norway	7	8	8	29
	Spain	4	8	12	35
	Sweden	18	22	32	127
	Switzerland	2	5	24	46
	UK	434	482	503	2993

Source: CMBOR an independent Research Centre founded by Touche Ross and Barclays Development Capital at the University of Nottingham.

FIGURE 1
VALUE OF BUY-OUTS AND
BUY-INS IN UK

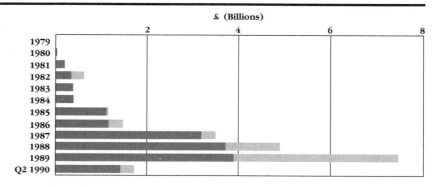

■ Buy-outs
▓ Buy-ins

TABLE 2 EUROPEAN BUY-OUT SOURCES, 1989 (% of total)		Sample	Local Div.	Foreign Div.	Family/ Private	Privat-isation	Going Private	Other	Total
	Austria	n.a.	n.a.	n.a.	n.a.	n.a.	n.a.	n.a.	100.0
	Belgium	8	37.5	50.0	12.5	-	-	-	100.0
	Denmark	29	58.6	27.5	10.3	-	3.4	-	100.0
	Finland	14	78.6	14.3	7.1	-	-	-	100.0
	France	58	20.7	10.3	44.8	3.5	15.5	5.2	100.0
	Germany	18	16.7	44.4	38.9	-	-	-	100.0
	Ireland	11	18.2	72.7	9.1	-	-	-	100.0
	Italy	18	5.6	33.3	50.0	11.1	-	-	100.0
	Netherlands	39	69.2	18.0	12.8	-	-	-	100.0
	Norway	3	66.7	33.3	-	-	-	-	100.0
	Spain	4	-	-	75.0	25.0	-	-	100.0
	Sweden	29	69.0	6.8	6.9	6.9	10.4	-	100.0
	Switzerland	21	52.4	19.1	28.5	-	-	-	100.0
	UK	350	56.0	6.8	29.7	4.3	2.6	0.6	100.0

Source: CMBOR an independent Research Centre founded by Touche Ross and Barclays Development Capital at the University of Nottingham.

for corporate control has until quite recently been almost completely dormant. Although France has recently seen its first successful hostile deals—and Germany its first hostile *attempts*—in both countries such transactions continue to be very difficult to accomplish. In France, for example, the ability to vary voting rights, the frequent existence of "loyal" (*noyau dur*) shareholders and interlocking shareholdings have tended to form an effective barrier to such transactions. In Germany, the power of managers and employees to frustrate unwelcome raiders, particularly by invoking their unusually protective employment contracts, amounts to an almost insurmountable barrier to takeover.[7]

It may also be true, however, that there is considerably less need for restructuring—or at least for one kind of restructuring—in countries like France and Germany. One consequence of having poorly developed corporate control markets is that there are few true conglomerates in the private sectors of these economies and, hence, few divestitures. Moreover, it is not only the absence of takeovers that has blocked the formation of conglomerates in Germany. Another part of the explanation has to do with the pivotal role of German commercial banks as stock owners and proxy stockholders.[8] Because German banks are well-diversified holders of corporate stocks, and thus obtain the benefits of portfolio diversification directly, they can be expected to offer far more resistance than widely dispersed shareholders to *corporate* diversification through merger.

For such reasons, then, the principal role of buy-outs in much of continental Europe has been confined to the financing of ownership transfers in the large private and family-run company sector. In France, for example, by the mid-1980s, thousands of family-run companies established in the post-war boom years found themselves with aging or infirm owner-executives. A traditional reluctance to cede control to an outsider, reinforced by the absence of an orthodox takeover market, led to specific legisla-

tion in 1984 to facilitate debt-financed transfers of control through buy-outs.[9]

Privatisations

Another important source of buy-outs in Europe has been activities chosen by state and local governments for privatisation. The level of such buy-out activity has, of course, been heavily influenced by individual countries' political commitments to privatisation as a means of restructuring industries, strengthening incentives, and improving control. Again, this activity has been at its most intense in the U.K. Between 1979 and 1990, the Conservative government of Margaret Thatcher used management buy-outs to sell off more than 100 smaller state-owned activities, particularly in transportation, shipbuilding, and metal and vehicle manufacturing.[10] A similar policy is now employed to encourage management buy-outs of locally provided services. Elsewhere in Western Europe, including France, Italy, Spain and Sweden, privatisations have tended to involve the divestment of subsidiaries from unwieldy groups and state-run holding companies.

Two present developments are likely to stimulate European restructurings in the near future. First, the momentous political changes and increased pressure for industrial efficiency in Eastern Europe have led to interest in the idea of the buy-out as a means of dealing with chronic control and incentive problems. Insofar as they replace passive state owners with active owners, buy-outs represent for many a superior alternative to various proposals for the free distribution of shares—all of which would continue to experience problems of diffuse and thus potentially ineffective ownership.[11]

As yet, however, there are severe practical difficulties in establishing who actually owns assets, in passing enabling legislation for privatisation, and in developing a financial infrastructure that, amongst other things, would include a basis for valuing assets. Another major obstacle to privatisation is the

7. See J. Franks and C. Mayer, "Capital Markets and Corporate Control: A Study of France, Germany and the U.K.," London Business School, mimeo, 1990.

8. See J. Cable, "Capital Market Information and Industrial Performance: The Role of West German Banks," *Economic Journal*, Vol. 95, 1985, pp. 118-32.

9. The specialist French buy-out legislation is outlined in C. Heuze, M. Wright, P. Dupouy, "Management Buy-outs in France," *Acquisitions Monthly—Buy-out Supplement*, November 1989.

10. See S. Thompson, M. Wright and K. Robbie, "Management Buy-outs from the Public Sector: Ownership Form and Incentive Issues," *Fiscal Studies*, August 1990, pp. 71-88.

11. The rationale for buy-outs as a key element in restructuring Eastern European firms is analysed in T. Buck and M. Wright, "Vertical Hierarchies, Soft Budgets and Employee Buyouts," *Economic Analysis and Worker Management*, forthcoming, 1990. A more sceptical view about buy-outs has been expressed in D. Lipton and J. Sachs, "Privatization in Eastern Europe: The Case of Poland," *WIDER*, Helsinki, September 1990. However, there appears to be general agreement about the need for managers and employees to have significant equity stakes in order to improve incentives and for close attention to be given to establishing clear mechanisms for corporate governance through strengthening financial institutions.

TABLE 3
BUY-OUTS OF QUOTED COMPANIES IN EUROPE*

	1985	1986	1987	1988	1989	1990 Q3
UK**	1	2	4	8	12	9
France	1	2	2	8	5	2
Sweden	-	1	-	2	2	9
Netherlands	-	-	-	1	0	-
Denmark	-	-	-	1	1	-
Switzerland	-	1	-	-	-	-

Source: CMBOR an Independent Research Centre founded by Touche Ross and Barclays Development Capital Ltd at the University of Nottingham.
*As recorded on CMBOR database
**Excluding partial buy-ins

need to disarm the perception of buy-outs as "asset-stripping" by members of the old regimes.[12] As in Western Europe, buy-outs are more likely to be experimented with in countries like Hungary, which has already taken considerable steps toward economic liberalization—and in Yugoslavia, where the relevant privatisation legislation places emphasis on this kind of transaction given the former self-management system in that country.

The other major development likely to stimulate restructuring activity in Europe is the expected creation of a Single Internal Market in 1992. In anticipation of a united Western Europe, there has been a very high level of cross-border merger and joint venture activity. And because these international link-ups tend to have high failure rates, we can predict with some confidence that many will be sold on to local management teams in subsequent years.

BUY-OUTS OF QUOTED COMPANIES

Leveraged buy-outs of publicly traded companies have been a major feature of U.S. corporate restructuring. Indeed, their success has even been viewed by some as foretelling the "eclipse of the public corporation"—at least in mature sectors of the economy.[13] In Europe, however, buy-outs of quoted companies have been much less prominent and have taken place in only six countries (see Table 3).

Hostile LBOs, moreover—or "management buy-ins" as they are called in the U.K.—are unknown to Europe outside the U.K.[14] And even the first successful hostile LBOs in the U.K. date from only as recently as 1988. Institutional shareholder support for the buy-in attempts was crucial in ensuring their success against defensive bids from incumbent management.[15] In continental Europe particularly, as noted earlier, poison pills and shark repellents have hitherto made successful hostile takeovers extremely difficult. Despite the move towards a single European market, progress in removing the barriers to a pan-European corporate control market is very slow. Although the European Community has now established merger referral guidelines and there has been some movement toward harmonising company law, individual countries still retain considerable scope for blocking what may be perceived as unwelcome takeover bids.

More common European practice has been for buy-outs of companies quoted on a stock market to involve friendly changes in ownership. In continental Europe, many quoted companies remain under family control. Buy-outs in such cases are often used to allow succession without control passing to an outsider. Moreover, the companies typically remain quoted. Several buy-outs in France have been of this kind. Buy-outs may also be a suitable means for a large shareholder to exit without destabilising the

---

12. The development of the necessary infrastructure is discussed for the case of Yugoslavia in T. Petrin, "Restructuring in Yugoslavia: The Role of Employee Buy-outs," University of Ljubljana, mimeo, 1990.

13. The arguments are eloquently set out by M. C. Jensen in "The Eclipse of the Public Corporation," *Harvard Business Review*, Sept/Oct 1989 and in "Active Investors, LBOs, and the Privatisation of Bankruptcy," *Journal of Applied Corporate Finance*, Vol. 2, No. 1, pp. 35-44, 1989. For a vigorous defense of the public corporation and a critical analysis of LBOs, see A. Rappaport, "The Staying Power of the Public Corporation," *Harvard Business Review*, Jan/Feb, 1990.

14. Even in the U.S., few LBOs are hostile; see, for example, G. Yago, "Corporate Restructuring in the US," in B. de Caires, M. Wright and S. Thompson (eds.) *Corporate Restructuring, Euromoney*, 1990.

15. Institutional support was especially in evidence in the Isosceles bid for Gateway Stores at £2.2 bn ($4bn) the largest in the U.K. to date and in that at Lowndes Queensway Stores which went into receivership in August 1990. In both of these cases, moreover, incumbent managers were widely considered to have underperformed.

Although the European Community has now established merger referral guidelines and there has been some movement toward harmonising company law, individual countries still retain considerable scope for blocking what may be perceived as unwelcomed takeover bids.

share price. And still another use for buy-outs is to provide entrepreneurs disenchanted with the stock market (or their shareholders) with the means of returning their quoted companies to private status. In such cases, in Europe as in the U.S., it is common for incumbent management already to own significant equity stakes. Examples of this practice in the U.K. include the MBOs of Virgin Group, Saga Group, and Really Useful Group.

The most controversial kind of buy-out of a quoted company has been the unforced opportunistic venture by incumbent management. Such buy-outs may be something of a double-edged sword for external shareholders. Despite evidence on both sides of the Atlantic showing that the premia to shareholders in such bids are generally above those for friendly takeovers,[16] buy-outs of quoted companies clearly hold the potential for incumbent managers to exploit inside information.

In response to this charge, however, defenders of MBOs argue that managers' inside knowledge may not necessarily be such that it could be made public or form the basis for an insider dealing strategy. Managers, for example, may believe that the company's activities could be reorganised profitably, but may be understandably reluctant to make major changes that would impose greater risks on themselves without an enlargement of their rewards. Existing shareholders, to be sure, would be better off if management made the necessary changes before the share sale takes place; but if the dispersed ownership of a public corporation creates a sufficiently intractable "free rider" problem, there may be no one with enough incentive to bring about beneficial change.

The existence of the buy-out also arguably makes it possible for the increased value to be released to the market to the benefit of current shareholders. And, to the extent a buy-out attempt does indeed signal the presence of unrealized value, it may trigger a competing bid, thus enlarging the already substantial premium to shareholders. (Such,

of course, was the outcome of the largest buy-out ever transacted—the $25 billion RJR-Nabisco deal.)

Despite such defenses of MBOs, increasing regulatory attention—especially in the U.K. but also in France—has been given to the potential for managers to engineer deals to their own advantage.[17] While a wide variety of valuation techniques may be used to arrive at objective fair value opinions, the possibility for significant gains to management in apparently short periods of time has led to such proposals as mandated auctions, retention of equity stakes, and ratcheted payment terms (i.e., "earn-outs"). In the U.K., moreover, the Takeover Panel in late 1989 issued a new set of rules governing buy-outs,[18] including the requirements that an independent adviser be appointed to the offeree board to evaluate all bids and that the information provided to prospective financiers of a buy-out be made available to all shareholders.[19]

But, as with many forms of financial market regulation, there is a danger that efforts to deal with this problem will lead to a more than offsetting loss of the benefits that such transactions bring. In particular, if the risk of failure to management rises greatly—whether from being outbid by outside purchasers or as a result of overpaying—managements may become unwilling to make a bid in the first place, thus depriving their shareholders of the possibility of significant gains. It can also be argued that rules to deal with potential abuses may militate unfairly against buy-outs compared with, say, transactions such as friendly, negotiated bids; in such cases shareholders may obtain a lower bid premium than if the company were submitted to an open auction.

FINANCING

In the U.K. and elsewhere in Europe, development capital firms have played the dominant role in the establishment of the buy-out market. Debt did not become an important source of finance in such

---

16. For a summary of the evidence in the U.S., see Y. Amihud (ed.), *Management and Leveraged Buy-outs*, (Irwin, New York, 1989), Chapter 1. For evidence on the U.K., see Wright et al, *Buy-outs and Buy-ins: New Strategies in Corporate Management*, (1990), cited in note 3.

17. In France, the Darty buy-out of 1988 attracted the attention of the *Commission d'Operations Boursiere* (COB) because of the treatment of minority shareholders.

18. See Takeover Panel, "Amendments to the Takeover Code: Management Buy-outs," The Panel on Takeovers and Mergers, 1989/27, 20 December 1989. In the U.K., this issue has also been extended to buy-outs from the public sector, with the appropriate bodies issuing guidelines; see, for example, Audit Commission, "Management Buy-outs: Public Interest or Private Gain?," Management Paper No. 6, 1990.

19. It is ironic that the deal which caused much controversy and probably provoked the introduction of the new rules, the buy-out of Magnet Group, was reputedly worth around half of the buy-out price less than one year after the transaction was completed, as a result of failing to meet profit projections.

TABLE 4
AVERAGE DEAL
STRUCTURES FOR
UK BUY-OUTS OVER
£25 MILLION*
(in £ millions)

Type of Finance	1985	1987	1988	1989	1990 Jan-June
Senior Debt	63.7	53.7	62.8	59.1	60.9
Mezzanine	3.1	8.3	6.8	18.7	10.8
Equity and Quasi-Equity	29.2	33.3	25.2	16.8	22.2
Loan Note	n.a.	n.a.	0.9	3.2	2.8
Other Forms	4.0	4.4	4.3	2.2	3.3
TOTAL	100.0	100.0	100.0	100.0	100.0
Sample Financing Value	671	2,350	2,322	2,225	608

Source: CMBOR an independent Research Centre founded by Touche Ross and Barclays Development Capital at the University of Nottingham.
*includes structures without mezzanine layers

transactions until the late 1980s, when subordinated debt was added to the traditional mezzanine layer of convertible and redeemable preference shares. In this period, debt levels in larger U.K. deals began to approach those seen in their counterparts in the U.S. (see Table 4). Deals in continental Europe also occasionally approached these levels.[20] Such a development was heavily influenced by the entry of U.S. banks. (A high yield bond market such as exists in the U.S. has yet to be established in Europe.[21])

The shift in fortune of the large end of the buy-out market in the last 18 months has been accompanied by significant changes in financing structures. After a resurgence of the senior debt element in larger buy-outs in 1988, 1989 witnessed a major growth in the use of mezzanine finance in the U.K. In 1989, 18.7% of the finance for buy-outs larger than $50 million was accounted for by mezzanine debt, almost three times the 6.8% recorded in the previous year. Correspondingly, the average percentage of equity and quasi-equity in large deals fell from 25.2% in 1988 to as little as 16.8%. In the first half of 1990, however, mezzanine finance experienced a major reversal to account for a little over 10% of the finance in larger buy-outs; and the share of equity and quasi-equity rose to over 22%.

Various factors have contributed to these changes. As the cost of debt has risen so dramatically, the *relative* cost of equity has fallen, which in turn appears to mean relatively lower discount rates and thus longer time horizons associated with equity capital. This position is reinforced both by the return to dominance in the U.K. of traditional venture and development capital firms, as well as the rise of a number of large specialist equity funds in the late 1980s (much of whose capital remains as yet to be invested). As the price earnings ratios at which deals can be completed have fallen, the acquisition premiums have been reduced. At the same time there has been a marked reluctance on the part of senior debt lenders to enter into highly leveraged deals to the same extent as seen in recent years.

While this has tended to mean continuing demand for mezzanine finance, mezzanine lenders have been reluctant to extend their positions. This reluctance stems in large part from problems with recent deals. By the same token, deal arrangers have been reluctant to use mezzanine finance because of the higher returns now required by mezzanine lenders to compensate themselves for what they perceive as increased risk. Association with the troubled U.S. junk bond market has also not helped the mezzanine market.

All these factors, then, have contributed significantly to the increased level of equity and quasi-equity seen in the first half of 1990. The proportion of finance accounted for by senior debt, however, has remained relatively constant throughout the turmoil, hovering around the 60% level in the last two and a half years.

20. See CEGOS, 'Enquete sur les Pratiques et Les Conditions de Reussite des RES en France', *CEGOS*, Paris, 1989.
21. For a very useful summary of current issues in the U.S. high yield debt market see, E. Altman, "Setting the Record Straight on Junk Bonds," *Journal of* *Applied Corporate Finance*, Vol. 3, No. 2, 1990, pp. 82-95. An exposition of the case for the development of a high yield bond market in Europe is contained in P. Molyneux, "US High Yield Debt and the Case for a European Market," *National Westminster Bank Review*, Feb, pp. 2-15, 1990.

The proportion of finance accounted for by senior debt has remained relatively constant throughout the turmoil, hovering around the 60% level in the last two and a half years.

The fluctuating importance of mezzanine finance is shown below.

Year	Number	Mezzanine Value (£m)	Total Value of Mezzanine Deals (£m)
1985	5	92.4	420.6
1986	10	104.2	503.2
1987	15	239.3	1,604.4
1988	20	172.0	1,220.8
1989	30	891.6	5,630.6
1990 Q2	11	89.2	658.8

Source: CMBOR an independent Research Centre founded by Touche Ross and Barclays Development Capital at the University of Nottingham.

Although mezzanine debt may contribute to the financing of smaller buy-outs, its main use has been in funding buy-outs with prices of at least £10 million ($20 million). The number of buy-outs in this larger category that included an element of mezzanine finance increased by 50% from 20 in 1988 to 30 in 1989. From 1988 to 1989, moreover, the value of mezzanine debt in buyouts larger than £10 million rose more than fivefold from £172 million to £892 million. In the first half of 1990, however, this trend was sharply reversed, with both numbers and values on a simple annualised basis returning to 1988 levels.[22] Mezzanine debt has been slower to develop in continental Europe principally because of the paucity of large transactions. The absence of (or at least lack of access to) accounting information of sufficient quality to establish the stability and viability of potential deals has also been an obstacle to mezzanine financing, as investors in at least one major deal subsequently discovered.[23] Nevertheless, pioneering deals have been completed in France, Germany, Sweden, and Belgium. A few domestic and cross-border European specialist mezzanine funds have also been established to add to the already significant number of specialist equity funds.[24]

These cross-border developments, along with joint ventures between institutions in different countries, reflect the anticipation of considerable restructuring opportunities by several types of institutions. U.S. commercial banks, as mentioned earlier, are also making strong bids to position themselves in Europe. At the same time, the development of local expertise in newly developed markets such as France, Denmark, and Sweden has enabled domestic players to engage in cross-border initiatives.

Such strategic moves have been conceived in part as approaches to the European Community's Single Market, with some institutions seeking to be Europe-wide leaders, and others niche players either in several countries, one country, or in a particular type of deal.[25] The full scope of these changes remains as yet to manifest itself, and will depend significantly on the future development of individual markets and on their ability to complete large transactions.

As in the U.S., large deals in the U.K. market are also now being adversely affected by variety of new regulatory factors. General economic and financial conditions in the U.K. have led to some caution amongst clearing bankers, which has been reinforced by expressions of concern by the Bank of England and the Bank for International Settlements about excessive bank exposure to highly leveraged transactions.[26] This issue has also been extended to France, the second most developed European market, where the Banking Commission has already voiced concern at exposure levels well below those of the U.S. and the U.K.

EXITS AND THE BUY-OUT LIFE CYCLE

There is currently a debate being waged on both sides of the Atlantic about the long-run economic significance of management buy-outs. Proponents argue that MBOs represent a new organisational form that will compete effectively with the corporation. Detractors claim that leveraged transactions are at best simply a means to achieve "one-time" efficiency gains and, at worst, a tool for

22. The size of the market meant that multi-layer mezzanine debt, reflecting the different levels of risk in a deal, made a notable contribution in only a small number of buy-outs (for example, Magnet) and buy-ins (the bid by Isosceles for Gateway stores) in 1989. Detailed discussion of mezzanine finance in the U.K. is contained in Wright et al, *Buy-outs and Buy-ins: New Strategies in Corporate Management*, footnote 3 above, chapter 6.

23. Despite the advent of the European Community Single Market, the harmonisation of accounting disclosure rules has yet fully to be achieved, so that levels of access comparable to the U.S. and the U.K. are by no means possible across Europe.

24. Detailed information on U.K. and continental European mezzanine funds is to be found in *Europe Buy-out Review*, cited in note 3 above.

25. An analysis of the strategic management issues facing banks as a result of the Single Market is contained in M. Wright and C. Ennew, "1992 and Strategic Bank Marketing," *International Journal of Bank Marketing—Special Issue on 1992*, Vol. 8, No. 3, 1990.

26. For an outline of the Bank of England's position, see Governor of the Bank of England, "Takeovers, Buy-outs and Standards in the City," *Bank of England Quarterly Bulletin*, Vol. 29, pp. 545-547, 1989. For the view of the Bank for International Settlements, see C. Borio, "Banks' Involvement in Highly Leveraged Transactions," Bank for International Settlements, mimeo, July 1990.

By the middle of 1990, over 70% of buy-outs completed between 1982 and 1987 with transactions prices in excess of £25 million ($50 million) had exited by means of a flotation, trade sale, or sale to another private investor or management group.

TABLE 5
EXITS FROM UK BUY-OUTS*

Type	1985	1986	1987	1988	1989	Jan-June 1989	Jan-June 1990
Sale of unquoted MBO to another company	12	33	38	49	81	35	27
Stock Market quotation	28	36	34	34	11	9	3
Receiverships	1	-	4	7	20	9	23
TOTAL	41	69	76	90	112	53	53

Source: CMBOR an independent Research Centre founded by Touche Ross and Barclays Development Capital at the University of Nottingham.
*Excludes Buy-ins

unscrupulous raiders to achieve "short-term" profits by "liquidating" corporate assets undervalued by the stock market.[27]

As evidence for their position, critics of LBOs in the U.S. invariably point to the number of companies that have gone private only to "cash out" a short time after by means of a public stock offering. To shed some light on this controversy, we have attempted to trace the fate of buy-out companies in the U.K.

As noted earlier, there have been few buy-outs of quoted companies in the U.K. Until the end of 1988, many buy-out companies returned to public status. But, after the U.K. stock market turned down sharply, a highly active takeover market—one that often gave investors the ability to realize price earnings ratios higher than those they originally paid—made sale of such companies to other firms the favoured exit route (see Table 5). Indeed, since the beginning of 1989, only two buy-outs of quoted companies in the U.K. have returned to the stock market.

In terms of the entire sample of U.K. buy-outs, as of October 1990 only about 30% completed between 1981 and 1985 had exited in some form (including receivership). (And roughly 80% of these exiting buy-out firms chose either a stock flotation or a trade sale to another company.) Larger buy-outs, however, have exited with far greater frequency. By the middle of 1990, over 70% of buy-outs completed between 1982 and 1987 with transactions prices in excess of £25 million ($50 million) had exited by means of a flotation, trade sale, or sale to another private investor or management group.

This pattern is being repeated in the newer European markets, which are only just beginning to witness exits by investors in bought-out companies. Continental European investors, in line with the traditionally less active capital and corporate asset markets, are often said to take a "longer-term" perspective. But there are signs that such attitudes are changing—although many of these exits, it should be noted, have involved the common continental European practice of industrial firms taking minority equity stakes in smaller firms.

What, then, does all this "exit" activity say about the contribution of buy-outs to the general economy. On the one hand, it supports the popular contention that the debt and intensified incentives present in buy-outs may force upon managers a short-term perspective that could end up depriving companies of the investment necessary for future growth and stability. Buy-outs can also be seen, however, as providing a legitimate transitional phase in the corporate lifecycle—one designed to squeeze inefficiencies, unproductive assets, and excess capital out of mature companies with low investment requirements. Some manager-owners and buy-out investors are understandably anxious to diversify their holdings after a period of, say, 5 years. But even such "short-term" restructurings, having once completed the necessary "downsizing" work, may actually prepare the way for renewed (but this time profitable) growth.

In the U.K., a substantial proportion of bought-out companies—especially those with development capital firm involvement—have discovered significant growth opportunities after the buy-out. Funding such projects requires substantial capital investment that can only be met from stock market flotation or sale to another group. In addition, what

27. See the articles by M. C. Jensen, "Eclipse of the Public Corporation," and A. Rappaport, "The Staying Power of the Public Corporation," cited in note 13. For perspectives on the U.K., see B. Chiplin, M. Wright, and K. Robbie, "Realisations of Management Buy-outs: Issues and Prospects," CMBOR Report, July 1989.

Buy-outs can also be seen as providing a legitimate transitional phase in the corporate lifecycle—one designed to squeeze inefficiencies, unproductive assets, and excess capital out of mature companies with low investment requirements.

TABLE 6
EXITS FROM BUY-OUTS: INTENTIONS AND ACTIONS

Actual Exit Route (at October 1990)	Intended Exit Route: Multiple	Secondary Market	Full Listing	Trade Sale	None Expressed	Total
Secondary Market	-	3	-	-	-	3
Full Listing	1	2	6	-	2	11
Reverse-in	2	-	-	-	-	2
Trade Sale	3	9	2	1	11	26
MBO/MBI	-	3	-	1	-	4
Receivership	1	1	-	-	4	6
No Exit	4	30	5	12	55	106
Total	11	48	13	14	72	158

Source: CMBOR survey and database.
Note: Two of the three buy-outs to enter the secondary market have subsequently been sold to other groups.

appears a stable, independent market position may change over time. This has become particularly evident as companies develop their strategies in relation to the European Community's Single Market. As a result, companies may suddenly see the need for significant change in their investment strategies, thus requiring a different capital structure from the one adopted in the buy-out.

One sign of such shifts in corporate investment and financing strategies are changes in the "exit" modes originally envisioned by buy-out companies. In 1987, we asked managers of 158 U.K. buy-outs completed in 1983-1986 to indicate their exit intentions. Three years later we compared those expressed intentions with the actions taken by such companies as of October 1990.

As summarized in Table 6, our findings reveal that the majority of all buy-outs (106 of 158) have not exited. Few of the companies that said they intended to exit by means of a trade sale have actually done so as yet. Those aiming for a full listing, however, were more likely to have done so. The most notable shift, however, has been the dearth of secondary tier market flotations. Prior to the Stock Market Crash of 1987, these markets provided a means for the management and institutions in smaller buy-outs to cash out at least part of their gains. While this had been by far the most popular intention (by 48 buy-outs), the subsequent drying up of these markets has meant that only three firms have actually taken this route. Trade sale or some form of restructuring has instead become the popular exit alternative, with 30 buy-outs having taken this route.

PERFORMANCE AND MANAGERIAL EQUITY STAKES

More than 20 serious studies of buy-out performance have now been completed in the U.S. and Europe.[28] The majority of systematic studies come from the U.S., and most such studies have addressed the short to medium term. In the U.S., it appears that buy-outs have improved most aspects of corporate performance including profitability, shareholder value, and productivity; the results with respect to employment and R&D spending have been mixed.[29] U.K. studies and the limited ones available for France and the Netherlands broadly support the U.S. picture. The longer-term effects, however, are much less clear—largely because of the newness of the phenomenon and the paucity of rigorous studies examining samples of sufficient size to provide reliable results.

The crucial question, of course, is to what extent the greater managerial equity stakes in buy-out companies lead to higher levels of performance. A recently published study of CEO compensation in the U.S. has concluded that management incentives

28. A detailed review of studies of buy-out performance, covering the U.S., U.K., and continental Europe is contained in Chapter 7 of Wright et al, *Buy-outs and Buy-ins: New Strategies in Corporate Management*, cited in note 3 above.

29. See, for example, S. Kaplan, "The Effects of Management Buy-outs on Operating Performance and Value," *Journal of Financial Economics*, Vol. 24, No. 2, October 1990.

30. See M. C. Jensen and K. Murphy, "CEO Incentives — It's Not How Much You Pay, But How," Harvard Business Review, May/June, pp. 138-149, 1990.

In our study of 28 U.K. buy-outs that were later floated on the stock market, we found that the increase in the value of the bought-out company between buy-out and flotation varied directly with management's percentage equity ownership.

TABLE 7
MANAGERIAL EQUITY
STAKES IN U.K. BUY-OUTS

Size Range	Period	Average Management Contribution (£'000)	Average Management Contribution as % Total Funding (%)	Management Equity Stake			
				Average (%)	Minimum (%)	Maximum (%)	Standard Deviation
Under £5m	1988	150	8.2	56.3	7.4	100.0	22.5
	1989	180	10.7	61.6	10.0	100.0	23.4
	1990Q2	120	7.1	61.0	1.0	100.0	22.9
£5-10m	1988	300	4.8	38.4	25.0	60.0	16.0
	1989	340	5.1	55.2	17.0	100.0	24.8
	1990Q2	510	9.4	47.5	15.1	100.0	28.3
£10-25m	1988	610	3.9	33.2	10.0	86.0	23.4
	1989	830	5.9	38.1	10.0	83.6	26.3
	1990Q2	160	1.0	30.6	10.0	52.0	14.7
Over £25m	1988	810	0.7	21.4	10.0	51.0	12.2
	1989	1,010	0.8	28.4	0	85.0	21.1
	1990Q2	850	1.1	31.4	5.0	51.0	17.8

Source: CMBOR an independent Research Centre founded by Touche Ross and Barclays Development Capital at the University of Nottingham.

in corporations with dispersed stockholder ownership are, on the whole, grossly inadequate—in large part because the average American top executive (of the largest 120 NYSE companies) today owns a negligible fraction (less than .03%) of his company's stock.[30] Moreover, conventional corporate practices such as the granting of stock options often fail to link effort, outcomes, and rewards, particularly in the case of divisional management. In this sense, the restructuring of ownership accomplished by management buy-outs dramatically amplify the risk-reward trade-off for managers.

Our research on U.K. buy-outs (summarized in Table 7) shows that managers in the smaller buy-outs are likely to hold more than half of the voting equity. In larger buy-outs (those with transaction prices in excess of £25 million [$50 million]), the average management stake was 31%. Such buy-outs, moreover, often include equity "ratchets" that provide for increases in management's equity stake when certain performance targets are met. In addition, other control devices such as institutional representation on the board of the buy-out and detailed informational requirements by institutions are frequently used to monitor the buy-out.

Our research on buy-outs also bears out that the size of the management equity stake is the most important systematic factor in explaining improvements in performance after buy-out. In our study of 28 U.K. buy-outs that were later floated on the stock market, we found that the increase in the value of the bought-out company between buy-out and flotation (adjusted for risk and general market movements over the same period—also known as the "excess return") varied directly with management's percentage equity ownership.[31]

CONCLUSIONS

Buy-outs of publicly quoted companies are infrequent in most European countries. With current high rates of interest, the prospects for further development in the foreseeable future seem limited—except in cases where incumbent management already hold signficant equity stakes and wish to take their company private.

30. See M. C. Jensen and K. Murphy, "CEO Incentives — It's Not How Much You Pay, But How," *Harvard Business Review*, May/June, pp. 138-149, 1990.

31. The detailed exposition of the methodology and results is in S. Thompson, M. Wright and K. Robbie, "Management Equity Ownership, Debt and Performance: Some Evidence from U.K. Management Buy-outs," CMBOR Occasional Paper 24, 1990.

As in the U.S., an "overshoot" in the extent and funding of highly leveraged deals also appears to have occurred in Europe, producing an increase in buy-out failures and a reassessment of strategy by many debt and mezzanine institutions. Nonetheless, the role of debt in funding large acquisitions and in bridging the divide between ownership and control has now been clearly established. The proposed LBO of BAT Industries—the highest ever takeover bid in the U.K.—is a prime example. Although the bid was ultimately blocked, it succeeded in forcing the company to restructure through divestments of a number of activities. And when the appropriate conditions return, as they surely will, the market for this kind of LBO is also likely to recover, though probably at more conservative levels of leverage.

Far greater roles in U.K. restructuring continue to be played by buy-outs of divested subsidiaries from diversified groups and privatisation of state-owned assets. In both cases, the introduction of managerial equity incentives and the control effects of debt and quasi-debt instruments appear responsible for significant gains in operating efficiency. Elsewhere in Europe leveraged buy-outs appear designed primarily to allow succession in family-owned firms. With an improvement in market conditions, however, this presently limited role is also likely to expand to include some hostile control transactions as continental capital markets become more developed.

Although the recent surge in takeover activity in Europe in advance of 1992 has been driven by companies' search for economies of scope and scale, subsequent restructuring through divestment and buy-outs is expected. Unwanted activities are still likely to have been acquired and cross-border takeovers are notoriously problematical, not least because of post-acquisition integration problems.

■ MIKE WRIGHT

is Professor of Financial Studies and Director of the Centre for Management Buy-out Research at the University of Nottingham, England. He has published widely in academic and professional journals on buy-outs, divestment, the market for corporate control, privatisation, financial services, and corporate restructuring in Eastern Europe. His books include *Management Buy-outs* (with J. Coyne), *The Logic of Mergers* (with Brian Chiplin), and *Divestment and Strategic Change* (with J. Coyne).

■ STEVE THOMPSON

is Senior Lecturer in Business Economics at the University of Manchester Institute of Science and Technology and an Associate of CMBOR. He is the U.K. Editor of *Managerial and Decision Economics*. He has published numerous academic papers in leading journals on internal organisation, buy-outs and divestment, agency theory, privatisation and competition in the newspaper industry. He is co-editor (with Mike Wright) of *Internal Organisation, Efficiency and Profit* and (with Mike Wright and Brian de Caires) of *Corporate Restructuring*.

■ KEN ROBBIE

is Research Fellow at CMBOR. He has wide experience in the banking and industrial sectors, having previously been involved in the practice of management buy-outs. He has published a number of articles on financial services, buy-outs and divestment. He is co-author (with Mike Wright and James Normand) of Touche Ross's *Management Buy-outs*, second edition, 1990. He is currently completing a major study of management buy-ins. All three are co-authors (with Brian Chiplin) of *Buy-ins and Buy-outs: New Strategies in Corporate Management* (in press).

PERSPECTIVES ON RESTRUCTURING IN EUROPE: INTERVIEWS WITH FOUR EUROPEAN EXECUTIVES

LWT DOES AN LCO: AN INTERVIEW WITH CHRISTOPHER BLAND

London Weekend Television, or LWT, is a producer of television programs for ITV, one of Britain's four television broadcasters. The 1989 Broadcast Bill introduced a number of changes to the television system in Britain. While BBC1 and BBC2 remained regulated providers of public service broadcasting, the other channels were subjected to varying degrees of deregulation. For LWT, the most significant change was that it was forced for the first time to bid for its heretofore government-granted franchise.

In response to this deregulation of broadcasting, LWT chose to undergo a leveraged restructuring known in the U.S. as a leveraged 'cash-out' (LCO). In return for surrendering their shares, the plan gave shareholders a large cash payment and preference shares convertible into equity. The distribution was financed with £50 million cash and £72.5 million new debt.

Another important feature of the LWT restructuring was that it provided management with a significant ownership stake, along with the opportunity to enlarge that initial stake through successful performance. Specifically, management purchased about 4% of the equity in the new LWT at market prices; and additional options will be granted them to the extent the company provides its outside investors (the preferred shareholders) with a compound annual rate of return that exceeds 20% over the next three years. For example, if the return to investors turns out to be as high as 40% per annum, management's ownership will increase from 4% to 15%.

In the interview that follows, Christopher Bland, Chairman of LWT, explains to Mark Gressle of Stern Stewart & Co. why he undertook such a dramatic restructuring.

CHRISTOPHER BLAND

MARK GRESSLE: Over the past few years, you have made two major changes in the organizational structure of LWT. One, you have sold all businesses unrelated to the production of television programming and thus greatly narrowed the company's focus. Two, you have dramatically changed the company's capital structure as well as its equity ownership structure. Why did you make these changes?

CHRISTOPHER BLAND: They were two different ways of achieving the same objective. They were all about focus and concentration and they were all related to the prospect of a more competitive environment in the 1990s.

Let's take the first one. We sold unrelated businesses because we brought nothing to them. We didn't aim to become a market leader in either publishing, travel, or Dynamic Technology (whatever that may be). So we've sold each of those three businesses. And with the benefit of hindsight, we have done dazzlingly well in the *timing* of our sales. For example, I don't know that we will ever again see multiples in the high 20s and low 30s for publishing companies. So, although we made what we feel was a good business decision, we were also aided in our timing by Dame Fortune.

GRESSLE: What sort of changes take place in an organisation as a result of pursuing a strategy of divestiture and focus?

BLAND: Well, divestiture per se didn't have a major change on how we ran our basic business. It did send signals both inside and externally, but that alone didn't bring about any fundamental change in behaviour.

There were three other factors, however, that brought about radical change. First was our decision to reform our industrial relations practices and reduce our staffing. That process commenced about two years ago and we now have 30% fewer people. We are now producing the same amount of programming hours with 400 fewer people, thus dramatically raising our productivity. And we accomplished all this without a day's industrial disruption.

Management's decision to "downsize" the organisation amounted to a reassertion of its right to manage the business—a right which, as in the printing industry, management had lost over time. And that decision changed everybody's behaviour and attitudes in the place. It was a careful, reasonable, well-argued case put to the staff. It was contested at first, of course; but in the end it was accepted and implemented. It was generously handled in the cases of those who took early retirement or redundancy. And, given the size of it, it was done remarkably well.

So that was the first thing that changed people's attitude. Management established the right to run the business. And the majority of the old practices that have long bedeviled this business went out the window.

The second thing that changed behaviour was the recapitalisation of the business, the substitution of debt for equity. We had a burden of debt that we had to pay off, we had covenants to meet, and we had the bidding for the franchise coming up. A combination of things that made people behave much more aggressively in their control of costs and in the way they ran the business. In the face of these combined pressures, top management was compelled to run this business as shareholders—and not as hired managers running it for absentee landlords. And that process has continued and intensified.

The third important change was the appointment of our new managing director. He was part of the recapitalisation, and he has led this revolution.

GRESSLE: The recap appears to improve management incentives by making managers into owners, which in turn seems to have affected performance. Am I right about this?

BLAND: Yes, you are. But strengthening management incentives wasn't the primary objective; it was only a secondary objective. The primary objective was to reduce the company's overall cost of capital by replacing equity with debt. Even at high rates, debt was a cheaper source of capital than equity. And that's historically been true, if you look at the rates of return we've had to promise our equity holders. Reducing your cost of capital is particularly important when you are bidding against large companies that effectively view—and mistakenly, in my opinion—their own retained earnings as "free" capital. Carried to its logical conclusion, this argument says you ought to reduce your equity capital to one pound; this way, provided you have met your interest payments, you will have achieved the maximum possible rate of return.

Of course, you don't have to leverage your companies to that extent to have significant gains—and, of course, most companies don't. Most companies in fact operate with very conservative capital structures. But, by God, when you're tendering for the right to remain in business—and when every pound of equity you tender with has got to come from someone with expectations of earning some 40-50% on investment per annum—then you make every effort to operate with as little equity as you possibly can. In this sense, financial structure really matters.

GRESSLE: With this heavy use of debt, do your outside investors feel that you're gambling the company?

BLAND: We're not gambling it. The Government has instructed us that we have to make the highest bid to win the franchise. So, sure, we're making a bet; but it's a very sensible bet. And our outside investors feel that we're in the best position to make a sensible bet—otherwise they wouldn't have committed their capital.

We (and they) are betting on our 10-year revenue forecast and, more generally, on our ability to run the business. And I think our outside investors—particularly the Americans, who best understood what we were doing—are confident about two things: they recognise the value and appropriateness of a highly leveraged capital structure in this case; and they recognise that it's particularly important to have a strong unity of interest between management and investors.

Without such an alignment of interests, we in management would face a temptation to overbid and thereby preserve our own high life in the broadcasting business—at the expense of our shareholders. But, given that we are now ourselves major shareholders, we have very strong incentives *not* to overbid for the franchise; we will bid on a basis that still leaves our shareholders (including ourselves) a reasonable rate of return. In theory, of course, that's how we should have been behaving *before* the recapitalisation; but I can assure you that our incentives—and thus our attitude to the shareholder—are now quite different from what they once were.

GRESSLE: Many critics of the use of debt finance claim that much of a company's future value is sacrificed in such recapitalisations in order to meet high debt service payments. Was that a concern for you?

BLAND: It can be true in certain businesses, particularly those that are research and development intensive. But our business is not R & D intensive, and thus we haven't been forced to cut back on any of our development projects or scripts and pilots. They've never been huge, but they're no less than they were. Our capital investment has gone down, but that's because much of our capital in the past was tied up in low-returning parts of our business like the studios and cameras. We were right to cut back on that capital. Those expenditures are now maintained at appropriate and essential levels. What has been stopped is the engineer-driven investment in the latest electronic toy.

GRESSLE: How do you see the role of institutional investors in this country?

BLAND: In the end our institutions supported us. It took a lot of hard work and argument and discussion—and I don't think that's unreasonable. Our restructuring was highly innovative. It had some features that on the face of it required a lot of explanation. And the institutions are understandably wary about the possibility that management could be enriching themselves at shareholders' expense. They gave this project very critical scrutiny. And I think that's absolutely right.

As a result of this scrutiny, the structure of the deal was changed in a number of respects and, I might add, for the better. For example, the institutions had an influence on the details of the way in which the "ratchet"—that is, the performance-based

awards of additional options to management—was to be calculated. They insisted that the incentive scheme should be based not on our earnings per share, but rather on market-based measures of performance like our share price. And they were right to do so. So, it was a very constructive dialogue.

Of course, there were one or two of our institutional investors that said within 24 hours of hearing about the scheme that they were not interested. But I think that was simply a typical, conservative, knee-jerk reaction. And, in the end, they were outvoted by those who supported the scheme.

GRESSLE: Do those institutions that owned the equity before the restructuring own the convertible preferred today?

BLAND: Yes, they all do, even the "knee-jerks."

GRESSLE: Your restructuring has been widely publicized and discussed. Yet it remains the only one of its kind. Why do you think that is so?

BLAND: Well, as you know, there's a psychological attitude toward debt finance today that is far more disapproving than a couple of years ago. And I also feel that we're especially well-positioned to bring off an innovative restructuring in the face of potentially difficult circumstances.

But, if you ask me, would I like to do it again, my answer would be: I wouldn't want to do it twice in a lifetime; I wouldn't do it again unless I had to. I believe that we had to do this restructuring in order to be competitive enough to win the franchise. Without the recap, I don't believe we would have made the changes that we have. Though we were beginning to change, we wouldn't have changed radically enough unless we did something like this.

So, if the government had not forced us to bid to retain our franchise, then we probably would not have under-

taken the restructuring. And we would likely not have made the difficult downsizing decisions that the restructuring forced upon us. People only do difficult, disagreeable things when they have to. And I would certainly classify some of the changes we made as difficult and disagreeable things.

GRESSLE: Well, yes, that may be true. But isn't 1992 going to bring about the same urgency, the same need for radical change for companies to remain competitive? It seems that many of the experiences you've faced in your industry are also confronting executives in other industries. With 1992 impending, isn't this the time for companies to get serious about narrowing the focus of their businesses, cutting excess costs, and perhaps using debt finance and equity incentives as a control device to bring about improvements?

BLAND: Yes, I agree. And, even without 1992, companies ought to have been moving in this direction. Nevertheless, in the U.K. there is an instinctive reluctance, even hostility, on the part of some institutions to leveraged restructurings that is much less in evidence in the States. I've found quite a different attitude amongst our American investors. Our major American investors grasped the scheme at once and said, "This is terrific, we fully support it." British institutions, it goes without saying, do not behave this way. Aside from a British distaste for enthusiasm of any kind, British institutions have also been slow to grasp the debt/equity argument and the importance of aligning management with shareholder interests. Convincing them was a much slower, harder process.◆

BENCKISER PURSUES A FOCUSED STRATEGY: AN INTERVIEW WITH MANFRED KLEIN

MANFRED KLEIN

Joh. A. Benckiser GmbH, based in Lugwigshafen, Germany, has pursued a strategy very different from that of most German companies. Since 1987, the company has divested a group of unrelated businesses and followed an acquisition strategy focused almost exclusively on one business—consumer household products. Between 1987 and 1990, Benckiser acquired the consumer products division of Ecolabs (U.S.) for $243 million, Panigal and Mira Lanza, household detergent producers in Italy, S.A. Camp, Spain's largest detergent company, for $282 million, and, more recently, the U.S. household products division ($106 million) and the European cosmetics business ($378 million) of Smithkline Beecham. Total acquisition costs have exceeded $1 billion. At the same time Benckiser has sold a group of unrelated businesses, some of which formed the company's traditional chemical business. Its growth has been financed from retained profits, disposals, and debt. The company has steadfastly remained private, claiming that going public would compromise its flexible management system and efficient decision-making.

In the interview below, Dr. Manfred Klein, Benckiser's Finance Director, explains the thinking behind the company's strategy.

GRESSLE: The strategy you have pursued is somewhat unique among German companies. What was your thinking behind this strategy?

MANFRED KLEIN: Our reasoning was very simple. We had a diversified corporate structure in Germany that originated in the 1960s. It was believed, at that time, that a company should have several different types of activities. We were also a very small conglomerate at that time with about $800 million in sales; but basically it was a diversified chemical business in a variety of different commodity markets. We eventually determined, however, that the only way to make this company profitable was to focus on one business.

GRESSLE: What kind of changes have you seen take place in the company as a result of following this strategy?

KLEIN: By divesting several businesses, we have taken a lot of complexity out of the company. This in turn has allowed us to develop a very decentralised organisation, thereby reducing overhead, selling costs, and administrative staff. All these fixed costs are governed by the complexity of the business and your organisational structure. So, instead of maintaining a highly centralised organisation with extensive monitoring by headquarters, we simply gave general managers full responsibility for the income statement and balance sheet in their different countries. And

we supported this approach with an aggressive profit-sharing plan. This kind of compensation structure is highly unusual in Germany. German companies typically pay most of an executive's compensation in fixed salary with only a small variable portion in the form of bonuses.

GRESSLE: What was the initial response of your managers when you sat down with them and said you would like to change your organisational structure?

KLEIN: They were very receptive because they wanted to take on greater responsibility. They wanted to have the freedom to act rather than being absorbed into a large organisation where they had to spend most of their time writing memos rather than making decisions.

Although our system is decentralised, our general managers do face a lot of pressure to perform. We start with a top-down planning approach in which targets are set by top management and then negotiated with the general managers that run our different international operations. By establishing clear targets, we can directly compare the performance of our GMs across countries and thus identify poor performers. For example, if our Austrian company achieves operating margins significantly different from those earned by our Swiss company, this difference provides an objective basis for challenging substandard performance. You can only use these comparisons to discipline management if you have comparable structures, which means that you have to narrow your focus on one business sector. If you have a company with many different businesses, the GMs will always find excuses for lagging performance. They will say, "But we are not comparable to the operation in that country because we have assets or products which you don't have in that country."

In our company, each GM and each company is effectively competing against all the others. Once a year we have a general managers' meeting in which the bottom-line performance of all GMs is measured against all other GMs'. So, a GM sitting amongst his colleagues will be forced to justify substandard performance. And that system really challenges managers to perform—not by instilling fear, but by stimulating a competitive spirit. It's a challenge in the sense of sport; and it makes everybody want to be the best. I have worked in several big companies in Germany, and none has focused on profit like Benckiser. **GRESSLE:** Much of your growth has come through acquisitions. What has

contributed most to the success of your acquisitions?
KLEIN: The management team we have built up in the last few years has been very effective in integrating acquisitions with the rest of our company. We have learned that if you wait a year to integrate a newly acquired business, you have clearly waited too long. When we acquire companies, we already understand how the acquisition will contribute to the rest of the company.

And that knowledge is, of course, the basis for the prices we pay to acquire companies. We made all our acquisitions in the household cleaning area in the past few years and in the range of 0.60 to 1.4 times annual sales. We are operating in a very mature, consolidating industry; and everybody in the industry has understood that the only profitable way to grow in such circumstances is through acquisition. For that reason, acquisition prices have gone very rapidly in the last 12 months. In the last acquisition by Clorox, for example, the price paid was more than 2.5 times sales. We will not pay those prices. In our industry, you can achieve levels of operating profitability that run as high as 25 percent of net sales; but that's more or less the upper limit. So, if you pay a multiple of 2.5 times on net sales, and you have an interest rate of 10 percent, you would have to make the business very, very profitable just to pay the interest.

The opposite has happened in the cosmetics industry, where 12 to 18 months ago we saw acquisition price multiples as high as 2.7 times sales. When we acquired the European cosmetics business of Smithline Beecham this year, prices had come down sharply, and we were able to buy the company for 0.7 times sales. **GRESSLE:** When you make an acquisition, do you generally keep the existing management team?

KLEIN: Our typical experience has been that when you buy a business that is undermanaged, the reason it is undermanaged is the management. So what is the natural conclusion? Don't keep the management. That's not true in all cases, but generally you know what you have to do if you want to integrate an acquisition very quickly and efficiently.

So, you have to have your own business plan. You have to have your own ideas about your business structure and you have to find the right people to implement it. And it has to be implemented *very quickly*. Otherwise you lose the opportunity to turn the business around. You then open the door to discussions about why your proposals for change will not work—typically because it has been done the old way for the last 15 years.

When you make an acquisition, you also create a situation in which everybody in the organisation tries to commit you to keep them. Everybody is ready to tell you what was wrong in the past and how they see it in the future. In the transition period, you have to try to get as much good information out of the company as you can. Then you use this new information to modify your plan, if need be, and make your final decision and say "You are the guy for this," "You are the guy for that," and this is the plan we are going to implement. You can only operate this way if you have focused on a business you understand.
GRESSLE: How do your acquisitions create value for your investors?
KLEIN: If you want to maximise the value for your shareholders, you finance every acquisition with as much debt as possible. This way, every penny you get over what you have to put into your P&L for the depreciation of intangibles and for interest costs goes to the equity holder. It also creates great pressure to perform. By

using debt, we have in effect forced ourselves to make a profit. And to the extent we earn a higher rate of return on investment than our cost of debt capital, we have significantly increased the return on equity for our shareholders. That's the story of leverage. And what we in fact have done amounts to an internal leveraged buyout.

As long as we can manage the company in this way, we have the right to pay no dividend. If we did not operate this way, then we would have to consider giving the money back to our shareholders. And that is a completely different approach from that of the typical German company. Unlike most companies in Germany, we begin by asking ourselves the question: Why do shareholders invest their money in companies in the first place? The answer is, to earn more on their invested capital than they could elsewhere. This means that corporate management's job is to earn a higher return on shareholder's equity than any other investment opportunity the shareholder might have.

For this reason, a company sitting on lots of excess cash and investing in government bonds is doing nothing for its shareholders that they cannot do for themselves; and unless management has a plan to reinvest that capital profitably, they should give it back to the shareholders.

GRESSLE: Is your viewpoint gaining support among German managers?

KLEIN: It is not a popular view. One reason for the problem is that German corporations are not permitted to buy back shares as you can do in the U.K. or the States. We can only return capital by means of dividend distributions.

That is one problem. Probably more important, however, in explaining German managers' attitude toward shareholders is the fact that there is

no real threat of takeover in Germany. And this stems in large part from differences in the identity of German shareholders. In Germany, you see large shareholdings by banks and other traditional institutional investors that have exerted little pressure for dividend distributions or higher share prices. They are interested primarily in just keeping their holdings.

So, corporate managements in Germany are not subjected to the same pressure to produce higher shareholder returns that they are in the States or the U.K. In Germany, shareholders feel that a company is performing well if it pays the same dividend as last year, or perhaps increases it by one Deutschemark per share. They do not go to companies and say, "What are you doing with your $5 million of excess liquidity? Why don't you distribute it to us?" German companies today are sitting on mountains of cash, saying to themselves, "We are playing it safe. We want this huge liquidity because there might be a recession in the future." They are not asking themselves, "What could I do with the money to help my shareholders?"

GRESSLE: It appears that the major German banks play a role that's quite different from banks in the U.S. and the U.K. For example, German banks own significant equity stakes in the companies they lend to and are thus able to influence corporate policy. Do you think they play a beneficial role that can enhance a company's performance?

KLEIN: German and also Swiss banks have a different attitude to their clients than U.S. banks—one that can be very positive. We have a few banks that we call "relationship banks" that have confidence in our management and in our strategy. They understand our objectives and they financed our acquisitions. They would not have

provided this financing unless they knew our company well. Unlike U.S. banks, which have become increasingly transaction-oriented, German banks like to establish long-term relationships with companies; and this means that they will stand by their companies in bad times as well as good times.

So that is the good news about German banks. The problem with our banks, however, is that they are still very conservative in their thinking. They are not often prepared to finance a strategy like ours. Although we have been able to convince some of our bankers to go along with us in financing our acquisitions, they clearly did not originate the idea; they are cautious by nature. But once you have convinced them that what you're doing is sensible, they are very, very good partners. Credit lending is confidence, nothing more than confidence in the management and in the strategy. So if you can prove with each step you take that you're improving the business, the banks will be with you.

GRESSLE: There are very few examples of companies like Benckiser in Germany; there are very few managements that have taken the path that you have taken, which is to borrow a lot of money and make big acquisitions. Could management compensation practices in Germany have anything to do with this conservatism? For example, if general managers are content with their current compensation and they see little to gain from changing how they operate, they too will resist changes that could benefit their shareholders?

KLEIN: You are completely right. Compensation systems for managers are very poor in this country. If you could give them stock options or establish some other direct link between pay and shareholder returns, you would see managers in this country behaving very differently. The compensation of German managers is fixed every year; it does not change with performance. You get paid even if you don't perform.

But changing the compensation plan would be very difficult to accomplish in most German companies. For example, to pay somebody in the third layer of management a bonus above his normal compensation is virtually impossible. You would go to the Personnel Department with your proposal and the Personnel Department would tell you, "You cannot do this. If we make an exception in one case, then everyone who comes in will want to do the same. If this happens, we will lose control over the process. Compensation must be looked at in the context of all the layers in the company," and so on and so on. It is this kind of bureaucratic thinking that makes large companies so inefficient. In a small organisation like Benckiser, we are flexible enough to make exceptions. This allows us to motivate our people. They understand that if they have performed well, they will instantly find something additional in their pockets. And believe me: Although money is not "the only thing," it is a very good motivator.◆

◆

DYNACTION BUILDS A SUCCESSFUL CONGLOMERATE: AN INTERVIEW WITH HENRI BLANCHET AND CHRISTIAN MORETTI

HENRI BLANCHET

CHRISTIAN MORETTI

At a time when financial markets and corporate advisers have been telling managements to shed their unrelated businesses and narrow the corporate focus, Dynaction has been demonstrating that the conglomerate form can be made to work. With interests in coated paper machines, electrical protection systems, mechanical engineering, and an assortment of other capital goods manufacturing operations, Dynaction has produced a tenfold increase in profits and market capitalization since 1985. Today, it generates about $27 million in operating profit on $855 million in sales.

The company was founded in 1982 by Henri Blanchet and Christian Moretti, when they purchased a subsidiary of Beatrice Foods for a token French franc. Since then, it has grown through acquisitions financed with a combination of modest amounts of debt together with equity raised by public offerings of equity interests in the subsidiaries. Today the company is comprised of eight major subsidiaries, four of which are separately quoted.

Besides this unusual financial structure, Dynaction's system of corporate controls also differs greatly from conventional conglomerates with their large headquarters. Its corporate office consists of four people—the two founders, a secretary, and an accountant. The executives who run the subsidiaries are given wide responsibilities in managing their businesses. Headquarters approval is required only for significant acquisitions and capital raising. The company also provides the subsidiary management teams with 25 percent of the equity in the subsidiary. The equity takes the form of warrants that management can eventually exercise either on the basis of a pre-set formula or in the event the subsidiary is taken public.

In the interview that follows, Blanchard and Moretti elaborate on their innovative corporate structure.

GRESSLE: Is there a common thread between the kinds of companies you have acquired in the past eight years?

HENRI BLANCHET: If you look at the companies we have today, you will see that there is some similarity. But it was not a question of our having a special interest in these kinds of companies. Rather, it was mainly the fact that these companies were overlooked. So we ended up acquiring companies in fields that were not crowded. For this reason the P/Es ratios we paid were low enough to provide us with a good return on investment.

GRESSLE: When you buy a company, do you typically do so with the expectation of making it more profitable than it was under its former owner?

BLANCHET: Well, there are two ways to make money on acquisitions. In some cases, we pay fair value and then improve the company's profitability. In other cases, we buy a company at a price that is lower than its real value. In that case, you don't have to improve the profit; you made your profit when you bought it. In many cases, of course, it is some combination of the two at work.

GRESSLE: When you expect to increase profits, where do you typically make your improvements? Is the company generally mismanaged or is it for some reason restricted in its ability to take full advantage of certain opportunities?

BLANCHET: We have bought about 40 companies, and it is difficult to generalize about them; each case has been a little different. We have sometimes encountered some very bizarre corporate behaviour. For example, the second company we bought was an excellently managed company. The problem was that the management team was fighting every day with the shareholders. The owner had a holding company whose chairman was a bit crazy—a nice guy, but difficult for everybody to live with. He wanted to make decisions instead of letting the managers in the company make the decisions. So people were fighting every day. All we did in that case was to buy the company and give the managers 25% of the shares. We then just let them do their work and the company went very well.

On the other hand, it may happen that we buy a company and then let all the management go. We change the management team because we think that the losing team should be thrown out. The team is usually tired and frustrated. In such cases, we bring in a new person at the top and allow him to assemble his own team.

Another type of situation where we have to replace management is when we buy a company facing a succession of ownership problem. In France today, there are some 40,000 companies employing between 50 and 1000 people. Many of these companies are family owned. Of these 40,000 companies, perhaps as many as 10,000 will face succession problems in the next three years. So this is the largest part of our market.

CHRISTIAN MORETTI: Finding a new general manager for a company in these circumstances is often very difficult. In fact, it may be the most difficult thing we have to do—matching the appropriate person with the management problem that needs to be solved. What we tend to do is to select an individual and make him an active participant in the evaluation and negotiation of the company. This enables us to get familiar with one another.

But once we decide to let him run the company, then he is given complete operating responsibility along with 25% of the company's shares both for himself and the rest of the management team he chooses. So we don't operate the companies ourselves. We find the best operators and let them do it.

GRESSLE: So choosing the operating head becomes very important, then?

MORETTI: Yes, it's the most important thing in our business. It is essential. When we negotiate a deal, we are liable to overpay by as much as 10% of the price, maybe even 20%. Such a mistake can be corrected over the long term. But if you choose the wrong man, then you are in trouble for a long period of time. Sometimes we find a very good individual, but one who is not appropriate for the company in question. So, it's like a marriage: you have to find not only the right person, but also the right person for that company.

But, let me also say that the profile of the people we are looking for has one constant: the entrepreneurial spirit. They can have different types of background—some are engineers, some are business school graduates, they come from all regions of France, and their ages range from 30 and 70 years—but they are all entrepreneurs.

GRESSLE: You must have made at least a few mistakes in your acquisition program?

MORETTI: Sure we've made mistakes, everyone makes mistakes. There are two types of mistakes. One is in the choice of the company itself. The second kind has to do with people, with the selection of management to run the business. As I mentioned before, in some cases we have found very good people who were simply not the right people for the challenge we were giving them—even though they're very good. In these situations, however, we have generally been lucky enough to detect the problem early. What has happened in such cases is that the company itself reacted negatively to the managers we put in. There's been a sort of rejection process which comes from within the company itself.

For this reason, when we buy a company, we are careful to observe how the integration process goes, and whether the new person works well with the company. Usually it works; but if it does not, there are strong signals from the company itself saying "this guy is not good at all." When we see this, we react quickly.

BLANCHET: To make the integration go smoothly, we have to be in close contact with the company in order to hear what the people have to say. Our information comes either from people within the company or from those around it. For example, the company's bankers or clients might come to us and say, "We have seen your person; he is strange." We have to be involved so we can get these signals.

MORETTI: We have also been wrong in our choice of companies. In one case, we bought a company from a crook! He sold us a company with false accounting information. And, even though we had our auditors go through the numbers, we got stuck. We won the law suit, but we lost time and money.

In another case, we misjudged the risk of a business. We bought a company that competed in a world market. The pricing for the raw material—which represented 80% of the added value in the finished product—was not set in France, but in world markets; and it was highly volatile. When the pricing situation went against us, we were in trouble and we couldn't do anything about it. So we closed the company. We understood quickly that we had no chance to turn it around, so we closed it down and paid everybody.

GRESSLE: You didn't mention overpaying for acquisitions as one of the pitfalls of an acquisitive strategy. You have never overpaid?

MORETTI: As Henri said earlier, if we overpay by 10%, that is not likely to be a serious problem over the long term. But I would also say that I don't think we've made many mistakes on pricing.

GRESSLE: Does that mean you've walked away from what were otherwise sound business deals because the price was too high?

BLANCHET: Oh yes, very often. Pricing for us is very important. In fact, we always try to buy companies from sellers who are not that interested in the price. And such situations arise more frequently than you might think. When you try to sell your house or your car, you try to maximise the price because it's very important to you. But, in the case of certain businesses, it may be different. For instance, if the company is owned by an elderly man who wants to sell it because he has no one in the family to take over, the price may not be so important. What is important is selling the company to someone who will ensure the future of the company he built. This process is very emotional, and the price often becomes secondary.

Another case where pricing may be less important to sellers is when major corporations attempt to sell off a marginal business. This is a problem for the big corporations because time for these guys is so important. Saving management time is a priority. The price is secondary.

MORETTI: In such cases, it is also important to recognize that management is spending other people's money. In France, we are more sensitive to this issue because we have nationalised companies. Here management doesn't want to sell their subsidiaries to a competitor. Also, they want each sale to be extremely well accepted by their employees. So it is very important for them to find the right buyer to ensure that the company will survive and grow.

GRESSLE: Let me follow up on your point that corporate management is not spending it's own money and therefore may not care about maximising price. Your own company is clearly very different in that sense. You have provided the managers with ownership in the company. Why did you decide to do it this way?

BLANCHET: It is a very important part of our strategy. Why did we decide to do it this way? There were two reasons. First, was our experience before starting Dynaction. We considered what was happening in France. When we started our company in 1982, we had each had more than 10 years' experience working for French companies and understanding their habits and rules. We saw things that appeared to us both unfair and unproductive. For instance, I used to work in a group which for 10 years had been losing money and which, in my opinion, was badly run. I went there more or less as a trouble shooter, and I was a controller when they appointed a new general manager. In two years, this general manager turned the company around completely and made it one of the most profitable companies. This guy was a whiz, but all he had to reward him was a good salary and nothing else. This we feel is wrong.

My second reason for making managers owners is not philosophical, just practical. If we can afford to give an individual an equity stake, then he wears our hat. He is a shareholder and he will drive his company with a long-term view—with *our* view—of what ought to be done.

GRESSLE: When the managers of one of your companies go out and buy other companies, can they do the same thing that you do? Can they give 25 percent ownership in the new affiliate to the new management team?

MORETTI: Yes, that's a rule in our company.

GRESSLE: Is this equity simply given to your managers?

BLANCHET: Nothing is given, nothing is a gift.

GRESSLE: Do they pay for it?

BLANCHET: No, what we give them is the opportunity to buy a shareholding. But the price they have to pay is the price we have paid.

They don't have to pay it all at once. In fact, they buy what amount to low-priced warrants. At the same time, we offer to buy back their shares, but not at the price they paid. Instead it is a price determined by a preset formula that reflects their success in adding value to the company.

MORETTI: We create liquidity for our managers on the basis of the formula. Let's say that it is a safety net, but it's nothing more. Our aim is to maximise the *long-run* value of the company, and we want our managers to share that aim.

BLANCHET: Based on our eight years of experience in running this company, I would say that it is very important for our operating managers to understand that they can become rich one day. But while it's certainly important for them to have this idea in mind, it is also, of course, important for them to enjoy themselves. What is finally most important is the challenge of the job and the way they lead their professional lives, the way they behave inside their companies, and the relationships they create with their team and with us. This is more important than to be rich. Because, once you're rich, all you have is just more money. It doesn't change anything. You still only eat three times a day.

MORETTI: The French way of life is different from the American. In the States when you are rich you have to show it. I mean nine times out of ten, you show it. It's a rule: You made it, so you show it. In Europe, it's different. Especially in France, you don't show it.

GRESSLE: To return to one of your earlier comments, it's not just giving somebody ownership that's important, it's giving the right person ownership.

MORETTI: Yes, if you were to go to a big French group and say to the head of each subsidiary, "We're going to give you the chance of getting 25% of the equity," some might say they're not interested, and many if not most would view the idea with great suspicion and distrust. It takes time for someone without an entrepreneur's mind to see the opportunity.

Let me give you an example. When we bought a subsidiary about three years ago, we told the people what we were going to do. Most people said it was too tough, and wouldn't do it. We said to their chairman, "Are you prepared to take the challenge with us?" And he said it was too difficult. He would rather go back to a big company with a golden parachute rather than take the risk.

I would say that only a few of the very big French groups are looking for larger profits. This is not the way management runs French companies. It's a matter of the French industry and the way the financial rewards to management are set up. Also, the fact that everyone owns everyone else is very important in limiting competition and takeovers. It is the political and social establishment in France. This is very important to understand.

Our method, by contrast, is very simple and has been very successful in adding value. It has nothing to do with the establishment. They stay on their own game, we on ours.◆

THE ECONOMIC IMPORT OF EUROPE 1992

by Alan C. Shapiro,
University of Southern California

B y December 1992, the last of some 300 directives designed to create a single European market for goods and services is set to be implemented. The objective of Europe 1992 is to tear down barriers to trade and commerce within Europe so that European nations can achieve economic prosperity. If and when the grand design of Europe 1992 comes to pass, goods, services, people, and capital will, for the first time, be able to move freely across European borders.

The economic unification of Europe contains a mix of good news and bad news for corporations, including those outside as well as inside the European Community. On the one hand, companies can cash in on the purchasing power of 320 million potential customers—a market larger than the United States and Canada combined. On the other hand, they will have to comply with new laws and regulations, some of which have protectionist overtones.

In this article, after briefly examining the causes and expected consequences of Europe 1992, I use the recent American experience with deregulation and corporate restructuring as a basis for speculating about the threats and opportunities a united Europe holds for multinational corporations. Perhaps the most important lesson for companies preparing for 1992 is that size and market share alone (achieved, say, through expensive acquisitions) may not be enough to guarantee survival in European markets, much less profitability. Far more critical are discriminating cost cutting and market segmentation based on a clear view of the company's competitive strengths, while firmly resisting the inefficiencies that tend to breed in large, especially diversified organizations.

BACKGROUND

Following the global recession of the early 1980s, the United States was creating millions of jobs and Japan was booming. But Europe was stagnant, with slow growth, a declining share of world trade, and unemployment hovering around 12%. Many economists and businessmen attributed this "Euro-sclerosis" to the structural rigidities resulting from the attempts of European governments to shield their constituencies—labor, management, local communities—from outside economic forces. In this view, the key to a revitalized Europe lay in dismantling the economic barriers that fragmented the European Community (EC). Supporters of a single market, pointing to the example of the United States, argued that economic integration would increase efficiency and stimulate growth by promoting competition within the EC and by enabling companies to attain greater economies of scale.

By 1986, the EC was sufficiently alarmed by its lagging economic performance and loss of competitiveness in the world economy that a decision to integrate its fragmented national markets became inevitable. On the basis of a study entitled "Completing the Internal Market"—now commonly referred to as "the White Paper"—the EC adopted a detailed program for creating a common market by 1992.

Integration of Goods and Services

The White Paper identifies three major types of barriers—*physical, technical,* and *fiscal*—each of which must be eliminated to integrate the 12 separate markets of the EC into a single European market for goods and services.

Physical barriers. Europe 1992 proposes to dismantle physical barriers at borders between EC nations such as customs posts, immigration controls, and passport and cargo checks. Some progress has already been made in reducing border controls. For example, a new policy adopted in 1988 permits truck drivers to pass through customs by showing a single document. Much work remains, however, to eliminate cross-border restrictions on communications, travel, and transport.

Technical barriers. Among the most restrictive technical barriers are those arising from differences in health, safety, and environmental standards for similar products among EC countries. By 1992, these different standards will be replaced by the principle of "mutual recognition," which says in effect that if a standard is good enough for one EC nation it is acceptable in all EC nations.

Protectionist public-sector procurement policies represent another type of technical barrier. Public-sector contracts, including those involving state-regulated utilities, represent a significant share—about 15%—of the EC's gross domestic product. Preferential treatment of domestic firms results in only 2% of these contracts being awarded to firms from other member countries. The White Paper calls for opening up the bidding process on public contracts by mandating common standards in the procurement process.

This is far from suggesting, however, that Europe is about to abandon all forms of protectionism by 1992. While aiming to increase competition among companies *within* the European Community, EC ministers are also insisting on "Buy Europe" provisions that would discourage outside competitors by allowing procurement officials to throw out bids involving less than 50% EC content.

Fiscal barriers. Finally, Europe 1992 aims to remove fiscal barriers, notably tax-related barriers to trade. For example, wide variation in value-added tax (VAT) rates now forces nations to control cross-border trade to prevent attempts at tax arbitrage. The White Paper proposes harmonizing VAT rates and excise taxes—by lowering them in high-tax countries and raising them in low-tax countries—to reduce paperwork and minimize tax-related national price differentials. Gaining agreement on tax harmonization, however, has proven very difficult, as countries that generate a lot of revenue from VATs continue to lobby vigorously against it.

Integration of Financial Markets

Besides removing the barriers to the free flow of goods and services, Europe 1992 seeks to integrate European capital markets and create a single market for financial services. By 1992, EC members must remove all capital market controls, liberalize capital flows between EC and non-EC countries, and permit EC-licensed banks to establish branches in any member state without obtaining permission from the local authorities. Moreover, as long as an EC bank's home country permits its banks to engage in an activity, then that bank can engage in that activity in another country, even if the activity is prohibited to domestic banks in the host country.

OBSTACLES TO EUROPE 1992

By the end of 1990, the 12 EC countries had agreed to only about two-thirds of the proposed measures. For reasons described below, getting agreement on the remaining third will prove tough going. And because some governments are now resisting implementation of EC decrees they have already consented to, even the two-thirds figure may overstate the rate of progress in overcoming intercountry conflicts.

Such resistance stems from the realization that Europe 1992 will reduce national sovereignty and imperil powerful and favored interest groups— notably, managers and employees of companies fostered by the state. Economic integration will force these less efficient and highly protected firms to make painful adjustments to heightened competition. These adjustments are likely to be reflected in:

1. Employment losses in sectors subject to rationalization. Shake-out and consolidation is inevitable in industries protected or subsidized by the state. Such industries, which often exhibit large potential economies of scale, typically suffer from overcapacity. For example, the tendency of the European public sector to procure goods and services from domestic firms is the principal reason there are ten turbo-generator manufacturers in the EC as compared to only two in the U.S., and eleven EC makers of telephone exchanges compared to four in the U.S.

2. Lower wages in some sectors. With national governments deprived of the levers of mercantilist (or "beggar-thy-neighbor") policy such as non-tariff barriers, subsidies, and preferential treatment of domestic firms, national competition for market shares and investment may increasingly take the form of competition over employee costs. Negotiations on wages and benefits, working hours, hiring and firing regulations, and who bears the costs of social security will reflect the consequences of allowing costs to get out of line after 1992.

3. Disruptions of the status quo of managers and other elites. Trade and regulatory barriers allow domestic firms to charge higher prices and subsidize inefficiency. Lowering these barriers will force such companies to become more competitive. The industries that suffer most will be those that supply the state or receive state subsidies. At the same time, the public elites who decide on subsidies, procurement policies, and regulation will lose power to the market—although there will be some gains to the "Eurocrats" who regulate that market.

4. Increasing national deregulation. Regulation in the service sector, allegedly designed for the "protection" of consumers, has created large islands of inefficiency in most European economies. Glaring examples include telecommunications, road and air transport, and financial services. Liberalization will lead to competition among regulatory systems as well as companies. As a result, perhaps the greatest economic impact of Europe 1992 will come from the national deregulation it brings about and the national competitive forces it unleashes.

Winners, Losers, and "Fortress Europe"

To summarize, the losers from economic integration will be sheltered companies and those who work for them. Such losses, however, will be dwarfed by the gains to the consumers of EC nations. Besides consumers, the other expected winners will be those companies that are already highly competitive within the EC but currently face substantial costs associated with EC market fragmentation. As a corollary, there will be a major redistribution of income from those with jobs in the sheltered sector of the economy to those with jobs in the competitive sector.

Inevitably, however, the protests of the losers will weigh more heavily with government officials than the benefits accruing to a dispersed majority. In response to such concentrated protest, the EC countries may try to offset some of the short-run costs associated with eliminating "protective" barriers among themselves by blocking competition from abroad. In fact, the EC may well end up deciding to erect trade barriers simply to keep all the benefits of Europe 1992 to themselves. In the words of the EC's president, Jacques Delors, "We are not building a single market in order to turn it over to hungry foreigners."

A Europe 1992 turned "Fortress Europe" would pose threats to some, but certainly not all U.S. companies. For companies with well-established European operations like GM, Ford, IBM, and DEC, European protectionism should present no particular worry because their EC affiliates are already largely independent of imports from the United States. Because imports from the U.S. are equal to only about 5% of the sales of their EC manufacturing affiliates, such companies should have no trouble complying with the expected 50% local content provision. So, when 1992 arrives, although companies such as IBM may end up reconfiguring their operations and decreasing the number of their manufacturing sites, they will not be shut out of Europe. If anything, they will prosper even more in the new environment.

Moreover, some companies that currently lack a significant EC presence are now in the process of moving production to Europe, in large part to avoid anticipated tariff barriers. Such a development simply reinforces the lesson provided by the experience of the American auto industry: Protectionism will not win EC firms a respite from competition. A decade after the imposition of auto quotas, the Japanese have developed the capacity to produce two million vehicles a year in the United States and are more competitive than ever.

The "Social Charter"

A more troubling prospect than EC protectionism may be the attempt to restrict labor market competition by imposing uniform economic policies on member states. In a free market, if one state taxes business too heavily or burdens it with excessive labor costs, companies can move to another state. This flexibility in turn sets a limit to the greed of workers or politicians.

Such an outcome of EC 1992, however, would be anathema to EC President Delors, an avowed socialist who has vigorously condemned what he calls "savage capitalism" (meaning unregulated markets). In response, the Delors Report has advocated adoption of the "Social Charter," which proposes the uniform imposition throughout the EC of expensive social programs (such as those specifying minimum wages and limits on work hours) based on the West German model.

At the same time, though, businessmen facing the prospect of fierce competition in less protected home markets are determined to water down the social-action program implementing the Social Charter. The Italian employer's federation, for example, has taken a tough stand in pay negotiations, citing Italian companies' declining competitiveness relative to the rest of European industry.

The hard fact is that no form of EC legislation will protect organized labor from the forces of global competition that have reduced union power so visibly over the past decade. Rather than a panacea for ailing European unions, the single market is likely to further weaken their power by making it easier for companies to invest anywhere in the EC. That will encourage companies to play off national unions—and even national governments—against one another in a battle to attract investment. Even those unions that manage to overcome national differences and bargain "pan-European" may be left empty-handed. By threatening to switch production to emerging markets in Eastern Europe, determined employers may try to call their bluff.

Moreover, any attempt by EC officials to regulate competition will also have to deal with those Europeans whose cooperation in the present negotiations rests on the understanding that Europe 1992 will be a free market of independent nations run by a non-interventionist central government. In the words of Margaret Thatcher, "We have not successfully rolled back the frontiers of the state in Britain only to see them reimposed on a European level."

LESSONS FROM U.S. DEREGULATION

Despite the enormous uncertainty surrounding Europe 1992, corporate management may want to look to the recent American experience with deregulation for guidance in entering uncharted territory. That experience shows clearly the competitive changes that take place when new entrants are allowed into once restricted markets. As such, it may provide valuable lessons for managers seeking to position their companies for the opening of the European market.[1]

Since 1975, the U.S. has deregulated various aspects of the securities industry, banking, airlines, trucking, railroads, and telecommunications. In all these industries, we can see the same set of competitive dynamics at work:

1. The industry becomes more competitive and profitability deteriorates rapidly as strong firms expand into formerly protected markets, while many new, low-cost suppliers enter the market. Falling profits spur staff reductions and other cost-cutting measures. In addition, the weak get weaker and many of them fail, but the strong do not get more profitable—not right away, at least. For example,

---

1. This section is based on Joel A. Bleeke, "Strategic Choices for Newly Opened Markets," *Harvard Business Review*, September-October 1990, 158-165.

trade barriers have allowed European banks to remain highly inefficient. Deregulation will shrink bank margins dramatically.

2. The most profitable market segments come under severe price pressure as competitors flock to them. Conversely, the least profitable segments before deregulation, which were typically cross-subsidized to hold down prices, become more attractive as the cross-subsidies are ended and many firms exit these markets. For example, the biggest changes in the banking industry will come in retail banking, which now provides as much as two-thirds of European bank profits and has served to cross-subsidize expansion into deregulated wholesale and investment banking.

3. Merger and acquisition activity accelerates. Initially, weaker firms combine to gain the size needed to compete with the giants of the industry. But the anticipated scale economies often don't materialize—and a wave of divestitures of at least some of the unwanted pieces obtained in such acquisitions typically follows. Later on, some of the strongest firms in the industry merge with each other. They also make selected acquisitions—and divestitures—to fill out gaps in their product portfolio or customer segments and to focus better on their core business.

4. Only a handful of firms survive as broad-based competitors. Those that succeed are companies that achieve, among other things, a precise understanding of their cost structures and pricing. With such an understanding, they are able to identify and eliminate cross-subsidies and create new price/service trade-offs for their customers. The rest are forced to narrow their product range to those in which they have a competitive advantage and to spin off noncore activities to survive. The result is much greater specialization and segmentation within the industry.

In short, the early years of deregulation are typically characterized by shake-outs, massive restructuring, and the consolidation of position among survivors. There is an important difference, however, between Europe 1992 and U.S. deregulation: Many of the new entrants into Europe are already mighty international competitors like American Airlines and Toyota. Thus the shake-out and consolida-

tion phases are likely to be even fiercer than they were in the U.S. during the 1980s. And, because reduced industry-wide profitability often forecloses the option of going to the capital markets, perhaps the biggest mistake many companies can make during the consolidation phase is to spend too much money on acquisitions, entry into new markets, or major capital investments—thus leaving themselves with too little cash to weather the profit drought.[2]

Besides conserving capital and maintaining financing flexibility, the *profitable* survivors are those companies that cut their costs substantially, find new ways of differentiating their products and services, and improve their pricing capability. For example, American Airlines established a two-tier wage structure to cut the cost of new flight crews and a hub-and-spoke system to capture customers and raise loads. It also introduced a frequent flyer program to gain the loyalty of business travelers and hired a staff of over 100 people to maximize revenue per flight by managing the mix of seats and fares. To cite two other cases, successful trucking companies used their investment in freight terminals and information systems to gain economies of scale; and some large securities firms escalated the role of risk capital in securities trading, as well as mergers and acquisitions.

Having weathered the widespead deregulation and restructuring of the 1980s, U.S. multinationals stand to benefit from their experience in highly competitive markets. As a result of such experience, they have acquired a greater readiness to organize their European activities along the most economically efficient lines and to redeploy assets aggressively across national boundaries. This willingness stems in part from the painful decisions many American managers had to make during the wave of corporate restructuring in the 1980s—along with the knowledge that these decisions were the more painful for having been so long delayed. Westinghouse, for example, is cutting back on mature products such as electrical equipment where it has decided it cannot add more value and focusing its resources instead on such growth areas as refrigerated trucking, defense electronics, and environmental controls. In so doing, the company has reduced its European work force by about 50% since 1980.

---

2. The trade-off is that companies with excess financial resources are insulated from the discipline exerted by the capital markets. However, the weakening of managerial incentives that tends to come with financial "slack" is primarily a problem when a company generates substantial amounts of free cash flow. A firm in a deregulating industry facing falling profits and a high degree of uncertainty is unlikely to have much money to squander.

Most such strategies represent nothing more substantial than managerial "leaps of faith"—investments of corporate time and capital whose principal aim at this point seems to be to provide companies with the flexibility to respond to whatever surprises 1992 may yield.

BUSINESS STRATEGY FOR EUROPE 1992

Although there remains considerable uncertainty about what agreements will survive the current negotiations over Europe 1992, companies inside and outside the European Community are acting on the assumption that the single market will be established and that it will mean stronger competition. Companies in industries as diverse as electronic engineering, packaged foods, and insurance are entering into cross-border alliances, merging with competitors, and otherwise restructuring their operations. Most such strategies, however, represent nothing more substantial than managerial "leaps of faith"—investments of corporate time and capital whose principal aim at this point seems to be to provide companies with the flexibility to respond to whatever surprises 1992 may yield.

Many of the moves are obvious ones. Those companies like IBM and Ford that have acted for three decades as if Europe were one market will realize large savings from market integration. They will no longer have to make alterations in their products to meet local standards, and transportation will be quicker and cheaper.

THE CASE OF PHILIPS

Similar gains will come to large European firms that operate in similar fashion. Consider Philips, the Dutch electronics firm that has long operated without much regard to national borders. Giant assembly plants take in components from Philips factories across Europe and dispatch finished products to distribution centers by way of a vast trucking network. A TV factory in Belgium, for example, gets tubes from Germany, transistors from France, and plastics from Italy. In theory Philips' system of centralized manufacturing should be a model of efficiency; in practice frontiers have made it cumbersome and expensive. Trucks spend 30% of their travel time idling in lines at customs posts. To avoid shutting down assembly lines when shipments are late, factories keep extra stock on hand. Philips' inventories are 23% of annual sales, as compared to about 14% for producers in the U.S. and Japan that can count on punctual deliveries. By eliminating delays at customs posts, Philips will be able to cut inventories, close warehouses, and reduce clerical staff and save several hundred million dollars a

year. Also, as local standards vanish, Philips intends to shrink its vast range of washing machines, fluorescent light bulbs, and, especially, TV sets (Europe currently has two standards for TV reception).

Besides opportunities for greater efficiencies in production and distribution, established multinationals may also be able to cut costs by centralizing and coordinating administrative and marketing functions. In dealing with a fragmented European market, many multinationals have evolved into collections of unrelated national subsidiaries, each serving its own local market. But, to serve pan-European customers, these companies will likely reorganize so as to coordinate production, marketing, and logistics across subsidiary boundaries and thereby present a common face to their customers. For example, IBM organizes its production by continent, but its sales by country. This structure may not suffice after 1992 because of customers' increased scope for arbitrage. Perhaps, as in the U.S., customers will buy where prices and VAT rates are lowest and then ship their computers in. Again, extrapolating from the American experience, they might prefer to deal with a Europe-wide IBM specialist for their industry rather than a less-specialized salesman in their own country. In general, companies redesigning their organizational structures to cope with post-1992 Europe must reckon with their customers' responses to the expanded choices they will have in an integrated European market.[3]

Those U.S. firms that are currently operating in a few protected local markets, such as medical supplies, may find that when regulatory barriers fall, they will face new competitors from other European countries. Companies like Philips, Siemens, and Thomson are committed to transforming themselves from "national champions" into global competitors. In responding to such competition, the choices available to U.S. firms include expansion in Europe through acquisition of moderate-sized European companies that appear to be for sale; the formation of strategic alliances, such as joint ventures or cooperation agreements for joint R&D or cross marketing of products; or sale to a competitor and withdrawal from Europe. The last may be the best option for those companies that don't realize much in the way of economies of scale and who may be

---

3. These challenges are described by John F. Magee in "1992: Moves Americans Must Make," *Harvard Business Review*, May-June 1989.

able to take advantage of an active seller's market. But, for those businesses that exhibit scale economies, the greater the growth potential and the weaker the ties between supplier and customer, the greater the opportunity to expand outward into a multinational position.

Those U.S. companies that are currently exporting to Europe may wish to consider producing there. The argument for manufacturing at home is that U.S. labor costs are generally lower and the cheap dollar makes American-made goods competitive. Yet simply staying home may be risky if a large share of the company's sales are in Europe and 1992 brings greater protectionism and competition from stronger European firms. Establishing production facilities abroad—through a start-up, acquisition, or joint venture—can improve relations with European customers, as well with U.S. customers now producing abroad, by demonstrating a deeper commitment to Europe. And producing abroad also provides a hedge against exchange risk.

Finally, U.S. companies that have focused exclusively on the domestic market should reconsider their options. The thrust of Europe 1992 is to allow European companies to build a market base that gives them the scale to compete globally. Ready or not, U.S. companies in many industries are going to face aggressive competition in the U.S. market from European multinationals. At the same time, U.S. companies that have stayed out of Europe because the EC market was too fragmented or the local producers too well protected may find that 1992 will create new opportunities for them. For example, deregulation has given American companies in industries like telecommunications and trucking years of valuable experience with innovative product and service concepts—experience that their European counterparts lack. An integrated EC market may also provide opportunities for U.S. retailers like Circuit City, Toys "R" Us, or Wal-Mart Stores to create new international distribution networks.

THE MYTH OF SCALE ECONOMIES

Underlying much of the planning for a single market is the conventional wisdom—shared by many corporate executives and European governments—that, come 1992, bigger will be better. In post-1992 Europe, national markets will become more like those in the American states, and the companies that prosper will be those that learn to compete according to the time-honored American formula for success: Exploit economies of scale and build up regional brands. This view has touched off a wave of cross-border mergers, as companies seek to gain the size necessary to compete in a borderless Europe and, indeed, a borderless world.

But if national differences across Europe run as deep as some observers maintain, 1992 will pose a much more difficult challenge to management than learning to think as big as Americans. For example, in both the U.S. and Japan, the white-goods business (large appliances like refrigerators and washing machines) is dominated by single brands that have economies of scale in both marketing and production. Europe, by contrast, has many national brands. Although the industry appears ripe for restructuring and consolidation, national brands continue to predominate. So far, widely varying national preferences, combined with the complexity of creating so many different machines, have overwhelmed economies of scale.

These difficulties are best exemplified by the experiences of Philips and Sweden's Electrolux, the first firms to try to create European-wide white-goods firms. Although they have operations in most countries, neither company dominates any national market, except for their small home markets (and in Italy, where Electrolux bought the leading local supplier, Zanussi). In recent years, the two companies have been among the least profitable European producers of washing machines. Much more profitable have been those local companies that have tenaciously defended their dominance of a single national market. Both Philips and Electrolux have found it difficult to realize scale economies through international expansion because of differences in languages, retail systems, and consumer tastes.

Moreover, the newest technologies—flexible manufacturing, faster computers, and better telecommunications—have reduced the optimal size of many businesses, and will probably continue to do so. Computer-controlled flexible manufacturing, which can produce batches tailored to changing customer needs, can now be just as profitable as mass production. Indeed, smaller runs may be necessary to keep up with fast-changing and increasingly specialized markets. For example, Electrolux has developed a flexible manufacturing system that can retool quickly enough to produce its entire range of 1,000 different types of refrigerators within a week.

The restructuring of corporate America during the 1980s indicates that many companies have become too large—that there are in fact signficant *diseconomies* of scale after a certain point.

The view that economies of scale are less important today will not surprise those who have seen GM, with its legendary economies of scale, lose the lead in profitability not only to much smaller Japanese companies but to smaller U.S. companies like Ford and Chrysler as well. Indeed, the restructuring of corporate America during the 1980s indicates that many companies have become too large—that there are in fact significant *diseconomies* of scale after a certain point. Such diseconomies stem from several sources: the growth of large bureaucracies that slow decision making, the increased likelihood of cross-subsidization in larger companies, and the greater administrative costs (including weakened management incentives) associated with managing unrelated businesses.

For example, Philips has cross-subsidized its ventures in computers and semiconductors with profits from its protected consumer electronics and lighting divisions. Such unprofitable businesses are prime candidates for restructuring or divestiture. Philips also spawned a bloated, complacent bureaucracy, weak marketing, and operations that are highly inefficient compared to its Japanese and American rivals. Its sales per employee in 1989 were $100,000, roughly half Matsushita's and Sony's and 25% below General Electric's.

The appropriate response is to weed out unprofitable products, production facilities, and activities. This means breaking down the entire business into the separate activities involved—purchasing, manufacturing, sales, distribution, R&D—and then figuring out how much each costs and how much value each adds. It also means examining every aspect of the business—product lines, customers, organizational structure—to identify those that create value and those that destroy it.

During the 1980s, this kind of value-based self-examination prompted many U.S. companies (or their acquirers) to "downsize" and divest unrelated business activities. In so doing, they were able to strip away superfluous management layers, thereby reducing expenses, speeding decision making, and improving incentives and initiative. At the same time, they were better able to recognize and eliminate hidden cross-subsidies.

Summing Up: A Healthy Skepticism About Scale Economies. Despite growing skepticism about the benefits of size, and the generally dismal experience of large mergers in the U.S., European mergers totaled a record $55 billion in 1989. Many of these mergers will likely fail because of the inability to bridge corporate culture differences and to make tough decisions on cost-cutting and strategy.

In short, companies should be highly selective in their pursuit of scale economies. Some computer makers, for example, have found that they can reap large economies only in R&D and component purchasing; so linking with other firms' R&D or purchasing divisions might be the best strategy. Automakers, by contrast, benefit from size in the centralized development of new engines, which explains why companies like Renault, Peugeot, and Volvo now develop their engines jointly.

Similarly, since many of the differences between the machines sold across Europe can be realized by combining the same parts in different ways, companies have found they can achieve economies of scale in component production, although not in producing and selling the end product. Electrolux, for example, wants to create a world-scale business in white-goods components, such as pumps and engines, as well as in the appliances themselves. It is also centralizing component purchasing and pooling research.

In sum, the surest route to pan-European efficiency is for corporate managements to subject every part of their business to a test of "critical mass." Since each activity—R&D, purchasing, manufacturing, marketing, and distribution—has its own optimal size, a merger that requires bigness across the board can be very inefficient. Megamerged companies joined together lock, stock, and barrel may find that they are too big in some areas—and not large enough in others. Instead companies should focus on growing only those areas where scale economies predominate. Corporate executives who associate size with competitive advantage may well have it backwards: Companies often become large because they are competitive, and not vice versa.

THE SOURCES OF COMPETITIVE ADVANTAGE

Corporate restructuring and "downsizing," of course, are not the answer to all corporate problems. In fact, they typically represent only the beginning stages of an ongoing process of adding value. Moreover, the large, "one-time" efficiency gains that tend to accompany major recapitalizations can generally be realized only by companies in mature industries with excess capacity and thus limited growth prospects. Such downsizings serve the general economic interest by releasing capital and other resources for redeployment in growth industries. But restructuring per se does not address the question of how to achieve future growth.

As Michael Porter has argued, in knowledge- and skill-based industries, the efficiency gains from restructuring matter far less than the ability to innovate and upgrade. Such competitive advantages, in turn, result not from a comfortable home environment but from intense competition. In short, the secret of competitive advantage is to compete.[4]

For example, fierce domestic competition is one reason the U.S. telecommunications industry has not lost its lead in technology, R&D, design, software, quality, and cost. Japanese and European firms are at a disadvantage in this business because they don't have enough competition in their home markets. U.S. companies have been able to engineer a great leap forward because they saw firsthand what the competition could do. Thus, for telecommunications firms like Germany's Siemens, Japan's NEC, or France's Alcatel, a position in the U.S. market has become essential.

Similarly, Porter points out that the most competitive European industries are those where capable national rivals challenge each other vigorously: German cars and chemicals; Swiss pharmaceuticals, heating controls, and flavorings; Swedish heavy trucks, paper products, and machinery; and Italian clothing and factory-automation equipment. Similarly, Japan's nine carmakers and fifteen TV manufacturers show how local rivals, each with only a small share of the home market, can prosper abroad through innovation and the constant pressure of global competition.

By contrast, the European construction industry, which does most of its business in protected home markets, is generally uncompetitive. Indeed, in 1986, American construction firms won $6 billion worth of public orders in Europe while all European firms together won only one-tenth as much in parts of the EC outside their home markets. Having grown fat and lazy through the system of preferential public procurement, local suppliers have little incentive—or ability—to expand abroad.

Although it may be stating the obvious to note that operating in a competitive marketplace is an important source of competitive advantage, this viewpoint appears to be a minority one today. Many companies are preparing for 1992 by seeking mergers, alliances, and collaboration with competitors. Some have gone further and are petitioning their governments for protection from foreign rivals and for assistance in R&D. But, to the extent companies succeed in sheltering themselves from competition, they endanger the basis of true competitive advantage and economic growth: dynamic improvement, which derives from continuous effort to enhance existing skills and learn new ones.

CANON DOESN'T COPY XEROX

The tribulations of Xerox illustrate the dynamic nature of competitive advantage.[5] Xerox dominates the U.S. market for large copiers. Its competitive strengths—large direct sales force that constitutes a unique distribution channel, a national service network, a wide range of machines using custom-made components, and a large installed base of leased machines—have defeated attempts by IBM and Kodak to replicate its success by creating matching sales and service networks. Canon's strategy, by contrast, was simply to sidestep these barriers to entry by (1) creating low-end copiers that it sold through office-product dealers, thereby avoiding the need to set up a national sales force; (2) designing reliability and serviceability into its machines, so users or nonspecialist dealers could service them; (3) using commodity components and standardizing its machines to lower costs and prices and boost sales volume; and, (4) selling rather than leasing its copiers. By 1986, Canon and other Japanese firms had over 90% of copier sales worldwide. And Xerox, having ceded the low end of the market to the Japanese, soon found those same competitors flooding into its stronghold sector in the middle and upper ends of the market.

Canon's strategy points out an important distinction between *barriers to entry* and *barriers to imitation*.[6] Competitors like IBM that tried to imitate Xerox's strategy had to pay a matching entry fee. Through competitive innovation, Canon avoided these costs and, in fact, stymied Xerox's response. Xerox realized that the more quickly it responded—by downsizing its copiers, improving reliability, and developing new distribution channels—the sooner it would erode the value of its leased

---

4. Michael E. Porter, *The Competitive Advantage of Nations* (Free Press: New York), 1990. See also his article on Europe 1992 titled "Don't Collaborate, Compete," *The Economist*, June 9, 1990, 17-19.

5. This example appears in Gary Hamel and C.K. Prahalad, "Strategic Intent," *Harvard Business Review*, May-June 1989, 63-76.

6. This distinction is emphasized by Hamel and Prahalad, cited in note 5.

> To the extent companies succeed in sheltering themselves from competition, they endanger the basis of true competitive advantage and economic growth: dynamic improvement, which derives from continuous effort to enhance existing skills and learn new ones.

machines and cannibalize its high-end product line and service revenues. Hence, what were barriers to entry for imitators became barriers to retaliation for Xerox.

Xerox's experience shows that even the most secure company is vulnerable to competitive innovation. And the absence of significant competitive pressure can increase that vulnerability by reinforcing the faith in accepted practice.

Lacking competitive pressure, dominant companies, or companies caught in a web of links with rivals, will not innovate and upgrade. And, because the expected efficiencies from mergers and collaboration often prove elusive in practice, those companies that seek to gain the size and strength to battle foreign competitors by dominating their home markets through mergers inevitably wind up as losers. Without serious domestic rivals and the constant pressure to excel, these "national champions" often lose their competitive edge and become vulnerable to intrusions by foreign firms.

FIAT'S STRATEGIC DILEMMA

Firms with high domestic market share and minimal sales overseas are vulnerable to the following strategic dilemma. Consider, for example, a Japanese company (call it Toyota) that cuts price in order to gain market share in Italy. If the dominant Italian producer (call it Fiat), with minimal foreign sales, responds with its own price cuts, it will lose profit on most of its sales. In contrast, only a small fraction of Toyota's sales and profits are exposed. Fiat is effectively boxed in: If it responds to the competitive intrusion with a price cut of its own, the response will damage it more than Toyota.

The local firm's correct competitive response is to cut price in the intruder's domestic market. Having such a capability will deter foreign competitors from using high home-country prices to subsidize marginal cost pricing overseas. But this requires investing in the domestic markets of potential competitors. The level of market share needed to pose a credible retaliatory threat depends on access to distribution networks and the importance of the market to the competitor's profitability. The readier the access to distribution and the more important the market to competitor profitability, the smaller the necessary market share.[7]

Companies that ignore these market realities—and most national champions seem to—must turn to government for protection. They then get hooked on government subsidies and become flabbier and less competitive still as protection diminishes the urgency for change. Ironically, domestic dominance typically does not benefit their shareholders, as employees and other special interest groups usually end up capturing any monopoly rents.

Nor are strategic alliances and cooperative research activity likely to be a panacea either. Collaboration can quash innovative design and produce indistinguishable "me-too" products. For example, to deal with Japanese car makers after 1992, European producers are engaged in a variety of collaborative efforts. The danger is that this will blunt competition and remove much of the pressure for innovation.

Identifying The Core Competencies

In many cases, then, companies will find they must develop internally the critical skills and assets they need to compete—the "core competencies" that spawn new generations of products and enable companies to adapt quickly to changing opportunities.[8] For example, 3M has applied its skills in adhesives and coatings across a broad range of products and markets: bandages and dental restoratives in health care; "Post-it" notes and Scotch tape in office supplies; reflective highway signs; diskettes and optical disks for personal computers; and videocassettes and audiocassettes in consumer electronics. What seems to be a highly diversified portfolio of businesses turns out to rest on a few shared capabilities. Similarly, Honda has leveraged its competence in small engine technology to expand from motorcycles into the automobile, lawn mower, marine engine, generator, and chain saw businesses. Unlike physical assets, which diminish with use, core skills are enhanced as they are applied; and they wither with disuse.

One way companies have found to sustain their competitive advantage is to emphasize manufacturing share in core products that embody these core competencies—like laser "engines" in printers or engines in cars—instead of focusing exclusively on

---

7. The notion of undercutting competitors in their home market is explored in Gary Hamel and C.K. Prahalad, "Do You Really Have a Global Strategy?" *Harvard Business Review*, July-August 1985, 139-148.

8. The concept and implications of core competence are discussed in Gary Hamel and C.K. Prahalad, "The Core Competence of the Corporation," *Harvard Business Review*, May-June 1990, pp. 79-91.

market share in the end products. For example, although Canon's share of the world market for laser printers is miniscule, it has a reputed 84% world manufacturing share in desktop laser printer engines. An important advantage of in-house manufacturing is that, by working with the production process on a daily basis, the firm has a better sense of the wider potential of the technology, of possible applications that it would not otherwise consider.

IN-HOUSE MANUFACTURING LEADS TO THE VCR

The history of the videocassette recorder shows how production know-how can yield important technical advances. Sony, along with Matsushita Electric and its partner, Japan Victor Corp. (JVC), redesigned a professional-use product from the U.S. that cost $20,000 or more and turned it into a $1,500 home product with a relatively small market. Japanese designers then worked closely with Japanese factories to make every VCR component smaller and less expensive. Cooperation between Matsushita's design teams and employees on the shop floor eliminated more than three-quarters of the product's cost while dramatically improving its quality. In the process, the company turned a niche product into the mass-market success story of the 1980s. Moreover, in ceding to the Japanese the development of VCRs, as well as laser video disk players, U.S. manufacturers lost more than these products alone. Each technology has since spawned entirely new, popular product lines from video cameras to compact disk players in which U.S. companies have been left with nothing to do beyond marketing the Japanese-made goods.

Modifying DCF Analysis to Accommodate Strategic Investment

Unfortunately, the growth options associated with investments in core products and competencies tend to be undervalued by the standard DCF analysis. To compensate for this bias, management must use an expanded net present rule that considers the costs of not making such investments. (Alternatively, they can use recent extensions of option pricing models to capture the value of strategic options.) Otherwise, as many American firms have discovered, they will wake up one day to find that their "partners"—who have invested in core skills and products—have metamorphosed into rivals who control essential product and process technologies.

IMPLICATIONS FOR U.S. BANKS

American banks should also benefit from a freer market in financial services. They will be able to branch throughout the EC while providing a greater range of financial services. The single license will enable all banks in Europe to realize a number of cost benefits, primarily by being able to operate throughout the EC using common distribution networks, managers, and support systems. A single banking license will also lower bank costs in Europe by eliminating overlapping or conflicting standards and regulatory procedures. The universal banking concept will also expand the powers of U.S. banks providing services in Europe.

Despite the potential cost advantages of establishing an EC-wide bank network, however, the empirical evidence suggests that the scope for economies of scale in banking is rather limited. Indeed, the correlation between size and profitability for the largest EC banks is either negative or minimal. Economies of scale in banking appear limited to instances where the bank's strategy involves common customers, information systems, skills, or processing facilities. One such business is credit cards, which benefits from economies of scale in issuance, centralized data processing, and design standardization.

Absent these commonalities, it seems unlikely that cross-border mergers between large institutions will create value: The cost of merging operations will probably exceed any economies of scale or scope they might achieve. Moreover, the ever-present danger is that as entry barriers start falling, new entrants might overpay in trying to get established and gain market share. Value-creating mergers are most likely to be between relatively small local banks in countries characterized by relatively low concentration ratios.

U.S. banks seeking to benefit from 1992 should focus on pursuing businesses in which they have a sustainable competitive advantage rather than competing directly against dominant local banks that have strongly entrenched positions in delivering basic banking services. For example, Citicorp's EC strategy has been to utilize a cadre of experienced professionals, with expertise in a number of product categories and management techniques, to develop and deliver products in multiple markets. Although each market presents a unique set of challenges, Citicorp employees have already experienced most, if not all, of these situations elsewhere in the world, and thus have ideas and procedures for dealing with them. Citicorp's large EC credit-card operation, for example, relies heavily on its extensive U.S. experience. It has also employed its experience in circumventing U.S. restrictions on interstate banking to build a 700-branch network throughout Europe.

SUMMARY AND CONCLUSIONS

Europe 1992 has enormous ramifications for European and non-European companies. European consumers will realize large gains, as will competitive corporations with access to the unified market. Those companies with an established European presence will have easier access to a bigger market and will be better able to integrate operations across borders, which in turn will help them to reap economies of scale and other efficiencies. They will also face tougher competition. Both factors should push down costs—partly by forcing companies to be more focused in their businesses and more demanding when dealing with unions.

Although consumers will benefit from all these effects, some producers will not. Competition may force them to shrink their businesses, sell out, or go under. Hardest hit by European integration will be those firms that currently enjoy monopoly power in local EC markets. Monopoly power is easy to identify: It shows up in significant price differences for similar products or services across countries. Based on the American experience with deregulation, eliminating entry barriers will allow efficient producers to arbitrage these price differences and lead to reduced profits for the local monopolists.

Those companies that are competitive will expand across Europe and grow much bigger. But companies seeking competitive advantage through size (by means of mergers, acquisitions, and collaborative arrangements) may find that they have put the cart before the horse. Experience suggests that corporate size (at least in unregulated markets) is far more the reflection of past profitability rather than a requirement for future competitiveness. Modern technology, the tendency for large organizations to breed administrative inefficiency, and variable consumer tastes have all reduced the efficient scale in many business activities.

Where scale economies exist, it may be preferable to realize them from worldwide sales rather than from expansion in a protected home market. Foreign competition tends to toughen companies and increase their competitiveness, improving their chances of becoming world-class competitors.

■ ALAN SHAPIRO

is Johnson Professor of Finance at USC's Graduate School of Business Administration. The focus of Dr. Shapiro's extensive research and writings is international financial management and, more recently, the link between corporate strategy and corporate finance.

CORPORATE GOVERNANCE CHANGES MAKE INROADS IN EUROPE

by Howard D. Sherman,
Institutional Shareholder Services

N ew codes of best practice concerning boards of directors, executive compensation, and takeovers within the European Union—each released within a few weeks of each other in the summer of 1995— mark a significant turning point in European corporate governance. The specifics of each code of best practice reflect compromise based on national and EU business practices, political pressures, and financial concerns. But what is common to each is a marked move towards greater transparency, shareholder empowerment, and director oversight—the basic tenets of U.S.- and U.K.-style corporate governance. These trends are likely to take hold over the next few years as privatization programs lure more U.S. and U.K. investors into continental Europe and as competition for listings among stock exchanges worldwide forces European companies to adopt more transparent disclosure standards and raise oversight standards for boards of directors.

How far this trend will develop may depend on another hotly debated issue in Europe. Governments throughout Europe, faced with aging populations and growing budget deficits, are trying to replace state-funded pensions in favor of private retirement systems. These governments face serious opposition from labor unions that fear change will result in reduced benefits and expose them to greater risk if a private sponsor goes bankrupt or misappropriates retirement funds. The transition to an employer-financed retirement system may result in plans more bent on promoting employees' interests than retirees' interests. These plans also could become closely aligned with the banks and other institutions that currently dominate the governance of European companies. Whether these plans will follow the U.S./U.K. pattern and become a new class of independent fiduciaries legally obligated to promote the interests of plan participants and beneficiaries is an unanswered question.

* Reprinted with permission from *Issue Alert* (September 1995), published by Institutional Shareholder Services.

CEPS ISSUES GOVERNANCE STANDARDS

The Centre for European Policy Studies is a research organization that provides an independent forum for debate and policy recommendations to the EU government. The CEPS is located in Brussels near many of the main EU institutions; it draws its participants from many levels of European business, government, and academia, and is a low-key but influential player in EU-wide issues. The CEPS laid the groundwork for governance reform in June 1995 when its Working Party on Corporate Governance issued a report entitled *Corporate Governance in Europe*.

The report stresses the areas in which European corporate governance differs from the U.S. model: where the U.S. model emphasizes shareholder value, European governance places greater emphasis on employee interests. The report's main thrust is that European companies will be increasingly subject to external forces, which will lead to a more open system of corporate governance.

The report also suggests that the U.S. and U.K. trends are likely to play an important factor in the development of European corporate governance: "American and British pension funds, in particular, which represent about 72 percent of total pension fund assets in the Western world, can be instrumental in changing corporate governance standards as a result of the active stance towards investment that is required by local laws and codes." While "a single market is gradually becoming a reality in the European Union," the report notes that "in the field of corporate governance, however, the achievement of a single area without borders is still a far way off."

To promote a more uniform approach, the CEPS Working Party proposed a set of Guidelines of Good Practice as a basic framework for governance standards in the EU. The Guidelines include the following recommendations:
■ There should be a one share, one vote standard unless shareholders approve a dual class structure.
■ Shareholders should be given the chance to vote in an informed and independent manner. At a minimum, they should be able to vote on the election of directors, auditors, dividends, capital authorizations, and company bylaws.
■ Minority shareholders should receive fair treatment in a takeover.
■ The board of directors in a unitary board system (and the supervisory board in the German system) should include outside directors who are capable of exercising independent oversight.

The Working Party did not recommend new legislation, but instead opted for a bottom-up approach: "To launch the initiative, [the EU] should constitute a core group of corporations that would subscribe to the Guidelines and give the necessary publicity to this initiative to foster adherence. An independent body could be appointed to guide the negotiations and later to monitor compliance." The Working Party also recommended that the EU continue to press for consistent international accounting standards.

Although the CEPS Code is liberal compared to current U.S. standards, compromise was the only viable solution to the many contentious issues to achieve a minimum set of standards. That a major EU-wide report has been published is an important step forward for the market. The next question is whether the bottom-up approach, and the recommendation to promote compliance with the Code, will further the development of corporate governance standards in the EU.

PAIRING UP ACCOUNTING STANDARDS

The International Accounting Standards Committee (IASC), comprising national accounting standards board representatives from major markets, and the International Organization of Securities Commissions (IOSCO), an organization designed to establish better coordination among the world's securities regulatory bodies, are two of the most important European organizations in establishing rules of conduct for cross-border securities transactions. In keeping with the CEPS recommendation, the IASC and the IOSCO issued a joint statement from Paris in July 1995 announcing their agreement on a program to develop uniform financial disclosure and accounting standards for companies seeking new capital and stock exchange listings outside their local markets. The program is targeted for completion by 1999.

The need for a uniform set of rules is clear. Multinational companies face an onerous paper and legal burden having to meet different standards each time they want to raise capital or list their shares in a new market. And, because disclosure and financial standards are different in the United States, many European companies that would benefit from a U.S. listing resist because they fear that complying with U.S. rules could alter their valuations and provide their competitors with previously undisclosed information. For example, when Daimler-Benz AG listed its shares on the NYSE in 1993, it reported a profit of DM 615 million under German accounting standards and a loss of DM 1.8 billion under GAAP.

The IASC/IOSCO announcement is a chance for all parties concerned to compromise enough to create a feasible set of accounting standards. One year ago, the same technical committee, which began to work on the project in 1988, failed to reach an agreement. Some observers believe the committee will release a set of initial core standards as early as next year at IOSCO's meeting. Many attribute the development to new pressure from German companies eager to raise capital outside Europe.

U.S. companies are concerned that if the SEC agrees to new IASC/IOSCO standards, they will face unfair competition because the Financial Accounting Standards Board's and the SEC's accounting standards for U.S. companies will remain more burdensome. From the perspective of European companies, however, this is welcome news: It could be their solution to an easier way to raise capital abroad. U.S. compliance with these new standards could lead to increased oversight from outside investors; European governance would separate from its traditional roots. Similar change may result from globalization of the securities industry itself. The EU Investment Services Directive, by promoting competition for cross-border business and listing standards among European exchanges, has already provided a push for more open disclosure within Europe.

GOVERNANCE REFORM IN FRANCE

Paris-based Franklin Global Investor Services and the Association for the Defense of Minority Shareholders have successfully raised the level of debate over French governance during the past few years. Recent shareholder campaigns at Navigation Mixte, Elf Aquitaine, and Compagnie de Suez (see sidebar stories) are examples of how French investors are starting to exercise their shareholder rights. These efforts have caught the attention of the French government and business community. With the ink barely dry on the CEPS report, France took an important step towards opening up its governance system with the release of the Viénot Report and an unprecedented address by the new finance minister.

Without a private pension system, the Paris Bourse (the French stock market) depends heavily on foreign investors. And, foreign investors, the majority of whom are U.S. and U.K. institutions, hold 30% of French equities. Fear of foreign shareholders gaining control of newly privatized companies has led the French government to establish a controlling group of cross-shareholders, termed the *noyau dur*. The emphasis of the noyau dur is on control and is reinforced by the fact that French companies' top executives are closely connected to one another through their attendance at one of France's select universities, the *grande écoles*. Business scandals, the need for new capital to feed the privatization program, and increasing competition for stock exchange listings and cross-border investing in the EU are important forces driving French companies towards a different style of governance.

On July 10, 1995, nearly 1,000 members of the French financial, corporate, and government elite met for a conference organized by Paris Europlace, a group established by the Paris Bourse to promote French business interests. Alain Madelin, the new Minister of Finance and the Economy, announced his intention to push ahead with France's privatization program and to support efforts to develop a private pension system. He noted that France would be implementing the requirements of the EU's Investment Services Directive by January 1996, meaning that the French securities industry and the Paris Bourse would face a more competitive market for stock exchange listings and cross-border securities operations. He also announced the government would look at the governance of state-owned companies.

That the topic of corporate governance made its way into Madelin's speech was news in itself—the subject is so new to France that the French have not yet decided on the proper terms for the debate. After Madelin's speech, Marc Viénot, chairman and CEO of Société Générale, introduced a report entitled, *The Boards of Directors of Listed Companies in France*—the first public document concerning governance standards for French business. The Viénot Report, with parallels to the U.K.'s 1992 Cadbury Report, outlines concepts of board independence familiar to most U.S. and U.K. institutions. The Viénot Report questions the prevalence of board interlocks and cross-holdings typical of French companies. Its recommendations include the following:

UNTIL COMPAGNIE DE SUEZ'S ANNUAL MEETING on June 14, shareholder revolts in France had been nonexistent. Suez shareholders had become increasingly critical of the company's large network of unrelated businesses and were arguing that Suez Chairman Gérard Worms had developed no coherent strategy for the future. Suez's performance was in a downward spiral; in 1994, the company posted losses of US$946 million. In November 1994, Banque Nationale de Paris Chairman Michel Pébereau approached Worms with a proposal to merge the two companies. What ensued was an eight-month battle among Suez's largest shareholders, which highlighted the fragile structure of French cross-shareholdings.

When Worms refused Pébereau's offer, BNP began increasing its stake in Suez. By March 1995, BNP had increased its stake to 5%, making BNP Suez's third largest shareholder behind Saint Gobain and Elf Aquitaine. Pébereau then suggested a three-way combination with Union des Assurances de Paris, another substantial shareholder; the two companies secretly approached Worms with their idea, which he again rejected. Feeling threatened by his large shareholders, Worms began searching for a "white knight." Soon thereafter, the French press began leaking stories of BNP and UAP's merger talks with Suez. Two days later, the press leaked details of merger talks between Suez and Pinault Printemps Redoute—Worms' white knight. The rumors infuriated UAP Chairman Jacques Friedmann, a Suez director who was unaware of Suez's discussions with Pinault. Such a merger would upset Suez's delicate shareholding structure and would give Pinault as much control of Suez as Suez's four largest existing shareholders combined.

At Suez's annual meeting, Friedmann attacked Worms for not informing shareholders of the company's strategy. In addition, the company was proposing a large share issuance request without preemptive rights; passage of the proposal would have given Suez the ability to complete a stock swap with another company without obtaining shareholder approval. At the meeting, the large shareholders forced through an amendment to the plan, prohibiting the use of the shares from the issuance request for a stock swap. Suez finally acceded to its investors' demands, and Worms later resigned under heavy criticism from shareholders.

■ French boards should include at least two independent directors.
■ Boards should establish independent audit, compensation, and nominating committees.
■ CEOs should not sit on one another's compensation committees.
■ Shareholders should have the right to vote on corporate divestitures.

Many considered the Viénot Report's suggestions radical. Yet the report stopped short of providing guidance on topics that others believe will be necessary over time. For example, it recommended that directors of publicly held companies be limited to five directorships, but did not include limits on directorships in privately held and subsidiary companies. Moreover, the report notes that "directors should at all times be concerned solely to promote the interests of the company." The choice of "interests of the company" rather than "interests of the shareholders" offers a glimpse of the differing perspectives between U.S.- and U.K.-style governance and French governance, where employee interests are held on a par with shareholders.

Neither Madelin's policy statement nor the Viénot Report are likely to bring about sweeping changes in the French market in the near term. In fact, not long after his speech, Madelin was forced to resign after French labor interests judged him too intent on reform. As a result, any real changes in French governance will have to come from the marketplace. On Sept. 4, 1995, the chairman of Lyonnaise des Eaux announced that he would, for the first time, disclose his salary and the amount of his stock options in the company's annual report. This move towards greater disclosure is a significant step for the French market and is indicative of where change is likely to occur.

THE U.K. PAY DEBATE

An interesting shareholder controversy this year concerned executive compensation at British Gas (see sidebar story). The issues at British Gas are indicative of growing criticism to reform pay practices in the United Kingdom. However, the overall level of executive pay packages in the United Kingdom pales in comparison with those

COMPAGNIE D'INVESTISSEMENTS DE PARIS'S JUNE 1995 annual meeting was the first time in France's history that a company was the target of a shareholder proposal. U.S. pension fund Elliott Associates submitted five separate shareholder resolutions calling for changes to company strategy and dividend policy. Elliott Associates had been disappointed at CIP's performance: Its shares had been trading at 40% to their net asset value, and for the five-year period ending December 1994, the company's shares had fallen 11% compared with a loss of 5% for the CAC 40 Index (the leading French index). CIP's parent, Banque National de Paris, held 82% of the company's capital and opposed the resolutions.

Disgruntled shareholders in France face more barriers in placing a resolution on a company's meeting agenda than do their U.S. counterparts: U.S. investors need only own $1,000 worth of a company's stock; French shareholders must own a larger amount, which varies depending on a company's size. Although the proposals failed, they set a precedent for future minority shareholder activism.

---

in the United States. According to a recent survey by Towers Perrin, average annual compensation for the CEO of a mid-sized American manufacturer is close to $925,000, compared to $480,000 for a British CEO. The real debate in the United Kingdom has less to do with the size of director pay packages and more to do with how these packages relate to company performance and employee wage levels. One of the hottest areas of concern is the sense that the managements of newly privatized companies have earned a windfall gain in recent years simply because they held options at the time of privatization. Because share prices typically rise after the initial public offering, critics charge that these managers' gains have nothing to do with their own performance. Critics also object to the additional grants the same executives often receive after privatization.

Another uniquely British issue involves "three-year rolling contracts" for directors, which refers to the standard three-year employment agreement for top management in the United Kingdom. The controversy is not the length of the contract, but that executives covered by such contracts are entitled to payment for the full three years even if they leave the company before their term expires. Active shareholders, led by Hermes Investment Management (formerly known as Postel), have campaigned to reduce executive contracts to one or two years to limit these post-employment payments.

In January 1995, the Confederation of British Industry organized a committee to study executive pay issues and provide recommendations for governance reform. On July 17, one week after the release of the Viénot Report in France, Sir Richard Greenbury, chairman of Marks & Spencer PLC, released a report concerning director compensation at publicly traded British companies entitled *Directors' Remuneration—Report of a Study Group Chaired by Sir Richard Greenbury.*

The Greenbury Report includes a Code of Best Practice that focuses on the "fundamental principles of accountability, transparency, and performance." The committee did not call for new regulations, but instead asked that the London Stock Exchange enforce the Code through its listing requirements. The Code includes the following recommendations:

■ Board remuneration committees should be established to handle management compensation decisions and should be comprised of independent, nonexecutive directors.

■ Committee membership should be disclosed in the proxy statement. The board should determine compensation for the nonexecutive directors.

■ Committee reports should be included as a separate section in the annual report and should fully disclose all elements of pay for all company directors, including base pay, incentive, and bonus plans and benefits. (Pension benefits are to be determined by the Faculty of Actuaries and the Institute of Actuaries). The report should also explain why the company is not in compliance with the Code of Best Practice.

■ Executive pay packages should "link rewards to performance" and should "align the interests of directors and shareholders in promoting the company's progress."

■ Management pay levels should be sensitive to employee wage levels.

■ Shareholders should be able to vote on all new long-term incentive plans, including share option schemes, and on existing pay packages that "have attracted controversy."

- Stock options should be granted in phases based on "challenging performance criteria," "should never be issued at a discount," and should not be exercisable for three years from the date of grant. Directors should be encouraged to own meaningful levels of stock.
- Options at newly privatized companies should not be granted for at least six months after the initial offering. Grants should be based on performance relative to other companies in the same industry and not on market-wide gains.
- Director contracts should be set for a maximum of two years.
- Stock option gains should be taxed as ordinary income rather than capital gains and should be taxed when exercised rather than when sold.

The British government immediately endorsed the committee's tax recommendations. However, both the government and Greenbury found themselves in an embarrassing situation. Under British law, taxpayers are entitled to a £6,000 exclusion on capital gains. While eliminating this exclusion would not affect a highly paid director, it would make a difference to a middle manager. Levying the tax at the time of exercise could force middle managers to sell their shares simply to pay the tax, thereby eliminating the purpose of option grants—to link manager and shareholder interests. Critics charged that these tax changes would unfairly penalize the more than 200,000 employees, middle managers, and entrepreneurs who participate in stock option plans in disproportion to the smaller cadre of top executives. Faced with these charges, both Greenbury and the government backed down within a few days and recommended that managers with income levels below a certain amount be allowed to retain their current tax preference for option grants.

With the arrival of the Greenbury Code of Best Practice and the 1992 Cadbury Code of Best Practice, U.K. investors now have standards of conduct for the two most important aspects of corporate governance: board independence and executive pay. With a sizable private pension system and a large number of U.S. institutional investors, there also appears to be a reasonably large and independent pool of capital to monitor these standards. And, the increasing number of British and international shareholder advisory firms to help institutions vote their proxies is advancing the growth of governance. Having established broad principles intended for most public companies, the United Kingdom is now worrying about a more practical problem—implementing the recommendations for independent directors and board committees common to both the Greenbury and the Cadbury Codes.

GERMANY GETS A TAKEOVER CODE

The debate over governance reform in Germany often centers on the rights of minority shareholders, who are usually treated differently from the controlling shareholders: The banks control the voting shares of most large German companies, and the system is plagued by a lack of transparency and a lack of basic legal protections for smaller shareholders. This not only affects their returns in corporate transactions, but can also adversely affect their shares' market valuation. For example, in 1994, minority shareholders at the Marz Group received $396 per share, versus the $528 per share that controlling shareholders received when the company sold off a brewery. The company's explanation was that the minority shareholders' shares were worth 25% less than the controlling shares.

To improve the situation, in July 1995 Germany introduced a set of governance standards designed to protect minority shareholders in the event of a takeover attempt. A takeover commission will monitor the code, which takes effect in October and is modeled in part on the U.K. takeover code and conforms with EU guidelines. The code states that any company acquiring more than 50% of another company must make an offer for the remaining shares within 18 months. The price offered to minority shareholders cannot be more than 25% below the price paid by the acquirer over the preceding six months.

Critics claim the new law does not go far enough, stating that a hurdle of 33% rather than 50% would provide more protection for minority shareholders. Critics have also denounced the 25% discount and 18-month time frame allowed the majority shareholder. On the other hand, supporters maintain that the code is a much-needed step to bring the German system closer to international standards.

Metallgesellschaft's near collapse in 1993 caused many to wonder if Germany's much-vaunted system provided the extra degree of supervision as advertised or whether the supervisory board was merely an extra layer of protection for entrenched managers. The Social Democratic Party has proposed various reforms in the wake of the Metallgesellschaft debacle, including proposals to increase the supervisory board's authority and to improve the links between the supervisory board and outside auditors. To promote an improved monitoring function for outside shareholders, the SDP has also proposed limiting German bank equity holdings and to separating German mutual funds from their bank parents. The German shareholders' association, DSW, has endorsed these proposals, but because the SDP is the opposition party, it will likely not win support for its reform measures. Nevertheless, Germany is clearly in the race for global capital. To stay there, concerns over voting rights and the board system will face tougher scrutiny.

A NEW ERA?

Market forces have made Europe's transformation towards improved corporate governance inevitable. One of Europe's greatest challenges now is how far local institutions will go to protect the rights of minority shareholders and exert meaningful pressure on entrenched management and controlling institutions. This question has much to do with the European private pension market.

Private pensions are now commonplace in the United Kingdom and the Netherlands as a result of increasing budget deficits and unfunded pension liabilities. Furthermore, European demographic trends, in which an aging population is putting demands on the pension system while the workforce is shrinking, are forcing the rest of Europe to move away from state plans to private retirement systems. According to Bloomberg Business News, European governmental retirement obligations now total more than $1 trillion. If these obligations were to be privatized, an enormous growth opportunity would develop for the

investment management and custody industry. The change might also create a new breed of European investor capable of challenging the traditional authority of banks and other controlling shareholders in Europe.

But the presence of large concentrations of new capital by itself is not sufficient to pressure traditional institutions to change. The U.S. experience suggests that without regulatory enforcement and changes to the law, private plan trustees will have a difficult time balancing the wishes of their corporate sponsors with their role as fiduciaries for private pensioners. To date, European governments have not shown a desire to enforce this independence through legislation or even persuasion. European governments face another obstacle in politically powerful labor unions, which are fearful of a change in benefits and guarantees and are resisting the move from state-funded to private plans.

As European corporate governance develops according to its own needs and culture, one result could be the development of a dual system, in which greater transparency, independent directors, and shareholder oversight become commonplace among multinational businesses, leaving the local firms to follow a more traditional European style of governance.

Only a few years ago, few Europeans had ever heard of corporate governance, let alone understood its meaning. However, the new codes of best practice from Viénot, Greenbury, and the CEPS, as well as other developments in Europe this summer, are evidence that the question is no longer whether European governance will face the issues with which the United States has been grappling for the last decade, but how and when its systems will evolve to meet the needs of the global market.

V. EVA: A NEW APPROACH TO CORPORATE GOVERNANCE

Deregulation, global competition, and the rush of technological change and new product development are all driving large organizations to push decision-making down through the ranks to managers and employees closer to the company's operations and customers. Companies that choose to decentralize must also change their performance-evaluation and reward systems to help ensure that operating managers and employees use their expanded decision-making powers in ways that increase the value of the firm. In this sense, decentralization, performance evaluation, and incentive compensation can be viewed as a "three-legged stool" of effective organizational design.

In *"The EVA® Financial Management System,"* my colleagues Joel Stern, Bennett Stewart, and I begin by describing the shortcomings of the top-down, EPS-based model of financial management that has long dominated corporate America. Next we explain the rise of hostile takeovers and the phenomenal success of LBOs in the 1980s as capital market responses to the deficiencies of the EPS model. In the second half of the article, we show how the EVA financial management system borrows important aspects of the LBO movement—particularly, its focus on capital efficiency and ownership incentives—but without the high leverage and concentration of risk that limit LBOs to the mature sector of the U.S. economy. We close by presenting the outlines of an EVA-based incentive compensation plan that is designed to simulate for managers and employees the rewards of ownership.

In *"Total Compensation Strategy,"* Steven O'Byrne argues that the design of the executive compensation plans found in most Fortune 500 companies contains a fundamental flaw. Even though a large proportion of an executive's *current year's* compensation may be "at risk," companies' commitment to maintaining "competitive" levels of compensation *in every year* effectively ensures that a large proportion of the executive's company-related *wealth* (that is, total expected compensation over the executive's entire tenure) is not really at risk. To create a total wealth incentive that replicates the incentives of a significant owner of the company's stock, total compensation strategy must be based on policies that make a substantial proportion of an executive's future compensation depend more heavily on current performance. These policies include (1) *front-loaded, fixed-share* option grants rather than the widely-used annual, variable-share option grants; and (2) formula-based rather than negotiated bonus plans.

THE EVA® FINANCIAL MANAGEMENT SYSTEM

by Joel M. Stern, G. Bennett Stewart III, and Donald H. Chew, Jr., Stern Stewart & Co.

T he information revolution, along with the pace of technological change of all kinds and the rise of a global economy, is leading to major changes in the structure and internal control systems of large organizations. Centrally-directed economies are failing, state-owned enterprises are being privatized, and non-profits are experimenting with new ways of motivating employees and "selling" their services. At the same time, the huge conglomerates built up during the 1960s and '70s—the epitome of central planning in the private sector—are being steadily pulled apart and supplanted by more focused competitors.

In each of these spheres of activity—private, public, and non-profit—the spread of powerful computer and telecommunications networks is contributing to a worldwide move toward decentralization or, to use the more fashionable term, "empowerment." With the flattening of management hierarchies, corporate decision-making is being driven down through the ranks to managers and employees closer to the company's operations and customers.

But, as organizational theorists have long understood, there are significant costs associated with decentralizing decision-making. Today's information systems may now be capable of providing top management with real-time monitoring of the revenues and profits of the most farflung operations. But what software is programmed to report opportunities lost by operating heads too comfortable with the status quo? And what accounting systems are capable of distinguishing reliably between profitable and unprofitable corporate investment decisions *at the time* the decisions are being made?

The answer, of course, is that this kind of information cannot be passed on by computer systems. Such information resides with experienced line managers and employees—those who are posi-tioned to serve as the nerve-endings of the organization—and it will be used to benefit the firm only insofar as those managers and employees are highly motivated and focused on the right goals.

And so, as some organizational theorists are now coming to understand, companies that push decision-making down into lower levels of the organization must also change their *internal control* systems. Such companies will typically find it necessary to rethink both their performance measurement and their reward systems to help ensure that operating managers use their expanded decision-making powers in ways that increase the value of the firm. In this sense, decentralization, performance measurement, and compensation policy constitute a "three-legged stool" of effective corporate control.[1]

In this article, we argue that for many large companies the top-down, earnings per share-based model of financial management that has long dominated corporate America is becoming obsolete. The most serious challenge to the long reign of EPS is coming from a measure of corporate performance called "Economic Value Added," or EVA. As Peter Drucker noted in a recent *Harvard Business Review* article, EVA is by no means a new concept. Rather it is a practical, and highly flexible, refinement of economists' concept of "residual income"—the value that is left over after a company's stockholders (and all other providers of capital) have been adequately compensated. As Drucker also observed, EVA is thus a measure of "total factor productivity"—one whose growing popularity reflects the new demands of the information age. For companies that aim to increase their competitiveness by decentralizing, EVA is likely to be the most sensible basis for evaluating and rewarding the periodic performance of empowered line people, especially those entrusted with major capital spending decisions.

---

1. The term is borrowed from James Brickley, Clifford Smith, and Jerold Zimmerman, "The Economics of Organizational Architecture," in this issue. For the original derivation of the concept, see Michael Jensen and William Meckling, "Specific and General Knowledge, and Organizational Structure," also in this issue.

EVA, moreover, is not just a performance measure. When fully implemented, it is the centerpiece of an *integrated financial management system* that encompasses the full range of corporate financial decision-making—everything from capital budgeting, acquisition pricing, and the setting of corporate goals to shareholder communication and management incentive compensation. By putting all financial and operating functions on the same basis, an EVA system effectively provides a common language for employees across all corporate functions, linking strategic planning with the operating divisions, and the corporate treasury staff with investor relations and human resources.

In the pages that follow, we begin by describing the shortcomings of the top-down, EPS-based model of financial management. Next we explain both the rise of hostile takeovers and the phenomenal success of LBOs in the 1980s as capital market responses to the deficiencies of the EPS model. The EVA financial management system, we go on to argue, borrows important aspects of the LBO movement—particularly, its focus on capital efficiency and ownership incentives—but without the high leverage and concentration of risk that limit LBOs to the mature sector of the U.S. economy. In the final section, we present the outlines of an EVA-based incentive compensation plan that is designed to simulate for managers and employees the rewards of ownership.

THE OLD SYSTEM: EPS-BASED FINANCIAL MANAGEMENT

As Alfred Chandler has argued, the centralized top-down approach to managing large corporations was well suited to the relatively stable business environment that prevailed during the first two or three decades after World War II. The principal challenge of top management then was to achieve the huge economies of scale in manufacturing and marketing that were available to firms finding opportunities for growth in the same or closely related businesses.

In this age of stability, the top managements of most large U.S. companies aimed to report steady increases in earnings per share by calling on each of their operating divisions to produce a given amount of profits each year. Because new capital appropriations for all the divisions (the total amount of which effectively determined the denominator in the EPS calculation) were usually tightly controlled from the top, a given amount of profits aggregated across all the divisions (the numerator) enabled top management to hit the target barring a sharp economic downturn.

The strategy of corporate diversification that became popular in the late 1960s and 1970s—that is, the acquisition of businesses in completely unrelated industries (which Chandler has called "both a disaster and an historical aberration")[2]—can also be explained in part as an attempt by top management to increase its ability to "manage" reported earnings. For one thing, the popular practice of buying companies with lower P/Es in stock-for-stock exchanges automatically boosted reported EPS (such "EPS bootstrapping," as the practice was called, was pure accounting artifice with no economic substance whatsoever). And, to the extent a portfolio of unrelated businesses produced less variable operating cash flows for the entire firm, such corporate diversification served to smooth reported earnings.[3]

Also contributing to top management's ability to deliver smoothly rising earnings—at least for a time—was the annual rite of negotiating divisional budget targets. In a time-honored practice known as "sandbagging," division heads with greater knowledge of their businesses' prospects than corporate staffers would underestimate the profit potential of their own units when negotiating their budgets with headquarters. And, having "low-balled" their estimates and negotiated easy targets, such operating heads also often found it in their own interest to "bank" excess profits for a rainy day—for example, by shifting revenues or costs.

This kind of "satisficing" behavior by division heads can be readily explained by standard features of the corporate reward system. In most companies, division heads' annual bonus awards were capped at a fairly modest fraction (say, 20-30%) of base salary, thus limiting their participation in exceptional profits. And really extraordinary divisional performance in any one year could have the unwanted

---

2. Alfred Chandler, in "Continental Bank Roundtable on Corporate Strategy in the '90s," *Journal of Applied Corporate Finance*, Vol. 6 No. 3 (Fall, 1993), p. 44.

3. Finance theory says that shareholders should be unwilling to place significant value on *corporate* diversification because they can achieve such diversification more cheaply on their own simply by diversifying their portfolio.

And the fact that unrelated businesses must be acquired at large premiums over their fair market value (which we like to describe as "charitable contributions to random passers by") tends to make corporate diversification a doubly losing strategy for the firm's shareholders.

effect of sharply raising future years' budgeted targets (as well as casting doubt on the integrity of the manager's forecasts).

But if the problems arising from budget negotiations were that obvious, then why didn't CEOs abandon the practice altogether and just give their division heads a fixed percentage of the divisional profits? After all, this system has reportedly served Warren Buffett well at a number of his companies.

As some economists and management experts have rightly pointed out, excessive reliance on divisional profit-sharing plans can discourage cooperation among divisions. Purely "objective" divisional performance measures have the potential not only to undermine attempts to exploit synergies among different business units (presumably the reason they are under the same corporate umbrella in the first place), they can even create internal conflicts that end up reducing overall firm value.

But another, more compelling explanation for the widespread use of negotiated budgets is that many top managements were content to tolerate, if not actually encourage, such counterproductive practices. For, besides making the life of division heads easier, the budgeting process also helped top management produce the smoothly rising EPS intended to satisfy shareholders. Thus, while division heads were "sandbagging" their estimates for headquarters, top managements were in some sense sandbagging their shareholders, managing investors' expectations while concealing the true profit potential of the business.

As Gordon Donaldson has argued, the understanding implicit in this management philosophy of the '60s and '70s was that a company's shareholders are only one of several important corporate constituencies whose interests must be served. Top managers saw their primary task not as *maximizing* shareholder value, but rather as achieving the *proper balance* among the interests of shareholders and those of other "stakeholders" such as employees, suppliers, and local communities.[4] In this view of the world, reporting steady increases in EPS was equivalent to giving shareholders their due. And, in fact, such a management approach worked reasonably well—at least as long as product markets were relatively stable, and international competitors and corporate raiders remained dormant.

....

THE CASE OF RJR NABISCO

In his last year as CEO of RJR Nabisco, Ross Johnson reportedly ordered John Greeniaus, the head of RJR's tobacco unit, to spend the excess profits of his division on additional advertising and promotion. Greeniaus later shared this information about the potential profitability of his unit with Henry Kravis of Kohlberg Kravis & Roberts, which reportedly played a major role in KKR's $25 billion bid for and eventual purchase of RJR Nabisco, the largest LBO to date.[5]

In the early 1980s, however, the deficiencies of the top-down, EPS-based system began to show in several ways. Strategically diversified conglomerates such as General Mills (which proudly called itself the "all-weather growth company"),[6] Northwest Industries, Beatrice Foods, and ITT saw their stock prices underperforming market averages even as the companies were producing steady increases in EPS. The operations of such diversified firms began to be outperformed by smaller, more specialized companies. And, as it became progressively more clear that large, centralized conglomerates were worth far less than the sum of their parts, corporate raiders launched the deconglomeration movement.

At the heart of the failure of the top-down, EPS-based control system was its refusal to empower divisional managers, to make them feel and act as if they were stewards of investor capital. One important consequence of this "lack of ownership" was that business units evaluated mainly on the basis of operating profits had little reason to be concerned with the level of investment required to achieve their profits. The primary incentive of operating managers was to achieve (moderate) growth in profits, which could be accomplished in two ways: (1) improve the efficiency of existing operations or (2) win more capital appropriations from headquarters. Because most corporate measurement systems did not hold corporate managers accountable for new capital, it did not take managers long to recognize that it was easier to "buy" additional operating profits with

---

4. See Gordon Donaldson, "The Corporate Restructuring of the 1980s and Its Import for the 1990s, *Journal of Applied Corporate Finance*, Vol. 6 No. 4 (Winter 1994).

5. Source: Brian Burrough and John Helyar, *Barbarians at the Gate* (Harper & Row, 1991), pp. 370-371.

6. See Gordon Donaldson, "Voluntary Restructuring: The Case of General Mills," *Journal of Applied Corporate Finance*, Vol. 4 No. 3 (Fall 1993).

capital expenditures—even if the investment did not promise anything like an acceptable rate of return[7]—than to wring out efficiencies with cutbacks.

This standard capital budgeting procedure led in turn to what might be called the "politicization" of corporate investment, a process in which persuasive and well-positioned business unit managers received too much capital while their less favored counterparts received too little. The top-down EPS system also tolerated the widespread practice of corporate cross-subsidization, in which the surplus cash flow of profitable divisions was wasted in futile efforts to shore up unpromising divisions or in diversifying acquisitions.[8] The result of this politicization of corporate decision-making was chronic overinvestment in some areas and underinvestment in others. In many cases, moreover, it was the potentially more profitable, but capital-starved business units that ended up being sold in LBOs to their own management teams, with the financial backing of outsiders like KKR and Clayton & Dubilier.

CORPORATE RAIDERS AND CAPITAL EFFICIENCY

As noted, the widespread corporate misallocation and waste of capital under the EPS-based system did not escape the attention of corporate raiders in the 1980s.[9] In making their own assessments of potential value, the raiders used a performance metric that was quite different from EPS. They were concerned primarily with companies' ability to generate cash flow (as opposed to earnings) and with their efficiency in using capital.

···

LESSONS FROM THE SAFEWAY LBO

Consider the following testimony from Peter Magowan, who was CEO of Safeway Stores both before and after the company's LBO by KKR in 1986:

"*When Safeway was a public company, our profits grew at 20% per year for five years in a row, from 1981 to 1985...*

We thought all the while that we were doing quite well. Our stock tripled during that period of time, we raised the dividend four years in a row, and 20% percent earnings growth seemed pretty darn good...

But we were still subjected to a hostile takeover [in 1986]—and deservedly so. We were not earning adequate rates of return on the capital we were investing to achieve that 20% growth. We were not realizing the values that were there for someone else to realize for our shareholders.... For this reason, and with hindsight, it now seems clear why outsiders could come in and see a way of buying our company for $4.2 billion—way above its then current market value—and improving it so it was worth $5.2 billion a few years later. And I think that's an important lesson for corporate America.[10]

In many cases, as takeover critics have argued, the push for capital efficiency led to cutbacks in corporate employment and investment. In the vast majority of such cases, however, "downsizing" was a value-adding strategy precisely because of the natural tendency of corporate management in mature industries to pursue growth at the expense of profitability, to overinvest in misguided attempts to maintain market share or, perhaps worse, to diversify into unrelated businesses.[11] This is why the vast majority of leveraged restructurings took place in industries with excess capacity—oil and gas, tires, paper, packaging, publishing, commodity chemicals, forest products, and retailing.

In an article published in this journal called "The Causes and Consequences of Hostile Takeovers,"[12] Harvard professor Amar Bhide compared the economic motives and consequences of 47 hostile takeovers of companies larger than $100 million attempted in 1985 and 1986 to those of a control group of 30 "friendly" takeovers in the same years. Whereas most of the friendly deals were designed to take advantage of vaguely defined "synergies" or to diversify the corporate "strategic" portfolio, the large majority of hostile deals were motivated by profits expected from "restructuring"—that is, from cutting

7. Just before KKR took over RJR, Ross Johnson reportedly approved a $2.8 billion dollar outlay for a state-of-the-art cookie manufacturing facility with a projected pre-tax rate of return of only 5%. (From Peter Waldman, "New RJR Chief Faces a Daunting Challenge at Debt-Heavy Firm," *Wall Street Journal*, March 14, 1989, p. A1:6).

8. The shareholder value destroyed by such unprofitable reinvestment of corporate cash flow has been described by Michael Jensen as the "agency costs of free cash flow." For the original formulation of this argument, see "The Agency Costs of Free Cash Flow: Corporate Finance and Takeovers," *American Economic Review* Vol. 76 No. 2, (May, 1986).

9. For estimates of the extent of the corporate misuse of capital and of the resulting gains from corprate control transactions, see Michael Jensen, "Corporate Control and the Politics of Finance," *Journal of Applied Corporate Finance*, Vol. 4 No. 2 (Summer, 1991).

10. Peter Magowan, "Continental Bank Roundtable on Performance Measurement and Management Incentives," *Journal of Applied Corporate Finance*, Vol. 4 No. 3, p.33.

11. See footnote 8.

12. Amar Bhide, "The Causes and Consequences of Hostile Takeovers," *Journal of Applied Corporate Finance*, Vol. 2 No. 2 (Summer 1989).

overhead, improving focus by selling unrelated businesses, and ending unprofitable reinvestment of corporate profits.

The targets of hostile and friendly deals were accordingly very different. Whereas the targets of friendly mergers tended to be single-industry firms with heavy insider ownership that had performed quite well (as measured by earnings growth, ROE, and stockholder returns), the targets of hostile deals were typically low-growth, poorly performing, and often highly diversified companies in which management had a negligible equity stake. (A *Fortune* magazine poll also ranked their managements as among the worst in their industries, as judged by their management peers.)

There were also notable differences between the *consequences* of friendly and hostile deals, although some differences were not as dramatic as they have been made out to be. Contrary to the claims of takeover critics, hostile deals did not typically lead to large cutbacks in investment or blue-collar employment.[13] And when they did—again, usually in consolidating industries with excess capacity—the cutbacks were roughly proportional to those made by other industry competitors not subjected to takeover. Those layoffs that did take place after hostile takovers tended to be concentrated in corporate headquarters and not on the factory floor. And, as for the R & D issue, the targets of hostile takeovers didn't spend much on R & D to begin with—and this was also true of LBO firms (as we discuss later).

So, if they were not laying off rank-and-file workers and gutting investment and research programs in the drive to make a quick buck, how were corporate raiders—after paying large premiums over market and hefty fees to lawyers and investment bankers—paying the rent? The answer Bhide offers is that, besides making cutbacks in overhead and unprofitable corporate reinvestment, the raiders played a "limited, but significant arbitrage role" in buying large diversified conglomerates, dismantling them, and then selling the parts for a sum greater than the value of the conglomerate whole. Of the 81 businesses sold by the 47 targets of hostile offers in Bhide's sample, at least 78 had been previously acquired rather than developed from within. And roughly 75% of those divested operations were sold

off either to single-industry firms or to private investment groups in combination with operating management. Which brings us to the subject of leveraged buyouts, or LBOs.

THE RISE OF THE LBO: AN INTERIM STAGE IN THE PUSH FOR A NEW CORPORATE GOVERNANCE SYSTEM

Contrary to popular opinion, LBOs are one of the remarkable success stories of the 1980s. So impressive were the results of the first wave of LBOs that Harvard professor Michael Jensen was moved to write an article in 1989 for the *Harvard Business Review* entitled, "The Eclipse of the Public Corporation." There Jensen observed that LBO partnerships like KKR and Forstmann Little, which acquire and control companies across a broad range of industries, represent a "new form of organization"—one that competes directly with corporate conglomerates. With staffs of fewer than 50 professionals, LBO partnerships were said to provide essentially the same coordination and monitoring function performed by corporate headquarters staffs numbering, in some cases, in the thousands. As Jensen put it, "The LBO succeeded by substituting incentives held out by compensation and ownership plans for the direct monitoring and often centralized decision-making of the typical corporate bureaucracy."[14] For operating managers, in short, the LBO held out a "new deal": greater decision-making autonomy and ownership incentives in return for meeting more demanding performance targets.

The Important Differences

Let's look more closely at the differences between LBO firms and the way most public companies were run in the 1980s.

First of all, as newly private companies, LBO firms no longer had any motive for *reporting* higher EPS. Thus, LBOs effectively increased their *after-tax* cash flow by choosing accounting methods that would *minimize* reported earnings—and hence taxes paid—for a given level of pre-tax operating profits. Many public companies, when confronted with the same choice, would routinely choose accounting methods designed to boost reported

13. For macro data that confirm this finding about the 1980s in general, see Michael Jensen (1992), cited above.

14. Michael Jensen, "Active Investors, LBOs, and the Privatization of Bankruptcy," *Journal of Applied Corporate Finance*, Vol. 2 No. 1 (Summer 1988).

earnings, even if this resulted in higher taxes and hence lower after-tax cash flow.[15]

More important, where operating managers in many large U.S. companies tend to treat investor capital as a "free" good, a major concern of LBO firms was to produce sufficient operating cash flow to meet their high required interest and principal payments. In the average LBO of the 1980s, the debt-to-assets ratio increased from about 20% to 90%. Such heavy debt financing had the effect of making the cost of capital in LBO companies highly visible and, indeed, *contractually binding*. Failure to service debt could mean loss of operating managers' jobs (as well as their own equity investment); and it would almost certainly mean a reduction of the LBO partnership's financial (and reputational) capital.

The heavy use of debt financing also provided what amounted to an automatic internal monitoring-and-control system. That is, if problems were developing, top management would be forced by the pressure of the debt service to intervene quickly and decisively. By contrast, in a largely-equity-financed firm, management could allow much of the equity cushion to be eaten away before taking the necessary corrective action.[16]

In addition to this explicit cost-of-capital target, operating managers were also provided—if not required to purchase—a significant equity stake. Such ownership was designed in part to encourage managers to resist the temptation, potentially strong in cases of high leverage, to produce "short-term" profits at the expense of the corporate future. For, even in those LBOs with exit strategies clearly defined at the outset, managers who are also significant owners have incentives to devote the optimal level of corporate capital—neither too much nor too little—to expenditures with longer-run payoffs such as advertising and plant maintenance. Regardless of how an LBO is eventually cashed out—whether by means of an IPO, a sale to another firm, or a recap involving another private investment group or management team—it is still true that the greater the level of *productive* investment undertaken by operating managers, the higher the value of their shares when traded in.

THE CASE OF DURACELL

Consider, for example, what Robert Kidder, CEO of Duracell, had to say about the firm's goals after it was purchased from Dart & Kraft by KKR in an LBO:

"The debt schedule is very effective in forcing management to attend to profitability in the near term. But, let me emphasize that another *important consideration—in some sense, more important than short-term cash flow—is carrying through on strategic commitments. There is a widespread public misconception that because you're an LBO, you have to do everything possible to generate short-term cash flow, and that LBOs thus simply represent a means of sacrificing future profit for immediate gain....*

Now, I don't mean to suggest that we don't do everything possible to reduce waste and cut costs. But, when I talk with Henry Kravis at lunch, we don't spend our time talking about cost reductions. We talk about how we're increasing the strategic value of the company—and by that I mean our long-term cash flow capability."[17]

In the average Fortune 1000 firm, as Jensen notes, the CEO's total compensation changes by less than $3 for every $1000 change in shareholder value. By comparison, the average operating head in an LBO firm in the '80s experienced a change of roughly $64 per $1000; and the entire operating management team owned about 20% of the equity, and thus earned close to $200 per $1000 change in value.[18] Moreover, the partners of the LBO firm itself (the KKRs of this world), which is the proper equivalent of a conglomerate CEO, controlled about 60% of the equity through their buyout funds.

Given such dramatic concentrations of ownership and improvements in the pay-for-performance correlation, researchers were not surprised to find major operating improvements in companies that were taken private through LBOs. There is now a large body of academic evidence on LBOs in the 1980s that attests to the following:[19]

■ *shareholders earned premiums of 40% to 50% when selling their shares into LBOs;*

■ *operating cash flow of LBOs increased by about 40%, on average, over periods ranging from two to four years after the buyout;*

---

15. Corporate managers persist in such EPS-boosting practices even in the face of academic evidence that the stock market rewards higher cash flow rather than reported earnings in cases—such as LIFO vs. FIFO inventory accounting and purchase vs. pooling accounting for acquisitions—where the two measures go in opposite directions.

16. For a demonstration of this point, see Jensen (1989), cited earlier.

17. "CEO Roundtable on Corporate Structure and Management Incentives," *Journal of Applied Corporate Finance*, Vol. 3 No. 3 (Fall 1990), pp. 8-9.

18. Jensen (1989).

19. For a review of research on LBOs, their governance changes, and their productivity effects, see Krishna Palepu, "Consequences of Leveraged Buyouts," *Journal of Financial Economics* 27, No. 1 (1990), 247-262.

- *in cases where LBOs later went public or were sold to another company or investor group, the average firm value (that is, the market value of debt plus equity) increased by 235% (96%, when adjusted for general market movements) from two months prior to the buyout offer to the time of going public or sale (a holding period of three years, on average).*
- *there is little evidence in LBOs of a drop in employment levels or average wages of blue-collar workers;*
- *LBO firms were not doing much R&D to begin with; only about 10% of LBO firms were engaging in enough R&D before the LBO to report it separately in their financial statements;*
- *LBO boards, with typically eight or fewer members, represent about 60% of the equity, on average.*

As the last finding suggests, however, it was not just better-designed performance measures and stronger ownership incentives that lay behind the success of LBOs. The LBO *governance* system is also fundamentally different from that of most public corporations. In fact, LBOs borrow several of the central governance features of venture capital firms.

Much as in venture capital firms like Kleiner Perkins, the boards of companies owned by LBO partnerships like KKR and Clayton & Dubilier are designed in large part to overcome many of the information problems facing boards of directors in public companies. The directors of a typical LBO don't merely represent the outside shareholders, they *are* the principal shareholders. Moreover, they have become the principal owners only after having participated in an intensive "due diligence" process intended to reveal the true profit potential of the business. And, as in the case of venture capital firms, the board members in LBOs also typically handle the corporate finance function, including negotiations with lenders and the investment banking community. If operating companies get into financial or operating difficulty, the board intervenes quickly, often appointing one of its members to step in as CEO until the crisis passes.

···

THE CASE OF THE BLACKSTONE GROUP

James Birle, General Partner of the Blackstone Group, comments as follows on the differences between the LBO governance process and that of most public companies:

"Unlike the boards of public companies, our board members come to the table already knowing a great deal about the operations and expected behavior of the businesses in various economic and competitive situations. This knowledge comes from the extensive due diligence process we have conducted just prior to the acquisitions. So we are able to determine when management has really gotten off the track far more quickly and confidently than most public company directors....

We [also] have a much tighter performance measurement system, by necessity, than most public companies I'm familiar with. The pressure to ensure that goals are being met is just far greater than that which exists in most public companies. At the same time, this sense of urgency does not prevent us from setting and pursuing long-term goals. Our goal at the Blackstone Group is maximizing shareholder value, and you can't command a high price for a business if all you've been doing is liquidating its assets and failing to invest in its future earnings power. And since management are also major equity holders in the company, we are confident that they are constantly attempting to balance short-term and long-term goals in creating value."[20]

What Went Wrong with the LBOs?

All this is not to suggest that the LBO movement was without flaws, or to deny that mistakes were made in structuring many of the deals. Beginning in 1989, there was a sharp increase in the number of defaults and bankruptcies of LBOs. Most of the problems, it turns out, came in the deals transacted in the latter half of the 1980s. Of the 41 LBOs with purchase prices of $100 million or more transacted between 1980 and 1984, only one defaulted on its debt. By contrast, of the 83 large deals done between 1985 and 1989, at least 26 defaulted and 18 went into bankruptcy.[21]

What went wrong with the later deals? Just as Jensen was the first economist to see the value-adding potential of LBOs, he was also the first to identify the source of the problems that were arising in the later transactions. Stated in brief, Jensen's analysis pointed to a "gross misalignment of incentives" between the dealmakers who promoted the transactions and the lenders and other investors who funded them. Such a "contracting failure" led to a

20. James Birle, "Continental Bank Roundtable on the Role of Corporate Boards in the 1990s," *Journal of Applied Corporate Finance*, Vol. 5 No. 3 (Fall 1992), pp. 68.

21. Steven Kaplan and Jeremy Stein, "The Evolution of Buyout Pricing and Financial Structure in the 1980s," *Journal of Applied Corporate Finance*, Vol. 6 No. 1 (Spring 1993).

Where operating managers in many large U.S. companies tend to treat investor
capital as a "free" good, the heavy debt financing in LBOs had the effect of making
the cost of capital highly visible and, indeed, *contractually binding*.

concentration of overpriced, poorly structured deals in the second half of the '80s.[22]

Jensen's diagnosis was supported, moreover, by an important study by Steven Kaplan and Jeremy Stein demonstrating that (1) buyout prices as multiples of cash flow rose sharply in LBOs completed in the period 1986-1988, especially in junk-bond-financed transactions; (2) junk bonds displaced much of both the bank debt and the private subordinated debt in the later LBOs, thereby sharply raising the costs of reorganizing troubled companies; and (3) management and other interested parties, notably the dealmakers, put in less equity and took out more money up front in later deals.[23]

The Limitations of LBOs

A private market correction to the contracting problem noted by Jensen and others was already underway when regulators intervened heavily in the summer of 1989. There was already a general movement toward larger equity commitments, less debt, lower transaction prices, and lower upfront fees when S&L legislation (FIRREA) and HLT regulations created a downward spiral in high-yield bond prices (and, some would argue, in business activity in general). And much tightened oversight by bank regulators made it virtually impossible to reorganize troubled companies outside of Chapter 11 (by contrast, low-cost, expeditious private work-outs were a common event for the first wave of LBOs during the severe recession of 1981-82).[24]

As a consequence, LBOs and other HLTs underwent a sharp decline during the early 1990s. But, in the past few years, LBOs have begun to show signs of a resurgence. Nevertheless, even with the contracting problems of the late '80s largely corrected, there are still inherent limitations in the LBO form that are likely to ensure them at most a fairly specialized role in the U.S. economy.

First, of course, is their reliance on high leverage. The role of debt financing in LBOs limits their use primarily to mature industries with modest capital requirements, tangible assets, and highly stable cash flows. Although some steady-state service companies may prove suitable for LBOs, high-growth and high-tech companies will generally not. In the latter case, the expected costs of debt financing in the form of lost investment opportunities are just too large.[25]

The second limitation of LBOs stems from one of their principal benefits: the concentration of equity ownership. Concentration of ownership also means a concentration of risk-bearing. One of the main advantages of the public corporation is its efficiency in *spreading* risk among well-diversified investors. At some point, increasing the "firm-specific" risk borne by the management team becomes self-defeating because such managers will require sufficiently higher compensating rewards (in the form of stock or profit sharing) that there will be less left over for shareholders, even after considering the incentive benefits of such concentrated ownership.[26]

It is this heavy concentration of risk, not managerial shortsightedness, that explains why so many LBOs return to public ownership in five years or less. When they enter into an LBO, both owners and operating managers are betting on their ability to increase the value of the organization. But, in order to limit the scope of their bet and minimize their exposure to risks beyond their control, they typically have an exit or cash-out strategy. In his study of "The Staying Power of Leveraged Buyouts," Steven Kaplan reported that, as of early 1993, roughly half of the large LBOs ($100 million or more) of the 1980s had reverted to public ownership. Even so, some 90% of the 2,500 LBOs (large and small) transacted since the late 1970s still remain private; and, as Kaplan also reported, those LBOs that had gone public through IPOs retained two distinguishing features of the LBO

22. See the comments by Michael Jensen in "The Economic Consequences of High Leverage and Stock Market Pressures on Corporate Management: A Roundtable Discussion," *Journal of Applied Corporate Finance* Vol. 3 No. 2 (Summer 1990), pp. 8-9. For a more formal elaboration of this argument, see Michael Jensen, "Corporate Control and the Politics of Finance," *Journal of Applied Corporate Finance*, Vol. 4 No. 2 (Summer, 1991), pp. 25-27.

23. As reported in Kaplan and Stein (1993).

24. See Michael Jensen, "Corporate Control and the Politics of Finance," *Journal of Applied Corporate Finance*, Vol. 4 No. 2, pp. 27-29. As Jensen writes, "Such regulations...reduced the flexibility of lenders to work with highly leveraged companies who could not meet lending covenants or current debt service payments. These changes, coming on top of the departure of Drexel, the principal market maker, caused a sharp increase in defaults."

25. Although some observers have predicted an extension of the LBO form to high-growth, high-tech companies, the lower leverage and greater dispersion of equity that is best suited to such riskier companies will ultimately work to undermine the very sources of financial discipline that have helped to make LBOs so effective. For a discussion of corporate debt capacity that bears on this issue, see Michael Barclay, Clifford Smith, and Ross Watts, "The Determinants of Corporate Leverage and Dividend Policies," *Journal of Applied Corporate Finance*, Winter 1995.

26. See the article in this issue by Randy Beatty, "Management Incentives, Monitoring, and Risk-bearing in IPO Firms," which shows that riskier IPOs actually tend to have lower percentage ownership.

form: (1) considerably higher leverage (though below buyout levels) compared to that of their public competitors; and (2) significantly more concentrated equity ownership by insiders (over 40%, on average).[27]

EVA: A NEW FINANCIAL MODEL FOR PUBLIC COMPANIES

The accomplishments of the LBO movement have some important lessons for the structure and governance of public companies. For most large public companies, of course, it will not make sense to raise leverage ratios to 90%. Nor will it generally be cost-effective to provide significant stock ownership for most operating managers. In such cases, top management must design a performance measurement and reward system that simulates the feel and payoff of ownership. This is the principal aim of an EVA financial management system.

Like LBOs, but without the costs of high leverage or excessive risk-bearing, an EVA-based performance measurement system makes the cost of capital explicit. In its simplest form, EVA is net operating profit after taxes less a charge for the capital employed to produce those profits. The capital charge is the required, or minimum, rate of return necessary to compensate all the firm's investors, debtholders as well as shareholders, for the risk of the investment.[28]

To illustrate, a company with a 10% cost of capital that earns a 20% return on $100 million of net operating assets has an EVA of $10 million. This says the company is earning $10 million more in profit than is required to cover all costs, including the opportunity cost of tying up scarce capital on the balance sheet. In this sense, EVA combines operating efficiency and balance sheet management into one measure that can be understood by operating people.

For operating heads and top management alike, EVA holds out three principal ways of increasing shareholder value:

■ First, increase the return derived from the assets already tied up in the business. Run the income statement more efficiently without investing any more capital on the balance sheet.

■ Second, invest additional capital and aggressively build the business so long as the return earned exceeds the cost of that new capital. (Targets based on rates of return such as ROE or ROI, incidentally, can actually discourage this objective when divisions are earning well above their cost of capital, because taking on some EVA-increasing projects will lower their average return.)

■ Third, stop investing in, and find ways to release capital from, activities that earn substandard returns. This means everything from turning working capital faster and speeding up cycle times to consolidating operations and selling assets worth more to others.

Besides making the cost of capital explicit, the EVA performance measure can also be designed to encourage tax-minimizing accounting choices and to incorporate a number of other adjustments intended to eliminate distortions of economic performance introduced by conventional accounting measures like earnings or ROE. For example, one notable shortcoming of GAAP accounting stems from its insistence that many corporate outlays with longer-term payoffs (like R & D or training) be fully expensed rather than capitalized and amortized over an appropriate period. While well-suited to creditors' concerns about liquidation values, such accounting conservatism can make financial statements unreliable as guides to going-concern values. More important, to the extent GAAP's conservatism is built into a company's performance measurement and compensation system, it can unduly shorten managers' planning horizon.

In setting up EVA systems, we sometimes advise companies to capitalize portions of their R&D, marketing, training, and even restructuring costs. In cases of other "strategic" investments with deferred payoffs, we have also developed a procedure for keeping such capital "off the books" (for internal

---

27. As Steven Kaplan has noted, there appear to be two distinct species of LBOs: (1) a "shock-therapy" variety, in which the LBO provides a vehicle for largely "one-time" improvements; and (2) a relatively permanent, "incentive-intensive" type, in which the company's investors and managers become convinced that the company is fundamentally more valuable as a private company than public. See Steven Kaplan, "The Staying Power of the Leveraged Buyouts," *Journal of Applied Corporate Finance*, Spring 1993. This article is a shorter, less technical, and partly updated version of another article with the same title published in the *Journal of Financial Economics* 29 (1991).

28. EVA is charged for capital at a rate that compensates investors for bearing the firm's explicit business risk. The assessment of business risk is based upon the

Capital Asset Pricing Model, which allows for a specific, market-based evaluation of risk for a company and its individual business units using the concept of "beta." In addition, the tax benefit of debt financing is factored into the cost of capital, but in such a way as to avoid the distortions that arise from mixing operating and financing decisions. To compute EVA, the operating profit for the company and for each of the units is charged for capital at a rate that blends the after-tax cost of debt and equity in the *target* proportions each would plan to employ rather than the actual mix each actually uses year-by-year. Moreover, operating leases are capitalized and considered a form of debt capital for this purpose. As a result, new investment opportunities are neither penalized nor subsidized by the specific forms of financing employed.

Even with the contracting problems of the late '80s largely corrected, there are
limitations inherent in the LBO form that are likely to ensure them at most a fairly
specialized role in the U.S. economy.

evaluation purposes) and then gradually readmitting it into the manager's internal capital account to reflect the expected payoffs over time. As these examples are meant to suggest, EVA can be used to encourage a more far-sighted corporate investment policy than traditional financial measures based upon GAAP accounting principles.

In defining and refining its EVA measure, Stern Stewart has identified over 120 shortcomings in conventional GAAP accounting. In addition to GAAP's inability to handle R&D and other corporate investments, we have addressed performance measurement problems associated with standard accounting treatments of the following: inventory costing and valuation; depreciation; revenue recognition; the writing-off of bad debts; mandated investments in safety and environmental compliance; pension and post-retirement medical expense; valuation of contingent liabilities and hedges; transfer pricing and overhead allocations; captive finance and insurance companies; joint ventures and start-ups; and special issues of taxation, inflation, and currency translation. For most of these accounting issues, we have crafted a series of cases to illustrate the performance measurement problem, and devised a variety of practical methods to modify reported accounting results in order to improve the accuracy with which EVA measures real economic income.

Of course, no one company is likely to trigger all 120 measurement issues. In most cases, we find it necessary to address only some 15 to 25 key issues in detail—and as few as five or ten key adjustments are actually made in practice. We recommend that adjustments to the definition of EVA be made only in those cases that pass four tests:

■ Is it likely to have a material impact on EVA?
■ Can the managers influence the outcome?
■ Can the operating people readily grasp it?
■ Is the required information relatively easy to track or derive?

For any one company, then, the definition of EVA that is implemented is highly customized with the aim of striking a practical balance between simplicity and precision.

To make the measure more user-friendly, we have also developed a management tool called "EVA Drivers" that enables management to trace EVA through the income statement and balance sheet to key operating and strategic levers available to them in managing their business. This framework has proven to be quite useful in focusing management's attention, diagnosing performance problems, benchmarking with peers, and enhancing planning. More generally, it has helped people up and down the line to appreciate the role they have to play in improving value. It can also help guard against an excessive preoccupation with improving individual operational metrics to the detriment of overall performance. For example, a drive to increase productivity—or, say, a single-minded obsession with winning the Malcolm Baldridge Award—could lead to unwarranted capital spending or to shifts in product mix that result in less EVA and value, not more. In the end, management must be held accountable for delivering value, not improving metrics.[29]

THE EVA FINANCIAL MANAGEMENT SYSTEM

As we suggested at the beginning of this article, the real success of business today depends not on having a well-thought-out, far-reaching strategy, but rather on re-engineering a company's business systems to respond more effectively to the new business environment of continuous change. Our contention at Stern Stewart is that just as this information revolution has created a need for business process re-engineering, it has also precipitated a need to re-engineer the corporate *financial management system*.

What do we mean by a financial management system? A financial management system consists of all those financial policies, procedures, methods, and measures that guide a company's operations and its strategy. It has to do with how companies address such questions as: What are our overall corporate financial goals and how do we communicate them, both within the company and to the investment community? How do we evaluate business plans when they come up for review? How do we allocate resources—everything from the purchase of an individual piece of equipment, to the acquisition of an entire company, to opportunities for downsizing and restructuring? How do we evaluate ongoing operating performance? Last but not least, how do we pay our people, what is our corporate reward system?

---

29. Nevertheless, our research suggests a remarkably strong correlation between a company's EVA performance, its shareholder value added (or "MVA"), and its standing in *Fortune's Most Admired* survey, a ranking based upon an assessment of such criteria as customer responsiveness, innovation, time-to-market, and management quality. See Bennett Stewart, "EVA: Fact and Fantasy," *Journal of Applied Corporate Finance*, Vol. 7 No. 2 (Summer 1994).

Many companies these days have ended up with a needlessly complicated and, in many respects, hopelessly obsolete financial management system. For example, most companies use discounted cash flow analysis for capital budgeting evaluations. But, when it comes to other purposes such as setting goals and communicating with investors, the same companies tend to reach for accounting proxies—measures like earnings, earnings per share, EPS growth, profit margins, ROE, and the like. To the extent this is true, it means there is already a "disconnect" between the cash-flow-based capital budget and accounting-based corporate goals. To make matters worse, the bonuses for operating people, as we noted earlier, tend to be structured around achieving some annually negotiated profit figure.

This widespread corporate practice of using different financial measures for different corporate functions creates inconsistency, and thus considerable confusion, in the management process. And, given all the different, often conflicting, measures of performance, it is understandable that corporate operating people tend to throw their hands in the air and say, "So, what are you really trying to get me to do here? What is the real financial mission of our company?"

With EVA, all principal facets of the financial management process are tied to just one measure, making the overall system far easier to administer and understand. That is, although the process of coming up with the right definition of EVA for any given firm is often complicated and time-consuming, the measure itself, once established, becomes the focal point of a simpler, more integrated overall financial management system—one that can serve to unite all the varied interests and functions within a large corporation.

Why is it so important to have only one measure? As we noted earlier, the natural inclination of operating managers in large public companies is to get their hands on more capital in order to spend and grow the empire. This tendency in turn leads to an overtly political internal competition for capital—one in which different performance measures are used to gain approval for pet projects. And because of this tendency toward empire-building, top management typically feels compelled to intervene excessively—not in day-to-day decision making, but in capital spending decisions. Why? Because they don't trust the financial management system to guide their

operating managers to make the right decisions. There's no real accountability built into the system, there's no real incentive for operating heads to choose only those investment projects that will increase value.

....

THE CASE OF BRIGGS AND STRATTON

At the annual shareholders' meeting in 1991, Chairman Fred Stratton of Briggs & Stratton noted that the company's stock was up 70% from the previous year, having outperformed the S&P 500 by about 40%. Stratton attributed the company's success in large part to the company's newly adopted "performance measurement and compensation system" based on EVA.

"Part of our problem in the early 1980s," comments president and chief operating officer John Shiely, *"was an antiquated functional 'top-down' structure. Nobody other than the CEO and the president was being held accountable for the profitability of our various lines. Under Chairman Fred Stratton's direction, we developed a plan to totally revamp the organization into discrete operating divisions. While the initial move was painful, the positive results were almost immediate. By pushing operating responsibility, including capital decisions, down to the level where they could be effectively managed, we accomplished a dramatic improvement in earnings and cash flow. Each of our seven new divisions now has its own functional management, resources, and capital. Each must develop very detailed strategic business unit plans. And each has an EVA incentive based on value created by the division."*

"Before moving to an EVA system, the company took pride in making almost all components in-house. We now buy premium engines, at significantly lower cost, from outside sources. Molded plastics and other components, once made in small batches in-house, now flow from suppliers in huge quantities. As a result, operating profits have risen while the amount of capital required to generate them has fallen sharply."

EVA is the internal measure management can decentralize throughout the company and use as the basis for a completely integrated financial management system. It allows all key management decisions to be clearly modelled, monitored, communicated, and rewarded according to how much value they add to shareholders' investment. Whether reviewing a capital budgeting project, valuing an acquisition, considering strategic plan alternatives, assessing performance, or determining bonuses, the goal of increasing EVA over time offers a clear financial mission for management and a means of improving accountability and incentives. In this sense, it offers a new model of internal corporate governance.

EVA AND THE CORPORATE REWARD SYSTEM

Incentive compensation is the anchor of the EVA financial management system. The term "incentive compensation" is not quite right, however, for in practice too much emphasis gets placed on the word "compensation" and not enough on the word "incentive." The proper objective is to make managers behave as if they were owners. Owners manage with a sense of urgency in the short term but pursue a vision for the long term. They welcome change rather than resisting it. Above all else, they personally identify with the successes and the failures of the enterprise.

Extending an ownership interest is also the best way to motivate managers in the information age. As the pace of change increases and the world becomes ever less predictable, line managers need more general as opposed to specific measures of performance to which they will be held accountable. They need more leeway to respond to changes in the environment. They need a broader and longer-range mandate to motivate and guide them. Maximizing shareholder value is the one goal that remains constant, even as the specific means to achieve it are subject to dramatic and unpredictable shifts.

Making managers into owners should not be undertaken as an "add-on" to current incentive compensation methods. Rather, it should replace them. In place of the traditional short-term bonus linked to budget and ordinary stock option grants, the EVA ownership plan employs two simple, distinct elements: (1) a cash bonus plan that simulates ownership; and (2) a leveraged stock option (LSO) plan that makes ownership real.

The EVA Bonus Plan: Simulating Ownership

The cash bonus plan simulates ownership primarily by tying bonuses to *improvements* in EVA over time. Paying for improvements in rather than absolute levels of EVA is designed mainly to solve the problem of "unequal endowments." This way, managers of businesses with sharply negative EVA can be given a strong incentive to engineer a turnaround—and those managers of businesses already producing large positive EVA do not receive a windfall simply for showing up.

Besides leveling the playing field for managers inheriting different circumstances, bonuses tied to improvements in rather than levels of EVA are also "self-financing" in the following sense: to the extent that a company's current stock tends to reflect current levels of EVA, it is only *changes* in current levels of EVA that are likely to be correlated with changes in stock price.[30] And, to the extent the managers of a given company succeed in increasing a company's EVA and so earn higher bonus awards for themselves, those higher bonuses are more than paid for by the increase in shareholder value that tends to accompany increases in EVA.

As with a true ownership stake, EVA bonuses are not capped. They are potentially unlimited (on the downside as well as upside), depending entirely on managerial performance. But, to guard against the possibility of short-term "gaming" of the system, we have devised a "bonus bank" concept that works as follows: Annual bonus awards are not paid out in full, but instead are banked forward and held "at risk," with full payout contingent on continued successful performance. Each year's bonus award is carried forward from the prior year and a fraction—for example, one third—of that total is paid out, with the remainder banked into the next year.

Thus, in a good year, a manager is rewarded—much like a shareholder who receives cash dividends and capital appreciation—with an increase in both the cash bonus paid out and in the bonus bank carried forward. But, in a poor year—again, much like a shareholder—the penalty is a shrunken cash distribution and a depletion in the bank balance that must be recouped before a full cash bonus distribution is again possible. Because the bonus paid in any one year is an accumulation of the bonuses earned over time, the distinction be-

---

30. Our own research indicates that the changes in companies' EVAs over a five-year period account for nearly 50% of the changes in their market value added, or MVAs, over that same time frame. (MVA, which is a measure of the shareholder value added by management, is roughly equal to the difference between the total market value and the book value of the firm's equity.) By comparison, growth in sales explained just 10% of the MVA changes, growth in earnings-per-share about 15% to 20%, and return on equity only 35%. For a description of this research, see Bennett Stewart, "Announcing the Stern Stewart Performance 1,000," *Journal of Applied Corporate Finance* Vol. 3 No. 2 (Summer 1990).

tween a long-term and a short-term bonus plan becomes meaningless.

When combined with such a bonus bank system, EVA incentive plans tied to continuous improvement also help to break the counterproductive link between bonuses and budgets that we described earlier. EVA targets are automatically reset from one year to the next by formula, not annual negotiation. For example, if EVA should decline for whatever reason, management will suffer a reduced, possibly negative bonus in that year. In the following year, however, the minimal standard of performance for the next year's bonus will be set somewhat lower—again, by a pre-set formula. This automatic lowering of expectations is designed to help companies retain and motivate good managers through bad times by giving them a renewed opportunity to earn a decent bonus if they can reverse the company's fortune. At the same time, however, it avoids the problem—inherent in the stock option "repricing" practices of so many public companies—of rewarding managers handsomely when the stock drops sharply and then simply returns to current levels.

In combination with a bonus bank, then, the use of objective formulas to reset targets eliminates the problems of "sandbagging" on budgets and encourages collaborative, long-range planning. Instead of wasting time managing the expectations of their supervisors, managers are motivated to propose and execute aggressive business plans. Moreover, because it compensates the end of creating value rather than the means of getting there, the EVA bonus plan is entirely consistent with the movement to decentralize and empower.

In sum, the banking of bonuses tied to continuous improvements in EVA helps companies to smooth cyclical bumps and grinds, extends managers' time horizons, and encourages good performers accumulating equity in their bank accounts to stay and poor performers running up deficits to go. In so doing, the EVA bonus bank functions as both a long-term and short-term plan at one and the same time.

Leveraged Stock Options: Making Ownership Real

The annual EVA cash bonus is intended to simulate an owner's stake. In many cases, however, it will often be valuable to supplement the bonus plan with actual stock ownership by management. Pursuit of that goal, however, runs headlong into this fundamental contradiction: How can managers with limited financial resources be made into significant owners without unfairly diluting the current shareholders? Showering them with stock options or restricted stock is apt to be quite expensive for the shareholders, notwithstanding the incentive for the managers. And asking the managers to buy lots of stock is apt to be excessively risky for them.

One approach we recommend to resolve this dilemma is to encourage (or require) managers to purchase common equity in the form of special leveraged stock options (LSOs). Unlike ordinary options, these are initially in-the-money and not at-the-money, are bought and not granted, and project the exercise price to rise at a rate that sets aside a minimal acceptable return for the shareholders before management participates.

Although managers' purchase of LSOs could be funded by them as a one-time investment, we typically recommend that managers be allowed to buy them only with a portion of their EVA bonuses. Besides providing even more deferred compensation, this practice helps ensure that only those managers who have added value in their own operations are allowed to participate in the success of the entire enterprise.

To illustrate how an LSO operates, consider a company with a current common share price of $10. The initial exercise price on the LSO is set at a 10% discount from the current stock price, or $9, making the option worth $1 right out of the gate. But instead of just handing the LSOs to management, managers are required to purchase them for the $1 discount, and that money is put at risk. Another difference between LSOs and regular options is that the exercise price is projected to increase at a rate that approximates the cost of capital (less a discount for undiversifiable risk and illiquidity)—let's say 10% per annum. In this case, over a five-year period (and ignoring compounding for simplicity), the exercise price will rise 50% above the current $9 level to $13.50. In sum, management pays $1 today for an option to purchase the company's stock (currently worth $10) for $13.50 five years down the road.

Only if the company's equity value grows at a rate faster than the exercise price will management come out ahead. Indeed, if the exercise price rises at a rate equal to the cost of capital (less the dividend yield), then the LSOs wll provide exactly the same incentives as an EVA bonus plan. It rewards management for generating a spread between the company's rate of return on capital and the cost of that capital (as reflected by the rate of increase in the exercise price) times the capital employed by management to purchase the shares.

Perhaps a better comparison, however, is between the incentives held out by LSOs and those provided by leveraged buyouts. LSOs can be seen as putting management in the position of participating in an LBO, but without requiring an actual LBO of the company. By virtue of their being purchased 10% in the money, LSOs effectively replicate the 90% debt and 10% equity that characterized the structure of the LBOs of this past decade. Companies ranging from Briggs & Stratton, Centura Bank, CSX, Fletcher Challenge (the largest industrial company in New Zealand), R.P Scherer, and Varity have adopted LSO plans.

At bottom, then, LSOs (and LBOs, as we have seen) also boil down to EVA, to the idea that management should participate only in those returns in excess of a company's required rate of return. But while conceptually identical to an EVA bonus plan, LSOs are likely to be an even more powerful motivator because they amplify the risks and rewards for management. Any improvement in EVA that investors think will be sustained is capitalized into the value of the shares; for example, a company with a cost of capital of 10% that increases its EVA by $1 million will see its value appreciate by $10 million. For managers holding the LSOs, such capitalized increases in value are themselves further leveraged 10 to 1, thus creating $100 of added managerial wealth for each $1 improvement in EVA. This leveraging effect makes LSOs a potent way to get management to concentrate on building EVA over the long haul.

....

BACK TO BRIGGS & STRATTON

Having tasted success with their initial EVA bonus plan, management's appetite was whetted for taking more risk in return for the prospect of an even greater return. In August 1993, the board approved a revised Stock Incentive Plan "to reward executives based on their ability to continuously improve the amount of EVA earned on behalf of shareholders." Under the new plan, the company's annual stock option grants were replaced with an equivalent increase in target EVA bonus awards, but with the requirement that one half of actual bonuses earned each year would automatically be used to purchase leveraged stock options (LSOs) at a cost equal to 10% of the company's prevailing stock price.

The net effect was to increase the cash portion of the EVA bonus, and to increase significantly management's interest in upside stock performance, but in exchange for taking more risk. In particular, LSOs are purchased only if earned (whereas before options were granted to management each year as a matter of course), and the LSOs will come into the money only after a significant appreciation of the stock price.

Investors reacted favorably to this restructuring of incentive pay. From a price of $65 a share at the close of the 1993 fiscal year (June 30), B & S's shares rose to $85 over a period of just several months as the market began to appreciate the powerful new incentives for management represented by the plan.

In sum, the EVA ownership plan replaces the traditional short-term bonus linked to budget and ordinary stock option grants with two components: (1) a cash bonus plan that simulates ownership; and (2) a leveraged stock option plan that confers actual ownership. The cash bonus plan simulates ownership by tying bonuses to sustained improvements in EVA over time, with a large portion of awarded bonuses held in escrow and subject to loss to ensure that improvements are permanent. The LSO plan corrects the deficiencies of normal stock option plans in two ways: the leverage factor allows managers to purchase significantly more stock for a given amount of dollars (thus replicating an LBO's effect on ownership); and a steadily rising exercise price ensures that managers win only if shareholders do.

IN CLOSING

An EVA financial management system represents a way to institutionalize the running of a business in accordance with basic microeconomic and corporate finance principles. When properly implemented, it is a closed-loop system of decision-making, accountability, and incentives—one that has the potential to make the entire organization and not just the CEO responsible for the successes and failures of the enterprise. It can result in a self-regulated and self-motivated system of "internal" governance.

As a concept, EVA starts simple, but in practice it can be made as comprehensive as necessary to accommodate management's needs and preferences. EVA is most effective, however, when it is more than just a performance measure. At its best, EVA serves as the centerpiece of a completely integrated framework of financial management and incentive compensation. When used in that manner, the experience of a lengthening list of adopting companies throughout the world strongly supports the notion that an EVA system can refocus energies and redirect resources to create sustainable value—for companies, customers, employees, shareholders, and for management.

The anchor of the EVA financial management system is a powerful incentive compensation plan that consists of two parts: (1) a cash bonus plan tied to continuous improvement in EVA, in which a significant portion of the awarded bonuses are carried forward in a "bonus bank" and held at risk; and (2) a leveraged stock option (LSO) plan, in which managers use part of their cash bonus awards to make highly leveraged purchases of company stock.

Such an EVA reward system holds out major benefits over more conventional compensation plans:
■ Rewarding managers for continuous improvement in (rather than levels of) EVA means that new managers neither receive windfalls for inheriting already profitable divisions, nor are they penalized for stepping into turnaround situations.
■ In contrast to compensation plans that continually revise performance criteria to provide "competitive" compensation levels *each year*, the EVA bonus plan has a "long-term memory" in the form of a bonus

bank that ensures that only consistent, sustainable increases in value are rewarded.
■ EVA bonuses are tied to a performance measure that is highly correlated with shareholder value, thus aligning managers' with shareholders' interests.
■ The strength of the correlation between changes in EVA and in shareholder value also means that the EVA compensation system is effectively "self-financing"; that is, managers win big only when shareholders are winning—and managers are truly penalized when shareholders lose.

Proper internal governance is certainly no guarantee of success, and it is no substitute for leadership, entrepreneurism, and hustle. But an EVA financial management and incentive system can help. We like to say that EVA works like the proverbial Trojan Horse: What is wheeled in appears to be an innocuous new financial management and incentive program, but what jumps out is a new culture that is right for times of rapid change and decentralized decision-making. By increasing accountability, strengthening incentives, facilitating decentralized decision-making, establishing a common language and integrated framework, and fostering a culture that prizes building value above all else, it significantly improves the chances of winning. That's all any shareholder can reasonably expect from governance in today's business environment of continuous change.

■ JOEL STERN

is Managing Partner of Stern Stewart & Co.

■ BENNETT STEWART

is Senior Partner of Stern Stewart & Co.

■ DON CHEW

is Executive Vice President, as well as a founding partner, of Stern Stewart.

EVA® is a registered trademark of Stern Stewart & Co.

TOTAL COMPENSATION STRATEGY

by Stephen F. O'Byrne,
Stern Stewart & Co.

"Total compensation shall represent competitive levels of compensation...

Performance-related pay shall be a significant component of total compensation

placing a substantial portion of an executive officer's compensation at risk."

T hese statements from a recent Compensation Committee Report aptly express the dominant total compensation strategy of public companies today. This strategy is widely accepted as the most reasonable way to limit retention risk and control shareholder cost while still providing a strong incentive for management to maximize shareholder value.

The commitment to competitive compensation levels limits retention risk—that is, the risk that key managers will leave the firm for a better offer elsewhere—because total compensation opportunities are not allowed to fall below competitive levels. The same commitment also limits shareholder cost because total compensation opportunities are not allowed to rise above competitive levels. The commitment to maintaining a substantial proportion of total compensation "at risk"—that is, in the form of bonuses, stock options, and other incentive compensation—is thought to provide a strong incentive to maximize shareholder value—an incentive comparable to that of an owner with a substantial proportion of his wealth in company stock.

This article argues that the dominant total compensation strategy is fundamentally flawed and can never provide incentives comparable to those of an owner/entrepreneur who holds a large proportion of his wealth in company stock. The critical flaw

in the strategy is that, even though a very large proportion of *the current year's* compensation may be "at risk," the commitment to maintaining competitive levels of compensation in all future years effectively ensures that a large proportion of the executive's *wealth* is not at risk. Incentives that approach entrepreneurial levels can be achieved only by total compensation strategies that make *the value of future compensation opportunities sensitive to current performance.*

But, strategies that provide strong wealth incentives will always lead to greater retention risk for poor performance or higher shareholder cost for superior performance than the dominant total compensation strategy. And this means that managers and directors who seek stronger wealth incentives must be prepared to make difficult trade-offs between stronger wealth incentives, greater retention risk, and higher potential cost to the shareholders. To help managers and directors in evaluating these trade-offs, this paper presents a new analytical framework—one that I call *total wealth incentive analysis.* This analytical framework can be used both to reveal the hidden and ill-considered trade-offs that typically underlie the dominant total compensation strategy, and to design compensation plans that provide strong, sustainable, and cost-effective wealth incentives.

TABLE 1		Competitive Percentile	Market Pay Mix	Target Pay Mix
Salary	$300	50	40%	30%
Target Bonus	$200		20%	20%
Target Cash Compensation	$500	60		
Target Option Value	$500		40%	50%
Target Total Compensation	$1,000	75		

THE DOMINANT TOTAL COMPENSATION STRATEGY

The foundation of the dominant total compensation strategy is the concept of annual recalibration to a competitive position target. The company adopts a competitive position target—say, the 75th percentile total compensation—and each year recalibrates its salaries, bonus plan targets, and number of option grant shares to provide a total compensation opportunity at the targeted percentile. Base salary and cash compensation can be targeted at the same percentile as total compensation, or, more commonly, at lower percentiles in order to provide higher leverage and a mix of pay that is more attractive to management and the directors than the market mix.

The company's total compensation strategy can be (and in fact often is) summarized in a table (much like Table 1) that expresses the company's target compensation percentiles and target pay mix. For example, in the case illustrated in Table 1, the firm has targeted the 50th percentile for salary, the 60th percentile for cash compensation, and the 75th percentile for total compensation. These targeted percentiles provide a targeted *pay mix* of 30% salary, 20% bonus, and 50% stock options. Despite the fact that these targets put 70% of total compensation at risk, the practice of annual recalibration, as I show below, leaves the company with a weak wealth incentive.

Recalibrating the total compensation program each year to maintain the target competitive percentiles requires adjusting the bonus plan performance target to a new level that represents current expected performance, and changing the number of option shares granted to reflect the current stock price. If, for example, the target operating profit for the first year is $10 million, but performance deteriorates to a level where the expected operating profit for the second year is only $5 million, the target operating profit for the second year must be reduced to $5

million to ensure that the target bonus is the expected value of the bonus. Similarly, if the initial option grant required to provide an expected value of $500K was 20,000 shares based on a stock price of $50 (and a Black-Scholes value of 50%, or $25 per option), and the stock price declines in the second year to $25, the number of option shares granted must be increased to 40,000 to provide an option grant with an expected value of $500K (because new at-the-money options are now worth only $12.50 per share). If performance improves instead of deteriorates, the target operating profit must be increased and the number of option shares reduced to maintain the expected value of the bonus and option grant at the targeted competitive level.

These annual adjustments required to maintain the target competitive position have two important consequences. The first, and intended, consequence is that the expected value of the total compensation opportunity remains at a competitive level. The second, unintended but unavoidable, consequence is that *poor performance is rewarded* by an increase in management's percentage interest in operating profit and stock price appreciation, while *superior performance is penalized* by a reduction in management's percentage interest in operating profit and stock price appreciation. When performance deteriorates and the target operating profit is reduced from $10 million to $5 million, the target bonus share of operating profit is increased from 2% ($200K/$10 million) to 4% ($200K/$5 million). When the stock price declines from $50 to $25, the number of option shares granted is increased from 20,000 to 40,000. When performance improves and the target operating profit is increased to $20 million, the target bonus share of operating profit is reduced from 2% ($200K/$10 million) to 1% ($200K/$20 million). When the stock price rises from $50 to $100, the number of option shares granted is reduced from 20,000 to 10,000.

As I demonstrate later, the "performance penalty" inherent in annual recalibration to competitive

The critical flaw in the dominant total compensation strategy is that, even though a
very large proportion of *the current year's* compensation may be "at risk," the
commitment to maintaining competitive levels of compensation in all future years
effectively ensures that a large proportion of the executive's *wealth* is not at risk.

compensation levels makes it impossible for the dominant total compensation strategy to provide incentives that approach those of an owner who holds a large portion of his wealth in the form of a *fixed* percentage interest in the dividends and stock price appreciation of the company. It can also lead, as the compensation history of John Akers at IBM illustrates, to huge discrepancies between management compensation and shareholder gain. In Akers' first year as CEO, the IBM board gave him an option on 19,000 shares exercisable at $145. In subsequent years, as the stock price declined, they gave him larger and larger option share grants to offset the decline in the stock price and maintain the value of his annual compensation package at a competitive level. In 1990, the Board gave him an option on 96,000 shares exercisable at $97. By the end of 1992, the Board had put him in a position where he would have realized an option gain of $17.6 million just for getting the stock price back to the $145 level at which he received his first option grant as CEO!

THE OBJECTIVES OF EXECUTIVE COMPENSATION

The dominant total compensation strategy is, as any total compensation strategy must be if it seeks to maximize the wealth of current shareholders, an attempt to balance four conflicting objectives:
- *Alignment:* giving management an incentive to choose strategies and investments that maximize shareholder value;
- *Leverage:* giving management sufficient incentive compensation to motivate them to work long hours, take risks, and make unpleasant decisions, such as closing a plant or laying off staff, to maximize shareholder value;
- *Retention:* giving managers sufficient total compensation to retain them, particularly during periods of poor performance due to market and industry factors; and
- *Shareholder cost:* limiting the cost of management compensation to levels that will maximize the wealth of current shareholders.

Each of these objectives is critical to the success of total compensation strategy, but every total compensation strategy must make trade-offs between leverage, retention risk, and shareholder cost. A strategy that relies on large stock grants can achieve substantial leverage with minimal retention risk, but only by accepting higher shareholder cost

than a strategy that relies on stock option grants. A strategy that relies on large stock option grants can achieve substantial leverage with limited shareholder cost, but only by accepting greater retention risk than a strategy that relies on stock grants. A strategy that relies on a high proportion of guaranteed compensation can achieve limited retention risk and limited shareholder cost, but only by accepting modest leverage.

Most companies and directors believe that the dominant total compensation strategy provides a reasonable balance between the four conflicting objectives of executive compensation. Indeed, the rationale for the dominant corporate compensation practice can be summarized as follows:
- It provides alignment because bonus and stock compensation is tied to operating and market measures of shareholder value;
- It provides substantial leverage because a large proportion of pay is at risk and gives the executive incentives comparable to those of an owner who holds a large proportion of his wealth in company stock;
- It provides retention because it gives the executive competitive compensation opportunities every year; and
- It controls shareholder cost because compensation opportunities are limited to a given percentile of the competitive pay distribution.

TOTAL WEALTH LEVERAGE

To understand why having a large proportion of the current year's pay at risk does not provide incentives comparable to those of an owner who holds a similar proportion of his wealth in company stock, we need to focus on the value of management *wealth*, as opposed to current *income*, and its relationship to shareholder wealth. Management wealth is the value of its investment capital plus the value of its human capital. In other words, management wealth is the sum of (1) the value of current stock and option holdings; and (2) the present value of expected future compensation, including (a) salary, (b) bonus, (c) long-term incentive grants, and (d) pension.

Managers, like shareholders, try to maximize their wealth, not their current income. The true measure of the wealth *incentive* provided by a compensation plan is the sensitivity of management wealth to changes in shareholder wealth. More specifically, for any given change in shareholder wealth, it is the ratio of the percentage change in management wealth to the percentage change in shareholder wealth. To illustrate, if a 10% change in shareholder wealth changes management wealth by 10%, management's *total wealth leverage* is 1.0. This is the total wealth leverage of a "pure" entrepreneur—one whose entire wealth is held in company stock; in such case, any percentage change in shareholder wealth causes the same percentage change in the entrepreneur's wealth.

If a 10% change in shareholder wealth causes a 7% change in management wealth, then management's total wealth leverage is 0.7. This would be the wealth leverage of a manager whose wealth consisted of 70% company stock and 30% the present value of future salary and benefits. This would also be the wealth leverage of an investor who holds a portfolio of 70% stock and 30% bonds in the same company. In this case, wealth leverage is easy to calculate. If the investor holds $700,000 of equity and $300,000 of debt, a 10% increase in shareholder wealth increases the value of the investor's equity by 10% to $770,000 and the value of the investor's portfolio by 7% to $1,070,000. The investor's total wealth leverage is 0.7 (= 7%/10%), which is equal to equity leverage (1.0) times the proportion of the investor's wealth held as equity, 1.0 × 70%.

The total wealth leverage of a typical executive, however, is more difficult to calculate because the executive holds a more complicated portfolio—one that includes stock options, future bonus payments, and future option grants. Before I illustrate the use of wealth analysis in total compensation design, it will be helpful to lay some groundowrk by first explaining:

■ the need to measure wealth leverage on a present value basis,
■ the leverage of options, and
■ the importance of expected future compensation in management wealth.

The Important Distinction Between Present and Future Values

Total wealth leverage must be measured on a present value basis since wealth is a risk-adjusted present value that reflects different discount rates for future stock and option gains as well as for future salary, bonus, and long-term incentive payouts. "Future value" wealth changes do not provide a meaningful measure of leverage.

To illustrate this point, suppose that an executive holds a ten-year option exercisable at the current market price of $50, and that the stock price increases by 10% over five years to $55. The value of the option at the time of grant is $31.82 (using the Black-Scholes model with a volatility of .350, a dividend yield of zero, and a risk-free interest rate of 8%), but declines by 17% to $26.33 at the end of five years. These two price changes over the five-year period imply that the option has a future value leverage of –1.7 since the 10% change in shareholder wealth reduces the option value by 17%. That is, option values appear to move in the opposite direction of shareholder value.

This paradoxical result arises because the future value leverage calculation ignores the fact that the option has greater risk, and hence a higher expected rate of return, than the stock. To calculate a meaningful measure of leverage, we need to compare the change in the present value of the option with the change in the present value of the stock. The present value of the $55 future stock price, assuming a 14% expected stock return, is $28.57, or 43% less than the initial $50 market price. The present value of the option, based on a 16.4% expected option return (from the Black-Scholes model), is $12.31, or 61% less than its initial value of $31.82.

This set of calculations reveals that the option's leverage is in fact a positive 1.4 (not a negative 1.7) since the percentage change in the present value of the option, –61%, is 1.4 times the percentage change in the value of the stock, –43%. This kind of present value analysis, unlike the future value analysis, confirms our intuitive sense that the option is more, not less, leveraged than the stock.

The Wealth Leverage Provided by Stock Options

The leverage of an option differs from the leverage of the stock in two basic ways. The leverage of an option can be much greater than 1.0 (and never less than 1.0), while the leverage of the stock is always 1.0. The leverage of the option also changes, unlike the leverage of the stock, as the stock price changes and also as the option comes closer to expiration. The leverage of an option declines as the option comes into the money and increases as the option falls out of the money and as the option comes closer to expiration. Table 2 shows the leverage of several different options for

The "performance penalty" inherent in annual recalibration to competitive
compensation levels makes it impossible for the dominant total compensation
strategy to provide incentives that approach those of an owner who holds a large
portion of his wealth in the form of company stock.

TABLE 2	Exercise Price	Market Price	Option Term	Option Leverage
	$50	$50	10	1.5
	$50	$50	5	2.0
	$50	$50	1	4.2
	$50	$40	1	5.7
	$50	$25	1	10.0

a company with an average volatility (.35) and dividend yield (3%).

The higher leverage of options plays a critical role in designing strong total wealth incentives because it makes it possible to design a total compensation program that offsets the effect of base salary (which has zero leverage) and provides total wealth leverage that equals or exceeds that of an entrepreneur. For example, if 30% of the executive's total wealth is the present value of future salary, but the remaining 70% is held in options with a leverage of 1.45, total wealth leverage will be 1.02 (= .7 × 1.45 + .3 × 0).

Incorporating the Present Value of Future Compensation

The present value of expected future compensation can be a very large component of management wealth. It includes the present value of total compensation for the executive's expected job tenure plus the present value of the executive's future pension. Assuming a 5% growth in competitive compensation levels (and a risk-free rate of 8%), the present value of ten future years of competitive total compensation is more than 8 times the value of current total compensation. Adding the value of a pension equal to 50% of cash compensation increases the present value of expected future compensation to more than 10 times the value of current total compensation.

The size of expected future compensation is important because the recalibration feature of the dominant total compensation strategy makes expected future compensation completely independent of current performance. That is, the wealth leverage of the present value of expected future compensation is zero. And, when the present value of expected future compensation is 10 times the value of current total compensation and the company's total compensation strategy makes the value of expected future compensation totally independent of current performance, total wealth

leverage will be very small even when current total compensation is highly sensitive to changes in shareholder wealth. For example, even if the leverage of current total compensation were designed to be 1.0, with annual recalibration *total wealth leverage* would be only 0.09 because current total compensation represents only 1/11, or 9%, of total wealth.

And this problem affects managers nearing retirement as well as those with longer time horizons. For, although the present value of total compensation for the executive's expected job tenure diminishes as she approaches retirement, the present value of the executive's pension increases. The present value of a pension equal to 50% of cash compensation can still be five times the value of current total compensation when an executive is close to retirement.

This basic analysis of the mix of management wealth and the leverage of options is helpful in understanding the fundamental flaw in the dominant total compensation strategy. But it is not powerful enough to guide the development of a new total compensation strategy. For that purpose, we need the ability to simulate the impact of *all* the key elements of total compensation strategy on total wealth leverage as well as their impact on retention risk and shareholder cost.

TOTAL WEALTH INCENTIVE ANALYSIS

To assess the leverage, retention risk, and shareholder cost implications of a total compensation program, we need to simulate the future payouts of the total compensation program across a set of future performance scenarios that reflect the range, variability, and probability of the company's stock price and operating performance and then calculate total wealth leverage as well as measures of retention risk and shareholder cost. In practice, we can do this by creating a Monte Carlo simulation of 100 (or more) five-year future performance scenarios and then simulating the five-year payouts

TABLE 3	Percentile of Future Shareholder Wealth	5th Year Shareholder Wealth	Percent Change in Shareholder Wealth	PV of Total Wealth	Percent Change in Management Wealth	Total Wealth Leverage
	30	$49		$3,050		
	50	$79	59%	$3,790	24%	0.41
	70	$123	57%	$4,670	23%	0.41

under the total compensation program for each scenario. The Monte Carlo simulations of future market value and operating performance are derived from—and thus are consistent with—the underlying assumptions of option pricing theory and discounted cash flow valuation.

For a company with a publicly traded stock, the future performance simulations are based on the current stock price, the historical volatility of shareholder return, the expected level of improvement in EVA® (that is, profit in excess of the cost of capital) reflected in the current stock price, and the historical volatility of year-to-year changes in EVA. For a private company or a business unit of a public company, performance simulations are based on the estimated market value of the company or business unit, the historical volatility of peer company shareholder returns, the level of the expected improvement in EVA that is reflected in the estimated market value, and the historical volatility of changes in EVA.

We use the future performance scenarios to simulate the future payouts under the total compensation program based on the actual bonus plan design and the specific provisions and grant guidelines of the stock option plan. We use the compensation simulations to measure *total wealth leverage* as well as *future retention risk* and *shareholder cost*. Total wealth leverage is based on a present value analysis using discount rates that reflect the risk of each element of the total compensation program. In some cases, especially where the expected job tenure of the management team is relatively short, our calculation of total wealth is based only on the present value of five-year total compensation. In other cases—for example, where the expected job tenure of the management team is much longer than five years and the company provides generous retirement benefits—our calculation of total wealth includes the present value of expected future compensation beyond five years as well as the present value of retirement benefits.

In either case, we measure *total wealth leverage* at each quintile or decile of the 100 future performance scenarios by calculating *the ratio of the percentage change in management wealth to the percentage change in shareholder wealth*. We measure future *retention risk* by calculating the expected value of total compensation at the end of the fifth year (based again on the actual bonus plan design and the specific provisions and grant guidelines of the stock option plan) and computing the *shortfall, if any, between expected and competitive compensation*. We measure *shareholder cost* by calculating *five-year total compensation* including salary, bonus, and long-term incentive payouts.

The Implications of the Dominant Total Compensation Strategy

These simulations allow us to assess the long-term implications of the dominant total compensation strategy. Let's assume, to begin, that the expected job tenure of the management team is relatively short and, hence, that the present value of five-year total compensation is a reasonable proxy for management wealth. Table 3 shows the total wealth leverage for the dominant total compensation strategy with a 30%/20%/50% mix of salary, bonus, and stock option value:

As shown in Table 3, the dominant total compensation strategy with 70% of pay "at risk" does not provide a total wealth incentive comparable to that of an owner who holds 70% of his total wealth in company stock. Under the most favorable assumptions, it provides a total wealth incentive comparable to that of an owner who holds only 40% of his wealth in company stock.

And if we lengthen the managerial time horizon, the plan provides even weaker wealth incentives. When we include the present value of expected future compensation for years 6-10 in the calculation of total wealth, the total wealth incentive provided by the same total compensation strategy (with 70% of

Managers, like shareholders, try to maximize their wealth, not their current income. The true measure of the wealth *incentive* provided by a compensation plan is the sensitivity of management wealth to changes in shareholder wealth.

TABLE 4

Percentile of Future Shareholder Wealth	5th Year Shareholder Wealth	Percent Change in Shareholder Wealth	PV of Total Wealth	Percent Change in Management Wealth	Total Wealth Leverage
30	$49		$5,770		
50	$79	59%	$6,510	13%	0.21
70	$123	57%	$7,390	14%	0.24

TABLE 5

Percentile of Future Shareholder Wealth	5th Year Shareholder Wealth	Percent Change in Shareholder Wealth	PV of Total Wealth	Percent Change in Management Wealth	Total Wealth Leverage
30	$49		$5,120		
50	$79	59%	$7,100	37%	0.62
70	$123	57%	$9,860	41%	0.72

TABLE 6

Percentile of Future Shareholder Wealth	5th Year Shareholder Wealth	Percent Change in Shareholder Wealth	PV of Total Wealth	Percent Change in Management Wealth	Total Wealth Leverage
30	$49		$4,550		
50	$79	59%	$6,890	51%	0.86
70	$123	57%	$10,880	58%	1.02

pay nominally "at risk") provides a wealth incentive comparable to that of an owner who holds only 20% of his total wealth in company stock (see Table 4).

Designing Entrepreneurial Incentives

To create a total wealth incentive that approaches entrepreneurial incentives, total compensation strategy must be based on policies that make a substantial proportion of management wealth sensitive to current performance. These policies include *front-loaded* option grants, *fixed-share* option grant guidelines, and formula bonus plans.

As shown in Table 5, substituting fixed-share annual stock option grants for the conventional fixed-dollar, variable-share grants provides a total wealth incentive that is comparable to that of an owner who holds 70% of his total wealth in company stock. Thus, just taking this step alone has the effect of tripling the proportion of management's wealth that is truly variable or "at risk."

This stronger incentive, however, comes with higher retention risk for poor performance and higher shareholder cost for superior performance. Retention risk increases for poor performance be-

cause the expected value of the fixed-share options will decline below competitive option grant values as the stock price declines. If a 24,500 share grant provides a competitive option grant value when the stock price is $50, it will only provide half of the competitive option grant value when the stock price is $25. Shareholder cost for superior performance will also increase because management will still get a 24,500 share grant when the stock is $100 or $200.

To demonstrate how an entrepreneurial incentive can be designed and to highlight the retention and shareholder cost implications of a strong wealth incentive, it will be useful to take our program redesign one step further and show the implications of a front-loaded option grant of 245,000 shares (in effect, granting 10 years' worth of options at the beginning of the manager's tenure). As shown in Table 6, a total compensation strategy based on a formula-driven, fixed-target EVA bonus and a front-loaded option grant can provide a total wealth incentive comparable to that of an entrepreneur whose total wealth varies in exact proportion to changes in shareholder value.

But what are the retention and shareholder cost implications of providing such an entrepreneurial

TABLE 7	Percentile of Future Shareholder Wealth	5th Year Shareholder Wealth	Year 6 Market Total Comp	Year 6 Expected Total Comp	Percentage Difference
	10	$28	$1,000	$610	−39%
	30	$49	$1,000	$830	−17%
	50	$79	$1,000	$1,260	+26%
	70	$123	$1,000	$2,030	+103%
	90	$208	$1,000	$3,610	+261%

TABLE 8	Percentile of Future Shareholder Wealth	5th Year Shareholder Wealth	5 Year Total Comp (A)	5 Year Total Comp (B)	Percentage Difference
	10	$28	$2,200	$1,800	−18%
	30	$49	$3,300	$2,700	−18%
	50	$79	$4,600	$7,700	+57%
	70	$123	$6,700	$18,100	+170%
	90	$208	$10,700	$38,200	+257%

incentive? If we assume that the front-loaded option grant vests pro-rata under this program, the expected value of total compensation in the sixth year is the sum of base salary, the target bonus, and expected value of the option shares vesting in the sixth year. And, as shown in Table 7, there are substantial differences between competitive total compensation and the expected value of the executive's total compensation in the sixth year. In fact, if the firm performs very poorly, and the stock price falls to $28 after five years, there will be an almost 40% difference between competitive levels and managers' expected total compensation.

Moreover, if we use the five-year sum of base salary and bonus payouts plus the spread on outstanding option grants as a measure of the total shareholder cost of the total compensation program, this alternative compensation strategy (column "B" in Table 8) has significantly higher shareholder cost than the dominant total compensation strategy (column "A" in Table 8). The higher cost will be incurred, however, when the shareholders are best able to afford it—when their shares have appreciated significantly.

As these comparisons of future retention risk and shareholder cost clearly show, there is no "free lunch" in total compensation strategy. The entrepreneurial leverage provided by the front-loaded option grant and EVA bonus plan implies both greater retention risk for poor performance and higher shareholder cost for average and superior performance. While future retention risk can be reduced by increasing the size of the initial option grant, an increase in the size of the option grant will increase the shareholder cost of the total compensation program. Such difficult trade-offs are unavoidable despite the illusions fostered by the dominant total compensation strategy. The real issue is how to make the trade-offs wisely—that is, in such a way that they will maximize the wealth of current shareholders.

A NEW APPROACH TO TOTAL COMPENSATION STRATEGY

The real issues in total compensation strategy are not competitive position targets and total compensation mix. The real issues are:
■ What are the wealth incentives created by the current/proposed program?
■ What is a desirable wealth incentive?
■ How should a stronger wealth incentive be "financed?"
  • Through greater retention risk?
  • Through higher shareholder cost?

We have already explained the analysis necessary to address the first issue, so let's now turn to the second and third.

In an ideal world, the determination of the optimal wealth incentive would be based on the empirical relationship between wealth incentive and shareholder return. This would identify the point at which the incremental cost of a stronger wealth incentive exceeds the incremental increase in shareholder wealth.

Unfortunately, there is no systematic research on this relationship, in large part because few companies publicly disclose their policies for adjusting performance targets and option grant levels. In the real world, decisions about optimal wealth incentives still require thoughtful director judgment about the expected effects of stronger incentives on management performance. While many directors are convinced that entrepreneurial leverage has a dramatic impact on management performance, others—particularly those with small stockholdings—remain skeptical that stronger incentives will make management work harder or smarter.

While there is no controlled statistical study that proves that entrepreneurial leverage has a dramatic impact on management performance, there is relevant evidence for these uncertain directors to consider. One important piece of evidence are the internal studies of chain restaurant companies that operate both company-owned and franchised units. These studies suggest that wealth incentives that approach or exceed entrepreneurial levels have a very significant effect on performance. More specifically, the studies show that franchised units, which provide wealth incentives at entrepreneurial levels, significantly outperform company-owned units with total compensation strategies tied to competitive pay objectives.

A second important piece of evidence in thinking about desirable wealth incentives is the wealth incentives agreed to in circumstances where there is substantial "arm's-length" bargaining over the terms of compensation. One important case of arm's-length bargaining occurs when outside directors and significant shareholders play the lead role in negotiating a long-term compensation contract for a new CEO hired from outside the company. In these situations, we often find compensation contracts that provide wealth incentives that approach or exceed entrepreneurial leverage. Consider, for example, Michael Eisner's original contract at Walt Disney. As I discussed in an earlier article in this journal ("What Pay for Performance Looks Like:

The Case of Michael Eisner," Summer 1992), Eisner was given a contract at the outset of his tenure that gave him a large front-loaded stock option grant and a bonus equal to 2% of Disney's profits after shareholders had been provided with a 9% return on equity. The total wealth leverage provided by the contract was 1.4. And, during a period in which the market value of Disney increased by $12 billion, Eisner received some $200 million.

Another instructive case of arm's-length bargaining is the determination of the general partner's compensation in private placement investment funds, such as leveraged buyout funds and venture capital funds. The general partner's compensation typically consists of a 1% management fee, based on the total assets invested by the limited partners, plus a 20% interest in the ultimate profits from the fund. In addition, the limited partners normally demand that the general partner make an equity investment in the fund. (KKR, for example, typically committed about 1-4% of the equity in the funds for which it served as general partner.) The management fee is essentially the general partner's "base salary" since it is based on the limited partners' initial investments rather than the current value of their investments. When we model the general partner's total wealth leverage, we find that it slightly exceeds entrepreneurial leverage even though the present value of the management fee represents 25% of the general partner's fund related wealth (including the value of a 20% profit interest and a 4% equity interest).

Making the Trade-Off

Once the directors come to a consensus about a desirable wealth incentive, they must decide what combination of greater retention risk and greater shareholder cost should be used to "finance" it. Unfortunately, it is difficult to generalize about the optimal way to "finance" a stronger wealth incentive. The optimal trade-off between retention risk and shareholder cost depends on the difficulty of replacing the management team and the shareholders' willingness to accept higher retention risk to limit the cost of management compensation.

To illustrate the process of making such trade-offs, consider the following case. The shareholders of a closely held corporation wanted to strengthen management incentives to ensure the continued success of the company as the original shareholders retired from active participation in management. The original shareholders had had very strong wealth incentives during the period they had built up the company, and they were eager to give the new management team a total compensation program that would make them feel, and act, like entrepreneurs. But entrepreneurial incentives were not the only objective of the shareholders. They didn't want to "give the company away" and felt that a 5% option interest was the most they should reasonably have to sacrifice to motivate the management team. They were also concerned about the volatility of the business and the retention risks of forcing management to make a big bet on the current value of the company.

Given these concerns, their initial preference was for a total compensation program that provided annual fixed-share option grants, building up to a 5% management team option interest over five years, plus an annual EVA bonus with a target opportunity of 30% of salary. To their surprise, however, our analysis showed that the total wealth incentives provided by this program were only half the level of entrepreneurial incentives. This finding created a difficult dilemma for the original shareholders. They could provide the new management team with a far weaker incentive than the one that had motivated them to build the business, but that was at odds with their basic objective of motivating management to replicate and extend their own success. Or they could increase the incentive by providing a much larger cash bonus opportunity, but they were afraid that management would then lose its focus on maximizing *long-term* shareholder value. Or they could reduce management's guaranteed compensation to enhance the relative impact of the stock option grants, but they immediately decided that that would alienate, not motivate, their management team. Or, finally, they could increase their "investment" in management compensation by agreeing to surrender more than a 5% option interest in the company.

After much thought, analysis, and discussion, they decided that the last alternative was the best.

CONCLUSIONS

The dominant total compensation strategy has a very strong appeal for "fiduciary directors" with small stockholdings because it minimizes the risk of highly visible failure. Total compensation strategy can fail to maximize shareholders' wealth because it fails to provide a strong wealth incentive, but highly visible failures (the great concern of the fiduciary director) almost always involve retention or shareholder cost. When key managers leave to join a competitor, it is hard to convince skeptical shareholders that the company's total compensation strategy was based on a reasonable decision to accept more retention risk to limit shareholder cost. When managers receive very large incentive compensation payouts, it is hard to convince a skeptical public that strong incentives played a key role in the company's success. But failures of leverage (or alignment) are rarely attributed to total compensation strategy; they are lost in a multitude of other explanations for poor performance—bad strategy, tough competition, product development failures, adverse market trends, etc.

Directors who are large shareholders are far more aware that inadequate wealth incentives can be a much greater threat to shareholder value than management turnover or large incentive compensation payouts. The successful history of LBOs and the entrepreneurs who leave big companies to start small ones is largely a history of inadequate wealth incentives. It is time for all directors to abandon the illusions of the dominant compensation strategy and face up to the difficult decisions required to create the strong wealth incentives needed to maximize shareholder value.

■ STEPHEN O'BYRNE

is Senior Vice President and head of Stern Stewart & Co.'s incentive compensation advisory practice.